CORPORATE INTERNAL INVESTIGATIONS

An International Guide

CORPORATE INTERNAL INVESTIGATIONS

An International Guide

Edited by

PAUL LOMAS

Freshfields Bruckhaus Deringer LLP

DANIEL J KRAMER

Paul, Weiss, Rifkind, Wharton & Garrison LLP

OXFORD
UNIVERSITY PRESS

Great Clarendon Street, Oxford ox2 6DP

Oxford University Press is a department of the University of Oxford.
It furthers the University's objective of excellence in research, scholarship,
and education by publishing worldwide in

Oxford New York

Auckland Cape Town Dar es Salaam Hong Kong Karachi
Kuala Lumpur Madrid Melbourne Mexico City Nairobi
New Delhi Shanghai Taipei Toronto

With offices in

Argentina Austria Brazil Chile Czech Republic France Greece
Guatemala Hungary Italy Japan Poland Portugal Singapore
South Korea Switzerland Thailand Turkey Ukraine Vietnam

Oxford is a registered trade mark of Oxford University Press
in the UK and in certain other countries

Published in the United States
by Oxford University Press Inc., New York

British Library Cataloguing in Publication Data
Data available

Library of Congress Cataloging in Publication Data
Data available

Typeset by Cepha Imaging Private Ltd, Bangalore, India
Printed in Great Britain
on acid-free paper by
CPI Antony Rowe, Chippenham

ISBN 978–0–19–955411–9

1 3 5 7 9 10 8 6 4 2

PREFACE

In a meeting in London in 2004 between partners and associates of our two firms, the conversation turned from securities litigation, the official topic, to what had become a common part of the professional lives of many of us: internal investigations. We had all seen the importance of well-organized investigations to clients, including major corporations and investment banks, which had benefited both from the corporate governance advantages and from managing their regulatory issues and legal risk through this technique.

We realized the extent to which we had shared similar experiences as the practice of investigations, particularly in the USA and the UK, had developed. It was also evident how expectations were evolving around Europe and in Asia.

It was clear then, as it is now, that this is an area that touches many fields of law. But also that it is a practical area: experience and judgement are critical; and there are important nuances between different jurisdictions and their cultures as to when, why and how such exercises are conducted. The idea developed, therefore, of pooling our respective firms' experience around the world, into a book, this book, which would be, perhaps, the first attempt to deal with this subject on an international basis. It has taken a little time in gestation, and we have never had the luxury of the languid few weeks that we promised ourselves, somewhere comfortable and tranquil, to write it.

We recognize that we touch on many issues without giving an exhaustive treatment of any. That is in the nature of internal investigations, particularly international examples. A detailed treatment of all regulatory powers and all the possible combinations of issues would be both unwriteable and unreadable. But we hope that this book is of use and that it offers some valuable guidance on how to conduct investigations and how to use them to manage risk and relationships.

This exercise would not have been possible without the enormous contributions of our colleagues, in both our firms, in the various jurisdictions covered in the guide: USA, UK, the Netherlands, Germany, Spain, France, Italy, Hong Kong, and Japan. It is their collective experience that is reflected in this guide. The authors are identified by chapter, but we should record here both their own efforts and those of the many others helping them.

Particular acknowledgements must also go to Rachel Couter, formerly at Freshfields Bruckhaus Deringer LLP and now a partner at Gibson Dunn & Crutcher and Paul Cohen, formerly of Paul Weiss and now with Dewey & LeBoeuf. Both were heavily involved in helping us to structure the project and personally contributed enormously to the UK and USA sections respectively. Their intelligent and focused participation was of great assistance.

Thanks are also due to Melanie Garson, an associate at Freshfields Bruckhaus Deringer LLP, who organized, project managed, critiqued and rewrote over a protracted period: without her work this book would not exist. Andrew Price, Lucy Onyeforo and Keren Azulay were a fantastic help in the final stages, researching, proofreading, checking and generally making sure that it happened.

Finally, we need to thank our partners, both the professional and the personal partners, for their support and encouragement throughout.

Paul Lomas and Dan Kramer
March 2008

CONTENTS—SUMMARY

CONTENTS

Contents

Contents

TABLE OF CASES

NETHERLANDS

SPAIN

UNITED KINGDOM

UNITED STATES

TABLE OF LEGISLATION

EC Legislation

LIST OF CONTRIBUTORS

Editors

Daniel J Kramer

Daniel J Kramer is a Partner in the Litigation Department of Paul, Weiss, Rifkind, Wharton & Garrison LLP, based in New York City, and Co-Chair of the firm's Securities Litigation and Enforcement Group. Mr Kramer is a leading trial lawyer with extensive experience in securities matters and internal investigations. He has handled complex litigations for some of the world's largest companies and has significant experience representing boards of directors on corporate governance issues and special committees in internal investigations. He lectures and writes extensively on securities litigation and corporate governance issues and is the co-author of *Federal Securities Litigation: A Deskbook for the Practitioner* and of *Regulation of Market Manipulation*. Mr Kramer has been selected as one of the leading securities lawyers in the USA by Chambers, as one of America's leading lawyers handling 'Bet the Company' litigation and commercial litigation by Best Lawyers in America, as one of New York's 'Top 100 Lawyers' by Super Lawyers, and as one of Lawdragon's '100 Lawyers You Need to Know in Securities Litigation'. Dan graduated from Wesleyan University and New York University School of Law, and served as a law clerk to Hon Wilfred Feinberg, the Chief Judge for the US Court of Appeals for the Second Circuit.

Paul Lomas

Paul Lomas leads the global commercial disputes group for Freshfields Bruckhaus Deringer LLP. He specializes in corporate crises, related litigation and governance issues, commercial litigation, cases with a strong economic or regulatory aspect and EU/competition law. He has appeared at all levels of the English courts, the European Court of Justice, the Court of First Instance, in US Courts and in arbitrations. He has acted in a large number of corporate governance crises, involving internal investigations into corporate conduct and related litigation including acting on the UN corruption allegations (Oil for Food and peacekeeping), allegations of malpractice in the art markets, in the retail insurance and consumer finance markets, in the advertising sector, insider dealing, market abuse in M&A transactions, SEC independence investigations, UK and US corruption investigations in a variety of countries and a considerable number of cartel investigations. He has represented, across the various areas in which he practises, world leading investment banks, industrial companies, energy companies, TMT businesses and professional services firms. He was educated at Emmanuel College, Cambridge and INSEAD. He has been a partner since 1990.

United States

Paul H Cohen

Paul H Cohen is an associate in the Litigation Department of Dewey & LeBoeuf, based in New York City. He specializes in criminal, regulatory and civil matters with an international or transactional aspect. Paul graduated from the University of Pennsylvania, received a PhD in political science from Oxford University and a JD degree from Columbia Law School.

Angela M Papalaskaris

Angela M Papalaskaris is an associate in the Litigation Department of Dewey & LeBoeuf, based in New York City. She has extensive experience in representing clients under internal investigation and/or investigation by state and federal government agencies. Angela graduated from Long Island University, CW Post and Benjamin N Cardozo School of Law.

Alex Young K Oh

Alex Young K Oh is a partner in the Litigation Department of Paul, Weiss, Rifkind, Wharton & Garrison LLP, based in the Washington DC office. She concentrates on white collar criminal and regulatory enforcement matters, including corporate internal investigations. Alex graduated from Williams College and Yale Law School, and served as a law clerk to Hon Paul V Niemeyer of the US Court of Appeals for the Fourth Circuit. Prior to joining Paul, Weiss, Alex served for nearly four years as an assistant US attorney in the US Attorney's Office for the Southern District of New York and was a member of the Securities & Commodities Fraud Task Force and the Major Crimes Unit.

United Kingdom

Rachel Couter

Rachel Couter* is a partner in Gibson, Dunn & Crutcher's London office, and practises in the firm's Dispute Resolution Group. Ms Couter has broad litigation and dispute resolution experience, with a focus on defending large corporate clients and financial institutions against high-value complex claims, often with an international angle or involving multiple jurisdictions. She has also represented a number of financial institutions and listed corporates in connection with investigations and disciplinary proceedings brought by various regulatory bodies, including the Financial Services Authority, the UK Listing Authority, the Department for Business, Enterprise and Regulatory (formerly, the Department of Trade and Industry) and the Securities and Exchange Commission.

* Rachel formerly worked at Freshfields Bruckhaus Deringer LLP.

Keith Wotherspoon

Keith Wotherspoon is a senior associate in the London office of Freshfields Bruckhaus Deringer LLP, specializing in transactional and advisory work on intellectual property and information technology issues. He has particular expertise in multi-jurisdictional data protection and e-commerce issues. He joined the firm in 1999 and has been on secondment to Freshfields' Tokyo office and BP's Digital Communications and Technology Group. Educated at Glasgow University, he is qualified as a solicitor in Scotland and in England & Wales. Prior to joining Freshfields, he was a lecturer at Aberdeen University and has written extensively on commercial, intellectual property (IP) and information technology law issues. He was a visiting lecturer in IT Law at Stellenbosch University in 2004 and has just finished serving as an external examiner in IP at Queen Mary, University of London (where he is now a visiting lecturer). Keith is the author of Chapter 2: 'Data Protection under European Community Law'.

Netherlands

Michael Broeders

Michael Broeders is a senior associate in the corporate group of Freshfields Bruckhaus Deringer LLP, based in the Amsterdam office. Michael's practice covers a wide variety of corporate advisory and corporate transactional involvements. Michael specializes in insolvency and restructuring. He graduated from Nijmegen University.

Wieke van Angeren-van den Elzen

Wieke van Angeren is a senior associate in the Intellectual Property and Information Technology (IP/IT) group of Freshfields Bruckhaus Deringer LLP, based in the Amsterdam office. Wieke specializes in outsourcing, IT transactional and e-commerce work and data protection. Wieke graduated from Utrecht University.

Paul Kreijger

Paul Kreijger is a counsel in the Anti-trust, Competition and Trade group of Freshfields Bruckhaus Deringer LLP, based in the Amsterdam office. Paul specializes in EU and competition law, regulatory matters, administrative law, public procurement and civil litigation. Paul graduated from the University of Amsterdam.

Brechje Nollen

Brechje Nollen is the head of the Amsterdam Employment, Pensions and Benefits group of Freshfields Bruckhaus Deringer LLP. Brechje was elected partner in 2008. Brechje specializes in all aspects of employment law including the employment, pension and benefits aspects of mergers, acquisitions and outsourcings, (collective) dismissals, executive remuneration and dismissals and works council matters. Brechje graduated from Utrecht University.

Jan Willem van der Staay

Jan Willem van der Staay is a partner in the corporate group of Freshfields Bruckhaus Deringer LLP, based in the Amsterdam office. He has wide experience in corporate practice, including internal investigations and specializes in mergers and acquisitions and corporate litigation. Jan Willem graduated from Utrecht University. He worked for the European Commission, the Dutch Ministry of Defence and the Dutch Ministry of Foreign Affairs from 1982 to 1984. He then joined the Dutch law firm Loeff & Van der Ploeg (later Loeff Claeys Verbeke), where he became a partner in 1990.

Max van Verschuer

Max van Verschuer is an associate in the corporate group of Freshfields Bruckhaus Deringer LLP, based in the Amsterdam office. Max specializes in mergers and acquisitions, securities laws and financial services. Max graduated from Groningen University.

Germany

Hanna Blanz

Hanna Blanz is an associate in the Frankfurt office of Freshfields Bruckhaus Deringer LLP. She is a member of the IP/IT practice group and specializes in the fields of data protection law, outsourcing, licensing and transaction related IP/IT issues. She studied law and German philology at the universities of Göttingen and Lausanne, Switzerland.

She spent part of her legal training in San Diego, California at the public legal prosecutor's office. After gaining her legal qualification, Hanna worked at the University of Bonn's Institute for Private and Comparative Law teaching foreign students of economics and social policies in the subjects of private, commercial and corporate law.

Alfried Heidbrink

Alfried Heidbrink, born 1964, studied law in Germany, Switzerland and the USA (in Bonn, Geneva and Miami respectively). He qualified as a German solicitor (*Rechtsanwalt*) in Germany in 1992. From 1992 to 2006, he practised law in the Frankfurt, New York and Berlin offices of Freshfields Bruckhaus Deringer LLP and its predecessor firms. Since 2006, he has been a partner at Lindenpartners in Berlin. His practise focuses on corporate and insolvency work as well as litigation. He has handled a number of complex internal investigations, including cases under the US Foreign Corrupt Practices Act.

Martina de Lind van Wijngaarden

Martina de Lind van Wijngaarden is a principal associate of Freshfields Bruckhaus Deringer LLP and works in the firm's Frankfurt office. She is a member of the dispute resolution practice group and specializes in financial services litigation and regulatory investigations.

She received her legal education at the universities of Passau, Cardiff and Münster. She worked as a research assistant at the University of Heidelberg, where she earned a Doctor of Laws (Dr iur) degree. She completed her Master of Laws (LLM) degree at the Columbia Law School, New York. She is admitted to the bars of Frankfurt and New York.

Anke Meier

Anke Meier studied law at the Ruhr University in Bochum, Germany, from which she holds a Phd degree (Dr iur) in legal history of insolvency law. From 2002 through 2007 she practised in the dispute resolution practice group of Freshfields Bruckhaus Deringer LLP, Düsseldorf, Germany. In 2006 she was seconded to Preston Gates & Ellis, Seattle, WA. She is currently an LLM candidate of Pepperdine University School of Law, Los Angeles, CA. Anke focuses on national and international arbitration and litigation. Her arbitration practice includes the representation of claimants as well as respondents in arbitration proceedings conducted under different rules such as ICC, Swiss, Uncitral, DIS, ad hoc. She advises clients in civil and commercial litigation matters, including securities litigation, products liability, and anti-trust related litigation. Her arbitration and litigation practice further focuses on international procedural law, amongst others, the international taking of evidence and recognition and enforcement of judgments and awards in foreign jurisdictions. Anke advises clients in the construction and energy sector as well as financial institutions and chemical industry enterprises.

Julia Strese

Julia Strese studied law at the universities of Heidelberg, Germany and Montpellier, France. She holds a Doctor of Laws degree from the University of Heidelberg and specializes in the fields of Civil Procedure, European and Private International Law.

Carolin Weide

Carolin Weide is a principal associate in the Düsseldorf office of Freshfields Bruckhaus Deringer LLP. She studied law at the University of Trier from 1995 to 2000. Between 2001 and 2003 she completed her legal traineeship (*Referendariat*) at the District Court of Duisburg. She specializes in litigation, contract law and (European) product liability and product safety law. She regularly advises on national and international product recalls, represents clients in civil proceedings and advises companies in building up a crisis management.

France

Jérémie Fierville

Avocat à la Cour, Jérémie Fierville joined Freshfields Bruckhaus Deringer LLP's dispute resolution group in September 2006, and was seconded for six months to the London office. He graduated from the University of Paris I Panthéon-Sorbonne (post-graduate degree in private international law and international commercial law), the University Paris II Panthéon-Assas (post-graduate degree in business law and tax), and from the French business school Ecole Supérieure des Sciences Economiques et Commerciales (ESSEC).

Elie Kleiman

Avocat à la Cour and Legal Consultant in the State of New York, Elie Kleiman is the head of the litigation team of the Paris office. Prior to joining the firm in August 2000, Elie was a partner in Jeantet & Associés, one of France's leading law firms, and was the managing partner of their New York office.

His experience includes advising and representing North American and European clients in complex international commercial disputes involving, in particular, corporate law, securities, M&A, joint ventures, banking, distribution, industrial risk and damage control, fraud and bankruptcy. He has trial experience before the courts of France and the European Court of Justice. Elie has significant experience in international commercial arbitration: he regularly acts as counsel in arbitral proceedings (including ICC and ICSID) and has also sat as an arbitrator. Elie graduated from the University of Paris X Nanterre (masters degree in private law) and the University of Paris II Panthéon-Assas (post-graduate degree in conflict of laws).

Pascale Lagesse

Pascale Lagesse is head of the employment, pensions and benefits (EPB) practice at Freshfields Bruckhaus Deringer LLP in Paris, which she set up in 2000. She advises on all aspects of employment law, including domestic plans, international and cross-border issues, and specializes in reorganization plans, collective redundancies, employees' representation, collective bargaining, employee share option plans, profit sharing schemes and international transfers (expatriation/secondment).

Pascale is an active member of various legal organizations, including the Conseil National des Barreaux (national bar council) to which she has been elected; International Bar Association, as vice-chair of the Employment and Industrial Relations Law Committee and editor of its Employment and Industrial Relations Law Newsletter from 2001 to 2005; Cercle Magellan (network of heads of human resources and international transfers) as an accredited expert; American Bar Association as a lecturer on discrimination, codes of ethics and whistle-blowing; the New York State Bar Association (NYSBA)—Chapter Chair (Paris), and European Lawyers Association. Pascale graduated from the University of Paris II (Maîtrise Carrières Judiciaires) and Paris I (DEA en Droit Privé).

Marine Lallemand

Avocat à la Cour, Marine Lallemand joined Freshfields Bruckhaus Deringer LLP's dispute resolution group in January 2005 after having spent three years as an associate in the litigation and arbitration group of a major American law firm's Paris office.

Marine has extensive experience in commercial dispute resolution (corporate law, shareholders agreements, joint ventures, commercial contracts) and financial services litigation. Her experience includes complex international commercial disputes and white collar crime. She advises investment managers and French companies in connection with sanction proceedings before the AMF (Autorité des Marchés Financiers). She graduated from the University of Paris II Panthéon-Assas (master's degree in private law), from the University René Descartes Paris V (post-graduate degree in private law) and also from the French business school HEC/ESCP-EAP (post-graduate degree in international law and management).

Nicolas Léger

Avocat à la Cour, Nicolas Léger joined Freshfields Bruckhaus Deringer LLP Paris in May 2005. Nicolas graduated from the University of Paris I Panthéon-Sorbonne (DEA en droit social and Doctorate). Nicolas has worked at the Paris Court of Appeal as a legal assistant and at the SCP Waquet-Farge-Hazan law firm in Paris. He taught labour law at the Universities Paris I, Paris VII and at the Institut d'Études Politiques of Paris and still teaches at the University Paris II.

Jérôme Philippe

Jérôme Philippe leads Freshfields Bruckhaus Deringer LLP's anti-trust, competition and trade (ACT) group in Paris. Before joining the firm in 2002, Jérôme was the head of the Office of Mergers and State Aids at the French competition authority (DGCCRF).

He primarily advises on French and EU merger control, cartel law, dominance cases, state aids and regulatory matters. He represents clients before the Conseil de la Concurrence, the DGCCRF, the European Commission, the European Court of Justice and French Courts. Jérôme has also been appointed as one of the non-governmental advisors for France to the International Competition Network (ICN).

In addition to being a lawyer, Jérôme received a PhD in economics from the University of Toulouse and also graduated as an engineer from Ecole Polytechnique and Ecole Nationale de la Statistique et de l'Administration Economique. He therefore has particular expertise in cases involving both legal and economic analyses.

Spain

Fernando Bedoya

Fernando Bedoya is an associate in the dispute resolution department of the Madrid office. He joined Freshfields Bruckhaus Deringer LLP in September 2005 and has completed four rotation periods in the tax, corporate, dispute resolution, and finance departments.

His practice covers advising both international and national clients with contentious and pre-contentious matters.

Fernando has a Degree in Law from Universidad Pontificia de Comillas (ICADE); a Degree in Business Administration obtained from Universidad Pontificia de Comillas (ICADE) and LUISS Guido Carli (Rome), and is a Member of the Madrid Bar.

Christian Castellá

Christian Castellá is a senior associate in the dispute resolution department in the Madrid office. Prior to joining Freshfields Bruckhaus Deringer LLP in March 2002, he worked in firms such as Baker & McKenzie where he acquired experience and know-how in the areas of commercial law, intellectual and industrial property.

His practice covers advising both international and national clients with contentious and non-contentious matters, relating to areas such as agency and distribution agreements, product liability, insurance claims and regulatory issues, including trade mark protection as well as unfair competition matters.

Christian has a Law Degree from the Universidad de Barcelona (Abad Oliba) (1996). He has a Masters Degree in Law from the Instituto de Empresa (Madrid, 1997) and an LLM in Intellectual Property from Queen Mary & Westfield College (London, 2000).

Rafael Murillo

Rafael Murillo is a partner in the dispute resolution department of Freshfields Bruckhaus Deringer LLP. He previously practised at the distinguished firm Hervada & Klingenberg.

Rafael specializes in the defence of both Spanish and foreign companies, in matters going before the courts and the arbitration authorities, as well as in pre-contentious matters. In particular he advises on contractual disputes and tort.

With a wealth of experience in public law, he has advised company groups and federations, as well as individual companies, on contesting administrative acts and provisions, and on the preparation of new regulations.

Rafael Murillo graduated in Law at the Universidad Pontificia de Comillas (ICADE).

Additional contributors include Raquel Florez, Javier Bau and Sergio Miralles.

Italy

Fabrizio Arossa

Fabrizio Arossa has acted or advised in connection with some of the most important financial scandals in Italy, also involving investigations, including the Ferruzzi-Montedison case in the 1990s and the Cirio-Del Monte and Parmalat cases in 2003 to 2004.

Fabrizio was educated in Italy, France and the USA. He was admitted to the Bar (Italy) in 1987 (Supreme Court, 2000) and has also been an adjunct professor of international trade and business law. He has been a partner of Freshfields Bruckhaus Deringer LLP since 1997.

Giovanni Barone

Giovanni Barone is an associate within the anti-trust department of the Rome office of Freshfields Bruckhaus Deringer LLP. He is involved in all aspects of anti-trust law, with particular reference to cartel proceedings (before both the European Commission and the Italian Anti-trust Authority), abuses of dominant position, state aids, merger control and competition-related litigation before civil and administrative courts.

Before joining Freshfields in 2004, he worked for a leading law firm in Turin as well as being an assistant professor in international and EU law at the University of Turin. He graduated in law (JD, summa cum laude) at the University of Turin in 2003, also attending periods of study at Georgetown University Law School (Washington DC) and McGill University (Montréal). In 2003, he won the Freshfields Prize as the Best Italian law student of the year. He was admitted to the Italian Bar in 2006.

Grazia Bonante

Grazia Bonante is a Rome based associate at Freshfields Bruckhaus Deringer LLP specializing in banking, financial markets and insurance law and regularly advises Italian and foreign intermediaries and institutions in connection with regulatory aspects of their activities and on financial and corporate law transactions.

She was involved in some of the major banking and financial transactions in the last years (including the Unicredit-HVB and San Paolo-Intesa aggregations and the acquisition of control of Borsa Italiana by the London Stock Exchange). She is member of the Legal Certainty Sub-group for the drafting of the directive on Clearing and Settlement.

She graduated in law (JD, summa cum laude) from the University of Rome 'La Sapienza' and is admitted to the Italian Bar. She graduated also from 'Universidad Complutense' of Madrid (Erasmus Programme) and holds a masters (LLM) in corporate and commercial law and law of international finance from the Queen Mary and Westfield College.

Andrea Marega

Andrea Marega is an Italian qualified lawyer at Freshfields Bruckhaus Deringer LLP based in the Rome office. He is a member of the Anti-trust, Competition and Trade group, in which context he is involved in most aspects of anti-trust law as well as in regulatory issues related to public utilities sectors. He gained experience as a trainee at the European Commission in Brussels, DG Information Society and Media, where he cooperated in the enforcement of a European policy of public procurement of R&D. He also worked as a trainee at the Italian Antitrust Authority in Rome, TLC Unit, being mainly involved in anti-trust cases in electronic communication sectors and misleading and comparative advertising issues. Before joining Freshfields Bruckhaus Deringer LLP in October 2007 he worked in an Italian law firm, dealing with local public services, public procurement contracts and competition law.

He graduated in law (magna cum laude) from the University of Pisa, also carrying out a period of study at University Carlos III Madrid (2001–2002). His thesis was awarded, by the Public Institute of Administrative Studies 'Umberto Borsi', the best thesis of the year 2004 in Administrative law competing against students at the University of Bologna, Firenze, Pisa and Siena. He then completed a Master of laws in company law at the University of Bologna. He is currently a PhD student in the public law of economics at the University of Pisa. He was admitted to the Italian Bar in 2007.

Elena Pagnoni

Elena Pagnoni is a senior associate at Freshfields Bruckhaus Deringer LLP specializing in corporate, securities and finance law. Her experience includes advising the primary business banks, financial intermediaries and insurance companies, both foreign and Italian.

Before joining the firm she worked for CONSOB for six years. She is the author of several publications on the subject, an editor of Previdenza e Assistenza pubblica e privata Law Journal and is often invited to give presentations in her field of practice.

She graduated in law (JD, summa cum laude) from the 'Libera Università Internazionale degli Studi Sociali' (LUISS) of Rome. She received a Master of Law Degree (LLM) from Harvard University.

Maria Tecla Rodi

Maria Tecla Rodi is a Rome-based associate at Freshfields Bruckhaus Deringer LLP. She specializes in corporate, banking and financial services law, advising on major M&A transactions in the banking and insurance sectors. Her experience includes participation in the team working on the business combination transaction between Unicredit and HVB-Hypovereinsbank.

She graduated in law (JD, summa cum laude) from the University of Rome 'La Sapienza' and was admitted to the Italian Bar.

Hong Kong

Patrick Swain

Patrick is a partner based in the Commercial Disputes Group of Freshfields Bruckhaus Deringer LLP, now based in London. Patrick has practised in London,

New York and, recently, for ten years in Hong Kong where he built up the Asia dispute resolution capability. He has extensive experience in a wide range of commercial disputes and investigations including advising clients on commercial fraud claims, M&A related and other shareholder disputes, contentious insolvency and professional negligence litigation.

His recent experience includes advising the majority of shareholders on cross-border litigation concerning control of a major investment in Vietnam; advising a major professional services organization in a SEC investigation focusing, in particular, on a major European jurisdiction; advising a US sportswear manufacturer in asset tracing and recovery litigation against former executives and associated entities and individuals; and carrying out an investigation into a principal investment fund involving issues of fraud and breach of fiduciary duty.

Patrick was educated at Corpus Christi College, Oxford and has appeared before Courts and tribunals in England and Wales and in Hong Kong at all levels and in New York, Singapore and in the Cayman Islands. He has been a partner since 2001. The same year he was appointed a member of the Hong Kong Chief Justice's Working Party reporting on Access to Justice.

Peter Yuen

Peter Yuen is based in the Hong Kong office of Freshfields Bruckhaus Deringer LLP. He advises regularly on a range of commercial disputes including China-related business disputes, regulatory and corporate compliance related investigations, banking related litigation, IP-related disputes and professional negligence litigation. He has acted for clients in High Court proceedings in Hong Kong, court proceedings in China as well as arbitration proceedings (both ad hoc and institutional) in a variety of venues.

Before studying law in England, Peter read chemistry at Oxford University, and he was a teaching fellow at Cornell University. He joined Freshfields in 1996, and is qualified as a solicitor in England and Wales and in Hong Kong.

Japan

Masashi Adachi

Masashi Adachi is counsel at Paul, Weiss, Rifkind, Wharton & Garrison LLP, LLM. He attended New York University School of Law (1993), MCJ, New York University School of Law (1992), BL, Tokyo University (1983), and is an editor of the New York University School of Law Journal of International Law and Politics; Practice Area; Corporate.

Masahide Fukuda

Masahide Fukuda is an associate at Freshfields Bruckhaus Deringer LLP Tokyo. Educated at the University of Tokyo, he specializes in M&A, general corporate, regulatory matters, and dispute resolution (especially corporate litigations).

Kazuki Okada

Kazuki Okada is a partner at Freshfields Bruckhaus Deringer LLP Tokyo. He was educated at Hitotsubashi University. He specializes in labour law, financial regulatory law and anti-trust law and is a lecturer at Hitotsubashi Law School.

Kaori Yamada

Kaori Yamada is an Associate at Freshfields Bruckhaus Deringer LLP Tokyo. She was educated at the University of Tokyo (Bachelor of Law), University of Oxford (Queen's College, MJuris), and London School of Economics (LLM). She specializes in competition law, M&A and general corporate matters.

Akiko Yamakawa

Akiko Yamakawa is senior counsel at Freshfields Bruckhaus Deringer LLP Tokyo. She was educated at the University of Tokyo and Harvard Law School (LLM). She specializes in financial regulatory matters, dispute resolution, employment law and anti-trust matters.

Additional contributors include Ryo Suzuki, Mieko Hosaka, Lisa Yano and Jennifer L Raisor.

INTRODUCTION[1]

It's 4pm on a Friday afternoon and your phone rings. The Chief Financial Officer, based in Germany, has noticed an unusual number of product returns from the company's Japanese customers, and a whistle-blower has been hinting at irregular business practices in that business. This is of particular concern because the CFO did not realize that the products at issue had a right of return, the CEO has had a difficult relationship with the business manager responsible for the Japanese market, and the company, which recently started trading depository receipts on the New York Stock Exchange, is scheduled to release its quarterly financial results in ten days.

The questions come fast and furious. How does the company figure out the number of returns, whether it is material, and whether something unlawful has happened? Should there be an investigation and, if so, who should undertake it? Will the review be privileged? What should the scope of the investigation be? Who should supervise it? Does the company need to be concerned about preserving documents? Are there laws that limit the company's ability to review the business manager's email, or to discipline him if there is a problem? Will the investigation delay the company's ability to issue its quarterly financial report? When should the Board of Directors or the Audit Committee of the Board be alerted to the issues? When should the company's external auditors be contacted? When does the company have an obligation to report the issue to the UK or US regulators, or to the company's shareholders? In short, how serious a problem is it?

This scenario, or something very similar to it, is increasingly familiar to general counsel and to those lawyers who represent public companies. The legal issues presented by corporate clients are increasingly multi-jurisdictional, as clients push to sell products and provide services all over the world. At the same time, the legal regimes that apply to international corporate conduct remain, to a very large extent, local in nature.

---

[1] Contributors: Paul Lomas and Daniel Kramer.

1

We wrote this book to help counsel, both in-house and at private law firms, take a broad, cross-border perspective in advising public companies that undertake internal investigations of potentially illegal, unethical or regulation infringing conduct. For many of our clients, the world has shrunk, as they raise capital, sell products and provide services in numerous countries around the globe more frequently and on a greater scale. As a consequence, in conducting internal investigations, we are increasingly called upon to consider legal issues and cultural norms in multiple jurisdictions. The process is becoming of steadily greater complexity and importance. In this introduction, we seek to identify some of the themes that have accompanied these developments.

When conducted properly, internal investigations are an effective means for management or the Board to learn quickly about potential illegal conduct by employees and to formulate an appropriate legal strategy. An internal investigation can reassure the corporation's various constituencies that the company is properly addressing its problems. It can recommend changes to prevent a reoccurrence of problematic conduct. It can also help ensure that companies receive lenient treatment from regulators. Of course, there are perils as well, and an investigation that is not properly thought through, or is poorly executed, can create more problems than it solves. For companies that operate in multiple jurisdictions, this means that the attorney conducting the investigation must also understand the nuances of the legal requirements in each country.

As we discuss in Chapter 3, the most highly regulated and legally developed country, in this respect, is the United States (US). These issues have been in development there for a long time. However, in the wake of the stock market decline that followed the burst of the dot-com bubble at the turn of the century, and the exposure of fraudulent activity at major companies such as Enron and World-Com, Congress, the Department of Justice (DoJ), state prosecutors, the Securities and Exchange Commission (SEC) and the US stock exchanges all responded with significant changes in legislation and rules governing corporate conduct intended to deter fraud and bring greater transparency to corporate decision-making and accountability to corporate managers, thereby bringing about a noticeable change in the environment.

The stakes have increased tremendously. The SEC, D of J and State Attorneys General have become more active in the past decade, expanding their resources and aggressively pursuing corporate officers, directors and general counsels and even the corporate entity itself. Fines can run into hundreds of millions of dollars for the largest companies with the most substantial problems. Individual offenders have received jail sentences that are measured in decades. And all of this has occurred against a backdrop of related private, civil litigation in the US that has cost companies millions of dollars to defend and billions of dollars to settle.

Although the reverse is sometimes seen, it is generally the regulators that have been driving this process, with the civil litigation following close in the wake. The increased vigilance and vigour of all the regulators have dramatically changed the risk profile of companies in the US and the circumstances in which, and frequency with which, they turn to investigations.

The US has been in the forefront of the trends that have led corporations to conduct internal investigations and to cooperate with governmental inquiries, but the procedures in the US are constantly evolving themselves. The pendulum recently has swung in the US from a general assessment, post-Enron, that there had to be more regulation and greater cooperation with regulators, to an emerging sense, more recently, that some of the regulations may need to be fine-tuned as they are too blunt to effect the desired changes, and may be too expensive and too intrusive.

At the same time, countries in Europe have been watching the American experience, and adopting some of the American approaches to internal investigations; to a greater extent in the UK and Germany, and a lesser extent in countries like Italy and Spain. Countries in Asia are just beginning to address these issues. This trend of learning from, and adopting aspects of, the American model is likely to accelerate as the capital markets become more and more global and more uniform. As this occurs, there will be higher expectations regarding the ethical standards for corporate conduct and the need for more independent and penetrating internal investigations to detect and remedy instances of fraudulent conduct.

It would be wrong to characterize the US as being the source of all technology in this field, either for regulators or companies, in terms of how they react to issues that might require an investigation. However, inevitably, the volume of cases and the sophistication of the parties involved have led to a deep experience there. Other countries are tending to encounter the inherent issues a little later. When this happens, a look at the US experience may not give the answer to a given problem, but it will almost certainly highlight the issues that are going to have to be explored under local law. Usually they will have been ventilated, if not, indeed, litigated, in the context of a US problem.

Regulators outside the US have made significant changes across recent years, while retaining their own, distinctive expectations about the appropriate response to suggestions of fraudulent conduct or regulatory infringement. As we discuss in the chapters that follow, similar trends, therefore, are seen, although attenuated, in other jurisdictions. Other regulators have been reluctant to allow the regulatory agenda to be set entirely by the US authorities. They have been learning from US experience, reacting to international treaties (like the OECD Anti-bribery Convention[2]) which are seeking to harmonize global standards, and responding to the changing policy imperatives of their own governments.

The precise details of how those regulators have been extending their powers vary by country. However, the uniform trend has been towards greater and more invasive regulatory powers, more comprehensive regulation, more adversarial treatment of companies and tougher sanctions. This has also led to changing regulatory relationships between companies and the agencies as they seek to come to terms with the evolving environment. This trend is marked. It is seen in all jurisdictions over the past ten years including such areas as financial markets, anti-trust, criminal behaviour, environmental issues and, increasingly, tax.

While the regulatory schemes in each country are distinct and independent, they are related and many countries follow closely the regulatory changes taking place around the world. For example, the requirements of the Sarbanes-Oxley Act of 2002 are widely discussed in boardrooms outside of the US, and its dictates often serve as the scale on which new regulation regarding corporate conduct is weighed. As discussed in Chapter 2, the standards of the most exigent relevant regime tend to dictate the approach that a multinational company must take in other jurisdictions.

Whether one views these changes as important advances in support of good corporate governance, excesses of ill-advised reforms, or something in between, they have imposed greater accountability for corporate conduct on company management, and increased their responsibility to prevent, detect, and deter unlawful practices. One of the principal tools that these corporate guardians increasingly use to fulfil their responsibilities, and to mitigate fines and penalties, is to initiate internal investigations to identify and address wrongdoing. This, in turn, has driven a growing need for lawyers who are skilled at conducting corporate internal investigations, and who can develop a comprehensive and sensible response to the issues facing the client. The increasing internationalization of corporate activities, and of any problems that emerge with it, requires those lawyers to be able to navigate the rules and expectations of regulators and courts in different jurisdictions, as well as ensuring that the investigation does not run foul of local laws on issues as diverse as self-reporting, export of confidential data, privacy, and employee rights.

---

[2] The OECD Convention on Combating Bribery of Foreign Public Officials in International Business Transactions.

Moreover, as investigations dig deeper, and regulators' expectations expand, these issues surface more often and in a more sophisticated fashion. This means that the lawyers involved in such exercises must constantly deepen and broaden their international skills.

For example, in an issue as mundane, but as important, as document collection, the substantive laws and the expectations of clients and their employees differ substantially from one country to another. They will often affect the scope of the documents the investigator is able to collect, the decision regarding where the documents should be reviewed, and whether relevant documents may be transported outside of the country of origin.

There is also a much greater use by regulators, and in internal investigations, of detailed document searches. This is a natural consequence of the value of email and IT meta-data information in establishing who was doing what, when and to whom. Regulators, lawyers and litigants are increasingly using sophisticated analytical tools in this area, including IT-based relevance and clustering software, to sort and order the vast amount of data that is available. Frequently, key search terms are agreed with regulators. This trend—the increasing importance of mining useful information from large document searches—will continue and will become more complicated. It is absolutely crucial that investigative counsel are experts in this area and up to date with the leading IT products. It is extremely dangerous if other parties, including regulators, have greater skills in this respect.

Conflicting statutes and a variety of cultural mores must often be considered in deciding when, and how, to interview company officers, employees and agents, and in determining how the company should treat persons suspected of wrongdoing. However, under the time pressures present in many international investigations (and with an increasing expectation that investigations will be conducted to equivalent levels of due diligence), some cultural sensitivities are having to give way to the exigencies either of 'head office' or of a foreign regulator. Thus, another trend is the slow harmonization, to a more invasive standard, of the expectations of employees in connection with investigations and the way in which the employees interact with their employer in such circumstances.

Regulators around the world also have different, and at times conflicting, views regarding whether and when companies should report to government officials suspicions of improper conduct, and the degree of transparency the company should allow the regulator into the workings and findings of the investigation. However, the success of, particularly, (i) the anti-trust leniency regimes in the EU and US and (ii) the requirements of financial service regulators to require self-reporting at an early stage of knowledge are informing regulators generally.

Where a matter touches the EU (generally in an anti-trust matter but also in some states in other matters) or the US in anti-trust or some wider regulatory, or particularly, criminal respects, the 'cooperation' guidelines or leniency rules have led many companies to self-report indications of potentially improper conduct at a very early stage. As a result, prompt self-reporting, and the culture associated with it, is becoming more common.

Moreover, capital markets and shareholders are changing their expectations of the governance standards of companies: more emphasis is being placed on companies 'doing the right thing' when faced with difficult situations, which often manifests itself in pressure to report issues early. Coupled with this, companies are developing more sophisticated relationships with regulators to provide the context in which such reports can be given. However, self-reporting cannot take place (and is actively dangerous) without a sufficient internal investigation to be confident that no one is being misled. Early self-reporting can easily result in incorrect information being transmitted at the beginning of an investigation when there is, inevitably, a fair amount of confusion and the facts, which seemed to be well settled, may well have been misunderstood. Accordingly, there must be a high degree of caution to avoid confusing or misleading any party to whom a report is made, including capital markets. This requires sensitive handling and a degree of transparency, including being prepared to admit uncertainties.

Finally, there is an established trend towards greater cooperation between regulators around the globe. This cooperation exhibits itself in cross-border assistance between governments that are investigating, prosecuting and settling the conduct that is the subject of investigations. It has generated a worldwide discussion regarding the degree to which corporations are expected to investigate and remediate their internal problems and the extent to which they will receive credit from regulators for taking those steps and sharing their internal reviews.

It is worth noting that, in the US, investigation practices have started to become more standardized, and a consensus is beginning to form on best practices in corporate internal investigations. We expect that the same phenomenon will occur in the UK and in continental Europe and, eventually, in Asia. All of this requires that lawyers and their clients stay on top of this area of practice so they can understand how the rules are developing and can achieve results that are appropriate in this multi-jurisdictional melange.

This book identifies the principal issues companies face in internal investigations within different jurisdictions. It suggests some concrete ways for working through the issues. We also hope that it will contribute to the ongoing discussion on global best practices for corporate internal investigations.

First, in Chapter 1, we provide an overview of managing multi-jurisdictional investigations. This chapter addresses, from an international perspective, issues regarding the organization of the investigation, data collection, protection and review, reporting issues, regulatory coordination, capital market issues, and privilege and waiver issues. In Chapter 2, we specifically consider certain issues of data protection (which are partially harmonized across Europe).

We then present a series of more detailed chapters on the laws and practices of different countries, and the concerns that may arise if investigations involve that jurisdiction. This includes separate chapters on the United States, the United Kingdom, Germany, Holland, France, Spain, Italy, Japan and Hong Kong.

Finally, in the Annexes we have proposed some short summaries of the practical points to consider in the areas of: initiating an investigation; disclosure obligations; privilege; document preservation; employee management; and publicity, drawing on the common themes of the preceding chapters.

We hope that this book will provide a useful desk reference for practitioners dealing with internal investigations particularly in an international context. With any luck, the next time a CFO calls you at 4pm on a Friday afternoon you will be ready and able to address the crisis with a comprehensive approach that takes into account the multi-jurisdictional issues that call raises.

Paul Lomas
Freshfields Bruckhaus Deringer LLP, London

Daniel J Kramer
Paul Weiss Rifkind Wharton & Garrison LLP, New York

1

INVESTIGATIONS WITH AN INTERNATIONAL DIMENSION

A. Introduction[1]

Three of the trends that have significantly affected risk (ignoring, for a moment, **1.01** US civil litigation risk[2]) for large companies over the past ten years are:

- the degree to which regulators not only have increased powers but cooperate with each other in the application of those powers to a particular company or practice which is of concern—ie globalization of the regulator regime;
- the increasing use of severe sanctions, particularly of a criminal or quasi-criminal nature, to control corporate behaviour; and
- the changing ethical environment and the expectations of 'stake-holders' as to corporate behaviour and as to what represents acceptable levels of governance in entities that are of increasing power and impact on all aspects of economic and social life.

Despite these factors increasing corporate risk, public and regulatory perception **1.02** has been that some companies, at least in some jurisdictions, continue to engage in infringing, and sometimes criminal, behaviour. It is unclear whether such continuing conduct is due to ignorance by those involved; a perception that the risks

---

[1] Contributor: Paul Lomas.
[2] However, the kinds of events that give rise to investigations will usually, if there is a sufficient connection with the USA, raise the risk of related US civil litigation.

of detection are small; or competitive and profit pressures incentivizing those involved to take the risks: in reality, it will be a mix of all three.

1.03   In some jurisdictions (Italy is an example), the reaction of the regulators has been a combination of being prepared to use large sanctions where they can and a clearly signalled expectation that companies should 'put their house in order'. The combination of the facts that (i) corporate behaviour is still often far from compliant; (ii) the invasive requirements of governance and regulators are increasing; and (iii) regulators have expectations that companies should be more proactive in taking affirmative responsibility for addressing their internal issues effectively; mean that the demand for internal investigations is set to increase. These factors come together particularly forcefully when one considers investigations with an international dimension.

1.04   In such cases, a wide variety of the issues addressed in the chapters that follow interact in a way that substantially complicates the picture and may, on occasions, produce conflicts. Those conflicts may go beyond simply tensions as to what is desirable in different jurisdictions into the area where compliance with obligations in one jurisdiction may actually create difficulties with legal obligations in another.

1.05   It is, clearly, not possible to cover all the possible permutations of issues and jurisdictions. However, there are some themes that are frequently encountered, and which can usefully be analysed, which provide indications as to how these matters can be addressed generally.

1.06   Albeit something of a sweeping generalization, it is nevertheless highly material that there is a steady convergence not only of the expectations of regulators but also those of wider stakeholders that companies will be applying consistent ethical and behavioural standards around the world. The idea that a company, particularly one with major global brands, can take the stance that a practice which is prohibited or unacceptable in its home jurisdiction, or in others where it has a major economic presence, is nevertheless appropriate in a given local environment is becoming increasingly unsustainable.

1.07   This is, perhaps, particularly the case in such general areas as corruption and related business practices, anti-trust or anti-competitive behavioural issues (there are increasingly few regions that do not have competition law requirements that are substantively aligned with EU/US standards), environmental standards, know your customer rules and control of the quality of counterparties. The proposition is perhaps less true in relation to highly regulated markets (like financial markets) where it may well be acceptable to follow a locally legitimate trading pattern even though it may be prohibited elsewhere. However, in relation to more general ethical and behavioural areas, the issue readily devolves to one of the integrity and quality of senior management, for example:

- did they know what was going on;
- if not why not;
- if they did, what view should regulators and stakeholders take of management that will permit behaviour that is unacceptable in their major markets because they think that they can 'get away with it' in local markets; and
- what does that say about their general approach to the business and the 'culture' of the organization?

From an investigation viewpoint, this has important implications. International **1.08** investigations need to consider what thresholds they should apply to behaviour: local; overall 'normalized' corporate standards; or world leading best practice. It also means that the management and control of the investigation process has to ensure that the quality of the investigation itself is aligned with the standard that the company sets for its behaviour generally. This does not necessarily mean direct head office control; but it will usually mean some supervision from an appropriately senior level in the company to ensure that the results are sensitive to these issues. This needs to be borne in mind when considering the issues discussed in this chapter.

B. Organization of an International Investigation

An international investigation must have one single point of management and **1.09** control. Without that, the process is likely to be chaotic and the output and conclusions may not be credible or reliable. Accordingly, it is important from the outset to decide the location from which it is to be led, and the individual who is to be accountable for it. This applies both to the overall strategic direction and to the day-to-day operational management.

Where a problem is potentially sufficiently serious, the location of that internal **1.10** accountability should usually be the audit committee or the management board, or a member of some such similar body involved in the governance of the company, one of the directors (usually an independent director) or any of the statutory watchdogs contemplated by some continental European jurisdictions, such as an Italian board of statutory auditors or the supervisory body. However, not all issues require that 'weight' and it may well be that responsibility can be allocated at a lower level in the organization, usually within the legal, compliance or internal audit function. Moreover, there are examples, which can work very successfully, of the appointment of a senior executive from an unrelated part of the business, perhaps with a taskforce, to address the issue in hand on behalf of the company.

1.11   The political reality is that, in an international investigation, there is likely to be defensive behaviour, whether between operating divisions, or, as is frequently the case, within business units in differing countries. Political sensitivities also arise when the company consists of formerly separate entities which have come together as a result of mergers or in the case of a joint venture. Such defensive behaviour can be extremely disruptive to the efficient conduct of an investigation, delaying the production of documents and the availability of witnesses, slowing the process and reducing the quality of the output. For example, where a company does not have a fully integrated email or document management system, it may not be physically possible to obtain the necessary data without physical access (never mind consent) to the IT systems of a particular subsidiary. It is surprising how long seemingly fulsome commitments to cooperation can take to turn into actual delivery of data. This tendency is common where businesses have grown by acquisition and there is not a uniform culture or sufficient degree of trust internally.

1.12   The natural concerns that any investigation can be used as a witch hunt, or to settle 'old scores', or as a lever to bring about other changes, become exacerbated in such circumstances. These are essentially management, and not legal, issues, but they require careful handling since they can significantly hamper, or even frustrate, an investigation. It is usually the case that such issues need to be addressed by a mixture of:

- strong commitment from a high level in the organization to a successful and properly resourced investigation;

- vesting appropriate authority in those concerned and making it plain, in sensitive terms, that undermining the investigation would be serious misconduct;

- bilateral conversations with those executives in charge of the business units that might be the sources of dysfunctional behaviour to ensure that they are brought 'on-side' and are supportive—and then also supported, as necessary;

- making plain, in the cultural context, that effective resolution of difficult issues is a necessary part of business life in successful and ethical organizations and that professional management does and should participate fully in such exercises, which should improve the quality of the business in which they all work; and

- ensuring that the investigation's conduct and modus operandi, and the messaging associated with it, clearly show that it is an independent and objective process and will not be used for political ends by any part of the organization, including senior management.

1.13   Once the right governance framework has been set for an investigation, it is important to consider the necessary operational aspects. Although the detailed processes will reflect the issues raised in the various national chapters discussed below (particularly in the UK and US sections), it is frequently the case in international cases that the flow of data is considerably larger (and may well give rise to language and translation issues). It is, therefore, particularly critical that there is a clear, organized and observed system for collecting information, across the various organizations involved, and holding it in one central location.

The data is usually held in a single database. Frequently, it will be in an external **1.14** law firm or outside vendor/service provider since they tend to have the technical and human resources (the demands can be considerable) to organize such an operation. It is extremely difficult to build chronologies, to analyse relationships, to create scenarios, to prepare the documentary evidence necessary for discussion with witnesses etc unless there is a single database.

Such a system is also fundamental for responding comprehensively to regulatory **1.15** enquiries. These enquiries may have short time frames, come from different sources and cut across each other. A well run investigation responds effectively to these requests, having the capability to produce accurate and complete responses and to maintain an audit trail of disclosures, by regulator, for the proper ongoing management of the regulatory relationship.

Ideally, the technology permits input direct from the various countries involved. **1.16** The ability to add know-how and secondary information into the database and to integrate it with the document management system for the project can be invaluable. In an investigation having a truly international dimension, a further important consideration is how to convert various documents made in respective local languages into a database in one common language (English in most cases) carefully but efficiently. One of the major challenges in a large investigation (as in a substantial piece of litigation) is how to extract the key story from a great deal of detailed and fine grained information where no one individual is familiar with all the material. The team organization and the IT systems must interoperate to make this process as effective as possible.

There are certain confidentiality and other benefits from having the evidential **1.17** material assembled in a law firm in a privileged relationship with the company. The degree of protection that is available to documents against regulatory attack varies across countries, but it is generally the case (particularly in civil law jurisdictions) that there is a particularly high degree of protection accorded to documents in the possession of outside lawyers.

An issue that is frequently of concern is whether, despite the value of a **1.18** single database, it is risky, in terms of a potential defence, to move documents into a jurisdiction where they may be more vulnerable to seizure or disclosure in any litigation. This is a judgement to be exercised on the specific facts. However, the following factors are usually relevant.

- Civil law jurisdictions do not generally have a discovery process or disclosure process. To the extent that they do, documents in the possession of external lawyers may be protected by the legal secrecy/privilege requirements as in the case of Spain or Italy—but this is not the case in Germany, where the protection only extends to documents that are subject to what is, in effect, client/attorney privilege.

- England and the US have a control-based test for disclosure,[3] rather than a strict geographic test. Analytically, the location of the documents is irrelevant—although caution in this area is common ('why take any risk?'). Theoretically, however, there is also the issue of whether assembling a database brings documents under the ultimate control of a different entity, say one lower down the corporate structure, which is, itself, likely to be the subject of litigation when the original controller of the documents was not. This is, in practice, a rather unusual circumstance, but may pertain to certain cases.[4] To the extent that this is not an issue, however, there is no reason why a database cannot be assembled in England or the US.

C. Self-reporting Issues

1.19 A clear and immediate tension arises on the threshold issue of self-reporting. Whilst, as discussed in the Introduction, the culture is progressively changing around the world, there are still big differences in the regulatory requirements associated with self-reporting. Perhaps more importantly, there are differences in the expectations, short of legal or regulatory requirements, as to whether it is attractive tactically or ethically for a company voluntarily to self-report.

1.20 This is critical because self-reporting is usually an immediate, or at least very early, decision. There is, generally, no retreat from a decision to self-report. It will strongly control the company's strategy on all future regulatory issues, and many other matters, including the litigation exposure.

1.21 A company must, moreover, proceed on the basis that self-reporting to one regulator constitutes self-reporting to all. With the exception, perhaps, of suspicious transaction reports under money laundering and anti-corruption legislation (which tend to be more of an administrative process), the working assumption has to be that

---

[3] *Lonrho Ltd v Shell Petroleum Co* [1982] AC 173.
[4] *Schlumberger Holdings Limited v Electromagnetic Geoservices AS* [2008] EWHC 56 (Pat), unreported.

regulators both within and across jurisdictions will communicate with each other, if not the actual text of any submissions or reports, the gist of the issue.

As described below, the gateways for the disclosure of information both within a **1.22** jurisdiction and internationally are generally very wide. There is very little inhibition on disclosures that are genuinely for the proper purposes of the relevant agencies' duties. Any corporate problem which is more general in scope, and particularly one that gives rise to issues regarding the integrity of the company and its management, is likely ultimately to be the subject of discussions at the regulatory level. Those discussions may not take place immediately but are likely, at some stage, to involve a consideration of whether a particular issue merits the allocation of internal resources by another regulator.

In the anti-trust field, self-reporting is essentially an issue of voluntarily seeking **1.23** leniency or amnesty. Almost invariably if a company faced with infringements in a multi-jurisdictional context seeks leniency in any one jurisdiction, it will be doing so in many. It will usually do so as close to simultaneously as it can, for technical reasons associated with the priority that it obtains by being first and the risks of prejudicing that position if information leaks. The principal exception to this approach is in the rare situation of an infringement operating only within the EU where there is a certainty that the European Commission will be the only regulator that will exercise jurisdiction over the matter.

Moreover, any disclosure to a regulator runs the risk of publicity, in due course, **1.24** leading to the risk of wider regulatory action at that later stage. Finally, it is usually regarded as simply not credible for a company to announce that it is cooperating with regulators in one country, but not to make the same commitment in relation to other jurisdictions.

The tension then arises where there is (i) a potential for there to be regulatory **1.25** interest in a country that has a strong expectation of voluntary self-reporting but (ii) a much stronger likelihood of penalties in a jurisdiction where there is no such tradition. An example might be a potential corruption issue for the Italian subsidiary of a US company.

As described below, a common reaction in the US would be to self-report, to **1.26** launch an effective investigation, to deal with matters as appropriate and to report the conclusions and actions to the Department of Justice (DoJ) or the Securities and Exchange Commission (SEC). In Italy, the culture has been different; regulators and prosecutors do not generally expect self-reporting; there are not the same regulatory benefits as in the US. Whilst the substantive internal actions may be the same for both the senior Italian and US management (cease the practice, take disciplinary action etc), the consequences of two different systems will differ. In the US, the self-reporting may well lead to a process that can be largely handled through internal investigation and the relationship with the regulator, albeit possibly leading to penalties. In Italy, the result of the US self-reporting may well be an external criminal investigation into the business with considerable disruption to it, impact on reputation and on business performance, quite apart from the issue of prosecution of those involved. Had the Italian management been able to conduct the matter under the usual procedures in Italy, the problem might well have been resolved in exactly the same way internally, in terms of remedial steps for the future, but without the same exposure for the past. This distinction can, self-evidently, cause enormous internal tensions (including engaging the personal exposure of individuals). It requires extremely sophisticated and well-considered responses from management.

D. Regulatory Coordination

1.27 The phenomenon of regulatory coordination goes beyond the simple transmission of information between regulators and the concerns associated with self-reporting into the active coordination between regulators. It also applies both to the allocation of responsibility and resources to deal with international problems and to the joint investigation and resolution (ie prosecution) of particular problems. It is almost a uniform refrain from regulatory agencies that this is (i) beneficial and (ii) set to increase further.

1.28 In some cases, the structure for this coordination is institutional. A classic example is the European Competition Network of the national competition authorities of the EC member states and the European Commission established under the modernization regime.[5] However, equally important are:

- the various associations of securities regulators looking at major issues affecting the securities markets; and
- the activities of the Organization for Economic Cooperation and Development which are particularly relevant in the anti-corruption field.

However, coordination is also happening at informal and bilateral levels with joint meetings, secondments of staff, exchange of data and the like. The authors have experienced regulators being quite open that their decision as to whether or not to take an interest in a matter would depend on discussions with another regulator in which context they would review each others' evidence to obtain a common understanding and then consider the priorities of, political pressures on, and resources available to, each before discussing which of them might pursue a particular topic.

---

[5] Council Regulation (EC) No 01/2003 of 16 December 2002.

A number of the most prominent corporate scandals of recent years have been the **1.29** subject of overt coordinated regulatory behaviour. Examples include:

- the joint resolution by the SEC and the FSA of the allegations against Shell in relation to the disclosures of its gas reserves. A solution was agreed with both regulators in a single process, concluded in London and then jointly announced;

- the coordinated announcement of early resolution of anti-trust investigations by the OFT and the DoJ against British Airways and Virgin in relation to the fuel surcharges price fixing and the coordinated criminal prosecutions in the marine hose cartel; and

- the coordination between the various criminal authorities around the world in relation to the United Nations Oil for Food corruption allegations and the arrangements whereby the criminal authorities for the home states of the various companies identified in the Report of the Independent Inquiry into the United Nations Oil for Food Programme (the 'Volcker Report') would decide how to take responsibility for investigating whether there had been corruption in relation to trading with Iraq under the programme.

This degree of coordination means that a 'divide and rule' strategy for addressing **1.30** the interests of regulators, if, indeed, it were ever very attractive, is becoming, increasingly, rarely of any relevance. Rather, what is needed is a coherent strategy which considers the actual or potential interests of the various regulators.

Such a strategy has always to take specific account of the likely approach **1.31** of US regulators given their resources and powers, particularly to project their activities and interests outside the borders of the US when there is the necessary relationship with matters of interest to them. However, one of the effects of the increasing degree of regulatory activity elsewhere in the world by non-US regulators (and the enhanced powers, and aggressive use of those powers in some areas, to impose very substantial fines) in that any such assessment has to be increasingly sensitive to the non-US exposure. Whilst criminal sanctions still lag behind US standards, in the anti-trust and financial areas the differentials are reducing if not disappeared.

Accordingly, one of the critical aspects of an international investigation, whether **1.32** in the context of regulatory action somewhere in the world or conducted on a wholly internal basis for governance reasons, is to consider what a balanced overall regulatory strategy would be as and when needed. It may, of course, well be the case that no self-reporting is appropriate and the issue is rather whether a regulator will take an interest in the matter for other reasons. But the issue of self-reporting needs to be considered from the view point of each potentially interested regulator and the resulting strategy needs to take account of the potential interests of all.

1.33   In practice, it is frequently the case that not only multiple self-reporting is appropriate but that large companies will want to be proactive in managing the resulting regulatory climate. This will mean not only selecting the regulator who is first approached, but developing a clear plan as to which other regulators might have an interest in the matter and defining an approach to them so that the exposure is controlled. This may well be in the interests of the company concerned. If there is a serious issue and a company may well have been at fault, it is often the case that there is an interest in resolving the issue as quickly and effectively as possible and that it is not in shareholders' interests for there to be rolling successive regulator processes. It may be highly attractive to seek to wrap the matter up in one resolution, with one PR and capital market impact, leading more quickly to reduced uncertainty as to the company's exposure and risk.

1.34   One of the trends that is of considerable assistance in this respect is the increasing frequency of institutions in Europe to reach settlements. This phenomenon still lags behind the very active practice in the US. But both as a matter of administrative convenience, pushing the limits of administrative powers, and also by virtue of change to the legal powers accorded to them, regulators in Europe are increasingly interested in reaching settlements. BA/Virgin and Shell (mentioned above) are two prominent examples. However, the anti-trust authorities in the UK are now actively interested in 'early resolution' approaches as seen at the end of 2007 in the case of the dairy cartel allegations.

1.35   Moreover, and again in the anti-trust field, the European Commission started, in late 2007, a consultation process on amendments to its own processes to provide a formal process for settling anti-trust investigations. The precise details of the approach are still being finalized at the time of writing. However, the central themes will include, at an appropriate stage in the process, the Commission agreeing to conclude an investigation on the basis of admissions by a company of infringements and the acceptance of a reduced fine. Settlement could be reached with some of the alleged infringers whilst others continued to defend the proceedings.

1.36   There are, naturally, many tactical issues associated with entering into such a process including:

- the nature of the disclosures made in any negotiation process and the risks thereby created;
- the vulnerability of submissions to third party discovery;
- the nature of the admissions that have to be made to reach a settlement, the factual statements that would be made by the regulator in any further process or decision and the possible scope for a 'plea bargain' with admissions on some matters and the regulator dropping its case on others; and

- the interrelationship of these matters with the substantive defence, particularly if a settlement 'fails', and/or the position of parties that chose not to settle.

These matters lie outside the scope of this book and are treated more fully in the texts focussed on the regulator concerned, for example dealing with anti-trust or financial services procedure.

However, this type of process clearly enhances the development of multi-jurisdictional regulatory settlements. In circumstances where the Commission has taken jurisdiction of a multi-jurisdictional cartel providing, to the extent possible, one regulatory interlocutor in Europe (in place of the many national competition regulators), there is the possibility of a single settlement for the whole of Europe and for the US. There is, increasingly, close liaison between the Commission and the DoJ. There are occasional high profile divergences of assessment, particularly in the merger control or behavioural field, but in the cartel investigation area, joint resolution is clearly now foreseeable, at least on a transatlantic basis. **1.37**

E. Capital Market Issues

A subtle tension can arise in relation to differing capital market reporting requirements. This is particularly sensitive: reporting to the capital markets and to shareholders is a critical aspect of governance and senior management's crucial relationships with the owners of the business. A failure to handle such disclosures properly can, itself, give rise to a separate infringement and a fresh 'satellite' investigation by regulators concerned about market transparency. **1.38**

The issue arises in the international context where a company's shares are quoted on different exchanges or it has other appropriately registered or listed securities, for example debt instruments or American Depositary Receipts (ADRs) which are subject to different reporting requirements. In a sense, this is no more than a manifestation of the inherent tensions in having more that one reporting regime that arise from accessing different capital markets. However, in the context of an 'out of the ordinary' event (like a possible accounting restatement, the discovery of possible corruption of a significant degree, cartel infringement or a serious ethical violation that impacts on the company's reputation for integrity), there can be particular issues associated with the speed and detail of any notification requirements. **1.39**

This issue needs to be considered on the precise facts, with sophisticated advice on the requirements of each market. Such advice will almost always include the views of the corporate brokers or investment bankers advising on securities listing issues for the company concerned. In the UK, a failure to follow the advice of that **1.40**

broker is, of itself, highly indicative of a breach of the UK disclosure requirements.[6] However, some general observations may provide overall guidance.

1.41 Within Europe, the disclosure requirements have been converging, partially as a
result of practice but largely as a result of EC Directives harmonizing the law in
this respect. The underlying policy is one of continuous update of the markets in
relation to price sensitive information, subject to limited short term protections
and safe harbours in appropriate circumstances—which will not normally apply
to issues of this nature.

1.42 Thus, the company will often be under an obligation in Europe to make a
disclosure as soon as possible, even if not all information is known and it is
possible that the markets may over-react. It is generally not an excuse that it is not
clear what should be announced because the investigation has not yet established
what may have happened. It is sufficient that the risk profile of the company in
relation to the particular issue has changed because of the (assumed to be
non-trivial) risk that there has been some such incident. However, this issue has
to be considered in each case. In Italy, for example, the position is a little more
liberal and the Consob will permit a degree of delay if insufficient information is
known or if it may change and there is a risk of market confusion or corporate
disruption.

1.43 A critical aspect is the precise wording of any announcement. Not only will markets (and their regulatory authorities) vary in the nuances of what needs to be
said, but it is important that announcements are phrased in terms that, given the
continuous update philosophy, do not then commit the company to issue frequent progress reports on the investigation, where it is going and what it is finding. It is simply not in the best interests of the company that the evolving risk
assessment (which is inevitable, as the facts are uncovered) should be conducted
under public scrutiny. Thus, the crafting of the announcements to ensure that
they disclose information to the markets properly, but do not put the company
in a position of having disclosed so much detail that it then has to publish changes
to that detail, is important.

1.44 However, within the US the position is different. The US has a system of periodic
disclosure, rather than continuous disclosure. As a general matter, the obligation
to notify the market is triggered by a periodic disclosure obligation (eg a quarterly
reporting obligation to the SEC), the need to correct a prior disclosure that was
incorrect when made, or the need to disseminate broadly material information
that was selectively disclosed to a smaller group. The result often is that the obligation to disclose information arises first outside of the US, forcing an earlier

---

[6] See the FSA decision of 9 December 2005 in the case of Eurodis Electron plc.

disclosure of the information in the US than would have occurred if other juris-dictions were not involved. Although these tensions are usually manageable in practice, they require careful consideration at a senior level.

F. Data Protection Issues

Data protection issues give rise increasingly to frustrating and diverting problems **1.45** for investigations. Not only has the legislation become more complex and varied, it has been more strictly enforced. As investigations become more international, the distinctions between the different regimes are more often being encountered. This topic is dealt with in each chapter and Chapter 2 gives an overview of the position across Europe.

Data protection issues pose inherent tensions for an investigation. The interests **1.46** of the company and, indeed, of a regulator in obtaining as quickly as possible, perhaps without prior notice (to minimize the risk of tampering), all of the rele-vant data, some of which may be of a highly sensitive nature, conflict directly with the principles of data protection law which is precisely about controlling the disclosure of sensitive personal data.

Since most of this law is derived from EU legislation, it might be hoped that it **1.47** would be consistent across Europe. Unfortunately, it is not. First, the EC Directive concerned is particularly general in its terms. Since directives are implemented by member states to achieve their objectives, but with a discretion as to the precise method and detail, there are inherent national differences in implementation. In this case, given the generality of the drafting of the legislation in question, there is particular latitude at a member state's disposal—and they have availed them-selves of it. Secondly, the directive is of a minimum harmonizing nature, such that member states are entitled to impose stricter criteria. This has led to consid-erable differences as those states which are politically more aligned with the pro-tection of the individual have passed stringent laws, whereas those of a more invasive culture have been less restrictive.

Moreover, the US does not have the same concerns. A major conflict automati- **1.48** cally arises, therefore, between the expectations of US regulators and European legislation protecting data. This is enhanced by the fact that, unlike Canada, the US is not regarded as having a sufficiently rigorous data protection regime to be accorded the necessary counter party status under the European regime.

The difficulties in this area have been recognized by the US agencies who have **1.49** described EU data protection law as one of the most serious procedural issues that they have to face when dealing with international investigations. Those issues surfaced in the SWIFT case in 2006, where the European authorities were in favour of protecting European data from being disclosed to the US even when sought in connection with terrorist investigations in the US.

1.50 As described elsewhere in this chapter, similar issues have been arising in US litigation. In *Société Internationale pour Participations Industrielles et Commerciales, SA v Rogers*,[7] the US Supreme Court recognized that criminal exposure (including for data protection reasons) was a valid factor to be taken into account when enforcing subpoenas. However, it is not the only factor that is considered and does not constitute a per se bar to enforcement.

1.51 The authors are aware of circumstances where European/US disclosure issues have been resolved by the use of anonymized data. However, the circumstances where this will be acceptable are limited. This is not a universal solution and will usually only be of assistance where an agency is engaged in a broader exercise rather than an analysis of specific infringements.

1.52 The position within Europe is complicated by inconsistent rules and expectations. Particularly critical is the issue of whether employees have given consent and, specifically, whether consent can be dealt with generically in an employee contract or has to be more specific (see the position in France for example). A cautious position is that, strictly, the individual consent of current employees affected is required in order to conduct internal investigations (including the collection and review of their emails and hard copy documents) unless the scope of that investigation is pursuant to a legal obligation and is strictly limited to such.

1.53 There are some country-specific issues that give rise to difficulties. In Germany it has been argued that where consent is required for disclosure, this means the consent of both the sender and the receiver of an email, which is usually highly impractical. Similar issues apply in Belgium, although the regulator seems to take a pragmatic attitude in practice, provided there are genuine needs for the data access and processing. However, there are also issues in Belgium as to whether the works council needs to be informed of the data collection.

1.54 In Holland, the usual interpretation is that prior consent from the Dutch regulator is required before data processing starts. This is unwieldy in practice and causes significant potential problems. France, theoretically, also has a prior notification scheme although it is unclear under French law whether it is necessary when the purpose of the data handling is bona fide for the company understanding its business rather than for the exploitation of the employee's personal data. Theoretically, large fines can be imposed, but the history has been of more pragmatic behaviour

---

[7] 357 US 197 (1958).

by the French authorities. French law also suggests that the employee should be entitled to review data before it is transmitted to the investigation to extract purely personal material. This, again, poses practical difficulties. France is one of the most complex jurisdictions (and one of the most favourable to employees) in this respect.

Particular problems occur in the case of Switzerland, which, of course, is not an **1.55** EU member state and not subject to the Directive. It is not a jurisdiction covered in this book but it, famously, has particular confidentiality legislation which impacts on data collection. Swiss legislation protects business secret information, according rights to the company concerned. It can be interpreted to apply to the disclosure even by a subsidiary to its parent company. It raises clear issues in relation to the disclosure to non-Swiss regulators. A solution, although it impacts on the efficient conduct of an investigation, is to hold the evidence in Switzerland, have the Swiss company instruct external lawyers to review the data and then to ask them to report in ways that avoid breaching Swiss law. However, that is not an attractive modus operandi.

As can be imagined, this web of data protection obligations gives rise to considerable **1.56** angst in the conduct of any investigation. These issues are not automatically resolved by being responsive to requests made by a regulator based in another member state and, as the following chapter discusses, can be strictly enforced against the activities of non-EU regulators. Moreover, and with reference to the defensive behaviour discussed above, there is considerable ability for a local business to deploy data protection arguments when it does not want to release data to an investigation. This can require enormous tact, management pressure and skill to ensure that data protection arguments are reduced to true legal points and not inflated for tactical reasons.

Data protection will often require specific specialist legal advice for the jurisdiction **1.57** in question, considering the issues in the context of the particular investigation. In practice, there have usually been solutions to data protection issues, albeit sometimes involving the company taking a difficult risk assessment when the position is unclear. However, it is an issue that always requires careful consideration for each investigation and, particularly, in international investigations.

G. Employee Issues

One of the most sensitive issues that arises in an international investigation is the **1.58** treatment of employees of different nationalities with different cultural expectations within a process that has to be of uniform quality and penetration. Very few companies have an international corporate culture that truly overrides national expectations in such delicate areas.

1.59   In the US, the tradition and expectations have generally been much harsher than elsewhere. In part, this comes from the frequent 'employment at will' basis of company/employee relationships. There is also a greater expectation of the need for companies to be seen to be taking quick and decisive action. This environment stems largely from the clearly articulated expectations of regulators, as reflected in the DoJ's Thompson Memorandum (albeit now partially superseded by the McNulty Memorandum in crucial respects) and the SEC's Seabord doctrine, which led companies to refuse to pay legal fees of staff subject to regulatory attack and to dismiss people early in the investigation rather than keeping them under the corporate umbrella.

1.60   That said, firing staff can have the effect of making it more difficult for the company or a regulator to have access to people with important information and make it harder to uncover, and fix, problems. It may, therefore, also be seen as adverse by some regulators as putting witnesses (particularly when they are outside the US) beyond the reach of the US regulators. It is not unknown to give a regulator prior warning of a dismissal of a key person so that the regulator has the opportunity to object to the company's proposal and/or to interview the individual first.

1.61   However, the pressures in the US may more frequently lead to:

- a prompt dismissal, or at least suspension, of potentially liable staff;
- much less support for the staff involved, in terms of legal fees and extending corporate protection;
- a much more formalized investigation process, with employees being more frequently and more formally given 'Miranda' or Upjohn style warnings (discussed below[8]), and therefore expecting them, and more adversarial interview processes; and
- a more legalistic relationship, with parties more frequently being separately represented or that separate representation occurring at an earlier stage in the process.

1.62   In the UK, the position is a little less formal. The civil litigation culture is (currently) significantly less aggressive than in the US and regulatory expectations are very different. Whilst it would be common (indeed, it is usually recommended) to suspend staff who might be at fault (or to put them on 'gardening leave'), the value of maintaining the employment relationship (with its benefits of cooperation, confidentiality and fiduciary duty) is highly rated. Save in clear and egregious cases, staff are not generally dismissed until the end of a formal disciplinary process which will usually follow a corporate investigation.

---

[8] See the discussion in sections 3.197 et seq and 4.288 et seq.

Whilst it may be necessary to recommend separate representation, it tends to happen at a slightly later stage in the development of a potential conflict of interest where it is actually clear that the witness concerned is making statements and admissions against his own interest which he would not do, particularly given the likely disclosure of that data more widely, if he were separately advised. There would more often be an arrangement that the company pays the legal fees, albeit sometimes with aggressive terms as to repayment in the case that dishonest behaviour or a failure to cooperate are established. There is, generally, a greater expectation of corporate support for the individual, particularly in cases where there is no evidence of any direct personal benefit (ie fraud against the company) but rather of someone, even if wrongly, seeking to enhance the company's position. **1.63**

In terms of conducting interviews, however, the process would usually be generally similar as regards the US and the UK, although perhaps a little less aggressive in the UK. Employees are prepared to accept, but may not like, questioning in some detail as to their behaviour, a thorough review of documents, an analysis of corporate performance and potential failings. Warnings as to the privileged and confidential nature of the conversation, the duties of the lawyers being to the company and not to the witnesses and the right of the company to use the information as it wishes are common practice. This reflects a certain overlap with the litigation tradition. As common law jurisdictions, with an emphasis on discovery/disclosure and on oral, or at least witness, evidence, there is generally a certain recognition of what an investigation process involves, of why it is necessary and of how it is fairly conducted. In Hong Kong, the culture broadly reflects the UK position. **1.64**

However, in continental Europe (for legal reasons) and Japan (for legal and cultural reasons) the approach is very different, being less invasive. Complex social legislation tends to entrench employee rights to a significant degree. It would be rarer that an employee would be separately represented, but much more common that legal costs would be paid. Summary dismissal or suspension is rare and the employee issues can take much longer to resolve. **1.65**

This difference reflects a number of issues. The social democratic norm over the past 50 years has created certain cultural expectations. Moreover, the litigation context is different, with a lower level of claims and for lower value—and less often targeting the individuals. Where there are claims, parties rely more heavily on their own internal documentary evidence to support their own positive case without there being a general obligation to reveal documents to the other side or cross-examination of witnesses. Regulators have tended to focus on companies and their responses to requests for information rather than going direct to individuals and expecting to interview them personally. This has tended to mean that **1.66** employees find an investigation process much more alien and intimidating than perhaps might be the case in the US or the UK. Their behaviour is more difficult to predict and the management of the process tends to require more care and attention. This requires considerable cultural sensitivity.

1.67   This emphasizes the enhanced need, reflected in some of the chapters below, to adopt an interview process that is aimed at winning the confidence of the employees concerned. In these jurisdictions, particularly, it is more effective to be jointly (with the employees) seeking information and understanding than to be engaged in an adversarial process to produce 'evidence'. An aggressive cross-examination technique aimed at forcing admissions and trapping an employee into inconsistencies and 'breaking' him as a witness is rarely the most sophisticated approach in an investigation, in any jurisdiction, but this is particularly so in those jurisdictions with a more employee-friendly legal system and tradition. It can be strongly counterproductive. That is not to say that the investigation does not 'have teeth' and that it is not necessary to be firm and committed in the questioning—but the style has to be highly sensitive to the cultural context.

1.68   These differences in approach have quite significant implications for the conduct of international investigations. It is necessary, so far as possible, to reconcile various objectives.

1.69   First, it is fundamental that the company gets to the truth of what occurred. That means that these cultural and legal issues cannot be used as an excuse for not investigating to a consistent level of detail. A regulator in the US or in the UK may accept that certain rights and powers of an employer do not exist in other jurisdictions (so that some things simply cannot be done) but will expect that a company will have used all the means at its disposal to establish all the relevant facts in an investigation. Moreover, it is suggested that credible senior management in an international business, being held to global ethical and governance standards, will have to impose similar requirements for gathering information and evidence around the world and can only take decisions based on full rather than partial data.[9]

1.70   Secondly, the effective conduct of an investigation is likely to require that local staff or external advisers conduct, or are involved in, the investigation in the jurisdiction concerned. Flying in 'an investigation team' from other jurisdictions, particularly without the necessary language skills and with different cultural expectations, runs a very significant risk of creating defensive and frustrating behaviour and producing highly sub-optimal results. Given the need for integration and the

---

[9]   Whilst not a legal issue, the internal organizational behavioural aspects of differing standards and the governance implications will usually be highly unattractive.

sharing of information, it may well be that a member of the central investigation team is present; but it is likely that the best results will be obtained with a significant 'local' contingent as part of the investigation. This is particularly the case as it will usually be better to conduct the investigation in the witness's mother tongue. It is, for obvious reasons, usually advisable to retain as appropriate, strong local counsel on employment, data protection and criminal law issues.

Thirdly, and consistently with the above, it is necessary to focus on equivalence **1.71** of result and output rather than becoming overly fixated on identical processes. Thus, a degree of pragmatism may be required.

Fourthly, whilst the disciplinary processes will have to follow local requirements, **1.72** it is often desirable to strive to achieve equivalent, and rationally related, sanctions across the different jurisdictions. This may well mean, so far as possible, a degree of normalizing of both interim sanctions (eg suspension, witholding of bonuses or promotion) as well as any final sanction, seeking to achieve a result that is right for the organization and non-discriminatory across jurisdictions rather than meeting each local expectation exactly.

H. Privilege Issues

A similar split is seen in the area of privilege (and the waiver of privilege) to that **1.73** observed in the area of employee issues. The US tends to have its own very sophisticated rules; the UK (and Hong Kong) have a similar common law approach but it is applied and operated in a rather different way to that seen in the US; and Continental Europe and Japan have a different philosophy—but it tends to lead, paradoxically, to what can be, in some cases, a higher degree of protection for lawyer-related communications. In the context of an international investigation, these differences manifest themselves in a number of respects.

Creation of privilege or confidentiality

Where an investigation is conducted in anticipation of litigation, a broad range **1.74** of communications, including with third parties, will usually attract privilege. However, care needs to be taken in a number of respects.

The US does not have an equivalent of the 'who is the client' issue that has arisen **1.75** in UK privilege law after the Court of Appeal decision in *Three Rivers DC v The Bank of England.*[10] In the UK, this means that, at a stage before litigation privilege is available, there is a risk that communications between lawyers and witnesses

---

[10] [2004] EWCA Civ 218.

who are not part of 'client team', although employees of the client company, may not attract legal advice privilege even if they are clearly for the purpose of giving legal advice to the company. This is particularly relevant in the context of the common UK practice of taking statements from witnesses which are sent back to them (sometimes many times) in draft for comment.

1.76 In this area, the degree of protection may be less than is available in the US. In the context of an investigation, in particular in a major transatlantic investigation, where a considerable amount of the output from the legal team is constituted by records of the evidence (or, at least, information) obtained from client employees in different jurisdictions, this can give rise to material having different levels of protection. Conversely, however, in the US, it is customary practice not to send employee witnesses draft statements of their evidence but for the legal team to keep a record in their own files. To enhance the protection of such output under the 'work product' doctrine, it is common for those notes not to simply be a transcript of the interview but expressly to incorporate the personal views of the legal team involved so that there is clearly legal work product incorporated as well as the purely factual record. Irrespective of whether this is also inherently a prudent practice in the UK, it is clearly a sensible precaution in a US/UK investigation.

1.77 In some senses, the position in Continental Europe and Japan is much more conducive to the efficient conduct of investigations. Here the doctrine is generally one of fundamental confidentiality of the lawyer's work and the inviolability of his records and work product whilst it is in his possession. The lawyer may not be able to waive that confidentiality even with the consent of the clients (although that is not always the case—see Germany). The protection is accorded a degree of respect (albeit varying) by regulators (and in litigation, to the extent that disclosure of documents is required). However, there are regulators that are known to take an aggressive line in this area such as the Italian Consob and IAA and this issue does need to be considered on a case-by-case basis. Nevertheless, in the classic situation of an investigation being conducted by a local law firm, with attorneys interviewing employees and considering the evidence, provided the work product is retained within the law firm, it is relatively safe from regulatory or litigation claims for disclosure. Contrast this with the US, where regulators often request that companies produce investigative reports and witness interview memoranda. Such production generally constitutes a waiver of privilege or work product protection as to those materials such that adversaries in civil litigation are subsequently able to obtain copies of those documents.

1.78 There is a difficult issue as to whether a document which is deemed privileged and immune from production in one jurisdiction will also be protected in the case of regulatory or litigation process in another jurisdiction which would not otherwise accord protection to the document. This is a sophisticated question and highly dependent on the procedural rigour of the requesting jurisdiction.

Under the Hague Convention on Taking Evidence Abroad in Civil or Commercial Matters[11] and most international criminal cooperation arrangements, where there are attempts for litigants or agencies to use the international mechanisms that have been put in place for the international gathering of evidence, the privilege of the requested state (the state of execution of the request) is recognized. It is usually the case, although not formally required by this Convention, that the requesting state will not seek material that is privileged under its own laws. This means, in effect, that only material that is protected under neither the privilege law of the requesting state nor the requested state will be transmitted. This provides a significant degree of protection. **1.79**

However, that result does not address the much more frequent situation where a regulator or a litigant takes proceedings against a party and directly uses its coercive powers on that party to produce material under its control wherever it may be in the world. **1.80**

In the litigation context, this is primarily an issue for the common law jurisdictions, given the general absence of discovery/disclosure under the civil law regimes. In the US, the position on disclosure of material that is privileged under US law, but not in the jurisdiction where it was created, is generally that it will not be disclosable. However, this issue is dependent on the venue in the US and is not a mandatory rule. **1.81**

The more controversial issue arises where material is not privileged under US law but does have a degree of protection under local law.[12] US courts generally enforce extraterritorial subpoenas to produce information. They tend to find that the interest of the US in law enforcement outweighs the interest of the foreign state **1.82**

---

[11] 18 March 1970, 23 847 UNTS 231—see Art 11.

[12] In the leading US Supreme Court decision on the conflict between US and foreign countries discovery rules, *Société Internationale pour Participations Industrielles et Commerciales, SA v Rogers* 357 US 197 (1958) the Court reversed a District Court decision to dismiss a complaint due to the claimant's failure to produce documents. The claimant alleged that such disclosure would violate Art 273 of the Swiss Penal Code and Art 47 of the Swiss Banking Law, and sustained the burden of showing good faith in its efforts to comply with the production order. The Supreme Court held that the failure to comply with the order was 'due to inability fostered neither by its own conduct nor by circumstances within its control'. Consequently, the Court ruled that the complaint should not be dismissed because of the claimant's inability to tender the documents. The Court found it 'hardly debatable' that the fear of criminal prosecution 'constitutes a weighty excuse for nonproduction, and this excuse is not weakened because the laws preventing compliance are those of a foreign sovereign'. However, the Court held that 'in the absence of complete disclosure by petitioner, the District Court would be justified in drawing inferences unfavorable to petition as to particular events'.

in preserving the information.[13] As a rule of comity, section 40 of the Restatement (Second) of Foreign Relations Law of the United States (1965) instructs courts to consider:

> moderating the exercise of [their] enforcement jurisdiction, in light of such factors as: (a) the vital national interest of each of the states; (b) the extent and the nature of the hardship that inconsistent enforcement actions would impose upon the person; (c) the extent to which the required conduct is to take place in the territory of the other state; (d) the nationality of the person; and (e) the extent to which enforcement by action of either state can reasonably be expected to achieve compliance with the rule prescribed by that state.

1.83 Section 442(1)(c) of the Restatement (Third) of the Foreign Relations Law of the United States (1987) provides a slightly modified balancing test, under which a court or agency ordering a person subject to their jurisdiction to produce documents, objects, or other information that is located outside the US should consider:

> the importance to the investigation or litigation of the documents or other information requested; the degree of specificity of the request; whether the information originated in the United States; the availability of alternative means of securing the information; and the extent to which noncompliance with the request would undermine important interests of the United States, or compliance with the request would undermine important interests of the state where the information is located.[14]

1.84 To prevent an improper assertion of extraterritorial power by US courts or agencies, section 442(2)(a) of the Restatement (Third) of the Foreign Relations Law of the United States instructs that a court or agency may require the person to whom an order to produce information is directed 'to make a good faith effort to secure permission from the foreign authorities' in order to make the information available.[15] However, while good faith efforts ordinarily would not result in the imposition of sanctions of content or dismissal,[16] under section 442(2)(c) of the Restatement (Third) of the Foreign Relations Law of the United States (1987), a court or agency may 'make findings of fact adverse to a party that has failed to comply with the order of production, even if that party has made a good faith

---

[13] See, eg, *United States v Field (In re Grand Jury Proceedings)* 532 F 2d 404, 407 (5th Cir 1976), certiorari denied, 429 US 940 (1976); *United States v The Bank of Nova Scotia (In re Grand Jury Proceedings)* 691 F 2d 1384, 1387 (11th Cir 1982), certiorari denied, 462 US 1119 (1983); *United States v First National City Bank* 396 F 2d 897 (2nd Cir 1968); *United States v Vetco Inc* 691 F 2d 1281 (9th Cir 1981), certiorari denied, 454 US 1098 (1981).

[14] See also, interpreting and applying the various factors, *Weiss v National Westminster Bank plc* 242 FRD 33 (DNY 2007).

[15] See, eg, *Montship Lines, Ltd v Federal Maritime Board* 295 F 2d 147, (DC Cir 1961).

[16] See Restatement (Third) of the Foreign Relations Law of the US, § 442 (1)(b): 'a court or agency should not ordinarily impose sanctions of contempt, dismissal, or default on a party that has failed to comply with the order for production, except in cases of deliberate concealment or removal of information or of failure to make a good faith effort in accordance with paragraph (a)'.

effort to secure permission from the foreign authorities to make the information available and that effort has been unsuccessful'.

In the UK, the courts (presently) treat as protected those communications that **1.85** satisfy the English law test for privilege, irrespective of how they would be treated in the court of any other jurisdiction.[17]

The position in relation to regulators is dependent on the regulators concerned. **1.86** In the UK, the same approach will seemingly be applied by regulators whose statutory powers to compel the disclosure of material are limited by reference to the common law concept of privilege,[18] since the relevant test is directly imported by the legislation. In a case where the protection is specifically statutorily defined (eg section 314 of the Financial Services and Markets Act 2000), there is no basis on which foreign privilege law could be applicable in any event. It is simply a question of whether the communications concerned fall within the protections proscribed by legislation. There is, however, no known specific UK authority or established practice on how the UK regulators would, in fact, seek to address the issue of communications not privileged under the relevant UK provisions but privileged, or otherwise protected, under another law. The practical experience has been consistent with regulators taking a relatively pragmatic position and not seeking to test the technical issue of the vulnerability of documents protected only under another legal system. The exception to this is the European Commission, or agencies applying Community anti-trust law on its behalf, when the Community's own law of privilege (which is more restrictive, but supervening) will be applied and local protections ignored.

There is a particular vulnerability in relation to disclosures within the EU in the **1.87** anti-trust regime. Because the detailed privilege rules do vary, material could be compelled in one country with a less protective privilege regime and could be disclosed under the cooperation arrangements between national regulators such that it would be in the hands of a regulator that could not have compelled it in its own jurisdiction. Since the EU has its own specific rules in the anti-trust area which apply across all member states, it has not been concerned to respect more protective regimes where the data is flowing within the inter-regulator system that the EU has established. If the anti-trust issue is subject to EU anti-trust rules, rather than national rules, the issue does not arise because the harmonized (limited) level of protection applies.

---

[17] *Bourns Inc v Raychem Corp* [1999] 3 All ER 154.
[18] See, eg, s 32 of the Competition Act 1998.

Waiver

1.88 A further complexity in this area is that of waiver. Here the rules and principles vary considerably.

1.89 As seen below, in some civil law jurisdictions, the lawyer generally cannot, even on instructions, waive privilege/confidentiality since he has a separate professional right and duty to maintain confidentiality. However, this is not true in Germany, where the privilege can be waived by the client putting the lawyer under an obligation to release the documents concerned to the regulator or litigant.

1.90 A client can choose not to assert a privilege, or right of confidentiality, over material in its (as opposed to the lawyer's) possession (if indeed, it is privileged—in some jurisdictions, it is not) and can release it to a regulator. Conversely, it has been the practice of regulators in Continental Europe to respect privilege and not to exert pressure on companies to waive it in the interests of a more harmonious and constructive relationship with the regulator concerned.

1.91 In the US, the position has been very different. It is not uncommon in the US for a regulator, in the context of a regulatory enquiry with which a company is cooperating, including by means of an internal investigation, to require access to, at a minimum, the witness interviews and investigative report created by counsel. This practice was encouraged by the DoJ's Thompson Memorandum and frequently advocated by representatives of the SEC's enforcement staff.

1.92 Since the redrawing of that approach in the McNulty Memorandum, the 'official' legal position of the DoJ has altered. However, in practice, it continues a to be the case in many investigations that privilege is not asserted in a cooperative relationship with a regulator. The only safe working assumption in relation to US regulators with whom there is to be any form of sophisticated cooperative relationship is that privilege may have to be conceded.

1.93 Within the US, this has profound consequences. In general, waiver of privilege to one regulator by the submission of privileged material constitutes a waiver of the protection not only against all regulators but also against all private litigants. This is despite the best efforts of some agencies and practitioners to persuade the courts otherwise in the hope of making it easier for companies to deal openly with them without prejudicing their position in civil claims.

1.94 In this area, the UK's position is perhaps the most attractive. As a general rule, regulators have not sought to persuade companies to waive their rights of privilege generally. Moreover, there is considerable authority that it is possible to give only a partial, or expressly limited, waiver of privilege. This has the attraction that it is possible to disclose to, and discuss with, a regulator a privileged document, such as the report of an investigation, such that the document is likely to remain privileged as regards not only other regulators but also private sector litigants.

It is open to debate (and not yet tested) whether the US courts (say) would recognize that, under English law, a waiver of privilege of a document created in, and privileged under the law of, England was limited and the client had maintained its rights as against other parties. As a matter of conflicts of law theory, one would have expected the sanctity of the privilege to be maintained since the detraction from it was specifically limited and did not have the impact of undermining it generally under the law governing both that privilege and that waiver. However, the likely position in the US is that its courts would not recognize a concept of limited waiver. A more sophisticated question is whether documents that had an inherently US connection and would otherwise be privileged under US law (say an investigation report by a US law firm, written in the US to the board of a US company) would lose its privilege by being disclosed to an English regulator even though the waiver, under English law, was limited. It is suspected that the US courts might well show considerably less sympathy in such circumstances. **1.95**

Equally, there must be a considerable risk that in private litigation in the UK, a US connected document would be disclosable if its privilege had been waived under US principles of privilege by disclosure to a US regulator, even if it would have been possible to have constructed a limited waiver under English law. **1.96**

A conservative position is consistently taken, in practice, in the case of disclosures to the European Commission, or national agencies, in anti-trust leniency applications. The perception is that the risk of the documents' consequent vulnerability to US civil claims is such that, whether the documents be originally US related documents or documents that had no particular relationship with the US, it will not willingly be accepted. This also means that strict steps are taken to avoid creating potentially disclosable documents in the context of the relationships with the regulators, including on leniency applications. There is, however, no escaping the impact of an agency in Europe applying EU rules on privilege (which, for example, do not protect communications with in-house counsel) requiring the disclosure of documents privileged under US law, but not within the EU, with the result that a US litigant would then argue that privilege had been waived by virtue of that disclosure. **1.97**

Applying this inconsistent set of approaches to an international investigation, perhaps in the teeth of multiple regulatory attacks, presents considerable problems. However, whatever the technical issues, the practical question usually resolves to the civil litigation exposure. It is, again, not generally credible that a company would seek to waive privilege by releasing to one regulator but seek to assert it against others. Such a position would look highly defensive and technical **1.98** and would be very difficult to justify in any credible regulatory strategy. It would also be likely to be self-defeating. Given the degree of coordination between regulators, it is likely that either the material disclosed or the gist of it will, in any event, be disclosed between different regulators.

1.99 However, it is a very credible concern that there is a sensitive internal report which a client would like to give to a regulator as part of its cooperation with that regulator but which it is inhibited from doing so by the prospect of rendering it vulnerable to litigation, particularly in the US. The process that is usually adopted to resolve such an issue tracks the procedure that is usually adopted in the US in such circumstances where the questions are purely national.

1.100 In such a case, the report is delivered orally to the regulator concerned in a meeting in which the relevant case officers are taken through the contemporaneous (and hence usually non-privileged) documentary evidence so that the necessary connections can be made and the context understood. In such a case, the case officers will usually take their own notes. However, it is generally considered that those reports, in the hands of foreign government or EC agencies are protected from US disclosure. There is, by definition, no document in the possession of the company over which privilege has been waived by the process of disclosing it to a regulator. The investigation report and related material remain privileged (assuming that they have attracted privilege) as between the lawyers and the client. This approach is almost uniform practice within anti-trust regulators in the EC and is becoming more frequently seen elsewhere when there is a risk of US litigation.

2

DATA PROTECTION UNDER EUROPEAN COMMUNITY LAW

Overview[1]

This chapter analyses the impact of data privacy laws on the conduct of internal **2.01** and regulatory investigations into the affairs of companies that have a presence in several EU countries. The focus is the relevant provisions of the EU Data Protection Directive[2] (the Directive), which is the source of much of the data protection requirements in Europe,[3] and their implementation into

---

[1] Contributor: Keith Wotherspoon.

[2] Directive (EC) 95/46 on the protection of individuals with regard to the processing of personal data and on the free movement of such data [1995] OJ L281.

[3] The E-Privacy Directive (Directive (EC) 2002/58 concerning the processing of personal data and the protection of privacy in the electronic communications sector [2002] OJ L201/37) and Retention of Communications Data Directive (Directive (EC) 2006/24 on the retention of data generated or processed in connection with the provision of publicly available electronic communications services or of public communications networks and amending Directive 2002/58/EC [2006]

national laws.[4] Consideration is given to the initial collection of information from or about employees and clients and the sharing or transfer of that information within the corporate group. This chapter also considers the data privacy law implications of sharing information with external advisers or consultants who are advising on the investigation and, ultimately, with regulators. The chapter assumes that the investigation could be either voluntary or be conducted in response to a regulator using coercive powers to require a company to provide information.

2.02 In some investigations, the affected employees or clients of the investigated company may be able to assert general privacy rights under national constitutional laws or Article 8 of the European Convention on Human Rights (ECHR) (in addition to data privacy rights under local law). The affected individuals may also enjoy common law or contractual rights of confidentiality—for example, clients of a bank that is the subject of an investigation will enjoy obligations of confidentiality that can be overridden in limited circumstances (or not at all under some national laws). Such general privacy or confidentiality rights that may impact on the collection and sharing of information are outside the scope of this chapter.

A. Data Protection Directive

Overview

2.03 The Directive requires substantive implementation by national legislation in the national laws of the 27 member states. It is, in effect, a minimum standards measure. This means that member states can introduce stricter privacy laws than the Directive requires, provided any stricter rules do not otherwise conflict with EU law. In addition, the Directive gives member states a discretion or 'margin for manoeuvre' in how they implement its requirements.[5] These two flexibilities mean that there are, despite the harmonization, considerable detailed differences within the EU.

2.04 The Directive aims to protect individuals whose 'personal data' is held or processed by 'data controllers'. In general terms, the Directive requires member states

---

OJ L105/54) are relevant to investigations involving live communications (unopened emails or voice mails) but are not considered in this chapter because it is assumed most investigations will be focusing on historical or opened communications.

[4] Increasingly, emerging markets such as Dubai International Financial Centre, Russia and China have adopted or proposed data privacy laws that are strongly influenced by the Data Protection Directive: see, eg, B Treacy, 'Current Data Protection Issues for Financial Institutions: Part 2—Global Businesses and Global Data Flows', *Privacy & Data Protection* (2007) 7(7), 3–5.

[5] Recital 9. One senior judge has expressed the view that the UK has 'in large measure' adopted the wording of the Directive: *Campbell v MGN Limited* [2003] 1 All ER 224 at para 96, per Lord Phillips of Worth Matravers MR.

to do so by requiring the introduction of various 'protection principles' into national law. The main principle that affects the conduct of internal and external investigations is the need to ensure fair and lawful processing of 'personal data' by data controllers.[6] It is left to the discretion of member states how the conditions for lawful processing are defined under national law.[7]

Personal data

The term 'personal data' covers any information that 'relates to' an identified or **2.05** identifiable individual.[8] The broad scope of this definition was curtailed by the English Court of Appeal's interpretation in 2003.[9] The Court was looking for information that was not only proximate and relevant to an individual (factors that were generally accepted as relevant); it now added a requirement that the information was only 'personal data' if it was also 'biographical in a significant sense' or had the individual as its focus (rather than some transaction or event in which that individual may have figured or had an interest).[10] The impact on this narrower interpretation of 'personal data' has been the subject of adverse review by the European Commission and is considered in more detail below.[11]

In the context of investigations, the Directive's broad scope for 'personal data' will **2.06** apply not only to private email addresses but also to corporate email addresses that incorporate an individual employee's or client's name.[12] 'Personal data' would also cover business or mobile telephone numbers for named employees or directors,[13] bank account details for individual clients[14] and sound or image data

---

[6] Art 6(1)(a).

[7] Recital 9.

[8] Art 2(a). To determine whether information renders an individual 'identifiable', Recital 26 indicates that account is to be taken 'of all means likely reasonably to be used by the controller or by any other person' to identify such an individual. The Directive also covers a sub-category of personal data that reveals 'racial or ethnic origin, political opinions, religions or philosophical beliefs, trade-union membership' and data 'concerning health or sex life' (Art 8(1)). The Directive's special rules dealing with the processing of these kinds of sensitive data are not covered here as they are unlikely to be relevant to most investigations.

[9] *Durant v Financial Services Authority* [2003] EWCA Civ 1746, followed by the English High Court in *Johnson v Medical Defence Union* [2004] EWHC 2509 (Ch).

[10] [2003] EWCA Civ 1746 at para 28, per Auld LJ.

[11] See paras 2.18 and 2.19 below.

[12] Eg if the investigated company has a client known as Acme Limited, email addresses that the company holds for Acme Limited will be caught as 'personal data' if they contain the names of Acme's employees or consultants (eg johannes.schmidt@acme.com).

[13] See European Court of Justice's preliminary ruling in *Lindqvist* [2004] 2 WLR 1398 at para 24 on a referral from the Swedish Court of Appeal that the term personal data 'undoubtedly covers the name of a person in conjunction with his telephone co-ordinates'.

[14] Ie it would not cover the bank account details of legal persons such as companies or limited liability partnerships.

relating to employees or clients.[15] While the focus of the Directive is on data relating to individuals, at least two member states have chosen to apply the protection principles to data relating to legal persons.[16] 'Personal data' can be held electronically or in a structured manual or paper filing system.[17]

Data controller

2.07 The concept of 'data controller' is similarly broad under the Directive. It covers any party that independently determines or co-determines with others what 'personal data' is collected or how it is used.[18] In the unanimous advisory Opinion of the Article 29 Working Party of EU privacy regulators, it was found that an entity that decides where it locates its facilities, what services are offered to clients and the standards of data processing that will be used is a data controller under the Directive (and not merely a data processor or agent).[19] In the context of investigations, the company that is the subject of the investigation will invariably be a data controller in respect of employee and client data that allows individuals to be identified.

Processing

2.08 The privacy protection afforded by the Directive is extended to the 'processing' of 'personal data'. As the English Court of Appeal has observed, the definition of 'processing' under the Directive and the UK's implementing legislation is 'very wide'.[20] Processing not only covers the obtaining of information and its subsequent

---

[15] Eg voice mail messages and CCTV footage are clearly covered as personal data (see Recital 14, referring to the need for the Directive to apply to sound and image data; also Recitals 16 and 17).

[16] Luxembourg's data privacy law covers individuals and legal persons. Italian law defines 'personal data' as 'any information related to individuals, legal persons, entities in general or associations that are identified or identifiable, even indirectly through other information' (Art 1.2(c) of the Law dated 31 December 1996, No 675).

[17] Arts 2(c) and 3(1). According to Recital 27, the content of a manual filing system that captures personal data must be structured according to specific criteria relating to individuals 'allowing easy access to the personal data'. In the controversial ruling in *Durant v Financial Services Authority* [2003] EWCA Civ 1746 at para 50, the English Court of Appeal held that the structure or organizing mechanism of manual files must have a 'sufficiently sophisticated and detailed means of readily indicating whether and where in an individual file or files specific criteria or information about the [individual] can be readily located'.

[18] Art 2(d).

[19] Opinion 10/2006 on the processing of personal data by the Society for Worldwide Interbank Financial Telecommunication (SWIFT) 01935/06/EN WP128. The opposite view has been taken on SWIFT's status by the Schleswig-Holstein data protection regulator in August 2006 which found that SWIFT was merely a data processor for German banks. The Spanish regulator also found in July 2007 that SWIFT 'acted, at all times, as the data processor, including when it transferred data to US authorities under US subpoenas': C Millard, 'Surprise Decision by Spain's Data Protection agency on SWIFT data processor status', *Privacy Laws & Business International Newsletter*, December 2007, 6.

[20] *Campbell v MGN* [2003] 1 QB 633 at 646, per Lord Phillips of Worth Matravers MR.

use but many other activities. This is relevant to investigations as it covers the initial collection of data relating to employees and clients (for example, where a company asks its in-house IT department to take a copy of the contents of an employee's hard drive held on that employee's office computer or laptop). Processing also covers the subsequent sharing, storage or other use of that data. In addition, the concept will capture the transferring of collected data between group companies located in the same country or other EEA countries and transferring it between EEA countries and non-EEA countries.[21]

As an illustration of the various layers of 'processing' that may occur in a multi-jurisdictional investigation, a US regulator may decide to investigate a Madrid headquartered bank with a US presence where group entities in the EU are alleged to have facilitated bank transfers for clients in contravention of US federal law. The bank may have branches or subsidiaries in many EU countries. As part of its internal investigation, the Madrid headquarters may ask Spanish and non-Spanish branches and subsidiaries to collect information held on local servers, desktop computers and laptops about named client relationship managers and their communications with named clients. The collected data may then be sent to Madrid for review by the bank's internal investigation team or the data may remain stored on local servers and made accessible to the Madrid team. The data may also be sent to the bank's external advisers in the UK for analysis and, later, to its US lawyers who will be dealing with the US regulator. Ultimately, it may be shared in some form with the US regulator. Each stage in the investigation just described will involve what the Directive would recognize as the 'processing' of 'personal data' relating to individual employees and clients. The only way of avoiding the Directive's application in these circumstances after the initial collection of data at local branch or subsidiary level is to anonymize the collected data so that it can no longer be correlated to individual employees or clients.[22]

2.09

Compliance

Assuming that an internal or external investigation involves the 'processing' of at least some personal or non-anonymized data, the main requirement of the Directive and national data privacy laws is to ensure fair processing of that data.[23] The Directive also requires that data controllers collect data for specified, explicit

2.10

---

[21] Art 2(b). The definition includes 'disclosure by transmission, dissemination or otherwise making available'. Processing would therefore cover, eg, giving employees of a group company located in the UK remote access to data held on a Luxembourg server for a Luxembourg entity in the group.

[22] See Recital 26. The initial collection of the data by local branches and subsidiaries would still need to meet the fair and lawful processing requirement under Art 6(1)(a) as that data would not be anonymized at the time of its initial collection for the purposes of the investigation.

[23] Art 6(1)(a).

and legitimate purposes and do not process or use that data in a way that is incompatible with those purposes.[24] In addition, the data that is collected should be relevant and not excessive to the purposes for which it was collected or is subsequently used.[25] There is also a requirement under the Directive that data controllers implement 'appropriate technical and organizational measures' to protect personal data against accidental loss or unauthorized disclosure or access.[26] This will be relevant where the initial data controller wishes to get other group companies and/or external advisers to hold or review the data on its behalf (see below).

2.11 There are various grounds on which personal data can be fairly processed. The most obvious ground is the prior consent of the affected individuals. The Directive requires consent to be unambiguous.[27] Consent must also be a freely given, specific and informed indication of the individual's wishes.[28] This consent might be found in the terms and conditions of the employment contract or client engagement that permit the company to review and disclose information in specified circumstances. The scope of what amounts to valid or true consent will depend on the provisions of national law. In the context of the employment relationship, some member states effectively operate a presumption that employee consent to curtailed privacy will not have been freely given because the employee is assumed not to have a genuine choice when contracting with an employer.[29]

2.12 In the absence of unambiguous employee or client consent to collect or share data for the purposes of an investigation, the Directive sets out various alternative grounds for fair processing that could be used by companies that are being directly investigated or those companies that wish to assist a group company which is being investigated.[30] These include: processing that is necessary for the purposes of the legitimate interests pursued by the data controller or by third parties to whom the data is disclosed except where interests are overridden by fundamental privacy rights of the affected individual;[31] processing that is necessary for the performance of a task that is carried out in the public interest or in the exercise of official authority vested in the data controller or in a third party to whom the data

---

[24] Art 6(1)(b).
[25] Art 6 (1)(c).
[26] Art 17(1).
[27] Art 7(a).
[28] Art 2(h).
[29] This view has also been expressed by the Article 29 Working Party of EU privacy regulators (Opinion 2093/05/EN WP114, point 2.1).
[30] Art 7.
[31] Art 7(f).

is disclosed;[32] or processing that is necessary for compliance with a legal obligation to which the controller is subject.[33]

In addition to the alternative grounds for fair processing where consent is absent, the **2.13** Directive permits member states under national law to override the fair processing requirement where restrictions on privacy protection are necessary in the public interest, including the investigation of crime or the exercise of a regulatory function.[34]

Sanctions

The Directive leaves the issue of sanctions to the discretion of member states pro- **2.14** vided they introduce 'suitable measures to ensure the full implementation' of the Directive.[35] In practice, many states have introduced criminal or administrative fines (which sometimes can be imposed on individual directors or senior officers, as well as on the data controller entities). For example, in the UK, offences carry a maximum fine of £5,000 per violation if prosecuted in the magistrates' court and an unlimited fine if prosecuted in the Crown Court. The Spanish regulator has a reputation for seeking heavy sanctions and recently had a fine of over €1m upheld by the Spanish Supreme Court.

The Directive also requires member states to give affected individuals judicial **2.15** remedies under national law for any processing that is carried out in breach of the Directive's protection principles but the type of remedy is left to their discretion.[36] The Directive specifies that individuals who suffer damage as a result of unlawful processing shall be entitled to receive compensation from the relevant data controller for the damage suffered. No minimum or maximum amount of compensation is specified in the Directive.

The remainder of this chapter examines in detail how the Directive's require- **2.16** ments can impact on the initial collection, later use and sharing of personal data at each potential stage in an internal and external investigation, including sharing with external consultants and domestic and foreign regulators.

B. Initial Collection

In a multi-jurisdictional investigation, the local data controller will be investigat- **2.17** ing itself or, perhaps more commonly, be responding to an investigation that has

---

[32] Art 7(e).
[33] Art 7(c).
[34] See Art 13(1), which permits member states to introduce restrictions that are 'necessary' to safeguard various public interest objectives.
[35] Art 24.
[36] Art 22.

been instigated by the parent company or corporate group headquarters. In either scenario, the compliance obligations under the Directive will fall on the local data controller in respect of an employee's or client's personal data held by it that is collected as part of the investigation. Where the local data controller allows or uses another group company or external consultants to assist in the initial collection of information, the local data controller still has compliance obligations under the Directive in relation to the process of initial collection because it is the original controller of the information.

Personal data

2.18 The local data controller's compliance obligations under the Directive will only apply if the information that is collected is regarded as 'personal data' relating to an identified or identifiable individual.[37] In most EU countries, the key issues to determine the status of information would be the proximity of the data to the individual and the relevance of the data to that individual. However, the UK's narrower interpretation of 'personal data' in the *Durant* case has introduced a test of whether information possesses a significant biographical element 'going beyond the recording of the [individual's] involvement in a matter or event which has no personal connotations, a life event in respect of which his privacy cannot be said to be compromised'.[38] The court also held that it was important to determine whether the information has the individual as its focus 'rather than some other person with whom he may have been involved or some transaction or event in which he may have figured or had an interest'.[39] So the fact that records refer to an individual does not mean that these records contain 'personal data' relating to that individual.

2.19 Following *Durant*, the UK Information Commissioner issued guidance on the scope of 'personal data'. In cases of uncertainty about whether information relates to an individual, the Commissioner stated that the data controller needs to take into account whether or not the information is capable of having an adverse impact on that individual's privacy. In the Commissioner's view, the inclusion of an individual's name will only be personal data where its inclusion in the information affects the individual's privacy. It is more likely that an individual's name will be personal data where the name appears alongside an address or telephone number. In the light of the European Commission's adverse scrutiny of *Durant*, it is probably safer for UK data controllers to proceed on the assumption that any data relating to an individual is 'personal data' and so needs to be assessed in terms

---

[37] Art 2(a).
[38] *Durant v Financial Services Authority* [2003] EWCA Civ 1746 at para 28.
[39] Ibid.

of proximity and relevance without applying additional tests dealing with the significant biographical element or focus of the information.

Fair processing

The Directive requires the local data controller to ensure fair processing of the **2.20** information relating to employees and clients. The grounds for fair processing include individual consent; pursuit of legitimate interests; and public interest.

In the case of individual employee consent to collect data, the starting point for **2.21** the local data controller is whether its local employment contracts or subsequent notices issued to employees are broad enough to provide the informed and unambiguous consent necessary to collect and review employee emails, documents and other communications where there is an internal or external investigation. A broad statement of the employer's information-gathering rights may meet the requirement for informed consent if it is made clear to the employee what type of communications will be reviewed and why.[40]

However, the Directive also requires consent to be freely given to be valid. This **2.22** will affect the obtaining of employee consent to the conduct of investigations in some EU states. For example, the privacy regulator in France has indicated that employees cannot freely give consent via an employment contract. There is no official guidance in Germany and academic opinion on valid consent is divided on whether employees can give genuine consent. In Spain, Italy and the UK, employees can give valid consent via employment contracts.

In the case of client consent to collect data, the local data controller will need to **2.23** look at its client's terms and conditions or subsequent notices issued to clients to determine if consent to data collection has been obtained for the purposes of carrying out an investigation. To be valid consent, the employer's statement will need to set out what communications will be reviewed and why.

If unambiguous and informed employee or client consent is not present, the local **2.24** data controller can use the Directive's 'legitimate interests' ground for fair processing unless these interests are overridden by the privacy interests of the affected individuals.[41] The relevant legitimate interests can be the interests of the local data controller or the third party to whom the collected data is disclosed—for example, the interests could be that of the parent company that is facing an external investigation and has asked the local data controller to assist it. The local data controller must

---

[40] If collected data will be transferred outside the EEA and/or shared with other group companies, the employer's statement also needs to refer to this specifically and explain why these transfers may be made.

[41] Art 7(f).

balance these interests against the objective impact of data collection on the privacy of employee and clients. In practice, this balancing of interests means the local data controller would be expected to ensure that certain privacy safeguards were built into the data collection process. For example, only a few members of the data controller's in-house IT team should be involved in taking images of hard disks containing employee or client data. In addition, where possible, data should be anonymized promptly after initial collection, with only one or two nominated individuals having the ability to unlock the identities of individual employees or clients in carefully prescribed circumstances. The legitimate interests ground for fair processing is qualified by a 'necessity' test. In effect, this means that some thought must be given by the local data controller as to the scope of the data that is going to be collected so that, as far as practicable, only data that is strictly necessary to the investigation is collected. For example, the data controller could ensure the necessary parameters are put in place by collecting only data that falls within certain dates fields that are likely to be relevant or restricting collection of employee communications to only identified clients. This does impose a theoretical problem in practice in that the acquisition of the data is usually done on a wide ranging basis and is then the subject of keyword searches to produce more relevant documents. Therefore, the initial trawl may be dependent on very strict limitations as to the people who have access to it. This is usually manageable because at that stage in the process it will usually be only one or two IT or forensic specialists who are involved and they are not reviewing the actual content prior to keyword searches being made.

2.25 Apart from consent and legitimate interests, the other relevant grounds for fair processing are processing that is necessary for the performance of a task that is carried out in the public interest or in the exercise of official authority vested in the data controller or in a third party to whom the data is disclosed;[42] or processing that is necessary for compliance with a legal obligation to which the controller is subject.[43] These grounds would allow data collection to take place where the local data controller has been issued with a subpoena requiring data to be handed over to a regulator or court. However, it will be important for the data controller to check the local law implementation of these grounds for fair processing as the legislation, case law and regulatory guidance may include elements that narrow or widen their potential scope. Clearly, it may be unattractive to invite a subpoena for the purpose of falling within this exception from the data protection obligations.

2.26 In addition to these public interest grounds, some member states[44] have introduced an 'obtaining legal advice' basis for fair processing provided the data processed is

---

[42] Art 7(e)
[43] Art 7(c).
[44] Eg UK and Ireland.

strictly necessary to obtain that advice. Some national laws may also recognize cooperation with regulators or criminal law investigations effectively as grounds for fair processing. The local data controller should verify the precise scope of these other grounds under national law and any guidance that has been issued by the regulator.

Processing contract

Where the local data controller uses another group company or external consultants or advisers to collect the data on its behalf, it should enter a data processing contract with them.[45] The prescribed content of the contract will depend on the detailed requirements of national data privacy laws in the EU. To comply with the Directive, the contract should provide that the data processor is only to act on the local data controller's instructions (and not act independently). In addition, the contract should require the processor to implement appropriate technical and organizational measures to ensure the collected data is held securely against unauthorized access or disclosure.[46] **2.27**

The contract should be used even if the group company or consultants are located in the same country as the data controller. **2.28**

Export outside the EEA

If the process of data collection will involve the local data controller giving remote access to other group companies or external consultants to employee or client data held on local servers, this will possibly involve an export of the accessed data if the accessing parties are located outside the EEA. This issue is dealt with in 2.35 below. **2.29**

C. Intra-group Sharing

The fair processing grounds for sharing collected data with other group companies are: individual consent; pursuit of legitimate interests; performance of a task carried out in the public interest; and legal obligation on the data controller. **2.30**

Consent

Employee or client consent to intra-group sharing may be found in the employment contract or client terms and conditions. To be effective, the consent must be informed, freely given and unambiguous (see 2.20 to 2.23). **2.31**

---

[45] Art 17(3).
[46] Art 17.

Legitimate interests

2.32　If consent is absent or ambiguous, the local data controller may seek to rely on the 'legitimate interests' ground (see 2.24). It may be difficult to show that privacy is not seriously prejudiced by sharing wholly or largely non-anonymized data with other group companies. This objection might be overcome if there is a necessity to share that data (for example, where the recipient is itself facing external investigation or will be instructing or coordinating liaison with external advisers) and the shared data is restricted to a few employees at the recipient entity. If there is no need for the recipient entity to know the identities of individual employees or clients, data should be anonymized by the local data controller (unless this is not practicable given the volume and complexity of data and the timescale in which the recipient entity needs to receive it in order to respond to the external investigation).

Other grounds

2.33　The other grounds for intra-group data sharing are set out in 2.25 and 2.26 above. Depending on the precise scope of the relevant nation law provisions, one or more of these grounds may apply to intra-group data sharing.

Data processing contract

2.34　Where data is shared with another group company, the local data controller should enter a data processing contract with the recipient where the recipient is acting as an agent or processor for the local controller (see 2.27 and 2.28). If the recipient will be carrying out purely independent use of the shared data, no processing contract is required. An example of independent use would include the recipient entity considering whether it had any independent, joint or subsidiary liability with the local data controller in respect of the matter being investigated internally or externally.

Export outside the EEA

2.35　Transferring collected data to another group company outside the EEA will involve a data export under the Directive. It is not clear from the Directive whether making data accessible outside the EEA can be considered an export as the Directive only refers to a 'transfer to a third country'.[47] The Advocate General has expressed the opinion that it does not matter whether the transfer is carried out by the sender sending the data or the recipient accessing the data remotely. This view was advanced on the basis that the data export protections in the

---

[47] Art 25(1). Because the three EEA countries (Iceland, Lichtenstein and Norway) have included the Directive in the EEA Agreement transfers to these countries are not treated as transfers to third countries ([1994] OJ L001, 3).

Directive would be avoided if the obligations were limited to transfers or data 'push' arrangements carried out by the sender.[48] The ECJ has accepted this view and so setting up data 'pull' arrangements that allow a non-EEA party to access data remotely from an EEA-located server will be regarded as a data export.

If an extra-EEA export to a group company is involved, the transfer must satisfy one of the export grounds under the Directive. The grounds that are potentially relevant are: consent from the affected individuals;[49] or the transfer is necessary or legally required on important public interest grounds or for the establishment, exercise or defence of legal claims;[50] or the transfer is made under appropriate contractual arrangements;[51] or the transfer is made to a non-EEA country offering adequate protection.[52] In addition to these grounds specified in the Directive, some member states may permit extra-EEA exports which are necessary to comply with a regulatory investigation or to assist with a criminal law investigation or to obtain legal advice. The precise scope of these other grounds will depend on the terms of national law and any regulatory guidance that has been issued. **2.36**

An individual's consent to extra-EEA export must be informed, unambiguous and freely given (see 2.21 to 2.23). Unless the employee or client contracts or terms and conditions contain a reference to the possibility that data collected during an investigation could be sent to group companies located outside the EEA, informed consent will be absent. Consent could be obtained separately once the need for the investigation is known. However, this is often not feasible in practice as individuals are likely to refuse to give consent or they will simply fail to respond altogether. **2.37**

In the absence of informed and unambiguous consent to extra-EEA export, the transfer can be made if it is required by law (ie complying with a subpoena or court order).[53] The Directive does not expressly tie the requirement of law obligation to the local data controller. It will be necessary for the local data controller to consider how the data privacy law in its country of establishment has implemented this ground for lawful export. In particular, the controller should check **2.38**

---

[48] Joined Cases C-317/04 and C-318/04 [2003] ECR I-4989 at para 91.

[49] Art 26(1)(a).

[50] Art 26(1)(d).

[51] Art 26(2) and (4).

[52] Art 25.

[53] Extra-EEA transfers that are necessary on 'important public interest grounds' are unlikely to be relevant to local data controllers as Recital 58 indicates that it was intended to cover transfers between governmental authorities (eg tax or social security authorities). In addition, local data protection laws or regulators where the local data controller is established may specify whether the public interest needs to exist in the member state rather than the non-EEA country—eg the UK Information Commissioner's view is that the public interest needs to be in the member state itself (Information Commissioner, 'The Eighth Data Protection Principle and International Data Transfers', 30 June 2006, para 4.4.2).

whether a foreign court order or subpoena or legal proceedings will be sufficient or whether a local court order or legal proceedings are also needed before the transfer is lawful. For example, the UK Information Commissioner does not distinguish between domestic and foreign court orders.[54] The controller should also check whether the order or legal proceedings need to have been made or raised against the controller itself or whether it is sufficient that another group company is the subject of the order or proceedings.

2.39 An extra-EEA transfer can be made to a group company if it is necessary to defend legal claims. The Directive does not define 'legal claims' but the term suggests civil liability rather than criminal liability. The local data controller should check how the Directive has been implemented in its country of establishment. It may, for example, cover the obtaining of legal advice in respect of any form of legal liability (civil, criminal and administrative). However, the extra-EEA transfer will need to be 'necessary' for the defence of legal claims and so the local data controller must consider whether all the information that would be transferred is strictly needed for the purpose of defending these claims.

2.40 An alternative ground for transferring to a non-EEA based group entity is the use of an approved form of contract between the local data controller and the recipient entity.[55] The European Commission has approved model sets of clauses for controller-to-controller and controller-to-processor transfers.[56] If these clauses are used in a substantially unamended form, the benefit of this ground will probably apply. The data controller will need to check with the regulator in the country of the controller's establishment to see whether anything beyond minor amendments to these model clauses will render the transfer illegal. As a general rule, any amendment that diminishes the rights of affected individual employees

---

[54] On the assumption that a court order or subpoena falls into the UK law category where the transfer is necessary for the purpose of, or in connection with, any 'legal proceedings': Information Commissioner, 'The Eighth Data Protection Principle and International Data Transfers', 30 June 2006, para 4.5.1.

[55] An alternative to the approved form of contract is to rely on an internally binding set of corporate rules (BCRs) that apply within the group to the export of employee and/or client personal data between the exporter and the importer. BCRs require prior approval by privacy regulators (the approval process is usually led by the national privacy regulator in the country where the group headquarters are established or where its group-wide data protection functions are managed). Regulators use a model checklist to assess the content of a BCRs application (Article 29 Working Party Working Document 05/EN WP 108) and an agreed procedure for cooperation between regulators (Working Document 05/EN WP 107). To date, it is understood that less than ten companies with a substantial presence in the EU have received BCRs approval for intra-group data transfers. If BCRs are in place, they will only cover intra-group transfers outside the EEA and will not cover sharing with external consultants or regulators located outside the EEA.

[56] Commission Decision (EC) 2001/497 of 15 June 2001 on standard contractual clauses for the transfer of personal data to third countries, under Directive 95/46/EC [2001] OJ L 181/19 as amended by Commission Decision 2004/915/EC17 of 27 December 2004 (controller-to-controller transfers); Commission Decision 2002/16/EC16 of 27 December 2001 (controller-to-processor transfers).

or clients is likely to nullify the effect of using the clauses. In some EU states, use of the model clauses may be supplemented by a requirement on the exporting data controller to obtain a data export permit or licence (eg the Netherlands). In other EU countries, the clauses used by the parties require to be checked by the privacy regulator or be the subject of a formal authorization procedure.[57]

Where the model clauses are used, these do not permit an onward transfer by the data importer (eg to a non-EEA regulator or legal adviser). In these circumstances, a separate contract would need to be put in place between the data importer and the new recipient. It is very unlikely that a non-EEA regulator would agree to enter into a contract that mirrors the European Commission's model clauses; US regulators in particular regularly refuse to do so. **2.41**

The final ground for lawful transfer to a non-EEA based group entity is where that entity is located in a country which the European Commission has declared to have adequate data privacy protection. To date, the countries that have been deemed to offer adequate protection are Argentina, Canada,[58] Guernsey, Isle of Man and Switzerland. These adequacy findings are reviewed every three years. The finding for Argentina is currently the subject of detailed discussion between the European Commission and the national regulator because of perceived inadequacies in local data privacy law. There is a risk that this adequacy finding may be withdrawn or limited if local law and practice in Argentina is not changed. **2.42**

D. External Advisers

The same considerations that apply to data sharing with other group companies also apply to allowing external consultants or advisers to collect or review personal data about employees or clients of the local data controller. **2.43**

Fair processing

The usual grounds for fair processing under the Directive will apply: individual employee or client consent; pursuit of legitimate interests; and public interest grounds. Some national laws may have introduced additional grounds that could be relevant (see 2.26). **2.44**

---

[57] Eg the Belgian regulator requires export contracts to be submitted for checking against the European Commission's model clauses (I Vereecken, 'Belgian Data Protection Rules', Privacy Laws & Business International Newsletter, February 2008, 18); the CNIL in France has an authorization procedure that takes two months unless extended (P Gelly, 'France's New Decree', Privacy Laws & Business International Newsletter, May 2007, 10–11).
[58] Where the importers are subject to the Canadian Personal Information Protection and Electronic Documents Act.

2.45   Consent to collection or use of data by external consultants will need to be informed, unambiguous and freely given consent (see 2.21 to 2.23).

2.46   The legitimate interests ground for fair processing can be satisfied if the processing by the external consultants is in the local data controller's interest (or the interests of another group company), provided there is no substantial impact on the privacy interests of the individuals involved (see 2.24).

2.47   The public interest grounds for fair processing are set out in 2.25 and other grounds that might exist under national law are set out in 2.26.

Data processing contract

2.48   If external consultants are engaged to collect or review personal data of employees or clients, the local data controller should enter into a data processing contract (see 2.27 and 2.28). The prescribed content of the data processing contract will vary depending on the country where the local data controller is established and can be incorporated into the terms of the engagement letter with the consultants.

Exports outside the EEA

2.49   If the external consultants receiving the data are located outside the EEA, or will be accessing it from outside the EEA, the local data controller must ensure that one of the grounds set out in 2.36 applies. The most straightforward way for the controller to comply is to put in place the European Commission's model export clauses with consultants (see 2.40).

E.   Regulators

2.50   This section considers whether the Directive permits the sharing of collected data about employees and clients with regulators based in the same country as the data controller or elsewhere in the EEA or outside the EEA.

Local regulator

2.51   If the regulator is located in the same country as the data controller, data collected by or on behalf of the data controller can be shared with the local regulator under the 'legitimate interests' ground (see 2.24). This ground involves balancing the legitimate interests of the data controller and/or regulator with the privacy impact on the affected employees or clients. In 2005, the Article 29 Working Party of EU privacy regulators issued a unanimous advisory Opinion in the SWIFT case which illustrates how the balancing of interests should be carried out. On the facts, it concluded that the data controller's interest in complying with subpoenas issued under US law[59] was outweighed by the privacy interests of the individual clients where data was sent to the US authorities in a 'hidden, systematic, massive and long term' manner. In the Working Party's view, the balance of interest should take into account issues of proportionality, the seriousness of the alleged offences that can be notified to the regulators and the consequences for the affected employees or clients.[60] The Belgian Information Commissioner issued an opinion in July 2006 that the relevant entity (SWIFT) was in breach of Belgian data protection law. The Swiss regulator found SWIFT in breach of Swiss data protection law in October 2006.

To comply with the 'legitimate interests' ground, the disclosure must be strictly **2.52** necessary for the purposes of the external investigation by the regulator. The local data controller should consider whether employee or client names or other identifying features should be anonymized before disclosure. It may be that only details of a core group of employees or clients needs to be disclosed for investigatory purposes.

Where the local regulator uses coercive powers to compel disclosure, what is dis- **2.53** closed must be strictly necessary to comply with the court order.

Other EEA regulators

The considerations in 2.51 to 2.53 apply to disclosure to a regulator in another **2.54** country but still inside the EEA.

Non-EEA regulators

Disclosure of data to a non-EEA regulator will depend on one of the conditions **2.55** for lawful export being met (see 2.36 to 2.42).

Where the non-EEA regulator is using coercive powers to compel disclosure, what is disclosed must be reviewed carefully to ensure that disclosure does not go wider than the information that is strictly necessary to comply with the terms of the sub poena or court order. However, in the light of the SWIFT case on compliance with US subpoenas, it would be advisable for the local data controller to check with the local privacy regulator whether compliance with a foreign subpoena or court order is permitted (see 2.51).

---

[59] The subpoenas were issued by the US Treasury's Office of Foreign Assets Control (OFAC) under the International Emergency Economic Powers Act 1977 to allow OFAC to scrutinize data in search of patterns that might indicate terrorist financing.

[60] Opinion 10/2006 on the processing of personal data by the Society for Worldwide Interbank Financial Telecommunication (SWIFT) 01935/06/EN WP128.

3

INVESTIGATIONS IN THE UNITED STATES

A. Introduction[1]

3.01 The dawn of the 21st century marked a new era of regulatory activism in the United States. The collapses of Enron and WorldCom brought revelations of corporate fraud that undermined investor confidence in listed companies and the financial markets. US lawmakers responded with new statutes, rules and regulations to enhance the oversight of listed corporations, and the Securities and Exchange Commission (SEC), Department of Justice (DoJ), and stock exchanges redoubled their efforts to enforce the federal securities laws. Now, more than ever, it is important for companies doing business in the US to be familiar with the US regulatory landscape, including who the key regulators are, and the scope and methods of their enforcement powers. It is also important to understand when and how companies should initiate investigations so they can identify and remediate problems and gain credit for cooperation with regulatory authorities.

3.02 Sections B and C of this chapter describe the principal national regulators which govern listed companies in the US. Sections D to F discuss the methods those regulators use to gather information and conduct investigations. Finally, sections G to J describe the law and practice of internal corporate investigations in the US. While there is no 'standard' internal investigation, this chapter aims to define the main characteristics of US internal investigations, and to provide useful guidance on the key issues companies are likely to face when conducting or considering whether to conduct an internal investigation.

B. US Regulatory Scheme

General background

3.03 The primary regulators for listed public companies doing business in the US are the Securities and Exchange Commission (SEC or 'Commission'), the

[1] Contributors: Paul J Cohen, Daniel Kramer, Alex Oh, Angela Papalaskaris. The authors wish to express their gratitude to Keren Azulay, Amir Weinberg and Mayur Saxena for their assistance in writing and editing this chapter.

Department of Justice, and member associations known as self-regulatory organizations (SROs). These regulatory agencies share broad, overlapping authority over listed companies to enforce compliance with US securities and corporate governance laws. This chapter provides an overview of these agencies and the laws that they enforce.

The Securities and Exchange Commission

The SEC is the primary federal government agency responsible for enforcing the federal securities laws and for regulating the securities industry.[2] The SEC was established by the Securities Exchange Act of 1934, five years after the stock market crash that led to the Great Depression.[3] The SEC's primary mission is to protect investors and to preserve the integrity of the financial markets in the US.[4] **3.04**

The SEC consists of four divisions: Corporation Finance, Market Regulation, Investment Management and Enforcement.[5] The Enforcement Division is charged with investigating possible violations of, and enforcing, the federal **3.05**

---

[2] The SEC consists of five commissioners and their staff. The President, with the advice and consent of the US Senate, appoints the commissioners for five-year terms. These terms are staggered. See About the SEC, *The Investor's Advocate: How the SEC Protects Investors, Maintains Market Integrity and Facilitates Capital Formation*, <http://www.sec.gov/about/whatwedo.shtml> (hereinafter *Investor's Advocate*). The composition of the SEC is mandated by statute: •

> Not more than three of such commissioners shall be members of the same political party, and in making appointments members of different political parties shall be appointed alternately as nearly as may be practicable. No commissioner shall engage in any other business, vocation, or employment than that of serving as commissioner, nor shall any commissioner participate, directly or indirectly, in any stock-market operations or transactions of a character subject to regulation by the Commission pursuant to this chapter.

15 USC § 78d(a). One of the Commissioners, also appointed by the President, serves as Chairman and the SEC's top executive. See *Investor's Advocate*. By federal agency standards, the SEC is relatively small. It has approximately 3,100 employees located in Washington, DC and among 11 district and regional offices across the country. See SEC Addresses, <http://www.sec.gov/contact/addresses.htm> (listing locations and contact information for all SEC offices).

[3] 15 USC § 78d (providing for the establishment of the SEC). 'Congress' primary contemplation was that regulation of the securities market might help set the economy on the road to recovery.' *United States v Naftalin* 441 US 768, 775 (1979).

[4] 'The mission of the [SEC] is to protect investors, maintain fair, orderly, and efficient markets, and facilitate capital formation . . . The SEC oversees the key participants in the securities world . . . [and] is concerned primarily with promoting the disclosure of important market-related information, maintaining fair dealing, and protecting against fraud.' *Investor's Advocate*. 'Typical infractions include insider trading, accounting fraud, and providing false or misleading information about securities and the companies that issue them.' Ibid.

[5] Each division has its own director. The responsibilities of each director and the duties of each division are set forth by federal regulations promulgated pursuant to the federal securities laws. See 17 CFR § 200.18 (Director of Division of Corporation Finance); ibid § 200.19a (Director of the Division of Market Regulation); ibid § 200.19b (Director of the Division of Enforcement); ibid § 200.20b (Director of Division of Investment Management).

securities laws.[6] Importantly, the powers of the Enforcement Division are civil in nature only. The SEC has no authority to bring criminal charges against individuals or corporations; however, the SEC can refer appropriate cases to the DoJ for criminal prosecution.[7]

3.06 The SEC's jurisdiction extends to all companies that are, or seek to be, listed on an American exchange, as well as to a certain class of people and entities—including investment advisers, investment companies and broker-dealers—that facilitate and mediate securities listings and/or trades by or for such listed companies.[8] Regulatory jurisdiction extends to foreign companies that register with the SEC to market and trade their securities in the US.[9]

3.07 The SEC administers the principal federal laws that regulate the securities industry in the US. These include the Securities Act of 1933, the Securities Exchange Act of 1934, the Public Utility Holding Company Act of 1935, the Trust Indenture Act of 1939, the Investment Advisors Act of 1940, the Investment Company Act of 1940 and the Sarbanes-Oxley Act of 2002 (SOX).[10]

---

[6] 17 CFR § 200.19b, in relevant part, provides that:
    The Director of the Division of Enforcement is responsible to the Commission for supervising and conducting all enforcement activities under the acts administered by the Commission. The Director recommends the institution of administrative and injunctive actions arising out of such enforcement activities and determines the sufficiency of evidence to support the allegations in any proposed complaint.

[7] See 17 CFR § 200.19b ('The Director supervises the Regional Directors and, in collaboration with the General Counsel, reviews cases to be recommended to the Department of Justice for criminal prosecution.'); ibid § 202.5(b) (granting the SEC discretion to refer willful violations of fraud to the DoJ for criminal prosecution but not allowing the SEC to prosecute directly).

[8] The SEC generally requires registration and regulation of these persons and entities. See Investment Advisors Act of 1940, 15 USC § 80b-3 (investment advisers); Investment Company Act of 1940, ibid § 80a-8 (investment companies); Securities Exchange Act of 1934, ibid § 78o (brokers and dealers).

[9] See 14 G P Lander, *US Securities Law for International Financial Transactions and Capital Markets* (2nd edn, 2005), § 2:1; see also 17 CFR § 240.12g3-2 (outlining registration requirements for foreign securities sold in US markets); *Itoba Ltd v LEP Group plc* 54 F 3d 118, 120 (2nd Cir 1995) (holding a foreign issuer with stocks traded on NASDAQ subject to the jurisdiction of US courts); *Pinker v Roche Holdings Ltd* 292 F 3d 361, 367–68, 372–73 (3rd Cir 2002) (holding that American Depository Receipts (ADRs) grant US courts jurisdiction over foreign companies and stating that ADRs are subject to SEC regulation). Like foreign broker-dealers and investment companies, above, foreign securities can be exempt from registration requirements provided they meet exacting criteria. See 17 CFR § 240.12g3-2 (allowing an exemption from registration requirements if the company has less than $10m in assets and fewer than 300 stockholders in the US). As a result of recent efforts to encourage participation in US markets, the SEC has eased rules for deregistration by foreign companies. See infra notes 75–76.

[10] See Lander (n 9 above), at §§ 1:3 to 1:9 (describing federal securities statutes administered by the SEC). See also 17 CFR § 200.1 (listing generally what is provided for by these federal securities laws).

The Securities Act of 1933,[11] also known as the 'Truth in Securities Act', requires, **3.08**
among other things, that the disclosure of financial and other information concerning companies whose securities are sold to the public be truthful.[12] Among
other things, the 1933 Act requires registration of securities that are being offered
for public sale.[13]

The Securities Exchange Act of 1934[14] is also known as the Exchange Act.[15] **3.09**
While the Securities Act regulates the initial public offering of securities, the
Exchange Act regulates secondary trading of securities on market exchanges.[16]
The Exchange Act empowers the SEC with broad authority to regulate all aspects
of the securities industry.[17]

Under the Securities Act and the Exchange Act, the SEC has the authority to pro- **3.10**
mulgate rules that have the force of law.[18] SEC rules are substantial in both number and effect.[19] Violations of the Securities Act and the Exchange Act, as well as
the rules promulgated thereunder, are enforced by the SEC.

---

[11] Securities Act, c 38, § 1, 48 Stat 74 (current version at 15 USC §§ 77a-77aa).

[12] See Lander (n 9 above), § 1:3.

[13] See *Investor's Advocate*. Investors who suffer losses as a result of purchasing registered securities
may be able to recover from the company if they can establish that there was insufficient or incorrect
disclosure of material information. US federal courts have jurisdiction in all cases brought to enforce
the Securities Act of 1933. See 15 USC § 77v.

[14] Securities Exchange Act, c 404, § 1, 48 Stat 881 (current version at 15 USC §§ 78a-78mm).

[15] In addition to creating the SEC, the Exchange Act transferred the administration of the
Securities Act to the SEC. See 17 CFR § 200.1. Formerly, the Securities Act was administered by
another US government agency, the Federal Trade Commission.

[16] See Lander (n 9 above), § 1:4.

[17] The SEC's Investor's Advocate lists the following as the powers given to the SEC by the
Exchange Act:
   This includes the power to register, regulate, and oversee brokerage firms, transfer agents,
   and clearing agencies as well as the nation's securities self regulatory organizations (SROs)
   . . . The Act also identifies and prohibits certain types of conduct in the markets and provides the Commission with disciplinary powers over regulated entities and persons associated with them. The Act also empowers the SEC to require periodic reporting of information
   by companies with publicly traded securities.
See *Investor's Advocate*. Importantly, 'the Exchange Act broadly prohibits fraudulent activities of any
kind in connection with the offer, purchase, or sale of securities'. Lander (n 9 above), § 1:4. § 27 of
the Exchange Act confers jurisdiction to US federal courts over all cases arising from the Exchange
Act, 15 USC § 78aa.

[18] Lander (n 9 above), § 1:12.

[19] The rules promulgated by the SEC can be found at Title VII, Chapter 2 of the US Code of
Federal Regulations. See ibid (describing the hierarchy of federal securities laws).

3.11   In addition to bringing civil charges against violators, the SEC can issue Reports of Investigation[20] and provide 'No-Action Letters',[21] among other types of formal and informal guidance regarding securities regulations. A Report of Investigation is used to alert the markets and issuers about certain conduct that the SEC finds objectionable, and to signal the government's intent to prosecute future potential violators who fail to take preventive measures or otherwise heed the SEC's concerns.[22] A 'No-Action' Letter may be issued by the SEC Staff in response to a request by an individual or entity seeking clarification as to 'whether a particular product, service, or action would constitute a violation of the federal securities law'.[23]

3.12   The SEC's jurisdiction is not intended to cover companies listed on a non-US securities exchange that merges with a US exchange. For example, in June 2006, the NYSE and Euronext NV, a foreign securities exchange, announced an agreement to merge.[24] In response to the fear that any such arrangement might extend

---

[20] See A C Flannery, 'Time for a Change: A Re-Examination of the Settlement Policies of the Securities and Exchange Commission' (1994) 51 Washington & Lee Law Review 1015, for a discussion of how the SEC uses these reports to shape securities laws. See, eg, SEC, Report of Investigation Pursuant to Section 21(a) of the Securities Exchange Act of 1934: Motorola Inc, Release No 46898/ November 25, 2002, <http://www.sec.gov/litigation/investreport/34-46898.htm> ('Here, before engaging in the conduct in question, Motorola officials sought the advice of in-house legal counsel. Counsel approved the conduct in question based on a determination that the information in question was not material or nonpublic. Counsel's determination was erroneous in both respects. Nevertheless, because it appears that counsel's advice was sought and given in good faith, and in light of the surrounding facts and circumstances, we are issuing this Report rather than bringing an enforcement action against Motorola or its senior officials.').

[21] See, eg, SEC, Handy Hardware Wholesale, Inc., No-Action Letter, June 28, 2006, <http://www.sec.gov/divisions/corpfin/cf-noaction/hhw062906.htm>.

[22] The SEC derives its authority to issue Reports of Investigation pursuant to § 21(a) of the Exchange Act. W H Volz and V Tazian, 'The Role of Attorneys Under Sarbanes-Oxley: The Qualified Legal Compliance Committee as Facilitator of Corporate Integrity' (2006) 43 American Business Law Journal 439, 444 n 22.

   [23] See SEC, No Action Letters, <http://www.sec.gov/answers/noaction.htm>:
   Most no-action letters describe the request, analyze the particular facts and circumstances involved, discuss applicable laws and rules, and, if the staff grants the request for no action, concludes that the SEC staff would not recommend that the Commission take enforcement action against the requester based on the facts and representations described in the individual's or entity's original letter.

   [24] In describing the proposed transaction, one commentator explained:
   Euronext will not register as a US exchange and will not offer its products directly in the US. Indeed, under this model, while the holding company for the markets will be under US jurisdiction and the NYSE will continue to be a US registered exchange, the non-US markets will not. As a result, there would not be mandatory registration of the non-US markets' listed companies in the US, nor would our federal securities laws necessarily apply to the non-US exchanges.

A L Nazareth, Commissioner, SEC, 'Speech by SEC Commissioner: Remarks Before the NYSE Regulation Second Annual Securities Conference' (20 June 2006) (hereinafter 'Nazareth Remarks'), available at <http://www.sec.gov/news/speech/2006/spch062006aln.htm>.

the applicability of US securities laws,[25] representatives from the exchanges have provided assurances to the contrary and have sought to structure the merger so as to avoid the reach of US regulators over foreign markets.[26]

The Department of Justice (DoJ)

In addition to the SEC, the DoJ is responsible for enforcement of the federal securities laws and for generally policing corporate behaviour in the US.[27] The DoJ operates through a number of subdivisions and subsidiary organizations, including the Federal Bureau of Investigation (FBI)[28] and the US Attorney's Offices (USAO).[29] While the FBI is the primary investigative branch of the DoJ,[30] the USAO is the frontline in the criminal prosecution of federal crimes, **3.13**

---

[25] See 'NYSE-Euronext merger deal may include anti-Sarbanes-Oxley break-up clause, <http://www.forbes.com/home/feeds/afx/2006/07/25/afx2901492.html> (25 July 2006).

[26] Ibid (noting that, in order to overcome fears amongst Euronext-listed companies and traders on its markets that US regulators might attempt to apply SOX corporate reporting rules to companies listed on non-US exchanges, lawyers and regulators are collaborating on a clause to include in the merger agreement that would end the deal if any attempt was made to apply SOX to any non-US exchanges based on any affiliation between NYSE and Euronext). Furthermore, British authorities have announced legislation designed to protect UK-listed companies from SOX rules. See J Eaglesham, N Cohen and J Grant, 'London Acts to Protect City from Threat of US Regulation', Financial Times (14 September 2006). One SEC Commissioner has remarked that 'Sarbanes Oxley would not apply to any market not registered in the US, nor would it apply to companies listed on that non-US market'. Nazareth Remarks.

[27] The DoJ was created in 1870, pursuant to the Act to Establish the Department of Justice, c 150, 16 Stat 162 (1870), which gave the DoJ control over all criminal prosecutions and civil suits that involved a federal interest. See About DoJ, <http://www.usdoj.gov/02organizations/index.html>. Its titular head is the Attorney General, a member of the President's cabinet, whose office had existed for nearly a century prior to the DoJ's creation. See Judiciary Act of 1789, c 20, § 35, 1 Stat 73, 92–93 (1789). In general, the DoJ's mission is:

> To enforce the law and defend the interests of the United States according to the law; to ensure public safety against threats foreign and domestic; to provide federal leadership in preventing and controlling crime; to seek just punishment for those guilty of unlawful behavior; and to ensure fair and impartial administration of justice for all Americans.

The DoJ has both civil and criminal authority.

[28] The FBI is the investigative arm of the DoJ. The general authority for the FBI is based on 28 USC § 533. In addition, there are other statutes, such as the Congressional Assassination, Kidnapping, and Assault Act (18 USC § 351), which give the FBI responsibility to investigate specific crimes. See Federal Bureau of Investigation <http://www.fbi.gov/priorities/priorities.htm>.

[29] The US Attorneys represent the federal government in US District Court, which is the trial court level; 28 USC § 547; see also US Attorneys' Manual (USAM) § 1-2.500 (November 2003) ('The United States Attorneys serve as the nation's principal litigators under the direction of the Attorney General. As such, the United States Attorneys conduct most of the trial work in which the United States is a party.').

[30] See DoJ, Federal Bureau of Investigation, Financial Crimes Report to the Public (May 2005), <http://www.fbi.gov/publications/financial/fcs_report052005/fcs_report052005.htm#a1> ('There are presently 405 Corporate Fraud cases being pursued by FBI field offices throughout the United States. This represents a 100 percent increase over the number of Corporate Fraud cases pending at the end of Fiscal Year 2003.').

including corporate crimes, and the USAO and the FBI often work together in the investigation and prosecution of federal crimes.

3.14   Federal statutes enforced by the FBI and DoJ under which corporate crimes can be prosecuted are too extensive to list in full here.[31] Such statutes include provisions relating to mail and wire fraud,[32] securities fraud,[33] making false statements to the federal government,[34] bank fraud,[35] money laundering,[36] counterfeiting[37] and obstruction of justice.[38]

3.15   The USAO also works with other federal investigative agencies to investigate potential violations of specific statutes, including the US Postal Inspection Service (eg violations of mail and wire fraud), the Secret Service (eg counterfeiting crimes), and the Internal Revenue Service (IRS) (eg tax evasion). For instance, the IRS employs special agents to carry out investigations into potential violations of the Internal Revenue Code, the Bank Secrecy Act and various money laundering statutes and can recommend criminal prosecutions to the DoJ.[39]

3.16   In addition to the FBI and the USAO, the DoJ's Antitrust Division is entrusted with enforcement of federal anti-trust laws. The principal anti-trust laws in the US are the Sherman Act and the Clayton Act.[40] Together, these laws apply broadly to prohibit various practices that restrain trade, such as price-fixing cartels, predatory acts aimed at monopolizing, either in part or in whole, an industry, and corporate mergers likely to result in stifled competition of particular markets. Depending on the violation of law, the Antitrust Division can seek criminal penalties or civil remedies, which may include monetary fines and injunctive relief.[41]

3.17   The authority of the DoJ was enhanced in the aftermath of the Enron scandal. In order to strengthen the DoJ's power to investigate and prosecute significant corporate crimes, President George W Bush established a Corporate Fraud Task

---

[31] For instance, the FBI has 'jurisdiction over violations of more than 200 categories of federal law'; see <http://www.fbi.gov/hq.htm>. A list of statutes currently administered by the DoJ's criminal division is set forth in USAM § 9-4.000 (January 2006).

[32] Mail and wire fraud are prohibited by 18 USC §§ 1341–43.

[33] Securities fraud is prohibited as a crime under 18 USC § 1348.

[34] The making of false statements to any agency of the federal government is a criminal offence pursuant to 18 USC §§ 1001-02.

[35] Bank fraud is prohibited by 18 USC § 1344.

[36] Money laundering is punishable as a crime pursuant to 18 USC §§ 1956-57.

[37] Counterfeiting and forgery are prohibited primarily by 18 USC §§ 471, 473–74.

[38] There are several provisions relating to obstruction of justice including: 18 USC § 1503 (influencing or injuring officer or juror generally); 18 USC § 1510 (obstruction of criminal investigations); 18 USC § 1512 (tampering with a witness, victim or informant); and 18 USC § 1519 (destruction, alteration, falsification of records in Federal investigations and bankruptcy).

[39] See IRS, 'How Criminal Investigations Are Initiated' <http://www.irs.gov/compliance/enforcement/article/0,,id=175752,00.html>.

[40] See Sherman Act, 15 USC §§ 1-7; Clayton Act, 15 USC § 14, 18, 19 and 20.

[41] See Overview of the Antitrust Division <http://www.usdoj.gov/atr/overview.html>.

Force by Executive Order No 13271 on 9 July 2002.[42] The Corporate Fraud Task Force consists of the Deputy Attorney General, Assistant Attorney General from the tax and criminal divisions of the DoJ, the Director of the FBI and US Attorneys from several districts.[43]

Parallel investigations

As noted above, the SEC has no power to pursue an individual or a corporation **3.18** for criminal violations of US securities laws.[44] Rather, that power rests with the DoJ. The SEC is only authorized to refer cases to the DoJ if it suspects criminal activity has occurred.[45] In addition, it is fairly common in the US for the SEC and the DoJ to conduct simultaneous—or parallel—investigations.[46]

Recently, courts have enforced limits on how regulators may conduct parallel **3.19** investigations. For example, the DoJ cannot use the SEC to gather evidence to be used in a criminal proceeding. In a recent opinion, a US District Judge dismissed an indictment filed against defendants who cooperated with an SEC investigation without having been told that the USAO was closely monitoring the SEC investigation, or that the SEC was passing along information gathered in its investigation to the federal prosecutors.[47] The court's rationale was that '[t]he strategy used [by the regulators] to conceal the criminal investigation from defendants was an abuse of the investigative process' and that '[t]he government's tactic to move forward under the guise of a civil investigation, violated defendants' due process rights'.[48]

---

[42] The Corporate Fraud Task Force is under the authority of the Attorney General. See Executive Order 13271—Establishment of the Corporate Fraud Task Force (11 July 2002) <http://frwebgate. access.gpo.gov/cgi-bin/getdoc.cgi?dbname=2002_register&docid=02-17640-filed.pdf>.

[43] In addition to DoJ members, there are several agency officials, including the Chairman of the SEC, who belong to the interagency group of the President's Corporate Fraud Task Force; see ibid. 'Since its creation, the Task Force has coordinated and overseen all corporate fraud matters under investigation by the Department of Justice and enhanced inter-agency coordination of regulatory and criminal investigations.' Corporate Fraud Task Force, Second Year Report to the President (20 July 2004) <http://www.usdoj.gov/dag/cftf/2nd_yr_fraud_report.pdf>.

[44] See nn 6 and 7 above.

[45] See SEC, E Tafara, Director, Office of International Affairs, Speech by SEC Staff: Remarks Presented at the IMF Conference on Cross-Border Cooperation and Information Exchange (7–8 July 2004) (hereinafter 'Tafara Remarks'), available at <http://www.sec.gov/news/speech/ spch070704et.htm> ('SEC staff may refer a matter to DOJ for investigation, and DOJ may conduct its criminal investigations parallel to the SEC's civil investigations.').

[46] Hence, companies often find themselves facing both regulators. See, eg, L Rohde, 'Time Warner Cuts DOJ Deal on AOL Case, SEC May Follow', The Industry Standard (4 April 2005) <http:// www.thestandard.com/internetnews/002585.php> (regarding certain accounting practices); DOJ News Release, 'Diagnostic Products Corporation Announces Settlements with the SEC and DOJ' (20 May 2005) <http://www.allbusiness.com/government/government-bodies-offices/5137356-1. html> (concerning compliance with the US Foreign Corrupt Practices Act).

[47] *United States v Stringer* 408 F Supp 2d 1083 (D Ore 2006).

[48] *Ibid* at 1088–89. Cf *United States v Scrushy* 366 F Supp 2d 1134 (ND Ala 2005). In *Scrushy*, the court found that the DoJ prosecutors and the SEC regulators acted improperly because the parallel investigations were 'inescapably intertwined', which 'negated the existence of parallel investigations'. Ibid at 1140. 'To be parallel, by definition, the separate investigations should be like the side-by-side train tracks

3.20 Parallel investigations are not limited to federal authorities. State authorities may also participate in parallel investigations along with federal regulators.[49] New York state, through its former Attorney General Eliot Spitzer, has used its authority to investigate and prosecute corporate misconduct.[50] In one instance, several different regulators, including the New York Attorney General, the SEC, and the DoJ, led an investigation into alleged conflicts of interest between the research analysis and investment banking divisions of various financial institutions, which led to an industry-wide global settlement.[51]

Self-regulatory organizations (SROs)

3.21 In addition to the SEC and DoJ, SROs are organizations that administer rules against their members based on federal securities laws.[52] The Exchange Act

that never intersect.' Ibid at 1139. Thus, upon the defendant's motion, his statements made during an SEC deposition were ordered to be suppressed and could not be used to criminally prosecute him.

[49] In the US, under the doctrine of dual sovereignty, the filing of federal charges does not preclude a subsequent filing of state charges based on the same facts. The doctrine of dual sovereignty can trace its roots back to the common law, where crime was considered to be a crime against the sovereignty of the government. See, eg, *Heath v Alabama* 474 US 82, 88 (1985). 'When a defendant in a single act violates the "peace and dignity" of two sovereigns by breaking the law of each, he has committed two distinct "offences".' Ibid. States are separate sovereigns with respect to the federal government and with respect to each other. See ibid at 89.

In addition, most states have laws regulating the offering and sale of securities. See Lander (n 9 above), § 1:10 ('Except where state law is specifically preempted, the various statutes under which the SEC operates all contain provisions generally preserving the jurisdiction of the state securities commissions. As a result, the federal and state governments have separate, independent securities laws.'). The state laws date largely from the era prior to federal legislation on securities and are commonly known as 'blue sky' laws. P G Mahoney, 'The Origins of the Blue-Sky Laws: A Test of Competing Hypotheses' (2003) 46 Journal of Law & Economics 229, 231. Thus, it is possible for a company to face both federal and state charges of securities fraud.

[50] For instance, during joint investigations of the mutual fund industry, a bank employee accused of alleged wrongdoing was facing New York state criminal charges as well as a federal civil enforcement action for his role in a scheme that involved the unlawful trading of mutual funds. See Press Release, Office of NYS Attorney General Eliot Spitzer, 'Attorney General Spitzer and Securities and Exchange Commission File Charges Against Bank of America Broker' (16 September 2003) <http://www.oag. state.ny.us/press/2003/sep/sep16a_03.html> (noting SEC Director of Enforcement Stephen M Cutler's remark: 'I am pleased that the staff of the Commission and Attorney General Spitzer were able to work closely and cooperatively in bringing today's important actions.'). Spitzer relied upon New York's blue sky law, New York General Business Law, §§ 352–359-h, also known as the Martin Act, which provides the Attorney General 'with what one commentator has characterized as "the broadest and most easily triggered investigative and prosecutorial powers of any securities regulator, state or federal"'. See *State v 7040 Colonial Rd Assocs Co* 671 NYS 2d 938, 941-42 (1998) (quoting Kaufmann, 'Introduction and Commentary Overview', 19 NY Gen Bus Law § 23-A, at 9). With the addition of criminal penalties in 1955, the Martin Act became a formidable weapon in the hands of a prosecutor willing to use it. See B A Masters, 'Eliot Spitzer Spoils for a Fight: Opponents Blast Unusual Tactics of NY Attorney General', *Washington Post* (31 May 2004), at A1 ('[Eliot Spitzer's] office has a history of picking cases that make imaginative, but legally supportable, use of New York's unusually strong anti-fraud laws.').

[51] For information about the Global Settlement, see Spotlight on the Global Research Analyst Settlement <http://www.sec.gov/spotlight/globalsettlement.htm>.

[52] See Lander (n 9 above), § 1:4 ('An SRO is a member organization that creates and enforces rules for its members based on the federal securities laws. SROs are overseen by the SEC and are the front line in regulating broker-dealers.').

empowers the SEC to register, regulate and oversee SROs.[53] The SROs include the various US securities exchanges, including, for example, NYSE (New York Stock Exchange) and NASDAQ (National Association of Securities Dealers Automated Quotations).[54]

All SROs have the ability, and indeed an obligation, to investigate and discipline members for non-compliance with their rules. The failure of an SRO properly to regulate its members may result in a sanction against the SRO itself.[55]   **3.22**

The NYSE traces its existence back over 200 years, and long pre-dates the Securities Act, the Exchange Act and the SEC.[56] The NYSE hosts, and regulates the conduct of, both members[57] and listed companies.[58]   **3.23**

---

[53] 15 USC § 78s (providing for registration, responsibilities and oversight of SROs).

[54] See ibid § 78f (providing for national securities exchanges). An exchange is defined broadly to include:

> any organization, association, or group of persons, whether incorporated or unincorporated, which constitutes, maintains, or provides a market place or facilities for bringing together purchasers and sellers of securities or for otherwise performing with respect to securities the functions commonly performed by a stock exchange as that term is generally understood, and includes the market place and the market facilities maintained by such exchange.

L Loss and J Seligman, *Securities Regulation* (3rd edn, 2004) § 7-B-1. All exchanges must be registered with, and are regulated by, the SEC; Lander, (n 9 above), § 1:4.

[55] For example, the SEC sanctioned the Philadelphia Stock Exchange for failing, from mid-1999 to early 2002, to enforce certain trading and order handling rules against certain specialists. One SEC official stated that '[i]t is essential that self-regulatory organizations vigorously enforce their own rules and the federal securities laws. This settlement will help strengthen [the Exchange's] regulatory function'. SEC Press Release, 'SEC Charges the Philadelphia Stock Exchange with Failing to Police Specialists' (1 June 2006) <http://www.sec.gov/news/press/2006/2006-84.htm (finding 'several deficiencies in [the Exchange's] surveillance programs to assure compliance with its own rules and the federal securities laws in both its options and equities markets').

[56] The NYSE, therefore, had extensive time to promulgate and refine rules of behaviour governing companies listed on and trading through it before the SEC was established. Many of the basic requirements set forth in the Securities Act and the Exchange Act already applied (albeit merely as a condition of membership) to companies listed on the NYSE. Rather than strip the NYSE and other such organizations of authority to make rules applicable to listed companies, the SEC allowed them to maintain an essentially self-regulatory function. See NYSE Group, <http://www.nyse.com/home.html>, for background and overview of the NYSE.

The NYSE regulates itself through a subsidiary, NYSE Regulation, Inc. See, About NYSE Regula-tion <http://www.nyse.com/regulation/about/1145313073247.html>. 'The rules are designed to prevent fraudulent or manipulative acts and practices, and provide a means by which NYSE Regulation can take appropriate disciplinary actions against its membership when rule violations occur.' Ibid <http://www.nyse.com/regulation/rules/1145486472038.html>. Because the NYSE is subject to SEC regulatory oversight, all rules and rule amendments proposed by the NYSE must be approved by the SEC. Ibid.

[57] A member organization is '[a] registered broker-dealer organized as a corporation, a partnership or an LLC, which is regulated by the Exchange. A member organization may, or may not, hold a trading license . . . [which] is required to effect transactions on the floor of the Exchange or through any facility thereof.' See <http://www.nyse.com/> (click 'Glossary' and under the letter 'M', click 'Member Organization'.

[58] NYSE-listed companies are wide-ranging in nature; these include all types of businesses from financial institutions (Bank of America) and investment firms (AllianceBernstein), to pharmaceutical companies (Pfizer) and retail stores (Wal-Mart). 'As of December 31, 2005, the NYSE listed approximately 2,672 issuers, which includes operating companies, closed-end funds and exchange

3.24   The National Association of Securities Dealers (NASD) is another prominent SRO in the US.[59] The NASD is a 'national securities association' established pursuant to section 15A of the Exchange Act,[60] and primarily regulates the conduct of broker-dealers in the US.[61]

3.25   In November 2006, in a move that was applauded by SEC Chairman Christopher Cox as a major improvement to self-regulation in the securities industry,[62] the NYSE and NASD announced that they would merge the regulatory arms of their respective operations by the middle of 2007.[63] The joint operation is the Financial Industry Regulatory Authority (FINRA).

3.26   As with the DoJ and state authorities, SROs also can and do conduct investigations parallel to the SEC.[64] While SROs do not have formal compulsory powers in an investigation,[65] as a practical matter they possess considerable authority to obtain cooperation from their members under threat of sanctions.[66] Failure to

---

traded funds.' NYSE Group <http://www.nyse.com/about/listed/1089312755443.html>. Note that NYSE listing standards vary for US and non-US companies. 'Domestic listing requirements call for minimum distribution of a company's shares within the United States.' NYSE Group <http://www.nyse.com/regulation/listed/1022221392369.html>. For non-US companies, '[t]he Exchange offers two sets of standards—worldwide and domestic—under which non-US companies may qualify for listing. Both standards include distribution and financial criteria. A company must qualify for both the distribution and financial criteria within that particular standard.' NYSE Group <http://www.nyse.com/regulation/listed/1147474807398.html>.

[59] The NASD 'oversee[s] the activities of more than 5,000 brokerage firms, approximately 170,328 branch offices and more than 658,400 registered securities representatives. In addition, [the NASD] provide[s] outsourced regulatory products and services to a number of stock markets and exchanges'. <http://www.nasd.com/AboutNASD/index.htm>.

[60] 15 USC § 78o-3; see also Restated Certificate of Incorporation of NASD <http://nasd.complinet.com/nasd/display/display.html?rbid=1189&element_id=1159000025>. Section 15A provides that 'an association of brokers and dealers may be registered as a national securities association' by filing an application for registration with the SEC. To become registered as a 'national securities association', the SEC must determine, inter alia, that the 'rules of the association are designed to prevent fraudulent and manipulative acts and practices'. 15 USC § 78o-3(b)(6).

[61] Broker-dealers are subject to regulation by the SEC as a result of the Exchange Act. Ibid § 78o.

[62] Speech by SEC Chairman, Christopher Cox, 'Statement at News Conference Announcing NYSE-NASD Regulatory Merger', <http://www.sec.gov/news/speech/2006/spch11280cc.htm> (Cox stated that '[t]his could make our self-regulatory system more efficient and more robust from an investor protection standpoint . . . we'll have a coordinated, integrated effort to keep our markets free of fraud and unfair dealing').

[63] G Farrell, 'Nasdaq, NYSE to Combine Regulators', *USA Today* (28 November 2006) <http://www.usatoday.com/money/markets/us/2006-11-28-watchdogs_x.htm>.

[64] This was, for example, the case with the research analyst investigations. Thus, the Global Settlement resolved actions by the NYSE and NASD. See n 51 above.

[65] See M I Steinberg and R C Ferrara, *Securities Practice: Federal and State Enforcement* (2nd edn, 2001) §14.5.

[66] Pursuant to its NYSE Rule 476, for example, the NYSE can impose the following types of sanctions: 'expulsion; suspension; limitation as to activities, functions, and operations, including

abide by SROs' rules or to cooperate with their inquiries can result in a fine and/ or censure, suspension, or possible delisting, which may have devastating consequences equivalent to those of governmental sanctions.[67]

Any disciplinary action instituted by an SRO is subject to review by the SEC.[68] **3.27**
Final orders of the SEC, in turn, are subject to review by the US Courts of Appeal.[69]

C. SOX and the Current Regulatory Environment

The aggressive regulatory response to the Enron and WorldCom scandals was **3.28**
exemplified by the enactment, on 30 July 2002, of the Sarbanes-Oxley Act (SOX).[70] Wide-ranging in scope, SOX was designed, among other things, to strengthen the autonomy of auditing firms; to improve the quality and transparency of financial reports and corporate disclosures; to enhance corporate governance; to increase the objectivity of investment analyst research; and to impose harsher penalties for violation of federal securities laws.[71]

Among SOX's principle provisions are the following: **3.29**

• **Certification requirements:** Sections 302 and 906 of SOX impose extensive new obligations upon all principal executive and financial officers of listed

---

the suspension or cancellation of a registration in, or assignment of, one or more stocks; fine; censure; suspension or bar from being associated with any member or member organization; or any other fitting sanction'. NYSE Rules <http://www.nyse.com/regulation/rules/1098571481177. html>.

[67] See, eg, NYSE News Release, 'NYSE Regulation Fines Deutsche Bank Securities, Inc. $1.275 Million In Two Disciplinary Actions' (8 February 2007) <http://www.nyse.com/ press/1170761886458.html>; NYSE News Release, 'NYSE Regulation Announces Decision to Suspend, Apply to Delist, Navistar International Corp.' (6 February 2007) <http://www.nyse.com/ press/1170156819548.html>.

[68] 15 USC § 78s(d). See, eg, *Shultz v SEC* 614 F 2d 561, 568 (7th Cir 1980); *Eichler v SEC* 757 F 2d 1066, 1070 (9th Cir 1985) (stating that the standard of review is de novo).

[69] 15 USC § 78y. *Shultz*, 614 F 2d at 568; *Eichler*, 757 F 2d at 1068 ('The findings of the Commission as to the facts, if supported by substantial evidence, are conclusive.') (quoting 15 USC § 78).

[70] President Bush signed SOX into law one month after the WorldCom fraud was publicly revealed. See J J Huber and J K Hoffman, 'The Sarbanes-Oxley Act of 2002 and SEC Rulemaking', in J J Huber, S Keller, V B Tsaganos and J Wolfman (eds), *The Practitioner's Guide to the Sarbanes-Oxley Act* (2004) I-3, n 2.

[71] See ibid at I-5 to I-7. Note that SOX was intended as 'a paradigm shift for all public companies, *both domestic and foreign*'. at I-5 (emphasis added). SOX provided the Enforcement Division of the SEC 'with significant new enforcement tools, including new causes of action, new remedies, and new regulators'. D B Bayless, 'Defending Your Client in the World of SEC Enforcement', Part I, 3 No 3 Sec Litigation Report 1 (March 2006).

companies to certify certain matters in periodic reports filed with the SEC.[72] In addition, pursuant to section 404, public companies subject to SEC reporting requirements must include in their annual reports a report of management on the company's internal control over financial reporting.[73]

- **Internal controls:** Reporting companies are required to maintain and provide disclosure relating to their internal procedures designed to ensure that information required to be disclosed is processed and reported within the required time period.

- **Independent audit committees and auditors:** Under section 301 of SOX, all listed companies must have independent audit committees. The audit committee hires and supervises the company's independent auditor. If the audit committee does not include a financial expert, the company must explain why not.[74] Additionally, section 202 of SOX prohibits auditors from providing to their audit clients specified services, including, for example, bookkeeping, appraisal or valuation services or management functions.

- **Disgorgement of CEO and CFO compensation following restatements:** Section 302 of SOX provides that if an issuer restates its financial statements due to material non-compliance with financial reporting requirements as the result of misconduct, the CEO and CFO must disgorge all bonuses and incentive-based compensation received during the 12-month period following the first public issuance or filing with the Commission of the document containing the non-compliant report.

---

[72] Section 302 requires a certification to be included in each annual or quarterly report filed with the SEC: (1) that the signing officer has reviewed the report; (2) that the report does not contain any material misrepresentations; (3) that the report accurately reflects the company's financial statements; (4) that the signing officer is responsible for establishing and maintaining internal controls to ensure that material information about the company is known to such officers during the reporting period, and that these controls have been evaluated within 90 days prior to the report, which also must include the signing officer's conclusions as to the effectiveness of its controls; (5) that the signing officer has made adequate disclosures to the company's auditors regarding the design or operation of its controls and any potential fraud involving anyone who has a significant role in the company's controls; and (6) whether there have been any significant changes to the company's internal controls since its last report. See SEC, 'Final Rule: Certification of Disclosure in Companies' Quarterly and Annual Reports', Release Nos 33-8124, 34-46427, 67 Fed Reg 57, 276 (28 August 2002) <http://www.sec.gov/rules/final/33-8124.htm>.

Section 906 provides for enhanced criminal penalties for failure to certify financial reports. Accordingly, violations of this provision are punishable by a fine up to $1m or imprisonment up to ten years, or both. See 18 USC § 1350(c)(1). For wilful violations, punishment can range up to a $5m fine or imprisonment up to 20 years, or both. Ibid § 1350(c)(2).

[73] See SEC, 'Final Rule: Management's Reports on Internal Control Over Financial Reporting and Certification of Disclosure in Exchange Act Periodic Reports', Release Nos 33-8238, 34-47986, 68 Fed Reg 36,635 (5 June 2003) <http://www.sec.gov/rules/final/33-8238.htm>.

[74] See E F Greene, L N Silverman, D M Becker, E J Rosen, J L Fisher, D A Braverman and S R Sperber, *The Sarbanes-Oxley Act: Analysis and Practice* (2003) 2–3.

- **Trading prohibitions during pension blackout periods:** Section 306(a) of SOX prohibits directors and executive officers of public companies from purchasing, selling or otherwise acquiring or transferring any securities of such company during any pension plan blackout period, if a director or executive officer acquired the securities in connection with his or her service or employment as a director or executive officer.

- **Prohibition on personal loans to executives:** Under section 402 of SOX, it is unlawful for an issuer to make, maintain or arrange for loans to executive officers and directors, except for certain types of loans approved by section 402(k)(2), such as loans for home improvements, margin loans by a broker-dealer to its employees, or loans by a depository institution subject to insider lending restrictions.

- **Real time issuer disclosure:** Section 409 of SOX requires issuers to disclose to the public, 'on a rapid and current basis', such information as the SEC may require relating to material changes in the issuer's financial condition or operations. These disclosures are to be presented in terms that are easy to understand, supported by trend and qualitative information or graphic presentations as appropriate.

- **Periodic SEC review of public company filings:** Section 408 of SOX establishes criteria the SEC should consider in scheduling periodic review of a public company's filings. Among the factors to be considered are: the volatility of stock price, whether the company issued material restatements of financial results, or whether the issuer's operations significantly affect any material sector of the economy. In any event, section 408 requires the review of a public company's filing at least once every three years.

- **The establishment of the PCAOB:** Sections 101–107 of SOX establish the Public Company Accounting Oversight Board (PCAOB), a quasi-regulatory body subject to the supervision of the SEC, which is responsible for establishing auditing, quality control, attestation and ethics standards for auditors.

- **Enhanced criminal and civil penalties:** Several SOX provisions enhance the criminal and civil liability for violations of various securities regulations. Among others, section 802 of SOX creates new crimes for destruction, alteration, or falsification of records in federal investigations and bankruptcy, and for destruction of audit records, which must be maintained for seven years; section 807 of SOX creates new criminal penalties for defrauding shareholders of publicly traded companies; and section 804 of SOX extends the statute of limitation for securities fraud claims.

3.30   To some extent, SOX sparked a backlash from critics and companies who con-
tend that compliance with the regulations makes it prohibitively expensive to do
business in the US.[75] In response, on 21 March 2007, the SEC issued new rules
for deregistration by public companies in the hope that 'by making it easier for
foreign companies to deregister, the US will be seen as a more favorable listings
venue'.[76] The SEC has announced it will consider taking steps to narrow the
scope of certain SOX regulations.[77] Other requirements imposed by SOX have
been challenged on various grounds in US courts.[78] In September 2006, a
commission was unveiled to study and recommend potential changes to SOX

---

[75] For example, s 404 has been the subject of intense debate. The Chairman and CEO of the
American Stock Exchange explained: 'While the intent was laudable, the new [SOX] regulations
made no distinction between a billion-dollar large-cap company and a $75 million small-cap one.
This has made it extremely difficult for smaller companies to compete and grow in this regulatory
environment.' N L Wolkoff, 'Sarbanes-Oxley Is a Curse For Small-Cap Companies', *Wall Street
Journal* (15 August 2005).

[76] J Grant, 'SEC Set to Ease Sarbanes-Oxley Rules', *Financial Times* (21 March 2007) (noting
that this will 'allow foreign companies to dodge compliance for the first time with the 2002 Sarbanes
Oxley corporate controls law'). See also SEC Press Release, 'SEC Posts Text of Rules Facilitating
Foreign Private Issuer Deregistration Under the Exchange Act' (27 March 2007) <http://www.sec.
gov/news/press/2007/2007-55.htm> ('Instead of counting the number of the issuer's US security
holders, the new benchmark will require the comparison of the average daily trading volume of an
issuer's securities in the United States with its worldwide average daily trading volume.'); P S Atkins,
Commissioner, SEC, Speech by SEC Commissioner: Comments on Final Deregistration Rules at
the SEC Open Meeting (21 March 2007) (remarking that the SEC's 'former deregistration rules,
which required a nose-count of US investors to determine if registration was required, was so beloved
by our foreign brethren that it gave rise to such kindly monikers as "hotel California", or the "roach
motel" or … the "Venus flytrap"').

[77] See, eg, J Rothstein, 'SEC Seeks Ideas on Sarbanes-Oxley Controls', *Reuters* (11 July 2006)
(regarding changes to provisions related to internal controls over financial reporting, also known as
Section 404); J Grant, 'SEC Proposes Move to Ease Sarbanes-Oxley Regulation', *Financial Times*
(10 August 2006) (offering to give companies a year's grace to comply with s 404); SEC Press
Release, 'SEC Votes to Propose Interpretive Guidance for Management to Improve Sarbanes-Oxley
404 Implementation' (13 December 2006), available at: <http://www.sec.gov/news/
press/2006/2006-206.htm>; SEC Press Release, 'Further Relief from the Section 404 Requirements
for Smaller Companies and Newly Public Companies' (15 December 2006), available at <http://
www.sec.gov/news/press/2006/2006-219.htm>. US lawmakers rejected a proposal that would
weaken SOX requirements by making it optional for certain companies (ie those with less than
$700m in total market value) to comply with s 404. See 'Senate Rejects Sarbanes-Oxley Change',
Reuters (25 April 2007) < http://www.insidesarbanesoxley.com/2007/04/senate-rejects-sarbanes-
oxley-change.html>.

[78] For example, the authority of the PCAOB was challenged on constitutional grounds in a US
District Court. See *Complaint, Free Enterprise Fund v Pub Co Accounting Oversight Bd*, Civ No 06-
217 (JR) (DDC, 7 February 2006); see also Press Release, 'SEC Joins Department of Justice in
Supporting Constitutionality of PCAOB' (1 September 2006) <http://www.sec.gov/news/
press/2006/2006-147.htm> (defending the PCAOB). The PCAOB was upheld as constitutional.
See D Reilly, 'Court Upholds New Auditing Board', *Wall Street Journal* (22 March 2007).

that would limit the impact of its reach.[79] Additional aspects of federal securities regulation have been challenged as overreaching.[80]

At the same time, the DoJ too has come under criticism for using overly aggressive methods to investigate and prosecute white collar crime. For example, the DoJ policies governing corporate cooperation were criticized in some quarters as interfering with individuals' right to counsel by pressuring companies not to advance legal fees to their employees who are targets or subjects of DoJ investigations, and eroding attorney-client privilege by pressuring companies to waive attorney-client or other privileges to curry favour with prosecutors.[81]

3.31

The DoJ's policies were attacked by a variety of sources.[82] In *United States v Stein*,[83] a federal judge in the Southern District of New York found the DoJ's

3.32

---

[79] The group, known as 'The Committee on Capital Markets Regulation', is chaired by former White House economic adviser Glenn Hubbard and former Goldman Sachs President John Thorton. See A Murray, 'Panel's Mission: Easing Capital Market Rules', *Wall Street Journal* (9 December 2006). The purpose of the committee is to suggest changes not only to SOX, but to other laws and regulations that the group concludes hinder the competitiveness of US capital markets. See ibid (noting that 9 of the 10 largest initial public offerings ('IPOs') of 2006, and all but one of the 25 largest IPOs in 2005, were done in foreign markets whereas in the 1990s most stock offerings were made in US financial markets). In late 2006, the Committee released an interim report that proposed an easing of regulation applicable to US securities markets. See Interim Report of the Committee on Capital Markets Regulation (30 November 2006) <http://www.capmktsreg.org/pdfs/11.30Committee_Interim_ReportREV2.pdf>. According to a March 2007 update, the Interim Report generated 'a great deal of media attention and public discussion of the Capital Markets competitiveness issues'. Committee on Capital Markets Regulation, Update (13 March 2007) <http://www.capmktsreg.org/latestnews.html>. Since 30 November 2006, 'various government agencies, including the SEC and PCAOB, Treasury Department, chairmen of Congressional Committees all have stepped up to address the competitiveness issues that were outlined in the Interim Report'. Ibid.

[80] In 2006, a US Court of Appeals ruled that the SEC's proposed hedge fund rule, which would have required hedge fund investors to be counted as clients of the fund's adviser for purposes of the fewer-than-15-clients exemption from registration under Investment Advisers Act, was invalid as conflicting with purposes underlying that statute. *Goldstein v SEC* 451 F 3d 873 (DC Cir 2006). This decision effectively limited the SEC's ability to register hedge funds. See Press Release, 'Statement of Chairman Cox Concerning the Decision of the US Court of Appeals in Phillip Goldstein, et al v Securities and Exchange Commission' (7 August 2006) (proposing new Commission initiatives concerning hedge fund regulations in light of the *Goldstein* decision).

[81] See text accompanying nn 361–62 below (acknowledging that the attorney-client privilege and the practice of advancing legal fees are important parts of the American legal framework).

[82] See Karen Mathis, President, American Bar Association, Statement before the Committee on the Judiciary of the US Senate concerning 'The Thompson Memorandum's Effect on the Right to Counsel in Corporate Investigations' (12 September 2006) <http://www.abanet.org/poladv/letters/attyclient/060912testimony_mathis-acpriv.pdf>; 'Letter from Former Senior Justice Department Officials to Attorney General Alberto Gonzales Regarding Proposed Revisions to Department of Justice Policy Regarding Waiver of the Attorney-Client Privilege and Work-Product Doctrine' (5 September 2006) <http://www.acc.com/public/attyclientpriv/agsept52006.pdf>; 'Submission by the Coalition to Preserve the Attorney-Client Privilege to the U.S. House of Representatives Judiciary Subcommittee on Crime, Terrorism and Homeland Security Regarding the Subcommittee's Hearings on "White Collar Enforcement (Part I): Attorney-Client Privilege and Corporate Waivers"' (7 March 2006) <http://www.acc.com/public/accapolicy/coalitionstatement030706.pdf>.

[83] 435 F Supp 2d 330 (SDNY 2006).

policy statement pertaining to the advancement of legal fees to be unconstitutional.[84] The Chairman of the Senate Judiciary Committee went so far as to propose a bill entitled the 'Attorney-Client Privilege Protection Act of 2006'.[85] In response to some of these concerns, on 12 December 2006, the DoJ announced revisions to its principles governing corporate cooperation.[86]

D. US Regulatory Investigations

How a regulatory investigation may be triggered

3.33 There are many ways in which a US regulatory investigation may commence. For example, the SEC may learn of improprieties through market surveillance, direct investor complaints, referrals from an SRO, or its own Office of Compliance Inspections and Examinations (OCIE). OCIE is the office by which the SEC conducts routine and periodic inspections of companies within its jurisdiction.[87]

---

[84] The United States District Judge in *Stein*, Judge Lewis A Kaplan, reaffirmed his findings in a subsequent decision in the same case. See *United States v Stein* 495 F Supp 2d 390 (SDNY 2007).

[85] The bill was introduced again on 4 January 2007 in the first session of the 110th Congress. See Attorney-Client Privilege Protection Act of 2007 (s 186) <http://www.acc.com/public/attyclient-priv/thompsonmemoleg.pdf>.

[86] See Prepared Remarks of Deputy Attorney General Paul J McNulty at the Lawyers for Civil Justice Membership Conference Regarding the Department's Charging Guidelines in Corporate Fraud Prosecutions (12 December 2006) <http://www.usdoj.gov/archive/dag/speeches/2006/dag_speech_061212.htm> (explaining that the revisions are meant to clarify the intent behind the DoJ's guidelines in connection with how prosecutors evaluate a company's cooperation in making their charging decisions).

[87] Federal regulation provides that:
> The Director of the [OCIE] is responsible for the compliance inspections and examinations relating to the regulation of exchanges, national securities associations, clearing agencies, securities information processors, the Municipal Securities Rulemaking Board, brokers and dealers, municipal securities dealers, transfer agents, investment companies, and investment advisors . . .

17 CFR § 200.19. OCIE monitors compliance with the securities laws. For minor deficiencies, OCIE issues a 'deficiency letter', which sets forth the problems that need to be corrected. OCIE then monitors the situation until compliance is achieved. OCIE, however, refers to the Division of Enforcement any violations that appear to be too serious for informal correction. *Investor's Advocate*. See also Mary Ann Gadziala, Associate Director, SEC, Speech by SEC Staff: The SEC Examination Perspective (6 May 2003) (describing four different types of examinations that the SEC may conduct of broker-dealers: comprehensive exams, special purpose exams, new rule compliance, and product reviews).

The DoJ, for its part, may follow leads from similar sources such as referrals from **3.34** one of its own agencies;[88] the SEC or other government agencies;[89] tips and public leads;[90] or directly through its own investigative efforts.[91]

A regulator may also launch a 'sweep' of an entire industry based upon findings or **3.35** suspicions of improper practices at one or more companies in the field.[92] Occasionally, a listed company may discover, investigate and voluntarily disclose to regulators the existence of accounting irregularities or other improprieties affecting its financial statements.[93] In this regard, SOX has imposed a requirement, under section 307, on all attorneys who appear or practice before the SEC, whether in-house or outside, to report 'evidence of a material violation of securities law', a 'breach of fiduciary duty', or a 'similar violation' to the chief legal counsel or chief executive officer.[94] If management fails to take appropriate action after being notified of such evidence, the attorney must 'report up' to the company's audit committee or board of directors.[95]

---

[88] For example, the Antitrust Division may refer an anti-trust investigation to the USAO. 'Once a United States Attorney's office accepts a referral, it will be primarily responsible for the investigation and prosecution of that case.' USAM, 7-1.100 (October 1997).

[89] The IRS, for example, can refer a case to the DoJ Tax Division or the USAO if, after conducting its own investigation it finds sufficient evidence to warrant criminal prosecution. 'If the Department of Justice or the United States Attorney accepts the investigation for prosecution, the IRS special agent will be asked by the prosecutors to assist in preparation for trial. However, once a special agent report is referred to for prosecution, the investigation is managed by the prosecutors.' See IRS, 'How Criminal Investigations Are Initiated' <http://www.irs.gov/compliance/enforcement/article/0,,id=175752,00.html>.

[90] The FBI encourages the public to report possible violations of federal criminal law. See 'FBI Tips and Public Leads' <https://tips.fbi.gov/> (providing form to be used in reporting suspected criminal activity to the FBI).

[91] The gathering and production of 'intelligence' is core to the FBI's mission. See Federal Bureau of Investigations <http://www.fbi.gov/intelligence/intell.htm>.

[92] The companies investigated in an industry-wide probe may find themselves at the centre or the periphery of the inquiry, depending upon their knowledge of and participation in the activity in question.

[93] In fact, this was the case with WorldCom. Beginning in 1999 and continuing through May 2002, the company used fraudulent accounting methods to hide its declining financial condition behind a false picture of sound financial health, which in effect artificially inflated the price of WorldCom's stock. An internal audit uncovered approximately $3.8bn of the fraud in June 2002 during a routine examination of capital expenditures. The company's external auditors were notified, and its internal audit committee and board of directors were alerted shortly thereafter. The company took action and the SEC promptly began an investigation on 26 June 2002. By the end of 2003, the WorldCom fraud was estimated to amount to approximately $11bn. See C Stern, 'King of the Bad-News Bulls: WorldCom's Distresses Are Investor David Matlin's Successes', *Washington Post* (10 October 2003); see also 'SEC Statement Concerning WorldCom' (26 June 2002) <http://www.sec.gov/news/press/2002-94.htm>.

[94] 15 USC § 7245 (SOX provision requiring the SEC to prescribe 'minimum standards of professional conduct for attorneys appearing and practicing before the Commission in any way in the representation of issuers'); 17 CFR §§ 205.1-205.7 (SEC rule containing such standards).

[95] See B D Brian and B McNeil, 'Overview: Initiating an Internal Investigation and Assembling the Investigative Team', in B D Brian and B F McNeil (eds), *Internal Corporate Investigations*

3.36 A 'whistle-blower' also may report allegations of improprieties at a company directly to a regulator.[96] Indeed, whistle-blowers may receive a bounty for reporting improprieties to the government under the federal False Claims Act.[97] In addition, section 806 of SOX provides protection for employees of publicly traded companies who report evidence of fraud.[98] SOX further directs the establishment of internal programmes at public companies to hear whistle-blower complaints about accounting and auditing issues.[99] Generally, employees who

---

(2nd edn, 2003), 2–3 (hereinafter '*Internal Corporate Investigations*') (explaining that the requirements of SOX, in this respect, radically alter the landscape for lawyers tasked with investigating and reporting possible wrongdoing).

[96] Both state and federal laws protect whistleblowers from retaliatory action by their employers for reporting alleged corporate misdeeds. See J F Coyne, Jr and C F Barker, 'Employees' Rights and Duties During an Internal Investigation', in *Internal Corporate Investigations* 173, 189–190; J Best and S N Auby, 'The Practitioner's Guide to Parallel Proceedings', in *Internal Corporate Investigations*, 227–228.

[97] False Claims Act, Pub L No 97-258, 96 Stat 978 (1982) (current version at 31 USC §§ 3729-33). See also DoJ Press Release, 'Schering-Plough to Pay $345 Million to Resolve Criminal and Civil Liabilities for Illegal Marketing of Claritin' (30 July 2004) <http://www.usdoj.gov/opa/pr/2004/July/04_civ_523.htm>. In the case of Schering-Plough Corp, three former employees filed a suit on behalf of the government under the False Claims Act regarding fraudulent pricing of the blockbuster allergy medication, Claritin. Notably, it was the filing of the whistleblower lawsuit that led to the subsequent criminal investigation of Schering-Plough by DoJ.

[98] See 18 USC §§ 1513, 1514A. See also K Day, 'Whistle-Stop Campaigns, Some Firms Are Trying to Limit Protection of Workers Who Expose Wrongdoing', *Washington Post* (23 April 2006) ('The law shields from retaliation any employee who tells superiors or federal officials of problems, about accounting or otherwise, that he or she thinks could hurt the company's investors—even if the claims turn out to be untrue.'). These provisions include criminal penalties for 'intentionally interfer[ing] with the lawful employment or livelihood of any person who provides truthful information to a law enforcement officer relating the commission or possible commission of any Federal offense'. S M Kohn, M D Kohn and D K Colapinto, *Introduction to Whistleblower Law* (2004), at xiii (quoting 18 USC § 1513(e), which prohibits retaliating against a witness, victim or an informant). One source reports that since the enactment of SOX, about 750 people have filed complaints with the Department of Labor alleging retaliation for revealing corporate problems, either to a superior within the company or outside the firm. See Day, ibid (stating further that practically all of these complaints have been for one reason or another unsuccessful).

18 USC § 1514A provides a civil remedy to protect whistleblowers against retaliation for providing evidence of fraud. See, eg, *Bechtel v Competitive Tech, Inc* 448 F 3d 469 (2nd Cir 2006) (action pursuant to 18 USC § 1514A). In *Bechtel*, the plaintiff alleged in a complaint to the Secretary of Labor that he was discharged only after raising concerns about his company's financial reporting. The Secretary ordered reinstatement. When the company refused to reinstate the plaintiff, he brought a complaint in district court seeking a preliminary injunction requiring the company to comply with the reinstatement order. The district court issued the preliminary injunction. The defendant company appealed, arguing that 18 USC § 1514A does not confer power on the district court to enforce the Secretary's order, which in this case was preliminary. The Second Circuit agreed with the corporate defendant and found that district courts have no power 'to enforce a preliminary reinstatement order as if the order were final', ibid at 473.

[99] See *Introduction to Whistleblower Law*,(n 98 above), describing corporate responsibility to receive whistleblower complaints.

blow the whistle before a body designated by such programmes to hear complaints cannot be retaliated against.[100]

SEC investigations and sanctions

SEC investigations are conducted by the Division of Enforcement.[101] A typical **3.37** SEC investigation may start with an informal request for testimony and/or documents from witnesses.[102] In the early stages of an investigation, the staff of the SEC is attempting to develop the relevant facts[103] and it may rely on voluntary cooperation from the witnesses and the corporation.[104]

If the level of cooperation is unsatisfactory, or for any other good cause, the **3.38** Division of Enforcement may seek an order from the Commission to conduct a formal investigation.[105] Once an investigation becomes formal, the SEC is empowered to use the process of subpoena to secure witness testimony and/or the production of documents.[106] 'Subpoenas issued by the Commission are not

---

100 In a case of first impression, the SOX whistleblower provisions were held not to protect 'foreign citizens working outside of the United States for foreign subsidiaries of covered companies'. *Carnero v Boston Sci Corp* 433 F 3d 1, 7 (1st Cir 2006), cert denied, 126 S Ct 2973. In Carnero, the court found that the employee, an Argentinean citizen and resident of Brazil who worked for two unlisted subsidiaries and whose whistleblowing regarded those companies' alleged improprieties in Latin America, could not sue the US parent corporation under SOX, 18 USC § 1514A.

101 Such investigations are carried out confidentially, meaning that the SEC typically does not comment on the targets of its investigation, or even confirm the existence of such investigation. See 17 CFR § 202.5(a) (providing that investigatory reports are for staff and Commission use only). There are, however, many scenarios in which shareholders may learn that an investigation is taking place. For instance, a company itself may disclose the fact of an investigation in public statements to shareholders or in public documents that are required to be periodically reported to the SEC.

102 'Investigative testimony is one of the primary methods the enforcement staff uses to get information. This testimony is similar to a civil deposition in that the witness is asked a series of questions and is often shown exhibits and asked about them.' K J Harnisch and N Colton, 'When the SEC Comes Knocking', *Business Law Today*, Vol 15, No 1 (September/October 2005) <http://www.abanet.org/buslaw/blt/2005-09-10/colton.shtml> (noting further that there are significant differences between providing testimony to the SEC and providing deposition testimony due to the fact that the Federal Rules of Civil Procedure do not govern the provision of testimony to the SEC). 'Although the details of the examination will vary, every witness must testify truthfully, fully and honestly. It is a federal crime to make a false statement or representation to any government official, including a member of the SEC.' M J Astarita, 'When the SEC Comes Calling' <http://www.seclaw.com/docs/597.htm>.

Typically, the SEC will seek 'a range of documents in investigations, including bank and brokerage records, telephone records, corporate records, Internet Service Provider records, audit work papers, and client identification records'. Tafara Remarks (n 45 above).

103 *Investor's Advocate* (n 2 above).

104 See D M Meisner, 'The ABCs of an SEC Investigation: 20 Essential Questions and Answers', 1492 PLI/Corp 981, 983 (May 2005) ('This sometimes puts defense counsel in a relatively good position to negotiate with the SEC regarding the volume and type of documents and/or testimony that will be provided.').

105 Ibid.

106 See Steinberg and Ferrara (n 65 above), at §§ 3.3-3.19 (discussing the distinction between preliminary SEC inquiries and formal SEC investigations). While the SEC is empowered to make

---

self-enforcing, and the recipients thereof are not subject to penalty for refusal to obey. But the Commission is authorized to bring suit in federal court to compel compliance with its process.'[107]

3.39 There is little practical difference between a formal and informal investigation for the company under investigation, except that 'once an investigation becomes formal, the enforcement staff is often less willing to terminate the probe'.[108] The length of an SEC investigation varies according to its subject matter and scope, and can last anywhere from months to years.[109]

3.40 At the conclusion of its investigation, the Division of Enforcement presents a memorandum of its findings to the Commission. If the staff's preliminary decision is to recommend an enforcement action for alleged violations of the federal securities laws, persons or companies that would be adversely affected by such a recommendation may be provided the opportunity to make a submission, known as a 'Wells' submission, in which they explain why an action should not be brought.[110] A Wells submission, once received, is forwarded for consideration

---

preliminary investigations by its own rules, it also has discretion to make formal investigations and authorize the use of process as it deems necessary. See 17 CFR § 202.5(a). The subpoena is a means of process necessary to compel cooperation with an investigation. The staff must make a request for the issuance of a subpoena in writing to the Secretary of the Commission, not to an individual Commissioner. Ibid §§ 203.8, 201.232.

[107] *SEC v O'Brien, Inc* 467 US 735, 741 (1984); *SEC v Higashi* 359 F 2d 550, 552 (9th Cir 1966) ('[SEC] subpoenas are only enforceable after the Commission has successfully applied to a United States Court for an enforcement order.'). Objections to a subpoena can be formally raised in a motion to quash or modify the subpoena; 17 CFR § 201.232(e). Failure to comply with a subpoena may lead to contempt charges. *United States v Ryan* 402 US 530, 532 (1971) ('[O]ne to whom a subpoena is directed may not appeal the denial of a motion to quash that subpoena but must either obey its commands or refuse to do so and contest the validity of the subpoena if he is subsequently cited for contempt on account of his failure to obey.').

[108] Harnisch and Colton (n 102 above). See also Meisner (n 104 above) ('Formal investigations generally assume a higher profile at the SEC and require the commitment of additional staff resources. Compared to informal investigations, fewer formal investigations are terminated without adverse action being taken against the party being investigated.').

[109] See Meisner (n 104 above).

[110] See SEC, 'Procedures Relating to the Commencement of Enforcement Proceedings and Termination of Staff Investigations', Release No 5310, 1972 WL 128568 (27 September 1972) ('The staff, in its discretion, may advise prospective defendants or respondents of the general nature of its investigation, including the indicated violations as they pertain to them, and the amount of time that may be available for preparing a submission.'). The Wells process usually begins with the Division of Enforcement informing a party that they are inclined to recommend that the SEC initiate enforcement proceedings for violations of the securities laws. The party is then afforded a period of time in which it can make a written submission outlining both factual and legal reasons why the enforcement action should not be brought. One commentator has observed that, post-Enron, the SEC's staff has become generally more demanding, which has affected the Wells process: 'Investigations are being done more quickly. Companies and individuals have less time to respond to ever more massive subpoenas for documents. The SEC is issuing Wells Notices . . . far earlier than it has historically with a shortened time to respond.'). See Bayless (n 71 above).

along with the Division of Enforcement's memorandum to the SEC, which makes the final decision on commencing an enforcement proceeding.[111]

The SEC has substantial discretion in deciding whether to bring an enforcement **3.41** action against a company (and any of its officers, executives or employees) following an investigation.[112] The written criteria by which the SEC will exercise its discretion on bringing enforcement actions against a corporation for civil violations will be discussed in detail below.[113]

Among the sanctions the SEC can seek in US courts are money damages for vio- **3.42** lations of federal securities laws.[114] The maximum damages award in federal court consists of the greater of the defendant's pecuniary gain or amounts ranging from $5,000 to $500,000 based on a three-tier system for individuals and business entities.[115] SOX added a provision allowing the SEC to pass penalties recovered to victims of the violation.[116]

The SEC may also seek an injunction in federal court when any provision of the **3.43** Securities Act or the Exchange Act has been or is about to be violated.[117] The SEC's injunctive authority extends to violations of SEC rules and regulations,

---

[111] Meisner (n 104 above).

[112] In fiscal year 2005, the SEC initiated 947 investigations, 335 civil proceedings and 294 administrative proceedings, and won more than $3bn in penalties and disgorgement. SEC, 2005 Performance and Accountability Report 7 (2005) <http://sec.gov/about/secpar/secpar2005.pdf>. In comparison, the SEC initiated 914 investigations, 218 civil proceedings and 356 administrative proceedings, and ordered more than $3.3bn in disgorgement and penalties during fiscal year 2006. SEC, 2006 Performance and Accountability Report 8 (2006) <http://sec.gov/about/secpar/secpar2006.pdf>. The number of civil actions and administrative proceedings initiated by the SEC was relatively the same in earlier years (ie 2000–2004). However, the amounts that the SEC recovered in penalties and disgorgement as the result of its investigatory efforts has increased sharply over the same time period:

Year	Penalties/Disgorgement
2000	$488m
2001	$522m
2002	$1.394bn
2003	$2bn
2004	$3bn
2005	>$3bn
2006	>$3.3bn

SEC, Annual Reports <http://www.sec.gov/about/annrep.shtml>.

[113] See Section G below.

[114] 15 USC § 78u(d)(1)(B).

[115] The first tier allows penalties of up to $5,000 for individuals and $50,000 for non-natural persons (ie business entities). Ibid § 78u(d)(3)(B)(i). The second tier requires some element of fraud or deceit and ranges up to $50,000 for individuals and $250,000 for business entities. Ibid § 78u(d)(3)(B)(ii). The third tier requires fraud or deceit and either substantial losses or the risk of substantial losses to third parties; penalties range up to $100,000 for individuals and $500,000 for business entities. Ibid § 78u(d)(3)(B)(iii).

[116] Sarbanes-Oxley Act, § 308, Pub L 107-204, 116 Stat 745 (Fair Funds provision).

[117] 15 USC § 77t(b); ibid § 78u(d)(1).

rules of an SRO, and rules of the PCAOB.[118] In addition to preventing or curtailing a violation, an injunction can include temporarily or permanently prohibiting an individual from serving as an officer or director of a public company.[119] The SEC can also seek to compel compliance with the rules of an SRO.[120] Other remedies that may be sought by the SEC include disgorgement, for example requiring the defendant to give up any profits gained from the violation.[121] Under the District Court's equitable inherent authority 'to effectuate relief granted in a securities fraud enforcement action', a defendant's assets may be frozen prior to disgorgement and may be subject to prejudgment interest.[122]

3.44 In addition to bringing actions in federal court, the SEC is empowered to initiate its own administrative hearings.[123] Available remedies in an administrative action following notice and a hearing[124] are disgorgement,[125] financial penalties,[126] and cease-and-desist orders.[127] While the disgorgement remedy is the same as in a federal court injunctive action, financial penalties in administrative proceedings are limited to the statutory amount.[128] Cease-and-desist orders can have the same effect as federal court injunctions, including barring individuals from serving as officers and

---

[118] Ibid. The PCAOB is, as mentioned in n 78 above, the Public Company Accounting Oversight Board.

[119] Ibid § 78u(d)(2) ('[T]he court may prohibit, conditionally or unconditionally, and permanently or for such period of time as it shall determine any person . . . from acting as an officer or director . . .').

[120] Ibid § 78u(e).

[121] *SEC v First City Financial Corp* 890 F 2d 1215, 1230 (DC Cir 1989) ('We see no indication in the language or the legislative history of the 1934 Act that even implies a restriction on the equitable remedies of the district courts. Disgorgement, then, is available simply because the relevant provisions of the Securities Exchange Act of 1934 . . . vest jurisdiction in the federal courts.'). Disgorgement is measured by the profits of the violator, not the damage to any victim or third party. See also *SEC v Tanner* 2003 US Dist LEXIS 11410 *3-4 (SDNY 2003). Since disgorgement is an equitable remedy, it cannot be used punitively and the property disgorged must be causally related to the violation. See *First City Financial Corp* 890 F 2d at 1231. In addition, because disgorgement is 'non-punitive' there is no double jeopardy when penalty damages are also sought. See *SEC v Monarch Funding Corp* 1996 US Dist LEXIS 8756 *33-35 (SDNY 1996); see also *Tanner* US Dist LEXIS 11410 at *6-8 (applying both disgorgement and third tier statutory penalties to defendant).

[122] *SEC v Hickey* 322 F 3d 1123, 1125 (9th Cir 2003) (freezing the assets of a non-party who was 'dominated and controlled by a defendant against whom relief has been obtained in a securities fraud enforcement action'); *Tanner* 1996 US Dist LEXIS 11410 at *5 (holding the disgorgement amount subject to prejudgment interest).

[123] 15 USC § 78u-2(a).

[124] See SEC, Rules of Practice and Rules on Fair Fund and Disgorgement Plans, Rule 200(a)(1) (March 2006) <http://www.sec.gov/about/rulesprac2006.pdf> (hereinafter 'Rules of Practice').

[125] 15 USC § 78u-2(e).

[126] Ibid § 78u-2(b)(1).

[127] Ibid § 78u-3(a).

[128] See n 115 above and accompanying text.

directors of public companies.[129] Finally, the SEC can issue temporary cease-and-desist orders where it finds 'that the alleged violation or threatened violation . . . or the continuation thereof, is likely to result in significant dissipation or conversion of assets, significant harm to investors, or substantial harm to the public interest . . . prior to the completion of the proceedings'.[130] Such temporary orders may be issued without prior notice and opportunity for hearing where the SEC 'determines that notice and hearing prior to entry would be impracticable or contrary to the public interest'.[131]

Companies in the US routinely settle SEC enforcement actions by agreeing to **3.45** pay a monetary penalty without admitting or denying liability.[132] A settlement may require the appointment of an independent monitor to review relevant practices and recommend enhancements,[133] restitution, and/or the imposition of a monetary penalty. In an administrative proceeding, the defendant may also submit an 'Offer of Settlement', consenting to a cease-and-desist order (and other monetary penalties) without admitting or denying the SEC's findings.[134]

In January 2006, the SEC issued a new set of guidelines, known as the McAfee **3.46** Release, setting forth the factors the SEC will consider before imposing a monetary penalty on a corporation.[135] The McAfee Release contains nine criteria to

---

[129] See 15 USC § 78u-3(a) (allowing cease-and-desist orders to prevent or curtail violations of the Securities Act), ibid § 78u-3(e) (accounting and disgorgement); ibid § 78u-3(f) (prohibiting individuals from serving as an officer or director).

[130] Ibid § 78u-3(a); Rules of Practice (Rule 512).

[131] Ibid § 78u-3(c)(1); Rules of Practice (Rule 513).

[132] See, eg, SEC Charges AIG with Securities Fraud, Litigation Release No 19560, Accounting and Auditing Enforcement Release No 2371 (9 February 2006) (without admitting or denying the relevant allegations, AIG agreed to 'pay $800 million, consisting of disgorgement of $700 million and a penalty of $100 million' as part of a $1.6bn global settlement to resolve claims related to improper accounting, bid rigging and practices involving workers' compensation funds).

[133] SEC settlements often include the appointment of independent monitors, whose subsequent advice to the company and/or its Board of Directors may prove to be quite influential. For instance, in 2004, former Judge Frederick Lacey was appointed by the SEC to monitor Bristol-Myers Squibb (BMS), after the SEC reached a settlement with the pharmaceutical company concerning accounting irregularities. Judge Lacey was again, in 2005, appointed as the company's 'Independent Adviser' under a deferred prosecution agreement with the New Jersey USAO. See S Saul, 'A Corporate Nanny Turns Assertive', *NY Times* (19 September 2006). After allegations of anti-trust violations against BMS surfaced in July 2006, the report of Judge Lacey greatly influenced the Board's decision to replace senior management of the company. See, eg, J Carreyrou and B Martinez, 'Bristol Myers Names New CEO', *Wall Street Journal* (12 September 2006) (reporting that, upon the advice of Judge Lacey, the board had little choice but to recommend firing the company's CEO and general counsel amid allegations of misconduct).

[134] See, eg, In re Raytheon Co, SEC Admin Proc No 3-12345, Release No 33-8715 (28 June 2006) <http://www.sec.gov/litigation/admin/2006/33-8715.pdf> (settling administrative proceeding alleging accounting irregularities).

[135] See 'Statement of the Securities & Exchange Commission Concerning Financial Penalties', Release No 2006-4 (4 January 2006) (hereinafter McAfee Release) <http://www.sec.gov/news/press/2006-4.htm>. The McAfee Release was issued in connection with the announcement of two settled actions against separate corporations: McAfee, Inc and Applix, Inc.

assist the SEC in evaluating whether a monetary penalty is warranted. The SEC emphasized that among the nine criteria, two weigh more heavily than others: whether there was a direct benefit to the corporation as a result of the violation, and whether a penalty is likely to recompense injured shareholders or merely to cause them greater harm.[136]

3.47 If no settlement is reached, once an SEC action is filed, it proceeds as any other civil or administrative action until there is a final order containing findings of fact and conclusions of law.[137]

DoJ investigations and sanctions

3.48 DoJ investigations may commence with the same purpose as an SEC investigation: to gather and develop the relevant facts by procuring testimony and/or documents from witnesses. The DoJ, however, has a broader range of investigative tools at its disposal than the SEC,[138] as it can obtain warrants from federal courts to monitor telephones[139] and conduct searches of specific premises.[140]

3.49 A federal prosecutor has broad authority to convene a grand jury with the power to issue subpoenas for documents and witness testimony.[141] The purpose of a

---

[136] The other criteria are: the deterrent effect of a penalty; the extent of injury to innocent parties; the breadth of complicity in the offence throughout the corporation; the level of intent of the perpetrators; the ease or difficulty in detecting the type of offence (a more subtle offence will more likely be punished because it will deter similarly difficult-to-detect schemes); the degree of remedial action taken by the corporation; and the extent of corporate cooperation in the investigation; McAfee Release, ibid.

[137] A final order is appealable to the US Circuit Court. See, eg, *Okin v SEC* 143 F 2d 960 (2nd Cir 1944).

[138] See Thomas C Newkirk, Assoc Dir, Div of Enforcement, SEC, Speech by SEC Staff: The Advantages of a Dual System: Parallel Streams of Civil and Criminal Enforcement of the US Securities Laws (19 September 1998) (explaining that the DoJ has 'the ability to tap phones and search for and seize evidence with the proper court authorization, conduct undercover operations, pay informants, [and] confer immunity from prosecution on reluctant witnesses').

[139] 18 USC § 2516 (providing that a USAO can authorize an application to a federal judge for an order authorizing or approving the interception of wire, oral or electronic communications by the FBI or other investigating agency). See also USAM § 9-7.000 (September 2004) (governing electronic surveillance).

[140] Fed R Crim P 41 (providing that any federal law enforcement agency or attorney may request a federal magistrate judge to issue a warrant to search for and seize a person or property located within that district). For example, Bristol-Myers, under investigation by the DoJ for allegedly concealing relevant information from federal regulators in order to secure federal approval of a settlement agreement, had its offices raided by federal agents in July 2006, after the government was tipped off about the terms of the settlement agreement. See S Saul, 'A Generic Drug Tale, With An Ending Yet to be Written', *NY Times* (15 August 2006), C1.

[141] US Attorneys derive the authority to conduct grand jury proceedings pursuant to 28 USC §§ 542, 547. '[T]he grand jury's principal function is to determine whether or not there is probable cause to believe that one or more persons committed a certain Federal offense within the venue of the district court.' USAM § 9-11.101 (August 2002). See also *United States v Williams* 504 US 36,

grand jury investigation is 'to assess whether there is adequate basis for bringing a criminal charge'.[142] A grand jury 'need not identify the offender it suspects, or even the precise nature of the offense it is investigating. The grand jury requires no authorization from its constituting court to initiate an investigation, nor does the prosecutor require leave of court to seek a grand jury indictment.'[143]

Failure to comply with a grand jury subpoena carries significant consequences.   **3.50** A witness may be held in contempt for refusing to comply with a grand jury subpoena, and may face possible jail sentence and/or fines.[144] In addition, where a witness refuses to comply with a grand jury subpoena to produce evidence, the government may obtain a warrant and seize the evidence itself.[145]

---

48 (1992) ('[T]he grand jury can investigate merely on suspicion that the law is being violated, or even because it wants assurance that it is not.'). In the context of anti-trust violations, Antitrust Division lawyers often open a grand jury investigation, since prior to obtaining FTC clearance and opening a preliminary inquiry or a grand jury investigation, they cannot contact individuals or firms on their own initiative. See ABA Section of Antitrust Law, *Antitrust Law Development* (6th edn, 2007) 739.

142 *United States v Williams* 504 US 36, 51 (1992).

143 Ibid at 48 (internal quotation marks and citations omitted).

144 Perhaps no recent case exemplifies the consequences of failure to comply with a grand jury subpoena better than that of Judith Miller. Ms Miller was a reporter for the *New York Times* who refused to comply with two grand jury subpoenas issued in connection with the investigation into whether government employees had violated federal law by the unauthorized disclosure of the identity of a CIA agent. See *In re Grand Jury Subpoena, Judith Miller* 397 F 3d 964 (DC Cir 2005). The subpoenas sought testimony and documents related to conversations between Ms Miller and a particular government official; Miller moved to quash them; ibid at 967. The motion was denied and the district court, finding that Miller's refusal to comply was without just cause, held her in civil contempt of court. Miller was sentenced to 18 months in prison for the contempt charge, but that sentence was stayed pending appeal. See C Leonnig, 'Journalist Cited for Contempt in Leak Probe', *Washington Post* (8 October 2004), A2. In July 2005, Miller was ordered to serve four of the original 18 months of her sentence, because that was all the time left in the term of the grand jury investigating the leak case. See A Liptak and M Newman, 'New York Times Reporter Jailed for Keeping Source Secret', *NY Times* (6 July 2005). Miller spent nearly three months behind bars before she was released, on 29 September 2005, after agreeing to testify in the grand jury investigation. See D Johnston and D Jehl, 'Jailed Times Reporter Freed After Source Waives Confidentiality', *NY Times* (29 September 2005).

145 *United States v Comprehensive Drug Testing, Inc* 2006 US App LEXIS 31850 (9th Cir 2006). In this case the US started with a grand jury investigation into illegal steroid use by professional athletes. The grand jury sought drug testing information for certain Major League Baseball (MLB) players. It, therefore, subpoenaed MLB, a third-party administrator that was hired to oversee MLB's drug use evaluation programme, and a medical laboratory that performed drug testing related to these players. After motions to quash the subpoenas were threatened, the government applied for and obtained search warrants that allowed federal agents to raid a Long Beach laboratory and seize several documents relating to its investigation. The Ninth Circuit found that the seizures were reasonable; ibid at 32 (there is 'no authority that simultaneous pursuit of search warrants and subpoenas in aid of an ongoing grand jury investigation constitutes a violation of the Fourth Amendment').

3.51   Individuals and companies under grand jury investigation are entitled to know their status. The DoJ therefore classifies those under investigation as targets or subjects:

> A 'target' is a person as to whom the prosecutor or the grand jury has substantial evidence linking him or her to the commission of a crime and who, in the judgment of the prosecutor, is a putative defendant . . .
>
> A 'subject' of an investigation is a person whose conduct is within the scope of the grand jury's investigation.[146]

3.52   The DoJ can also call witnesses who are not targets or subjects to testify before the grand jury. A witness is a person with little or no risk of criminal exposure. On occasion, federal prosecutors interview individuals outside the grand jury; these interviews are sometimes called 'proffer sessions'.[147]

3.53   A DoJ investigation may culminate with the filing of a criminal indictment or information in federal court.[148] Felony prosecutions generally require an indictment.[149] Misdemeanours, however, may be charged through a document known as an information, and do not require grand jury action.[150] Once an indictment or information is issued, a prosecutor must seek court permission to dismiss the action.[151]

---

[146] USAM § 9-11.150 (September 2006). There are three principal considerations in making a determination whether to approve a subpoena for a target: (1) whether the testimony is important to the success of the grand jury's investigation; (2) whether the testimony can be obtained by other witnesses; and (3) whether the testimony would be protected by a valid claim of privilege.
Note that the Antitrust Division, which derives its authority to conduct grand jury proceedings pursuant to 28 CFR § 0.40(a), follows the DoJ's general practice of informing individuals that they are targets of an investigation and advising such individuals that they may appear voluntarily before the grand jury. There is no similar opportunity for corporate entities to appear before the grand jury. As a practical matter, counsel for corporate entities should ordinarily be advised if the USAO is contemplating an indictment against an organization. USAM, § 7-1.200 (October 1997).

[147] In a typical proffer session:
> a participant in the wrongdoing—or his attorney—will hypothetically indicate to [investigators] the kind of information he has and is willing to provide in testimony, in exchange for immunity or leniency as to his own role in the crime. Under what is colloquially called a 'Queen-for-a-Day' arrangement, prosecutors may allow a witness to speak in such a session without risk of his own words being used against him except for purposes of impeachment.

See Newkirk (n 138 above).

[148] Fed R Crim P 1, 2.

[149] Ibid 7(a), (b). Any offence punishable by imprisonment of more than one year must be charged by an indictment unless the defendant waives the requirement; ibid; see also US Const amend V ('No person shall be held to answer for a capital or otherwise infamous crime, unless on a presentment or indictment of a Grand Jury.'); *United States v Ellsworth* 783 F 2d 333, 334 (8th Cir 1984) (defining a serious offence under the Rules as a felony).

[150] Fed R Crim P 7(a)(2), 58(b)(1). A misdemeanour can be charged using an indictment but it is not necessary; ibid at 58(b)(1).

[151] Fed R Crim P 48(a); USAM § 9-2.050 (December 2006) (governing dismissal of indictments and informations).

In some cases, the DoJ may file charges but also enter into a so-called deferred **3.54** prosecution agreement.[152] A deferred prosecution agreement may allow a company ultimately to avoid criminal indictment, but typically requires the company to make admissions of guilt.[153]

Non-prosecution agreements are another possible means of concluding a DoJ **3.55** investigation.[154] The use of non-prosecution agreements signals leniency on the part of the government.[155] One study found that non-prosecution agreements were more likely than deferred prosecution agreements 'to mention an internal investigation, and were more likely to underscore the key role an internal investigation played in the government's willingness to enter into the agreement'.[156] The fact that the corporation is willingly conducting an internal investigation may affect the conclusion of the DoJ's investigation, as is further discussed in section E.

A DoJ investigation may also be terminated by a declination of prosecution.[157] **3.56** For example, in 2005, the DoJ decided not to prosecute Royal Dutch/Shell after investigating the company regarding its recategorization of proved oil and gas reserves.[158]

---

[152] Deferred prosecution is most readily conceived of as a form of corporate probation. Certain conditions, such as a fine and the implementation of structural changes (usually including a compliance programme), may be imposed. In exchange, the DoJ agrees not to prosecute the company unless it violates the terms of the agreement. See, eg, Deferred Prosecution Agreement, *United States v Computer Assoc. Int'l, Inc* Crim No 04-837 (EDNY 22 September 2004); Deferred Prosecution Agreement, *United States v America Online, Inc* Crim No 1:04-M-1133 (ED Va 14 December 2004).

[153] See S A Resnik and K N Douglas, 'The Rise of Deferred Prosecution Agreements', New York Law Journal (18 December 2006) ('Notably, these agreements require corporations to admit the unlawful conduct and toll statutes of limitation, so in the case of a breach by the corporation, the prosecutor is virtually guaranteed to obtain a conviction.').

[154] See, eg, Letter from the DOJ Enron Task Force to Robert Morvillo, Esq, and Charles Stillman, Esq Re: Merrill Lynch & Co, Inc (17 September 2003) <http://www.usdoj.gov/dag/cftf/charging-docs/merrill_lynchagreement.pdf> (agreeing not to prosecute Merrill Lynch in connection with its activities relating to the Enron scandal).

[155] See generally N Kestenbaum and J P Criss, 'Credit Where Credit Is Due? The Role of Internal Investigations In the Outcome of Government Investigations', 1564 PLI/Corp 121, 128 (August 2006).

[156] Ibid (finding 'a correlation between government citations to a company's internal investigation and relatively lenient treatment of the company by the government').

[157] USAM § 9-2.020 (December 2006) (declining prosecution provision). A declination is maintained in the prosecutor's files and generally does not require the approval of either the referring agency or a superior in the DoJ; see ibid. There are certain statutory exceptions to this authority, including: a referral from a bankruptcy court or trustee; or declining to prosecute for national security reasons; ibid § 9-2.111.

[158] News Release, 'Shell Confirms Conclusion of US Department of Justice Reserves Investigation: No Further Action Against Companies' (30 June 2005) <http://www.shell.com/home/Framework?siteId=investor-en&FC2=/investor-en/html/iwgen/news_and_library/press_releases/2005/zzz_lhn.html&FC3=/investor-en/html/iwgen/news_and_library/press_releases/2005/reserves_investigation_30062005.html>.

3.57 Criminal prosecution of a corporation can have serious repercussions. For example, Arthur Andersen effectively collapsed after it was criminally indicted in 2002.[159] The collapse of Arthur Andersen, in turn, reduced the number of full-service accounting firms, which had a detrimental effect on the entire accounting industry. The devastating consequences of Andersen's criminal indictment may have influenced the government's perceived willingness to enter into a resolution short of indictment, that is, a deferred prosecution agreement, with another accounting company under subsequent investigation for tax fraud.[160]

E. Compulsory Process: Subpoenas

Authority to issue subpoenas

3.58 The ability of regulators and federal prosecutors to force compliance with government investigations stems from their authority to issue subpoenas.[161] U.S. regulators can obtain information from within the United States and from abroad through the use of such subpoenas. The authority to issue a subpoena seeking information from abroad may arise under an express grant of power from a statute or a grant of power implied from statute by judicial decision.

3.59 As a general matter, courts will presume that a statute does not have extraterritorial effect unless the statutory text evinces some intent to authorize extraterritorial reach.[162] Even where an agency's statute does not explicitly confer the authority to issue administrative subpoenas seeking information abroad, some courts have found implied grants of extraterritorial subpoena power.[163]

---

[159] For its role in connection with the Enron scandal, a jury found Arthur Andersen guilty of obstructing justice in violation of 18 USC § 1512(b)(2)(A) and (B). This verdict was upheld on appeal. See *United States v Arthur Andersen, LLP*, 374 F 3d 281 (5th Cir 2004). The Supreme Court ruled in 2005, however, that the conviction of Arthur Andersen was tainted by an improper jury instruction and reversed the judgment. See *Arthur Andersen, LLP v United States* 544 US 696 (2005). The decision came two years too late for the company, which had already dissolved.

[160] KPMG entered into a deferred prosecution agreement with federal prosecutors in order to end a DoJ investigation regarding the company's design, marketing, and implementation of fraudulent tax shelters. See KPMG Deferred Prosecution Agreement (26 August 2005) <http://www.usdoj.gov/usao/nys/pressreleases/August05/kpmgdpagmt.pdf> . See also C Johnson, 'KPMG to Admit Role in Tax Shelters; No Criminal Charges Expected', *Washington Post* (28 August 2005), A8 (regarding KPMG, 'senior Justice Department officials, concerned about the potentially fatal impact such a move would have on the firm, pushed negotiations'). The government's decision not to prosecute KPMG was reportedly influenced by the fact that such a prosecution would have had a disastrous impact upon what remained of the accounting industry after the demise of Arthur Andersen. See A Sloan, 'KPMG Partners Lucked Out—Thanks to Enron and Arthur Andersen', *Business Week* (6 September 2005).

[161] See section B above.

[162] *Foley Bros v Filardo* 336 US 281, 285 (1949) ('[L]egislation of Congress, unless a contrary intent appears, is meant to apply only within the territorial jurisdiction of the United States.').

[163] *Montship Lines, Ltd v Fed Maritime Bd* 295 F 2d 147, 154, 156 (DC Cir 1961); see also *SEC v Minas De Artemisa, SA* 150 F 2d 215, 218 (9th Cir 1945) (analysing the legislative history of s 19(c)

Personal jurisdiction and power to enforce subpoenas

A court must have jurisdiction over the person to whom a subpoena is directed in **3.60** order to enforce the subpoena. Thus, '[a] federal court's jurisdiction is not determined by its power to issue a subpoena; its power to issue a subpoena is determined by its jurisdiction'.[164] As a general matter, a court may assert jurisdiction over a foreign person or corporation if that person or corporation has sufficient minimum contacts with any part of the US.[165] If the foreign person or corporation challenges the court's jurisdiction, the issue becomes 'how much of a jurisdictional showing the Government [can] make in order to warrant the issuance of [a] subpoena'.[166]

Courts have exercised jurisdiction over, and therefore enforced subpoenas against, **3.61** foreign companies with parent corporations, offices, agents, or subsidiaries located in the US.[167] For example, a court asserted jurisdiction over a Swiss corporation that did not have any offices in the US, but that did have a wholly-owned subsidiary doing business in New York, where the same persons were directors of both companies, and where there was an alleged 'conspiracy among all of these parties to evade [US] tax laws'.[168]

When the corporation to which the subpoena is directed does not have sufficient **3.62** contacts with the US, however, courts have refused to assert jurisdiction.[169] For example, where a foreign corporation had no offices or employees in the US and conducted no business here, a court refused to assert jurisdiction 'merely because [the corporation] transfers funds and maintains a bank account here'.[170]

---

of the Securities Act of 1933 and concluding that the statute was designed to authorize the SEC to serve subpoenas abroad).

For instance, in the absence of explicit authority, a court concluded from the 'coverage and the purposes of the Shipping Act' that if the Federal Maritime Board's 'investigatory powers were limited to the territorial confines of the United States, regulation of foreign flag carriers would be hampered to a substantial degree', and thus refused to 'read into [the Act] a territorial limitation which appears to be contrary to the purposes of the Shipping Act'.

[164] *Marc Rich & Co v United States (In re Grand Jury Proceedings)* 707 F 2d 663, 669 (2nd Cir 1982).

[165] Ibid at 667.

[166] Ibid at 669.

[167] See, eg, *In re Grand Jury 81-2*, 550 F Supp 24, 27 (WD Mich 1982) (asserting jurisdiction over a German bank because of its 'maintenance . . . of an active branch office in New York'); *Doe v Unocal Corp* 248 F 3d 915, 926 (9th Cir 2001) (finding that where the parent and its subsidiary 'are not really separate entities', or where 'one acts as an agent of the other, the local subsidiary's contacts with the forum may be imputed to the foreign parent corporation' (quotation omitted)).

[168] *Marc Rich & Co v United States (In re Grand Jury Proceedings)* 707 F 2d 663, 667 (2nd Cir 1982).

[169] See, eg, *In re Sealed Case* 832 F 2d 1268, 1272–74 (DC Cir 1987) (refusing to enforce a subpoena where the foreign corporation did not have sufficient contacts with the US and noting that the presence of the corporation's custodian of records in the US did not confer jurisdiction over the corporation), abrogated on other grounds by *Braswell v United States* 487 US 99 (1988).

[170] *In re Arawak Trust Co (Cayman) Ltd* 489 F Supp 162, 165 (SDNY 1980).

3.63 The US Supreme Court has, over several decades, articulated and developed a constitutional doctrine requiring a defendant to have reasonably foreseen the possibility that his or her actions might lead to a lawsuit in the US.[171] Hence, certain acts by putative defendants abroad, even if they involve companies listed on an American exchange, will be beyond the pale of US jurisdiction.

3.64 For example, in *SEC v Alexander*,[172] the district court rejected the SEC's attempt to sue the Italian mother of an officer of an Italian public company with American Depositary Receipts (ADRs)[173] listed on the New York Stock Exchange. The mother had allegedly received inside information based on which she sold stock and avoided considerable loss. Unbeknown to the mother, who traded the stock in Italy through her Italian bank, the sale was effectuated through the company's ADRs. Notwithstanding this connection to the US, however, the mother successfully argued that she 'did not purposefully avail herself of the privilege of conducting activities in the United States and it would be unfair to require a 65-year-old non-English speaking person to defend insider trading charges arising from a single transaction, initiated in Italy and involving the securities of an Italian company'.[174]

Subject matter jurisdiction

3.65 Apart from the question of whether a court can assert personal jurisdiction over a subpoenaed entity or person to enforce the subpoena, there is a separate question of whether the subject matter itself is within a US court's jurisdiction. Congress can, and in certain cases does, prescribe extraterritorial application for its legislation.[175] Absent any such pronouncement in the legislation, however, the presumption is that the statute is intended to have solely or principally

---

[171] See *World-Wide Volkswagen Corp v Woodson* 444 US 286, 297 (1980) (holding that a US court has personal jurisdiction over a defendant whose 'conduct and connection with the forum State are such that he should reasonably anticipate being haled into court there').

[172] 160 F Supp 2d 642 (SDNY 2001).

[173] 'An ADR is a negotiable receipt usually issued by a United States bank, which certifies that a stated number of shares of a foreign private issuer have been deposited in the bank or in its foreign affiliate or correspondent.' Loss and Seligman (n 54 above), § 2-E-2.

[174] *Alexander* 160 F Supp 2d at 655. The court agreed, holding that it could not exercise personal jurisdiction over her. Such a finding in connection with foreign defendants who purchase stock listed on an American exchange is an exception rather than the rule. See, eg, *SEC v Unifund SAL* 910 F 2d 1028 (2nd Cir 1990) (affirming the lower court finding of personal jurisdiction over Lebanese and Panamanian companies trading stock in Lebanon and Switzerland, through American brokerage firms, of an American public company listed on the New York Stock Exchange); *SEC v Euro Sec Fund, Coim SA* No 98 Civ 7347, 1999 US Dist LEXIS 1537 (SDNY 17 February 1999) (denying motion to dismiss for lack of personal jurisdiction and holding that the SEC could sue Swiss-based defendant in the US for insider trading where defendant had traded significant amounts of Dutch company stock listed exclusively on the New York Stock Exchange).

[175] See *EEOC v Arabian Am Oil Co* 499 US 244, 248 (1991).

domestic effect.[176] Neither the Securities Act nor the Exchange Act—the foundational statutes of the modern federal securities regime[177]—explicitly refers to extraterritoriality.[178] The presumption, therefore, is against it.

Over the years, however, federal courts nonetheless have permitted the extraterritorial application of the US securities laws under certain circumstances.[179] The criteria applied by these courts have been distilled into two, mutually compatible tests: the 'conduct' test and the 'effects' test. [180] The tests apply to SEC enforcement actions and lawsuits by private litigants alike.[181] **3.66**

Under the conduct test, a defendant perpetrating a securities fraud in another country is subject to the jurisdiction of a US court if that individual or entity took substantial action in connection with the fraud in the US.[182] Such action must have been more than 'mere[ly] preparatory' to the fraud;[183] it must be shown 'directly [to have] caused losses to foreign investors abroad'.[184] The conduct test may permit foreign private litigants to sue foreign companies for alleged losses concerning stocks not listed in the US—provided that some allegedly fraudulent conduct relating to the fraud occurred in the US.[185] The rationale for permitting such suits is to prevent the US from becoming a haven for fraud committed elsewhere.[186] **3.67**

---

[176] See ibid. See also *American Banana Co v United Fruit Co* 213 US 347, 356-57 (1909); *Foley Bros, Inc v Filardo* 336 US 281, 285 (1949); *Argentine Republic v Amerada Hess Shipping Corp* 488 US 428, 440-41 (1989).

[177] See text accompanying nn 10–19 above.

[178] See *Alfadda v Fenn* 935 F 2d 475, 478 (2nd Cir 1991) ('The Securities Exchange Act is silent as to its extraterritorial application').

[179] See D J Kramer and M E Murray, 'The Extraterritorial Application of United States Securities Laws to Punish Insider Trading', Sec & Commodities Reg Vol 35, No 7 (10 April 2002), for a concise survey of the extraterritorial scope of US securities laws.

[180] Stated another way, US courts 'have consistently looked at two factors: (1) whether the wrongful conduct occurred in the United States, and (2) whether the wrongful conduct had a substantial effect in the United States or upon United States citizens'; *SEC v Berger* 322 F 3d 187, 192 (2nd Cir 2003). The point of the foregoing inquiry is meant to determine 'whether Congress would have wished the precious resources of United States courts and law enforcement agencies to be devoted to' investigating such wrongful conduct.

[181] *In re Yukos Sec Litig* 2006 WL 3026024, *9 (SDNY 25 October 2006) (declining to exercise subject matter jurisdiction over certain foreign defendants in the context of a securities class action after applying both the conduct and effects tests).

[182] See, eg, *Continental Grain (Australia) Pty, Ltd v Pacific Oilseeds, Inc* 592 F 2d 409, 420-21 (8th Cir 1979) (finding significant conduct to justify imposition of subject matter jurisdiction).

[183] *IIT v Vencap, Ltd* 519 F 2d 1001, 1018 (2nd Cir 1975).

[184] *Alfadda* 935 F 2d at 478.

[185] See, eg, *Leasco Data Processing Equip Corp v Maxwell* 468 F 2d 1326, 1334-35 (2nd Cir 1972) (finding that subject matter jurisdiction existed in a case brought by British plaintiffs against a British defendant listed on the London Stock Exchange, where there were allegations of substantial fraudulent conduct in the US).

[186] 'We do not think Congress intended to allow the United States to be used as a base for manufacturing fraudulent security devises for export, even when these are peddled only to foreigners.'; *AVC Nederland BV v Atrium Inv P'ship* 740 F 2d 148, 153 (2nd Cir 1984) (quoting *Vencap* 519 F 2d at

3.68   Under the effects test, a US court may exercise subject matter jurisdiction 'where illegal activity abroad has a "substantial effect" within the United States'.[187] This doctrine therefore permits the SEC (as well as private litigants)[188] to invoke the long arm of US law across the world, if need be, in order to call to account those deemed to have harmed the interests of American shareholders.

3.69   The DoJ also may extend its reach beyond the borders of the US in cases where criminal activity affecting the US has occurred.[189] Certain criminal statutes explicitly grant the DoJ the ability to operate and prosecute outside the US.[190] Others, by their subject matter or language, do so implicitly.[191]

3.70   An example of a US law routinely applied by the DoJ to conduct occurring outside the US is the Foreign Corrupt Practices Act of 1977 (FCPA).[192] The FCPA prevents US individuals and listed companies—including foreign companies listed on American exchanges—from bribing foreign officials for the purpose of obtaining or retaining business, and from falsifying records that would reflect such payments.[193] The law by definition concerns itself with activity that occurs exclusively abroad.[194]

1017); see also *In re Royal Dutch/Shell Transport Sec. Litig* 380 F Supp 2d 509, 539 (3rd Cir 2005) (rejecting the argument 'that the United States was not the location of "substantial and material" conduct by the Companies because the Companies are European companies with a largely European shareholder base that run their most vital operations from their respective European headquarters').

[187] *Alfadda* 935 F 2d at 478.

[188] Federal securities laws generally include provisions that allow for actions by private litigants. See, eg, Loss and Seligman (n 54 above), §§ 11-C-1 to 11-C-8.

[189] See DoJ Press Release, 'Korean Company—Hynix—Agrees to Plead Guilty to Price Fixing and Agrees to Pay $185 Million Fine for Role in Dram Conspiracy' (21 April 2005) ('This case illustrates the international scope of our criminal investigations and underscores the importance of looking beyond our nation's borders to prosecute and deter cartels that harm American consumers.'); see also DoJ Press Release, 'Samsung Agrees to Plead Guilty and to Pay $300 Million Criminal Fine for Role in Price Fixing Conspiracy' (13 October 2005).

[190] See, eg, 18 USC § 1956(f) (providing extraterritorial jurisdiction in certain circumstances for money laundering); ibid § 1513(d) (providing extraterritorial jurisdiction for the crime of retaliating against a witness, victim, or an informant).

[191] 'There is no constitutional bar to the extraterritorial application of penal laws.' *United States v King* 552 F 2d 833, 850 (9th Cir 1976) (involving a case wherein the federal statute was expressly aimed at having extraterritorial effect, but defendants protested that its attempted reach was unconstitutional). When 'a statute is silent as to its territorial reach, and no contrary congressional intent clearly appears, there is generally a presumption against its extraterritorial application.' *Carnero v Boston Sci Corp* 433 F 3d 1, 7 (1st Cir 2006) (citing *Arabian Am Oil Co* 499 US at 248) cert denied, 126 S Ct 2973 (2006). Nevertheless, there have been cases where a court has found extraterritorial intent without explicit statement in the text of a statute or its related legislative history. See, eg, *United States v Bowman*, 260 US 94, 98 (1922); *Schoenbaum* 405 F 2d at 206.

[192] 15 USC §§ 78m, 78dd-1 to 78dd-3, 78ff.

[193] See DoJ, <http://www.usdoj.gov/criminal/fraud/fcpa/>, for extensive information regarding the FCPA.

[194] The FCPA has garnered attention as regulators and federal prosecutors use this law to crackdown on overseas bribery of foreign officials. See S McNulty and B Masters, 'Baker Hughes Settles', *Financial Times* (27 April 2007) (announcing that Baker Hughes, the US oil fields products and services provider, entered into a settlement with regulators that will require the company to pay a

Similarly, the DoJ also may seek to criminalize activity occurring entirely abroad if **3.71** such activity affects American consumers.[195] In this context, as well as others involving a federal statute that is silent as to its extraterritorial application,[196] the conduct and effects tests have been applied to determine the question of subject matter jurisdiction. These include cases involving alleged anti-trust and RICO violations.[197]

Proper service of subpoenas

Even if a court has jurisdiction over the person subpoenaed, the subpoena remains **3.72** unenforceable unless it is properly served. Courts have generally looked to the Federal Rules of Civil Procedure[198] in order to determine the manner in which subpoenas seeking documents abroad must be served.[199]

Individuals may be served anywhere in the US even if they are only transitorily **3.73** present in the country.[200] In addition, US nationals or residents may be served

---

$44m fine, the largest ever in a regulatory settlement involving overseas bribery); M Esterl and D Crawford, 'Siemens Investigations Gain Scope', *Wall Street Journal* (27 April 2007) (reporting that the US investigation into corruption at Siemens AG was intensifying).

[195] See, eg, *United States v Nippon Paper Indus Co, Ltd*, 109 F 3d 1, 9 (1st Cir 1997), cert denied, 522 US 1044 (1998) (holding 'that Section One of the Sherman Act applies to wholly foreign conduct which has an intended and substantial effect in the United States' in a criminal case).

[196] See *Alfadda* 935 F 2d at 479. ('Like the Securities Exchange Act, the RICO statute is silent as to its extraterritorial application.').

[197] The Racketeer Influenced and Corrupt Organizations Act, 18 USC § 1961 et seq. See, eg, *Nippon Paper* 109 F 3d at 6 (involving federal anti-trust laws); *North South Fin Corp v Al-Turki* 100 F 3d 1046 (2nd Cir 1996) (involving RICO allegations); *Ayyash v Bank Al-Madina* 2006 WL 587342 *4 n3 (SDNY 9 March 2006). The *Ayyash* court, citing *North South Finance Corp v Al-Turki* 100 F 3d 1046 (2nd Cir 1996), upon which it relied, made an interesting point:

> The *Al-Turki* court recognized that the application to RICO of [the conduct and effects] tests, drawn from the securities and antitrust contexts, may be inappropriate, stating '[we] do not assume that congressional intent in enacting RICO justifies a similar approach to the statute's foreign application.' 100 F 3d at 1052. The Court nevertheless applied those tests because, as in this case, the parties assumed that those tests were applicable. *Id.* To date no other test has been proposed.

Ibid at *4 n 3.

[198] See Fed R Civ P 4(f) (providing for service upon individuals in a foreign country), (h) (providing for service both in the US and abroad upon foreign corporations, partnerships, or associations); see, eg, *United States v Toyota Motor Corp* 569 F Supp 1158, 1160 (CD Cal 1983) (relying on Rule 4(h)); *In re Elec & Musical Indus, Ltd* 155 F Supp. 892, 893 (SDNY 1957) (relying by analogy on what is now Rule 4(h)); *United States v Danenza* 528 F 2d 390, 391–92 (2nd Cir 1975) (relying on what is now Rule 4(f)).

[199] One court, however, referred instead to Rule 45, which governs domestic civil subpoenas and requires service by hand. See *FTC v Compagnie de Saint-Gobain-Point-à-Mousson* 636 F 2d 1300, 1324 (DC Cir 1980) (refusing to enforce an FTC subpoena directed at a French company because it was served by direct mail to the French company, a method not permitted by Rule 45, but noting that 'personal service upon the president, an officer, or a director of [the company] within the territorial boundaries of the United States' would be appropriate); see also Fed R Civ P 45(b)(1) (requiring personal delivery).

[200] *United States v Field (In re Grand Jury Proceedings)* 532 F 2d 404, 405 (5th Cir 1976) (enforcing a subpoena served on a Canadian citizen in the Miami Airport lobby); see also S Sun Beale et al,

with a grand jury subpoena in a foreign country using any method provided for in the Federal Rules of Civil Procedure.[201] In contrast, courts refuse to expand the reach of subpoenas by permitting their service upon *foreign* citizens in foreign countries without clear congressional authorization.[202] For example, a court rejected a Commodity Futures Trading Commission (CFTC) subpoena served upon a Brazilian citizen in Brazil because the statute authorizing CFTC subpoenas did not authorize 'enforcement of an investigative subpoena served upon a foreign citizen in a foreign nation'.[203]

3.74   Service of a subpoena upon a multinational corporation gives rise to more complex issues because such service may be made upon various persons in either its US or foreign offices. First, a subpoena that is directed at a corporation may be served upon 'an officer or a managing or general agent of the corporation named'.[204] Second, a subpoena directed at, and served upon, a US corporation may demand production of documents located abroad in possession of a foreign subsidiary or office.[205] Similarly, a subpoena directed at a foreign corporation

---

Grand Jury Law and Practice (2nd edn, 1997) § 6.6 (noting that although '[a] prospective foreign witness who did not reside in the United States could not be subpoenaed abroad,' '[t]ransitory presence' in the US is sufficient to accomplish service).

201   *United States v Danenza* 528 F 2d 390, 391–92 (2nd Cir 1975) (enforcing a subpoena served on an American citizen in Milan and delivered by the American consulate to Italian authorities who left the subpoena with the subject of the subpoena's concierge, who placed it in his mailbox).

202   See US Department of State, 'Service of Legal Documents Abroad' <http://travel.state.gov/law/info/judicial/judicial_680.html> ('There are no provisions for service [of subpoenas] upon non-US nationals or residents.'); Beale (n 200 above), § 6.6. However, Congress has attempted to authorize direct foreign service of grand jury subpoenas by amending the anti-money laundering statute. See Combating Money Laundering and Terrorist Financing Act of 2006, S 2402, sec 103, 109th Cong, 2d Sess, 13 March 2006 (currently before the Senate Judiciary Committee, amending 31 USC § 5318(k)(3) to broaden the existing administrative subpoena power and to grant a new power to issue 'a grand jury or trial subpoena' abroad. 31 USC § 5318(k)(3)(A) allows for the service of a 'subpoena' upon 'any foreign bank that maintains a correspondent account in the United States and request records related to such correspondent account' only 'if the foreign bank has a representative in the United States, or in a foreign country pursuant to any mutual legal assistance treaty, multilateral agreement, or other request for international law enforcement assistance'.

203   *CFTC v Nahas* 738 F 2d 487, 493 (DC Cir 1984).

204   *In re Elec & Musical Indus, Ltd* 155 F Supp. 892, 893 (SDNY 1957) (relying by analogy on Fed R Civ P 4(h)) ('This agent may be an individual, a partnership, or another corporation.'); see also *United States v Toyota Motor Corp* 569 F Supp 1158, 1160 (CD Cal 1983) (enforcing an IRS summons directed at a Japanese corporation but served in California on the president of its US subsidiary who was also the managing director of the parent, and whom the court found to be a 'managing agent' under Fed R Civ P 4(h)); *SEC v Minas De Artemisa, SA* 150 F 2d 215, 217 (9th Cir 1945) (enforcing an SEC subpoena directed at a Mexican corporation served upon its president, a US citizen resident in Arizona).

205   See, eg, *United States v First National City Bank* 357 US 197 (2nd Cir 1968) (enforcing a subpoena served upon a New York bank demanding the production of documents in the possession of its Frankfurt branch); *In re Grand Jury Subpoena* 218 F Supp 2d 544 (SDNY 2002) (enforcing a subpoena served upon a New York bank demanding the production of documents in the possession of its foreign branch).

demanding production of documents located abroad may be served upon its US subsidiary or office.[206]

Federal statutes may also create further requirements for proper subpoena serv- **3.75**
ice. For example, courts have interpreted the Clayton Act to limit service of grand jury subpoenas issued under the Act to districts within the US where the person named in the subpoena may be 'found'.[207]

Enforcement of subpoenas over conflicting foreign privacy laws

Most courts have enforced US subpoenas extraterritorially even if their disclosure **3.76**
requirements conflict with foreign laws prohibiting such disclosure, and even if compliance could result in criminal liability to the party producing the information. Courts have applied a balancing test, weighing US and foreign enforcement interests along with other factors,[208] and some courts have required that the party

---

206 See, eg, *United States v Bank of Nova Scotia (In re Grand Jury Proceedings)* 691 F 2d 1384, 1385 (11th Cir 1982) (enforcing a subpoena seeking documents from a Canadian Bank's Bahamian branch, served upon the Bank's Miami agency); *In re Grand Jury* 81-2, 550 F Supp 24, 27 (WD Mich 1982) (finding that service of subpoena directed at a German bank was proper on its New York branch); *Marc Rich & Co v United States (In re Grand Jury Proceedings)* 707 F 2d 663, 667 (2nd Cir 1982) (enforcing a subpoena directed at a Swiss corporation but served on its wholly owned subsidiary doing business in New York); *FTC v Compagnie de Saint-Gobain-Point-à-Mousson* 636 F 2d 1300, 1323 (DC Cir 1980) (refusing to imply the authority to serve a foreign corporation by direct mail and concluding that 'the best reading of congressional intent with regard to permissible modes of subpoena service was one authorizing the FTC to use all customary and legitimate methods of service of compulsory process commonly employed by American courts and administrative tribunals').

207 *In re Elec & Musical Indus, Ltd* 155 F Supp 892, 894 (SDNY 1957) ('Like other process issued pursuant to the anti-trust statutes, a subpoena may be served only in a district in which the person named is "found".'); see also *In re Grand Jury Subpoenas Duces Tecum Addressed to Canadian Int'l Paper Co* 72 F Supp 1013, 1020 (SDNY 1947) (enforcing a Sherman Act subpoena served upon the New York Deputy Secretary of State and directed at a Canadian corporation because the corporation was 'found' there, as evidenced by payment of rent for a New York office, maintenance of an active bank account, shipping of products into New York, and having several executive officers resident in New York).

208 See Restatement (Second) of Foreign Relations Law § 40 (1965) (listing the factors to be used in the balancing test: (1) the most important factor, the vital national interests of each of the states; (2) the extent and nature of the hardship that inconsistent enforcement actions would impose upon the person named in the subpoena; (3) the extent to which the required conduct is to take place in the territory of the other state; (4) the nationality of the person; and (5) the extent to which enforcement by action of either state can reasonably be expected to achieve compliance with the rule prescribed), cited in *United States v Bank of Nova Scotia (In re Grand Jury Proceedings)* 691 F 2d 1384, 1387 (11th Cir 1982); *United States v Vetco* 691 F 2d 1281, 1288 (9th Cir 1981); *United States v Field (In re Grand Jury Proceedings)* 532 F 2d 404, 407 (5th Cir 1976); *United States v First Nat'l City Bank* 396 F 2d 897, 903 (2nd Cir 1968). Note that the Restatement (Third) of Foreign Relations § 442 presents a modified test that has been applied by at least one court so far: 'The Restatement (Third) of the Foreign Relations of the United States, section 442(1)(c), further directs courts to consider the importance of the documents requested to the underlying litigation, the availability of alternative means of disclosure, and the degree of specificity of the request.' *In re Grand Jury Subpoena* 218 F Supp 544, 554 (SDNY 2002).

seeking enforcement show that the party refusing to comply with the subpoena failed to make a good faith effort to seek permission from the foreign authorities to obtain an exemption from the foreign law.[209]

3.77 In general, '[c]ourts consistently hold that the United States interest in law enforcement outweighs the interests of the foreign states in bank secrecy and the hardships imposed on the entity subject to compliance'.[210] In *United States v Bank of Nova Scotia*,[211] for instance, the court held in contempt a Bahamian bank's Miami agency that refused to comply with a federal grand jury's subpoena in connection with a tax and narcotics investigation on the basis that such disclosure would violate Bahamian bank secrecy law.[212] The court first found that the US government's request for an 'order of judicial assistance' was not a necessary prerequisite to its issuing a grand jury subpoena.[213] The court then balanced the 'vital role of a grand jury's investigative function to our system of jurisprudence and the crucial importance of the collection of revenue to the financial integrity of the republic' against the Bahamian bank secrecy law, which it found to be 'hardly a blanket guarantee of privacy' because a 'Bahamian court would be able

---

[209] See, eg, *Montship Lines, Ltd v Fed Maritime Bd* 295 F 2d 147, 154, 156 (DC Cir 1961) (finding with regard to an administrative subpoena, that '[p]rior to demanding whether these foreign laws do in fact forbid the production of documents such as those required by the [Federal Maritime] Board's order and, if so, what effect this should have on compliance, the appropriate procedure is to require these petitioners to make a good faith attempt to obtain a waiver of such restrictions from their respective governments') (citing *Société Internationale Pour Participations Industrielles et Commerciales, SA v Rogers* 357 US 197, 208 (1958)); *United States v First National Bank of Chicago* 699 F 2d 341, 346 (7th Cir 1983) (remanding to determine 'whether to issue an order requiring First Chicago to make a good faith effort to receive permission from the Greek authorities to produce the information specified in the summons').

[210] *In re Grand Jury Subpoena* 218 F Supp 2d 544, 554 (SDNY 2002). See also *United States v Bank of Nova Scotia (In re Grand Jury Proceedings)* 691 F 2d 1384, 1391 (11th Cir 1982) (noting that the 'vital role of a grand jury's investigative function' and the 'crucial importance of the collection of revenue' in the US outweigh the interests underlying the Bahamian bank security law, which is 'hardly a blanket guarantee of privacy' because it 'would allow a Bahamian court . . . to order production of these documents'); *United States v Vetco* 691 F 2d 1281 (9th Cir 1981) (enforcing an IRS summons against Swiss subsidiary of US corporation because '[t]here is a strong American interest in collecting taxes from and prosecuting tax fraud by its own nationals operating through foreign subsidiaries' and noting that the Swiss interest in privacy of business records is 'diminished in this case, where the parties are subsidiaries of American corporations'); *United States v Field (In re Grand Jury Proceedings)* 532 F 2d 404, 408 (5th Cir 1976) (holding that the interests underlying the Cayman Bank Secrecy Act did not outweigh the '[significant] restrict[ion] [of] the ability of the grand jury to obtain information which might possibly uncover criminal activities of the most serious nature'); *United States v First Nat'l City Bank* 396 F 2d 897, 903 (2nd Cir 1968) (holding that the interests underlying a grand jury's investigation of a violation of anti-trust laws, which 'have long been considered cornerstones of this nation's economic policies', outweighed the interests underlying German bank security law, which 'Germany considers . . . simply a privilege that can be waived by the customer' and 'not even required by statute').

[211] 691 F 2d 1384 (11th Cir 1982).

[212] Ibid at 1386–87.

[213] Ibid.

to order production of these documents'.[214] Finding it 'incongruous to suggest that a United States court afford greater protection to the customer's right of privacy than would a Bahamian court', the court enforced the order of contempt.[215]

Similarly, in *In re Grand Jury Subpoena*,[216] a grand jury investigating a New York corporation under the FCPA for bribery of foreign officials served the corporation with a subpoena demanding production of documents from its foreign branch.[217] Balancing the interests, the court noted that the United States' 'strong national interest in combating international bribery' was 'at least arguably share[d]' by the unnamed foreign nation, which was 'widely perceived to suffer from corruption', and that '[t]his alignment of interests distinguishes an FCPA investigation from other crimes where international discovery is sought'.[218] The court then found the hardship to the corporation to be insubstantial because of the foreign government's lack of 'enforce[ment] by any active prosecution' and the fact that the document production required would be 'relatively straight forward'.[219] The court concluded that 'the United States interest in investigating suspected violations of its criminal laws outweighs the Republic's interest'.[220]   **3.78**

In contrast, in *United States v First National Bank of Chicago*[221] the court remanded an order enforcing an IRS summons. There, the IRS sought disclosure of certain customers' bank records in possession of First Chicago's branch in Athens, Greece. First Chicago refused to furnish the requested information in order to avoid incurring criminal penalties under the Greek Bank Secrecy Act.[222] The IRS thereafter filed a petition in the district court to enforce the summons, and the court ordered compliance, which First Chicago challenged. On appeal, the court balanced the competing interests at stake and concluded that 'it was an abuse of discretion to enter an unqualified order compelling production'.[223] Specifically, the court considered Greece's interest in maintaining its bank secrecy law, as well as the potential hardship of the bank employees who would be exposed to criminal penalty in Greece. Ultimately, the court remanded to determine whether First National should be required to make a good faith effort to seek an exception from   **3.79**

---

214 Ibid at 1391 (internal quotations omitted).
215 Ibid.
216 218 F Supp. 2d 544 (SDNY 2002).
217 Ibid at 547.
218 Ibid at 555, 562.
219 Ibid at 563.
220 Ibid at 564.
221 699 F 2d 341 (7th Cir 1983).
222 Ibid at 342.
223 Ibid.

Greek authorities and to determine whether it was possible to 'coordinate efforts to collect delinquent taxes through diplomatic means'.[224]

Power of court to quash or modify subpoenas

3.80 The power to obtain disclosure through a subpoena is limited by courts' ability to 'quash or modify the subpoena if compliance would be unreasonable or oppressive'.[225] Courts have quashed subpoenas in the following circumstances.

3.81 First, courts have generally found subpoenas that purport to reach materials privileged under US law to be unreasonable.[226] When deciding whether to enforce subpoenas demanding disclosure in violation of foreign privileges, however, courts have engaged in the balancing analysis described above, and, in some cases, have enforced such subpoenas.[227]

3.82 Second, courts have quashed as unreasonable subpoenas that request documents not in the possession, custody, or control of the person to whom the subpoena is directed. Control means not only the physical ability to obtain the documents, but also the legal right to have the documents disclosed.[228] Although a mere parent-subsidiary relationship may not itself establish control,[229] when an entity has or shares 'practical and actual managerial control' over its affiliate, courts have found such control sufficient, 'regardless of the formalities of corporate organization'.[230]

---

[224] Ibid at 346.

[225] Fed R Crim P 17(c); Fed R Civ P 45(c)(3)(A).

[226] See, eg, *In re Grand Jury* 821 F 2d 946, 958 (3rd Cir 1987) (remanding district court order limiting a subpoena to determine whether the US deliberative process privilege applies); *In re Zuniga* 714 F 2d 632, 639–40 (6th Cir 1983) (recognizing the existence of US psychotherapist-patient privilege as applied to grand jury subpoenas but deciding that it did not apply to the case facts).

[227] See, eg, *United States v First Nat'l City Bank* 396 F 2d 897, 899, 903 (2nd Cir 1968) (enforcing a subpoena that violated a German bank secrecy law that 'was in the nature of a privilege that could be waived by the customer but not the bank'). Note that sovereign immunity is not subject to balancing as a 'privilege' provided by foreign law, but rather is protected by US law. See Foreign Sovereign Immunities Act, 28 USC §§ 1603(a), 1604 (providing that a 'foreign sovereign' or 'agency or instrumentality' thereof is 'immune from the jurisdiction of the courts of the United States', with certain exceptions). Courts have found that 'individuals acting in their official capacities as officers of corporations considered foreign sovereigns' are immune under the act. See, eg, *Keller v Cent Bank of Nigeria* 277 F 3d 811, 816 (2002). But see *Southway v Cent Bank of Nigeria* 198 F 3d 1210, 1214–16 (10th Cir 1999) (finding that the FSIA provides no immunity against criminal proceedings).

[228] *Marc Rich & Co v United States (In re Grand Jury Proceedings)* 707 F 2d 663, 667 (2nd Cir 1982) ('The test for the production of documents is control, not location.').

[229] See *Wasden v Yamaha Motor Co, Ltd* 131 FRD 206, 209 (MD Fla 1990).

[230] *In re Uranium Antitrust Litig* 480 F Supp 1138, 1145 (ND Ill 1979) (noting that 'the issue of control is more a question of fact than of law'); see, eg, *In re Investigation of World Arrangements with Relation to Prod, Transp, Refining & Distrib of Petroleum* 13 FRD 280, 285 (DDC 1952) ('[I]f a corporation has power, either directly or indirectly, through another corporation or series of corporations, to elect a majority of the directors of another corporation, such corporation may be deemed a

Courts also have found subpoenas that request documents outside the scope of **3.83** the investigation to be unreasonable.[231] In the grand jury context, some courts have even required a preliminary showing by affidavit of the subpoena's 'proper purpose'.[232] In the administrative context, however, the courts have interpreted the relevance requirement broadly, giving wide discretion to agencies to determine themselves what is a proper subject of their subpoenas.[233]

Sanctions for non-compliance with subpoenas

Under the rules of civil and criminal procedure and the various agency statutes, a **3.84** court may issue an order holding in civil or criminal contempt a party disobeying a subpoena.[234] For example, a court sanctioned a Swiss corporation for failing to

---

parent corporation and in control of the corporation whose directors it has the power to elect to office. If any corporation herein under the subpoena duces tecum has that power it has the control necessary to secure the documents demanded by the Government.').

231 See, eg, *United States v Powell* 379 US 48, 57–58 (1964) (requiring that the subject of an administrative subpoena must be 'relevant' to a 'legitimate purpose' of the agency, must not demand information already in the agency's possession, and must properly follow agency procedures); *In re Grand Jury Proceedings (Schoefield)* 507 F 2d 963, 965 (3rd Cir 1975) (requiring material demanded by a subpoena to be 'relevant to an investigation being conducted by the grand jury'). Grand jury subpoenas in anti-trust investigation are usually challenged on constitutional and non-constitutional grounds. Constitutional grounds invoke the judiciary's supervisory authority over the grand jury. Other grounds include unreasonable burden, relevancy, lack of authority to conduct the investigation, procedural irregularities in issuing the subpoena, and improper purpose behind the subpoena. See ABA Section of Antitrust Law, (n141 above), at 743–744 and the cases cited there.

232 Cf *In re Grand Jury Proceedings (Schoefield)* 507 F 2d 963, 965 (3rd Cir 1975) (requiring such a showing), with *United States v Bank of Nova Scotia (In re Grand Jury Proceedings)* 691 F 2d 1384, 1387 (11th Cir 1982) (not requiring such a showing).

233 *SEC v Brigadoon Sch Dist* 480 F 2d 1047, 1053 (1973) ('[The SEC] must be free without undue interference or delay to conduct an investigation which will adequately develop a factual basis for a determination as to whether particular activities come within the Commission's regulatory authority.').

234 See, eg, Fed R Crim P 17(g) ('The court . . . may hold in contempt a witness who, without adequate excuse, disobeys a subpoena issued by a federal court in that district.'); Fed R Civ P 45(e) (substantially same); 28 USC § 1784(a)–(b) ('The court of the United States which has issued a subpoena served in a foreign country may order the person who has failed to appear or who has failed to produce a document or other thing as directed therein to show cause before it at a designated time why he should not be punished for contempt . . . The court . . . may direct that any of the person's property within the United States be levied upon or seized . . . and held to satisfy any judgment that may be rendered against him.'); 15 USC § 78u(c) (2000) ('In case of . . . refusal to obey a subpena [sic] issued [to] any person, the Commission may invoke the aid of any court of the United States within the jurisdiction of which such investigation or proceeding is carried on, or where such person resides or carries on business . . . [to] issue an order requiring such person to appear before the Commission or member or officer designated by the Commission, there to produce records, if so ordered, or to give testimony touching the matter under investigation or in question; and any failure to obey such order of the court may be punished by such court as a contempt thereof . . . Any person who shall, without just cause, fail or refuse to attend and testify or to answer any lawful inquiry or to produce [documents] . . . shall be guilty of a misdemeanor and, upon conviction, shall be subject to a fine of not more than $1,000 or to imprisonment for a term of not more than one year, or both.').

disclose documents demanded by an IRS subpoena.[235] Noting that the 'terms of an enforcement order rest within the discretion of the district court', the court upheld an order requiring production of the documents in Los Angeles, not Switzerland, '[g]iven the previous difficulties of securing production voluntarily, and the infeasibility of on-site inspection'.[236] The court went on to uphold the district court's order of contempt, issued upon the Swiss corporation's refusal to comply with the subpoena, imposing a fine of $500 per day until compliance.[237] Note, however, that if a party fails to comply with a subpoena on the basis that production would violate a foreign secrecy law, courts often decline to impose sanctions if the party made a good faith attempt to seek an exemption from that law.[238]

F. Alternative to Subpoenas: International Agreements and Diplomacy

3.85 'Since foreign nationals residing in . . . foreign countries are not subject to the subpoena power of United States courts, their attendance can be obtained only on a voluntary basis. Obtaining testimony from foreign nationals is often a delicate matter, and care must be taken to avoid offending the sovereignty of the foreign country involved.'[239] Because of the potential for international friction, the US has

---

[235] *United States v Vetco* 691 F 2d 1281 (9th Cir 1981).

[236] Ibid at 1283, 1291.

[237] Ibid at 1284, 1291. Courts have enforced contempt orders using both physical confinement and monetary fines. See, eg, *In re Sealed Case* 832 F 2d 1268, 1272 (DC Cir 1987) ('The court ordered the Witness confined for the life of the grand jury or until he complied with the District Court's order . . . unless the Witness sought an immediate appeal.'), abrogated on other grounds by *Braswell v United States* 487 US 99 (1988); *In re First Nat'l City Bank* 285 F Supp 845, 848–49 (SDNY 1968) (ordering the individual respondent to be confined to jail 'until he shall have complied with the Court order, but not in excess of sixty days from the date of commencement of the commitment' and levying a fine on the bank for '$2,000 a day until it shall have complied with the Court order').

[238] See, eg, *United States v Bank of Nova Scotia (In re Grand Jury Proceedings)* 691 F 2d 1384, 1388–89 (11th Cir 1982) (court imposed sanction finding that foreign bank had not made a good faith effort to comply with the grand jury subpoena by seeking waiver of privacy laws from its government); *United States v Vetco Inc* 691 F 2d 1281, 1287 (9th Cir 1981) (citing *Société Internationale Pour Participations Industrielles v Rogers* 357 US 197, 205–206 (1958) (finding that imposing sanction of dismissal of suit where Swiss holding company refused to comply with a US court order demanding disclosure in contravention of a Swiss penal law violated due process because the company sought waiver of the law from the Swiss government in good faith)).

[239] USAM § 3-19.320 (October 2002); see also Restatement (Third) of Foreign Relations Law § 442 rep n 1 ('No aspect of the extension of the American legal system beyond the territorial frontier of the United States has given rise to so much friction as requests for documents in investigation and litigation in the United States . . . The common theme of foreign responses to United States requests for discovery is that, whatever pretrial or investigative techniques the United States adopts for itself, they may be applied to persons or documents located in another state only with the permission of that state.'); USAM § 9-13.510 (December 2006) ('Because virtually every nation enacts laws to

increasingly sought to obtain information abroad through treaty-based measures, voluntary agreements or by using other alternatives to compulsory process.[240]

The following methods have been employed to obtain disclosure of information in the possession of individuals and corporations overseas, even where a US court's exercise of jurisdiction would not be deemed proper: (1) requests based on treaties and executive agreements; (2) letters rogatory; and (3) diplomatic cooperation.[241]   **3.86**

Requests based on treaties and executive agreements

States may obtain evidence through treaty-based obligations—such as those created by mutual legal assistance treaties (MLATs) and the Hague Conventions—as well as through interim executive agreements. The primary advantage of MLATs is flexibility, as they may 'provide for a wide variety of assistance, including servicing [sic] documents, providing records, locating persons, taking testimony or statements of persons, producing documents, executing requests for search and seizure, forfeiting criminally-obtained assets, and transferring persons in custody for testimonial purposes'.[242]   **3.87**

---

protect its sovereignty and can react adversely to American law enforcement efforts to gather evidence within its borders as a violation of that sovereignty, contact the Office of International Affairs initially to evaluate methods for securing assistance from abroad and to select an appropriate one.'); ibid, Title 9, Criminal Resource Manual § 268 (October 1997) ('Generally, foreign cooperation depends on the existence of articulable facts indicating that evidence is located in a particular jurisdiction. The prosecutor should be prepared to provide that information.').

240 See R M Olsen, 'Discovery in Federal Criminal Investigations', 16 New York University Journal of International Law and Policy 999 (1984) ('[L]itigation [caused by subpoena disputes] has raised a plethora of questions about the necessity and wisdom of compulsory process.').

241 See USAM, Title 9, Criminal Resource Manual § 274 (October 1997). None of these methods is the exclusive means of taking evidence in foreign countries. See, eg, Mutual Assistance in Criminal Matters, art 38, § 1, 25 May 1973, US-Switzerland, 27 UST 2019, TIAS No 8302 (stating that the treaty is not the exclusive means by which the states parties can procure evidence from each other); *United States v Vetco* 691 F 2d 1281, 1286 (9th Cir 1981) (enforcing IRS summons upon Swiss subsidiary of US corporation despite bilateral US-Swiss treaty because '[t]he treaty does not state that its procedures for the exchange of information are intended to be exclusive'); Hague Evidence Convention, Art 27 ('The provisions of the present Convention shall not prevent a Contracting State from (a) declaring that Letters of Request may be transmitted to its judicial authorities through channels other than those provided for in Article 2; (b) permitting, by internal law or practice, any act provided for in this Convention to be performed upon less restrictive conditions; (c) permitting, by internal law or practice, methods of taking evidence other than those provided for in this Convention.').

242 B Zagaris, 'Developments in International Judicial Assistance and Related Matters', 18 Denver Journal of International Law & Policy 339, 352 (1995); see, eg, Treaty on Mutual Assistance in Criminal Matters, 25 May 1973, US-Switzerland, 27 UST 2019, TIAS No 8302; Treaty on Extradition and Mutual Assistance in Criminal Matters, 7 June 1979, US-Turkey, 32 UST 3111, TIAS No 9891; Treaty on Mutual Assistance in Criminal Matters, 19 March 1986, US-Thailand, S Treaty Doc No 100-18; Treaty Concerning the Cayman Islands Relating to Mutual Legal Assistance in Criminal Matters, 6 July 1986, US-United Kingdom of Great Britain and Northern Ireland, S Treaty Doc No 100-8; Treaty on Mutual Legal Assistance, 8 August 1987, US-The Bahamas, S Treaty Doc No 100-17.

3.88 In addition to the typically bilateral treaty obligations created by MLATs, the Hague Convention on the Service Abroad of Judicial and Extra-Judicial Documents in Civil and Commercial Matters,[243] and the Hague Convention on the Taking of Evidence Abroad in Civil and Commercial Matters,[244] create multilateral treaty obligations.

3.89 The Hague Service Convention, incorporated by reference into the Federal Rules of Civil Procedure, designates a Central Authority in each state party—the Civil Division of the DoJ in the US—to receive service of judicial documents from foreign countries.[245] If the Central Authority of the receiving state considers the request for document service to comply with the requirements of the Convention, it must serve the document upon the person designated in the request, unless the recipient consents to informal delivery.[246] The Convention does not apply to information sought in criminal investigations, as it only applies to civil or commercial matters.[247]

3.90 The Hague Evidence Convention also operates through the Central Authorities, authorizing them to receive letters of request—which are binding upon signatories of the treaty—seeking evidence abroad.[248] Letters of request may only seek evidence 'intended for use in judicial proceedings, commenced or contemplated', and only in civil or commercial matters.[249]

3.91 As an alternative to treaty-based requests, states have begun using interim executive agreements with increasing frequency:

> Interim executive agreements of one form or another are currently in force with a number of countries. Most apply to investigations arising from illegal narcotics trafficking. Some require the Attorney General to certify to the attorney general of the other nation that specified records located in the other country are required in connection with a pending investigation of criminal conduct that is covered by the agreement.[250]

---

[243] 20 UST 1361, 658 UNTS 163 (1965).

[244] 23 UST 2555, TIAS 7444 (1970).

[245] See Hague Service Convention, Art 2.

[246] Ibid Art 5.

[247] Ibid Art 1.

[248] See Hague Evidence Convention, Art. 2.

[249] Ibid Art 1. For further information on both Hague conventions, see generally US Department of State, Circular: Hague Service Convention (2006); US Department of State, Circular: Hague Evidence Convention Operations Authorities (2006); see also Hague Conference on Private International Law <http://hcch.e-vision.nl/index_en.php> (click 'Authorities' (per convention), click on Statute of the Hague Conference on Private International Law).

[250] USAM, Title 9, Criminal Resource Manual § 277 (October 1997).

Letters rogatory

US courts may issue letters rogatory in civil or criminal investigations requesting **3.92** foreign courts to obtain certain specified evidence.[251] Unlike letters of request under the Hague Evidence Convention, compliance with letters rogatory is voluntary, and only effective if the producing country has a similar provision allowing for the execution of letters rogatory or some similar type of order.

Some courts, in the interest of comity, have refused to enforce subpoenas unless the **3.93** party seeking disclosure first attempts to send the foreign court letters rogatory.[252] More recent decisions, however, have held that issuing letters rogatory is not mandatory because they are not sufficiently similar to subpoenas.[253] Accordingly, US regulators have used letters rogatory with less frequency.[254]

Diplomatic cooperation

States may also use other cooperative measures to procure evidence from abroad. **3.94** These methods include: (1) persuasion of foreign authorities to share information from their own investigations; (2) requests through diplomatic channels; (3) voluntary depositions at US embassies and consulates; (4) treaty-type requests when no treaty is in force but the foreign government is likely to cooperate; (5) informal police-to-police requests through US law enforcement agents stationed abroad; and (6) requests through Interpol for information obtainable by foreign police without an official request.[255]

---

[251] See 28 USC § 1781 (2000).

[252] See, eg, *Ings v Ferguson* 282 F 2d 149, 152–53 (2nd Cir 1960) (denying enforcement of a subpoena requiring production of documents in Canada until the party seeking the documents first attempted to procure the documents using letters rogatory because '[w]hether removal of records from Canada is prohibited is a question of Canadian law and is best resolved by Canadian courts').

[253] See, eg, *United States v Vetco* 691 F 2d 1281, 1290 (9th Cir 1981) (where Swiss government refused to execute letters rogatory in a tax investigation, court rejected letters rogatory as a 'substantially equivalent alternative' to IRS summons because 'letters rogatory will not be honored in Switzerland where they seek records for litigation involving fiscal matters'); *In re Grand Jury* 81-2, 550 F Supp 24, 29 (WD Mich 1982) ('The United States has chosen subpoenas as the preferred method of obtaining the records . . . Recognizing the availability of letters rogatory, nevertheless, the court will not second-guess the grand jury. The possibilities offered by letters rogatory do not render the subpoena alternative invalid or otherwise improper.'); cf *United States v Bank of Nova Scotia (In re Grand Jury Proceedings)* 691 F 2d 1384, 1390 (11th Cir 1982) (refusing to require the investigators to file an 'order of judicial assistance permitting disclosure from the Supreme Court of the Bahamas' because it is 'not a substantially equivalent means for obtaining production because of the cost in time and money and the uncertain likelihood of success').

[254] See, eg, US Department of State, Service of Legal Documents Abroad <http://travel.state.gov/law/info/judicial/judicial_680.html> ('Letters rogatory are a time consuming, cumbersome process and should not be utilized unless there are no other options available. If the laws of the foreign country permit other methods of service, the use of letters rogatory is not recommended given the habitual time delays of up to a year or more in execution of the requests.').

[255] USAM, Title 9, Criminal Resource Manual § 278 (October 1997).

3.95   US regulators prefer these methods because they often avoid international friction. For example, in anti-trust investigations, the DoJ will first seek disclosure either voluntarily or through international anti-trust assistance agreements. If the entity under investigation wishes to send a representative to the US, the DoJ will provide assurances that the representative will not be served with compulsory process while in the US. The DoJ takes this approach partly because it 'will be in a stronger litigating and diplomatic posture in ultimately invoking compulsory process if it has first exhausted more conciliatory avenues'.[256]

3.96   The US investigation of Jacob 'Kobi' Alexander provides an illustration of how US regulators might employ the methods discussed above. Alexander was a CEO who was charged in the US with securities fraud, and who went into hiding in Namibia, a nation with which the US does not have an extradition treaty. Nonetheless, Alexander was arrested by Interpol and Namibian police on a warrant issued at the request of US authorities. After Alexander's arrest, Namibia amended its laws governing extradition to allow the rendering of fugitives to the US.[257] The US then formally requested Alexander's extradition, and a Namibian magistrate set a date for the extradition hearing.[258] Should the Namibian courts grant the US request for an extradition order, Alexander could then be extradited and would thus be subject to the full scope of US investigatory power.[259]

G. Conducting Internal Investigations in the United States— Background and Recent Trends

What is an internal investigation?

3.97   An internal investigation is an inquiry conducted by, or on behalf of, a company and/or its board of directors in an effort to discover facts relating to possible improper acts or omissions that may have occurred at the company. There is no standard 'internal investigation', and internal investigations come in all shapes and sizes. An internal investigation can be a critical means for a company to uncover and address misconduct that poses risks to the company's reputation or that may generate civil or criminal liability.

---

[256] Spencer, Weber and Waller, *Antitrust and American Business Abroad* (3rd edn, 1997) §§ 14:2–3.

[257] See A Dodds Frank and B Van Voris, *Former Comverse Chief Alexander Arrested in Namibia*, Bloomberg (27 September 2006) <http://quote.bloomberg.com/apps/news?pid=20601087&sid=aJHBHVHTD2JE>.

[258] Associated Press, 'April Hearing Set for Ex-Comverse CEO', *Miami Herald* (17 November 2006) <http://www.redorbit.com/news/technology/735208/april_hearing_set_for_excomverse_ceo/index.html>.

[259] The hearing has been postponed a number of times. See John Grobler, 'Extradition of Former Comverse Chief Delayed in Namibia', *NY Times* (26 April 2007).

Internal investigations are a fact of life for corporations in today's regulatory **3.98** enforcement environment. Given their broad authority to enforce compliance with the laws that they administer—coupled with the expansive reach of their jurisdiction and authority to issue subpoenas—the chance of encountering the DoJ and/or the SEC is a real concern for anyone doing business in today's global marketplace.

Historically, the DoJ and the SEC pursued a reactive approach to business crime **3.99** and regulatory actions.[260] When wrongdoing was exposed, law enforcement and regulators typically addressed it by conducting extensive inquiries and meting out appropriate sanctions. Today's regulators, however, expect companies to conduct proactive internal investigations as a way of demonstrating their cooperation with regulators. As then General Counsel of the SEC, Giovanni P Prezioso, commented, '[t]he strong incentives for cooperation, in both criminal and Commission investigations, appear to have greatly increased the number of independent investigations undertaken by companies presented with evidence of potential misconduct'.[261] Understanding how to conduct internal investigations is key to navigating today's regulatory landscape in the US and, when under regulatory scrutiny, obtaining the best possible outcome in a related government investigation.[262]

The enactment of SOX has imposed on companies an obligation, under certain **3.100** circumstances, to conduct internal investigations. Among other things, SOX requires corporations to adopt effective compliance programmes and initiate internal investigations to address allegations of misconduct.[263] Directors of public companies may face personal liability for failure to exercise their fiduciary and oversight roles properly. Accordingly, there is a greater expectation that independent directors, including members of audit committees, will discharge their duties by demanding that companies retain independent counsel to conduct internal investigations when intimations of serious misconduct arise concerning the company.

As previously mentioned, cooperation with US government investigators may **3.101** avoid or mitigate charges or penalties. While the nature and seriousness of the

---

[260] See, eg, S M Cutler, Dir, Div of Enforcement, SEC, Speech by SEC Staff: Remarks Before the District of Columbia Bar Association (11 February 2004) (hereinafter Cutler, Remarks Before DC Bar) <http://www.sec.gov/news/speech/spch021104smc.htm>.

[261] Giovanni P. Prezioso, Gen Counsel, SEC, Speech by SEC Staff: Remarks Before the Vanderbilt Director's College (23 September 2004) <http://www.sec.gov/news/speech/spch092304gpp.htm>.

[262] Kestenbaum and Criss (n 155 above), *125 ('General wisdom is that a company under investigation—or which discovers possible wrongdoing on its own—achieves a better result from the government if it conducts an internal investigation.').

[263] See Sarbanes-Oxley Act, Pub L No 107-204, §§ 301, 304, 404, 116 Stat 745 (2002).

underlying conduct and its pervasiveness within a corporation will always be the dominant concerns for regulators in the US, cooperation with regulatory authorities is the next most important factor affecting the outcome of any investigation.

3.102   A former Director of the SEC's Division of Enforcement has explained that cooperation is currently assessed using a 'more graduated scale' and that the Commission takes into account both cooperation, and the lack thereof, in making charging decisions.[264] Similarly, federal prosecutors 'now take a harder look at whether the company is really [fully] cooperating' in deciding whether to bring charges.[265]

3.103   Moreover, as discussed above, while this is an area that is very much in flux today, the government often expects companies to waive the attorney-client privilege and work-product protection as part of a company's full cooperation.[266] Such expectations have come under heavy criticism in recent years.[267] The DoJ, in response, 'adjusted' and 'clarified' its stance on the waiver of the attorney-client privilege and work product protections.[268] The SEC has been asked to do the same.[269]

---

[264] Cutler, Remarks Before DC Bar (n 260 above).

[265] Christopher A Wray, Assistant Attorney General, Crim Div, Remarks to the ABA White Collar Crime Luncheon (25 February 2005).

[266] See M Coyle, 'Waiving Privilege a Crucial Sentencing Issue', National Law Journal, 29 August 2005, at 6 ('In practice, companies are finding that they have no choice but to waive these privileges whenever the government demands it.').

[267] Indeed, in recent years, there have been extensive lobbying efforts aimed at changing the government's position on waiver. Notable in this regard were the efforts of the Coalition to Preserve the Attorney-Client Privilege, which presented a comprehensive statement to Congressional lawmakers regarding the potential impact of the DoJ's policies regarding privilege waivers. Coalition members included: American Chemistry Council, American Civil Liberties Union, Association of Corporate Council, Business Civil Liberties, Inc, Business Roundtable, National Association of Criminal Defense Lawyers, National Association of Manufacturers, and US Chamber of Commerce. See Submission to the US House of Representatives Judiciary Subcommittee on Crime, Terrorism and Homeland Security Regarding the Subcommittee's Hearings on 'White Collar Enforcement (Part I): Attorney-Client Privilege and Corporate Waivers' (7 March 2006) <http://www.acc.com/public/accapolicy/coalitionstatement030706.pdf>. Another source of pressure upon the government has been exerted by the American Bar Association (ABA). See Letter to Attorney General Alberto Gonzales Regarding Proposal for Revising Department of Justice Attorney-Client Privilege and Work Product Doctrine Waiver Policy (2 May 2006); Letter to Attorney General Alberto Gonzales Regarding Proposed Revisions to Department of Justice Policy Regarding Waiver of the Attorney-Client Privilege and Work-Product Doctrine (5 September 2006).

[268] See Memorandum from Paul J McNulty, Deputy Attorney Gen, to Heads of Dep't Components & US Attorneys (12 December 2006) (hereinafter McNulty Memorandum) See <http://www.usdoj.gov/opa/pr/2006/December/06_odag_828.html> (DoJ press release announcing McNulty's Revised Charging Guidelines for Prosecuting Corporate Fraud); For text of the memorandum, see <http://news.findlaw.com/hdocs/docs/doj/121206mcnultymemo3.html> >.

[269] Letter to Christopher Cox, Chairman, SEC, Regarding Proposal for Revising the Commission's Policy Regarding Requesting Waiver of Attorney-Client Privilege, Work Product, and Employee Protections (5 February 2007) (providing suggested new language to amend and supplement the Seaboard Report).

Nevertheless, the government still insists that its ability to root out corporate **3.104** wrongdoing is of paramount importance and that 'a company's disclosure of privileged information may permit the government to expedite its investigation'.[270] Thus, it remains that corporations ignore regulators at their peril, and it has become more important than ever for attorneys representing companies to understand how to conduct internal investigations.

What events trigger an internal investigation?

There is no rule of thumb on when a company should conduct an internal inves- **3.105** tigation. Events that typically trigger an internal investigation include the following:

- The company discovers, on its own or through its outside auditors, that there are errors or irregularities affecting the company's financial statements.
- The company receives whistle-blower or anonymous allegations concerning purported misconduct by company executives or employees.
- The company receives notification from a regulatory authority that an investigation has commenced or is imminent.
- The company is served with a civil complaint, including derivative claims and whistle-blower lawsuits, alleging misconduct at the company.
- The company discovers an inappropriate business practice that may lead to litigation exposure, such as price-fixing, bid rigging, misleading public disclosure or payments of bribes.
- The company is informed by (outside) counsel of evidence of a material violation of securities law, or breach of fiduciary duty or a similar violation.
- Allegations of misconduct appear in the press.

Why should a company conduct an internal investigation?

There are many reasons why a company should conduct an internal investiga- **3.106** tion. Corporate officers and directors need to understand if unlawful conduct is occurring so they can stop improper conduct and institute remedial action. In addition, US regulators often expect companies promptly to undertake an internal investigation when faced with indications that unlawful conduct is occurring.[271]

---

[270] McNulty Memorandum (n 268 above).

[271] According to one SEC spokesman, 'internal reviews "are not a substitute for SEC investigations" but "can accelerate the pace of investigations and bring faster results for investors"'. M Esterl, D Crawford and N Koppel, 'Siemens Internal Review Hits Hurdles', Wall St J, at A18 (23 January 2008).

3.107   Both the DoJ and the SEC have issued written guidelines setting forth their clear expectation that a company faced with any of the above triggering events would be wise to undertake a prompt internal investigation to determine whether any wrongdoing, in fact, has occurred, and to take remedial measures.[272]

3.108   The SEC's Seaboard Report contains a list of factors that are used to determine 'whether, and how much, to credit self-policing, self-reporting, remediation and cooperation'.[273] The Seaboard Report currently provides that waiver of the attorney-client and work-product protections are not necessary to show cooperation through the sharing of information with regulators. Nonetheless, the

---

[272] The DoJ's latest policy statement on cooperation is formally entitled 'Principles of Federal Prosecution'. This statement of principles is commonly known as the McNulty Memorandum, for its author Deputy Attorney General, Paul J McNulty. See McNulty Memorandum (n 268 above). The McNulty Memorandum is the third version of the DoJ's policy on cooperation. See Memorandum from Larry D Thompson, Deputy Attorney General, to Heads of Department Components, United States Attorneys (20 January 2003) <http://www.usdoj.gov/dag/cftf/corporate_guidelines.htm>; Memorandum from the Deputy Attorney General to All Component Heads and United States Attorneys, 'Bringing Criminal Charges Against Corporations' (16 June 1999) <http://www.usdoj.gov/criminal/fraud/docs/reports/1999/chargingcorps.html>.

The SEC's guidelines regarding cooperation are contained in a Report of Investigation and Commission Statement, which is familiarly known as the 'Seaboard Report'. See Report of Investigation Pursuant to Section 21(a) of the Securities Exchange Act of 1934 and Commission Statement on the Relationship of Cooperation to Agency Enforcement Decisions, Exchange Act Release No 44969, Enforcement Release No 1470, 2001 SEC LEXIS 2210 (23 October 2001).

In addition to the DoJ and the SEC guidelines, the recently revised US Sentencing Guidelines for Organizations set forth additional criteria that credit corporate cooperation. See United States Sentencing Commission, *Guidelines Manual* § 8C2.5(g) (November 2006).

The NASD and the NYSE have similar guidelines. See, eg, NASD, Sanction Guidelines (2006) <http://www.nasd.com/web/groups/enforcement/documents/enforcement/nasdw_011038. pdf>; NYSE, Memorandum to All Members, Member Organizations and Chief Operating Officers Regarding Factors Considered by the New York Stock Exchange Decision of Enforcement in Determining Sanctions (7 October 2005) (hereinafter Factors Memorandum) <http://apps.nyse.com/commdata/PubInfoMemos.nsf/AllPublishedInfoMemosNyseCom/85256FCB005E19 E8852570920068314A/$FILE/Microsoft%20Word%20-%20Document%20in%2005-77. pdf>; NYSE, Memorandum to All Members, Member Organizations and Chief Operating Officers Regarding Cooperation (14 September 2005) (hereinafter Cooperation Memorandum) <http://apps.nyse.com/commdata/PubInfoMemos.nsf/vwAllPubInfoMemosNumberWeb/852 56FCB005E19E88525707C004C6DE0/$FILE/Microsoft%20Word%20-%20Document% 20in%2005-65.pdf>.

[273] These factors include: (1) the nature of the misconduct; (2) the events and circumstances that gave rise to the misconduct; (3) where in the organization the misconduct took place; (4) the duration of the misconduct; (5) any harm caused by the misconduct; (6) how, and by whom, the misconduct was detected; (7) the amount of time it took to implement an effective response after the misconduct was discovered; (8) how the company reacted after it learned of the misconduct; (9) processes used by the company to address these issues; (10) whether the company fully and expeditiously committed itself to learn the entire truth; (11) whether the company shared with regulators comments and information regarding the misconduct and the company's ensuing investigation; (12) any assurances that the misconduct is unlikely to recur, and (13) whether the corporation has changed as a result of a merger or bankruptcy reorganization. Ibid at *5–9.

Seaboard Report considers waiver as a 'means (where necessary) to provide relevant and sometimes critical information to the Commission staff'.[274]

The DoJ's McNulty Memorandum similarly encourages cooperation by stating **3.109** certain factors that must be considered in determining whether to charge a corporation. In particular, out of the nine factors the McNulty Memorandum sets forth as the circumstances in which companies will receive credit for taking appropriate action, three address cooperation and compliance:

4. the corporation's timely and voluntary disclosure of wrongdoing and its willingness to cooperate in the investigation of its agents;
5. the existence and adequacy of the corporation's pre-existing compliance program; [and]
6. the corporation's remedial actions, including any efforts to implement an effective corporate compliance program or to improve an existing one, to replace responsible management, to discipline or terminate wrongdoers, to pay restitution, and to cooperate with the relevant government agencies[.][275]

The General Principle set forth in Part VII of the McNulty Memorandum **3.110** explains that cooperation is multifaceted:

In gauging the extent of the corporation's cooperation, the prosecutor may consider, among other things, whether the corporation made a voluntary and timely disclosure, and the corporation's willingness to identify the culprits within the corporation, including senior executives.[276]

The McNulty Memorandum also warns corporations:

Another factor to be weighed by the prosecutor is *whether the corporation, while purporting to cooperate, has engaged in conduct intended to impede the investigation* (whether or not rising to the level of criminal obstruction). Examples of such conduct include: overly broad assertions of corporate representation of employees or former employees; overly broad or frivolous assertions of privilege to withhold the disclosure of relevant, non-privileged documents; inappropriate directions to employees or their counsel, such as directions not to cooperate openly and fully with

---

274 Ibid at *8, n 3. The SEC states further that 'in certain circumstances, the Commission staff has agreed that a witnesses' production of privileged information would not constitute a subject matter waiver that would entitle the staff to receive further privileged information'. This principle, known as selective waiver, has been generally rejected by US courts. *Westinghouse v Republic of the Philippines* 951 F 2d 1414 (3rd Cir 1991) (no exception exists to allow parties to disclose communications to government agencies without waiving the attorney-client privilege); *In re Grand Jury Investigation of Ocean Transp* 604 F 2d 672, 675 (DC Cir 1979) ('An intent to waive one's privilege is not necessary for such a waiver to occur.'); *In re Penn Central Commercial Paper Litig* 61 FRD 453, 463 (SDNY 1973) (attorney-client privilege was waived with respect to documents produced and as to matters on which testimony was provided during SEC hearing).
275 The other factors to be considered are as follows: '(1) the nature and seriousness of the offense; (2) the pervasiveness of the wrongdoing within the corporation; (3) the corporation's history of similar conduct . . . (7) any collateral consequences; (8) the adequacy of the prosecution of any culpable agents; and (9) the adequacy of alternative remedies.' McNulty Memorandum (n 268 above).
276 Ibid VII.A.

the investigation including, for example, the direction to decline to be interviewed; making presentations or submissions that contain misleading assertions or omissions; incomplete or delayed production of records; and failure to promptly disclose illegal conduct known to the corporation.[277]

3.111 Anti-trust regulations provide the corporation, that suspects that an anti-trust violation has occurred, with a special incentive to conduct an internal investigation. The Corporate and Individual Leniency Policies[278] accord leniency to 'corporations reporting their illegal antitrust activity at an early stage, if they meet certain conditions'.[279] 'Leniency' means that the corporation will not be criminally charged for the activity being reported. The policy is also known as the corporate 'amnesty' or 'immunity' policy.[280]

3.112 The Corporate Leniency Policy offers two types of leniency. 'Type A' leniency is accorded to a corporation automatically, if it comes forward before the Antitrust Division has initiated an investigation of the reported conduct, and, if six conditions are met: (1) at the time the corporation comes forward, the Division has not received information from any other source; (2) when the corporation discovered the illegal activity, it took prompt and effective action to end its involvement in the activity; (3) the corporation reports the wrongdoing completely and with candour, and provides full, continuing and complete cooperation to the Division throughout the investigation; (4) the confession of the wrongdoing is a corporate act, as opposed to isolated confessions of individual executives or officials; (5) the corporation, when possible, makes restitution to injured parties; and (6) the corporation did not coerce another party to participate in the illegal activity and clearly was not the leader in, or originator of, the activity.[281]

3.113 'Type B' leniency was created for corporations that come forward after an investigation has begun. Although Type B leniency is not granted automatically, it also provides a strong incentive for corporations to conduct an internal investigation to assess whether the corporation participated in an illegal activity, be the first to come forward, and qualify for leniency. Type B leniency may be granted if:

> (1) The corporation is the first one to come forward and qualify for leniency with respect to the illegal activity being reported; (2) The Division, at the time the corporation comes in, does not yet have evidence against the company that is likely to

---

277 Ibid VII.B.4 (emphasis added).

278 See the Department of Justice Corporate Leniency Program <http://www.usdoj.gov/atr/public/guidelines/0091.pdf>.

279 Ibid.

280 Type A amnesty will be accorded to all directors, officers, and employees who come forward and admit wrongdoing with the corporation and agree to cooperate in the investigation. Type B amnesty will be accorded to directors, officers, and employees, under consideration of the Antitrust Division, in exchange for full cooperation. See ABA Section of Antitrust Law (n 141 above), at 756.

281 See the Department of Justice Corporate Leniency Program (n 278 above).

result in a sustainable conviction; (3) The corporation, upon its discovery of the illegal activity being reported, took prompt and effective action to terminate its part in the activity; (4) The corporation reports the wrongdoing with candor and completeness and provides full, continuing and complete cooperation that advances the Division in its investigation; (5) The confession of wrongdoing is truly a corporate act, as opposed to isolated confessions of individual executives or officials; (6) Where possible, the corporation makes restitution to injured parties; and (7) The Division determines that granting leniency would not be unfair to others, considering the nature of the illegal activity, the confessing corporation's role in it, and when the corporation comes forward.[282]

The Antitrust Division has a 'marker' policy under which a corporation can **3.114** secure its place as the first to report the illegal activity by putting down a 'marker'. The policy was designed to encourage corporations to come forward as quickly as possible—even before they complete the internal investigation. Once the Division puts down a 'marker', the corporation will be given a certain period of time—depending on the stage of the internal investigation—to complete its investigation and report its findings to the Division.[283]

Waiver of attorney-client privilege

The most significant departure of the McNulty Memorandum from its predecessor, **3.115** the Thompson Memorandum, concerns its detailed provisions governing the waiver of attorney-client and work-product protections. Generally, a prosecutorial request for waiver of attorney-client privilege or work-product protection must now be approved by the US Attorney in consultation with the head of the Criminal Division at the DoJ. In addition, requests for waiver of the attorney-client privilege must, with limited exceptions, be approved by the Deputy Attorney General, and requests for waivers must be made in writing to the corporation. In order to obtain permission from the DoJ to seek waivers, the McNulty Memorandum states that a prosecutor must establish a 'legitimate need' for the privileged material.[284]

The McNulty Memorandum states that a prosecutor requesting permission to **3.116** seek a corporation's waiver of the attorney-client privilege or work-product protection must assess the following factors in determining whether there is a 'legitimate need' for the requested information: (1) the likelihood and degree to

---

[282] Ibid. The Antitrust Division has two more plans called 'Amnesty Plus' and 'Penalty Plus', which complement the general leniency program.

[283] See ABA Section of Antitrust Law (n 141 above), at 757.

[284] The second major change outlined in the McNulty Memorandum is an instruction to prosecutors that—absent extraordinary circumstances—they should not consider a corporation's advancement of attorney's fees to its employees in deciding whether to charge the corporation. The Memorandum provides for an exception to this rule 'in extremely rare cases' when 'the totality of circumstances show that [the advancement of attorneys' fees] was intended to impede a criminal investigation', VII.B.3, n 3.

which the information sought will benefit the government's investigation; (2) whether the information sought can be obtained from alternative sources without seeking the waiver; (3) the completeness of voluntary disclosures already made; and (4) collateral consequences to the corporation of the waiver.[285] The McNulty Memorandum distinguishes between requests for waivers of the work-product protection and waivers of the attorney-client privilege, noting that waivers of the attorney-client privilege 'should only be sought in rare circumstances'.[286]

3.117 Another source that clarifies the government's expectations of cooperation through internal investigation and remedial measures is the US Sentencing Guidelines for Organizations.[287] In the introductory commentary, the US Sentencing Commission explains that '[t]hese guidelines offer incentives to organizations to reduce and ultimately eliminate criminal conduct by providing a structural foundation from which an organization may self-police its own conduct through an effective compliance and ethics program'.[288]

3.118 Section 8C2.5 of the Organizational Guidelines sets forth, in subsection (g),[289] entitled 'Self Reporting, Cooperation, and Acceptance of Responsibility', a downward adjustment of varying amounts if the organization self-reports wrongdoing, 'fully cooperate[s] in the investigation', and accepts responsibility for its actions.[290] The application notes clarify, in relevant part, that:

> [t]o qualify for a reduction under subsection (g)(1) or (g)(2), cooperation must be both timely and thorough. To be timely, the cooperation must begin essentially at

---

[285] McNulty Memorandum, VII.B.2.

[286] Ibid. The legal community's reaction to the DoJ's efforts has been lukewarm, with ABA President Mathis noting that the new guidelines 'fall far short of what is needed to prevent further erosion of fundamental attorney-client privilege, work product, and employee protections during government investigations . . . [and] are but a modest improvement'. See E Abramowitz and B A Bohrer, 'Defending Corporate America: The Year in Review', NYLJ (2 January 2007).

[287] See US Sentencing Guidelines ch 8 (November 2006) (hereinafter USSG).

[288] Ibid ch 8 intro comment.

[289] USSG § 8C2.5(g) provides:

(1) If the organization (A) prior to an imminent threat of disclosure or government investigation; and (B) within a reasonably prompt time after becoming aware of the offense, reported the offense to appropriate governmental authorities, fully cooperated in the investigation, and clearly demonstrated recognition and affirmative acceptance of responsibility for its criminal conduct, subtract 5 points; or

(2) If the organization fully cooperated in the investigation and clearly demonstrated recognition and affirmative acceptance of responsibility for its criminal conduct, subtract 2 points; or

(3) If the organization clearly demonstrated recognition and affirmative acceptance of responsibility for its criminal conduct, subtract 1 point.

Ibid § 8C2.5(g).

[290] Ibid USSG § 8C4.1 provides credit, similar to USSG § 5K1.1, to a corporate defendant that 'has provided substantial assistance in the investigation or prosecution of another organization that has committed an offense, or in the investigation and prosecution of an individual not directly affiliated with the defendant'.

the same time as the organization is officially notified of a criminal investigation. To be thorough, the cooperation should include the disclosure of all pertinent information known by the organization. A prime test of whether the organization has disclosed all pertinent information is whether the information is sufficient for law enforcement personnel to identify the nature and extent of the offense and the individual(s) responsible for the criminal conduct.[291]

3.119 Moreover, the Organizational Guidelines punish, or provide for an 'upward departure', where a corporation obstructs justice and impedes a government investigation.[292]

3.120 In addition, the NYSE encourages cooperation through the Factors Memorandum and the Cooperation Memorandum. Cooperation is but one factor that the NYSE considers in determining sanctions.[293] The Factors Memorandum provides that NYSE members:

> have a responsibility to cooperate with the Exchange's regulatory program and are expected to comply with requests for documents, testimony and other information. No additional credit will be given for doing what is required by Exchange Rules. However, where a respondent can demonstrate a record of disclosure and cooperation that is proactive and exceptional, the Enforcement Division will, in appropriate circumstances, give this factor weight in its consideration of a sanction. Conversely, a respondent's failure to cooperate fully and completely will support an increased sanction.[294]

---

[291] Ibid § 8C2.5, comment (n 12) (emphasis added).

[292] Ibid § 8C2.5(c).

In a significant development, the US Sentencing Commission voted unanimously on 5 April 2006 to delete the following sentence from the applications notes (which had been added to the notes only two years earlier):

> Waiver of attorney-client privilege and of work product protections is not a prerequisite to a reduction in culpability score under subdivisions (1) and (2) of subsection (g) unless such waiver is necessary in order to provide timely and thorough disclosure of all pertinent information known to the organization.

The proposed change took effect on 1 November 2006.

This action by the Sentencing Commission followed public hearings in March 2006 at which the Commission heard testimony urging repeal of the language in question. Also in March 2006, the House Judiciary Subcommittee on Crime, Terrorism and Homeland Security heard testimony from organizations urging Congress to use its oversight powers to restrain prosecutors from routinely seeking privilege waivers as part of corporate cooperation. Along with the changes announced in the McNulty Memorandum, this amendment to the Guidelines commentary may relieve some of the pressure that corporations have felt to waive privilege in connection with government investigations.

[293] The NYSE also considers the following criteria in determining sanctions: (1) the nature of the misconduct/degree of scienter; (2) the harm caused by the misconduct; (3) the extent of the misconduct; (4) a company's prior disciplinary record; (5) its acceptance of responsibility; (6) the implementation of corrective measures and restitution; (7) enrichment and/or deceptive conduct; (8) neglect or disregard of 'red flags'; (8) effectiveness of operational, supervisory, and compliance controls; (9) the company's size and financial resources; (10) training and education; (11) reliance on professional advice; and (12) other discipline. See Factors Memorandum (n 272 above).

[294] Ibid.

3.121   The Cooperation Memorandum elaborates upon the notion of 'proactive and exceptional' cooperation by stating, in general, that 'what constitutes an "extraordinary" case is not susceptible of generalization'.[295] Among the eight factors that the NYSE will consider in assessing a firm or individual's cooperation are the company's 'prompt, full disclosure coupled with thorough internal review' and the 'waiver of attorney-client privilege'.[296]

3.122   Thus, the SEC, the DoJ, the US Sentencing Commission and SROs such as the NYSE both reward and expect cooperation. Significant credit is given to organizations that get the facts out and aid the government in its investigations, and that have instituted compliance and ethics procedures. Indeed, failure to cooperate may increase the likelihood of criminal charges being brought and more severe penalties being pursued.[297]

The role of auditors

3.123   Another important force in play in today's regulatory and enforcement landscape in the US is the outside auditor. While the federal government and market regulators wield the threat of regulatory sanctions to motivate corporations to conduct searching internal reviews, the independent audit firms also wield substantial leverage over companies to conduct internal investigations.

3.124   Auditors have a statutory duty to report illegal acts to management and the board, and, if necessary, to the SEC. Section 10A(b) of the Exchange Act establishes a reporting and disclosure framework that outside auditors must follow when they become aware of information indicating possible wrongdoing.[298] When auditors first discover evidence of a suspected violation during an audit, they must promptly inform management and the audit committee.[299] After informing the audit committee, if the auditor determines that (1) the illegal act has a 'material effect' on the financial statements, (2) senior management has not taken, or the

---

[295] Cooperation Memorandum (n 272 above).

[296] The other six factors are candour with the Exchange; breadth, depth and timeliness of remedial action; responses to investigative requests; aiding the jurisdiction of the Exchange; culture of compliance; and partnering with the Exchange to uncover wrongdoing.

In exchange for extraordinary cooperation, the NYSE may reduce the number or types of charges, seek a reduced sanction, obviate the need for an undertaking, include language in the documents that resolve enforcement proceedings to mitigate the severity of the charges and/or credit the level of cooperation, include a public acknowledgement of the level of cooperation in a press release, and, in the exceptional case, take no enforcement at all.

[297] See E. Lawrence Barcella, Jr et al., 'Cooperation with Government Is a Growing Trend', Nat'l LJ (19 July 2004), S2 (noting 'emerging trend in the prosecution and defense of corporate crime: Cooperating with the government—not by choice—is often the only road to survival for both corporations and their executives').

[298] 15 USC § 78j-1.

[299] Ibid § 78j-1(b)(1).

board has not caused management to take, 'appropriate remedial action', and (3) 'the failure to take remedial action is reasonably expected to warrant departure from a standard report of the auditor, when made, or warrant resignation from the audit engagement', then the auditor must apprise the board of its conclusions.[300]

Within one business day of receiving an auditor's report, the board must notify **3.125** the SEC of the problem and provide the auditor with a copy of the notice given to the SEC. If the auditor does not receive this notice within the one-day period, then the auditor is required to either (1) 'resign from the engagement', or (2) provide the Commission with a copy of the report it prepared.[301] If the auditor chooses to resign, it still must furnish the SEC with its report.[302]

While section 10A imposes an escalating reporting requirement on auditors, in **3.126** practice, it is exceedingly rare that the SEC actually learns of corporate wrongdoing from the auditor because of a company's failure to take remedial action. Rather, the section 10A reporting-out mechanism exists as a last resort. When an auditor becomes aware of suspected wrongdoing, it will often insist that the company conduct an internal investigation, generally at the direction of the company's audit committee. This internal review, in turn, can lead to a company's self-reporting and cooperating with the government.

Given the requirements of section 10A and the regulatory expectations in this **3.127** area, audit firms have used their ability to withhold or qualify audit opinions to induce companies to conduct investigations, institute remedial measures, and even to alter management. In situations where a section 10A investigation has been undertaken and evidence of an illegal act has been detected, audit firms will often demand that any potential problems be examined and resolved before they are willing to issue an unqualified report on the company's financial statements.

The role of directors

Under state law, officers and directors of companies have certain duties of **3.128** due care, loyalty, and good faith. These duties encompass the obligations to consider and react with requisite process to reasonably available material information, to act in the best interests of the corporation and to prioritize the interests of the corporation, to act when there is a known duty to act, and not to act with intent to violate applicable positive law.[303] As a part of their fiduciary obligations,

---

[300] Ibid § 78j-1(b)(2).
[301] Ibid § 78j-1(b)(3).
[302] Ibid § 78j-1(b)(4).
[303] See *In re Walt Disney Co Derivative Litig* No Civ A 15452 2005 WL 1875804, at *35 (Del Ch 9 August 2005) (describing fiduciary duties under Delaware law); see, eg, *In re Enron Corp Sec,*

directors have the specific duty to investigate red flags.[304] Corporate charters, bylaws and other internal policies and procedures can impose additional obligations on directors. They may require directors to receive reports of wrongdoing[305] and, where appropriate, to conduct investigations. They may also assign certain investigative obligations to committees of the board of directors such as the audit committee. Where a designated committee or director fails to fulfil its oversight responsibilities, it is possible that a violation of the duty of care has occurred.[306]

How can an internal investigation affect the company—benefits of internal investigations

3.129 An internal investigation, properly handled, can be beneficial to the company. Some of the benefits of a well-handled investigation include:

- Evaluating liability: An internal investigation can assist a company in determining the extent of potential criminal or civil liability—including whether individuals should be disciplined or separated from the company.

- Shaping a response: Information gathered in the course of the investigation can assist in forming an effective response to the government and may uncover evidence that can be used to persuade the government that its investigation can be narrower or less extensive than it might otherwise be.

- Controlling expenses: By quickly and effectively investigating its own misconduct, a company may persuade the government to rely on the findings of the internal investigation, or to forgo a separate investigation entirely. It can also give the company more control over the nature and focus of the government investigation.

Derivative & ERISA Litig 284 F Supp 2d 511, 657-58 (SD Tex 2003) (finding that plaintiffs had stated a claim as to breach of fiduciary duty for failure to act, despite having access to material information about the actual financial condition of Enron).

[304] See *In re Caremark Int'l, Inc* 698 A 2d 959, 970 (Del Ch 1996) ('[A] director's obligation includes a duty to attempt in good faith to assure that a corporate information and reporting system, which the board concludes is adequate, exists, and that failure to do so under some circumstances may, in theory at least, render a director liable for losses caused by non-compliance with applicable legal standards.'); see also *In re Citigroup, Inc S'holders Litig* Civ A No 19827, 2003 Del Ch LEXIS 61, at *6-7 (Del Ch 5 June 2003) (describing failure to provide oversight claim under *Caremark*); cf *In re WorldCom, Inc Sec Litig*, No 02 Civ 3288DLC, 2005 WL 638268, at *8 (SDNY 21 March 2005) ('[D]irectors . . . may not fend off liability by claiming reliance where "red flags" regarding the reliability of an audited financial statement, or any other expertised statement, emerge.'); *In re WorldCom, Inc Sec Litig* 346 F Supp 2d 628, 684 (SDNY 2004) ('If red flags arise from a reasonable investigation, underwriters will have to make sufficient inquiry to satisfy themselves as to the accuracy of the financial statements, and if unsatisfied, they must demand disclosure, withdraw from the underwriting process, or bear the risk of liability.').

[305] Section 307 of SOX and various listing standards currently require audit committees of public companies to regularly receive reports of wrongdoing. Sarbanes-Oxley Act of 2002, 15 USC § 7245 (Supp IV 2005).

[306] Cf *Walt Disney Derivative Litig* 2005 WL 1875804, at *35 (describing violation of fiduciary duty claim where directors fail to act in the face of a legal obligation to act).

- Minimizing regulatory liability: By conducting a thorough investigation and cooperating with the government, a company may persuade regulators not to bring claims against the company.

- Discharging legal obligations and minimizing liability: A company's executives or its board of directors may have a legal duty to investigate misconduct. The fiduciary duty to the corporation may include the duty to investigate when there are indications of misconduct.[307] In addition, the fact that, upon uncovering red flags, a company promptly undertook an internal investigation and implemented appropriate remedial action can assist a company in arguing against the imposition of civil penalties.[308]

- Managing disclosure: An investigation, regardless of the ultimate findings, allows the company to control the disclosure of information, rather than wait for regulatory findings. In addition, the fact of an investigation can be used to the company's advantage to show that the company is not engaged in a cover-up, but rather is moving ahead to correct a difficult situation.

- Public relations: An investigation demonstrates a company's good faith in doing the right thing, which may help maintain or restore investor confidence.

An illustration of how a well-conducted, independent investigation can inure to the benefit of the company may be found in the investigation of the Dutch food giant, Royal Ahold, which launched an internal investigation after learning of possible improprieties involving its subsidiary, US Foodservice (USF). While certain individuals in this matter ultimately were charged by the DoJ, the government declined to file any charges against Royal Ahold, explaining that: **3.130**

> Ahold self-reported the misconduct and conducted an extensive internal investigation, including an investigation of misconduct beyond that at USF. It made its personnel available for interviews by Government investigators, including bringing witnesses to the United States from abroad, and made available to the Government the factual results of its internal investigation. In addition, Ahold terminated employees responsible for the wrongdoing at USF.

> Because Ahold has cooperated fully with the Government's investigation, has settled the SEC enforcement action, and has made substantial restitution to victims through the $1.1 billion class action settlement, the public interest has been sufficiently vindicated. Moreover, criminal prosecution of Ahold would likely have a severe and unintended disproportionate economic impact upon the many innocent Ahold employees worldwide. Accordingly, [the US Attorney] stated that, after carefully balancing all of the factors set forth in the Thompson Memorandum, criminal prosecution of Ahold would not serve the public interest.[309]

---

307 See *Hoye v Meek* 795 F 2d 893, 896 (10th Cir 1986).
308 See *United States v Phelps Dodge Indus, Inc* 589 F Supp 1340 (SDNY 1984).
309 USAO Press Release, SDNY, 'US Reaches Non-Prosecution Agreement with Royal Ahold, NV' (28 September 2006) <http://www.usdoj.gov/usao/nys/pressreleases/September06/aholdnonprospr.pdf>.

3.131 As one commentator noted, 'Ahold [was] among a growing number of companies that have avoided prosecution or received leniency from the Justice Department and the SEC because they agreed to cooperate with investigations'.[310]

3.132 In another case—that of Royal Dutch/Shell—following an announcement by the company that it would recategorize approximately 3.9 billion barrels of oil equivalent of its reported 'proved' reserves, the Shell Group Audit Committee (GAC) disclosed that it was conducting an independent investigation of the facts and circumstances surrounding the recategorization. As part of the investigation launched by the GAC, there were approximately 130 interviews of over 90 witnesses and hundreds of thousands of pages of hard copy documents reviewed, in addition to the electronic files of approximately 50 individuals and server data and back-up tapes for select individuals.

3.133 Ultimately, the DoJ decided not to bring criminal charges against Royal Dutch/Shell.[311] The company also entered into an unprecedented settlement agreement with the SEC and the UK's Financial Services Authority, simultaneously, without admitting or denying the regulators' findings.[312]

Costs of internal investigations

3.134 While internal investigations provide substantial benefits to companies, as described above, they are not without consequences. This section describes some of the costs of conducting internal investigations for companies.

H. Potential Waiver of Privilege and Exposure to Civil Liability

3.135 One drawback to conducting an internal investigation is the possibility that the findings of the company's internal investigation will be used against the company in civil litigation. As detailed above, regulators routinely expect companies to turn over the findings of an internal investigation as part of cooperation; such disclosure of the findings to regulators may result in a waiver of applicable privileges—such as attorney-client privilege and/or work-product protection—with respect to third parties. As such, the findings—including any written reports, memoranda of witness interviews and other related materials—may be subject to discovery in civil

---

[310] 'Ahold to Avoid US Prosecution', CFO.com (29 September 2006) <http://www.cfo.com/article.cfm/7989249/c_7988012?f=home_todayinfinance>. Other examples include Fannie Mae, the government-sponsored mortgage lending giant that avoided DoJ prosecution by, in part, retaining independent outside counsel, to conduct a thorough internal investigation under the direction of the Board of Directors and by cooperating fully with the investigation.

[311] See n 158 above.

[312] SEC Press Release, 'Royal Dutch Petroleum Company and the "Shell" Transport and Trading Company, PLC Pay $120 Million to Settle SEC Fraud Case Involving Massive Overstatement of Proved Hydrocarbon Reserves' (24 August 2004) <http://www.sec.gov/news/press/2004-116.htm>.

litigation.[313] Such findings likely would provide a 'roadmap' to civil plaintiffs of the facts at issue.

Recently, regulators have been increasingly willing to enter into non-waiver or **3.136** limited waiver agreements, whereby the privilege is ostensibly waived only as to the regulators.[314] The SEC appears to support limiting the waiver of the work-product protection when parties disclose to it confidential documents prepared by counsel. In *McKesson HBOC Inc v Superior Court*,[315] the SEC filed a brief in support of the corporation's efforts to maintain the work product privilege over an audit committee report and interview memorandum prepared by outside counsel during an internal investigation. The SEC argued that allowing parties to provide protected documents to it without waiving the work-product protection served the public interest by enhancing the SEC's ability to conduct investigations more effectively and expeditiously. The court, however, determined that the corporation's disclosure to the government resulted in a waiver of the attorney-client privilege and work-product protection.[316] In general, US courts have been reluctant to recognize the limited waiver exception and the majority of courts have held that the privilege, once waived as to regulators, is waived as to all.[317]

The determination of whether to waive is a critical one for the corporation. **3.137** Although waiver poses clear disadvantages, it may be necessary for the company to obtain credit for full cooperation from the government, and avoid either a criminal charge or hefty civil penalties. For a corporation faced with true wrong-doing, there may be no practical alternative to fully disclosing the findings of the internal investigation and risk a waiver.

---

[313] See, eg, *In re Leslie Fay Sec Litig* 161 FRD 274 (SDNY 1996); *In re Kidder Peabody Sec Litig* 168 FRD 459 (SDNY 1996); *In re Subpoena Duces Tecum Served on Willkie Farr & Gallagher* No M8-85, 1997 WL 118369 (SDNY 1997). But see *In re Woolworth Corp Sec Class Action Litig* No 94 Civ 2217, 1996 WL 306576 (SDNY 7 June 1996) (disclosure of report does not waive privilege in underlying materials).

[314] A similar privilege issue exists as to auditors. Many outside auditors demand access to attorney work product from internal investigations as a precondition to signing off on outstanding audits and continuing to work with the client. A client is often torn between the likelihood that attorney work product, including interview memos, will be discoverable by future civil litigants and the auditor firm's demand that it satisfy itself with respect to the scope and results of the internal investigation before it will issue a report on the company's financial statements.

[315] 9 Cal Rptr 3d 812 (Cal App 1 Dist 2004).

[316] Ibid at 821.

[317] See, eg, *In re Royal Ahold NV Sec & ERISA Litig* 230 FRD 433 (D Md 2005) (holding that limited confidentiality agreement under which interview memos were disclosed to the government was not sufficient to preserve confidentiality of interview memos from class action plaintiffs); see also *In re Columbia/HCA Healthcare* 293 F 3d 289 (6th Cir 2002) (rejecting concept of selective waiver); *In re Natural Gas Commodity Litig* 03 Civ 6186, 2005 US Dist LEXIS 11950, at *22-33 (SDNY 25 June 2005) (collecting cites—good discussion of case law in the area of non-waiver agreements). But see *Saito v McKesson HBOC, Inc* Civ A No 18553, 2002 Del Ch LEXIS 125 (Del Ch 25 October 2002) (holding that 'the corporation did not waive the work product privilege when it gave documents to the SEC and the USAO under [a] confidentiality agreement').

3.138   Public disclosure of an internal investigation report may also be a viable option for the company wishing to clear its name of any wrongdoing. For example, when the pharmaceutical company Merck's announcement on 30 September 2004 that it was voluntarily withdrawing from the market Vioxx, a widely used prescription pain medication, over concerns that the medication increased patients' risks of heart attacks and strokes, triggered immediate, extensive and at times negative comments in the media that the company was aware of these risks and concealed them from patients. In response, a special committee of the board of directors of the company launched an internal investigation, which included 115 witness interviews and lasted 20 months. The findings of that investigation concluded that Merck acted properly.[318]

3.139   There may however be situations where a decision not to disclose the entire findings of the internal investigation makes more sense given the potentially devastating consequences to the company of civil litigation exposure. Under such circumstances, it may be prudent to provide the government with only a portion, or a summary, of the internal investigation report.[319]

3.140   Companies may be pressured to disclose the results of internal investigations not just to the government, but to other entities as well. For example, if the company's outside auditor demands access to the work product of counsel, there may be no choice but to accede because one of the risks of refusal may be that the auditor cannot certify the company's financial statements. This was the case with Royal Dutch/Shell.[320]

3.141   Indeed, in the current regulatory climate, few auditors will agree to an engagement that would entail restricted access to the company's books and records and the large auditing firms have generally refused to accept such limitations in their engagement letters. Nevertheless, there may be circumstances where it is neither in the corporation's nor the auditor's interest for work product to be produced to the auditor.

---

[318] The report was published on the company's website, as well as the website of the law firm that the company retained to lead the investigation. See Statement of William G Bowen, Chairman of the Special Committee of Merck & Co, Inc, to Interested Parties (6 September 2006) <http://www.merck.com/newsroom/vioxx/pdf/bbowen_to_interested_parties_090606.pdf>.

[319] Royal Dutch/Shell, for example, only published the executive summary of its report to the company's GAC. See Report of Davis Polk & Wardwell to the Shell Group Audit Committee, Executive Summary (31 March 2004) (hereinafter Davis Polk Report]) <http://www.shell.com/static/investor-en/downloads/gac_report.pdf>; see also 'Can Shell Put Out this Fire?', *Business Week* (3 May 2004) (reporting that Shell released the summary of its investigation in the hopes of dampening the media scandal regarding its recategorization of reported 'proved' reserves).

[320] See Davis Polk Report (n 319 above), at 1.

In the end, the benefits of conducting and disclosing the results of an investiga- **3.142**
tion often outweigh the risk that those findings ultimately may be disclosed to
civil plaintiffs, and that such disclosure may increase the company's potential
civil liability.

I. Conflicts of Interest

Another cost of conducting an internal investigation is the possibility that the **3.143**
investigation will not be viewed as fully independent, or will be criticized as a
'whitewash', or otherwise compromised by conflicts of interest.

Indeed, the Seaboard Report in considering whether 'the company committed to **3.144**
learn the truth, fully and expeditiously', finds it relevant to consider also whether
company employees or outside counsel performed the internal review. In the case
where the company uses outside persons, the Seaboard Report asks whether they
'had done other work for the company', whether 'management previously
engaged such counsel', whether 'scope limitations [were] placed on the review',
and '[i]f so, what were they'.[321]

An example of an internal investigation that is often described as having suffered **3.145**
from a conflict of interest is the investigation of allegations raised by a whistle-
blower at Enron. After the whistle-blower raised allegations of impropriety to
then-CEO Kenneth Lay, Enron's general counsel retained Vinson & Elkins to
investigate. Vinson & Elkins, however, was the long-standing regular outside
counsel to Enron and was heavily dependent on Enron's business. Indeed,
approximately 7 per cent of Vinson & Elkins' annual billings related to Enron
matters.

Once it was retained to look into the whistle-blower allegations, Vinson & Elkins **3.146**
limited the scope of its investigation as follows: '[It] was decided that our initial
approach would not involve second-guessing the accounting advice and treatment provided by [Arthur Andersen], that there would be no detailed analysis of
each and every transaction and that there would be no full-scale discovery-style
inquiry'.[322] After conducting an investigation subject to such limitations, Vinson
& Elkins concluded that 'the facts disclosed through [its] preliminary investigation did not . . . warrant a further widespread investigation by independent counsel and auditors', and found significant that Ms Watkins (the whistle-blower)

---

[321] Seaboard Report (n 272 above), at *7-8.
[322] See Letter from Max Hendrick, III, Partner, Vinson & Elkins, to James V Derrick, Jr, Exec VP
& Gen Counsel, Enron Corp. (15 October 2001) available at D Ackman, 'Enron's Lawyers: Eyes
Wide Shut?', Forbes (28 January 2002) <http://www.forbes.com/2002/01/28/0128veenron.html>.

'acknowledged that she had no personal, first hand knowledge of [her] allegation[s] [which were] based solely on rumors that she heard'.[323]

3.147 After the scope of improprieties that occurred at Enron came to light and the company was forced into bankruptcy with many of its highest level executives under criminal indictment, Vinson & Elkins was sued by Enron shareholders and employees. Furthermore, the independent counsel who was retained by the Board of Directors of Enron to conduct an investigation in the aftermath of the scandal criticized Vinson & Elkins for an 'absence' of 'objective and critical professional advice'.[324] Commentators noted a 'beneath-the-surface struggle' between Vinson & Elkins and Enron's CFO Andrew Fastow concerning questionable transactions, with Enron's outside counsel consistently backing down.[325] Vinson & Elkins' former managing partner later explained that he had been warning Enron's in-house attorneys about the transactions all along, and that he did not believe that his firm 'should have gone around Enron's in-house lawyers and their executives directly to the board'.[326]

3.148 In June 2006, Vinson & Elkins settled with Enron's bankruptcy trustee for $30m, and agreed to forgo another $3.9m in legal fees that it claimed was still owed by Enron.[327]

Cross-border investigations

3.149 Cross-border investigations may raise additional problems, as illustrated by the investigation of engineering giant, Siemens AG ('Siemens').

3.150 Siemens came under intense regulatory scrutiny in a number of jurisdictions, including the US, following a raid of its corporate headquarters in late 2006 amid revelations of bribery and corruption.[328] The company announced that, as a result of its own internal investigation, it had unearthed $1.9bn in questionable payments made by Siemens to third parties around the world from 2000 to 2006. At that time, the company already had spent $500m on its internal investigation and reportedly still had 'a long way to go'.[329]

---

[323] Ibid

[324] E J Pollock, 'Enron's Lawyers Faulted Deals but Failed to Blow the Whistle', Wall St J (22 May 2002).

[325] Ibid.

[326] Ibid.

[327] See 'Enron's Last Mystery', *Business Week* (12 June 2006) <http://www.businessweek.com/magazine/content/06_24/b3988056.htm>.

[328] Although Siemens is a German company, it lists its shares on the NYSE and has extensive operations in the US and, therefore, is subject to the provisions of the Foreign Corrupt Practices Act. See J Ewing, 'Siemens Braces for a Slap from Uncle Sam', *Business Week* (26 November 2007).

[329] Ibid.

According to one account citing sources close to the probe, the internal investiga-   **3.151**
tion at Siemens had been hampered by 'the absence of subpoena powers,
wary Siemens employees and its lawyers' own missteps'.[330] Some commentators
noted that US-based lawyers had difficulty in getting access to information from,
and the investigative files of, foreign authorities. The company's lawyers also
had to deal with 'Anti-American sentiment'. '[E]mployees questioned why
information should be shared with private investigators that will be handed over
to US authorities who would then fine the company.' In response, the law
firm circulated a slide-show presentation to the company's employees aimed at
dispelling negative perceptions of the internal investigatory process. Reportedly,
employees are now cooperating more with the firm. In addition, to manage
the growing costs of its investigation, Siemens has recently taken more of
an active role in gathering evidence directly, rather than relying on its lawyers to
do so.[331]

While a high-ranking Siemens official continued to praise the work of the com-   **3.152**
pany's law firm, the long duration of the internal investigation has resulted in
uncertainty for shareholders.[332]

J. How to Conduct an Internal Investigation

Determining who should supervise the investigation

After determining that an internal investigation is required, the first issue   **3.153**
presented is who should direct the investigation. The most common alternatives
are: (1) the audit committee (or other committee of the board composed of independent directors); or (2) the management of the corporation (often the general
counsel or a lawyer in his or her office).

In many cases, it will be in the company's best interest to have non-management   **3.154**
directors oversee an investigation. Various regulators have expressed their preference for investigations run by outside board members because such directors
usually are independent from management. Such a course may be best followed
where the conduct under inquiry is widespread and/or may involve the company's senior management. Indeed, investigations run by non-management directors are often a sensible and cost-efficient path because it is frequently difficult to

---

[330] See Esterl, Crawford and Koppel (n 271 above).
[331] By the summer of 2007, the company's lawyers identified activities in 65 countries that
required further investigation. Ibid.
[332] Ibid.

determine at the outset of the inquiry whether senior management had a role in any alleged wrongdoing. If properly performed, an investigation supervised by non-management directors may eliminate the need for regulators or the outside auditors to conduct their own parallel investigations.

3.155 Choosing the wrong person to oversee the investigation may lead to increased cost, delay and loss of credibility if it turns out that the alleged wrongdoing is more extensive, or that senior management is implicated in the wrongdoing. In such circumstances, a board committee of outside directors may be forced to redo the investigation, after hiring its own counsel.

3.156 This is not to suggest, however, that an investigation led by senior management is never appropriate. The use of management and in-house counsel to lead an investigation may offer great efficiency and cost savings for the corporation and its directors. This is particularly true where, for instance, misconduct appears to be localized within a confined area of the company. For example, the allegations of wrongdoing may involve only a foreign affiliate of a US-based corporation or only conduct that occurred in the past and under the watch of a different management team. In such a case, current management or the chief legal officer may be the most appropriate entity to supervise the investigation. Likewise, where there is a premium on speed in conducting an investigation and high-level management does not appear to be involved, a corporation may well rely on its general counsel or in-house counsel to conduct the investigation.

3.157 In a management-led investigation, a company may choose to report its findings to either its general counsel's office or directly to management. Reporting to a representative of the general counsel's office will enhance the position that the purpose of the investigation was to render legal advice, a necessary element in asserting privilege over the report and supporting interview notes.[333] A report to management, in contrast, may threaten the assertion of privilege over the investigation

---

333 To assert a testimonial privilege such as the attorney-client privilege:
   (1) The communication must originate in an *expectation* that it will not be disclosed.
   (2) The element of *confidentiality* must be essential to the full and satisfactory maintenance of the relationship between the parties.
   (3) The *relationship* must be one that, in the opinion of the community, ought to be carefully *fostered*.
   (4) The *injury* that would inure to the relationship by the disclosure of the communications must be *greater* than the *benefit* that would be gained for the correct disposal of litigation by virtue of the disclosure.

J Wigmore, *Evidence* (McNaughton rev edn, 1961) § 2285, at 527, cited in E Selan Epstein, *The Attorney-Client Privilege and the Work-Product Doctrine* (3rd edn, 1997), 4.

because a court may find that the investigation was conducted for business reasons, not to render legal advice.[334]

Where senior management is chosen to supervise an investigation, counsel **3.158** should regularly revisit that decision as the investigators learn more about the nature and scope of the conduct being investigated. The decision initially to launch an investigation led by management does not foreclose a later decision that the outside directors or the board are the best individuals to supervise the investigation.

Selecting investigative counsel: who should conduct the investigation?

After the individuals who are supervising the investigation are chosen, investiga- **3.159** tive counsel must be chosen. With few exceptions, the company has broad discretion over who it *may* choose. The law does not dictate that a corporation must hire a particular lawyer or even a particular type of lawyer. The more complicated question is whom it *should* choose. The typical choices include: (1) in-house counsel and other company employees such as internal auditors; (2) outside counsel with whom the company has a pre-existing relationship; and (3) independent counsel.

In some cases, in-house counsel may be best equipped to handle certain business **3.160** related issues and whistle-blower complaints. Again, however, the credibility of an in-house counsel investigation will be impaired if there is any question of whether the in-house counsel is implicated in the facts or issues raised by the investigation, or if the in-house counsel reports to business people who are implicated in the conduct under inquiry. Even if the in-house counsel is not involved in the issues being investigated, or does not report to the persons under review, he or she may not have the resources to meet the demands of the investigation.

Hiring outside counsel with whom the corporation has a pre-existing relationship **3.161** may solve both of these problems. Choosing outside counsel may bolster the credibility of the investigation, a factor that may be important if there is a chance that regulatory agencies could become involved or if senior executives are implicated. Additionally, outside counsel is more likely to have experience with certain issues, such as those arising in criminal matters, and may be better able to structure and conduct the investigation in a manner that best preserves attorney-client

---

334 See, eg, *In re Leslie Fay Sec Litig* 161 FRD 274 (SDNY 1995). In Leslie Fay, the court held that attorneys' notes of employee interviews were not protected as work product because the investigation was conducted primarily for business reasons. In making this determination, the court found significant that the investigative report was used by company management to implement new financial controls, and to reassure lenders, trade creditors, customers and stockholders that the wrongdoers were being rooted out and that the conduct would not be repeated.

privilege and work-product protection. Further, in contrast to independent counsel, outside counsel, if knowledgeable of the company and its personnel, and familiar with the regulatory and factual framework, will have a shorter learning curve, will get up to speed more quickly and efficiently on a matter, and presumably will be better suited to evaluate evidence in context than counsel who lacks this background.

3.162 These same considerations, however, can also work to a company's disadvantage as it considers the potential regulatory reaction to an internal investigation. Outside counsel who are too close to the company may be deemed insufficiently independent from it. One factor in the decision of who should conduct the investigation is assessing how regulators will view the independence of prospective investigative counsel. Often regulators express scepticism regarding the independence of an investigation and the reliability of its results if the investigation has been conducted by counsel who has recently defended the corporation before a regulatory agency or as an advocate in litigation.[335]

3.163 Likewise, regulators might well question the independence of an investigation conducted by a company's regular outside counsel, or by any counsel that does a significant amount of work for the client or its officers or directors.[336] An example is the close relationship between Enron and Vinson & Elkins, discussed above, where the law firm was criticized for an 'absence' of 'objective and critical professional advice', partly because Enron was the firm's biggest client and the two were 'intertwined in Houston's corporate community'.[337]

3.164 There are thus costs to hiring outside counsel who is, or is perceived to be, too close to current management. If management is implicated in wrongdoing, counsel with ties to such management is not going to be viewed as the most objective investigator. While there is no clear rule stating that, in such circumstances the outside counsel with ties to management should not be hired, if the company chooses the wrong counsel, the failure to hire independent counsel to conduct

---

[335] There has been such criticism of investigative counsel's role in the accounting scandal in the city government of San Diego, California. There, counsel led two internal investigations, the first of which was characterized by an outside auditor as 'insufficient', because counsel is defending the city of San Diego before the SEC. The SEC told city officials that the second internal investigation also lacked independence, since counsel had provided some information to employees in advance of their interviews. See D Solomon, 'Lost City: After Pension-Fund Debacle, San Diego Is Mired in Probes', Wall St J (10 October 2005), A1.

[336] The representation of outside counsel in the Enron and Global Crossing scandals implicated these concerns. See T E Hoeffner and S M Rabii, 'Maintaining the Integrity of Internal Probes', Nat'l LJ (23 June 2003), 19; J Mason, 'Houston Law Firm Probed for Role in Fall of Enron', *Houston Chronicle* (14 March 2002) A13; S Pearlstein, 'Corporate Counsel Gone Astray', *Washington Post* (19 March 2003), E01; C Stern, 'Report Criticizes Global Crossing's Outside Counsel', *Washington Post* (11 March 2003), E05.

[337] Pollock (n 324 above).

the investigation can be expensive.[338] Even where there is no possibility of senior management involvement in wrongdoing, management may sometimes choose to hire independent outside counsel to conduct the investigation in the first place rather than subject themselves to second-guessing by the board or regulators simply because an investigation is conducted by regular outside counsel.

When a company faces a situation where the findings of an internal investigation   **3.165** must be above reproach—for example when allegations of widespread misconduct are critical to the company's survival, or implicate senior management or the general counsel's office—then it would be wise to select an independent outside counsel with significant experience and background in internal investigations.

Determining the scope of the investigation

After determining who should supervise an investigation and which counsel   **3.166** should be retained, the next step is to define the scope of the investigation. Ideally, at the outset of the investigation, the parties should prepare a formal document authorizing the investigation and broadly outlining the scope of the investigation (and confirming the privileged nature of the inquiry). This documentation may consist of a resolution of the board of directors, a resolution of the audit committee, an engagement letter, or a memorandum issued by senior management or the general counsel. Such documentation should instruct the investigators to conduct a confidential internal investigation, define the scope of the investigation, outline appropriate document retention instructions, instruct company personnel that they are to cooperate in the investigation, and specify (if appropriate) that the investigation is being conducted in anticipation of litigation and for the purpose of obtaining legal advice.

The scope of the investigation usually is, and should be, resolved by the corpora-   **3.167** tion in consultation with investigative counsel; however, other parties may also have an effect on the scope of the investigation, such as the outside auditor, the board, the regulators, or any whistle-blowers. As the investigative counsel, it is important to balance carefully the objectives and needs of each of the involved parties, while satisfying each that the investigation will be thorough and complete.

There are several factors that should be considered in determining the proper scope   **3.168** of an investigation. The guiding principle is the need to discover whether there is unlawful activity and, if so, to stop it. At a minimum, the investigation should

---

[338] See Cooper Companies Report, Exchange Act Release No 35082, 58 SEC 591, 594-96 (12 December 1994) (faulting internal investigation where co-chair and CFO of company had refused to cooperate with outside counsel's investigation, and the board of directors did not act).

address the actual allegations of wrongdoing that prompted the investigation and other possible violations that are uncovered during the course of the investigation.

3.169 Investigative counsel should periodically reassess the breadth of the engagement and recommend expanding (or contracting) the scope of the investigation as circumstances warrant. Counsel should consider whether the scope of the investigation is broad enough to accomplish the varying objectives of the investigation, including taking appropriate remedial actions, formulating defence strategy, and determining the extent to which personnel should be disciplined. Further, both the investigative counsel and the company should be mindful that limitations in scope may lead regulators, auditors, lenders, or other important constituents to discount the findings and conclusions of the investigation.

3.170 The relevant guideposts on appropriate scope of an internal investigation may be found in state corporate fiduciary duty law and federal securities law, among others. For example, directors, under state corporate law, have an obligation to investigate 'red flags',[339] and assure themselves that 'information and reporting systems exist in the organization that are reasonably designed to provide to senior management and to the board itself timely, accurate information sufficient to allow management and the board, each within its scope, to reach informed judgments concerning both the corporation's compliance with law and its business performance'.[340] Such an obligation to investigate 'red flags' may also be imposed by an SRO.[341]

3.171 In addition, under the federal securities laws, a corporation is liable to investors if it intentionally or recklessly makes a material misstatement.[342] Such liability may extend to persons who make or participate in the making of the misstatement.[343] Accordingly, officers and directors of companies should diligently pursue red flags that may affect the company's public statements, including financial statements. While '[d]irectors are entitled to rely on the honesty and integrity of their subordinates until something occurs to put them on suspicion that something is wrong', if red flags go unheeded, 'then liability of the directors might well follow'.[344]

---

[339] See, eg, *In re John A Chepak* Release No 42356 (24 January 2000).

[340] *In re Caremark Int'l* 698 A 2d 959, 970 (Del Ch 1996).

[341] See Factors Memorandum (n 272 above).

[342] See *Ernst & Ernst v Hochfelder* 425 US 185 (1976) (requiring allegations of more than negligence alone to sustain a 10b action for failure to make proper inquiry); see also *In re WorldCom, Inc Sec Litig* No 02 Civ 3288, 2005 WL 638268 (SDNY 21 March 2005) (describing 'the standards for imposing liability on directors of public companies under Section 11 of the Securities Act . . . and under the controlling person provisions in the Securities Act and the Securities Exchange Act').

[343] In particular, s 302 and 906 of SOX impose extensive new obligations upon all principal executive and financial officers of listed companies to certify certain matters in periodic reports filed with the SEC. See n 72 above).

[344] *Graham v Allis-Chalmers Mfg Co* 188 A 2d 125, 130 (Del 1963); see also *In re WorldCom, Inc Sec Litig* 2005 WL 638268, at *8 (articulating strict liability standard applicable to corporations under the 1933 Act).

By the same token, internal investigations must be carefully supervised by the **3.172** company or its board to ensure they are conducted efficiently and effectively. Internal investigations are often costly, and companies have an obligation to ensure that they are properly focused.

It is usually very important that an internal investigation be conducted expedi- **3.173** tiously, efficiently and effectively, especially if the company's financial statements are being delayed pending the outcome of the investigation, or the regulator is threatening to conduct its own investigation because the company's investigation is taking too long. The timing of the investigation is often a critical factor, as extended investigations may have negative collateral consequences for a company, such as causing the company's stock to be delisted from a stock exchange, triggering an event of default under loan agreements or significant contracts, depressing the price of the company's stock, generating low employee morale, hampering employee recruitment or the company's ability to obtain new contracts, and prolonging regulatory investigations. In addition, facts discovered through the investigation, even where there is no wrongdoing, may serve as fodder for litigation against the company.

In the end, decisions regarding the proper scope of the investigation should be **3.174** the subject of discussion. And, whatever the decision, the scope of the investigation, including its limitations, should be clearly expressed to regulators, auditors, and other interested parties.[345]

Hiring forensic experts

If the investigation involves allegations relating to financial and accounting irregu- **3.175** larities or misconduct, the company should consider hiring a forensic accounting expert to assist counsel in the investigation. The forensic accountant should work under the direction of investigative counsel in conducting the financial aspects of the investigation and assisting in providing technical analysis of the issues. Other forensic experts who typically may play a role in an investigation include electronic discovery experts who can ensure the collection and review of all relevant electronic materials at the company, including any 'deleted' files in computers and other electronic storage media, and corporate investigative firms that can perform background checks on individuals or companies. For purposes of maintaining all appropriate privileges and protections over the forensic expert's work, they are often retained directly by the investigative counsel and not by the company.

---

[345] Many of the risks inherent in limiting investigative scope materialized into an unmitigated disaster for the first law firm that investigated Enron's accounting practice. There, investigative scope was severely limited as to persons interviewed and material reviewed, and was subject to an extremely tight time deadline. See Hoeffner & Rabii (n 336 above).

3.176 Because the forensic expert plays a critical role in the investigation, it is important to retain the right firm. Multiple candidates should be researched and interviewed before hiring the right firm. Among the factors the investigative counsel should consider are: (1) the firm's background and experience in the subject matter at issue; (2) the resources the firm has available to dedicate to the investigation, including any foreign offices, depending on the needs of the investigation; (3) any potential or actual conflicts of interest in view of the firm's previously published opinions, if any, concerning the subject matter under inquiry; and (4) whether any member of the expert firm may be a testifying witness in any proceedings as a result of the investigation. Finally, it is important for investigative counsel to have an understanding of the costs that may be incurred by hiring the forensic expert, and to communicate the anticipated costs to the company, which will ultimately be responsible for paying the bill.

Document preservation and collection

3.177 Proper document preservation and collection are becoming an increasingly important part of any investigation in the US, and in litigation generally. Documents often play a key role in proving or refuting allegations of misconduct, and can be used to confirm or contradict the statements of key witnesses. For the investigative counsel—and the company on whose behalf the investigation is undertaken—the ability to say, at the conclusion of the investigation, that all known relevant documents have been collected and reviewed is critical to the credibility of the investigation.

3.178 The first order of business for any company faced with the events that trigger an internal investigation is to seek to preserve all relevant documents so that there can be no allegation down the road of destruction of documents. The company should not wait until the details of the internal investigation are resolved. One of the first questions likely to be posed by regulators, assuming a regulatory investigation follows the triggering event, is whether all relevant documents have been preserved. Regulators will be very nervous about waiting for the company to conduct an internal investigation if the answer to that question is anything but a resounding 'yes'.[346]

3.179 Examples of steps that may be taken to preserve all relevant documents include a memorandum from the Office of the General Counsel to employees in all areas of the company that may have potentially relevant information, which explains the situation and instructs employees not to destroy or delete any relevant

---

[346] In fact, regulators often will issue a subpoena for documents to the company upon learning of a triggering event as a 'placeholder'. The subpoena serves as an official notice to the company that all relevant documents must be preserved.

documents, including electronic data. Another example is to suspend any automatic or routine recycling of electronic data at the company. Other steps may include copying or imaging the hard drives of all employees who are implicated in the wrongdoing or who may have information relevant to the subject matter under investigation. Once the investigative counsel is retained, such counsel may seek to review the adequacy of the company's document preservation efforts to determine whether all information required by the investigative counsel has been preserved.

Once all documents have been preserved, the next step is to collect and review the documents. Both the company and the investigative counsel must carefully consider who should conduct and supervise the document preservation and collection efforts, whether it should be in-house counsel, outside counsel, an outside vendor, or individual employees. The decision often will depend on the specifics of the matter, including the scope of the investigation, the time frame under which the documents must be collected and reviewed, and whether employees who possess the documents are themselves under inquiry. In certain cases, the allegations of misconduct may involve the legal department; in such a case, the investigative counsel or the company may determine that the legal department should not be involved in document preservation or collection efforts lest the investigation's methodology be open to criticism.

3.180

Document preservation

With the exception of certain types of companies that have affirmative document preservation obligations,[347] it is not unusual for typical document retention policies to mandate that various classes of documents be periodically and systematically destroyed.[348] Preserving documents for an investigation, however, will most likely mean overriding any such standing document retention policies.[349]

3.181

A regulatory inquiry or internal investigation requires a prompt suspension of any procedures that mandate or permit the destruction of documents. In the

3.182

---

[347] Broker-dealers registered with the SEC, for example, must preserve certain records for a three-year period. The failure by several broker-dealers to do so has resulted in steep fines by the SEC. See SEC Interpretation: Electronic Storage of Broker-Dealer Records, 17 CFR pt 241 (2003).

[348] The advent of email has created new issues concerning document preservation. Because companies routinely archive employee emails on back-up servers, an immense volume of material is available for review by regulators and investigatory counsel. A demand by regulators or a request by investigators to retrieve and review these emails often necessitates Herculean efforts by a company's IT department. Such efforts can be managed by hiring outside consultants who specialize in the retrieval and sorting of electronic information for litigation and investigation purposes.

[349] Although document retention is now fairly routine in the context of litigation, companies sometimes respond less formally to internal investigations. Whatever choices are made by the company, the investigative counsel must be confident that the documents pertaining to the areas within the scope of the investigation are preserved.

regulatory context, document destruction, if seen as wilful, can constitute obstruction of justice, and can expose the company to criminal liability. For example, Arthur Andersen was convicted of obstruction of justice after an in-house lawyer 'reminded' employees of the company's document retention policy—which included routine destruction of certain files—following reports of accounting irregularities at its client, Enron. This reminder resulted in a dramatic spike in document destruction in Arthur Andersen's Houston office that continued until the company received a subpoena.[350] In another case, Frank Quattrone, a former investment banker, was convicted of obstruction of justice for endorsing a reminder of the company's document retention policy to employees and recommending that they 'clean up those files'. Quattrone's conviction was later reversed on appeal.[351]

3.183 Even if documents are not in fact destroyed, the failure properly to supervise the retention production of documents that are subject to litigation may result in sanctions. For example, in a recent case, Morgan Stanley repeatedly asserted in court that it had lost a substantial number of email backup tapes that may have been relevant to the litigation. As it turned out, the company's legal department had been on notice that the backup tapes, in fact, existed. Once the discrepancy came to light, the court imposed drastic sanctions on Morgan Stanley by shifting the burden of proof at trial against Morgan Stanley to prove that it did *not* commit fraud.[352]

3.184 Investigative counsel therefore must conduct enough due diligence to be confident that the company has taken measure to preserve all relevant documents.

Document collection

3.185 Once documents are preserved, the next task is to collect and review all documents that may be relevant to the investigation. The investigative counsel should ensure that his or her team maintains a detailed record of all incoming and outgoing documents; it is also useful for the company to designate a person at the company to act as a liaison to the investigative counsel to handle document requests.

---

[350] See *Arthur Andersen LLP v United States* 544 US 696 (2005).

[351] *United States v Quattrone* 441 F 3d 153, 165 (2nd Cir 2006). Both convictions were ultimately reversed when courts found that the jury instructions at both trials imposed a kind of strict liability for document destruction. See *Arthur Andersen* 544 US at 707-08. The Supreme Court held that innocent document destruction that impedes a government investigation is not in itself criminal. There must be some finding of corrupt intention and some nexus between the corrupt activity and a foreseeable proceeding. Ibid at 707-08 (noting that 18 USC § 1512, does not require a pending proceeding, but does require the proceeding be foreseeable); *Quattrone*, 441 F 3d at 170-71 ('A defendant's awareness that a subpoena seeks documents, coupled with his actions taken to place those documents beyond the grand jury's reach clearly would meet the hemming function of the nexus requirement.').

[352] See *Coleman Holdings v Morgan Stanley* No CA 03-5045 AI, 2005 WL 674885 (Fla Cir Ct 1 March 2005).

Because requests may come from several different parties over the course of the investigation—including regulators and parties in private civil actions—investigative counsel and the company should coordinate to develop an organized process for requesting and responding to document requests.

Another important decision involving documents is how the documents relevant **3.186** to the investigation should be collected. The investigative counsel must choose whether to ask the company's employees to gather relevant documents themselves or have the lawyers from the investigative counsel's firm or other third party do so.

The principal advantage of having a company's own employees search for docu- **3.187** ments is economy: it is expensive to send attorneys and paralegals to the office of every employee, especially for international companies that may have relevant documents in far-flung corners of the world. Moreover, the attorneys and paralegals will be far less familiar with the location of documents and the company's filing system than employees. Further, the presence of unfamiliar attorneys and paralegals at the company to collect files, may be disruptive and disconcerting to the employees.

A document collection conducted by investigative counsel, however, has advan- **3.188** tages that may outweigh the burden on the company. If employees are implicated in allegations of wrongdoing, regulators will question the integrity of an investigation that relied only on documents selected as relevant by such employees. Also, the disruption created by lawyers and paralegals searching through files may be no greater than the disruption caused by employees having to set aside time to search through their own files.[353] Finally, investigative counsel likely will have a better understanding of the legal issues associated with the investigation, including issues of privilege and relevance.[354]

---

[353] Deciding between collection by employees or lawyers is less difficult for electronic documents. The technical nature of electronic storage media generally requires the company's information technology department or an outside consultant to gather the documents.

[354] Employees may be concerned that some documents in their possession contain personal or private information. In the US, courts assume that materials kept at work, including emails on a company server, are property of the company. Companies thus generally retain the right to search and inspect all documents in the employee's custody. See *Muick v Glenayre Elecs* 280 F 3d 741, 743 (7th Cir 2002) (holding that employee had no right to limit access to files or email on a computer owned by his employer). But see *Leventhal v Knapek* 266 F 3d 64, 74 (2nd Cir 2001) (holding employees may have a right to privacy of materials on employer's computer if employer does not reserve the right to inspect). In contrast, in some foreign jurisdictions, employees can preserve the privacy of such communications by placing them within a private sub-folder and designating them as such. See K Eltis, 'The Emerging American Approach to E-Mail Privacy in the Workplace: Its Influence on Developing Caselaw in Canada and Israel: Should Others Follow Suit?' (2003) 24 Comparative Labor Law & Policy Journal 487, 493.

3.189 For investigations involving a large number of documents in electronic format, the company or investigative counsel should consider hiring an outside vendor to assist with some part of the document collection and review process. Such outside vendors can assist in many capacities, including locating and collecting data; implementing search terms or concepts through the collected data to find items that may be relevant to the issues in the investigation; staging or hosting data on an Internet website for review by several parties; and conducting forensic analysis of data to determine whether any files have been deleted or destroyed. In cases involving millions of pages of electronic documents, it is fairly common for vendors to house documents electronically on one Internet site and enable multiple parties to log in with their own security codes to view the documents. Also, given that many investigations may result in private civil litigation against the company, it is cost effective for the company to have the data available in an electronic format so that if the need arises to reproduce the data to others in the future, such productions can be made with relative ease.[355]

3.190 One note of caution for using a vendor to process electronic data: because parties with divergent interests often share a vendor's website to upload and review documents, it is critical for the vendor to have a functionality to provide each party with its own secure space where the party can make notes on the electronic documents (eg designating the relevance or significance of the document) without any risk that such notes may be visible to others who also have access to the documents. Many electronic vendors currently are able to provide such functionality.

3.191 As with forensic consultants, discussed above, the client must research, prescreen, and interview potential document vendors to find one that fits its specific needs. Electronic vendors are expensive to retain, so it is important to get a cost estimate before work begins, and if that is not feasible, to get a sense of what the vendor costs generally to host and process stock quantities of electronic documents. In addition, it is important to ensure that the electronic vendor understands the importance of confidentiality and/or deadline sensitivity. Another factor in choosing between document vendors, it is important to understand the experience such a vendor has had in handling internal investigations and/or litigations, and the resources the vendor is willing or able to put into the task at hand.

---

[355] It is also not uncommon for adverse parties in private litigation to share the costs of uploading and hosting documents on electronic vendors' Internet sites.

Conducting witness interviews

In addition to documents, witness interviews are an important part of the investi-   **3.192**
gative process. This section addresses the steps and issues involved in conducting
witness interviews.

Preparing for and conducting interviews

Investigative counsel must first decide whom to interview. The initial list, often   **3.193**
compiled with the help of company management, need not be exhaustive because
the first several interviews are likely to generate names of additional witnesses
who may have relevant information. It is usually helpful to select someone from
the company—usually a member of the in-house counsel staff—to act as a liaison
between investigatory counsel and the company employees selected for interview. The liaison will be more familiar to the employees, and also can advise the
employee of the general nature of the interview.

It is not unusual for investigative counsel to request that no one from the com-   **3.194**
pany (other than the employee who is being interviewed and his or her counsel,
if any), attend the interview. Such a request typically is made in an effort to create
an atmosphere for the employee where he or she will feel freer to speak about the
conduct of other employees. One can imagine how a lower-level employee may
be 'chilled' from discussing any questionable conduct of a higher-level employee
in front of a company representative for fear of retaliation.

Nonetheless, employees sometimes feel more comfortable with a familiar face   **3.195**
from the company (such as in-house legal counsel) present. In such a case, the
decision whether to include the company representative should be made by
the investigative counsel in view of the circumstances of the investigation. To the
extent that it is important to maintain the independence of the investigation, it
may be reasonable for investigative counsel to make a bright-line decision not to
include any company representatives in witness interviews. In other situations, it
may be perfectly appropriate, and even helpful, to include company in-house
counsel in the witness interview.

It is important that investigative counsel create an accurate record of the sub-   **3.196**
stance of the statements made by witnesses during interviews. Such a record of
the interview can be reflected in a variety of ways: a transcript prepared simultaneously by a court reporter; handwritten or typewritten notes of interviews taken
by an attorney or a paralegal; or after-the-fact summary memoranda of interviews
prepared from notes taken during the interviews. The mode in which one prepares
the record of the interview can be determined by the investigative counsel. One
factor that may be relevant to how one prepares the record of the interview may

be whether the final product has, or should have, any privileged status. An interview memorandum prepared after-the-fact that contains an attorney's mental impressions may be protected from further disclosure by the attorney work-product doctrine. A mere transcript of the questions and answers, however, may not be entitled to similar protection.

3.197 Under the Supreme Court's decision in *Upjohn v United States*, memoranda of witness interviews prepared by counsel for the purpose of rendering legal advice to the client are protected as attorney work-product or by the attorney-client privilege.[356] To best preserve the privilege, the following statements, often known as '*Upjohn* warnings', should be made to the witness prior to beginning the interview:

- Investigating counsel represents the company (or the committee of the board of directors of the company overseeing the investigation), and not the individual.

- The investigation is being conducted to provide the company (or the committee) with legal advice relating to specified matters.

- The interview is protected by the attorney-client privilege of the company and, as a result, the employee is not authorized on his or her own to waive that privilege, and therefore, should keep confidential the subject matter of the interview. The privilege belongs to the company (or the committee), not the individual.[357]

- The company (or the committee) therefore may decide, without the employee's consent, to disclose the contents of the interview to regulators or other persons outside the company.

- It is very important that the employee be truthful in providing his or her answers.[358]

---

[356] See *Upjohn v United States* 449 US 383, 397, 401–02 (1981). *Upjohn* provides the following guidelines for assessing the applicability of the attorney-client privilege: (1) whether the communications were made for the corporation to obtain legal advice; (2) whether senior management directed the employees to cooperate with the investigation; (3) whether the communications concerned matters within the scope of an employee's employment; and (4) whether the information was unavailable from senior management. Ibid at 394-97.

[357] If the investigating attorney informs the employee that the attorney represents the company, and that the attorney-client privilege belongs to the company, the employee may not assert a privilege over interview memoranda provided by the company to the SEC. *In re Grand Jury Subpoena: Under Seal* 415 F 3d 333 (4th Cir 2005).

[358] Guilty pleas of three Computer Associates employees for obstruction of justice were based on the theory that lying in interviews to the law firm handling an internal investigation misled the government. See DoJ Press Release, 'Former Computer Associates Executives Indicted on Securities Fraud, Obstruction Charges' (22 September 2004).

When preparing a record of the interview, it is important to keep in mind that the **3.198** record may be produced to regulators or to parties adverse to the company in private civil actions, or even to the media. A lawyer preparing a record of the interview also may be called to testify as to the meaning of his notes or memoranda. It is, therefore, in the preparer's interest to be as accurate as possible. To enhance accuracy, it is important that a memorandum of the interview be prepared as soon after the interview as practicable.

Interviewing witnesses with their own representation

Some employees may decline to be interviewed, citing the potential risk of regu-   **3.199** latory exposure. The employee may decline to be interviewed, but doing so may be viewed as a failure to cooperate with the company's internal affairs and may have consequences. Depending on what employment agreements or understandings, if any, the company has with such an employee, the company may be entirely within its rights to take appropriate actions against the employee for failure to cooperate with the company's investigation.[359]

Employees who do agree to speak to investigative counsel about alleged or poten-   **3.200** tial wrongdoing at the company nevertheless may have concerns about their exposure to potential regulatory actions or the confidentiality of their statements. The investigative counsel is in no position, however, to give any assurances of confidentiality to such an employee because he must preserve the ability to disclose the information provided by that employee to the client (the board committee or management), regulators, and potentially to other employees. Further, because it represents the company, there is a potential conflict of interest in investigative counsel providing any legal advice to employees. Thus, it is not uncommon for companies to offer, for employees who are sufficiently concerned about their role or status in the internal investigation, the option of retaining individual counsel.[360]

---

[359] The United States Constitution's Fifth Amendment right against self-incrimination, like other constitutional protections for individuals, is a right against government action (federal, state, or local), not private action. See *Johnston v Herschler* 669 F 2d 617, 619 (10th Cir 1982); *Confederation of Police v Conlisk*, 489 F 2d 891, 894-95 (7th Cir 1973). If the employee is not an 'at-will' employee, however, he or she may still resort to contractual remedies against the company. Although even an 'at-will' employee may not be terminated for a capricious or discriminatory reason, termination for failure to cooperate with an internal investigation is not viewed as either. State law may also provide protections for non-cooperating employees. The company and investigating counsel should take care to determine whether any such state law protections would apply to non-cooperating employees.

[360] Because certain employees may have interests that substantially diverge from the interests of their fellow employees, it may be useful to have more than one lawyer or law firm available to represent individual employees.

3.201   Because retaining separate counsel may be prohibitively expensive for some employees, companies may, in appropriate circumstances, advance the employee's legal fees in connection with the investigation. Further, under certain circumstances as determined by state law, companies may even indemnify employees for their expenses incurred in defending against any litigation arising out of the investigation. Many states permit a company to indemnify its officers and directors who are being sued or who are under threat of suit in connection with actions they took or failed to take in the course of their professional duties. For example, Delaware law allows for the indemnification of any director, officer, or employee 'who was or is a party or is threatened to be made a party to any threatened, pending or completed action, suit or proceeding, whether civil, criminal, administrative or investigative'.[361] An internal investigation falls within this rubric if it occurs in connection with a regulatory inquiry. If the investigation preceded any such inquiry, however, the statutory indemnification might not apply. Nonetheless, a separate statutory provision states that the indemnification criteria set forth above are not exhaustive, and that the company may expand them.[362] The charters and bylaws of many corporations have expanded indemnification rights to provide for indemnification of employees in internal investigations.

3.202   The company can also, however, reclaim legal fees it has advanced to employees who prove to be implicated in the misconduct under investigation. For example, Delaware law provides that the company need only indemnify a director or officer who 'acted in good faith and in a manner the person reasonably believed to be in or not opposed to the best interest of the corporation, and, with respect to any criminal action or proceeding, had no reasonable cause to believe his conduct was unlawful'.[363] Company bylaws generally set forth the criteria determining whether an employee has met this standard, usually consisting of a vote by the board or a special committee of board members.

3.203   If the employee accepts the company's offer of separate representation, ethical guidelines mandate that any communication with the employee concerning the investigation occur through his or her lawyer.[364] In dealing with represented employees' counsel, it may be wise for investigative counsel to develop a practice early on concerning what information, if any, to provide to employees or their counsel in advance of interviews. It is also a good practice to keep records of communications with employees' counsel in the event of later disagreements or to

---

361   8 Del C § 145(a) (2006).

362   Ibid § 145(f).

363   Ibid § 145(a).

364   See Model Rules of Prof'l Conduct R 4.2 ('In representing a client, a lawyer shall not communicate about the subject of the representation with a person the lawyer knows to be represented by another lawyer in the matter, unless the lawyer has the consent of the other lawyer or is authorized to do so by law or a court order.'). The same rules apply if the employee selects his or her own counsel.

document the level of cooperation of a particular employee so that later on, when asked by the company and/or the board of directors, the investigative counsel can provide an assessment of the level of cooperation received from various employees.

Certain employees may be reluctant to be interviewed without a joint defense **3.204** agreement. The utility of a joint defense agreement is that it may enhance the likelihood that the exchange of facts and legal theories between the company and the employee will not waive the attorney-client privilege and will be subject to other protections from disclosure. Privileged information shared with a party pursuant to a joint defence agreement remains protected from disclosure, and all parties to the agreement must concur before any one party is permitted to waive the privilege.[365]

Where the company is cooperating with a regulatory investigation, however, a **3.205** joint defence agreement may prevent the company from being able to disclose certain facts to the regulators, and accordingly, may be viewed as inconsistent with cooperation.[366] This is because a company in a joint defense agreement with an employee often may not, without the employee's consent, disclose any information about the investigation that it gathered from that employee. A joint defense agreement between a company and its employees who are under a regulatory investigation, therefore, is less common than it would be in private civil litigation.

Dealing with regulators

A critical issue for companies and investigative counsel is whether and when to **3.206** report the possibility of unlawful activity to regulators. Regulators invariably take the view that prompt self-reporting of wrongdoing and full cooperation with regulatory investigations are always in the company's best interests. For example, the Thompson Memo warns: 'In determining whether to charge a corporation, that corporation's timely and voluntary disclosure of wrongdoing and its willingness to cooperate with the government's investigation may be relevant factors.'[367] In light

---

[365] *United States v Under Seal* 902 F 2d 244 (4th Cir 1990); *Sobel v EP Duton, Inc* 112 FRD 99 (SDNY 1986).

[366] McNulty Memorandum (n 268 above), VII.B(3).

[367] Ibid II.A. Similarly, the Seaboard Report includes, as a factor, whether the company promptly reported the results of its review to the SEC. *Seaboard Guidelines* (n 272 above). In the US Sentencing Guidelines for Organizations, punishment is mitigated based on a company's efforts in self-reporting, cooperation with authorities, and acceptance of responsibility. See USSG § 8C. The CFTC states that it considers the company's good faith in uncovering and investigating misconduct, the company's cooperation with Division staff in reporting misconduct, and the company's actions with respect to Division staff. See Cooperation Memorandum (n 272 above). The NASD likewise states that it considers whether the company accepted responsibility to a regulator prior to intervention by the regulator, whether the company voluntarily employed corrective measures, prior to detection or intervention by the regulator, to revise general and/or specific procedures to avoid recurrence of

of these regulatory pronouncements, clients often ask investigative counsel whether and how to report a problem.[368]

3.207 Legal rules and ethical considerations do not always mandate full, real-time disclosure of all potential problems to regulators, although they do mandate truthful disclosure when disclosure is actually made. When considering whether to self-report, a client should weigh the following, among other relevant factors:

- the nature and extent of possible wrongdoing and the circumstances of its discovery;
- whether the possible wrongdoing is in the past or is ongoing;
- the cost and collateral consequences of reporting;
- the possibility of harm to the corporation, its shareholders, or other constituencies;
- the persons alleged to have engaged in wrongdoing; and
- whether there are or will likely be other investigations with respect to the possible wrongdoing or related matters, including by a regulatory body.[369]

3.208 The client should more generally consider whether failure to disclose will be viewed as a failure to cooperate such that the government's later discovery of corporate wrongdoing would lead to a penalty or even indictment. Where the possibility of wrongdoing is high-level, widespread, or ongoing, establishing a satisfactory compliance programme is essential, and therefore, prompt and full disclosure of the problem will often be the only sensible course.

How to report the findings of the internal investigation

3.209 One of the most important decisions to be made in the course of an internal investigation is how the final product of the investigation will be presented. Will there be a written or oral report? What should the investigative counsel and/or the company share with the government (and therefore, potentially, with litigants)? Factors to consider in making the decision include:

- Is the government likely to require a written report as part of cooperation? A written report may be more useful to the government when the matters under inquiry

---

misconduct, and whether the company voluntarily and reasonably attempted, prior to detection and intervention, to pay restitution or otherwise remedy the misconduct. See Factors Memorandum (n 272 above). NYSE Rule 351 and NASD Conduct Rule 3070, go even further, requiring companies to promptly report any violation of securities laws or regulations.

[368] This does not apply to ongoing illegal activity, such as the improper destruction of documents, which constitutes obstruction of justice. Outside counsel has an affirmative obligation to try to ensure preservation of relevant documents to the potential wrongdoing.

[369] Ass'n of the Bar of the City of NY, 'Report of the Task Force on the Lawyer's Role in Corporate Governance' (November 2006) <http://www.abcny.org/pdf/report/CORPORATE_GOVERNANCE06.pdf>.

are complex or technical. Is the company or the board willing to deal with the waiver of privilege that producing the written report to the government will raise?

- Does the client have a preference for a written report for business reasons? Written reports are easier for company management and others to analyse and evaluate.
- Is a written report more likely to restore investor, consumer and employee confidence in the company? If a written report is given to the company or its auditors, the company should anticipate that the government will expect that the report be produced to them.
- Does the investigation warrant the added cost of a written report?
- What is the report likely to contain? Will it provide an unwanted or unnecessary roadmap for criminal or civil charges for the client?

As discussed above, production of a written report (or written interview memoranda) may result in a waiver of attorney-client privilege or work-product protection over such materials. Even with a non-waiver agreement, however, the production of a written report to the government may result in its availability to civil litigants, often providing them with a roadmap to the best evidence against the company. Provision of a written report to third parties, such as an auditor, likewise will result in waiver of the privilege. **3.210**

Finally, if the investigating law firm issues a written report, the content of that report will depend in large part on the type of investigation conducted and the mandate given to the investigator. Some sections to consider including are: **3.211**

- a description of the circumstances that prompted the investigation and a description of the scope of the investigation;
- a description of the methodologies utilized in the investigation (the documents collected and reviewed, witnesses interviewed);
- an executive summary of findings and recommendations;
- for each issue investigated, a summary of the relevant background facts (a chronology of the relevant events, a description of the relevant individuals and entities, and an outline of the relevant agreement and/or transactions);
- a discussion of the evidence;
- a summary of the relevant law, if applicable;
- an identification of the corrective measures that should be considered (or have been taken) as a result of issues uncovered during the investigation; and
- an analysis of the materiality of the misconduct (if any) to the company's business.

4

INVESTIGATIONS IN THE
UNITED KINGDOM

A. Introduction[1]

4.01   The UK has developed into a sophisticated regulated market for corporates. The level of regulation of all aspects of corporate life has been increasing over the past years. This includes not only securities markets but also regulation of operational parts of corporate activities. This is seen in the expansion of the government and regulatory affairs units of companies and in the significant increase in the regulatory advisory and defence resources of law firms in the UK.

4.02   There are a number of reasons for this change in regulation. In part, it is the result of the substantial privatization programme, which started in the 1980s, and which introduced sector regulators and increased powers of regulation in relation both to privatized industries and to other businesses that operated in the same industrial sectors.

4.03   A substantial part of the regulation flows from European Community legislation as it harmonizes markets across Europe. This has ranged from requirements in relation to securities, listing and, prospectuses, into transactions in financial markets, and to many operational matters, particularly in the anti-trust field. It is important to note, in this respect, that much of the enforcement of this regulation is left to national regulators and not conducted at the European level.

---

[1] Contributors: Paul Lomas and Rachel Couter.

Thirdly, there has been an increase in the powers of all competition-related agen- **4.04** cies as UK policy has strongly endorsed free competition, rather than industrial policy, as the route to improving UK competitiveness.

Finally, and not surprisingly in the light of historical and cultural contacts, UK **4.05** regulators and policy-makers have been influenced by experiences in the US. In a number of areas, agency behaviour now looks considerably more US in style than was previously the case. This is seen not only in the nature and career aspirations of the individuals employed by the regulators, but also in the regulators' powers and the way in which they are exercised, in the increasing use of higher (including criminal) sanctions, in the vesting of responsibility in senior people and in the requirements to operate systems and controls that reduce the risk of infringement. However, the 'lighter touch' style of regulation in the UK still means that it is a less aggressive market than the US.

This more critical regulatory environment, coupled with a series of reports and **4.06** commentaries on corporate governance, has lead to a corporate culture that is much more highly sensitized to governance issues. Both regulators and non-executive directors require ever higher standards, irrespective of the views of executive management (which is also highly interested in the light of its clearer and more direct responsibility). Moreover, the capital markets themselves, assisted by the close scrutiny of the financial and trade press, are increasingly exigent in their expectations. Accordingly, corporate responses to actual and anticipated regulator concerns and to the uncovering of issues which might lead to regulatory interest or simply reflect poorly on the ethical or legal compliance culture within organizations have become much more acute.

Thus, thorough investigations into the nature and cause of, and accountability **4.07** for, any issues are now frequently seen. Standards of due diligence and quality in this respect are steadily increasing. Recognized ways of undertaking such exercises are developing, leading to expectations on the part of stakeholders as to the appropriate way of responding.

B. Regulators

Key regulators

There are a number of UK statutory regulatory bodies and authorities primarily **4.08** relevant to investigations into listed corporations. These are briefly described below.

The Financial Services Authority (FSA) assumed responsibility for regulating **4.09** financial market activity and corporate entities listed on (or applying for listing on) the London Stock Exchange (listed corporates) on 1 December 2001. The FSA's broad investigatory and disciplinary powers are derived from the Financial Services and Markets Act 2000 (FSMA 2000).[2] All in all, the FSA is responsible for 30,000 firms and 165,000 individuals.

4.10 The FSA is responsible for regulating all financial market activity, including banking, securities, retail investment services, insurance and mortgages. Further, in its role as the United Kingdom Listing Authority (UKLA), the FSA is also responsible for the regulation of listed corporates and, in particular, their compliance with the applicable rules and regulations, namely the UK Listing Rules, Disclosure Rules and Transparency Rules, and Prospectus Rules[3] (all contained within the FSA Handbook). The FSA's listing principles came into force on 1 July 2005. They set out general principles to ensure that listed corporates pay due regard to the fundamental role they play in maintaining market confidence and ensuring fair and orderly markets.

4.11 This creation of a single regulator, together with the impact of corporate scandals such as Enron, WorldCom and Parmalat, have led to stricter regulation and closer supervision of listed corporates and their personnel. However, regulatory scrutiny in the UK has still not reached the same level as in the US. For example, the UK has no equivalent to the US Sarbanes-Oxley Act of 2002.

4.12 In 2006/2007, the FSA commenced a total of 267 new investigations and closed a total of 219 cases during the course of the year. Of the new investigations, 43 related to market abuse, insider dealing, and misleading statements and practices. Eighty-nine enforcement cases were started during the period, out of which there were 71 cases of disciplinary or enforcement action. The FSA imposed 32 financial penalties totalling approximately £13m, most of which were associated with some form of market abuse.[4] Only one investigation related to breaches of the Listing Rules.[5]

4.13 The Financial Reporting Review Panel (FRRP), a subsidiary of the Financial Reporting Council,[6] is responsible for ensuring that listed corporates (and other

---

2 The UK comprises three separate jurisdictions, each with its own laws. This chapter deals with the laws of England and Wales only. For the avoidance of doubt, references to England and English law are references to England and Wales and the laws of that jurisdiction.

3 These rules replaced the previous rules on 1 July 2005 to reflect European directives, in particular the Prospectus Directive (Directive 2003/71/EC), Market Abuse Directive (Directive 2003/6/EC), and Transparency Directive (Directive 2004/109/EC) and the outcome of a fundamental review of the rules applicable to listed corporates conducted by the UKLA. The detailed requirements of the Listing Rules, Disclosure Rules and Transparency Rules, and Prospectus Rules are beyond the scope of this chapter.

4 Appendix 5 to the FSA Annual Report 2006/7.

5 Appendix 5 to the FSA Annual Report 2006/7.

6 The UK's independent regulator for corporate reporting and governance.

public and large private companies) comply with the financial reporting requirements of the Companies Acts[7] (including applicable accounting standards).[8]

The Department for Business, Enterprise and Regulatory Reform (BERR), **4.14**
formerly the Department of Trade and Industry, deals with various issues, in
particular, relating to compliance with the Companies Acts[9] to ensure confidence
is maintained in corporate Britain.

The Serious Fraud Office (SFO) is an independent government department **4.15**
that investigates and prosecutes serious or complex fraud.[10] The law has been
enhanced by the Fraud Act 2006, which came into force on 15 January 2007.[11]
The UK also created the Serious Organised Crimes Agency (SOCA), which has
wide-ranging investigation powers. SOCA has taken over the National Criminal
Intelligence Service's responsibility for receiving disclosures about suspicious
transactions, including where corporates have been handling the proceeds
of crime (possibly innocently) and fall under duties of disclosure. Importantly,
these bodies are responsible for investigating overseas corruption under the
wider jurisdiction introduced with effect from February 2002.

The Crown Prosecution Service (CPS)[12] has the responsibility for taking over **4.16**
the conduct of all criminal proceedings instituted by the Police.

The London Stock Exchange regulates trading on that exchange (and AIM (the **4.17**
Alternative Investment Market)), including deciding whether to permit trading
in any listed security and setting, monitoring and enforcing the procedures and
standards applicable to admission to trading.

The Office of Fair Trading (OFT)[13] has primary responsibility for the enforce- **4.18**
ment of competition law in the UK, including conducting highly invasive
investigations into behaviour (anti-competitive agreements and abuse of dominant position) or market structures and making references to the Competition
Commission. It can also act on behalf of the European Commission in connection
with cross-border competition issues.

---

[7] Primarily the Companies Act 2006.

[8] The powers of the FRRP derive from the Companies Act 2006 and the Companies (Audit,
Investigations and Community Enterprise) Act 2004.

[9] Primarily the Companies Act 1985.

[10] Under the Criminal Justice Act 1987.

[11] The new act creates a general offence of fraud and three ways of committing it through either:
false representation; failure to disclose information; or abuse of position. It also formally introduces
plea bargaining into the UK criminal system for the first time.

[12] Or, in Northern Ireland, the Director of Public Prosecutions in Northern Ireland.

[13] The Enterprise Act 2002 abolished the office of the Director General of Fair Trading, created
the OFT, and transferred the former's powers to it.

4.19 The Competition Commission[14] is an independent public body with statutory powers and responsibilities to conduct in-depth inquiries into mergers, markets and the regulation of the major regulated industries, such as water, gas and railways, on reference by the OFT, the Secretary of State, or industry-specific regulators. Since its activities tend to be market structure or merger orientated and it does not deal with behavioural infringements, it is less relevant for current purposes.

4.20 Industry-specific regulators exercise some competition powers concurrently with the OFT and include:

- the Office of Gas and Electricity Markets (Ofgem), which is the regulator for gas and electricity industries in England, Scotland, and Wales, operating under the direction and governance of the Gas and Electricity Markets Authority;[15]
- the Office of Water Services (Ofwat), which is the regulator for water and sewerage services in England and Wales;[16]
- the Office of Communication (Ofcom), which is the regulator for the communications industries in the UK, with responsibilities across television, radio, telecommunications, and wireless communications services;[17] and
- the Office of Rail Regulation (ORR), which is the regulator of the rail network infrastructure and operations in Great Britain.[18]

4.21 Her Majesty's Revenue and Customs (HMRC) is responsible for the collection and management of all taxes and duties and National Insurance contributions.[19] HMRC has extensive investigatory and information gathering powers, which it is exercising more fully in its enquiries into the tax affairs of large corporates, which are themselves becoming more common.

Concurrent investigations

4.22 Although the FSA/UKLA is the primary regulator for listed corporates, there may be circumstances where more than one regulator has jurisdiction over, and is interested in, a particular matter. For example, in the case of financial crime and/ or regulatory misconduct, one or more of the FSA (which would encompass the

---

[14] Established by the Competition Act 1998.

[15] Ofgem's powers derive from the Gas Act 1986 and the Electricity Act 1989, both as amended by the Utilities Act 2000, and also the Competition Act 1998 and the Enterprise Act 2002.

[16] Ofwat's powers derive from the Water Industry Act 1991, the Competition Act 1998, and the Water Act 2003.

[17] Ofcom's powers derive from the Communications Act 2003.

[18] ORR's powers derive from the Railways Act 1993 (as amended by the Transport Act 2000), the Railways and Transport Safety Act 2003, the Competition Act 1998, and the Railways Act 2005.

[19] Under the Commissioners for Revenue and Customs Act 2005, s 5; the Taxes Management Act 1970, s 1; and the VAT Act 1994, para 1 to Sch 11.

UKLA), the SFO and BERR may have jurisdiction (indeed, the FSA has the power to prosecute criminal offences related to certain financial crimes). Alternatively, different regulators may pursue different parties (eg individuals and companies) for their involvement in the same set of facts. Similarly, for example, in circumstances where a listed corporate's statutory accounts are not in compliance with the requirements of the Companies Acts[20] (including applicable accounting standards), as well as the FRRP, the UKLA will also have jurisdiction to investigate, because the failure may also constitute a breach of the Disclosure Rules and Transparency Rules.[21] However, the fact that another regulatory body is proposing to take action (or has taken action) against a listed corporate for a breach is a consideration taken into account by the UKLA (or the FSA) in determining whether or not to institute formal disciplinary proceedings.[22]

Guidelines[23] have, therefore, been agreed between the FSA and various other bodies, including the SFO, BERR and the CPS, to assist them to: **4.23**

- decide which of them should investigate such cases, in an attempt to ensure that only the body with the most appropriate functions and powers will commence investigations;
- cooperate with each other, particularly in cases where more than one body is investigating;
- prevent unnecessary duplication of effort by reason of the involvement of more than one body; and
- prevent the subjects of proceedings being treated unfairly by reason of the unwarranted involvement of more than one body.

---

[20] Primarily in the Companies Act 2006.

[21] The requirement that a listed corporate's annual report and accounts be prepared 'in accordance with the national law of the EEA State in which the issuer is incorporated': FSA Handbook at DTR 4.1.6(2).

[22] For example, in the *Indigo Capital LLC* final notice (21/12/04), the FSA took into consideration the fact that Indigo Capital had previously been publicly censured by the Takeover Panel in determining whether or not a penalty for market abuse should be imposed. Ultimately, the FSA decided that it was appropriate to exercise its own powers under the market abuse regime because the Takeover Panel's censure had been in respect of violations of the City Code on Takeovers and Mergers, which had occurred prior to the events the subject of the market abuse, and had been committed by different behaviour.

[23] FSA Handbook at EG Annex 2. See also:
   1. The Memorandum of Understanding between the FRRP and the FSA (6 April 2005);
   2. The Operating Guidelines between the FSA and the Takeover Panel (29 November 2001, as amended. In these circumstances, the FSA has made it clear that it does not expect to use its investigative powers while a takeover bid is current, subject to exceptions. See also FSA Handbook at DEPP 6.2.22-6.2.28 and EG generally); and
   3. The joint statement of the FSA and the OFT (July 2007). See <http://www.oft.gov.uk/shared_oft/oft941.pdf>.

4.24 These guidelines do not, however, eradicate the possibility of multiple investigations by different bodies in appropriate circumstances. Indeed, the guidelines recognize that, in certain circumstances, concurrent investigations may be the quickest, most effective and most efficient way to deal with the matter.

Relationships with overseas regulators

4.25 There is nothing to prevent UK regulators from conducting an investigation or bringing enforcement proceedings against a listed corporate in circumstances where the listed corporate is already being (or may be) investigated by an overseas regulator.[24] However, the fact that an overseas regulator is already investigating may be a relevant factor in determining whether enforcement proceedings should be brought. Moreover, the UK authorities have entered into a number of Memoranda of Understanding with overseas enforcement agencies, including the SEC, which set out channels of communication and procedures for cooperating and sharing information.[25]

4.26 The OFT, as with all other European Competition regulators, is party to the European Competition Network, which acts as a forum for discussion and cooperation to ensure an efficient division of work and effective and consistent application of the EU competition rules. The EU Commission and the European regulators cooperate inter alia through informing one another of new cases and envisaged enforcement decisions; coordinating investigations, where necessary; helping each other with investigations; and exchanging evidence and other information. The OFT is also a member of the International Competition Network which promotes cooperation to ensure more efficient and effective anti-trust enforcement worldwide.

4.27 The SFO has extensive relationships with overseas regulators (some 65 per cent of its cases have an international dimension). It liaises with authorities in many

---

[24] Indeed, concurrent investigations were brought by the FSA and the SEC against Shell (see *Shell* final notice: 24/8/04) in relation to the misstatement of gas resources. In the case of CSFB International, the FSA conducted an investigation despite the fact that the majority of the relevant events occurred in Japan and the primary charges were that CSFB engaged in conduct designed deliberately to mislead the Japanese regulatory and tax authorities and failed to organize and control its activities in Japan in a responsible manner: *CSFB International* final notice (11/12/02).

[25] The Memorandum of Understanding between the Department of Trade and Industry, now BERR, the Securities and Investment Board (responsibility transferred to the FSA), the SEC and the US Commodity Futures Trading Commission, dated 25 September 1991; the Memorandum of Understanding between the Investment Management Regulatory Organization (responsibility transferred to the FSA) and the SEC, dated 1 May 1995; the Memorandum of Understanding between the FSA, the Bank of England, the SEC and the US Commodity Futures Trading Commission, dated 28 October 1997; the Multilateral Memorandum of Understanding concerning consultation and cooperation and the exchange of information, dated May 2002; Internal Organization of Securities Commission and the Memorandum of Understanding between the SEC and the FSA, dated 14 March 2006.

national jurisdictions and with supra-national bodies such as the European Anti-Fraud Office (OLAF). In order to deal with the many requests from overseas jurisdictions, the SFO has formalized its working relationships with foreign counterparts in various Mutual Legal Assistance Treaties whose operation is controlled by the Home Office rather than the SFO direct. The SFO will provide overseas prosecutors and investigators with assistance in obtaining evidence including using various coercive powers requiring individuals to produce documents and answer questions, or conducting searches where there is a suspicion that evidence could be destroyed if warning is given. The SFO does not require reciprocity in other jurisdictions in order to assist overseas investigators.[26]

C. Powers of Regulators

Motivations for investigations

Matters may come to a regulator's attention from a variety of routes including media reporting, information received from another regulator, a complaint by an investor, competitor or customer, or even from the company itself, possibly seeking leniency, or from a whistle-blower. **4.28**

The UKLA also conducts its own monitoring of share price movements and, in particular, the reaction of a share price to a public announcement: if a listed corporate's share price drops sharply following any announcement, the corporate may receive a letter of enquiry from the UKLA. The OFT usually launches investigations based on complaints received and informal discussions with the complainant or where it has reasonable grounds for suspecting that an infringement of the competition provisions has occurred. Such a suspicion can arise from policy concerns as to markets where infringements are likely to be found and econometric evidence as to the movement of prices and the commercial behaviour of undertakings active in that market. Similarly, the SFO conducts investigations based on referrals, most often from the various police forces, or from private applicants who can demonstrate that the case meets the SFO's acceptance criteria.[27] The SFO will also launch an inquiry independently if it has reason to believe that a major or complex fraud has been committed. **4.29**

---

[26] For further information on requesting SFO assistance, see <http://www.sfo.gov.uk/international/evidence_uk.asp>.

[27] The SFO only investigates major or complex frauds, which usually meet one or more of the following criteria:
- the value of the alleged fraud exceeds £1m;
- there is a significant international dimension;
- the case requires highly specialized knowledge, eg of financial markets; and
- there is a need to use the SFO's special powers, eg the Criminal Justice Act 1987, s 2, requiring people to answer or supply documents.

4.30 The FSA, in its wider supervisory capacity, also conducts 'themed visits', namely industry-wide reviews of a particular risk affecting the industry in question, which involve the cooperation of certain regulated entities 'invited' to take part, even where there is no suspicion of any wrongdoing on the part of a particular entity involved. Other regulators including the competition authorities and the sector regulators have policies to review and investigate particular sectors of the economy which may lead them to take specific investigative or enforcement action.

Levels of regulatory scrutiny

4.31 Most of the key regulators in the UK will operate some type of informal investigations procedure as well as having recourse to formal investigation powers to ascertain whether a breach has occurred and the type of action it should take.

4.32 It is, however, less common for the competition authorities to engage with undertakings at an informal level on behavioural matters; they prefer to conduct an internal consideration of the position, perhaps with cooperation from a leniency applicant or a whistle-blower and then to use their formal powers. However, where the undertakings concerned are applying for leniency, the extensive obligation in relation to cooperation mean that the corporate is, in practice, undertaking a full internal investigation, under the exigent attention of the regulator, precisely to maintain its leniency relationship. A similar position applies in relation to the SFO, which tends, given the criminal remit, to rely on formal powers when it is interacting directly with companies. A corporate is, therefore, placed in the similar position of having no choice but to conduct precisely the same kind of investigation to ensure that it understands the issues that it faces, as well as it can, in advance of the SFO. Thus, whilst the circumstances may be a little different (particularly as to the 'constitution' of the investigation), the operational aspects are very similar.

4.33 However, other regulators generally operate on a more flexible basis and it is possible to have a more nuanced relationship with them based on voluntary cooperation by the corporate, reflecting the voluntary proffer of information based on an internal investigation.

4.34 In particular, the UKLA can investigate potential breaches of the Listing Rules, Disclosure Rules and Transparency Rules, or Prospectus Rules by either conducting an informal investigation to obtain information utilizing its de facto power arising from its role in connection with those rules, or by using its statutory powers to conduct a formal investigation. If the listed corporate is also an 'authorised person', the FSA has further powers to conduct various levels of investigation ranging from investigating the matter itself, requiring the 'authorised person' to commission a report by an independent skilled third party on the matter,[28] or working with the corporate which undertakes internal fact-finding and disclosure exercises without being subject to formal powers.

If fraud is not suspected, HMRC will also usually initiate an informal investigation procedure, requesting a corporate to provide information and documents. Failure to cooperate with an informal investigation results in HMRC exercising its more onerous formal information powers. HMRC deals with most tax fraud cases by means of its Civil Investigation of Fraud (CIF) procedure. A decision is taken at the outset in most cases to use CIF rather than to mount a prosecution.[29] **4.35**

Investigation tools

The UK regulators all have a wide range of investigation tools at their disposal, including statutory powers to search premises and seize documents.[30] These powers are often extremely broad and there is little scope for a corporate to avoid compliance. The precise detail of each of the specific powers is outside the scope of this book, but some examples may help to show the scope. **4.36**

The UKLA has powers under the Listing Rules and the Disclosure Rules and Transparency Rules to obtain information from listed corporates for enforcement purposes. This information includes any information that the UKLA considers appropriate in order to protect investors or ensure the smooth operation of the market; and any other information or explanations that the UKLA may require to verify compliance with the Listing Rules and/or the Disclosure Rules and Transparency Rules. Such information must be provided as soon as possible following a request and there are no express limits on the type of information that can be requested.[31] **4.37**

The UKLA also has formal investigation powers under FSMA 2000, Part VI, which allows it to appoint an investigator to conduct an investigation.[32] **4.38**

---

[28] FSMA 2000, ss 165–68.

[29] HMRC has issued two codes of practice, COP8 which applies where less serious frauds are suspected and COP9 which applies to more serious frauds.

[30] For powers of the UKLA, see 4.37 and 4.38; for HMRC, see 4.39; for the OFT, 4.40; and for the SFO, see 4.41.

[31] FSA Handbook at LR 1.3.1 and DTR 1.3.1. The requirements of DTR 1.3.1 also apply to 'persons discharging managerial responsibility' and their 'connected persons'. 'Persons discharging managerial responsibility' primarily comprise directors and senior executives, who have a role involving access to 'inside information', while their 'connected persons' primarily comprise close relatives and other companies of which the 'person discharging managerial responsibilities' or his or her connected persons is a director or senior executive: FSMA 2000, s 96B.

[32] The UKLA may only appoint an investigator if there are circumstances suggesting that:
1. There may have been a breach of the requirements imposed by the provisions of FSMA 2000, Part VI;
2. There may have been a breach of the Listing Rules (or Disclosure Rules and Transparency Rules or Prospectus Rules);

The hurdle for initiating an investigation is extremely low[33] and it is, de facto, within its discretion as to whether an investigation should be commenced. Investigators appointed by the UKLA[34] have broad powers to interview the person under investigation, and any person connected with that person[35] and require them to provide materials as requested,[36] as well as to require any person to provide specified documents at a specified time and place.[37]

4.39 HMRC has even more draconian information gathering powers where it suspects the commission of a serious tax fraud and believes documents evidencing the suspected fraud are held on premises.[38] It can obtain from a judge a warrant authorizing a dawn raid on the premises[39] or those of a third party on notice.[40] Anyone who destroys, conceals, falsifies or disposes of relevant documents may be imprisoned. It also has extensive investigatory and information gathering powers in the indirect tax field.[41]

4.40 The OFT has similarly broad investigation powers where it has reasonable grounds for suspecting that there has been an infringement of the competition provisions, although the OFT cannot generally compel statements from individuals as is the

---

3. A person who was at the material time a director (which includes shadow directors and de facto directors: FSMA 2000, s 417) of a listed corporate or applicant for listing has been 'knowingly concerned' in a breach of the Listing Rules (or Disclosure Rules and Transparency Rules or Prospectus Rules) by the listed corporate or applicant; or
4. A criminal offence under FSMA 2000, s 85 may have been committed.
Note that the FSA has additional powers against directors who are also 'approved persons' and corporates which are also 'authorised persons'. See FSMA 2000, s 97 and FSA Handbook at EG 3.10.

[33] It need only 'appear to [the UKLA]' that there are 'circumstances suggesting' one of the criteria is satisfied (and, in two of the three, only circumstances suggesting that there 'may have been'). There do not need to be, for example, reasonable grounds for suspecting that a breach has occurred.

[34] He or she is treated as though he or she were appointed under FSMA 2000, s 167(1): FSMA 2000, s 97(3)(a).

[35] The meaning of 'connected persons' in this context broadly includes not only affiliated companies, controllers and partnerships of which the person under investigation is a member, but also the company's employees, agents, appointed representatives, solicitors, bankers, auditors and/or actuaries (and those of other group members): FSMA 2000, s 171(4).

[36] Insofar as he or she reasonably considers the material to be relevant to the purposes of the investigation: FSMA 2000, s 171 and FSA Handbook at EG 3.

[37] Unless the investigation is into whether one of the criminal offences in FSMA 2000, s 85 may have been committed, only documents can be obtained from unconnected third parties, not information or answers to questions: FSMA 2000, s 172 applied by FSMA 2000, s 97(3).

[38] HMRC is reviewing its powers with a view to strengthening them significantly. It is intended that VAT-style inspections will be adopted in the direct tax field (eg unannounced visits to taxpayers in order to make 'real time' checks on their tax records). HMRC's information powers are likely to be extended (eg to enable it to require a company to prepare new documents or provide explanations). Civil penalties will be stiffened.

[39] Taxes Management Act 1970, s 20C.

[40] Taxes Management Act 1970, s 20BA.

[41] VAT Act 1994, Sch 11. Many of these mirror, but some are more extensive than, those that apply to direct taxes (eg a right to enter premises with or without a warrant in order to carry out an inspection).

case for some other regulators. The OFT has civil powers of investigation under the Competition Act 1998 and criminal powers of investigation under the Enterprise Act 2002. Utilizing its civil powers, the OFT can require the production of documents on written notice,[42] carry out an on-site investigation of business premises without a warrant,[43] or carry out an on-site investigation of both business and domestic premises with a warrant.[44] If the OFT has reasonable grounds for suspecting that a cartel offence has been committed and has 'good reason' to exercise its investigatory powers it can conduct a criminal investigation in which it can require individuals to answer questions, produce documents and provide information on written notice, as well as carry out on-site investigations of business and domestic premises with a warrant.[45]

As expected, the SFO has the most complete powers, in particular based on section 2 of the Criminal Justice Act 1987, to compel the production of any kind of evidence. This includes the attendance of individuals to be examined. These formal powers are routinely used in any investigation.   **4.41**

Extra-territorial jurisdiction

UK regulators are generally restricted to operating within the UK and can only operate extra-territorially through the cooperation of the relevant authorities in other countries. However, acts taking place overseas may still fall within the jurisdiction of UK regulators, either because they have sufficient impact within the UK (eg anti-competitive agreements entered into overseas in relation to UK markets) or because they are sufficiently within extra-territorial provisions (eg the extension of the jurisdiction in relation to overseas corruption brought about by the Anti-Terrorism, Crime and Security Act 2001).   **4.42**

For example, the UKLA has jurisdiction over corporates that have a listing in the UK irrespective of the nationality of the company.[46] If a corporate that is listed in   **4.43**

---

[42] Competition Act 1998, s 26. This requires that the person produces specified documents or specified information. The notice must indicate the subject matter and purpose of the investigation and the offences committed for failure to comply. The OFT may take copies of the documents and require explanations of the documents.

[43] Competition Act 1998, s 27. Although OFT officers exercising these powers can enter the premises, they do not have the power of search or to take away any original documents.

[44] Competition Act 1998, ss 28 and 28A. These permit OFT officers to enter premises, by force if necessary, search for relevant documents and take away originals of documents.

[45] Enterprise Act 2002, ss 193–94.

[46] A listed overseas company must comply with the requirements of the Listing Rules, Disclosure Rules and Transparency Rules and Prospectus Rules so far as (i) information available to it enables it to do so; and (ii) compliance is not contrary to the law in its country of incorporation: FSA Handbook at LR 1.4.2.

the UK commits a breach outside the UK, such as a failure to disclose 'inside information', it will be treated as if the act was committed inside the UK.

4.44 The FSA's jurisdiction is even broader than that of the UKLA if a corporate is also conducting specific regulated activities (eg a financial services institution, such as an investment business, bank or building society).[47] The obligation for 'authorised persons' to cooperate with the FSA[48] is not restricted to matters within the UK.[49]

4.45 In addition, market abuse can be committed by foreign corporates if the relevant events occur within the jurisdiction.[50] Even behaviour that takes place outside the UK may amount to market abuse in a variety of situations, for example, if activities on a non-UK market constitute behaviour that occurs in relation to qualifying investments on a UK prescribed market, such as where the price of the overseas investment is expressed by reference to the investment traded on a UK prescribed market. In these circumstances, it may be that an overseas regulatory authority will also have jurisdiction and both regulators may have an interest in pursuing enforcement action. In such circumstances, the FSA will work with the relevant overseas authority to coordinate effective enforcement action.

4.46 As a general proposition, the coordination between UK regulators and their overseas counterparties has dramatically increased.

- The SEC and the FSA are frequently cooperating (see for example the joint settlement and announcement in connection with the investigation into the misstatement of gas reserves by Royal Dutch Shell).

---

[47] Known as 'authorized persons': FSMA 2000, s 31(2)—permission to conduct regulated activities is given by the FSA. There may also be wider regulatory consequences for certain individuals within those 'authorized persons' who are performing certain functions within the organization, known as 'controlled functions', who need to have specific approval from the FSA for the performance of those functions. Such individuals are known as 'approved persons': FSMA 2000, Part V, particularly s 59. It is a criminal offence for unauthorized persons to conduct regulated activities: FSMA 2000, Part II to IV.

[48] Principle for Business 11 states: 'A firm must deal with its regulators in an open and co-operative way, and must disclose to the FSA appropriately anything relating to the firm of which the FSA would reasonably expect notice': FSA Handbook at PRIN 2.1.1. There is a similar obligation on 'approved persons' in Statement of Principle for Approved Persons 4: FSA Handbook at APER 2.1.2.

[49] In the case of CSFB International, the FSA disciplined CSFB despite the fact that the majority of the relevant events occurred in Japan and the primary charges were that CSFB engaged in conduct designed deliberately to mislead the Japanese regulatory and tax authorities and failed to organize and control its activities in Japan in a responsible manner: *CSFB International* final notice (11/12/02).

[50] For example, in the *Indigo Capital LLC* final notice (21/12/04), a limited liability company incorporated in New York was disciplined for market abuse in connection with the shares of a company listed on the London Stock Exchange.

- The OFT and the US Department of Justice (DoJ) cooperated in connection with the settlement with British Airways for competition infringements on fuel surcharges.
- The DoJ and the SFO have been cooperating in relation to corporate involvement in the various corruption issues arising at the United Nations.
- The FSA has been cooperating extensively with other European financial regulators in relation to various market abuse issues.
- The OFT is part of the European Competition Network, the collection of EU-wide competition agencies created by the European Commission to assist in the rational and coordinated combating of cross-border competition law offences in Europe.

The UK regulators have wide powers to release information to, and to coordinate **4.47** with, overseas regulators and the only basis upon which a corporate can operate when faced with an investigation is to assume that there will be disclosure to other regulators both within the UK and overseas when it is deemed appropriate.[51]

Protections

The protections available when a corporate or individual is under investigation **4.48** vary between the regulators. It is worth noting from the outset that the common law privilege against self-incrimination, comprising, inter alia, the right to silence, which enables a person to refuse to answer any question if the answer thereto would expose the person to any criminal charge or penalty (etc), is generally excluded in the context of investigations conducted pursuant to statutory powers, although varying degrees of statutory protections restricting the use which can be made of the compelled answers replace it.[52]

When under investigation by the UKLA or the FSA, there is no general right to **4.49** refuse to answer questions on the ground of privilege against self-incrimination,[53] even if it is a formal investigation being conducted pursuant to its statutory powers and the relevant individual has been compelled to attend an interview.[54] There is some limited statutory protection in terms of the use of a compulsorily obtained interview if the relevant individual is later charged with a criminal offence or subject to market abuse proceedings.[55] Any such compulsorily

---

[51] Considered further from 4.255.

[52] The statutory protections generally aim to ensure compliance with the decisions of the ECHR on the right to a fair trial under the European Convention on Human Rights, which UK courts are required to take into account under s 2 of the Human Rights Act 1998. See, for example, *Saunders v United Kingdom* [1996] ECHR 19187/91 and *Shannon v United Kingdom* (2006) 42 EHRR 31.

[53] FSMA 2000, s 174.

[54] Pursuant to, for example, FSMA 2000, s 171 and FSA Handbook at EG 3.

[55] FSMA 2000, s 174.

obtained statements cannot be used against the relevant individual although they can be used to obtain evidence through other means to be used in those proceedings.

4.50 Likewise, when under investigation by the SFO, the privilege against self-incrimination cannot be relied upon,[56] but limited statutory protections prevent statements obtained by a person in response to a requirement imposed by the SFO from being used in any criminal proceedings against the person making them[57] (except in very limited circumstances).

4.51 There are more protections available in the context of OFT investigations. The OFT can only take copies of documents within the scope of the investigation. Further, the OFT cannot require an undertaking to answer a limited class of incriminating or leading questions, or questions unconnected to the subject matter of the investigation. Statements given to the OFT during a civil investigation[58] cannot be used in a criminal prosecution brought against that person.[59] However, any documents obtained by the OFT during its civil investigation may be admissible in any subsequent criminal proceedings.

4.52 In all investigations in the UK, there are protections available for privileged documents, as discussed in Section I below. As elsewhere, in certain instances, it may be advantageous to corporates to waive privilege, at least to some extent, to demonstrate full cooperation and transparency.

Sanctions for failure to cooperate

4.53 Although a corporate may attempt to negotiate with regulators to try to protect its interests whilst under investigation, it will usually be the right advice, given the width of the regulators' formal powers, the continuing relationships with the regulators and the wider reputational position, that corporates cooperate with regulatory investigations, irrespective of whether there is a specific cooperation obligation. Cooperation will also usually assist the corporates in seeking reduced or mitigated penalties. The UK regulators generally have far-reaching powers to enforce cooperation with investigations, the application of which tend to be more detrimental to the corporate's position than willing cooperation.

4.54 The proactive duty of cooperation is a key obligation for 'authorised persons' and 'approved persons' within those entities, which are financial institutions.

---

[56] The SFO has broad information requesting powers under the Criminal Justice Act 1987, s 2.
[57] Criminal Justice Act 1987, s 2(8) and (8AA).
[58] Under the Competition Act 1998.
[59] Under the Enterprise Act 2002 or the Criminal Justice Act 1987.

The duty expressly includes an obligation to self-report breaches.[60] Failure can, itself, lead to enforcement proceedings.[61]

However, other listed corporates also have an obligation to deal with the FSA and **4.55** the UKLA in an open and cooperative manner, breach of which could expose the corporate, or any directors 'knowingly concerned' in the breach, to sanctions.[62] The sanctions available to the UKLA (or the FSA) for a failure to cooperate with a regulatory investigation are the same as for a breach of any other of the Listing Rules (or Disclosure Rules and Transparency Rules or Prospectus Rules).

Failure to comply with a requirement imposed by an investigator may carry a **4.56** number of other consequences including a court treating the person as though he or she were in contempt of court;[63] the FSA obtaining a warrant to search the premises;[64] or the corporate and its directors or employees being charged with criminal offences.[65] If the relevant person is also an 'authorised person' or an 'approved person', it could lead to wider regulatory repercussions, for example the variation of the listed corporate's permission[66] or the withdrawal of the individual's approval.[67]

---

[60] The obligation of cooperation imposed on 'authorized persons' (and 'approved persons' within those entities) is to 'deal with its regulators in an open and co-operative way, and must disclose to the FSA appropriately anything relating to the firm of which the FSA would reasonably expect notice' (Principle for Business 11 set out in the FSA Handbook at PRIN 2.1.1 and Statement of Principle for Approved Persons 4 set out in the FSA Handbook at APER 2.1.2). Not only does the obligation of cooperation include an express obligation to self-report breaches of the regulatory obligations of the 'authorised person' but the duty to cooperate is not restricted to the FSA or to matters within the jurisdiction, but extends to an obligation to cooperate with all of its regulators, including overseas regulators. Hence, a failure by an 'authorized person' to cooperate with one of its overseas regulators could give rise to enforcement proceedings by the FSA in the UK (and this is expressly set out in the case of 'approved persons' in the FSA Handbook at APER 4.4.2). The obligation to self-report is considered further from 4.124.

[61] It is important to note that cooperation does not necessarily mean acceptance of the regulator's view of there having been a breach of the rules, nor acceptance of any proposed penalty. (However, if the listed corporate settles disciplinary action early, a discount will be applied to the financial penalty imposed.) The corporate can contest both these issues (even as far as the Financial Services and Markets Tribunal) but still cooperate in other ways.

[62] Listing Principle 6, introduced with effect from 1 July 2005: FSA Handbook at LR 7.2.1. In addition, there are specific rules requiring listed corporates, 'persons discharging managerial responsibilities' and 'connected persons' to provide information to the UKLA when requested to do so: FSA Handbook at LR 1.3.1 and DTR 1.3.1.

[63] FSMA 2000, s 177, applied by FSMA 2000, s 97(3)(a).

[64] FSMA 2000, s 176, applied by FSMA 2000, s 97(3)(a).

[65] Such as knowingly or recklessly providing false or misleading information in purported compliance with a requirement imposed during a statutory investigation (FSMA 2000, s 177(4), applied by FSMA 2000, s 97(3)(a), and s 398) (although a simple failure to provide information ought not, without more, of itself constitute a criminal offence); and falsifying, concealing, destroying or otherwise disposing of a document (or causing or permitting another to do so) that the person knows or suspects is or would be relevant to an investigation which he or she knows or suspects is being or is likely to be conducted by the UKLA (FSMA 2000, s 177(3), applied by FSMA 2000, s 97(3)(a)).

[66] FSMA 2000, s 45.

[67] FSMA 2000, s 63.

4.57 If a corporate is invited by HMRC to make full disclosure of all irregularities and it does so, it can avoid prosecution. However, failure to comply with HMRC investigations, and/or the destruction, concealment or falsification of documents can have severe consequences for a company and its employees resulting in imprisonment and detriment to the company's relationship with HMRC.[68]

4.58 Failure to comply with an OFT investigation that is conducted through either its civil or criminal powers[69] is a criminal offence for which both the corporate and its officers can be liable.[70] Penalties for failure to comply with the investigation; obstructing an authorized officer carrying out an inspection with or without a warrant; destroying, concealing, falsifying documents; or providing false or misleading information can be as severe as unlimited fines or imprisonment. Similar penalties apply for a failure to comply with an SFO investigation.

D. Voluntary Investigations

Benefits and risks of voluntary investigations

4.59 Aside from conducting an investigation 'defensively', in the teeth of regulatory enforcement activity, corporates in the UK commonly investigate a potential problem for two principal other reasons.

4.60 First, as part of a proactive relationship with a regulator, it may well be a highly appropriate way of managing the regulatory interest in the issue. This is particularly so if there is a self-reporting obligation, or incentive,[71] where not only is it necessary to investigate sufficiently to report appropriately and accurately but, typically, the corporation is required to give full (and very extensive) ongoing cooperation, with the resolution of further questions raised by the regulator being undertaken by the corporation, to a high standard, internally. This is typically the case in leniency situations.

4.61 Secondly, even if there is no self-reporting obligation (or incentive) or anticipated regulatory interest, it may be substantive good corporate governance to investigate. Compliance standards are generally regarded as increasing in this area in the UK. The circumstances could range from a major corporate scandal, raising possible issues of dishonesty, malpractice or reckless risk-taking, to matters of poor

---

[68] Taxes Management Act 1970, s 20BB.

[69] Under the Competition Act 1998 or under the Enterprise Act 2002.

[70] Competition Act 1998, s 42. Officers in this context mean a director, manager, secretary or other similar officer of the company or a person purporting to act in such capacity.

[71] Considered further from 4.124.

judgement or internal failures to meet more subtle ethical or behavioural standards. The benefits include being seen by stakeholders (including shareholders, capital market opinion formers (and the press), counterparties, customers and employees) as having enforced high standards of behaviour and being prepared to improve them for the future. However, they also extend substantively to: improving the corporation's systems and controls, and thereby managing its risk profile; the intangible benefits of the enhancements to the brand from high standards of governance; and the impact on the internal culture as to the behavioural standards that are expected to be observed.

It does not follow that there should be publicity for such an investigation: that **4.62** may or may not be the case, depending on the facts. Some of these internal benefits do not, in fact, require external publicity and it may be much more appropriate to act discreetly. Moreover, if there were subsequently to be publicity, or a further event which resulted in previous experiences being considered by an agency (particularly a criminal one), the behaviour of the corporation in dealing with earlier issues (the so-called 'wake-up calls') can be critical to the public and regulatory reaction to the later event. Appropriate action, and documentation of such action, may be critical in obtaining a sympathetic view of regulators in the future and in managing and mitigating penalties risks.[72]

Non-executive directors frequently have a close interest in such matters, given **4.63** their responsibilities for the governance of the company and the potential impact on their personal reputations from their actions when faced with such issues. This type of wholly private internal investigation is increasingly being seen in the UK.

There is no express formal or regulatory requirement on a listed corporate to **4.64** conduct an investigation when it identifies that there might be a rule breach or other problem.[73] However, Listing Principle 6, requires that 'a listed corporate must deal with the FSA in an open and co-operative manner'.[74] Whilst this falls short of the full self-reporting obligation to the FSA of regulated entities[75] if the UKLA asks the listed corporate to undertake an internal investigation, it would be expected do so.

---

[72] Particularly in the US, this prior conduct is highly relevant in the case of a later incident.

[73] Note that the FSA has the power to require an 'authorised person' to produce a report on any matter reasonably required in connection with the exercise by the FSA of its statutory functions: FSMA 2000, s 166. The person appointed to produce the report must be nominated or approved by the FSA and appear to the FSA to have the skills necessary to make a report on the matter concerned (known as a 'skilled person').

[74] FSA Handbook at LR 7.2.1.

[75] Considered further from 4.124.

4.65 Moreover, the listed corporate will want to consider what, if any, steps it should take to ensure that the problem does not reoccur in the future. It is important to establish not only what happened, but why it happened. The corporate's response to an issue is of itself a part of the corporate's systems and controls; and they, in turn, are a specific regulatory requirement as a result of Listing Principle 2. This requires that a 'listed corporate must take reasonable steps to establish and maintain adequate procedures, systems and controls to enable it to comply with its obligations'.[76]

4.66 Addressing any issue properly, 'fairly and squarely' (and making sure it should not reoccur) is likely to be an important part of demonstrating that a listed corporate takes reasonable care to establish and maintain adequate procedures, systems and controls to enable it to comply with its regulatory obligations. If there may have been improper practices somewhere in a company's activities, it is very important that senior management, and particularly the non-executive directors, can be confident that it has accurate and unbiased information as to what has occurred and clear advice on the steps necessary to remedy the problem properly for the future. Senior management needs to be able to give shareholders and regulators sufficient confidence that the company is meeting high standards of behaviour and is under proper control.

4.67 Moreover, directors can incur liability for knowing involvement in rule breaches. To date, this provision has only been applied in more extreme cases, in particular when a director was not informing a market efficiently and promptly of price sensitive information.[77] However, the concept of director liability has been established. Further, the practice of UK regulators generally has been to focus on breaches of general principles and, particularly, reporting and controls, rather than specific or detailed breaches. Accordingly, an increasing focus on senior management's high performance in investigating and resolving potential issues is likely to become more and more influential in deciding whether to sanction either the corporate or a given individual.

4.68 Conducting an internal investigation does not necessarily mean that the UKLA will not conduct its own investigation. However, it may be that, by means of its internal investigation, the corporate will be able to persuade the UKLA that no breaches of the relevant rules have occurred or, if they have, that, in less severe cases, no enforcement proceedings should be brought because the matter has been comprehensively addressed voluntarily by the undertaking.

---

[76] FSA Handbook at LR 7.2.1.

[77] The FSA first used its statutory powers to fine a director for being 'knowingly concerned' in a corporate's breach of the Listing Rules in 2004. *Sportsworld Media Group/Geoffrey John Brown* final notice (29/03/04); *Universal Salvage PLC/ Martin Christoper Hynes* final notice (19/05/04).

Common events triggering a voluntary investigation

A common trigger, in the UK, for an investigation is regulatory action, in partic- **4.69**
ular a sudden transition, or threatened transition, into enforcement (which dramatically increases management's focus on an issue), or a dawn raid or other
unforeseen hostile action by a regulator. Regulatory derived action may also come
from more routine themed visits, and the like, in the supervisory context whereby
a concern comes to light in a less threatening way.

However, a wider variety of other causes may be relevant. Whistle-blowers are **4.70**
increasingly prevalent (whether they have good or bad motives) and are protected
to a significant degree by legislation,[78] whether they are whistle-blowing internally or externally. It will be rare that a well-run company with high standards of
governance will not want to investigate any whistle-blower action which is not
clearly spurious. Not least, it will want to be able to say later that any allegations
have been investigated properly and appropriate action taken.

Unusual trading patterns, particularly in the financial services or securities **4.71**
sector, frequently give rise to a need for an investigation, particularly given the
self-reporting obligations and the close ongoing nature of the relationship with
the FSA. For example, there have been recent examples of regulatory interest in
Payment Protection Insurance, the mis-selling of consumer financial products,
and the holding of 'orphan' financial accounts or of credit balances to
customers who were not collecting their assets (in the case of non-financial sector
entities) to name but a few. The raising of such matters can, and arguably should,
prompt proper internal action by a well-governed corporation. It may not be
under regulatory scrutiny itself, but is aware of the issue because attention
has fallen on its competitors. Prudent management takes stock of whether its
company might have a related exposure in the light of its knowledge of its own
operations.

Apart from governance and general reputational issues, there are more general, **4.72**
but powerful, reasons under criminal law why appropriate investigations should
be undertaken. There is an increasing criminalization of corporate malpractice
under UK legislation. It is important to ensure that neither the company (which
can, in certain circumstances, incur criminal liability) nor its employees are
exposed to criminal investigation. Such processes are highly invasive and divisive.
The spectre of criminal liability is highly damaging and can have a profound
effect on a corporate's reputation and the trust reposed in its management. Two
areas are particularly relevant in the UK.

---

[78] Considered further from 4.270.

4.73 The Proceeds of Crime Act 2002 (POCA), which came into force in February 2003, extended the scope of money-laundering offences and introduced various reporting requirements in respect of money-laundering. POCA introduced three principal offences arising from involvement in acts that may constitute part of the money-laundering process.[79] The offence of money laundering is committed unless those concerned go through a disclosure and consent process from SOCA[80] before they carry out the relevant act. The particular relevance of this legislation is that it now encompasses overseas corruption, with the result that agencies can allege that either dividends remitted or intra-group payments from subsidiaries that have been engaged in corruption are proceeds of crime and infect the treasury operations of the wider group. This can bring about a de facto self-reporting obligation in relation to overseas corruption. In addition to the principal offences, offences may be committed when someone in the 'regulated sector'[81] fails to disclose knowledge or suspicion that another person is involved in money laundering. The penalties for breaches of POCA include fines and up to 14 years imprisonment.

4.74 As another example, the Theft Act 1968 expressly brings wrongfully retained property within its scope.[82] This is of particular relevance to, for example, trading companies, where they receive funds in excess of those required to satisfy a customer's account as a result of that customer's mistake. If such funds are, for example, not recorded as a liability of the company but instead transferred to the company's income statement in circumstances where there is no attempt to make restitution to the customer or notify it of the mistake, then the company may be charged with theft. This is because property 'belonging to another' is broadly defined to expressly include property received by another's mistake where there exists an obligation to make restoration of the property or the value thereof.[83] In such circumstances, an intention not to make restoration to the customer might be regarded as an intention to deprive the customer of the property or proceeds. By keeping or dealing with such property as owner (in this example by

---

[79] Broadly speaking an offence is committed by doing one or more of the following:
  • acquiring, using, or having possession of criminal property;
  • concealing, disguising, converting, transferring criminal property, or removing it from any part of the UK; and
  • becoming concerned in an arrangement that facilitates the acquisition, retention, use or control of criminal property.

[80] The Serious Organised Crime Agency. For further information about the disclosure and consent process, see <http://www.soca.gov.uk/financialIntel/disclosure.html>.

[81] Members of the regulated sector include, among others, lawyers involved in financial or real property transactions, and anyone advising on deals in investments.

[82] Theft is defined by the Theft Act 1968 as 'dishonestly appropriat[ing] property belonging to another with the intention of permanently depriving the other of it': s 1(1).

[83] Theft Act 1968, s 5(4).

recording it as a profit of the company) notwithstanding that the property was come by innocently, might be regarded as an appropriation of that property.[84]

However an investigation will not automatically follow any possible concern. Investigations incur cost, disrupt (at least to some degree) the usual running of a business and set in train a process which can have unintended consequences. It is a matter of judgement in each case, depending on such considerations as:

- the degree of concern;
- the size of the issue;
- the risk of regulatory action or stakeholder interest (in context: might it be the sort of issue which, in the light of other concerns, might have increased impact or might suggest a culture of inappropriate behaviour?);
- the prospects of any possible disposal requiring the giving of warranties as to the business concerned which might have significant later financial consequences;
- the seniority of those potentially involved or responsible;
- the possibility for the matter to be 'the tip of an iceberg', with much wider ramifications;
- the capacity of line management to deal fully with the issues; and
- the cultural impact (positive and negative) of an investigation with its potentially invasive and disruptive impact.

However, a properly constituted and effective investigation is one of the range **4.75** of possible appropriate management reactions to possible compliance breaches and an option that should be specifically considered, even it is then rejected on a reasoned basis. It may, indeed, be appropriate and beneficial, from a governance perspective, expressly to have considered and rejected the possibility.

Structuring an internal investigation

If it is decided to conduct an investigation, it is important to establish it on a **4.76** proper, and sometimes quite formal, basis. In the UK, this will usually involve a consideration of the following factors:

- Who should comprise the sponsoring group within the company, which will be responsible for overall control and direction?
- How can the process be isolated from internal political sensitivities or interference?
- What is the scope of the process, how are excursions from scope monitored and controlled (the investigation should not become an end in itself nor fall victim

---

[84] Theft Act 1968, s 3(1). Dishonesty would still need to be established.

to the trap of becoming unfocused roving enquiry) and what procedures are in place to deal with appropriate refinements of scope?

• What is the source of corporate authority that will be necessary to ensure full and effective cooperation with the investigation process?

• Who is supplying the resources to ensure an effective process, particularly internally?

• What is the operational, and final, reporting structure?

• Is there an effective division and relationship between (i) the detailed fact finding and legal analysis and (ii) the taking of wider decisions as to the appropriate corporate conduct such as communications, self-reporting, dismissing/suspending staff, dealing with customers' reactions, changes to practices etc?

4.77 The answers to such issues will be very fact specific and will to a large extent depend on the culture of the company concerned and the management style of those executives involved. However, within the UK environment, the factors discussed below commonly feature in these decisions.

The sponsoring group

4.78 It will be essential, as a basic rule of good governance, that the sponsoring or controlling person or body cannot have had responsibility for the events being investigated. If it were not the case, there would simply be no credibility for the process. Whatever the actual quality or benefit of the work, it would have little value for external parties and is likely to have its value undermined. It could also lead to the corporation's and individual's reputation for good governance being damaged. An alleged 'cover-up' can be more damaging than the underlying event.

4.79 This, means ideally, that the ultimate responsibility for the process should lie outside line management and certainly line management that has had any responsibility for the matters at issue. This does create issues since it will frequently be impossible to say, at the outset, that the line management (possibly senior line management) cannot have had any responsibility for any malpractice, given its responsibility for setting standards, creating the right ethical climate and instituting systems and controls. However, this is ultimately a matter of degree and judgement. If the circumstances are such that someone in line management should be the sponsor of the process, it may well be sensible to support that line manager with some independent party (either an external adviser, or a senior internal person) to protect the line manager from any later allegations that his or her judgement might have been affected by the prospect of any level (possibly very small) of responsibility for what might have occurred.

4.80 In the UK, the audit committee, or its chairman, or the senior independent director, or a non-executive director who has specific skills or an interest in the relevant area would frequently be an appropriate choice to lead the process. It is not unknown for specific committees to be set up, perhaps involving prominent external parties with no prior involvement with the corporate concerned. This is particularly so where the issues are significant and important and could affect senior management, or issues of culture, ethics or systems that go to the heart of the organization. Where that is not the case, alternatives include the General Counsel, the Head of Compliance, the Finance Director/Chief Financial Officer, the Head of Internal Audit or a senior executive in an unrelated division of the business.

Naturally, it is critical that the individual taking such a position has the resources **4.81** (particularly time) to fulfil the role properly. It is also important to ensure that the responsibility, authority and accountability are clearly vested in that individual from the outset. If the matter has an external profile, it is particularly important to consider whether the person would be an appropriate public face for the company. There can be enormous value in having the investigation under the ultimate authority of (say) a non-executive director of recognized authority and integrity who can credibly represent to stakeholders, without necessarily disclosing confidential matters and thereby potentially damaging the interests of the company or its customers, that the matter has been properly and fully investigated, what has been said publicly is an accurate and fair reflection of the results and that the action taken has been appropriate with nothing further being necessary. In such circumstances, non-executive directors can 'come into their own' and provide great value to the company.

The sponsor, or those supporting and advising him or her, must be able to predict **4.82** political reactions within the company and take steps to ensure that they do not undermine the process. It is not unknown for powerful divisions within a corporation, often led by charismatic or strong leaders, to reject 'interference' with 'their' business in the sense of an investigation and to act to undermine it. The senior part of the project team needs to be able to anticipate such disruption and defuse it.

The scope of the investigation

There is often a value in having a clearly defined scope for an investigation, **4.83** possibly even with written terms of reference in appropriate cases. This may seem like bureaucracy or excessive process and terms can be difficult to define bearing in mind that the extent of the issue is likely to be unclear at the beginning of an investigation. However:

- it can be an excellent discipline;
- an investigation is likely to be ineffective unless it is targeted;

- it can provide clear internal authority;
- it focuses the minds of both the investigation team, and perhaps more critically, senior management on the precise issues of concern, and the objectives of the investigation process;
- it controls 'mission creep'; and
- if there is likely to be any external interest, whether at the outset, or at a later stage, it is likely that it will be necessary to state clearly exactly what has been investigated.

4.84 The exact scope of the investigation is key. If the scope is too narrow, or artificial, the investigation risks having no value on the basis of a suspicion that it has been manipulated to avoid the issue and by being characterized as simply a ruse by management to delay or deflect attention. If is too wide, it may be impossible for the process ever to be completed properly to the required detail. This can have the result that any report is so qualified that it raises more doubts than it resolves and that it is impossible honestly to announce an end to the process.

4.85 It is also the case that a change of scope is often sensitive, particularly where a matter is in the public eye. Indeed, it may be the case that where the fact and/or results of an investigation are price sensitive and have to be announced to the capital markets [85] that a change of scope will also have to be announced. It is extremely unattractive to have to announce a change in scope because it will almost inevitably be perceived as an increase in scope and as indicating further or bigger 'problems' than had first been suspected. This will have a negative effect on share price and reputation.

4.86 However, where scope is formally defined, it is important for the integrity of the process that there is a mechanism for the investigation team to revert to the sponsors if they have found matters which seem to be of concern but which go outside the defined scope. A typical example would be emails or oral evidence indicating that similar activities occurred in another part of the business. It is critical for corporate governance purposes that there is a proper process for deciding whether those other matters should be examined. This would usually involve the sponsor, or sponsor group, reviewing a recommendation from the investigation team, consulting as necessary, and reaching a reasoned (and probably recorded) decision on whether any amendment to scope, at the relevant time, was required.

4.87 It is, therefore, good practice to include in the terms of reference a clear statement that they are based on the *ex ante* assessment of the issues and that the investigation team is charged with raising any issues that it identifies which may require further investigation but, conversely, that it is not authorized to investigate such matters on an independent or self-authorized basis. Not only can unfettered authority be very

---

[85] Considered from 4.132.

threatening and disruptive internally, it also makes it very difficult to present conclusions or results clearly: it is difficult to claim that a job that needed doing, but which was not defined, has ever been done, never mind done well.

Finally, defining the scope and roles of those involved may well have an impact **4.88** on the degree of legal privilege available to an investigation. Privilege looks at the substance of the relationships and then at whether communications are protected.[86] It is not possible to 're-badge' an exercise to give it privilege. However, accurately defining the actual nature of the relationships and work being done and advice given is important to ensuring that such privilege as is available is available and evidenced.

Appropriate corporate authority

There is a close link between scope and authority. It is fundamental that any **4.89** investigation must be granted sufficient authority to enable it to achieve its purpose. It might well be that the sponsor does not have the necessary authority, *ex officio*, within the organization, but that authority can be supplied by an appropriate individual, like the Chief Executive Officer, confirming that the process has his or her personal backing and requiring full compliance with the requirements of the investigation from all staff. Sufficiently empowering the investigation is essential because, even with the best and most sensitive investigative processes, it should not be underestimated how defensive parts of organizations can become if they sense that they personally, or by comparison with others, are under threat. This defensiveness manifests itself in presenting difficulties in releasing documents, delaying tactics, partial answers to interviews etc. Whilst there are sound investigation techniques for addressing such issues, the best way to clear any such obstacles is to have high authority and support, within the company, for the process. Such authority can only appropriately be given by a responsible senior officer where the scope is properly defined.

Resources

A proper consideration of resources at the outset is important. Investigations are **4.90** usually done under considerable time pressure. The volumes of documents to examine may be very considerable, particularly given the inevitable email searches. Obtaining and reviewing electronic material and assembling databases (which is almost always appropriate) requires specialist skills and software (particularly if the full value is to be obtained). The review process can be time consuming and it is helpful to have access to experience in the analysis of documents and the building of scenarios, chronologies, patterns of relationships, flows of information

---

[86] Considered from 4.207.

and so forth that make it possible to form some sensible assessment of the fact pattern that the documentary record will (usually only partially) reveal.

4.91 Moreover, any investigation is likely to involve interviews with employees on sensitive matters. It is important to have people with the necessary skills for, and experience of, conducting such interviews and who know how to prepare for them and obtain the best from them. There are also a variety of different interview techniques: the best interviews are not necessarily hostile or cross-examining type, even when there are reasons to suspect the motives of the witness.

4.92 Corporations may have these skills in-house, particularly within the legal department or the internal audit teams. However, the necessary resource does need to be fully available and committed, even though the total size of the task may be difficult to predict at the outset.

4.93 Whether the resources are primarily internal or external, it is usually invaluable (and a considerable saving of cost) to have as, at least, one member of the investigation team a sufficiently senior individual from within the corporation. The institutional knowledge that such an individual can bring, together with the understanding of culture and relationships can dramatically enhance the quality of an investigation. Issues (and non-issues) can be much more rapidly identified with the benefit of 'insider' knowledge.

Reporting structure

4.94 The reporting and control systems for any investigation will be highly context-specific. It will usually be essential, however, for the operational investigation team to have in place processes for considering the information that they are gathering on an evolving basis and reporting regularly. The regular control may well be at a level below that of the sponsor (indeed that will often be the most effective). However, it will usually be helpful for there to be higher level reporting sessions at the sponsor level so that the sponsor's understanding of the issues evolves as the investigation proceeds. In this way, the sponsor is in a position to redirect effort, to adjust the position and actions of the corporation accordingly and to anticipate the likely outcome and conclusions and to prepare the way for them. This role can be critical to an investigation which is successful not just in the sense that it reaches the right answers but also in that it has a beneficial impact on, or for, the company.

4.95 It is almost inevitable that those conducting the investigation get very close to the precise issues and there is a risk that they can become personally quite committed to particular concepts or individuals. Where an investigation is into matters that are of serious concern for the company, it is usually invaluable to ensure that, at the sponsor level, there is senior expertise that can exercise a more independent, or second, judgement. The issues which are likely to arise for that judgement are the seriousness of the findings, and their implications for the corporation, the nature of any conclusions or recommendations (or the comment on them if they are not to be the views of the sponsor but, say, of an external professional firm), communications strategy, the resulting governance or systems and controls changes and the implementation of recommendations.

As important, is the ability of the sponsor to decide when an investigation is **4.96** reaching diminishing returns. Investigations tend to develop a momentum and purpose of their own. To a point, this is good and necessary to ensure that they are effective. However, there needs to be senior oversight to ensure that they do not progress to the level where they are investigating for their own sake. There will inevitably be a stage when, even if every detail is not clear, there is sufficient certainty for appropriate management action to be determined and for it to be possible for the corporation to take a view that all necessary steps to conclude a matter have been taken or can be defined and a proper programme to implement them agreed. At some point, it will be necessary for the corporation to 'draw a line' and 'move on'. In practice, it is usually fairly clear when less information is being obtained and the investigation is filling in detail, rather than changing the picture. But it may not be very clear to the investigation team itself.

Where there is an active regulatory interface, of course, the requirements of the **4.97** regulator need to be borne in mind and may well affect precisely where that line is to be drawn. However, even the most aggressive regulator will eventually accept that the answers to its outstanding questions are simply not available from within a corporation's resources and that the regulator must use its wider powers to seek information from third parties if it is to make progress. It is, therefore, valuable to ensure that the sponsor is able to take control of this relationship, interfacing, or controlling the interface, with the regulator to prevent wasted effort and, possibly, damage being done to the operations of the organization for no further benefit to the investigation or the regulator.

In essence, it is critical that, in such circumstances, there is credibility for the con- **4.98** clusion that there is nothing more that is material that is likely to be discovered. This will flow from the quality of the work and the hard evidence of the process, as well as the authority of those exercising the judgement on this delicate issue.

It is critical that the sponsor level for the investigation has proper communications **4.99** with, and can invite into the process, other parties closely affected by any investigation. The identity of such parties will depend on the nature and size of the issues, but could easily include legal advisers, the investor relations team, senior human resources support, audit committee or non-executive board members, as well as the corporation's brokers or auditors.

'First day' steps

4.100   Irrespective of the actual structure of the investigation, there are a number of 'first day' steps to be considered which are of high importance.

4.101   It will be crucial that appropriate steps are taken to preserve evidence at the outset.[87] An investigation, obviously, can be frustrated by evidence destruction. However, whether deliberate or accidental, it is potentially catastrophic as regards the views of any regulators, the courts or stakeholders (as encouraged by the press). The object lesson of the collapse of Arthur Andersen only serves to illustrate that the impact of the destruction of evidence may outweigh the underlying issue. Inevitably, the worst inferences are drawn.

4.102   Although the position in the UK may not yet be quite as serious as in the US, it is of enormous value to be able to show that all the usual steps have been taken to preserve evidence. Failure to do so, irrespective of whether destruction can be shown to have occurred, also undermines the credibility of those charged with the responsibility for the matter and may well affect the wider view taken by the authorities of the ethics and reliability of those concerned. It is wholly acceptable in UK practice to send strongly worded memoranda and take quite forceful action, including locking down IT systems, to ensure that the documentary record is protected. This is frequently done without seeking any internal consents of those involved (although the employee relations implications need to be considered). There is no difficulty with (accurately) presenting this as part of the usual and appropriate corporate process and not carrying any particular stigma or admission of guilt but rather as being best practice. There are, naturally, issues as to how wide such processes should go, and for how long they should remain in place. Whilst these are matters for judgement, on advice, on the specific facts, a corporation is usually justified in being very conservative in this area and would be reckless to take risks.

4.103   Further issues to be considered at the outset of any matter, again on the specific facts, include whether:

- it is necessary to notify insurers where there is relevant cover. This may be necessary either because of notification requirements in the policy providing any relevant cover or in the context of disclosures on renewal of cover;
- it is necessary to notify any regulators[88] or make a market announcement;[89]
- any conduct needs to be stopped or suspended immediately given its possible consequences (particularly if it might be criminal). It is sometimes tempting to

---

[87] Considered from 4.152.
[88] Considered from 4.124.
[89] Considered from 4.132.

continue the conduct for a short period to keep it under surveillance and understand its nature and the responsibilities involved, but this clearly, needs very careful advice and control;[90]

- any steps need to be taken to secure any assets, relationships or individuals in any way;
- there are customers or counterparties who should be informed (which may raise, at an early stage, issues of restitution);
- any action taken by the company might give rise to publicity which is actively unhelpful to the investigation—although this is rarely a long-term issue in practice, because the fact of an investigation rapidly becomes known; and
- any action could amount to tipping off parties.[91.]

It will almost always be necessary to consider both internal and external communications. If an announcement to the capital markets is required,[92] then the issue of external communications is immediately engaged. However, even if not required, a corporation may well decide that it is appropriate proactively to say something about an investigation or the underlying circumstances. At the least, given the risk of leaks, it is usually appropriate to brief the communications team and to have prepared a defensive press release so that in the event of publicity surrounding an issue, an appropriate response can be made. **4.104**

As important, perhaps more important, are the internal communications. Not only do they need to be consistent, both amongst themselves and with external communications, but they offer an important opportunity to send the right signals to the organization about culture, ethics, support for individuals, a lack of tolerance of certain forms of behaviour and so forth. Moreover, good internal communications ensure that customers and counterparties receive consistent messages as to the position from the people that they know within the corporation. This can be an important part of controlling the message (or the way that it is interpreted). **4.105**

---

[90] Considered further from 4.121.

[91] Proceeds of Crime Act 2002, s 333 (now repealed and replaced with s 333A) introduced the offence of tipping off. Tipping off applies in the regulated sector and is committed if, knowing that a disclosure of information relating to a possible money laundering offence (where that information came to the person making the original disclosure in the course of a business in the regulated sector) has been made under POCA to the law enforcement authorities, a person makes a disclosure which is 'likely to prejudice any investigation' (again, where the information so disclosed came to the person in the course of a business in the regulated sector). In practice, this would include, in the regulated sector, making any kind of communication which could make people involved aware that concerns about money laundering had been raised with SOCA. There are some limited exceptions between lawyer and client in regards to privileged information; however it is recommended that advice is sought before discussing any issue associated with a SOCA disclosure.

[92] Considered from 4.132.

Using external advisers

Is there any need to use external advisers at all?

4.106   As already noted, a company may well conduct its own internal investigation. However, there are a number of reasons why it may be advisable to bring in external advisers to be part of the investigation team or, as is often the case, to run the investigation under the direction of the sponsor. The relevant external advisers are typically external counsel or forensic accountants. However, the company may also have to consider whether it requires the assistance of other advisers such as external auditors, experts on discrete matters associated with the investigation, or private investigators. Advisers with specialist forensic IT (particularly) and accounting skills will usually be required. It is also frequently the case that it is helpful to understand the background to individuals or relationships or matters external to the company where private investigators are better placed to be able to efficiently provide information. There are constraints, however, under the law on their doing so and great care must be exercised when instructing them, in order to ensure that they do not gather information illegally.

4.107   Good external advisers often have greater experience than the company itself in conducting investigations and can efficiently project manage an investigation as well as provide the additional resources and manpower necessary to conduct an investigation quickly. Large law and accountancy firms have cross-border capabilities which can be of great use to companies if the investigation has any multi-jurisdictional element. External advisers will usually have greater experience in key areas such as witness interviews, gathering and the analysis of evidence, and report writing, which a corporate will not maintain as part of its internal resources. Indeed, if they do not bring these skills, it is questionable whether they should be retained.

4.108   For matters entirely within the UK, there is no legal reason why the choice between internal and external legal advisers should have any impact on the extent to which privilege is available to protect any communications. However, there are two critical reasons why external legal advisers may offer a higher degree of protection. First, as a general rule, internal legal advisers are not regarded by civil law systems as having the necessary degree of independence for the related concept of confidentiality (which fulfils some of the same functions as privilege under the common law system) to apply. This is particularly critical in the anti-trust area where the application of EU competition law does not recognize privilege for internal legal advisers.[93] Accordingly, in an increasingly international context

---

[93] In *155/79 AM & S v Commission* [1982] ECR 1575, the ECJ held that, in the context of investigations by the European Commission into allegedly anti-competitive conduct, privilege only protects written communications between lawyers and clients if the following conditions are met:
- the communications in question were made for the purposes and in the interests of the client's rights of defence and

where matters may easily attract the attention of regulators or litigants in other jurisdictions, there is a greater degree of security associated with communications with external legal advisers. Secondly, as a matter of practice, there is usually a clearer definition of the role of an external adviser than an internal one and, in circumstances where, say, an internal lawyer has wide-ranging responsibilities, it may be easier to evidence the privileged nature of a communication if it is coming from an external adviser specifically retained on an identified matter.

Further, engaging external advisers can often boost the credibility and authority **4.109** of an internal investigation particularly with regulators, senior management, shareholders, and the public. It reflects the company's commitment to address seriously and vigorously any allegations or issues and to rectify any potential misconduct.

External advisers can also often act as a contact point for any criminal or external **4.110** investigating authorities, managing the flow of information and providing professional support to the corporate and lending a degree of distance and objectivity to the corporate/regulator relationship.

Essentially, the company is gaining support for its internal process from the **4.111** reputation and professional responsibilities of the external firm. This creates some inherent tensions. The external firm owes client duties to the corporate but is being placed in a position where its own reputation is directly impacted and where it may have to formulate conclusions which are critical of the actions of its client. It is no longer acting purely as an adviser or representing the client as an advocate. The relationship has delicate points. However, provided this is fully understood at the outset and the value of maintaining the objectivity of the view of the external firm is fully recognized, it can still be an effective relationship.

If external advisers are used, who should they be?

There is no fundamental reason why, if it is decided to retain an external adviser **4.112** to lead the process, that adviser has to be a law firm. It is important to consider the nature of the exercise and the skill set required. However, a law firm will generally offer the following advantages:

• privilege protection;[94]

• the communications emanate from independent lawyers, that is, those not bound to the client by a relationship of employment.

This decision was, broadly, followed recently by the CFI in Joined Cases T-125/03 and T-253/03 *Akzo Nobel Chemicals and Akcros Chemicals v Commission.*

[94] Considered from 4.207.

- higher level of expertise in the areas of interviewing, interpreting facts and building and testing scenarios since these are inherent parts of the litigation process in which lawyers are trained and law firms have deep skill sets;
- to the extent that there is any possibility of any interface with any regulators:
  — the benefits of the skill sets and experience associated with conducting regulatory defence work;
  — the advantages of having those steeped in the investigation facing up to the regulators;
  — thereby meeting the usual expectations of regulators that they will be dealing with a law firm on behalf of the client in such circumstances; and
- the reputation benefits of the firm concerned.

4.113 The overwhelming experience in the UK has been that, where external advisers are involved, the matter has been led by a law firm, bringing in such external other parties as may be appropriate, in much the same way as a piece of litigation would be organized.

4.114 If it is decided to instruct an external law firm, there remain subtle issues as to which firm to use. They flow from the value of, and need for, objectivity in the external advisers' analysis and views. In particular, there must be no question that the external firm might have moderated its views or the conduct of the investigation in relation to the actions or responsibilities of senior management because of the relationship that it has with them, either historically or with expectations of future work.

4.115 Clearly, any firm that has any direct prior involvement in the circumstances in issue is likely to be in a difficult, if not impossible, position. Even if there is no reason to doubt the actual objectivity of their work, insofar as the matter is likely to be public, then press and capital markets may be sceptical, although regulators tend to be a little more pragmatic, in practice.

4.116 However, it does not follow that, at least in UK practice, the external adviser need have no prior relationship with the corporation whatsoever. It is frequently seen that a firm with a relationship with the corporation is selected. In this respect, the approach is a little different from the US where market expectations are stricter. Whether it is appropriate is a difficult question of judgement.

4.117 There are clearly advantages to having individuals who have some prior knowledge of the corporation, and its business, and have the trust and confidence of the senior executives. This is usually reflected in lower cost, higher quality and faster progress. It is also the case that the learning and understanding of the business, personalities and 'family history' of the corporation that the external adviser will inevitably gain during an investigation may be of most value to the corporation nested in the minds of those who will be continuing to advise it in the future.

Additionally, insofar as the circumstances may lead to litigation or regulatory **4.118** action, the company may prefer to have its regular and trusted advisers in place. It is not unknown for the investigation to be carried out by one firm and the representational work by another but it can, obviously, be expensive and lead to considerable duplication and even different views being advanced (albeit in different fora) by different firms.

Since the true interests of the corporation, the client, lie in identifying issues **4.119** properly and addressing them, it can often fairly be said that there is no underlying conflict of interest in using the corporation's existing law firm. Additionally, it may well be the case that that external adviser has the market and professional reputation and authority to be trusted as to its conclusions, despite having a prior relationship with the corporation. This is particularly the case where the source, scope and nature of its instructions reinforce the necessary objectivity and independence of view (eg it is reporting to non-executive board members who have, to a degree, similar issues to consider, in that they are not entirely external).

However, there is no single 'right' answer to such a question. It very much depends **4.120** on the facts. Where necessary for the integrity of the investigation and to ensure a return on the money invested in it, it may be appropriate for a corporation to instruct a wholly independent external firm, or at least one which does not have the 'house' advisory relationship.

Managing illegal activity during investigations

When a company first becomes aware of allegations of misconduct, there may be **4.121** a temptation to allow the activity to continue in order to collect further evidence or to identify all those who may be involved. Whether this is appropriate (and if so for how long) is a sophisticated judgement call based on all the facts, including the degree of knowledge (as opposed to concern or suspicion), the impact on third parties and the time that would be taken to obtain a better assessment of the position. However, as a starting point, if the activity could constitute a criminal or regulatory breach, the company should take prompt action to stop that activity.[95] If necessary, this may involve suspending a suspect employee or removing him or her from a sensitive position in accordance with the company's disciplinary procedure.

The major general exception to this approach is where an undertaking is seeking **4.122** leniency and, in conjunction with the regulator and with the benefit of its protection, allows a pattern of conduct to continue for a period whilst it is investigated.

---

[95] Unless (in the regulatory sector) the broadly defined crime of money laundering is suspected and stopping the activity would constitute tipping off for the purposes of the Proceeds of Crime Act 2002, s 333A.

This may be relevant in the competition field where leniency is particularly sophisticated and it may be difficult for the regulators to obtain the evidence that they seek without the cooperation of a participant in the infringing practice.[96]

4.123 If the company does not ensure that the illegal conduct is halted, there may be various and serious implications. First, a regulator may consider that the company (and its directors) is acting in concert with the employee and is therefore guilty of the same breach. Secondly, although the adequacy of the company's systems and controls may be brought into question by the fact that the illegal conduct originally occurred,[97] the fact that it was not stopped is likely to cause further concern for regulators.

E. Self-reporting

Duty to self-report

4.124 As a general rule, openness with regulators is beneficial and instances in which companies have uncovered breaches and reported them to regulators are usually viewed favourably by regulators and can impact on any subsequent regulator action.

4.125 Some of the UK regulators have principles that unambiguously include an obligation to self-report misconduct. For example, in the financial services industry, there are general principles[98] which expressly impose the requirement that 'authorised persons' and 'approved persons' 'disclose to the FSA appropriately anything relating to the firm of which the FSA would reasonably expect notice',[99] which includes any breach of a rule of which the 'authorised person' or 'approved person' becomes aware.[100] The FSA believes that self-reporting is crucial to its aim of maintaining clean financial markets. Its policy has been that if staff engage in

---

[96] Note that such an arrangement does not exempt a corporation from the civil exposure associated with any infringement.

[97] For example, Listing Principle 2 requires listed corporates to 'take reasonable steps to establish and maintain adequate procedures, systems and controls to enable it to comply with its obligations', FSA Handbook at LR 7.2.1.

[98] Principle for Business 11: FSA Handbook at PRIN 2.1.1 and Statement of Principle for Approved Persons 4: FSA Handbook at APER 2.1.2.

[99] Or 'any information of which the FSA would reasonably expect notice' in the case of an 'approved person'.

[100] There are also four specific rules in the FSA Handbook at SUP 15 requiring 'authorised persons' to report: (i) matters having a serious regulatory impact; (ii) breaches of rules and other requirements under FSMA 2000; (iii) civil, criminal or disciplinary proceedings against that 'authorised person'; and (iv) fraud, errors and other irregularities. Persons in the regulated sector are also obliged to report any knowledge or suspicions of the broadly defined crime of money laundering to SOCA: Proceeds of Crime Act 2002, s 331.

misconduct, and firms know it has happened, it requires a firm to inform then. If a firm has good systems and controls and can show it is complying with them, it may not pursue the firm in an enforcement action, and will pursue the individual instead.[101] However, this approach needs to be kept under close review as it is clearly subject to the specific facts and changing policy needs.

Other UK regulators have rules that may ambiguously imply an obligation to self-report misconduct. For example, Listing Principle 6 imposes an obligation on listed corporates to be open and cooperative with the UKLA. However there is no express obligation on listed corporates to self-report breaches of the Listing Rules (or Disclosure Rules and Transparency Rules or Prospectus Rules). The UKLA has in the past proposed including an express obligation on listed corporates to self-report any breach of the Listing Rules (or Disclosure Rules and Transparency Rules or Prospectus Rules)[102] but that has not been adopted and is not currently the law.[103] However, whether or not the breach was brought to the attention of the UKLA is one of the factors to be taken into account by the UKLA in determining whether to take disciplinary action at all[104] and, if so, what penalty to impose.[105] **4.126**

Although there is no formal obligation to self-report in the competition arena, the OFT (and EU) leniency programmes provide incentives for companies that may be members of a cartel to self-report any abuses or misconduct. This can include total immunity from financial penalties for companies that are the first member of a cartel to provide relevant information, if the information is provided before the OFT has commenced its investigation and when it does not then have sufficient evidence to establish that the cartel exists.[106] **4.127**

Culture of self-reporting

As corporates are rapidly learning about the potential benefits of self-reporting globally, the culture of self-reporting has increased in the UK. This is particularly noticeable in the competition sector where companies such as Virgin Atlantic **4.128**

---

[101] Speech by Sally Dewar, Director of Markets Division, FSA Wholesale Conference, QEII Conference Centre, 17 May 2006 <http://www.fsa.gov.uk/pages/Library/Communication/Speeches/2006/0517_sd.shtml>.

[102] FSA Consultation Paper 100 (*Proposed Changes to the Listing Rules at N2*), June 2001.

[103] Note that the UKLA might still seek to argue that the obligation to self-report is implicit in the obligation to cooperate with the UKLA, with the result that it may attempt to argue that a failure to self-report is a breach of Listing Principle 6.

[104] FSA Handbook at DEPP 6.2.1(2)(a).

[105] FSA Handbook at DEPP 6.5.2(8)(a) and DEPP 6.4.2(4).

[106] Whether to seek leniency in a competition matter is a complex issue with potentially dramatic consequences requiring specialist advice and a properly informed decision at the right level of authority within the corporate.

managed to take advantage of both the OFT's and the DoJ's leniency programmes through self-reporting its involvement in fuel fixing surcharges and thereby avoiding heavy fines.[107]

4.129   Self-reporting is one of a number of factors that regulators, particularly financial regulators, will take into consideration when considering whether to trust a corporate. However, self-reporting is only a start. Most regulators will not be satisfied without regular updates and evidence of remedying the issue: self-reporting is the beginning of a process and not a conclusion.

4.130   Moreover, self-reporting (absent a specific obligation to do so) is not an automatic decision but depends on an assessment of the risk and incentives. In appropriate circumstances, a corporate may take all the necessary steps to deal with a matter to the highest level but still consider that it is not appropriate, in the circumstances, to self-report.

4.131   In the UK, it is important, when considering whether to self-report, to be mindful of the impact of POCA referred to above[108] and the prospect of a separate criminal offence being committed by the handling of funds which are the proceeds of crime without having made the necessary notification.

F. Announcements and Public Relations Strategies

External communications

4.132   When facing a regulatory investigation or when conducting its own internal investigation, a corporate has to decide whether it is required to make any announcements to the markets.

4.133   A listed corporate's disclosure obligations are governed by the Listing Rules (in particular the Listing Principles) and the Disclosure Rules and Transparency Rules. As a general overarching principle, Listing Principle 4 requires a listed company to communicate to the markets in such a way as to avoid the creation or continuance of a false market. The key specific rules are set out in chapter 2 of the Disclosure Rules and Transparency Rules in the FSA Handbook.

---

[107] In August 2007, British Airways was fined £121.5m and $300m by the UK OFT and the DoJ respectively for its part in colluding with Virgin Atlantic and fixing fuel surcharges on both passenger and cargo flights. This was the highest fine that the OFT has ever imposed. In the US, a judge is expected to uphold British Airways's $300m fine and decide whether the personnel involved will face criminal prosecution. If the DoJ were to prosecute, the relevant personnel could be extradited to the US and, if convicted, jailed or fined. Virgin Atlantic prompted the investigation by approaching the OFT with incriminating information and will avoid sanctions as a result. This sends a particularly clear signal from the OFT encouraging businesses to self-report and blow the whistle on fellow cartel members. See also Christies, self-reporting in the Auction Houses Commission Cartel.

[108] At 4.73.

A listed corporate is required to disclose any 'inside information' to the market as   **4.134**
soon as possible.[109] The fact that a corporate is facing a regulatory investigation
or is the subject matter of an internal investigation may constitute 'inside information'. This is particularly the case if there might be risks of material fines or
damages or if there might be an impact on the corporate business model, the
position of its senior management, possible disbarment from certain areas of
business, critical client relationships, or the reputation of the corporate generally
impacting on its future revenue.

Whether the information is 'inside information' will depend not only on its   **4.135**
nature but also on the materiality to the corporate and the likely impact on share
prices.[110] This is a complex issue on which specific advice should be sought from
external legal advisers and, critically, the corporate brokers concerned. As recent
FSA decisions[111] show, it is very important that the brokers' advice is then followed and not ignored. In practice, such decisions are time consuming, urgent
and fraught. They are, however, critical.

A critical consideration is that the same questions may arise on the identification of   **4.136**
the underlying facts, whether or not a regulator is threatening to take steps. Since
the obligation to notify the market is immediate, it is not sufficient to wait to see if
there is regulatory interest. Management's perception of the risk to the business is
affected by the information that has come to light and in appropriate circumstances, this may trigger an obligation to notify the market. Clearly, an announcement to the exchanges will be equivalent to self-reporting in that it is putting the
matter in the public domain and it will come to the attention of regulators.

There is an exception to the requirement to notify where early disclosure would   **4.137**
prejudice the company's legitimate interests, for example, if early disclosure of the
fact of an investigation or the underlying issues might be prejudicially premature
because the company is still trying to ascertain the extent of the problem.[112]
However, this exception is restrictively construed.

There is an inherent tension in that early or inaccurate disclosure might also poten-   **4.138**
tially mislead the market. It may be appropriate to delay briefly whilst the corporate
puts itself in a position to be able to make a proper and accurate announcement.
However, any such delay would have to be extremely short. It is not permitted to
wait for an appropriate moment (say interim results) for an announcement.

---

109 FSA Handbook at DTR 2.2.
110 'Inside Information' is, broadly, information of a precise nature, which:
    (a) is not generally available;
    (b) relates, directly or indirectly, to the listed corporate or its shares; and
    (c) would, if generally available, be likely to have a significant effect on the price of the shares
        or on the price of related investments: FSMA 2000, s 118C.
111 *Eurodis Electron plc*, final notice (9 December 2005).
112 FSA Handbook at DTR 2.5.

4.139   Moreover, the delay itself must not be likely to mislead the public.[113]

4.140   One of the conditions for delaying disclosure to allow the company to clarify the situation is that the listed corporate can ensure the confidentiality of the 'inside information'.[114] If the company believes that there is a danger of inside information leaking before the facts and their impact can be confirmed, the company should make a holding announcement.[115]

4.141   Provided that confidentiality can be and is maintained, there is no obligation on a listed corporate to respond to and/or correct market rumours. However, if market rumours become sufficiently precise so as to suggest a leak of 'inside information', which might affect the listed corporate's share price, an announcement will be required.[116] Once an investigation is underway, it is difficult to ensure secrecy and it is possible that disclosure will be required.

4.142   If a regulator, such as the UKLA, has requested that the investigation be kept confidential, it would be advisable to consult with it before public disclosure is made.

4.143   It is important to note that failure to comply with disclosure obligations can result in fines for directors as well as public censure.

4.144   Even if there is no regulatory obligation to make an announcement, consideration should be given to the benefits of doing so, given the inherent risk that details of an investigation, whether regulatory or internal, could be leaked and the (negative) interest that this could generate. An announcement of an investigation that is being conducted thoroughly and independently with the aim of rectifying the problem will protect the company's reputation more than any defensive statement made after the investigation has been leaked to the press. It is also helpful to be able to show that the corporate has been taking action independently before the press interest, rather than reacting to it.

4.145   If a company decides to make an announcement it is critical to coordinate it with a tight media plan to control any speculation that could cause lasting damage to the company's reputation. To this end, it is important that the legal team, whether in-house or external advisers, are working closely with the public and investor relations teams from the outset of the investigation.

---

[113] FSA Handbook at DTR 2.5.1(1).
[114] FSA Handbook at DTR 2.5.1.
[115] FSA Handbook at DRT 2.2.9. The holding announcement should:
  • detail as much of the subject matter as possible;
  • set out the reasons why a fuller announcement cannot be made; and
  • include an undertaking to announce further details as soon as possible.
[116] FSA Handbook at DTR 2.7.2.

It is also crucial to identify stakeholders, whether shareholders, the media, cus- **4.146** tomers, suppliers or business partners, who may require reassurance or information, and the best strategies for managing such communications. This is especially acute if public notifications are being made or if there is press speculation. Strategies can include involving senior management in talking to customers and partners, particularly to those whose business it is important to retain, and maintaining good relationships with analysts who are feeding information to the markets. In all cases it is important that the company is putting out a consistent message that is open and informative and assists in preserving the company's reputation. It is also critical that any such activity is clearly within the FSA rules (and those of any other relevant exchanges) as to what can be said against the background of any stock exchange announcement that has been made.

It is important to remember that regulators can often have their own media **4.147** agenda, and therefore if an investigation is being conducted in the public eye, the regulators will be courting the press to their own advantage. This can cause even greater problems when multiple regulators are involved, possibly with each trying to boost its individual reputation.

In order to try to manage the consequences of each regulator's publicity aims it is use- **4.148** ful to maintain open channels with the regulators to gain an indication of the type of information that they are planning to publicize. It is also sometimes possible to agree a 'no surprises' arrangement with a regulator such that there is a prior warning from the regulator (even if it is limited both as to time and content) that it will be making an announcement so as to enable the corporate to manage the impact of any announcement on its own public position in a responsible manner. As much as possible, the company should put in place an effective external communications strategy on its own terms rather than have to communicate with the public from a reactive position.

Internal communications

At the beginning of an investigation, a company's natural inclination is to con- **4.149** tain internal communication to only those who are required to know of the investigation. Some regulators (such as the UKLA) do not publicize investigations, unless and until they determine that a penalty should be imposed for a breach. Therefore it can often be a decision for the company (unless a regulator has requested otherwise or there is an obligation to make an announcement to the market) as to whether, and to the extent to which, the company decides to keep the fact of the investigation confidential from its employees and only disclose it to certain relevant employees on a 'need to know' basis.

However, it is likely that a number of employees will soon become aware of the **4.150** investigation as it is likely that their cooperation will have been sought in relation to complying with a regulator's requests. Further, if there has been any type of communication to employees regarding document retention or document destruction policies (as there almost inevitably will be), the employees are likely to deduce that some type of investigation is underway. Moreover, as soon as the fact of an investigation becomes public, employees will discuss between themselves and are likely to be asked by customers and counterparties what is going on. In these circumstances, it is important that they know how to react. Therefore, to control the spread of rumours and the possibility of leaks, it is usually appropriate for employees to be informed of the existence of an investigation and to be required to observe a policy covering confidentiality and of not responding to any media enquiries. Further, it is not unknown for a speaking note of key issues to be circulated, particularly to staff with outward facing roles, to make sure that there is accuracy and consistency in what is said externally, even if its contents are very limited, or 'no comment'.

Key points for Public Relations strategies

4.151 The precise nature of any PR strategy will be very fact specific and depend closely on the company's wider approach to, and style in, PR matters. However, there are certain general factors that are usually seen in well-managed responses.

- The company has good sources of information to identify potential PR angles early and to plan a response.
- There is a central point of decision-making to ensure the consistency and credibility of message.
- There is good consultation, including with external advisers (principally lawyer, brokers and PR agencies) to ensure that legal risks, factual issues and market reactions are considered.
- There is an effective system for handling press enquiries which can be highly intense at peak periods.
- Senior people, particularly at board level, do not brief externally privately.
- Public statements are made in good time, limited in scope and considered from the perspective of the future—it is essential to remember that the understanding of the facts may well change and it is therefore important to ensure that earlier statements, made in good faith, do not subsequently look misleading, over-confident or incompetent.

G. Best Practices in Document Gathering and Preservation

Expectations of regulators and courts

4.152 Whilst there is no express requirement on a company to preserve documents for the purposes of regulatory or internal investigations, companies have other statutory obligations that require them to retain certain documents for specified periods of time. For example, the Companies Acts require companies to preserve records of registers, charges, minutes and resolutions for at least ten years, and in some cases the life of the company.[117] Similarly HMRC expects companies to retain relevant tax records for periods of up to six years,[118] and accounting records must be retained for between three to six years depending on whether it is a private or public company.[119] In the financial services industry, FSA regulated entities are required to 'take reasonable care to make and retain adequate records of matters and dealings (including accounting records) which are the subject of requirements and standards under the regulatory system'.[120] This is generally held to be at least five years, and possibly longer in exceptional circumstances.[121] Companies should also be aware of other international document preservation limitation periods which can often differ dramatically from the UK and make provisions accordingly.[122]

Once an investigation is underway, all relevant documents should be preserved as **4.153** regulators such as the OFT, SFO, the FSA in market abuse investigations, and the UKLA can bring criminal charges against those who falsify, conceal, destroy or otherwise dispose of documents or (allow such to happen), which the individual knows or suspects are relevant to the investigation.[123] Failure to preserve documents may also be seen by the regulators as a failure to cooperate which could give rise to further sanctions or penalties.[124] A deliberate decision to destroy relevant documents when civil proceedings are imminent or in contemplation could also involve the criminal offence of obstructing or perverting the course of justice or contempt of court.

Further, irrespective of the legal position, there are important strategic, govern- **4.154** ance and presentational issues associated with preserving evidence. Whilst the levels of presumption are not, perhaps, quite as high as in the US, failure to

---

[117] Under the Companies Act 1985 and 2006.

[118] VAT Act 1994, s 58 and Sch 11, para 6 requires VAT documents to be retained for six years. Finance Act 1998, Sch 18, paras 21–23 require corporation tax self-assessment records to be retained for six years from the end of the year of assessment. Businesses not subject to corporation tax are required to retain returns for five years from 31 January following the year the return was made (Taxes Management Act 1970, s 12B(2)(b)). PAYE documentation must be retained for at least three years after the end of the relevant tax year (Income Tax (PAYE) Regulations 2003, reg 97).

[119] Companies Act 2006, ss 386–89: public companies must retain accounting records for six years, private companies for three years. A listed corporate must also ensure that its annual financial report remains publicly available for at least five years: FSA Handbook at DTR 4.1.4.

[120] FSA Handbook, SYSC 3.2.20 (1).

[121] Commission Directive 2006/73/EC, Art 51.

[122] For instance, whilst the maximum document limitation period in the UK for some documents is six years, in the Netherlands it is 20 years, and in France 30 years.

[123] FSMA 2000, s 177(3), applied by FSMA 2000, s 97(3); Criminal Justice Act 1987, s 2(16); Enterprise Act 2002, s 201(4).

[124] The UKLA is likely to view a failure to preserve documents as a breach of Listing Principle 6 (duty to cooperate), and as a failure of the company's systems and controls under Listing Principle 2. See FSA Handbook at LR 7.2.1.

preserve documents, and to be seen to have taken adequate and demonstrable steps to preserve documents, is very likely to increase suspicion with regulators, courts and parties. This has enormous potential not only to expose the company to embarrassment, but to cause substantive damage to its legal position. It is almost always in a company's interest to take strong action to ensure that documents are preserved and gathered effectively. Regulators may also view good document retention and management practices as evidence to prove that the company has acted appropriately and has adequate systems and controls in the face of issues. Management that permits evidence destruction has little chance of gaining any sympathy from any regulator on any aspect of leniency or future trust and it may well be treated as aggravating behaviour and increase fine exposures.

4.155 Moreover, a good evidential record can assist the company in carrying out its own review. Evidence that looks bad may still be of assistance, particularly if it shows the company's position to have been less bad than would be assumed in its absence, once the surrounding facts are clearer.

4.156 Despite the fact that there is no standing duty to preserve all documents at all times, it is recommended, therefore, that companies do adopt and adhere to a structured document management policy. Such a policy would, for instance, set out the length of time for which documents should be kept before destruction and should also contain provisions allowing for it to be quickly suspended in a clear and demonstrable process in the event of an investigation being started.

Rights to documents

4.157 Regulators in the UK have wide-ranging powers to access documents, which may be shared with other regulators. Indeed, given the general commitment for cooperation between regulators,[125] documents could be shared with other regulators and that should be the usual working assumption.

4.158 The UKLA has the statutory power to require any person to produce at a specified time and place any specified documents or documents of a specified description it reasonably considers to be relevant for the purposes of its investigation.[126] Further, as employees of the listed corporate are 'connected persons', the UKLA has the statutory power to require them to provide any other information it reasonably considers to be relevant to the purposes of the investigation.[127] The physical location of such material, in the possession of an individual, is immaterial.

---

[125] Considered from 4.242.

[126] Note that 'document' is defined widely to include information recorded in any form: FSMA 2000, s 417(1). This includes information held electronically, including emails and tapes of telephone calls.

[127] FSMA 2000, s 171.

In its wider regulation of the financial sector, the FSA has extensive powers to **4.159** compel the production of documents both from regulated entities and more widely. These powers are constantly in use as part of its regulatory activities. It also has powers to enter premises and obtain documents in appropriate circumstances, which are, however, rarely used. Given the strength of the FSA's regulatory powers over financial institutions, it would only be appropriate in the most extreme circumstances.

The Competition Act 1998 and Enterprise Act 2002 provide the OFT with far- **4.160** reaching powers of investigation. In particular the OFT can, on written notice, require the production of specified documents and specified information which it considers relate to any matters relevant to the investigation.[128] The OFT also has the power to carry out, on notice, an on-site investigation of business premises without warrant in which the OFT can require any person on the premises to produce any document that is considered relevant to the investigation and provide an explanation of the document, or require any person to state to the best of his or her knowledge and belief, where any relevant document is to be found.[129] The OFT can take copies or extracts of any documents produced. Under these powers the OFT investigators can also require any relevant information which is stored electronically and is accessible from the premises to be produced in a form in which it can be read and taken away. Whilst a company is under investigation, the OFT can take any steps that it sees fit in order to preserve the documents and prevent interference with them such as sealing offices, files and cupboards.[130]

Finally, the OFT investigators have the so-called 'dawn raid' powers (which are **4.161** increasingly frequently used, particularly in conjunction with Commission Officials in cartel cases) to enter premises with a warrant, and to search for and remove relevant documents.[131] Again, they can require a person to provide an explanation of documents and require the production of electronically held information. Further, in a criminal investigation, an individual can be required to answer general questions that are not limited to any document or information that has been requested. It is important to note that the OFT can use any information obtained during a criminal investigation under the Enterprise Act in civil investigations under the Competition Act.

---

[128] Competition Act 1998, s 26 (civil investigation) and Enterprise Act 2002, s 193 (criminal investigation).

[129] Competition Act 1998, s 27.

[130] OFT guidance provides that this time period should not be longer than 72 hours.

[131] Competition Act 1998, s 28 (civil investigation) and Enterprise Act 2002, s 194 (criminal investigation).

4.162 If the SFO is conducting an investigation, it can issue a notice requiring an individual to produce documents and provide information. It can take copies or extracts of the documents and require an explanation of any document produced.[132] In addition, the police authorities have extensive search and seize powers, acting under warrant, under various criminal statutes.

4.163 In all these procedures, there has traditionally been room to contest the scope of the powers of the agency concerned and to restrict access to material that did not fall within the scope of the particular decision or warrant or other document authorizing the procedure. Similarly, it can be possible to challenge certain requests as not sufficiently specific or 'fishing' or moving outside the area within which the agency has satisfied the necessary evidential basis for launching its investigation (in that, say, 'reasonable suspicion' of an infringement in one area is not a legal basis for an investigation in another). However, agencies have become more skilled at avoiding these problems with experience and more robust about insisting on their view of their powers. Moreover, if the company is intending to cooperate or apply for leniency, it is difficult to take too strong a stance on such an issue without risking not cooperating as fully as such regimes require.

H. Data Protection

Overview

4.164 This section analyses the impact of UK data privacy laws on the conduct of internal and regulatory investigations.

4.165 A company established in the UK or a non-EEA established company using a UK located server will be subject to the Data Protection Act 1998 (DPA) in respect of personal data relating to employees and clients.[133] The DPA implements the EU Data Protection Directive (the Directive).[134]

4.166 The UK's implementation of the Directive is currently being investigated by the European Commission. Several areas of implementation are believed to be of concern to the Commission but none of the grounds for concern have been confirmed publicly. It is possible that the UK may need to amend the DPA in the light of the Commission's review.

---

[132] Criminal Justice Act 1987, s 2.

[133] The test under s 5 of the DPA is whether the company is 'established' in the UK and the data is processed in the context of that establishment (where establishment includes local incorporation or maintaining an office, branch or agency). A non-EEA established company is caught by the DPA if it uses a UK server unless the server is only used to transit data through the UK.

[134] Directive 95/46/EC.

This section only considers the main DPA implications of investigations.[135] Any **4.167** Article 8 ECHR privacy rights or contractual or common law confidentiality rights that might apply to affected employees and clients are outside the scope of this section.

Key issues

The DPA aims to protect individuals whose 'personal data' is held or processed by **4.168** 'data controllers'.

Personal data

The term 'personal data' covers any information that 'relates to' an identified or **4.169** identifiable individual.[136] The broad scope of this definition was curtailed by the Court of Appeal's controversial interpretation in the *Durant* case in 2003.[137] The court was looking for information that was not only proximate and relevant to an individual (factors that were generally accepted as relevant); it now added a requirement that the information was only 'personal data' if it was also 'biographical in a significant sense' or had the individual as its focus (rather than some transaction or event in which that individual may have figured or had an interest).[138] This narrower interpretation of 'personal data' has been the subject of adverse review by the European Commission. Because the Commission may require the UK government to amend the law so that *Durant* is effectively overruled, it is submitted that UK data controllers should proceed on the cautious assumption that 'personal data' is not restricted by the tests introduced by the Court of Appeal.

In the context of investigations, the term 'personal data' will apply not only to **4.170** private email addresses but also to corporate email addresses that incorporate an individual employee's or client's name.[139] 'Personal data' would also cover business or mobile telephone numbers for named employees or directors,[140] bank

---

135 The laws restricting the 'monitoring' of emails and voice mails (Regulation of Investigatory Powers Act and Telecommunications (Lawful Practices) (Interception of Communications) Regulations 2000) are not considered because monitoring involves live review of unopened emails or voice mails. It is assumed that most investigations will be focusing on stored emails and voice mails that have already been opened by the intended recipient. In the UK Information Commissioner's view, the rules on monitoring only apply to active or live monitoring.

136 DPA, s 1(1).

137 *Durant v Financial Services Authority* [2003] EWCA Civ 1746, followed by the High Court in *Johnson v Medical Defence Union* [2004] EWHC 2509 (Ch).

138 [2003] EWCA Civ 1746 at para 28, per Auld LJ.

139 Eg if the investigated company has a client known as Acme Limited, email addresses that the company holds for Acme Limited will be caught as 'personal data' if they contain the names of Acme's employees or consultants (eg johannes.schmidt@acme.com).

140 See European Court of Justice's preliminary ruling in *Lindqvist* [2004] 2 WLR 1398 at para 24 on a referral from the Swedish Court of Appeal that the term personal data 'undoubtedly covers the name of a person in conjunction with his telephone co-ordinates'.

account details for individual clients[141] and sound or image data relating to employees or clients.[142] 'Personal data' can be held electronically or in a structured manual or paper filing system.[143]

4.171   Where data is anonymized so that it cannot readily be correlated to an individual employee or client, it will no longer be personal data from the time of anonymization.[144]

Data controller

4.172   The DPA recognizes 'data controller' as a broad concept. It covers any party who independently or jointly or in common with others determines the purposes for which and the manner in which any personal data are, or are to be, processed.[145] In the context of investigations, the company will invariably be a data controller in respect of employee and client data that allows individuals to be identified.

Processing

4.173   As the English Court of Appeal has observed, the definition of 'processing' under the Directive and the DPA is 'very wide'.[146] Processing not only covers the obtaining of information and its subsequent use but many other activities. This is relevant to investigations as it covers the initial collection of data relating to employees and clients (for example, where a company asks its in-house IT department to take a copy of the contents of an employee's hard drive held on that employee's office computer or laptop). Processing also covers the subsequent sharing, storage or other use of that data. In addition, the concept will capture the transferring of collected data between group companies located in the UK or other EEA countries and transferring it between EEA countries and non-EEA countries.

---

[141] Ie it would not cover the bank account details of legal persons such as companies or limited liability partnerships.

[142] Eg voice mail messages and CCTV footage would be covered as 'personal data' in s 1(1) of the DPA. See also Recital 14 of the Directive, referring to the need for the Directive to apply to sound and image data; also Recitals 16 and 17.

[143] According to Recital 27 of the Directive, the content of a manual filing system that captures personal data must be structured according to specific criteria relating to individuals 'allowing easy access to the personal data'. In the controversial ruling in *Durant v Financial Services Authority* [2003] EWCA Civ 1746 at para 50, the Court of Appeal held that the structure or organizing mechanism of manual files must have a 'sufficiently sophisticated and detailed means of readily indicating whether and where in an individual file or files specific criteria or information about the [individual] can be readily located'.

[144] The test under s 1(1) of the DPA is whether a living individual can be identified from information which is in the actual possession of the data controller or is likely to come into its possession.

[145] S 1(1).

[146] *Campbell v MGN* [2003] 1 QB 633 at 646, per Lord Phillips of Worth Matravers MR.

Compliance

The main DPA obligation on data controllers is to comply with various data pro- **4.174**
tection principles.[147] The key principle that affects the conduct of internal and
external investigations is the need to ensure fair and lawful processing of 'personal
data'. The grounds for fair processing include the prior consent of the affected
individuals;[148] processing of data in pursuit of legitimate interests where this does
not cause unwarranted prejudice to the privacy interests of the affected individuals;[149] processing that is necessary for compliance with any non-contractual legal
obligation to which the data controller is subject;[150] or processing that is necessary for the administration of justice.[151]

The other main principles that are relevant are the need to ensure that data proc- **4.175**
essors (eg other group companies or external consultants) are placed under certain contractually binding data security obligations and that data is not exported
outside the EEA in the absence of a DPA gateway permitting extra-EEA export.

Sanctions

The DPA is enforced by the UK Information Commissioner. The Information **4.176**
Commissioner can issue formal enforcement notices or seek undertakings as to
future conduct (where the Commissioner audits compliance and will convert
into an enforcement notice if the undertakings are breached). Both forms of
sanction are publicized by the Information Commissioner. Where an enforcement notice is ignored, the Information Commissioner can bring a prosecution.
Fines in the magistrates' court are up to £5,000 per offence but unlimited fines
can be imposed in the Crown Court. Data controllers can be sued by affected
individuals under the DPA for quantifiable damage caused by a breach of the
legislation.

The rest of this section examines how the DPA's requirements can impact the ini- **4.177**
tial collection, later use and sharing of personal data at each potential stage in an
internal and external investigation, including sharing with external consultants
and UK and foreign regulators.

Initial collection

The initial collection of employee or client data by a UK data controller will need **4.178**
to comply with the DPA's requirement for fair processing. The grounds for fair

---

[147] S 4(4). The eight data protection principles are set out in Sch 1, Part I.
[148] Sch 2, para 1.
[149] Sch 2, para 6(1).
[150] Sch 2, para 3.
[151] Sch 2, para 5(a).

processing are: individual consent; pursuit of legitimate interests; processing that is necessary for the administration of justice; or processing that is necessary for compliance with a legal obligation to which the data controller is subject.[152]

Consent

4.179 To be valid, consent must be informed consent. To determine if there is individual informed employee consent to collect personal data, the UK data controller should review its local employment contracts or subsequent notices issued to employees. The relevant clauses or notices may contain references to the employer's gathering of information to carry out an internal investigation and/or to respond to an external investigation. It would need to be made clear to the employee what type of communications will be reviewed and why. If the UK data controller intends to share the gathered information with other group companies or to send it outside the EEA, this would need to be set out in the relevant clauses or notices.

4.180 In the case of client consent to collect data, the UK data controller will need to look to its letter of engagement with clients or subsequent notices issued to them to determine if consent to data collection has been obtained for the purposes of carrying out an investigation.

Legitimate interests

4.181 In the absence of employee or client consent, the UK data controller may be able to use the 'legitimate interests' ground.[153] The 'legitimate interests' can be those of the UK data controller. They could also be the interests of another group company which is facing an external investigation and has asked the UK data controller to assist it. The UK data controller must balance these legitimate interests against the impact of data collection on the privacy interests of employees and clients. In practice, this balancing of interests means the UK data controller would be expected to ensure that certain privacy safeguards were built into the data collection process. For example, only a few members of the data controller's in-house IT team should be involved in taking images of hard disks containing employee or client data. In addition, where possible, data should be anonymized promptly after initial collection, with only one or two nominated individuals having the ability to unlock the identities of individual employees or clients in carefully prescribed circumstances.

4.182 The legitimate interests ground for fair processing is qualified by a 'necessity' test. In effect, this means that some thought must be given by the UK data controller

---

[152] Sch 2.
[153] Sch 2, para 6(1).

as to the scope of the data that is going to be collected so that, as far as practicable, only data that is strictly necessary to the investigation is collected. For example, the UK data controller could ensure the necessary parameters are put in place by collecting only data that falls within certain dates fields that are likely to be relevant or restricting collection of employee communications to only identified clients. In practice, an initial trawl for information will usually be done on a wide-ranging basis and then narrowed using keyword searches to produce more relevant documents. The initial trawl should therefore involve very strict limits on the number of people who have access to it. This is usually manageable because at this stage only one or two IT or forensic specialists will be involved and they will not be reviewing the actual content of documents or communications prior to keyword searches being made.

Administration of justice

This ground would apply where a court order or subpoena requires the UK data **4.183** controller to provide information.[154] The collected data would need to be limited to data that was 'necessary' to comply with the court order.

Legal obligation

This ground applies where the UK data controller is under a statutory obligation **4.184** to collect or report data (eg to notify suspicious financial transactions).[155] The data collected must be strictly necessary to meet the controller's statutory obligations.

Intra-group sharing

The fair processing grounds under the DPA that might be relevant for the UK **4.185** data controller sharing collected data with other group companies are also: individual consent; pursuit of legitimate interests; processing that is necessary for the administration of justice; or processing that is necessary for compliance with a legal obligation to which the data controller is subject.[156]

Consent

Employee or client consent to intra-group data sharing may be found in the **4.186** employment contract or client terms and conditions. Individuals will only have given valid consent if they have been informed (at least generically) about what data might be shared and why.

---

154 Sch 2, para 5(a).
155 Sch 2, para 3.
156 Sch 2.

Legitimate interests

4.187   If consent is absent or ambiguous, the UK data controller may seek to rely on the 'legitimate interests' ground (see 4.181 to 4.182). It may be difficult to show that privacy is not seriously prejudiced by sharing wholly or largely non-anonymized data with other group companies. This objection might be overcome if there is a necessity to share that data (ie where the recipient is itself facing external investigation or will be instructing or coordinating liaison with external advisers) and the shared data is restricted to a few employees at the recipient entity. If there is no need for the recipient entity to know the identities of individual employees or clients, data should be anonymized by the UK data controller (unless this is not practicable given the volume and complexity of data and the timescale in which the recipient entity needs to receive it in order to respond to the external investigation).

Administration of justice

4.188   This ground would apply where a court order or subpoena requires the UK data controller to provide the information.[157] The collected data would need to be limited to data that was 'necessary' to comply with the court order. It is unlikely that this ground would apply to intra-group data sharing by the UK data controller.

Legal obligation

4.189   This ground applies where the UK data controller is under a statutory obligation to collect or report data (eg to notify suspicious financial transactions).[158] The data collection must be strictly necessary to meet the controller's statutory obligations.

Data processing contract

4.190   Where the data is shared by the UK data controller with another group company, the UK data controller should enter into a data processing contract with the recipient entity where that recipient will be acting as an agent or processor for the UK data controller. The contract should require the recipient only to process the data on the UK data controller's instructions and to take appropriate technical and organizational measures to keep the data secure.[159] If the recipient entity will be carrying out purely independent use of the shared data, no processing contract is required. An example of independent use would include the recipient entity considering whether it has any independent, joint or subsidiary liability with the UK data controller in respect of the matter being investigated.

---

[157]   Sch 2, para 5(a).
[158]   Sch 2, para 3.
[159]   Sch 1, Part II, paras 9–12.

Exports outside the EEA

Transferring collected data from the UK data controller to another group com-   **4.191**
pany outside the EEA will involve a data export. The transfer must satisfy one of
the export grounds under the DPA. The grounds that are potentially relevant
include: consent from the affected individuals; or the transfer is made under
appropriate contractual arrangements; or the transfer is made to a non-EEA
country that has been declared by the European Commission to offer adequate
protection; or the transfer is necessary in connection with legal proceedings or to
obtain legal advice.

Consent of affected individuals[160] may be contained in employment contracts or   **4.192**
client engagement letters. The UK Information Commissioner has emphasized
the need for 'clear evidence' of consent and that the individual was informed
about the extra-EEA transfer.[161] Consent could be obtained separately once the
need for the transfer is known. However, this is often not feasible in practice as
individuals are likely to refuse to give consent or they will simply fail to respond
altogether.

An alternative ground for transferring to a non-EEA based group entity is the use   **4.193**
of an approved form of contract between the UK data controller and the recipient
entity.[162] The European Commission has approved model sets of clauses for
controller-to-controller and controller-to-processor transfers.[163] The UK
Information Commissioner's guidance indicates that none of the model clauses
may be amended but the parties are free to include other clauses provided they do
not contradict the model clauses.[164]

---

[160] Sch 4, para 1.

[161] Information Commissioner, 'The Eighth Data Protection Principle and International Data
Transfers', 30 June 2006, para 4.2.1, referring to the requirement in Art 2(h) of the Data Protection
Directive that consent must be 'any freely given, specific and informed indication' of the individual's
wishes.

[162] Sch 4, paras 8 and 9. An alternative to the approved form of contract is to rely on an internally
binding set of corporate rules (BCRs) that apply within the group to the export of employee and/or
client personal data between the exporter and the importer. BCRs require prior approval by privacy
regulators (the approval process is usually led by the national privacy regulator in the country
where the group headquarters is established or where its group-wide data protection functions are
managed). Regulators use a model checklist to assess the content of a BCRs application (Art 29
Working Party Working Document 05/EN WP 108) and an agreed procedure for cooperation
between regulators (Working Document 05/EN WP 107). To date, it is understood that less than
ten companies with a substantial presence in the EU have received BCRs approval for intra-group
data transfers. If BCRs are in place, they will only cover intra-group transfers outside the EEA and
will not cover sharing with external consultants or regulators located outside the EEA.

[163] Commission Decision 2001/497/EC15 of 15 June 2001 as amended by Commission
Decision 2004/915/EC17 of 27 December 2004 (controller-to-controller transfers); Commission
Decision 2002/16/EC16 of 27 December 2001 (controller-to-processor transfers).

[164] Information Commissioner, 'The Eighth Data Protection Principle and International Data
Transfers', 30 June 2006, para 3.2.5.

4.194 Where the model clauses are used, these do not permit an onward transfer by the data importer (eg to a non-EEA regulator or legal adviser). In these circumstances, a separate contract would need to be put in place between the data importer and the new recipient. It is very unlikely that a non-EEA regulator would enter into a contract that mirrors the European Commission's model clauses; US regulators, in particular, regularly refuse to do so.

4.195 Another ground for lawful transfer to a non-EEA based group entity is where that entity is located in a country which the European Commission has declared to have adequate data privacy protection. To date, the countries that have been deemed to offer adequate protection are Argentina, Canada,[165] Guernsey, Isle of Man and Switzerland.

4.196 Another ground for lawful export outside the EEA is where the transfer is strictly necessary in connection with UK or foreign legal proceedings (or prospective legal proceedings) or for the purposes of obtaining legal advice.[166]

External advisers

4.197 The considerations that apply to data sharing with other group companies also apply to allowing external consultants or advisers to collect or review personal data relating to employees or clients of the UK data controller (see 4.185 to 4.189).

Data processing contract

4.198 If external consultants located in the EEA are engaged to collect or review personal data relating to employees or clients, the UK data controller should enter into a data processing contract with the consultants or include appropriate terms in the consultants' letter of engagement. The DPA requires the UK data controller to ensure that the consultants will only process the data on the controller's instructions (and not act independently when processing it) and that the consultants will take appropriate organizational and technical measures to ensure that the data is kept secure.[167]

---

[165] Where the importers are subject to the Canadian Personal Information Protection and Electronic Documents Act.

[166] Sch 4, para 5(a) and (b). The UK Information Commissioner has indicated that the legal proceedings or prospective legal proceedings can be in a non-EEA state: Information Commissioner, 'The Eighth Data Protection Principle and International Data Transfers', 30 June 2006, para 4.5.1.

[167] Sch 1, Part II, paras 9–12.

Exports outside the EEA

If the external consultants receiving the data are located outside the EEA or will **4.199**
be accessing it from outside the EEA, the UK data controller must ensure that
one of the grounds set out in 4.191 to 4.196 applies. In practice, the most straightforward approach would be for the UK data controller to put in place the
European Commission's approved model export clauses.

Regulators

This section considers the DPA's requirements for the sharing of collected data **4.200**
relating to employees and clients with regulators in the UK or elsewhere in the
EEA or outside the EEA.

UK regulator

If the regulator is in the UK, the UK data controller can share collected data with **4.201**
that regulator if the 'legitimate interests' ground is satisfied.[168] This will involve
the UK data controller balancing its interests in making a disclosure to a UK regulator with the potential impact of that disclosure on the privacy interests of
employees or clients. In the unanimous advisory Opinion of the Article 29
Working Party of EU privacy regulators, the Working Party concluded that the
balance of interest should take into account issues of proportionality, the seriousness of the alleged offences that can be notified to the regulators and the consequences for the affected employees or clients.[169]

To comply with the DPA's 'legitimate interests' ground, the disclosure should be **4.202**
strictly necessary for the purposes of the regulator's investigation. The UK
data controller should consider whether employee or client names or other identifying data should be anonymized before disclosure. It may be that only details
of a core group of employees or clients needs to be disclosed for regulatory purposes and that remaining disclosures can be made on a generic or anonymized
basis.

Where the UK regulator uses coercive powers to compel disclosure, the UK data **4.203**
controller should give careful thought to what is disclosed in response as the disclosure should be restricted to what is strictly necessary to comply with the court
order.[170]

---

[168] Sch 2, para 6(1).

[169] Opinion 10/2006 on the processing of personal data by the Society for Worldwide Interbank
Financial Telecommunication (SWIFT) 01935/06/EN WP128.

[170] See Sch 2, para 3 (processing necessary for compliance with any legal obligation to which the
data controller is subject) and para 5 (processing necessary for the administration of justice).

Other EEA regulators

4.204 The factors discussed in 4.201 to 4.203 will also apply to voluntary or compelled disclosure to a regulator in another part of the EEA.

Non-EEA regulators

4.205 Disclosure of data to a non-EEA regulator will depend on one of the conditions for lawful export being met (see 4.191 to 4.196).

4.206 Where the non-EEA regulator is using coercive powers to compel disclosure, what is disclosed must be reviewed carefully to ensure that disclosure does not go wider than the information that is strictly necessary to comply with the terms of the subpoena or court order.[171]

I. Dealing with Privileged Documents

General rules on privilege

4.207 As outlined above, regulatory investigations commonly involve the compulsory production of documents and the giving of oral evidence. Privilege entitles a person to withhold both documentary and oral evidence during legal proceedings and regulatory investigations. Under English law, there are four broad types of privilege: legal advice privilege and litigation privilege (which are, together, commonly known as legal professional privilege); common interest privilege;[172] and 'without prejudice' communications.[173]

4.208 A fifth form of immunity from disclosure, although not strictly a privilege, is Public Interest Immunity (and a not dissimilar doctrine relating to European Community matters) which applies to certain limited categories of (usually, but not exclusively, government related) documents, which public policy requires should be protected from disclosure. This is rarely encountered in investigations (save insofar as it is relevant to certain categories of communications with the European Commission) and is outside the scope of this book.

---

[171] Sch 4, para 5(a) (processing necessary for purpose of, or in connection with, any legal proceedings).

[172] This is a subset of legal professional privilege, which arises in certain circumstances in the case of communications between parties with similar interests. The scope of its application in the context of investigations (eg between financial institution under investigation for similar activity or parties accused of participating in the same cartel) is complex and outside the scope of this book. A specialist work on the law of privilege should be consulted.

[173] This covers documents evidencing a genuine attempt to settle a matter. The fact that a document is marked 'without prejudice' does not conclusively or automatically render it privileged. A court may seek to ascertain for itself whether the document concerned was genuinely a negotiating document: *Buckinghamshire County Council v Moran* [1990] 1 Ch 623, Court of Appeal and *South Shropshire District Council v Amos* [1986] 1 WLR 1271, Court of Appeal.

Legal advice privilege (which bears some resemblance to US attorney-client privilege), protects confidential communications between a client and its legal adviser[174] sent or received for the purpose of seeking or obtaining legal advice. It applies irrespective of whether litigation is contemplated or pending. **4.209**

Advice in this context has been defined as not only telling the client the law, but providing 'advice as to what should prudently and sensibly be done in the relevant legal context'.[175] It has been accepted that consulting lawyers with regard to preparing and conducting an investigation would constitute a relevant legal context and should attract legal advice privilege.[176] However, it is important that there is a legal context. In particular, it is crucial that the terms of reference, if they are formally drafted (or the engagement letter of the legal advisers) reflect that it is a legal analysis that is sought and not merely a factual enquiry. **4.210**

When claiming legal advice privilege, it is crucial to remember that, in the UK, it can only attach to communications between the person(s) in the client's organization with responsibility for obtaining the legal advice and the organization's lawyers and not to communications between those lawyers and other employees of the organization, no matter how senior.[177] There can be some uncertainty, therefore, as to who is the client for the purposes of legal advice privilege, and it cannot be assumed that all communications between legal advisers and employees of a company will be protected by the privilege. In order to try to ensure that legal advice privilege will apply it is critical to clarify and evidence at the outset exactly who constitutes the client. It may be useful, in the context of an investigation, to designate a particular body or group of individuals, including the board of the company, as the client so that all discussions with those parties would remain privileged. **4.211**

A company should also bear in mind that communications between a company or its legal advisers and third parties, for example, in which information is sought from third parties, are unlikely to be legally privileged, unless they are produced **4.212**

---

[174] In the UK (unlike in other parts of Europe), privilege generally attaches to communications with in-house lawyers (save in certain anti-trust areas) as well as communications with external lawyers. It does not, however, attach to communications with people who do not hold a legal qualification, such as compliance officers or company secretaries, or those who, irrespective of a legal qualification, are not employed as a lawyer or acting in that capacity.

[175] *Balabel v Air India* [1988] 1 Ch 317, 330.

[176] Lord Brown: 'I would go so far as to state as a general principle that the process by which a client seeks and obtains his lawyer's assistance in the presentation of his case for the purposes of any formal inquiry—whether concerned with public law or private law issues, whether adversarial or inquisitorial in form, whether held in public or in private, whether or not directly affecting his rights or liabilities—attracts legal advice privilege': *Three Rivers District Council and Others v Governor and Company of the Bank of England (No 5)* [2004] UKHL 48, House of Lords.

[177] *Three Rivers District Council and others v Governor and Company of the Bank of England (No 5)* [2004] EWCA Civ 218, Court of Appeal.

for the purposes of existing or reasonably contemplated legal proceedings (see below). This is an important limitation in practice and, for example, means that a report prepared by accountants for legal advisers is unlikely to be privileged unless litigation is contemplated.[178]

4.213   Further, the company should remember that the purpose for which the document was produced is critical. Material produced internally to enable the company to take legal advice[179] may well be privileged, provided it is in fact provided to the company's lawyer and advice is taken. However, companies should be wary of creating purely internal documents analysing what went wrong since these will be unlikely to be privileged unless they are prepared by lawyers or directly to enable the company to take legal advice.

4.214   *Litigation privilege* (the broad equivalent of attorney work-product protection) protects:

* communications between a client and its legal adviser made confidentially for the dominant purpose of obtaining or seeking legal advice for use in existing or reasonably contemplated legal proceedings; and

* communications between a client or its legal adviser and a third party made confidentially for the dominant purpose of seeking or providing information or evidence to be used in or in connection with existing or reasonably contemplated legal proceedings.

4.215   The circumstances that give rise to an investigation may also give rise to the risk of litigation. In these circumstances, documents may be created both for the purpose of the investigation itself and to combat the perceived risk of litigation. Documents that do not otherwise attract legal advice privilege will only be privileged if prepared for the dominant purpose of litigation.

4.216   The predominant purpose test requires an examination of motive. Whether litigation (as opposed to legal advice) privilege attaches depends highly on the facts.

4.217   A purely internal investigation will not constitute litigation. However, if it is conducted for the purpose of defending genuinely anticipated claims, and not as a free standing exercise (eg where there are purely internal ethical or governance concerns), the purpose of the document creation could genuinely be the anticipated litigation such that privilege would be available.

---

[178] *Price Waterhouse v BCCI Holdings (Luxembourg) SA* [1992] BCLC 583.

[179] Legal advice is interpreted fairly widely, to include all communication within the continuum aimed at keeping legal adviser and client informed, but it may not include the legal adviser's advice on purely commercial or business matters: *Three Rivers District Council and others v Governor and Company of the Bank of England)* [2004] UKHL 48, House of Lords.

A regulatory investigation, particularly in its initial or informal stages, is also **4.218** unlikely to be treated as litigation. The precise time at which such a process becomes sufficiently adversarial to be treated as litigation has not been considered judicially. It will be dependent on the process in question but the 'litigation status' is likely to be triggered by the service of a formal document by the relevant regulator stating its legal case against the company and not by the agency using its evidence gathering powers as part of an investigation of the facts that give rise to the concern.[180]

Accordingly, documents created for the purpose of defending (or, indeed, cooper- **4.219** ating with) a regulatory process (ie prior to formal adversarial steps being taken) risk not attracting litigation privilege. In reality, where such an external investigation is underway, it will usually be impossible to prove that the predominant purpose of the document creation was, in fact, the litigation that might subsequently flow from the events giving rise to the regulatory interest.

Further, there is also an in-built tension. The interests of the company will usually **4.220** be to forestall a formal investigation by cooperation and conducting a voluntary process. However, that is precisely the situation where litigation privilege would not normally apply and the sole measure of protection is legal advice privilege. In addition, even if litigation privilege does apply, extreme care must be taken not to waive that privilege by disclosing privileged material prepared for the purposes of litigation in the context of the related inquiry.

Ultimately, the risk is usually manageable in practice. It is only relevant to docu- **4.221** ments created in the context of the investigation, since original documents will not usually be privileged and do not become so by becoming evidence in the investigation. Moreover, since legal professional privilege will apply to communications between lawyer and client, it does not impact on those documents.

The main areas of impact are on communications with other advisers, say foren- **4.222** sic accountants, environmental experts, private investigator agencies and with witnesses who would not be considered 'the client'. This is likely to mean, for example, that statements of witnesses prepared for the purposes of an internal investigation (as opposed to a lawyer's private notes) will not be privileged, even if those statements are prepared by lawyers and even if litigation proceedings, such as a claim by a shareholder, may be brought as a consequence of the problem that gave rise to the internal investigation. It is in these areas that every party needs to proceed with caution.

---

[180] Proceedings before the Financial Services and Markets Tribunal are almost certainly legal proceedings and material produced for the purposes of those proceedings should therefore be privileged, provided it fulfils the other requirements for 'litigation privilege'.

Statutory rules on privilege

4.223 In reflecting privilege issues, the legislation granting powers to the various investigatory agencies either simply preserves privilege as it operates under general English law or, in some cases, specifically redefines the protection in statutory form (with the result that there is little or no case law interpreting it and the substantial body of authority on the common law position referred to above is of relatively little assistance).

4.224 For example, if subject to an investigation by the UKLA, FSMA 2000 provides statutory protection for privileged documents against the obligation to disclose them to the UKLA. Such documents are termed 'protected items' and are:[181]

- communications between a professional legal adviser and his or her client (or a person representing his or her client) made:
  — in connection with the giving of legal advice to the client; or
  — in connection with, or in contemplation of, legal proceedings and for the purposes of those proceedings; or
- communications between any of a professional legal adviser, his or her client or a person representing his or her client and any other person made in connection with, or in contemplation of, legal proceedings and for the purposes of those proceedings; or items:
  — enclosed with or referred to in any of the above communications; and
  — made:
    in connection with the giving of legal advice to the client; or
    in connection with, or in contemplation of, legal proceedings and for the purposes of those proceedings; and
  — in the possession of a person entitled to possession of them.[182]

4.225 Communications or items are not 'protected items' if held with the intention of furthering a criminal purpose.[183]

4.226 Whilst the definition of 'protected items' does not precisely mirror the test for English legal professional privilege, as a matter of general law, 'protected items' are broadly the same as those items covered by English legal professional privilege and it is currently unclear whether the differences are material. Note that 'protected items' do not specifically include 'without prejudice' communications.

---

[181] FSMA 2000, s 413.

[182] It is not wholly clear what this is intended to cover, but it may be intended to address the principle that a non-privileged document does not become a privileged document simply because it is enclosed with a privileged document.

[183] FSMA 2000, s 413(4).

In addition, there is extremely limited statutory protection against the obligation **4.227** to disclose documents to the UKLA for documents subject to a duty of banking confidentiality.[184] Such protection does not apply if:

- the person owing the obligation of confidentiality is the person under investigation or is a member of that person's group;
- the person to whom the obligation of confidence is owed is the person under investigation or a member of that person's group;
- the person to whom the obligation of confidence is owed consents to the disclosure or production; or
- the imposing of the requirement to disclose such information or document has been specifically authorized by the FSA (or, if appropriate, the Secretary of State).

Conversely, if the OFT is investigating, section 30 of the Competition Act 1998 **4.228** expressly protects documents on the grounds of privilege where they would be protected in the High Court. This directly imports the common law position.

Waiving privilege

As a general rule once a document is privileged, it is always privileged. However, privi- **4.229** lege will be lost if a document loses confidentiality by entering the public domain.

Legal professional privilege can also be waived by: **4.230**

- the party holding the privilege, or his lawyer, agreeing to waive privilege;
- selective waiver of part of a privileged document;
- waiving privilege over one document, which in certain circumstances can lead to waiver over a class of documents, such as where one document refers to another document;
- references to privileged documents in pleadings, witness statements, expert reports and correspondence which can lead to the production of the privileged documents being ordered; and
- inadvertent disclosure.

As a general rule, disclosure of a privileged document to a regulator will amount **4.231** to a waiver of privilege on the basis that the disclosing party is clearly not asserting the privilege but allowing the document into the hands of a public body. However, this is subject to the position on limited waiver discussed below.

---

[184] FSMA 2000, s 175(5).

Limited waiver

4.232 The basic English rule is that, where privileged material is produced by one party to another within a confidential relationship, then, provided there is no intention to waive privilege, the privilege should be maintained against other third parties.[185] As a result, there is a good argument that, depending upon the precise situation and the terms on which the material is disclosed, privileged items can remain privileged as against any other party, including third parties who might bring civil claims against the company, even after certain disclosures, including to a regulator in appropriate circumstances.

4.233 If a company is communicating a privileged document or privileged information it should try to ensure that the recipient will treat it as privileged and confidential. Specifically it should consider imposing terms on the recipient:

- to treat the communication as confidential and not to disclose all or any of its contents to any third party and in particular not to take any step or action that could constitute a waiver of confidentiality or privilege in relation to this communication;

- not to use the communication or its contents for any purpose other than a stated purpose; and

- to alert the other party immediately if there is any request from a third party for disclosure of all or any of the contents of the communication and, upon request, to join in asserting against any third party that the communication and its content are protected by privilege and that, as against such third party, that privilege has not been waived.

4.234 Note, however that, as most regulators have the right or obligation to disclose material gathered to other regulators, there can be no guarantee that, ultimately, the privilege will not be determined to have been waived or the information will not ultimately leak out, such that confidentiality (and therefore the privilege) will in any event be lost.

J. Managing Regulators

Dialogue with regulators

4.235 When facing the threat of regulatory investigation, it is generally advisable to maintain open lines of communication with regulators. It is often appropriate for a company to be proactive in this respect. Engaging with the regulators effectively can

---

[185] *City of Gotha v Sotheby's* [1998] 1 WLR 114 and *(1) B and Others (2) Russel McVeigh McKenzie Bartleet & Co v (1) Auckland District Law Society and (2) Gary J Judd* [2003] PC 38 on appeal to the Privy Council from the Court of Appeal in New Zealand.

reduce the risk of 'surprises' that may be difficult to manage, will usually result in a more sophisticated relationship with the regulator, may help to reduce the scope of any area that is under suspicion and can lead to a regulator being satisfied with some form of internal investigation rather than using its own investigatory powers.

A corporate may appoint its general counsel, compliance officer or a member of **4.236** senior management to be the contact point with the regulator and to manage the communications. This is particularly the case where the company has staff with the appropriate skills or pre-existing relationships with the regulator.

However, these communications are frequently managed through an external law **4.237** firm. The specialist skills of the law firm (coupled, often, with the lawyers' personal knowledge of the individuals in the regulator, based on frequent dealings) can assist considerably with optimizing the company's position in the procedural stages and providing a degree of distance and detachment for the company from the aggressive aspects of the regulator's activities. In addition, the law firm's broader and more frequent relationship with the regulator, coupled with its own professional responsibilities, may mean that the regulator is prepared to operate on the basis of a greater degree of trust and informality that can be beneficial for all concerned.

However, regulators will usually require a company's senior management to have **4.238** some oversight of the investigation. This is, generally, to evidence the corporate's commitment to the process, to provide accountability and to allocate responsibility for the implementation of any remedial steps.

Where the company is investigating internally and a regulator is involved and **4.239** aware of the position, it is likely that the regulator will want to be aware of the extent and progress of the investigation being conducted, so that it can be made comfortable that the investigation is thorough and be satisfied with the investigation's scope, methodology and timing. The corporate may also have to demonstrate to the regulator the measures taken to ensure that the investigation is sufficiently independent. Usually, the regulator will want to be kept informed of material action taken in relation to employees and counterparties. If it has been possible to avoid a full regulatory investigation, it is almost inevitable that the regulator will want to be satisfied as to the quality and depth of the internal investigation work and will want to have a detailed understanding of the corporate's proposed remedies and why they are sufficient to alleviate any possible regulatory concerns.

As a general rule, regulators will want an investigation to take a holistic and com- **4.240** prehensive view, examining the problem and identifying its root causes. This is likely to cover the following issues:

- What precisely happened and during which periods?
- Who was involved: internally and externally?
- Who was responsible, both directly and at a higher management level?

- Is there evidence of wider unethical conduct or wrongdoing? Could similar fact patterns occur in other areas of a company's operations?
- Were there systems, controls, reporting, cultural or management failures that were implicated?
- What was the company's previous history in relation to similar fact patterns and what internal compliance culture had been created?
- What are the potential regulatory, criminal or civil exposures?
- What is the appropriate remedial action?

4.241 In appropriate circumstances, the scope of activity in these areas may well be specifically defined internally and, possibly, in discussion with the regulator concerned.

Use of information by regulators

4.242 The various regulators each have different levels of confidentiality in relation to information disclosed and the extent to which they are obliged or able to share that information with other regulators.

4.243 Most regulators will, and will be obliged to, share information regarding material criminal activities with SOCA.

Statutory restrictions on disclosure by regulators

4.244 The FSA (including the UKLA) has very specific rules regarding the use of information disclosed to it. The general rule is that information obtained in the discharge of its regulatory functions or by any person obtaining the information directly or indirectly from the FSA, which relates to the business or affairs of any person (ie it is 'confidential information'), may not be disclosed without the consent of:[186]

- the person from whom the FSA obtained the information; and
- if different, the person to whom the information relates,

unless the information has already been made public (unless that disclosure was made contrary to the prohibition) or the information is in the form of a summary or collection of information so framed that it is not possible to ascertain from it information relating to any particular person.

4.245 It is a criminal offence for a person to disclose 'confidential information' in breach of the statutory restriction.[187]

---

[186] FSMA 2000, s 348. Since the prohibition applies to 'confidential information' received directly or indirectly from the UKLA, it applies to 'confidential information' received from the UKLA by the company under investigation, unless that information was *both* obtained by the UKLA *from* the company itself and relates *only* to the company itself (in which case the company is entitled to consent to the disclosure, thereby effectively releasing itself: FSMA 2000, s 348(1)).

[187] FSMA 2000, s 352.

It is immaterial whether or not the 'confidential information' was received by the **4.246**
FSA under a requirement to provide it imposed by or under FSMA 2000 or whether
it was received for other purposes in the discharge of any functions of the FSA.[188]

Similarly, confidential information[189] obtained by the OFT cannot be disclosed **4.247**
during the lifetime of the individual or business to which it relates, unless consent
has been obtained either from the person who provided the information or to
whom it relates. Therefore it is generally recommended that all confidential information is clearly marked as such[190] before it is shown to investigators and that its
confidentiality is confirmed in writing during or soon after the investigation.

Exceptions to the statutory restrictions on disclosure

Gateway regulations

The statutory restriction on disclosure of information obtained by the FSA/UKLA **4.248**
is subject to certain exceptions, most notably the ability to make disclosures permitted under the so-called Gateway Regulations made by HM Treasury.[191]

The key exceptions under the Gateway Regulations include: **4.249**

- the UKLA may disclose 'confidential information' to the FSA for the purpose
  of enabling or assisting it to discharge its wider regulatory functions.[192] It is
  therefore prudent for those subject to an investigation to assume that information provided to the UKLA will, where relevant, be shared within the FSA;
- the FSA may disclose 'confidential information' to, among others:[193]
  — a UK recognized investment exchange, such as the London Stock Exchange;
  — the Takeover Panel;
  — various other UK regulatory bodies, for example, the FRRP; and
  — various types of overseas regulatory authorities for the purpose of:
      enabling or assisting such bodies to discharge their functions as such;
      criminal investigations or proceedings;[194] and

---

[188] FSMA 2000, s 348(3).

[189] This is defined as commercial information the disclosure of which would, or might, significantly harm the legitimate business interests of the undertaking to which it relates or information
relating to the private affairs of an individual, the disclosure of which might significantly harm his
or her interests.

[190] It is usually recommended that all such documents as a general rule should be marked 'confidential—contains business secrets.'

[191] The Financial Services and Markets Act 2000 (Disclosure of Confidential Information)
Regulations 2001, SI 2001/2188.

[192] And vice versa: Gateway Regulations, regs 3 and 12 and Sch 1.

[193] Gateway Regulations, reg 12 and Schs 1 and 2.

[194] Gateway Regulations, reg 4.

— among other things, civil proceedings arising under or by virtue of FSMA 2000 (and certain other legislation), proceedings before the Financial Services and Markets Tribunal, any other civil proceedings to which the FSA or UKLA is (or is proposed to be) party, proceedings under the Company Directors Disqualification Act 1986 and certain proceedings under the Insolvency legislation.[195]

4.250 Further, there are other important caveats:

- if the material has been used in open court, for example in proceedings before the Financial Services and Markets Tribunal in public relating to enforcement action that the UKLA or FSA has taken, then it is unlikely to be confidential any more and will not therefore be protected from disclosure.[196] This may be an important caveat in practice, because civil legal proceedings may follow the conclusion of the regulatory enforcement process; and

- it is likely that the statutory protection does not preclude a court from ordering disclosure of the material by a person where that disclosure would be permitted under the Gateway Regulations.[197.]

4.251 It is important to note that, where an exception exists, there is no requirement to inform the person to whom the 'confidential information' relates of the disclosure.

4.252 Furthermore, the FSA is under a statutory obligation to take such steps as it considers appropriate to cooperate with other persons (whether in the UK or elsewhere) who have functions similar to those of the FSA or in relation to the prevention or detection of financial crime.[198] Thus, the possibility of the FSA sharing information with overseas regulators is a definite and real possibility and a statutory requirement if requested. In this regard, there are a number of Memoranda of Understanding between UK regulators and overseas regulators, as well as between regulators within the jurisdiction, in which the various regulators have agreed to cooperate with regulatory investigations and enforcement

---

[195] Gateway Regulations, reg 5.

[196] FSMA 2000, s 348(4).

[197] But not otherwise: *Bank of Credit and Commerce International (Overseas) Ltd (in liquidation) and others v Price Waterhouse (a firm) and others (Abu Dhabi and others, third parties) (Bank of England intervening)* [1997] 4 All ER 781, in relation to an equivalent provision in the Banking Act 1987, s 82, on the basis that a court cannot compel a person to commit a criminal offence.

[198] FSMA 2000, s 354. Moreover, FSMA 2000, s 169 gives the FSA general information gathering and investigative powers on behalf of overseas regulators and contains the considerations the FSA must take into account in determining whether to give assistance to overseas authorities by using its statutory powers, such as (i) whether the overseas authority would be in a position to help the FSA if necessary; (ii) whether the overseas authority has a similar regulatory system; (iii) the seriousness of the case and its importance to persons in the UK; (iv) whether it is in the public interest; and (v) the costs.

proceedings, including the sharing of information to the extent they are not restricted from doing so.[199] Significant examples are:

- the Memoranda of Understanding between the FSA and the SEC;[200]
- the Memorandum of Understanding between the FSA and the FRRP;[201]
- the Partnership Agreement between the FSA and the National Criminal Intelligence Service,[202] now SOCA;
- the Memorandum of Understanding between the FSA and HMRC;[203] and
- the Memorandum of Understanding between the FSA and the City of London Police.[204]

The OFT, by virtue of its membership of the European Competition Network **4.253** shares certain information as to its activities with the European Commission and with other national competition authorities in the European Community. This is for the express purpose of enhancing the quality and consistency of competition law enforcement across Europe. There are also arrangements to exchange information with other regulators, for example in North America. Due to the duties of confidentiality owed by those regulators, the agencies will ask for the permission of the company concerned to disclose specific information derived from the company to other regulators. Where a company is in a leniency situation, such a request can be difficult to refuse, given the duty of cooperation. However, it can and has been done in appropriate circumstances, without obviously incurring retribution from the agency in the process. Further, since s 241A of the Enterprise Act 2002 came into force from 17 April 2007, SI 2193 means that, from effect from 1 October 2007, the OFT can disclose, without consent, certain limited information for use by consumers and intellectual property litigants in civil litigation (and in taking advice in connection with such litigation). However, most information obtained under the competition related investigation powers is excluded.

---

[199] The Memorandum of Understanding between the Department of Trade and Industry, now BERR, the Securities and Investment Board (responsibility transferred to the FSA), the SEC and the US Commodity Futures Trading Commission, dated 25 September 1991; the Memorandum of Understanding between the Investment Management Regulatory Organization (responsibility transferred to the FSA) and the SEC, dated 1 May 1995; the Memorandum of Understanding between the FSA, the Bank of England, the SEC and the Commodity Futures Trading Commission, dated 28 October 1997; and the International Organization of Securities Commissions Multilateral Memorandum of Understanding concerning consultation and cooperation and the exchange of information, dated May 2002.

[200] The Memorandum of Understanding between the SEC and the FSA, dated 14 March 2006. Indeed, in relation to the disciplinary proceedings brought by the FSA against Shell, the FSA specifically commented in its press release that: 'The swift resolution of this case was made possible by the excellent co-operation the FSA has enjoyed with the [SEC]': FSA/PN/074/2004.

[201] 6 April 2005.

[202] 27 July 2001. The FSA is in the process of agreeing a Memorandum of Understanding with SOCA.

[203] March 2004.

[204] 23 July 2003.

4.254 The SFO has wide powers to share information with other criminal authorities. The only assumption that can be made in the context of an international investigation is that, where it will assist the prosecution of potential criminal activity, there will be a positive sharing of information, particularly amongst European and North American police authorities, and related cooperation and coordination of activities.

Freedom of Information Act 2000

4.255 The UKLA and the FSA are both public authorities within the meaning of the Freedom of Information Act 2000 (FOIA), which came fully into force in England on 1 January 2005. From that date, individuals and companies (including private civil litigants) have two principal rights under the FOIA (subject to certain exemptions): the right to be informed in writing whether a public authority holds specified information (*the existence right*) and, if it does, the right to be provided with that information (*the access right*).

4.256 Thus, the UKLA (and the FSA) has a duty to disclose documents (or the information contained in them) to individuals or businesses that make a request for them under the FOIA, unless an exemption applies. The original owner of the document has no automatic right to be consulted or informed before such information is handed over to a third party.

4.257 Information does not have to be provided in response to an existence right or access right request if the information is exempt information. Circumstances in which information or documents are subject to an absolute exception include:

- information or documents provided in confidence;[205] and
- information or documents subject to the statutory restrictions on disclosure in FSMA 2000, section 348.[206]

4.258 In certain other circumstances, information or documents are subject to a qualified exemption on disclosure. In these circumstances, the public authority is only required to disclose such information or documents if disclosure is in 'the public interest'.[207] Circumstances in which information or documents are subject to such a qualified exemption include:

- information or documents containing information that may be used for investigations (including regulatory investigations) or criminal prosecution where disclosure would prejudice their outcome;[208]

---

[205] FOIA, s 41.
[206] FOIA, s 44. This exemption would similarly apply to any other legislation prohibiting disclosure.
[207] FOIA, s 2.
[208] FOIA, s 30.

- information or documents, the release of which would be likely to prejudice effective law enforcement, including the prevention or detection of crime;[209]
- information or documents, which are subject to legal professional privilege;[210] and
- information or documents containing trade secrets.[211]

Whilst the absolute and qualified exemptions should protect most information **4.259** and documents provided as part of a regulatory investigation from FOIA-related disclosure, particularly if the company providing that information or documents expressly ensures that the information is provided in confidence and/or expressly explains that the information or documents contain commercially sensitive information, this is not an absolute guarantee. For example, the UK's Information Commissioner has recently ordered the FSA to disclose the identities of certain entities, which had been investigated, but not ultimately disciplined, by the FSA pursuant to a FOIA request.[212] There is, therefore, a risk that cannot be excluded that at least some documents produced may have to be disclosed in response to a FOIA request by a private litigant.

Private litigation

A frequent and major concern is whether documents in the possession of a regu- **4.260** lator will be vulnerable to third party disclosure applications in private litigation. The documents in which, as part of a leniency application or settlement, a company 'confesses' or gives highly prejudicial evidence would clearly be of great value to a litigating party.

English law has given a degree of protection to such documents.[213] However, **4.261** litigation in the US has tended not to be reassuring in this respect.[214]

This creates a natural tension. The agencies will want as full a disclosure to them **4.262** as possible, and would not want the company to be inhibited in doing so by the impact on its private litigation exposure. As a general rule, the concern focuses on communications between the company and the agency rather than the regulator's internal documents.

The usual, albeit unwieldy, resolution of this issue is a theatrical exercise whereby **4.263** the lawyer representing the company will give a presentation based on his privileged

---

209 FOIA, s 31.
210 FOIA, s 42.
211 FOIA, s 43.
212 7 August 2007. The FSA is currently appealing that decision using the appeal procedure in the FOIA.
213 At least at the European Commission level: see *Trouw (UK) Ltd v Mitsui (UK) Plc* [2006] EWHC 863.
214 See 3.135ff.

notes (often a script agreed in detail with the client) accompanied by original documents (which are vulnerable to disclosure in any event and which do not become more so by this process). The agency will then create its own notes of that presentation which remain its own documents, on its own files, and which will usually be protected from disclosure. The mechanics of undertaking this exercise are burdensome as are any further procedural steps associated with the information thereby conveyed, but it offers the highest degree of protection at the moment.

4.264 This process is less relevant for the FSA, which will usually perform its own interviews with individuals, using its statutory powers. However, similar issues do arise in relation to the delivery of any investigation report to the FSA.

Managing multiple regulators

4.265 A substantial problem is likely to attract the interest of multiple regulators, not only, say, within the UK but also internationally. For example, unless the circumstances are such that the European Commission takes jurisdiction, an international cartel will involve parallel dealings with different national competition agencies. Similar situations frequently occur in other areas such as corruption or securities market issues.

4.266 The only assumption can be that the regulators will cooperate at least at the level of sharing information, even if they do not actually coordinate their activities. On occasion, they can almost seem to be competing with each other, particularly to be seen to be taking action and being forthright in their handling of issues. It is, therefore, critical that there is a single, all encompassing strategy to manage the portfolio of regulators that might be involved. This will involve:

- ensuring that consistent explanations are given, and approaches taken, to each (this may well involve a standard 'script' narrating the parts of the story that are common to different regulators);

- having a clear view as to the relative interests of the different regulators, both as to what their likely timetables might be and how it may be possible to have that timetable adapted to a more rational approach;

- being prepared to take a strong stance on the respective jurisdictions of the various regulators and to avoid risks of 'double jeopardy' or '*ne bis in idem*', (being punished twice for the same wrong);

- assessing which regulators are likely to be 'opinion forming' on particular issues and prioritizing appropriately how to address their particular concerns; and

- coordinating between the various external advisers to ensure that the implementation of the company's approach is consistent and effective (bearing in mind that it will usually be the case that local staff or advisers will be best placed to deal with agencies in their jurisdiction).

It is in such circumstances that the management of investigations becomes most **4.267** complex and nuanced. A detailed understanding of the approach and objectives of the various regulators is critical to forming the right strategy.

K. Managing Employees During Investigations

Aside from the often substantial task of comprehensively gathering, data-basing **4.268** and analysing the documents (physical and electronic), the critical, and delicate, task will be that of obtaining information from employees. This task is fraught with pitfalls including:

- will people cooperate, what powers are there to compel them and is it wise to use them;
- will they give accurate evidence when they are worried that they might incriminate either themselves or their colleagues;
- what happens when the people concerned are exposed, themselves, to personal risk;
- when can they claim a right not to answer questions, or to separate legal representation;
- should they be suspended, or dismissed, and how is their status described internally;
- in what order should employees be interviewed;
- is it possible to prevent employees speaking to each other about the interview process and/or clarifying 'their story';
- what is the interface with disciplinary procedures;
- should anonymity or amnesty be offered;
- how are people protected from fears of internal retribution; and
- can, or should, legal fees be paid by the employer on behalf of the employee?

These are subtle issues and matters of judgement in each case, to be assessed in the **4.269** light of the particular problem in hand and the culture of the organization. It is part of the skill of a well-conducted investigation. However, there are some general propositions which are usually relevant.

Protection of whistle-blowers

It is worth recalling at the outset that UK legislation protects whistle-blowers **4.270** from being the subject of retribution. Such protection is afforded by the Public Interest Disclosure Act 1998 (PIDA), which inserted new provisions into the Employment Rights Act 1996 (ERtsA). Under PIDA, whistle-blowers are protected provided that their disclosure constitutes a 'protected disclosure'.

4.271 An employee can complain to the employment tribunal if he or she suffers a detriment as a result of making a protected disclosure[215] or is dismissed, in which case an employee will be regarded as having been unfairly dismissed if the reason or principal reason for a dismissal is the making of a protected disclosure.[216] In the latter case, there is no limit on the amount of the compensatory award the tribunal can make.[217]

4.272 Disclosures covering past, present or even anticipated failures may qualify as protected disclosures.[218] Such failures include crimes, miscarriages of justice, failure to comply with legal obligations, risks to health and safety, damage to the environment and the covering up of any of these.[219] It is immaterial whether the relevant failure occurred, occurs or would occur in the UK or elsewhere, and whether the law applying to it is that of the UK or of any other country or territory.[220]

4.273 The employee making the disclosure must have a reasonable belief that the disclosed information 'tends to show' the failure in question.[221] Consequently, it may not be a defence available to an employer that, unbeknownst to the employee, the allegations were untrue, provided the employee reasonably believed them to be so.

4.274 In addition, to be protected under PIDA, the disclosure should be made to:

- the employee's employer[222] or other responsible person,[223] in good faith;[224]
- the employee's legal adviser;[225]
- a person prescribed by the Secretary of State in respect of the failure in question,[226] provided that the employee makes the disclosure in good faith[227] and reasonably believes, inter alia, that the information disclosed, and any allegation contained in it, are substantially true; or

---

[215] ERtsA, s 47B.
[216] ERtsA, s 103A.
[217] ERtsA, s 124(1A).
[218] ERtsA, s 43B(1).
[219] ERtsA, s 43B(1).
[220] ERtsA, s 43B(2).
[221] ERtsA, s 43B(1).
[222] If the employer has a whistle-blowing procedure which authorizes disclosure to a third party, ie a regulator, disclosure under that procedure to the third party is treated the same as disclosure by the worker to the employer: ERtsA, s 43C(2).
[223] ERtsA, s 43C.
[224] In the reasonable belief of the worker, a person to whose conduct the failure solely or mainly relates or who solely or mainly has legal responsibility for the matter to which the failure relates.
[225] ERtsA, s 43D.
[226] ERtsA, s 43F.
[227] Where good faith on the part of the worker is required, consideration of the worker's motive is necessary—notwithstanding that the substance of the allegation is true, if the worker makes the disclosure with improper purpose, he may not have protection. See Butterworths, *Harvey on Industrial Relations & Employment Law* at A7D[673] at <http://www.lexisnexis.com>.

- in limited circumstances, other persons,[228] provided that various conditions are met and that the employee makes the disclosure in good faith, he or she reasonably believes that the information disclosed, and any allegation contained in it, are substantially true, does not make the disclosure for purposes of personal gain and in all the circumstances of the case, it is reasonable[229] for him or her to make the disclosure.

Any provision in an agreement which purports to preclude the employee from making a protected disclosure is void.[230] This includes provisions in any agreements, not just the employment contract, and expressly includes provisions in compromise agreements.   **4.275**

Note that a disclosure of information is not a protected disclosure if the person making the disclosure commits an offence by making it.[231]   **4.276**

Cooperation by the employee

It is an implied term in English employment contracts that employees will cooperate with reasonable instructions from their employers. This extends to requests to cooperate with internal investigations.[232] However, in cases where it is arguable that the request is not reasonable (such as where the employee may not be important to the conduct of the investigation or where the employee has valid reasons not to cooperate), the question of whether he or she can be compelled to cooperate will depend upon the express terms of the employee's contract of employment. If the requirement to cooperate is within its terms, or the terms can be interpreted so that a failure to cooperate could be deemed to be misconduct, then such a failure could result in the company having the power to dismiss the employee.   **4.277**

In practice, it is extremely rare in an investigation that any relationship with an employee is conducted on the basis of the strict nature of his or her legal obligations. A potentially 'guilty' employee who chooses not to cooperate, whether formally denying liability or not, is very unlikely to be compellable, in practice, under his or her employment contract, not least because the sanction of dismissal is one that he or she already faces in connection with the substantive issue. The relationship will have moved beyond such issues.   **4.278**

---

228 ERtsA, s 43G (other cases) and s 43H (exceptionally serious failures).
229 For example, it will rarely be reasonable to make a disclosure to the press.
230 ERtsA, s 43J.
231 ERtsA, s 43B(3).
232 If the employee is also an 'approved person', he or she will have a separate, general duty to the FSA to be open and cooperative with the FSA and to disclose appropriately any information of which the FSA would reasonably expect notice under Statement of Principle for Approved Persons 4: FSA Handbook at APER 2.1.2.

4.279 Even in relation to employees not so implicated, formal compulsion is virtually never the best route to obtaining information or evidence. If it is necessary to threaten the use of the employment obligations or, indeed, do more than merely acknowledging in response to a question on duties that there is, in fact, such an obligation of cooperation, it is likely that the relationship is already damaged and the process is unlikely to be productive. Note that, if the company does threaten an employee with dismissal for failure to cooperate, he or she may consider that he or she has been constructively dismissed and may accordingly resign.[233] Accordingly, it is necessary to proceed cautiously.

4.280 It is usually the case that a clear management direction that the company's interests require that the investigation understands fully and properly the factual position and the employee is requested to answer fully and frankly all questions put to him or her will be sufficient to obtain cooperation without formal pressure. An employee will usually consider that, however painful the process may be, his or her long term future interests at the company are best served by positive cooperation rather than dysfunctional behaviour. However, it is important that the employee perceives the investigation process as objective and fair; there will be considerable, understandable, reluctance to participate in a politically driven exercise which could be abused.

4.281 However, it is often appropriate to make it plain that actively lying to, or misleading the investigation will be treated as misconduct and subject to disciplinary action if appropriate. It is critical that there is the necessary degree of confidence in the employee's evidence. The company has to take significant and difficult decisions as to how to react to the issue that is being investigated. If the investigation is misled, there is an increased risk of the wrong decisions being taken and the company's position being damaged as a result. It can be made plain that this would be a very serious issue for the company and for the employee concerned. Companies may well also explain that they will do all that they can to support and protect employees who are cooperating fully with the investigation (subject to the inevitable constraints discussed below), providing a 'carrot', to contrast with the threat associated with any deception. Moreover, save in the case of an employee who is a 'potential guilty party', it may well not be in the employee's own interests to mislead. Should the matter later come to the attention of a regulator or a prosecutor, any dissimulation would be regarded with considerable concern and could amount, in certain circumstances, to an offence itself.[234]

---

233 Generally the test will be whether a reasonable listener would have interpreted the threat as amounting to constructive dismissal, see Butterworths, *'Harvey on Industrial Relations & Employment Law'* at DI2C(1)[229].

234 For example under FSMA 2000, s 177(4) and s 398.

In practice, it is usually most productive to structure the investigation as a coop- **4.282**
erative process with the employees and not as an adversarial one. It can fairly be
said that the subject of the investigation is a shared problem that both employees
and the company need to understand as fully as possible and the employee's
support is encouraged. This has implications for the interview process which
should usually, where possible, be collaborative, seeking information rather than
in the form of a 'cross-examination' seeking admissions and confessions. In most
circumstances, the former approach is much more efficient and informative.

Representation

Whether or not employees should be independently represented at an interview **4.283**
or otherwise in an investigation ultimately depends upon the circumstances, for
example, whether there is any suggestion that the breach may have resulted from
deliberate action by the employee, whether there is a risk of the employee facing
a criminal prosecution or whether there is a risk that the interests of the employee
and the interests of the company may conflict.[235] In any event, if the individual
asks to bring a lawyer to an interview, at his or her own cost, it is usually difficult
to refuse.

A more difficult, and frequent, issue is whether, and if so when, a lawyer comes **4.284**
under an ethical obligation to advise an employee that he or she should have separate representation and terminate the interview until that has occurred.

Rule 10 of the Solicitors' Code of Conduct 2007 provides that, in its dealings **4.285**
with third parties, a solicitor must not use its position to take unfair advantage of
anyone either for its own benefit or for another person's benefit. Particular care is
advised when solicitors deal with a person who does not have legal representation. A balance has to be struck between doing what is best for the client, in this
instance the employer, and not taking unfair advantage of the unrepresented
employee. The Code of Conduct recognizes the tension present in this balancing
exercise and states, 'to an extent, therefore, [Rule] 10.01 limits [a solicitor's] duty
to act in the best interests of [its] client'.

Consequently, at the outset of any interview with an employee who is suspected **4.286**
of being culpably involved in the matter under investigation, the employee
should be cautioned about the potentially incriminatory nature of the interview.
During the interview, the employee should be 'cautioned' when the solicitor
first has reason to believe that it is required.

---

[235] If there is no conflict, or no significant risk of conflict, one counsel may act for both a listed
corporate and its employees: The Solicitors' Code of Conduct 2007 at Rule 3.

4.287 In addition, as soon as the possibility of incrimination on the part of the employee does in fact arise, the interview should be suspended and he or she should be advised to obtain legal representation. If the employee declines representation (having been given reasonable time to consider it), then the solicitor should conduct the interview in a manner so as not to take unfair advantage of the employee, even if this means not extracting the most out of the interview from the employer's perspective.

The conduct of the interview

4.288 An interview is usually a tense process, particularly for the employee. It is now common practice, and prudent, to give the employee a clear statement as to the 'ground rules' for the interview, particularly when conducted by outside lawyers. This includes explaining that:

- the lawyer acts for the company and not for the employee and is, therefore, not in a position to advise him personally;
- that the meeting is confidential in every respect and is not to be discussed by the employee with any other party (save for his or her lawyer, if he or she has one)—but that the confidentiality may be waived by the company where it is appropriate, for example in defending regulatory proceedings or civil litigation; and
- where appropriate, the communications in the meeting are legally privileged, explaining the meaning of the term, but that the privilege is that of the company, which it may also decide to waive.

4.289 Since these messages can easily seem intimidating, or officious, to the employee, considerable tact is required to ensure that this position is understood without damaging what would otherwise be a useful interview. This is more easily done in the context of a cooperative process.

4.290 It is also good practice to explain whether notes will be taken (as they usually will) and if so, whether the employee will be allowed to view those notes. If the interviewer is a lawyer, it should be explained to the employee that any personal notes of the interviewer will be subject to a claim for privilege and will be treated confidentially and that, accordingly, the employee will not be able to see them.[236] Care must be taken not to mislead the employee: whether such notes are privileged depends on (a) whether the conversation itself is privileged[237] and (b) whether the notes contain added legal comment and analysis (which usually will be privileged)

---

[236] Depending on the circumstances, showing the notes to the employee has a risk of waiving privilege over them.

[237] Considered from 4.207.

or are just a verbatim record. If in doubt, it should be assumed that notes of interviews will not be privileged.

It is not common for investigation interviews to be recorded although this **4.291** does sometimes happen. Whilst it is helpful in terms of having an exact record, as discussed above, there may be a lesser degree of privilege protection for such a recording. Moreover, it is an invasive process and has a chilling impact on people's willingness to express themselves freely. It is often the case that more is discovered in a meeting that is not being recorded when it is possible to discuss the issues in a more open way.

Whether the employee should see the note, leaving aside privilege issues, is a **4.292** more complex matter. It would be common not to disclose it, leaving the note as an internal document. However, sometimes, and particularly where legal or regulatory proceedings are anticipated at which the employee might be a witness, it may be appropriate to prepare a formal statement working in conjunction with the employee. This process, although time consuming, usually has the benefit of refining considerably the nuances on a witness's evidence; surprising levels of detail can come to light in the process of moving from a note of a meeting to a carefully considered statement that an employee is prepared to endorse. Such a 'hard' document has considerable value in the future in assisting the employee to prepare for any interview and to remain clear on his evidence. Care needs to be taken, however, to ensure that litigation privilege[238] will protect the drafting process and, indeed, until used, the final statement. Again, if in doubt, it should be assumed that notes of interviews or draft witness statements will not be privileged.

The interview process itself requires skills and subtlety and is best done by people **4.293** with experience. It requires the ability to understand in detail the factual matters in issue; an understanding of the legal and regulatory aspects (so as to focus the questioning on key issues); the skill of adapting to new information, fitting it into the existing pattern and turning the interview to follow new relevant lines of enquiry, practice at posing and following up on questions to elicit information, some feel for the psychology of the employee and a degree of emotional intelligence as to how the process is managed.

Detailed preparation is essential and should be undertaken unless the time pres- **4.294** sures are so overwhelming that it is simply not possible. This may be the only opportunity to interview a particular witness, particularly where it becomes clear in the interview that someone who was not thought to be seriously involved is potentially guilty and the nature of the relationship then changes.

---

[238] Considered from 4.207.

Disciplinary process and amnesties

4.295 Employees frequently, and understandably, seek reassurance as to their personal position. This raises fact specific issues, reflecting also the corporate culture concerned. Some general points can, however, be addressed.

4.296 The investigation cannot be conflated with a disciplinary process. If it is necessary to begin any such process, it needs to be conducted entirely separately under the formal procedures established by the company. Clearly, what is said in an investigation process may be relevant to a disciplinary procedure, or to the decision to begin one, but the disciplinary process must establish the facts for itself and follow its own proper due process.

4.297 It is not possible to offer an employee a general amnesty. It needs to be clear that the company can give no protection against regulators or any personal civil or criminal liability. However, it is possible to offer a waiver of any possible disciplinary process but it needs to be considered with considerable circumspection. It would be prudent to exclude from that waiver certain categories of behaviour, which may come to light in the future and which would make any waiver seem ill-judged and inappropriate such as: any acts of dishonesty or knowing breaches of regulatory rules (eg in the financial services sector) or, importantly, misleading the investigators. It is also important to bear in mind that reaching a resolution with a regulator, or the company's wider image and reputation for strong corporate governance, may make it necessary to dismiss staff with a certain level of involvement in the matter.[239] This becomes dramatically more difficult if assurances have been given. Moreover, if the employee is an 'approved person' and regulatory proceedings take place, it is possible that the FSA will withdraw the individual's approval[240] in which case the person may not be able to do his or her previous job.

4.298 The FSA has indicated that it expects entities to deal adequately with any individuals who are responsible for misconduct, in order to foster a culture of zero tolerance to regulatory wrongdoing. In particular, the FSA has indicated that it expects serious regulatory misconduct to be a ground for summary dismissal and that dealing decisively with the relevant individuals will be taken into account in mitigation of any penalty the FSA (or the UKLA) might impose. This may also ensure that the breach is not repeated and may be viewed by the FSA or UKLA as a positive step taken by the company to protect the evidence.

---

[239] 'Enforcement priorities and issues for 2006', speech by Margaret Cole, Director of Enforcement, FSA, 18 January 2006.

[240] FSMA 2000, s 63.

In many cases it may be appropriate to take immediate action to suspend the **4.299** employee in question or remove him or her from any sensitive positions pending the completion of the investigation. This is very likely to be the case where the employee in question is an 'approved person' and is therefore carrying out a function which requires FSA approval and a certain level of fitness and propriety—if not suspended, such an individual should usually be moved to an unregulated position whilst the investigation is ongoing. The company's employee handbook and contract should be checked to confirm that the company has the power to suspend the employee.

Suspension is a delicate matter. It can, of course, be extremely disruptive to the **4.300** business and for the individual. It is more frequent in the financial services industry and in firms with a US culture (reflecting common practice in the US). However, it is very important to establish clearly, particularly in the minds of colleagues, that this is not a conclusion on responsibility or 'guilt' but rather prudent good governance, common in such circumstances, to ensure that the investigation and the handling of the company's business in the meantime are wholly presentable externally.

As a general rule, suspension is preferable to dismissal even where there is strong **4.301** evidence that serious breaches have occurred. Whilst the employment relationship is maintained, there are much closer links with the employee who continues to owe wider fiduciary duties to the company including confidentiality and cooperation with the investigation. There is, de facto, a higher degree of commercial leverage in any discussions with the individual, who may well depend on the company for his or her income and other benefits and may also have aspirations (depending on the facts) for some form of severance package, if he or she is ultimately dismissed. Finally it postpones what can be the very sensitive issue of the terms of any severance. There would not generally be any criticism in the UK of the company for imposing a protracted suspension, in the context of either an internal investigation or wider regulatory action or litigation.

If it is necessary to terminate an employment relationship with an employee, it **4.302** may be worth including specific cooperation and confidentiality wording in any severance arrangement.[241]

---

[241] Where an employee is dismissed for misconduct and that employee has been performing a controlled function, the company will need to notify the FSA of that fact on Form C within seven business days after the person ceases to perform that function. The company is obliged to make full disclosure of a suspected misconduct issue even in cases where the employee has resigned before the issue has been investigated or fully investigated. If the company has reasonable grounds for believing it will submit a qualified Form C, it has an obligation to notify the FSA as soon as practicable, and ideally within one business day of becoming aware of the facts. A Form C will be qualified if:

  (a) the company reasonably believes that the information contained in the form may affect the FSA's assessment of the approved person's fitness and propriety;
  (b) the company dismisses or suspends an approved person from employment;

Specific issues relating to interviews by regulators

4.303   When dealing with regulators such as the UKLA or FSA, which require a company to deal with it in an open and cooperative manner, the regulator may well expect the company to take reasonable steps to ensure that its employees assist with any investigation.

4.304   Interviews by regulators of employees raise a wider set of issues than interviews by the company itself or the investigation team. The precise powers and approach will depend on the regulator and the nature of the matter in issue. However, the following features would be common.

- The employee is accompanied by lawyers, often the company's legal team, to protect both his or her interests and the company's. The lawyers have the ability to intervene, particularly on scope or due process issues to ensure fair play, but they are not there as advocates for the witness and can play only a limited role.

- Legally privileged discussions remain protected but self-incrimination defences are not necessarily available (albeit that most regimes include a 'Saunders' protection).[242]

- The interviews are normally recorded. The witness will usually be told, on the record, that misleading answers can give rise to independent offences.

- The interviewers will have some documentary evidence which they will 'put to' the witness, seeking his or her views.

- Although the scope is confined to that of the investigation, it can be difficult to prevent the questioning becoming quite wide-ranging, since the regulator is in a position of some considerable legal strength particularly when, as would usually be the case, the employee is being interviewed under compulsory powers.

- In most cases, although stressful, such interviews are more inquisitorial, seeking information, understanding and evidence, rather than adversarial processes of hostile cross-examination using leading questions and similar techniques. They are not always conducted with rigour and there are risks that a regulator can misunderstand a position because, although in control of the questioning process, the relevant facts are not established with sufficient precision. A key role for any adviser present is to seek to anticipate and prevent such conceptual errors, whilst not interfering with an interview process that he or she does not control.

- Although a transcript is often made available to the witness to review and correct, this is not always the case and it depends on the regulator and its approach

---

(c) an approved person resigns while under investigation by the company, the FSA or any other regulatory body: FSA Handbook at SUP 10.13.6–10.13.7.

[242] To the effect that the witness does not have the right to refuse to answer questions the answers to which might incriminate him or her, but those answers cannot be used as evidence against him in any subsequent personal proceedings that there might be against him or her, after *Saunders v United Kingdom* [1996] ECHR 19187/91. See also FSMA 2000, s 174. See also 4.48 above.

(despite it usually being good practice, not least for the regulator in having a more accurate result). Substantive 'corrections' or changes to the individual's evidence can also be used against the individual by the regulator as evidencing inaccurate testimony initially.

• It is customary, and often essential, to prepare an employee for such a process, observing carefully applicable ethical guidelines to ensure that the preparation is to enable the witness to give his evidence clearly and succinctly and not to assist him in giving misleading or evasive evidence.

Challenges posed by ex-employees

From time to time an employer may wish to interview or otherwise obtain infor- **4.305**
mation from an ex-employee for the purpose of the employer's own internal investigation.

Unlike a current employee (whose terms of employment—both express and **4.306**
implied—may require him or her to cooperate with a reasonable request from the employer), an ex-employee is generally under no obligation to cooperate with a former employer. This position may be varied by the terms of any termination or compromise agreement governing the terms on which the ex-employee's employment ended. It is common practice among many regulated firms for these agreements to impose an obligation on the ex-employee to provide such assistance as may reasonably be required by the former employer with any investigation, internal or external. However, in the absence of such an agreement, an ex-employee's cooperation will be on a voluntary basis only. This will often be the case where the ex-employee's employment ended by reason of his or her resignation in circumstances wholly unconnected with the matters under investigation.

Relationships with separately represented employees

Joint defence agreements, whereby parties with a common interest in a particular **4.307**
matter agree that they may exchange confidential and privileged information for their mutual benefit, without waiving either the confidentiality or the privilege, are, in general, permitted by English law. Formal contractual documents have not been common but are more frequently being considered.

A formal agreement is not necessary to create a common interest between two **4.308**
parties; nor is it necessary to preserve confidentiality and privilege over documents exchanged between them: if there is a common interest, a document privileged in the hands of one party will not lose its privilege by disclosure to the other party[243] (although one party cannot assert that privilege any longer against the other).[244]

---

[243] *The World Era (No 2)* [1993] 1 Lloyds Rep 363.
[244] Although privilege will be retained as against the other in respect of any documents or information not disclosed.

However, a formal agreement, which identifies the common interest and provides expressly that the documents are being shared under the protection of common interest privilege, may assist in evidencing the common interest and therefore limiting the risk of any privilege having been considered to have been waived by exchanging the documents or information.

4.309 Privilege created in such a process is held jointly. It is unclear, however, if it can be waived one party alone. This may cause a problem if, for example, the company, but not the employee, wishes to waive privilege in a document protected by common interest privilege.

4.310 Moreover, it is not clear how effective and robust joint defence agreements are in the context of regulatory investigations. For example, it has been argued, in the anti-trust field, that the risk that one party might go for leniency and give evidence against another means that there is insufficient common interest for the privilege to apply. On the other hand, that risk, or something similar to it, applies in many circumstances where there is an adversarial legal process and has not operated to prevent the privilege applying.[245]

4.311 Whilst the position remains unclear on the authorities, care needs to be exercised as to disclosures to former employees and third parties in the teeth of a regulatory investigation. However, this is a risk assessment and there are many occasions where a degree of communication, perhaps orally between external legal advisers, is desirable and wholly appropriate. Generally speaking, regulators in the UK have not sought to probe such communications nor have they obviously been adversely influenced by the fact that they have occurred provided, of course, that there is no suggestion that false evidence has been given or that any duty of confidence owed to the regulator has been breached.

4.312 As there is a risk that waiver by one of the interested parties of the common interest privilege could constitute waiver by all, the value of the privilege in the context of joint defence is uncertain, particularly where there is an incentive for a party to cooperate with a regulatory authority to the detriment of the other(s).

Payment of legal fees/indemnification/fee advances

4.313 Employees (including directors) may be indemnified against the costs of defending regulatory enforcement action and against any costs that they may be ordered

---

[245] As Rix J commented in *Svenska Handelsbanken v Sun Alliance and London Insurance plc* [1995] 2 Lloyd's Rep 84:
[I]t is clear that the fact that differences may arise between parties of whatever closeness of interest, such as to prevent them from at all times using the same lawyers, or such as may indeed even cause them to find themselves ultimately on opposite sides of litigation, does not necessarily mean that they cannot be parties with a common interest for the purpose of this concept . . .

to pay to regulators, if it is in the best interests of the company to do so.[246] Note, however, that companies are prohibited from indemnifying directors against financial penalties imposed by regulators.[247] Moreover any obligation to indemnify an employee against the penalties arising from criminal behaviour or regulatory breaches is likely to be unenforceable as a matter of public policy.[248]

Employees (including directors) may also be advanced fees for representation by separate legal counsel. In the case of directors, the director must be obliged to repay these fees if he or she is subsequently convicted of any offence in any criminal proceedings.[249]   **4.314**

Whether it is appropriate to enter into these types of arrangements is, again, a matter of delicate judgement. In the UK (contrasting the position in the US), it has generally been the case that employees are treated as 'innocent until proven guilty' and support of this nature is frequently extended so long as the employee is cooperating and keeping lines of communication open and effective (whilst, of course, protecting his or her own position) and the evidence against him or her is not such that support is clearly inappropriate in governance and PR terms. Clearly, where it is appropriate, support of this nature is reassuring to all staff and, again, engenders a degree of commitment and loyalty from the employee that may make it easier to manage the company's own position.   **4.315**

L. Concluding an Investigation

The question of when, and how, to conclude an investigation can be surprisingly subtle.   **4.316**

In practice, most investigations do hit a stage of diminishing returns when incrementally less information is coming out from the process. The main issues are relatively clear, even if there remain details that are not fully understood. Where an investigation is purely internal, conducted, for example, as a matter of good   **4.317**

---

[246] In the case of directors, any decision should be taken by disinterested members of the Board only.

[247] Companies Act 2006, ss 232–34. Similarly, 'authorised persons' are prohibited from indemnifying any persons against financial penalties imposed by the FSA: FSA Handbook at GEN 6.1. Companies are also prohibited from exempting a director from or indemnifying a director against any liability incurred in defending any criminal proceedings in which he or she is convicted, or against any liability incurred in defending any civil proceedings brought by the company in which judgment is given against him or her: Companies Act 2006, ss 232–34.

[248] *Askey v Golden Wine Co* [1948] 2 All ER 35. However, where the employee is convicted on the basis of strict liability in circumstances in which he or she was not in any way culpable he or she may succeed in recovering fines and costs in a civil action (*Osman v J Ralph Moss* [1970] 1 Lloyd's Rep 313).

[249] Companies Act 2006, s 205. Note that neither the obligation to repay any loan granted to cover the costs of defending any proceedings nor the prohibition against indemnity apply in the case of proceedings brought by third parties, such as class actions brought by shareholders.

corporate governance, it may well be that, in such a case, there is sufficient certainty as to what occurred (and who should be held responsible) for senior management to be comfortable that it can take the right management action without further work being undertaken on the specific facts. In such cases, it may well be entirely consistent with good governance to draw a close to a process relatively early.

4.318 However, where regulators are involved, it is likely to be the case that the investigation will have to probe deeper and the point at which it is disproportionate to continue is postponed. This is for the following reasons.

- If the investigation is to provide information and evidence to enable the company to defend its position in regulatory or criminal proceedings, there is a need for detailed evidence to support a technical legal position. This is likely to require a more fine-grained understanding of the facts.

- Where the investigation is being conducted to be disclosed to a regulator as part of managing an issue which is of supervisory or regulatory concern, the regulator is, in a sense, outsourcing the work to the company (or its external advisers at the company's expense). It is easy for a regulator to be exigent in demands for detail. Additionally, it is important for the credibility of the process that the company has drilled down to the appropriate level and can demonstrate that it has done so. Tactically, it is unattractive to have to prepare supplemental reports (particularly in an area that has already been represented to have been addressed) and there is, therefore, a strong incentive to investigate to a detailed level.

- Where a company has a difficult history in a particular area, it may well be that considerably more work needs to be done both to satisfy a regulator generally and to deal with the issues raised by the current problem in the context of what may have previously occurred. In essence, the company has ground to make up and will likely have to invest more effort in the process.

- Finally, where a company has sought leniency, for example in the anti-trust area, there is an ongoing obligation of cooperation to maintain the value of the leniency discount. Agencies can be forceful in applying that pressure to seek more and more information forcing a process of a rolling investigation over a protracted period. This is particularly the case where the agency's own investigation into other parties produces new information which forces a re-examination of issues in the company from a new perspective.

4.319 In general, no investigation should cease short of the point where:

- the scope of the issue is clear and there can be confidence that there are no other related or similar issues elsewhere in the organization;

- management can be confident that 'the bottom of the problem' has been reached (as far as possible);
- the parties responsible have been identified and it is possible to take a reasoned view on any necessary disciplinary measures;
- systems, controls and related management and reporting failures have been identified; and critically
- management can be confident that remedial measures can be identified which are sufficient properly to address the issue for the future and can be presented appropriately.

Where an investigation is a matter of public interest, there are particular stake-holder and PR issues to be considered. There will, inevitably, be cynicism by critical or hostile observers (or simply those seeking to create a story) that any process did not go far enough. There needs to be a careful strategy, perhaps using the authority of senior non-executive directors or external advisers, to ensure that any decision to terminate an investigation is presentable and will be viewed externally as an example of good, rather than poor, governance. This requires careful PR planning, including managing the expectations of external parties appropriately. Ideally, it is possible to address these issues within the context of the remedies that have been applied, without having to explain any such decision with reference to the facts that were uncovered. **4.320**

A common issue is whether a report should be prepared. In the case of an investigation that is conducted in conjunction with regulatory action, it may well be unavoidable. The regulator will usually insist on formal output that it can keep in its files. **4.321**

However, the inevitable difficulty is that any such document is highly sensitive. Unless the investigation has established that there was no wrongdoing (which is rare, given that it is predicated on a high degree of concern that there was misbehaviour) such a document is likely to contain findings of fact against the company which would be highly valuable admissions in the hands of a third party, in particular in civil litigation. This is particularly relevant in the anti-trust field (and in situations of leniency) where the communications with the regulator are frequently the subject of disclosure activity from damages-seeking litigants. In this area, the practice of giving oral evidence, by outside lawyers, recorded by the agency in its own private records, to give the maximum amount of protection, has become common.[250] **4.322**

Conversely, senior management will usually feel more comfortable having reviewed, and minuted the receipt and approval of, a report explaining the results **4.323**

---

[250] Considered from 4.260.

of the investigation. Not least, many senior executives regard it as appropriate given the (often substantial) costs of such an exercise to see some 'hard' output from the process.

4.324 Privilege may be available for such a report, particularly insofar as it analyses the company's legal position. However, that may not always be the case. A company can come under pressure to waive privilege, particularly if there is also regulatory action in the US. A claim of privilege can look very defensive in relation to a key-note document such as a final report.

4.325 Finally, once a final report exists, it can become a focal point for claims for disclosure in either a full or abridged version whether from regulators (in future matters), litigants (who will want the full version!), the press or shareholders. The very fact of such a tangible document creates the call for publicity. The natural and justifiable refusal to disclose, however, automatically creates an impression of defensiveness or guilt, cover-up, a lack of transparency and poor governance, even if wholly unjustified.

4.326 A frequent solution to this issue is a compromise that may work well in practice. Senior management, or the board, as appropriate, receives a detailed oral presentation from the external legal team, with visual aids as necessary. The text and details of that presentation are kept with the law firm conducting the investigation. The presentation includes explaining the contemporaneous evidence, in detail, and its relevance (such material exists anyway and the company's position is not usually materially worsened by its being presented). The presentation would include clear proposals (usually discussed in detail with senior management in advance) as to what remedial measures would be appropriate. The company then appropriately records the process that was adopted, that (hopefully) the board or senior management approved the process, the factual conclusions and, critically, the remedial measures, which may then be recorded in some detail.

M. Litigation Risks

4.327 A driving concern for companies undergoing an investigation is often their broader litigation risk. The litigation exposure faced by a company in such situations includes regulatory proceedings leading to administrative sanctions, criminal proceedings against either the company or, more likely, individuals, and civil litigation from private parties. As a general rule, the management of all these risks is assisted, but clearly not excluded, by an investigation. Its main impact is to bring greater certainty. This is usually valuable in bringing about an early settlement of any any litigation issues and may also assist in doing so at a lower cost. This will generally have considerable management and shareholder benefits.

Criminal litigation by regulators

Clearly, not all investigations conducted by regulators will result in a criminal **4.328** prosecution. Regulators generally follow a specific set of criteria to determine whether or not it is appropriate to commence criminal litigation.

The FSA will only pursue[251] a criminal prosecution where appropriate.[252] In **4.329** deciding whether it is appropriate, the FSA applies the two general, criminal tests set out in the Code for Crown Prosecutors.[253]

First, the FSA will commence criminal proceedings only where it is satisfied that **4.330** the evidence is such that a jury or a bench of magistrates (properly directed in accordance with the law) is more likely than not to convict the defendant of the charge alleged. In deciding whether there is enough evidence to prosecute, the FSA will consider whether the available evidence can properly be used in criminal proceedings and is reliable. It is important to note that many regulators, such as the FSA, will not generally be able to use, or refer to, in criminal proceedings a statement made by the defendant in compliance with the regulator's compulsory powers of investigation.[254]

Secondly, where the evidential test is satisfied, the FSA will also consider whether **4.331** a prosecution would be in the public interest. This will depend on the circumstances of each individual case. The FSA will balance the factors for and against prosecution, for example, if a conviction is likely to result in a significant sentence, the defendant was in a position of authority or trust or there is evidence that the offence was premeditated, this will favour prosecution. Only if the FSA determines that criminal prosecution is in the public interest will it proceed to prosecute.

A criminal prosecution does not preclude a regulator from taking other civil or **4.332** regulatory action in relation to the same matter. The expectation would be, however, that the civil or regulatory proceedings will lag the criminal proceedings if there is any real risk of prejudicing the criminal proceedings (eg because both proceedings involve adjudication of the same issues).[255]

---

[251] The FSA can also issue a formal caution, rather than pursuing a criminal prosecution. However, in accordance with Home Office guidance, it will not administer a caution unless it is satisfied that (i) there is sufficient evidence of the person's guilt to give a realistic prospect of conviction if prosecuted; (ii) the person admits the offence; and (iii) the person understands the significance of a caution and gives informed consent to being cautioned: FSA Handbook at EG 12.5.

[252] FSA Handbook at EG 12.2.

[253] See FSA Handbook at EG 12.2.

[254] FSMA 2000, s 174.

[255] The factors that will be taken into account in deciding whether to take civil or regulatory action where criminal proceedings are possible are set out in the FSA Handbook at EG 12.4. These factors reflect the legal position that courts may intervene to prevent injustice where the continuation of one

4.333   For example, it is quite possible to envisage circumstances in which instances of market misconduct may arguably involve a breach of the criminal law (eg the offences of insider dealing and/or misleading statements and practices) as well as market abuse for which regulatory sanctions can be imposed. In these circumstances, it is the FSA's policy not to impose a sanction for market abuse where a person is being prosecuted for market misconduct or has been finally convicted or acquitted of market misconduct in a criminal prosecution arising from substantially the same allegations.[256]

4.334   Conversely, it is the FSA's policy not to commence a criminal prosecution where it has brought, or is seeking to bring, disciplinary proceedings for market abuse arising from substantially the same allegations.[257] If the circumstances give rise to potential criminal and civil sanctions, it may be that the FSA will prefer to proceed down the market abuse route.[258] A prosecution may be harder to prove and take longer to get to trial: the FSA would have to prove its case beyond reasonable doubt in front of a jury.

4.335   All of the criminal offences that can be committed by a company can also be committed by individuals, whether directors, former directors or employees of companies (or, for example, in the case of market abuse, even if the individual is totally unconnected with the company). The same policy and criteria are applied by the FSA in determining whether to pursue criminal prosecutions or market abuse proceedings against a company.

4.336   Similar issues arise in the context of criminal cartel behaviour under the Enterprise Act 2002 where there are also wider regulatory investigations into infringements under Chapter 1 of the Competition Act 1998 or Article 81 issues. It would be expected to be clear from the very early stages of a competition investigation whether the OFT was seeking a criminal prosecution or not. At the time of writing, the first criminal prosecutions are starting to be seen and experience of agency

---

set of proceedings may prejudice the fair trial of other proceedings, but will only do so where there is a real risk of serious prejudice that may lead to injustice: Per Neill LJ in *R v Panel on Takeovers and Mergers, ex p Fayed* [1992] BCC 524 at 531.

256 FSA Handbook at EG 12.10. Although the FSA may apply to the court for an injunction to prevent market abuse continuing or to require the person to take steps to remedy the consequences of the abuse or may impose or apply to the court for a restitution order in relation to profits accrued to the person or loss suffered by others as a result of the market abuse: FSA Handbook at EG 12.4.

257 FSA Handbook at EG 12.10, although it may still apply to the court for an injunction to prevent market abuse continuing or to require the person to take steps to remedy the consequences of the abuse or impose or apply to the court for a restitution order.

258 And history suggests that it does so, although the FSA has obtained criminal convictions for misleading statements and practices against the former CEO and finance director of the call centre software firm, AIT (on 16 August and 18 August 2005 respectively), for recklessly making a misleading statement to the London Stock Exchange.

practice in this area will develop. However, it is critical that, if the OFT is seeking criminal enforcement, the procedures that it uses for its investigation process will be to the necessary criminal standard, including interviewing people under caution. Other cases where a company or its staff are exposed both to regulatory and criminal risks are in tax or environmental investigations.

Any threat of criminal proceedings accentuates heavily the conflict of interest **4.337** issues discussed above between the company and its relevant employees,[259] and almost always mandates separate representation. This inevitably complicates the management of the company's position enormously. However, it is usually in such situations that a fully effective internal investigation comes into its own. Not only will the company have a factual understanding that is ahead of that of the regulator, it may be able to deploy the investigation, particularly by an outside firm, to demonstrate to a regulator that there is not the necessary evidential basis, and never will be, to justify criminal proceedings, or not on all aspects of a particular matter. This is the paradigm case of the benefits of this form of risk management.

Civil/regulatory or other action by regulators

Regulators have a wide variety of tools at their disposal to address breaches of **4.338** their rules and regulations, short of formal proceedings, and certainly criminal proceedings.

The UKLA (and the FSA as a whole) takes a risk-based approach to disciplinary **4.339** proceedings, selecting cases according to their seriousness and how they fit in with the UKLA's priorities. Often the key driver will be the deterrent effect of publicly disciplining companies for breaches of relevant rules and the belief that an increased public awareness of regulatory standards may also contribute to the protection of investors.[260]

The policy in determining whether to take disciplinary action is to consider the **4.340** full circumstances of the case, in particular, taking account of a number of factors (the list of which is expressly non-exhaustive), namely:[261]

- the nature, seriousness and impact of the suspected breach, including:
  — whether the breach was deliberate or reckless;
  — the duration and frequency of the breach;
  — the amount of any benefit gained or loss avoided as a result of the breach;

---

[259] Considered from 4.283.
[260] FSA Handbook at EG 2.1 and EG 7.1.
[261] FSA Handbook at DEPP 6.2.1.

— whether the breach reveals serious or systemic weaknesses of the management systems or internal controls relating to all or part of a person's business;

— the impact or potential impact of the breach on the orderliness of markets including whether confidence in those markets has been damaged or put at risk;

— the loss caused, or risk of loss, to consumers or other market users;

— the nature and extent of any financial crime facilitated, occasioned or otherwise attributable to the breach; and

— whether there are a number of smaller issues, which individually may not justify disciplinary action, but which do so when taken collectively;

• the conduct of the person after the breach, including the following (and thereby directly demonstrating the value of an effective internal investigation and pre-emptive action by the company concerned):

— how quickly, effectively and completely the person brought the breach to the attention of the FSA or another relevant regulatory authority;

— the degree of cooperation the person showed during the investigation of the breach;

— any remedial steps the person has taken in respect of the breach;

— the likelihood that the same type of breach (whether on the part of the person under investigation or others) will recur if no action is taken;

— whether the person concerned has complied with any requirements or rulings of another regulatory authority relating to his behaviour (eg where relevant, those of the Takeover Panel or a regulated investment exchange); and

— the nature and extent of any false or inaccurate information given by the person and whether the information appears to have been given in an attempt to knowingly mislead the FSA;

• the previous disciplinary record and compliance history of the person including:

— whether the FSA (or any previous regulator) has taken any previous disciplinary action resulting in adverse findings against the person;

— whether the person has previously undertaken not to do a particular act or engage in particular behaviour;

— whether the FSA (or any previous regulator) has previously taken protective action in respect of a firm, using its own initiative powers, by means of a variation of a Part IV permission or otherwise, or has previously requested the firm to take remedial action, and the extent to which such action has been taken; and

— the general compliance history of the person, including whether the FSA (or any previous regulator) has previously issued the person with a private warning;

- whether the UKLA has given any guidance on the conduct in question;[262]
- where other regulatory bodies propose to take action in respect of the same or a similar breach, whether that action would be adequate to address the UKLA's concerns and whether it would be appropriate for the UKLA to take its own action; and
- action taken by the FSA in previous similar cases.

When deciding whether to take action for market abuse or requiring or encour- **4.341**
aging it, the FSA may consider the following additional factors:

- the degree of sophistication of the users of the market in question, the size and liquidity of the market, and the susceptibility of the market-to-market abuse;
- the impact, having regard to the nature of the behaviour, that any financial penalty or public censure may have on the financial markets or on the interests of consumers, including whether a penalty may bolster market confidence, deter future market abuse and improve standards of conduct or, in the context of a takeover bid, whether the use of its powers may have an adverse effect on the timing or outcome of that bid.[263]

The UKLA has indicated that it regards the listed corporate as having primary **4.342**
responsibility for ensuring compliance with its own regulatory obligations and, therefore, any disciplinary action for breach of the Listing Rules (or the Disclosure Rules and Transparency Rules or the Prospectus Rules) will normally be taken in the first instance against the listed corporate itself.[264] However, where a director was 'knowingly concerned' in the listed corporate's breach, the UKLA may take action against the director. It may also do so where it does not consider it appropriate to seek a disciplinary sanction against the listed corporate.[265]

Note that the UKLA has also given detailed guidance as to the factors it will take **4.343**
into account in determining which (if any) of the relevant penalties should be imposed.[266]

---

[262] The UKLA will not take action against a person for behaviour that it considers to be in line with guidance, other materials published by the FSA in support of the Handbook or FSA-confirmed Industry Guidance, which were current at the time of the behaviour in question.

[263] FSA Handbook at DEPP 6.2.2. If the FSA considers that the proposed use of its powers may have such an adverse effect, it will consult the Takeover Panel and give due weight to its views.

[264] FSA Handbook at DEPP 6.2.10.

[265] FSA Handbook at DEPP 6.2.11. The FSA has additional disciplinary powers against directors who are also 'approved persons', for example, it has the power to discipline 'approved persons' for breaches of the Statements of Principle for Approved Persons (FSMA 2000, s 66 and FSA Handbook at APER 2.1.2), although, in broad terms, the FSA's policy is to discipline 'approved persons' only where there is evidence of personal culpability: FSA Handbook at DEPP 6.2.4.

[266] See, for example, FSA Handbook at EG 7.10 in respect of private warnings; DEPP 6.4 in respect of public censures and financial penalties; DEPP 6.3 for market abuse; LR 5.1 in respect of

4.344 In the UK, the FSA and the UKLA have been the most sophisticated regulators in setting out their policy in this respect. The position in relation to other regulators is much more nuanced. The issue clearly does not arise in the context of the criminal authorities. The anti-trust authorities certainly prioritize (usually on a publicly disclosed basis) the areas that they think are the most appropriate use of their resources which, in turn, gives some indication of whether they will pursue substantial remedies, thereby requiring a greater allocation of their resources.

4.345 In 'hard core' areas, including price fixing, market sharing, bid rigging or market foreclosure issues, it will usually be the case that the regulators will use the full force of their powers, even in quite small markets. These issues are seen as critical to the type of competitive economy that the UK seeks to create. However, in other cases, in particular behavioural issues, perhaps relating to the application of licence conditions in the regulator sectors (eg telecommunications, energy), to particular practices by a dominant company (say on discounting or bundling) or on issues relating to the impact of particular contract terms or conditions or transparency practices, it is possible to resolve matters by less formal means. Indeed, the OFT has specific powers to accept undertakings from companies as a way of terminating an investigation. It has rarely done so to date, but there have been specific cases where this has occurred and it is quite possible that the practice will increase.

Risks of private civil litigation

4.346 Frequently, the facts and matters that give rise to possible breaches of applicable regulatory requirements will involve a breach of a legal obligation owed to shareholders, competitors or counterparties, which has caused them financial loss such that they seek compensation.

4.347 In the case of listed companies, breaches of their regulatory obligations will not usually give shareholders or other third parties a direct means of obtaining redress for their loss as a result of that breach. This is in sharp contrast to the position in the US and in some other European countries. The position in the UK is still governed by the rule in *Foss v Harbottle*[267] to the effect that the right claimant for damage done to the company is the company itself and not its shareholders. Although the new, currently unused, derivative action contained in the Companies Act 2006 will enhance shareholder rights, it does not undermine that fundamental principle.

---

suspension of listing; LR 5.2 in respect of cancellation of listing; EG 10 in respect of injunctions; and EG 11 in respect of restitution orders.

[267] (1843) 2 Hare 461, 67 ER 189.

Thus, in normal circumstances, a private litigant who has suffered loss will have to establish that the company is liable to him or her under general legal principles (eg for breach of contract under the Memorandum and Articles of Association of the company if the private litigant is a shareholder or for negligent misrepresentation). These tend to be high tests. Thus, even if the company has to concede that it committed a regulatory breach, for example to reach a settlement with the UKLA on disciplinary or other enforcement issues, it does not necessarily follow that shareholders or other third parties will be able to bring a private action as a result of that breach. **4.348**

English law recognizes a claim in tort, known as breach of statutory duty, based on a person's breach of an obligation imposed on him or her under statute. However, a breach of statutory provisions does not necessarily give rise to a claim for damages for breach of statutory duty.[268] The key to such a claim is to show that, as a matter of construction, the statutory duty was imposed on the person for the protection of a limited class of the public and the English Parliament intended to confer upon the members of that class a private right of action for breach of that duty.[269] **4.349**

If it is possible to overcome this hurdle, and show that the relevant provision is capable of giving rise to a claim for breach of statutory duty, then the person concerned must also show that: **4.350**

- the damage is of a type that the legislation was intended to protect against and that the claimant is within a class of persons that was intended to be protected by the statute;
- the relevant statutory duty was breached;[270] and
- the breach of duty caused the loss.

Of course, there may be defences available to the company. **4.351**

There are other ways in which a private litigant could be compensated for any losses it has suffered outside the court processes. For example: **4.352**

- the regulator may apply to the court[271] to impose a restitution order on the company;[272]

---

[268] See *Leon Carty (by his litigation friend, Dorothy Brown-Carty) v London Borough of Croydon* [2004] EWHC 228 (QB).

[269] See *X (Minors) v Bedfordshire County Council* [1995] 2 AC 633, House of Lords (and the appeal to the ECHR in *Z v UK* [2001] 2 FLR 612). Whether or not such a right exists is a matter of construction of the statute concerned.

[270] This depends upon the construction of the relevant provision. For example, some duties imposed by statute require the person to take reasonable care while others are to be applied with strict liability.

[271] In the case of market abuse or where the entity or individual is an 'authorised person' or an 'approved person', the FSA can impose a restitution order without obtaining a court order: FSMA 2000, s 384.

[272] FSMA 2000, ss 382 and 383 and FSA Handbook at EG 11.

- the regulator may apply to the court for an injunction requiring the company to remedy its breach;[273] and/or
- the company itself may decide voluntarily to compensate shareholders (or other third parties) as part of the negotiation process with the regulator, to demonstrate cooperation and mitigate any fine.[274]

4.353 So far as procedure is concerned, English law does not, currently, have US-style class actions. There are, however, three specific procedures by which multiple claimants, such as shareholders, can bring claims against the company or, for example, its directors.[275] The closest English equivalent to a class action is the group litigation order.[276] An English court may make a group litigation order where there are multiple claims giving rise to 'common or related issues of fact or law'.[277] Whilst those group litigation orders that have hitherto been made have tended to relate to personal injury and taxation, they remain a possibility in cases of claims against listed corporates.

4.354 Another option for multiple claimants is the representative action.[278] This allows actions to be started by one or more persons as representatives of a larger group of persons who have the 'same interest' in the claim. The 'same interest' requirement is narrower than the need for 'common or related issues of fact or law' for a group litigation order to be granted. This means that representative actions rarely occur in practice. In addition, as noted above, English law has a specific procedure called derivative actions, by which a claim is brought by one or more shareholders of a company in name of and on behalf of the company, for example, against its directors, to claim a remedy for the company.[279]

4.355 While a decision by a regulator and a corporate on a particular matter of fact or law is binding as between the corporate and that regulator,[280] so as to prevent the same issue from being relitigated between them in any other forum, it is not normally binding as between the company and any third party.[281] However, since the

---

[273] FSMA 2000, ss 380 and 381 and FSA Handbook at EG 10.

[274] Although this will not necessarily prevent individual civil litigants from seeking alternative redress.

[275] The details of these procedures are beyond the scope of this book. There are also a number of proposals, particularly in the competition arena, to allow private litigation to be brought more easily in England.

[276] Civil Procedure Rules, Part 19, Part III.

[277] Civil Procedure Rules, Part 19, Rules 19.10 and 19.11.

[278] Civil Procedure Rules, Part 19, Part II.

[279] Civil Procedure Rules, Part 19 at Rule 19.9.

[280] For example, an order of the Financial Services and Markets Tribunal may be enforced as if it were an order of a county court: FSMA 2000, s 133(11). Further, an appeal from the decision of the Tribunal may only be made on a point of law: FSMA 2000, s 137.

[281] Note that, in the competition arena, an infringement decision of the OFT or European Commission is binding in the event of a damages claim being brought by a person who has allegedly suffered injury as a result of the infringing action: Competition Act 1998, s 47A.

relaxation of the English law of evidence on hearsay, such material is admissible as evidence and will be highly persuasive.

Even if there is little UK tradition of shareholder or bond holder litigation against **4.356** a company experiencing problems giving rise to an investigation or regulatory action, there are considerable exposures to customers and competitors.

In the anti-trust area, so-called 'follow on' actions seeking compensation on the **4.357** basis of a regulatory finding of infringement are becoming extremely common. Under the provisions of Council Regulation 01/03,[282] the Competition Act 1998 and the Enterprise Act 2002, and related case law, English courts are effectively bound by decisions of the Commission; the specialist tribunal, the Competition Appeal Tribunal which awards damages in cartel cases does so based on the decision of either the Commission or the OFT, which is determinative of liability; and tribunals will, even where not formally bound, accord enormous evidential weight to the views of the specialist agencies on matters within their jurisdiction. Thus, decisions of regulators in the anti-trust area are highly, if, indeed, not completely, determinative of matters within their scope.

In the financial services area, there have been high profile cases of compensation **4.358** being paid, for example to those who were mis-sold retail financial products. There are a number of routes where this may occur under the provisions of the FSMA 2000, including a compensation plan being agreed as part of a settlement of an investigation and the involvement of the Financial Ombudsman Service. As indicated above, the FSA also has the power to seek restitutionary remedies.

More widely, civil litigation can follow in the wake of criminal investigations **4.359** where there are allegations of fraud or other malpractice, particularly where counter-parties or competitors have suffered loss. Equally, investigations giving rise to product recalls will always give rise to a consideration of the potential exposure to civil litigation although, of course, the terms and nature of the recall will usually be such as to diffuse that risk.

Relevance of investigation report

As discussed above regulators are generally bound either through statutory **4.360** duties or confidentiality agreements from disclosing a corporate's internal investigation reports (or other information provided by the corporate to the regulator) to others, except in such circumstances as to other regulators and law enforcement agencies.[283] Nonetheless, a regulator could use the results of an internal

---

[282] 1/2003 Council Regulation of 16 December 2002 on the implementation of rules on competition by the Commission pursuant to Arts 81 and 82 of the EC Treaty.
[283] Discussed at 4.244.

investigation as a springboard for its own investigation which could be publicly disclosed and its results would be admissible in litigation proceedings.

4.361 As noted above, Courts, even if not formally bound, are likely to treat the findings of regulators as highly persuasive in third party proceedings. Further, if a corporate has made any admissions during a settlement process with a regulator, it will be difficult for it to distance itself from such admissions should they be cited by civil litigants in a claim. Listed corporates should bear this carefully in mind when considering the nature and scope of any admissions they may make. This is in addition, of course, to the risk of having to disclose to third parties, in any such legal proceedings, any documents prepared in the course of the investigation and enforcement process, whether by the company or the regulator (unless those documents are protected by legal professional privilege or a statutory restriction on disclosure[284]) any of which may be damaging to the company or of help to a third party.

4.362 However, a finding by a regulator (or an admission) that the corporate committed a regulatory breach (or a finding by a court that the corporate committed an offence) is likely only to be one element of a civil claim. The other necessary elements of a civil claim, such as the amount and extent of any losses that were suffered by the particular third party and whether those losses are referable, in legal terms, to the corporate's actions, are unlikely to be an important factor in the regulatory proceedings. The resolution of the regulatory enforcement issues should not affect the company's ability to argue any issues that were not raised in the regulatory proceedings.

N. Settlement with Regulators

Process

4.363 The possibility of resolving disciplinary issues by agreement between regulators and a corporate is becoming an important feature of the UK regulatory regime. Increasingly, the regulators view settlement as an effective means of enforcing the regime without the need to devote the resources that would be required if every disciplinary case were fought. It also relieves regulators of the uncertainty inherent in the outcome of proceedings before tribunals and commissions and therefore

---

[284] In *Real Estate Opportunities Limited v Aberdeen Asset Managers and Others* [2007] EWCA Civ 197, the Court of Appeal confirmed that documents created by regulators are not always protected by the statutory restrictions from production in court proceedings, when those documents only contained information already known to the company: it could not be said, therefore, that the information contained therein was information 'obtained' from the FSA within the meaning of FSMA 2000, s 348.

the prospect of losing enforcement cases. From the company's point of view, settlement allows it to put the issue behind it and move on, and to avoid incurring the substantial cost and significant amount of management time that would be involved in taking a case to its conclusion. Settlement can be reached either by means of normal negotiations or by means of mediation. The precise process is highly dependent on the regulator concerned. The prospects of an acceptable settlement depend on a variety of factors including the strength of the evidence, policy objectives, the possibility of other regulatory action and the nature of the regulatory relationship.

Some regulators such as the FSA and the OFT have developed relatively formal-   **4.364**
ized settlement schemes. For example, the FSA (including the UKLA) operates a settlement discount scheme, by which a negotiated settlement will be subject to a reduction in the financial penalty imposed by a fixed percentage, according to the stage in the process at which agreement is reached.[285] For example, if the issue is settled at a very early stage of the investigation process, a reduction of 30 per cent will be applied to any settlement figure agreed between the FSA or the UKLA and the person who is the subject of the investigation, with a reduction of 5 per cent to settlements reached at a much later stage.[286]

The OFT leniency regime offers a reduction in and in some cases total immunity   **4.365**
from, financial penalties for those admitting breaches and cooperating with cartel investigations. Moreover, the OFT is now starting to operate an 'early resolution' process whereby it is prepared to accept reduced fines, on a negotiated basis as part of obtaining a decision, effectively final, at the Statement of Objections stage.

England has not traditionally accepted plea bargaining in criminal cases, although   **4.366**
it is fair to say that some understandings were not unknown in relation to some prosecutions. However, the Fraud Act 2006 specifically introduces such powers. It is therefore very likely that more sophisticated arrangements will be reached with the criminal authorities in the future in appropriate cases.

Is an admission necessary?

In the anti-trust area, admission to an infringement is effectively required to   **4.367**
benefit from the leniency regime. Moreover, the new 'early resolution' process is currently only being operated on the basis of formal admissions. The HMRC generally requires admissions before allowing for any type of settlement.

---

[285] This is separate from any reduction in the proposed penalty being achieved as a result of the listed corporate's cooperation with the UKLA during the course of the investigation, such as the listed corporate's willingness to establish the facts, to make changes to its systems to prevent the recurrence of mistakes or to make prompt and full arrangements to compensate any affected third parties: FSA Handbook at, inter alia, DEPP 6.5.
[286] FSA Handbook at DEPP 6.7.

4.368 The FSA/UKLA used to require admissions to be made in agreeing a settlement;[287] however, it seems that that practice may be changing in appropriate cases. For example, following the settlement of the FSA's market abuse proceedings against Shell,[288] the company issued a press release stating that it had come to a settlement with the FSA 'without admitting or denying the findings and conclusions in the FSA's Final Notice'.[289] The FSA did not go as far as the SEC, however, which included the company's lack of admission or denial in its cease and desist order.[290]

4.369 Short of formal admissions, it has been the practice of the FSA (including the UKLA) to insist that the person who has been disciplined agrees not to dispute the facts and matters contained in the final notice as a condition of agreeing to a settlement, with the terms to that effect being embodied in the settlement agreement with the FSA.

Impact if under investigation by multiple regulators

4.370 As regulators are often investigating under a mandate specific to that regulator, settlement with one regulator does not necessarily create settlement opportunities with all regulators.[291] Furthermore, settlement by a company with a regulator for the company's behaviour can still leave individuals exposed to action.

4.371 The FSA has indicated that it may take action under the Listing Rules or Disclosure Rules and Transparency Rules (in its capacity as the UKLA) against one person (eg against the company) and take action (in its wider capacity) under the market abuse regime against a different person (eg a director).[292] Equally, the FSA can theoretically take action under the Listing Rules or Disclosure Rules and Transparency Rules (in its capacity as the UKLA) at the same time as taking action (in its wider capacity) under the market abuse regime against the same

---

[287] And the FSA publicized such admissions in the ensuing final notice. For example, the *CSFB International* final notice (11/12/02) states: '[CSFB] has admitted those facts and matters and agrees to settlement on that basis'. It has also been the FSA's policy to insist that disciplined persons should agree not subsequently to cast doubt on whether they were in breach or to dispute the findings of fact made by the FSA as a condition of settlement.

[288] *Shell* final notice (24/8/04).

[289] *Shell News & Media Release* (24/8/04). Similarly, when 18 of the firms that the FSA had been investigating in relation to the sale of split capital investment trusts contributed to a £194m fund for distribution to investors, those contributions were expressed in an FSA press release to be 'without admissions': FSA/PN/114/2004 (although the agreement that was reached with the FSA was without the instigation of the formal disciplinary procedure and the FSA has stated that this settlement was highly exceptional and should not be treated as a precedent for 'without liability' resolutions in future investigations).

[290] Complaint H-04-3359.

[291] If a corporate is subject to a joint OFT/SFO investigation for breaches of the Enterprise Act 2002 or the Criminal Justice Act 1987, there is greater scope for joint settlement arrangements.

[292] FSA Handbook at DEPP 6.2.21.

person in relation to the same conduct.[293] However, in practice, if the FSA wishes to pursue the company for market abuse, it is unlikely that the UKLA will also pursue it for a fine for breach of the Listing Principles or Disclosure Rules and Transparency Rules (as this might involve the listed company being fined twice), although it might want publicly to censure it for that breach or to take other action, in extreme cases, such as suspending listing of the company's shares.[294]

Since market abuse and regulatory action for breach of the Listing Rules (or Disclosure **4.372** Rules and Transparency Rules or Prospectus Rules) involve different procedures, difficulties may arise in running the different proceedings in tandem. Issues might therefore arise about which process should be pursued first and whether one might prejudice the other[295] and, from the company's perspective, it would be important to be aware of the potential effect of its actions in one context upon its potential liability in the other. For example, to settle the disciplinary case against it by admitting a breach of the Listing Rules (or Disclosure Rules and Transparency Rules or Prospectus Rules) might cause it great difficulty in defending the market abuse proceedings.

In the case of criminal cartel issues, the OFT and the SFO are obliged to operate **4.373** in tandem so there is automatic coordination, to the extent that there may be any prospect of settlement. However, as regards other multiple regulatory investigations, each has, in the UK, traditionally had to be treated on its own merits. Although it has to be assumed that regulators are increasingly coordinating behind the scenes in the UK, 'composite settlements', whereby a company can achieve a single resolution of all the concerns, with multiple regulators, who have different processes and different responsibilities, have not yet been seen.

O. Conclusion

The UK has a complex and evolving regulatory regime, world-leading capital **4.374** markets, a highly active financial press and increasingly active shareholders and consumers. It also has close transatlantic business, regulatory and professional connections.

Not surprisingly, therefore, there has been considerable growth in the focus on **4.375** corporate governance and behaviour. Expectations of the standards to be observed

---

[293] For example, see *Shell* final notice (28/8/04).

[294] In the *Shell* final notice (28/8/04), the FSA fined the company £17m for market abuse, but simply issues a public censure in relation to the breach of the Listing Rules (now the Disclosure Rules and Transparency Rules).

[295] For example, there is a privilege against self-incrimination in market abuse proceedings but not in proceedings in relation to breaches of the Listing Rules (or Disclosure Rules and Transparency Rules or Prospectus Rules).

have risen steadily. Regulatory and criminal sanctions have increased, as have the readiness of third parties to take action and the legal structures to assist them to do so.

4.376 There has, consequently, been a steady increase in the use of internal investigations to control these risks. They are becoming more valuable to companies, providing both independent support for management as they seek to understand fact patterns and risks and also guidance as to how to respond properly to ethical, governance or regulatory issues. Inevitably, they are becoming more sophisticated as 'accepted' practices become more established. They are also, to an extent, becoming more invasive and thorough, as companies need to understand issues at a more detailed level.

4.377 It is likely that this trend will continue since there is no reason to think that any of the underlying drivers for this change will weaken. Properly managed and properly used, internal investigations will be a valuable part of a company's weaponry, not only for defensive purposes, but used positively to manage the inherent business risk and enhance the levels of corporate ethics and governance that are seen in the UK.

5

INVESTIGATIONS IN THE NETHERLANDS

A. Introduction[1]

5.01 As in many European jurisdictions the strengthening of the regulatory framework and enforcement has been high on the agenda of Dutch lawmakers over the past few years. The implementation of European directives accompanied by a number of high-profile scandals, such as the accounting fraud at Ahold, the cartel and bid-rigging investigations as well as the parliamentary inquiry into the Dutch construction sector, the bankruptcy of the Dutch bank 'Van der Hoop Bankiers' and insider trading investigations involving high profile members of the Dutch business community, have further expedited this process.

5.02 Whilst economic and financial criminal law still plays an important role, administrative enforcement by independent regulators and other governmental agencies and authorities is on the rise. A clear example of this trend was seen in the decriminalization of competition law which, as of 1 January 1998, is enforced by the Dutch Competition Authority whose powers of investigation and sanctioning are governed by administrative law. This development has led to the introduction of numerous due process rules and principles under administrative law enforcement. A legislative proposal that seeks to codify these principles, which are already common under criminal law, in the General Administrative Law Act[2] is expected to be enacted by 1 January 2009.[3]

---

[1] Contributors: Jan Willem van der Staay, Paul Kreijger, Michael Broeders, Max van Verschuer, Brechje Nollen and Wieke van Angeren-van den Elzen.

[2] *Algemene wet bestuursrecht.*

[3] According to the legislative calendar issued by the Ministry of Justice on 15 February 2008.

Over the past few years the Netherlands has restructured its supervisory frame- **5.03**
work in order to better reflect market trends and market realities. As in various
other jurisdictions, the Dutch financial sector has come to be dominated by a few
very large financial conglomerates operating across sectoral lines. An example of
this is the range of increasingly complex financial products on offer which do not
fit neatly into traditional sectoral classifications.

The reform of the financial supervision legislation in the Netherlands was **5.04**
completed with the entry into force of the Financial Supervision Act (Wft)[4] on
1 January 2007. It has replaced seven supervision acts, taking a more functional
approach as compared to the traditional sectoral approach.

In this respect the Wft contains a clear division between the tasks of the Dutch **5.05**
Central Bank (*De Nederlandsche Bank NV*) (DNB)—in the area of prudential
supervision—and the tasks of the Financial Markets Authority (*Autoriteit
Financiële Markten*) (AFM)—relating to market conduct or conduct of business
supervision. Furthermore, some of the requirements which must be met by
financial services providers have been simplified, resulting in a reduction of the
administrative burden caused by financial supervision. In certain areas this has
been achieved by introducing one cross-sectoral rule which replaces various differing rules contained in the previous supervision Acts.

Both DNB and AFM conduct their own investigations within their respective **5.06**
area of supervision. In 2007, the AFM launched a total of 701 supervisory
investigations.[5] Breaches were established at all the institutions inspected, of
which 18 were serious. In the same year DNB investigated 45 cases of enterprises
allegedly offering financial services without a licence.[6] DNB further conducted
investigations into reinsurance risk control at insurance groups and a number of
specific investigations into the activities of financial institutions in the field of
hedge funds, private equity funds and real estate.[7]

As in many other European jurisdictions, competition law enforcement also **5.07**
figures prominently on the agenda. Since its inception on 1 January 1998, the
Dutch Competition Authority (NMa)[8] has been very active, both in examining
a number of high-profile mergers as well as in imposing multi-million euro fines
on cartel participants. Its powers of investigation and sanctioning were significantly increased since the new legislation of 1 October 2007. As of 2001, the
NMa has applied a leniency programme that introduces incentives (ranging from

---

[4] *Wet op het financieel toezicht.*
[5] 2007 Annual Report AFM, 158.
[6] 2007 Annual Report DNB, 89.
[7] 2007 Annual Report DNB, 67–91.
[8] *Nederlandse Mededingingsautoriteit.*

full immunity to important reductions in fines) for members of a cartel to disclose their misconduct to the authorities and to cooperate fully with them.

B. Regulators

Key regulators

The Dutch financial markets authority (AFM)

5.08 The AFM is the principal supervisor of the Dutch financial markets. It is responsible for regulating market activity in the areas of savings, loans, investment, securities and insurance. The AFM derives its authority from the Wft and its accompanying regulations.

5.09 Under the Wft the Secretary of Finance[9] is charged with exercising the supervisory and regulatory powers granted by the Wft, however these have substantially been transferred to the AFM, a regulatory body which essentially operates independently. The Secretary of Finance remains politically responsible for the AFM but has limited influence on day-to-day affairs and the manner in which the AFM operates and performs its tasks.

5.10 The AFM is responsible for the following:

- granting licences to institutions or persons that wish to operate in the Dutch financial markets; this includes verifying whether the private individuals in charge of a financial institution are sufficiently qualified and of good standing;
- protecting the orderly operation of the Dutch financial markets by supervising the official stock exchanges in the Netherlands, approving prospectuses for the issuance of securities, supervising public takeovers and the correct and timely publication of price sensitive information;
- investigating insider trading and market-abuse; and
- protecting consumers of financial products.

5.11 The AFM is also charged with supervising due compliance with the rules with respect to the notification of capital and voting interests in listed companies. Pursuant to the relevant rules in the Wft,[10] a person is required to inform the AFM of changes in its shareholdings in a Dutch public company[11] listed on an

---

[9] *Minister van Financiën.*
[10] Ss 5:38—5:45 Wft.
[11] *Naamloze Vennootschap* or *NV.*

official stock exchange within the European Union if and when certain thresholds are crossed upwards or downwards.

The AFM is furthermore charged with the supervision of annual accounts of companies incorporated in the Netherlands and listed on an official stock exchange within the European Union.[12] In that regard the AFM has the authority to request the Enterprise Chamber, a specialized division of the Amsterdam Court of Appeals, to order a company to provide the AFM with additional information in respect of its financial statements and documents that formed the basis for these financial statements. In principle, the relevant request of the AFM will not be publicly disclosed and the information that the AFM receives in response to its request must be treated confidentially. However, once the AFM requests the Enterprise Chamber to order a company to provide information, the AFM involvement will be in the public domain. Following receipt of the requested information the AFM may make certain recommendations to a company concerning its annual accounts; the company may or may not follow such recommendations. However, if the company were to deviate from the recommendations, the AFM could commence legal proceedings before the Enterprise Chamber to enforce its recommendations.   **5.12**

Finally, the AFM is charged with supervising certified auditors.[13]   **5.13**

The AFM may investigate allegations of a number of acts and crimes, including forgery of documents;[14] distribution of deceitful communications, aimed at inflating or decreasing the price of securities or commodities;[15] fraud with respect to balance sheets and profit and loss accounts;[16] fraud;[17] and more generally any failure to comply with the Wft, all of which are subject to administrative sanctions, but are also criminally sanctioned under the Economic Offences Act (WED).[18] Criminal liability is equally incumbent on accessories and co-perpetrators.[19] The Public Prosecutors Office (OM)[20] has the statutory monopoly to prosecute criminal cases.[21]   **5.14**

---

[12] Act on the supervision of financial reporting (*Wet toezicht financiele verslaggeving*).

[13] Act on the supervision of accounting organizations (*Wet toezicht accountantsorganisaties*).

[14] *Valsheid in geschrifte*, s 225 Dutch Penal Code. This is punishable with a maximum prison sentence of six years and a maximum fine of €74,000.

[15] *Leugenachtig bericht*, s 334 Dutch Penal Code. This is punishable with a maximum prison sentence of two years and a maximum fine of €74,000.

[16] *Bedrog met balans en winst- en verliesrekening*, s 336 Dutch Penal Code. This is punishable with a maximum prison sentence of one year and a maximum fine of €74,000.

[17] *Oplichting*, s 326 Dutch Penal Code. This is punishable with a maximum prison sentence of three years and a maximum fine of €74,000.

[18] *Wet op de Economische Delicten*. See ss 1 and 1a.

[19] *Medeplichtigen*, medeplegers.

[20] *Openbaar Ministerie*.

[21] Section 4 WED.

5.15 Under the Wft, the AFM is provided with an extensive set of instruments to take action against a person that fails to comply with the Wft.[22] The AFM has discretionary power in utilizing these instruments. Under the provisions of the Wft, the AFM has practically unrestricted access to any information in the possession of a financial institution (or a third party) which it deems necessary for the performance of its supervisory duties. Violation of almost every single provision of the Wft may lead to sanctions.[23] Depending on the nature of the violation or the nature and extent of non-compliant behaviour, the AFM may take punitive action (eg withdrawal of consent or authorization, imposition of fines) or corrective action (such as the requirement to observe a certain line of conduct by a set date). The formal set of corrective and/or punitive instruments available to the AFM consists of (i) giving instructions in respect of the course of action to be pursued as of a set date;[24] (ii) the appointment of a (silent) receiver;[25] (iii) the imposition of a fine or a cease and desist order enforced by recurring penalty payments;[26] (iv) withdrawal of the authorization pursuant to section 15 of the Wft; or (v) a report to the public prosecutor or to other authorities responsible for the enforcement of legal standards (eg the FIOD-ECD in the case of violation of the WED).

The Dutch central bank (DNB)

5.16 The DNB also plays an important role in the supervision of Dutch financial institutions. The DNB supervision complements the AFM supervision. In general terms one could say that the DNB supervision focuses on the solvency and integrity of financial institutions, whereas the AFM focuses on the 'behavioural' conduct of financial market participants.

5.17 The DNB is responsible for ensuring that financial institutions meet the relevant capital and solvency requirements. Under the Wft, the DNB is also charged with granting banking licences to credit institutions[27] and supervising compliance of credit institutions with the Wft and the terms of the licences granted under the Wft. The DNB also supervises insurers in a similar way.

5.18 Under the Wft the DNB has the same investigatory powers and the same set of instruments at its disposal as the AFM, as outlined above.

---

[22] Sections 1:75 through 1:88 Wft.
[23] Sections 1:75 through 1:88 Wft.
[24] *Aanwijzing.*
[25] *Stille curator.*
[26] Section 1:81 Wft.
[27] *Kredietinstellingen.*

The Dutch competition authority (NMa)

The NMa is a significant regulator that conducts corporate investigations in the **5.19** Netherlands. The authority of the NMa is based on the Dutch Competition Act[28] and the EC Treaty (Articles 81 and 82). Its key functions include the enforcement of the prohibition on anti-competitive agreements and concerted practices and preventing abuses of market-dominant positions; monitoring M&A transactions in cases where the offeror and the target have combined worldwide annual sales of €113,450,000 or more and individual sales of €30m in the Netherlands and prohibiting such transactions where they are likely to significantly impede competition on the Dutch market.

The NMa also applies European competition law under Regulation 1/2003 and **5.20** the case allocation criteria set out therein.

The NMa has the power to impose fines for a range of infringements of the **5.21** Dutch Competition Act. These fines may amount to a maximum of the higher of €450,000 or 10 per cent of the annual revenues for material infringements or 1 per cent for procedural infringements (eg failure to submit all necessary information for a merger notification). Fines are further established in accordance with the policy guidelines of the NMa that were last revised on 9 October 2007.

Since its inception on 1 January 1998, the NMa has been actively pursuing com- **5.22** petition law infringements and has imposed significant fines in a number of sectors. Apart from the investigation in the construction sector (which was unique in terms of scale and number of undertakings involved), high fines have been imposed on, among others, bicycle manufacturers, mobile telecoms operators, trade associations, banks, energy and telecoms infrastructure operators, clothing manufacturers and agricultural companies. Since 1 October 2007, the NMa's authority to impose fines was extended to natural persons actively involved in the infringements (eg directors). The NMa also has the authority to conclude a binding settlement with companies subject to an investigation, which will allow prior termination of an infringement procedure in return for specific undertakings to avoid future infringements.

Public prosecutor's office (OM)

A large number of infringements of regulatory legislation (varying from environ- **5.23** mental, health and safety legislation, financial regulations, customs and tax to food safety and traffic regulation) are enforced and penalized under criminal law (competition law, which is only enforced under administrative law, being a

---

[28] *Mededingingswet.*

notable exception). The central institute in criminal law is the OM which has the statutory monopoly to prosecute criminal cases before the courts and has considerable discretion in deciding whether to prosecute cases or settle them out of court. This discretionary authority is balanced by the statutory 'complaint' provision that allows for any decision not to prosecute to be submitted to legal review at the request of interested parties (eg victims of the alleged criminal act).

5.24 The OM is also charged with prosecuting cases of corruption and bribery. In that regard, sanctions for private, that is, non-government, corruption have existed since 1967.[29] Sanctions for the bribery of government officials and civil servants were included in the Dutch Penal Code in 2000 in light of the Convention on Combating Bribery of Foreign Public Officials in International Business Transactions (the Convention)[30] issued by the Organization for Economic Co-operation and Development which was signed by the Netherlands in December 1997.[31]

5.25 A broad distinction can be made between general criminal law provisions as codified in the Dutch Penal Code and the specific provisions under the WED. The WED, which dates from 1951, enumerates a large number of specific provisions from other statutes, the infringement of which constitutes an economic offence to be investigated and sanctioned under the special regime of the WED. The WED introduced broad investigatory powers and specific sanctions, including a separate regime for fines and interim measures such as cease and desist orders, to be imposed by the OM. Depending on whether a violation qualifies as a misdemeanour (*overtreding*) or a crime (*misdrijf*) the criminal sanctions under the WED[32] vary from a maximum prison sentence of six months or a fine of €74,000 for a misdemeanour to a maximum prison sentence of six years or a fine of €740,000 for a criminal offence. For legal entities the maximum fine is €740,000.[33]

5.26 Both ordinary police officers as well as officers of the FIOD-ECD (the special investigations unit for tax and economic offences) investigate economic offences, though in practice ordinary police officers rarely investigate infringements of the WED—with the exception of environmental crimes. Economic criminal law has thus become a specific branch of criminal law.

---

[29] Section 328*ter* Dutch Penal Code.
[30] Available from <http://www.oecd.com>.
[31] Particularly sections 117, 177a, 178 and 178a Dutch Penal Code.
[32] Under the WED an act will qualify as a criminal offence if it is committed intentionally (*opzettelijk*) and as a misdemeanour if this is not the case (s 2 WED). For intent to be present it does not need to be proven that the perpetrator's intention was aimed at committing the crime. For intent to be present it is sufficient that the perpetrator should have realized that his actions were prohibited. In case of an economic action, intention will often be deemed included in the nature of the action.
[33] Section 2 WED in conjunction with s 6 WED in conjunction with s 23 Dutch Penal Code.

Civil sanctions

Although the concept of civil monetary penalties or punitive damages is unknown **5.27** in the Netherlands, failure to comply with certain statutes may trigger civil law liability. As such, a type of civil sanction may supplement administrative and/or criminal sanctions. For instance, a failure to comply with the Wft rules relating to the notification and disclosure of capital and voting interests in listed companies may result in a suspension of voting rights. Also, as outlined above, both the AFM and DNB have the authority to appoint an administrator[34] over institutions under their supervision.[35] A failure to comply with instructions of an administrator appointed by DNB may expose directors to personal liability. In addition, commercial contracts entered into by financial institutions, for instance credit agreements or the purchase or sale of securities, may be void or subject to cancellation by the counter-party if the relevant credit institution or broker did not comply with provisions of the Wft, as is outlined in section 3:40 of the Dutch Civil Code (DCC).[36] Other civil sanctions include the suspension of voting rights in respect of a shareholding in a financial institution if the acquisition of such shareholding by the new shareholder was not approved by DNB or AFM.[37] Also, in some cases the OM has the authority to seek 'disgorgement'[38] of criminal gains; one of the measures available under the WED is the seizure of the proceeds of the criminal act.[39]

Although competition law enforcement in Europe has always been predomi- **5.28** nantly a public matter, the infringement of the prohibition on anti-competitive agreements and abuse of dominant positions may also have important consequences under civil law, that is, nullity of agreements and exposure to claims from third parties (eg suppliers and/or purchasers) who claim to have been damaged by cartels or abuse. Over the past few years, private enforcement followed by litigation (damage claims following a cartel fine by the Commission or the NMa) is becoming increasingly common. The Commission has recently imposed a series of multi-billion euro fines and has also put private enforcement of competition claims high on the political agenda. A dedicated 'plaintiff bar' is developing, with law firms advertising for claimants to bring damages actions, both individually and via collective claims. The Netherlands is no exception and companies involved in competition law infringements may find themselves exposed to civil actions in the Dutch courts.

---

[34] *Bewindvoerder.*
[35] Section 1:76 Wft.
[36] *Burgerlijk Wetboek.*
[37] Section 3:95 Wft.
[38] *Ontneming.*
[39] Section 36c Dutch Penal Code and s 8 WED.

Other regulators

5.29 There are a number of industry-specific regulators in the Netherlands. These include individual regulators for the agricultural sector, data and privacy protection, the food industry and workers safety. Some of the key industry specific regulators include the following agencies:

- The Office of Energy Regulation (DTe)[40] is a separate chamber of the NMa and is responsible for implementing the Electricity Act[41] and the Gas Act,[42] as well as supervising compliance with these Acts. DTe has extensive powers, including the authority to impose substantial fines.

- The Dutch Telecommunications Authority *(OPTA)*[43] independently regulates compliance with legislation and regulations in the areas of postal and telecommunications services. The legislation and regulations are intended to promote competition on these markets. OPTA is a non-departmental agency that is under the auspices of Department of Economic Affairs.[44]

- The Transportation Chamber[45] is a branch of the NMa which derives its authority from the Act on Public Transportation 2000.[46] The Transportation Chamber supervises the various public transportation operators in the Netherlands.

Concurrent investigations

5.30 As mentioned above, an increasing volume of regulatory legislation is enforced through administrative sanctions, including administrative fines. In many cases, infringements of such legislation may well also constitute a criminal offence under the WED or the Dutch Penal Code, attracting concurrent enforcement actions.

5.31 Though the WED formulates the principle that economic offences should only be sanctioned in accordance with the WED, the legislator has in many cases abandoned this principle. Thus, non-compliance with statutes or regulations may lead to both administrative enforcement actions and sanctions by the relevant regulator as well as criminal enforcement, prosecution and criminal sanctions. Such accumulation of enforcement action may give rise to complicated questions which have not been fully resolved to date. Essentially, it is more or less accepted

---

[40] *Directie Toezicht Energie.*
[41] *Elektriciteitswet.*
[42] *Gaswet.*
[43] *Onafhankelijke Post en Telecommunicatie Autoriteit.*
[44] <http://www.opta.nl>.
[45] *Vervoerkamer.*
[46] *Wet Personenvervoer 2000.*

that the *una via* principle (according to which either criminal or administrative enforcement can be applied, but not both) implies that an administrative fine cannot be imposed following a criminal sanction or transaction for the same infringement. Many administrative acts already explicitly contain provisions to this effect. Likewise, the imposition of an administrative fine will not be possible in the case of an earlier administrative fine for the same infringement. Even after the codification of this key principle in the General Administrative Law Act, numerous questions and problem areas remain, among others the issue of accumulation of Dutch punitive measures and foreign punitive measures and the question when certain behaviour qualifies as 'the same' infringement to which only one type of enforcement should be applied. Moreover, accumulation of punitive measures (eg fines) and non-punitive measures (eg cease and desist orders) is generally considered possible.

Although regulators do not have the power to prosecute crimes, regulators can, **5.32** and in practice do, file reports with the OM based on information collected through the exercise of their investigatory powers. In practice, more complex cases—such as insider trading, accounting fraud or price fixing—are often dealt with through the criminal justice system. This is most likely because the criminal justice system is felt to offer more elaborate means to investigate facts and also because these cases tend to be 'high profile' (ie involving large companies and high paid executives) resulting in more public attention and indignation and thus in a greater pressure to prosecute. A well-known example was the Ahold case, which was investigated by the AFM but was also the subject of a criminal case brought by the OM against several former executives of Ahold.[47] The AFM, the FIOD-ECD and the OM have discussions on a regular basis, in the so-called *tripartite overleg* (tripartite consultation) in order to discuss the manner in which particular infringements should be dealt with.

Relationships with overseas regulators

The AFM is represented in European and global cooperative bodies that address **5.33** issues relating to the supervision of conduct on the financial markets. Within the European Union (EU) the AFM participates in the Committee of European Securities Regulators (CESR), which is both an advisory body for the European Commission and a cooperative body for the securities regulators involved. At global level the Netherlands is a member of the technical committee of the International Organization of Securities Commissions (IOSCO).

---

[47] In this case Ahold's Columbia food distribution unit, US Foodservice Inc, and other subsidiaries had fraudulently inflated earnings by nearly $830m between 2000 and 2002.

5.34 International cooperation between regulators mainly revolves around the exchange of supervision information between regulators. This bilateral exchange of information is supported by a system of memorandums of understanding (MOUs). Overall MOUs have been established in the context of CESR and IOSCO, while supervisory authorities also make arrangements among themselves about exchanging information. In total, the AFM has made such arrangements with 14 foreign supervisory authorities. In 2006, the AFM received 127 requests to provide supervisory information to fellow supervisory authorities in other jurisdictions. In addition to specific matter-linked information, many of these requests involve general information, such as information on the day-to-day exercise of supervision, the interpretation of regulations and internal organization. This is done via questionnaires or specific questions. In 2006, the AFM received and replied to 97 requests for information, as against 57 in 2005. A large number of these requests concern the practical application of European regulations.[48]

5.35 In case of criminal investigations, the international cooperation is governed by international treaties.

5.36 As of 1 May 2004, the application and enforcement of European competition law has been 'decentralized' significantly. As of this date, the Commission no longer has the sole jurisdiction to grant exemptions from the prohibition on anti-competitive agreements (such exemption can no longer be obtained) and national competition authorities can directly apply European competition law in their jurisdictions. As the application of the same substantive law by a range of different regulators may well lead to undesirable divergence of interpretation and enforcement among EU jurisdictions, coordination mechanisms between national authorities and the European Commission have been reinforced and extended. The NMa is required to keep the Commission informed on its application of EU competition law, and all information and evidence may circulate freely between the Commission and national competition authorities. The NMa may be asked to obtain evidence in the Netherlands for the benefit of investigations in other jurisdictions and vice versa. The NMa cooperates closely with the European Commission and other competition authorities in the context of the European Competition Network (ECN), which streamlines and enhances the coordination between various authorities. The ECN provides the forum for authorities to discuss general matters as well as specific cases, which can be allocated (European competition law only applies in cases that potentially impact cross-border competition) to the best-placed authority. Though the ECN has no formal decision-making powers, its activity does lead to enforcement convergence in the application of EU

---

[48] 2006 AFM Annual Report.

competition law between EU member states. It should be noted that the exchanged information and evidence may only be used for competition law enforcement and information provided by leniency applicants will only be exchanged with their consent (though may be used without their consent for punishment of other cartel participants). The NMa is also member to the International Competition Network (ICN), a platform for competition agencies around the world to discuss developments and best practices. More or less similar international organizations exist for telecommunications (Independent Regulators Group and European Regulators Group, in which OPTA participates) and energy (the Council for European Energy Regulators, the European Regulatory Group for Electricity and Gas, the Madrid Forum and the Florence Forum, in which DTe participates).

C. Powers of Regulators

Motivations for investigations

The NMa and the AFM have in recent years become significantly more aggressive in conducting investigations into possible violations of applicable regulations. The NMa has been active in large investigations involving entire industry sectors in the Netherlands. More recently the AFM also conducted investigations on a larger scale, such as into the sale of a particular financial product by various financial institutions to retail investors that invested in a risky leveraged investment product offered by Dexia Bank called 'Legiolease' and suffered €1bn-plus damages following the downturn of the securities market in the Netherlands in 1999 and 2000.   **5.37**

Regulatory investigations can be triggered in various ways. A regulator can commence an investigation on its own accord, or as a result of reports such as those received by financial institutions and listed companies who are obliged under the Wft to report any transactions to the AFM of which there is a reasonable suspicion of insider trading or market abuse.[49] In addition, the AFM may choose to initiate an investigation following complaints of investors or routine audits. Furthermore, any institution subject to the Wft is obliged to inform the AFM of certain events relating to the integrity of its employees which may trigger an investigation.[50]   **5.38**

The NMa may initiate an investigation following complaints filed by competitors or consumer associations, anonymous tips from whistleblowers, or following   **5.39**

---

[49] Section 5:62 Wft.
[50] Section 29 Decree on supervision of conduct of financial institutions Wft (*Besluit Gedragstoezicht financiële ondernemingen Wft*).

NMa observations of market failures in specific markets. The NMa has developed policy guidelines for dealing with informers who wish to remain anonymous and not file a formal complaint. Whilst the NMa cannot completely guarantee that anonymity will be maintained, its stated policy is to undertake all efforts to maintain anonymity. The NMa has the discretion to set priorities in its enforcement activities (and lack of priority may be a reason to dismiss a complaint). Each year, the NMa publishes an annual agenda in which its sets out its priorities for that year. The financial sector, energy sector and media and telecommunications sector regularly feature in the annual agendas.

5.40 Important information on cartel behaviour is offered to the NMa by companies who apply for immunity or reduction of fines under the leniency programme that the NMa has operated since 2001. Participants to illicit agreements and practices who provide the NMa with relevant and new information that allows the NMa to conduct an investigation, may qualify for immunity if they are the first to report and subsequently cooperate fully with the investigation. Reductions are available to participants who are not the first to report but nevertheless provide information with added value and/or cooperate with the investigation. The purpose of the programme is to incentivize cartel participants to disclose their infringements and thus significantly facilitate enforcement. In order to benefit from the leniency programme, the cartel participants have to collect and present all relevant information to the NMa, underlining the practical relevance of internal investigations in this field. Preparing a leniency application is often an intensive exercise requiring substantial investigation work, as failure to produce all relevant information may be considered a lack of cooperation and jeopardize immunity or reduction.

5.41 Further to the extended leniency programme introduced by the European Commission,[51] the NMa adopted a revised leniency programme on 9 October 2007.[52] This revised programme takes into account the new power to impose fines on individual persons for cartel participation. Companies who file for leniency may also ask leniency for their employees. The NMa also proposes to allow individuals to file for leniency. This may be problematic, as an individual application only protects the applicant and not the company he or she works for, thus creating a potential conflict of interests between the company and its employees who were involved in the cartel behaviour. Likewise, the position of former employees is also problematic, because the company cannot extend the scope of

---

[51] European Commission Leniency Programme of 1996 OJ C207, 18 July 1996, 4; European Commission Leniency Programme of 2002 OJ C45, 19 February 2002, 3; European Commission Leniency Programme of 2006OJ C298, 8 December 2006, 17.

[52] Available at <http://www.nmanet.nl>.

its leniency application to former employees. This is especially problematic as in many cases cartel participation of a company consists of the participation of just a few persons (eg directors, sales executives) whose cooperation may be crucial for the preparation of a complete leniency statement. The NMa also proposes the introduction of a 'marker' system, where a participant in a cartel can contact the NMa and declare its willingness to cooperate to keep its position in the queue until it files an application for leniency and submits the relevant information. This is important, as only the first participant to file for leniency is eligible for full immunity and it now no longer has to wait for the completion of the internal investigation with the associated risk that another participant is first to file.

Levels of regulatory scrutiny

The various statutes—with the exception of the Dutch Competition Act, which **5.42** distinguishes two phases in the merger approval trajectory[53]—do not make a formal distinction with respect to the various levels of regulatory scrutiny, nor do they use some type of formal announcement when an investigation is commenced. In practice the relevant regulator may just appear and request certain information for review and analysis, which at a later stage may be used as evidence for administrative sanctions. However, once the investigation has progressed to a stage that it has become reasonable to expect that a punitive sanction may be imposed, the regulator will have to caution the persons involved as regards their rights against self-incrimination.

The OM may commence a criminal investigation when there is a 'reasonable **5.43** suspicion' that a crime (eg fraud) has been committed. Depending on the severity of the crime the OM may seek the opening of a judicial investigation in which case an investigative judge may be appointed which may hear witnesses and which may order the deployment of criminal investigative tools such as seizure of documents, electronic files, and the interception of data-traffic.

Investigation tools

The general legal framework for investigation powers of regulators is provided in **5.44** the enforcement provisions of the General Administrative Law Act, though specific legislation (such as the Wft or the Dutch Competition Act) often qualifies or extends these powers. An important feature of the regulatory regime in the Netherlands is the statutory right generally granted to regulators to obtain information in order to perform their regulatory tasks.[54] This right is mirrored by the

---

[53] Sections 34, 35 and 37 Dutch Competition Act.
[54] Section 5:16 and 5:17 General Administrative Law Act and s 1:72 Wft.

statutory obligation for persons—in case of a company the obligation rests both on managing directors, officers and ordinary employees of the company—to cooperate with regulators.[55] Non-cooperation is a criminal offence and may also lead to administrative fines or other sanctions depending on the applicable legislation.

5.45 The regulator's right to obtain information includes access to business documents, electronic records, archives and offices. If necessary in some instances, if access is refused, access can be obtained by regulators with the help of law enforcement without any prior court approval being required.[56] The right to obtain information can even include access to information held by third parties.[57] It also includes the right to ask questions from employees and management. Under the Wft, the AFM also has the authority to request the appearance of managing directors and other policy-makers of the company for questioning.[58] Under the Dutch Competition Act, the NMa can impose fines for non-cooperation and may search private homes with a court order. The NMa may seal off premises or parts thereof (eg closets, drawers, rooms) during an on-site inspection and the breaking of such seals carries penalties.

5.46 The investigation powers in the context of criminal offences are regulated by the Code of Criminal Procedure[59] and the WED. FIOD-ECD officers can exercise their powers under the WED regardless of whether there is a 'reasonable suspicion'. Actually, if there are indications that the WED has been infringed, the FIOD-ECD officers are even required 'in the interest of prosecution' to use their investigation powers under the WED to verify whether any offence has been committed.[60] They have the ability to copy or seize documents, computer files and other information and are entitled to access to company premises, if required to perform their statutory duties.[61] Cooperation with the FIOD-ECD is mandatory.[62] Similar powers of investigation may be exercised by NMa officials, if they can show a reasonable suspicion. The NMa has developed the practice of copying entire servers and searching them separately with forensic imaging software (which retrieves deleted items) at their offices.

---

[55] Section 1:72 Wft in conjunction with s 5:20 General Administrative Law Act.
[56] Section 1:72 Wft and s 5:15 General Administrative Law Act.
[57] Section 1:74 Wft.
[58] Section 1:74 Wft.
[59] *Wetboek van Strafvordering.*
[60] Kamerstukken II 1968/69, 9608, nr 5, p 2.
[61] Section 18 and 19 WED.
[62] Section 24a WED.

Extra-territorial jurisdiction

In principle, Dutch law does not grant Dutch regulatory authorities jurisdiction **5.47** over parties or in respect of conduct outside the Netherlands. The Wft and the Dutch Penal Code, however, do allow for extra-territorial jurisdiction to some extent.

For instance, the provisions of the Wft related to insider trading,[63] price-sensitive **5.48** information and directors' dealings apply whenever the relevant securities are listed on a Dutch stock exchange, regardless of whether the issue or conduct in question is based or takes place in the Netherlands. If this conduct takes place in a member state of the EU or a contracting state of the European Economic Area (EEA), the AFM will ask the competent regulatory authority of the relevant state to conduct the investigations and to transmit the information which is suitable and necessary for the AFM to meet its statutory tasks. Also, the AFM may request the foreign regulatory authority to allow AFM personnel to participate in the investigations of the foreign authority. If the conduct takes place outside the EU or a contracting state of the EEA the AFM may generally enter into ad hoc discussions with the relevant regulators to achieve similar cooperation as outlined above.

The Dutch Penal Code generally applies the principle of *lex locus delicti*, meaning **5.49** that the application of the Dutch Penal Code is limited to acts committed within the territorial jurisdiction of the Netherlands. However, jurisdiction extends to certain criminal offences committed outside the Netherlands, either by Dutch nationals or others, in a number of specifically circumscribed situations. These offences include corruption-related offences (eg bribery of government officials).

Furthermore, case law of the Dutch Supreme Court allows the prosecution by the **5.50** OM of criminal acts in their entirety if at least one element of the relevant criminal act (eg preparatory work) took place in the Netherlands.

Protections and due process

Dutch administrative and criminal law recognize the *nemo tenetur* principle, that **5.51** is the right to avoid self-incrimination by refusing to answer questions from regulators. Regulators are required to caution subjects of an investigation once it becomes clear that the investigation may be expected to culminate in an administrative or criminal sanction. It is not always clear when this point in time has been reached—though quite crucial as evidence gathered prior to this moment is

---

63 *Handelen met voorwetenschap*; s 5:56 Wft.

outside the scope of protection of the *nemo tenetur* principle. Moreover, evidence which is not dependent on respecting the *nemo tenetur* (such as documents or records obtained during a search) is also not protected.

5.52 The exercise of regulators' powers is subject to the principle of proportionality and must be reasonably necessary for the purpose of the investigation. However, as the exact scope of the investigation is normally not disclosed in full, it is in practice often difficult to assess if, and to what extent the boundaries are overstepped. An instruction from a regulatory authority to provide information or the exercise of other powers cannot be appealed in administrative courts (though civil actions remain possible) and any failure of directors or employees to cooperate may be attributed to the institution or company that is the subject of the investigation and may result in monetary penalties being imposed for failure to cooperate. The NMa may also impose fines for non-cooperation on natural persons.

Sanctions for failure to cooperate

5.53 Cooperation with regulators acting within their powers is mandatory.[64] A failure to cooperate may result in administrative fines being imposed on the company, as any failure to cooperate by any of the persons involved will be attributed to the company. Under the Dutch Competition Act, administrative sanctions for non-cooperation can be imposed on natural persons as well. Failure to cooperate is also a criminal offence under section 184 of the Dutch Penal Code, which carries a maximum prison sentence of three months or a fine up to a maximum of €3,350. In situations of failure to cooperate with FIOD-ECD officers section 24a to 26 WED provides a maximum prison sentence of two years or a fine up to a maximum of €74,000.

D. Voluntary Investigations

Risks and benefits of voluntary investigations

5.54 Internal investigations are routinely carried out by institutions and corporates that are subject to self-reporting obligations. Also, internal investigations may be carried out as part of the general risk and compliance policy of corporates, including ethical codes of conduct and, obviously, in the event that 'issues' have been spotted, voluntary investigations may be carried out defensively, in order to understand and address the issue.

---

[64] Section 25 General Administrative Law Act.

Regulators in the Netherlands do not have an established attitude towards internal **5.55** investigations. However, voluntary internal investigations may demonstrate good faith on the part of the company and may be a valuable source of information, assuming that the company will share its findings with the regulator.

Regulators will not allow internal investigations to replace their own investigations **5.56** completely. Nevertheless, regulators may use the findings of internal investigations as a helpful source of relevant data.

Moreover, companies sometimes conduct an internal investigation before any **5.57** regulatory activity has been initiated; particularly in cases of suspected anti-trust violations. The company will then keep the internal report on file so that it can be handed over to the NMa if, and as soon as, the latter initiates an investigation. The intended result is that the NMa curtails the scope and intensity of its own investigation and lets itself be guided to some extent by the findings of the internal investigation.

Thorough internal investigations are crucial if the company considers submitting **5.58** a request for leniency (either to the European Commission or the NMa), as one of the key conditions for obtaining immunity or fine reduction requires the company to disclose all relevant facts. If at a later stage it appears that the company was not able to fully disclose the facts, this may seriously jeopardize the chances for a successful leniency application, whilst the information that was provided may still be used as evidence.

Events triggering considering conducting a voluntary investigation

In the banking industry, there are express legal requirements to conduct what might **5.59** be referred to as ongoing internal investigations. Banks are under a statutory obligation to maintain internal auditing and risk-control departments. If any gross misconduct is detected by any of these departments, an internal investigation is the logical step in order to get to the bottom of the problem.

In general, any expectation of regulatory intervention warrants a preceding inter- **5.60** nal investigation, so as to avoid surprises and prepare the defence or, in case of competition law infringements, enable the company to decide whether to apply for leniency.

Structuring an internal investigation

If a company decides to conduct a voluntary investigation, there are no general **5.61** legal principles that apply. However, as a matter of course, the company has to comply with all general provisions relevant for its business, for instance, statutory rights of its employees or statutory disclosure obligations.

5.62 As a general rule it is of utmost importance to investigate the issues at stake as quickly as possible while being as comprehensive as possible. Therefore, the company's decision-makers must decide within a short period of time as to whether a voluntary investigation should be conducted and define its purpose.

5.63 The success of an internal investigation largely depends upon the effective structuring and management of the investigation process. First, it will be necessary to clearly define the scope and purpose of the investigation and determine who shall become part of the team conducting this investigation. Almost every internal investigation will require the involvement of the legal department, and possibly external legal advisers, since there are inevitably a number of legal questions at stake. Also, it will be helpful—and sometimes necessary—for the team to have a sponsor or, even, an ultimate leader at the highest corporate level, for example a member of the Supervisory Board. Once the team is established, it will be necessary to allocate precise roles and functions within the team and determine a team leader who will supervise the entire investigation and assume overall responsibility for managing the team effectively. The ultimate responsibility for the investigation should obviously lie outside the group of people that may be involved in or may have responsibility for the matters at stake. In accounting matters, this could be the chairman of the Audit Committee. In governance-related matters, one of the senior members of the Supervisory Board (ie the non-executives) would be the appropriate choice to lead the process. If the matters at stake seem to be relatively isolated (eg certain business units or certain jurisdictions with no potential involvement of top level management) the Chief Financial Officer or General Counsel could assume the lead of the investigation.

5.64 It is also critical at the start of an investigation to establish the channels of communication between the investigation team and the management. Depending on the sensitivity of the issues at stake the company must consider to what extent and at which point in time written reports which outline the results of the investigation are to be submitted. It is important to bear in mind that, as described below, the company's internal documents in most cases will not be privileged even if external counsel is involved in the investigation.

5.65 As a matter of best practice, one of the very first steps to be taken is to preserve evidence. Failure to do so may heavily undermine the credibility of the investigation. Instructions to preserve evidence would normally be given to employees that may have been involved in the matters at stake or, in the event of a wider issue, even to all employees. In addition, further action to ensure that the documentary record is protected may be warranted.

5.66 An internal investigation should be organized in such a manner that the defined aim of the investigation can be achieved, taking into account available resources.

This includes considering such factors as whether it is necessary to review documents or examine a whole range of employees. In many cases, a large volume of documents will be relevant and material to the investigation. Consequently, it is necessary to implement a well-functioning document management system from the outset and designate a team member as responsible for all questions concerning document management including dealing with sensitive or secret documents. Such person must be experienced in handling large numbers of complex data and documents.

During the course of the investigation it is advisable regularly to review whether **5.67** the aim of the investigation can actually be achieved by the means that have been identified at the beginning of the investigation or if it has become necessary to utilize other means or redefine the scope and purpose of the investigation. Regular review of the provisional results reduce the risk of being sidetracked or spending too much time on irrelevant points. Ideally, in order to avoid such problems, an investigation should be structured in different phases which are executed one after the other. Upon completion of each phase, an assessment would need to be made whether the aim of that particular part of the investigation has been reached and whether any interim conclusions could be drawn from the results to date.

Once the investigation has been concluded it may be worth considering whether **5.68** its conclusions may have further benefits for the company beyond the particular investigation itself and whether there are any general conclusions the company may draw from the particular issue, for instance, whether there are, in general, certain processes that could be optimized or whether there are other tools that could be implemented to avoid misconduct or irregularities at a very early stage. The company should then consider implementing or improving a compliance system which aims to ensure that relevant statutory provisions are observed and misconduct of single individuals be avoided, or, at least, that potential irregularities be discovered at an early stage.

Using external advisers

Dutch public companies commonly have a two-tier board system. The **5.69** board of managing directors[65] is charged with day-to-day management of the company. It is the duty of the board of supervisory directors[66] to advise and supervise the board of managing directors. By virtue of its function and position, the board of supervisory directors is best placed to retain external advisers to conduct an investigation. It has become an established practice for the board of supervisory directors to retain independent external counsel to conduct investigations into

---

[65] *Bestuur.*
[66] *Raad van commissarissen.*

matters in which members of the Management Board may have been involved and may have failed their statutory or fiduciary obligations (eg Royal Dutch oil reserves).

5.70 External legal advisers have the added advantage of being subject to statutory confidentiality restrictions and related legal privilege. In contrast to the members of the company's legal department, an external lawyer has the right to refuse testimony in court proceedings. Furthermore, external lawyers typically are experienced in determining as to how evidence that was obtained during the investigation can be used in subsequent proceedings before courts or any competent authorities. The involvement of external lawyers may also be helpful in cases which reveal that preliminary measures before the courts become necessary, eg provisional seizure of assets. Finally, from an operational perspective, external counsel may have a higher level of expertise in the areas of interviewing, interpreting facts and building and testing of scenarios. International law firms will have access to regulators in the relevant jurisdictions. Engaging external counsel can contribute to the credibility of the investigation.

5.71 The Dutch Corporate Governance Code in section III 1.9 specifically states that the Supervisory Board may separately retain external advisers to assist the board in performing its duties. To the extent that a Dutch company has a one-tier board, the provisions in relation to the Supervisory Board equally apply to the non-executives on the Management Board.

5.72 No practice has yet developed among corporates in the Netherlands as to the criteria that should be applied when selecting counsel. Depending on the specific circumstances of the presupposed breach, the company's regular counsel may continue to be involved. However, a 100 per cent 'clean hands' approach would favour the involvement of an independent law firm; this would often be the preference of the Supervisory Board.

Managing illegal activity during investigations

5.73 If an investigation uncovers illegal acts, these should in principle be stopped immediately. To the extent that illegal conduct causes damages to third parties, continuing illegal conduct may expose the company to civil liability.

5.74 Illegal acts may only continue if required by the OM and the relevant regulator and when in the interest of the company, for instance if a lower fine would be the result. In the context of a leniency application with the NMa or the Commission, immediate termination of the applicant's participation in a cartel may forewarn the other members of the cartel and jeopardize the investigation. Continued participation during the investigation may thus be allowed under certain conditions.

E. Self-reporting

Duty to self-report

Under the Wft, financial institutions are obliged to self-report certain incidents **5.75** to regulators.[67] These include:

- any criminal offences by its employees which it has reported to the police or OM;
- any events that may jeopardize the continuity of the operations of the institution; and
- any events or circumstances which may generate public attention.

Furthermore, section II.1.6 of the Corporate Governance Code requires companies **5.76** to put in place whistle-blowing procedures for employees enabling them to report irregularities of a general, operational or financial nature to the chairman of the Supervisory Board or to an officer especially designated for this purpose.

Culture of self-reporting

The self-reporting of an offence to the relevant regulator before a regulatory investi- **5.77** gation has started, may sometimes prove more beneficial for a company than remaining silent hoping that its offence may go unnoticed. Indeed, self-reporting and subsequent cooperation with the regulator may be rewarded with a reduction of the otherwise applicable sanctions and may also prevent a regulator from making the matter at stake public. In assessing the reduction of sanctions, the regulator will generally also take into account factors such as the nature and severity of the offence, the timing of the reporting and the level of subsequent cooperation with the regulator.

In practice, offenders indeed regularly self-report voluntarily. Reporting by finan- **5.78** cial institutions of internal violations or fraud cases to DNB or the OM is also common in the Netherlands. Companies also voluntarily report competition law infringements to the NMa or the Commission under the applicable leniency programmes. A self-reporting, due to its secretive nature, takes place behind closed doors; there are no specific examples that can be referred to here.

F. Announcements and Public Relations Strategies

Regulatory investigations

External communications

Dutch listed companies are required to publish price sensitive information **5.79** concerning their business without delay in order to ensure an orderly and fair market.[68] The Wft defines price sensitive information as 'information of a precise

---

[67] Section 29 Decree on supervision of conduct of financial institutions Wft.
[68] Section 5:59 Wft.

nature relating directly or indirectly to an issuer of financial instruments, or to trading in those financial instruments, which information has not been made public and which, if it were made public, would be likely to have a significant effect on the price of the relevant financial instruments'.[69] Therefore, if a regulatory investigation is launched into a Dutch listed company, such a company may be obliged to report this to the market when the impact of the investigation might be significant.

5.80 In the case of investigations relating to a defective product or other dangers, the company may be under a civil law obligation to report the potential defect to its customers or the public at large and alert them to potential risks.

5.81 A company should therefore have an emergency plan in place on how to deal with the media and requests for information in case the public, shareholders or customers become aware of the investigation.

Internal communications

5.82 Under Dutch law, there is no general duty to inform employees of regulatory or criminal investigations. However, the works council[70] of the company should be informed. Time and scope of any such communication should be determined on the basis of the circumstances of the relevant matter at stake.

5.83 Although there is no general duty to inform employees of regulatory or criminal investigations, it might still be advisable to do so if they could otherwise hear of the investigation from other sources. By communicating that an investigation is underway and explaining the strategy as to how to deal with the situation, management can demonstrate leadership and prevent rumours and insecurity among employees. In practice, the works council would be informed at an early stage if a significant number of employees were involved or if the anticipated outcome of the investigation were to require measures affecting the work force or the structure of the company. Often these early stage communications would be on an informal and fully confidential basis, through communications between management and the chairman of the works council.

G. Voluntary Investigations

External communications

5.84 In the event that an internal investigation conducted by a Dutch listed company falls within the scope of price sensitive information under the Wft, such company

---

[69] Section 5:53 Wft.

[70] *Ondernemingsraad*, an employee consultation body that has certain rights with respect to information, advice and co-determination.

will, in principle, be obliged to expeditiously disclose this information to the market, as outlined above.[71] If, on that basis, a company has to disclose the circumstances that gave rise to the internal investigation, it will usually make sense to disclose the fact that an internal investigation has been launched at the same time

To the extent that the investigation or the facts which are being investigated **5.85** are price sensitive, postponement of disclosure is permitted when it is in the legitimate interest of the company. Postponement of disclosure of price sensitive information is only allowed if and for as long as three requirements are met:

- postponement would serve the legitimate interest of the company;
- postponement would not give reason to fear that the public/investors would be misled; and
- the confidentiality of the information can be ensured.

The Wft prescribes that confidentiality must be ensured by disclosing the price **5.86** sensitive information only to those persons within the organization that have a need to know. In voluntary (internal) investigations, the company is more likely to be 'in control' of the process and therefore more likely to be in a position to ensure confidentiality—which in turn may entitle the company to postponement of disclosure.

Once rumours or false information are starting to float around in the market, **5.87** companies will need to publicity disclose and/or 'correct' such information.[72].

Internal communications

In the era of modern mass communication it is likely that information communi- **5.88** cated to employees (particularly in large organizations) will very quickly reach the public domain. Informing employees at large will, in practice, happen shortly before the company is obliged to make a public disclosure about the investigation pursuant to the Wft. If the company were to postpone making an announcement, usually only a limited number of employees would be informed so as to ensure confidentiality.

A company's decision on whether and when to inform its employees about an **5.89** upcoming or ongoing internal investigation will usually be driven by the objectives of the internal investigation. If the primary objective is to provide information to a regulator or a prosecutor's office, it may be wise to conduct the investigation with

---

[71] Price sensitive information is any knowledge which is specific and that directly or indirectly pertains to the company that issued the securities or to the trade of such securities, which has not been disclosed and which may have a significant influence on the price of the securities or on the price of derivatives of the securities. Section 5:53 Wft.

[72] Section 5:47 sub-para 3 Wft.

as much secrecy as possible, at least during the initial stages. If, by contrast, the investigation is predominantly aimed at maintaining or re-establishing the company's reputation as a 'good' corporate citizen, it would seem natural for the company to communicate the fact that the investigation is under way to the employees and to the general public at a much earlier stage. The same consideration applies to the extent that the investigation serves other publicity purposes, such as paving the way for the company's new management to pursue claims against former management.

5.90 Even if the purpose of the internal investigation calls for more, rather than less secrecy, the company may determine that it will be impossible to keep the investigation completely confidential. This may prompt the company to disclose to its employees the fact that an investigation is being conducted.

Key points for Public Relations strategies

5.91 The public disclosure of price sensitive information may be part of a wider PR strategy. Listed companies have some discretion as to the manner in which price sensitive information is published, for as long as it is accessible to everyone and is presented in such a manner that investors are in a position to assess the information fully, correctly and in time.

5.92 In order to clarify its views on publication of price sensitive information the AFM has published a special brochure.[73] It requires that the publication of the price sensitive information be effected by publication of an official press release in a combination of general and specific financial media.[74] The contents of the press release must be clear and should obviously not be misleading.

5.93 It is recommended that a specific headline is included that clearly summarizes the announcement. The press release may not be combined in any potentially misleading fashion with advertisements for the business's activities.

5.94 The listed company must have a website and must place the announcement on that website immediately, where it must be accessible for at least 12 months (the AFM recommends keeping such announcements there for a longer period of time). In order to meet the disclosure requirement, it would, however, not be sufficient to place the publication only on the company's own website.[75]

---

[73] AFM brochure 'Publication of price-sensitive information' <http://www.afm.nl>.
[74] The Transparency Directive provides more specific information regarding press releases in general.
[75] AFM brochure 'Publication of price-sensitive information', 10.

A company should have a designated emergency team and an emergency plan in **5.95** place on how to deal with the media and requests for information in case of a crisis and/or investigation. The emergency team should consist of members of the senior management of the company, and be available to be activated on short notice. The email addresses, addresses, and telephone numbers of the team members should be kept up to date at all times(ie at weekends, during vacations, business trips etc). Only persons designated by the emergency team should engage in any internal or external communications. Ideally, only these persons should exclusively perform the entire communication to demonstrate that the company is focused and the responsibilities are clear.

If the company does not have a special PR department, obtaining profes- **5.96** sional PR support from outside consultants should be considered. Together with the company's legal counsel PR advisers could help create a legally correct and media-suitable concept of communication which could avoid negative publicity.

Further, no statement should be issued prior to a proper first analysis of the situa- **5.97** tion. Even if journalists are aware of a search of the company's premises and bluntly confront management with questions, management should not give in to such pressure. Rather, nothing spontaneous should be said and reference should be made to a press statement that would be in the process of being prepared. In addition, the company's employees should be explicitly asked to refrain from any public statements. In critical situations, the company may consider having its employees sign written confidentiality agreements.

Any statement by the company's spokesperson should be brief and comprehensible **5.98** and should contain only confirmed facts. The emergency plan should list the most dangerous mistakes of conduct such as:

- complete silence;
- giving of 'no comment' answers;
- hesitation;
- defending oneself; and
- minimizing of the problem.

H. Best Practices in Document Gathering and Preservation

Expectations of regulators and courts

Under Dutch law, there is no general statutory obligation for companies or individu- **5.99** als to preserve every single piece of evidence once a regulatory or internal investigation has begun or is likely to be initiated. However, a company under investigation has a general duty to cooperate with authorities once an investigation has commenced—which may in turn prevent the destruction of documents.

5.100   Also, there are certain statutory provisions that give regulatory authorities the power to specifically demand that certain documents be preserved. Furthermore, certain statutory provisions require companies to preserve certain types of documents for certain periods of time regardless of whether an investigation has commenced, or is likely to do so. For example, the management board of a Dutch legal entity is obliged to preserve all (financial) records of the legal entity that are relevant for ascertaining its duties and liabilities for a period of seven years.[76] Likewise, the Identification Provision of Services Act[77] requires banks and insurers to verify their clients' identity, and to preserve their records of such verification. A failure to comply with the WID constitutes a criminal offence[78] and may also attract administrative fines, depending on the applicable legislation.

5.101   Irrespective of the formal legal position, there are strong arguments for a company to adopt a structured document management policy, including standby emergency instructions to immediately suspend regular document destruction if and when an investigation is initiated or announced. Any suspicion of deliberate destruction of 'bad' documents is likely to ruin the company's position vis-à-vis the regulators and to cause irreparable embarrassment.

Rights of documents and confidentiality

5.102   Regulators generally have wide-ranging powers to demand documents and emails from companies, employees and relevant third parties. Failure to comply constitutes a criminal offence.[79]

5.103   The FIOD-ECD and police officers can seize original records and documents; this includes electronic files and even personal email files. They may also request access to data and documents or other data carriers. Regulators must be granted access to business records, including electronic records within reasonable limits, but do not have the authority to actually seize originals. They must be allowed to take copies. Regulators may only take originals with them for a short period to make copies if copies cannot be made on site.[80]

5.104   If documents are about to be seized or copied on site, it should be ensured that a list of the seized documents is prepared. This list should be as detailed as possible.

---

[76] See s 2:10 DCC.
[77] *Wet identificatie bij dienstverlening.*
[78] See s 5:17 General Administrative Law Act.
[79] See s 184 Dutch Penal Code.
[80] Section 5:17 General Administrative Law Act.

For example, the list should contain a description of the content of each individual binder. In addition, if possible, photocopies of the seized documents should be made.

Data protection

When gathering documents and submitting information to authorities, the company must be aware that such information may contain data related to one or more identified or identifiable natural persons ('personal data'). This data is protected under the Dutch Data Protection Act (DPA)[81] and may even be protected under the Dutch Telecommunications Act (DTA).[82]   **5.105**

The processing of personal data and its transmission to requesting authorities must comply with both the DPA and the DTA. The DTA is only of secondary importance as it only contains minimal obligations to be observed in this respect.   **5.106**

When assessing compliance with the DPA in the context of data processing pursuant to a regulator's request, one must differentiate between requests of authorities situated within the Netherlands, requests of authorities from within EU countries[83] and requests of authorities from outside the EU.   **5.107**

By way of general background, it should be noted that the DPA stipulates that, prior to any processing of personal data, data controllers (eg employees) in the Netherlands must notify the Dutch Data Protection Authority of such (intended) processing.[84]   **5.108**

The definition of personal data is very broad. Pursuant to the DPA, all data that could lead to the identification of a natural person (eg including names in email addresses, IP addresses etc) qualifies as personal data. In addition, data that does not directly relate to a natural person but to a product or (production) process qualifies as personal data in case it indirectly provides information about a natural person (eg the productivity of an individual). Personal data does not, however, include data regarding a legal entity.[85]   **5.109**

---

[81] *Wet Bescherming Persoonsgegevens.*

[82] *Telecommunicatiewet.*

[83] Please note that the processing and transfer of personal data in all EEA countries is treated equally as in EU countries. Norway, Liechtenstein and Iceand (the EEA countries) have implemented Directive 95/46/EC on the protection of personal data.

[84] For the categories of data which can be processed without notification please see the Exemption Decree (*Vrijstellingsbesluit*). Note that where data will be transferred to non-EU countries, notification is always required.

[85] The scope of the DTA is broader; pursuant to the DTA, companies which control public electronic communications networks have a duty of care with regard to protection of personal data and, under circumstances, with regard to data regarding legal entities (s 11.2 DTA).

5.110 The DPA contains an exhaustive list of grounds on the basis of which the processing of personal data is legitimate.[86] One of the legitimate grounds is that the processing of personal data is necessary for compliance with a legal obligation to which the data controller is subject. If and to the extent information containing personal data is requested by Dutch authorities on the basis of such a legal obligation,[87] the processing of personal data by the requested data controller and its transmission to the requesting authority is permissible.[88] The requested data controller may only process and transfer personal data to the extent necessary for the fulfilment of the legal obligation.[89]

5.111 In the event that an employer intends to voluntarily cooperate with a regulator, then the above-mentioned exception would not be available as there would not be a legal obligation to cooperate with the authorities. In such circumstances, there are two alternative grounds on the basis of which the processing and transferring of personal data would be legitimate:

- **Ground 1**: the processing is necessary for the performance of a task carried out in the public interest or in the exercise of official authority vested in the data controller or in a third party to whom the information is disclosed (this ground will not often be relevant in regulatory investigations); or

- **Ground 2**: the processing is required to serve the legitimate interest of the data controller or the third party to whom the information is disclosed, except where such interests are overridden by the fundamental rights of the relevant individual.[90]

5.112 The assessment of the applicability of the 'legitimate interest' ground (Ground 2 above) requires a balancing of interests on a case-by-case basis, as it can only be relied on if and to the extent that the employee's legitimate interests prevail over the relevant individual's legitimate interests.[91]

5.113 Under the DPA the relevant employee may raise objections against the processing and/or transferring of his or her personal data. The employer must then inform

---

[86] See s 8 DPA.

[87] Please note that the provision of personal data to Dutch Authorities in the context of a criminal investigation against a data subject falls outside the scope of the DPA.

[88] See s 8(c) DPA.

[89] In a situation in which a data controller can also comply with the statutory obligation by alternative means, the processing and transfer of personal data is not permissible.

[90] See s 8(f) DPA.

[91] In some cases, a third party could be deemed to have a legitimate interest for obtaining personal data. For example, recent Dutch case law confirmed that in certain circumstances, an Internet provider is entitled (even obliged) to provide the contact details of a website owner acting unlawfully against a third party (eg by offering unlawful content).

the relevant individual as to whether it accepts or rejects the objection.[92] The relevant individual is entitled to claim damages in case the employer continues to process and transfer personal data after a court has confirmed that the objection of the relevant individual is valid.

In addition, the Dutch Data Protection Authority has the authority to impose **5.114** administrative fines for violation of obligations set out in the DPA. In case of continued violation, the Dutch Data Protection Authority may even refer the matter to the OM, which may prosecute the relevant data controller and may seek criminal sanctions.

However, that is not to say that companies will generally abstain from processing **5.115** and/or transferring personal data without the consent of the relevant individual under all circumstances. The need for the company to conduct an internal investigation in order to prevent sanctions may far outweigh the potential risk of claims for damages by the relevant individual. Therefore, in most cases it will be a judgement call for a company whether or not it is in the best interest of the company to take the risk of processing and/or transferring personal data without first obtaining the consent of the relevant individual.

If a company is confronted with a direct request for personal data from an EU **5.116** authority (ie not through a Dutch authority), then such a request is typically based on a legal obligation in that EU member state. According to the Dutch Data Protection Authority,[93] such a foreign legal obligation does, however, not qualify as a 'legal obligation' as referred to in section 8 of the DPA.[94] If, instead, the company invokes the 'legitimate interest' exception, it will need to anticipate that the Dutch Data Protection Authority has ruled that the mere existence of a foreign legal obligation does not in itself satisfy the 'legitimate interest' test.

Therefore, in order for a company to rely on the 'legitimate interest' criterion, it **5.117** should actually consider for each case whether its legitimate interest (associated with its compliance with the foreign obligation) should prevail over the interests of the relevant individual(s) (eg intrusion into the employee's private life).

With respect to requests from non-EU authorities, there will be the additional **5.118** complication of export of personal data, as it involves the transfer of personal data to a jurisdiction outside the EU. Any such export of information would be prohibited unless the third country to which the information would be exported were to ensure an adequate level of protection.

---

[92] See s 40(1) and (2) DPA.
[93] *College Bescherming Persoonsgegevens.*
[94] Only Dutch legal obligations qualify as such.

5.119   The EU Commission has issued guidelines as to which non-EU member states are deemed to have an adequate level of protection; these guidelines are also followed in the Netherlands. The EU Commission guidelines only include a small number of non-EU member states.[95] In principle, unless the data receiver in the US has committed itself to the Safe Harbor Principle,[96] the US is not deemed to ensure an adequate level of protection.

5.120   If the relevant third country does not ensure an adequate level of protection, then the DPA only allows the export of personal data if the company has obtained unambiguous consent from the relevant individual;[97] the transfer is necessary or legally required on important public interest grounds, or for the establishment, exercise or defence of legal claims; or the data controller has obtained an export permit from the Dutch Minister of Justice.

Unambiguous consent

5.121   Apart from the practical difficulties that arise when having to obtain the unambiguous consent from the relevant individual,[98] it should be noted that the relevant individual has the right to withdraw such consent at any point in time. Consequently, this is not an ideal ground on which to base the export of personal data.

Transfer legally required for defence of legal claims

5.122   This exemption is, in principle, available in cases such as the export of information in connection with (anticipated) legal proceedings against the data controller or export of information to a debt collection agency. The extent to which this exemption is available would, however, need to be assessed on a case-by-case basis. In the SWIFT case,[99] the Dutch Minister of Finance confirmed that this exemption is only available in exceptional cases and cannot be a basis for regular data exports.[100]

---

[95] Pursuant to s 25(6) of the EU Data Protection Guideline, the Commission may determine that a third country provides for an appropriate level of protection.

[96] 'Safe-Harbor' is a data protection package negotiated by the Commission with the US Ministry of Trade, obliging the recipient vis-à-vis the US authority in charge to comply with certain principles of data protection.

[97] See s 77(1)(a) DPA.

[98] The word *unambiguous* means that consent to transfer personal data to non-EU authorities is not sufficient; the consent should be aimed at the transfer to a specified authority in a specified country. Consent must be given on a case-by-case basis.

[99] SWIFT is a Belgian organization which arranges international payments for banks all over the world. Despite SWIFT's efforts to arrange for certain safeguards in respect of transferring personal data to US authorities, the Belgian Committee for Data Protection ruled in September 2006 that by processing data to the US, SWIFT had breached the Belgian rules on Data Protection.

[100] Report on the provision of personal data by banks to US authorities, commissioned by the Minister of Finance in March 2007.

Export permit

The data controller could also obtain an export permit for the transfer of personal **5.123** data to non-EU authorities from the Dutch Minister of Justice. The Minister will only grant the permit if the envisaged processing (including the intended export) is in line with the principles set out in the DPA and, particularly, only if the fundamental rights of the relevant individual are adequately protected.

It should be noted that, in principle, the strict rules in relation to export of per- **5.124** sonal data would equally apply to internal investigations if within one group of companies personal data were to be shared with persons (eg group compliance departments) outside the Netherlands.

As referred to above, a data subject can initiate civil proceedings in the event that a **5.125** data controller breaches its DPA obligations towards such data subject. A data controller may be held liable for damages caused by the continued processing and the transfer of personal data in the event that the unlawfulness has been established in court. A data controller may also run the risk of negative publicity as a result of any publications, press releases etc that may be associated with the civil proceedings.[101]

Practical considerations

Whatever the legal obligation, as discussed above, a company facing an investiga- **5.126** tion or initiating a voluntary internal investigation should ensure that no documents be destroyed that may be relevant for the investigations, and issue instructions accordingly. Likewise, when creating documents, the scope for speculation, exaggeration or misinterpretation should be kept to a minimum. This caution extends to internal emails and notes, not just formal memos and letters. Records should be kept of decisions taken by the company in investigating the issue/situation and formulating its follow-up action. The company should also at all times be able to see itself 'through the eyes of the regulator' (ie be aware of what a regulator would expect the company to do or not to do in anticipation of or during an investigation).

I. Dealing with Privileged Documents

General rules on privilege

The concept of legal privilege with regard to documents is not specifically addressed **5.127** in Dutch legislation. The central concept in Dutch law is the exception for certain professionals (eg external legal counsel, medical professionals, accountants) to the

---

[101] In the Netherlands, civil proceedings are in principle open for public and in many cases the judgment will be published.

general duty to testify in court and/or cooperate with regulatory investigations. This right to refrain from giving testimony is extended to the work product of external legal counsel, as well as their communications with their clients. Effectively, these are therefore privileged under Dutch law and cannot be seized according to the relevant provisions of the Code on criminal procedure.[102]

5.128 Section 5:20 of the General Administrative Law Act exempts lawyers admitted to the bar from the obligation to cooperate with regulatory authorities. As a result attorneys may refuse cooperation and/or access to documents that they have in their possession insofar as covered by their confidentiality obligation vis-à-vis the client.[103] As a general rule this obligation covers any information that the client has provided to his counsel in order to enable his counsel to determine the legal position of the company. The Dutch Competition Act extends this exemption to legal advice provided by an external counsel to a company on the regulatory position of the company that is on file with the company.[104]

5.129 Under Dutch law the position of in-house lawyers who are admitted to the bar is similar to the position of external legal counsel. Bar membership for in-house counsel is conditional upon him or her having some degree of autonomy in the corporate organization. In the recent *Akzo*[105] judgment of the Court of First Instance it was, however, established that in-house counsel do not enjoy legal privilege under EC competition law, regardless of whether they are members of the bar.

5.130 Lawyers are obliged to keep confidential all information that has been obtained in the course of professional activities for a specific client, regardless of the nature of the information or the manner in which they obtained it. All such communications are privileged.

5.131 There is no concept of pre-trial discovery or disclosure under Dutch law. There is no general obligation for a party to civil proceedings to disclose documents. For general litigation purposes, the legal privilege exception is therefore less crucial than in certain other jurisdictions. There is, however, a—be it relatively limited—procedural opportunity for a party to a legal relationship to request access to certain documents related to that legal relationship (eg a contract) from the party holding such documents.

---

[102] Section 218 and 98 Code of Criminal Procedure.
[103] Section 51 Dutch Competition Act and s 5:20 General Administrative Law Act.
[104] Section 51 Dutch Competition Act.
[105] CFI 17 September 2007, joined cases T-125/03 and T-253/03, not yet reported.

Waiving privilege

Privilege can in principle only be waived by external legal counsel or any other **5.132** person covered by professional privilege.

Once a civil law litigant has lawfully gained access to privileged information or **5.133** work product, such civil litigant is free to use such information or work product in the litigation and is not restricted by the privilege. Obtaining such information directly from the company under investigation would, however, be very difficult because there is no concept of US style discovery in Dutch civil proceedings.

Where the prosecutor's office conducts an investigation, the file is in principle **5.134** only accessible to the defendant and his legal counsel.[106] However, information from the file may be given to third parties if this is necessary to serve the statutory tasks of the OM and is required to pursue by an important general interest or to defend a right in court, including a civil damages claim that is already pending. The purpose of any such information exchange is limited to, among other things, the prevention or investigation of criminal offences, maintenance of public order, the support of victims and others involved in a criminal offence and the adoption of administrative decisions. Access is granted at the discretion of the OM[107] which has for this purpose developed strict policy guidelines. Regulators and private parties who suffered damages are among the categories of possible recipients of information.

When the NMa conducts infringement proceedings, it is obliged to consolidate **5.135** its findings and intended sanctions in a report (similar to the 'statement of objections' under EU competition law) that sets out the charges against which the company has to defend itself. The company itself as well as interested third parties are invited to submit their views in writing and/or during a hearing. The report and all other relevant documents are made available for all interested third parties for a period of four weeks. Business secrets of the company under investigation are excluded from such access rights.[108] Nevertheless, obtaining access to the files of the NMa can be a powerful tool for preparing a civil law action for damages.

The Public Information Act[109] allows anyone (regardless of purpose or interest) to **5.136** file a request for access to information with respect to, essentially, governmental

---

[106] As well as a third party who challenges a decision not to prosecute a case and the victim, to the extent its interests so require.

[107] Section 39e of the Act on judicial and criminal records (*Wet justitiële en strafvorderlijke gegevens*) and Guidelines on judicial and criminal records (*Aanwijzing justitiële en strafvorderlijke gegevens*).

[108] Section 60 Dutch Competition Act.

[109] *Wet openbaarheid van bestuur.*

affairs with public authorities who hold this information. The obligation to disclose is subject to exceptions, including the protection of business secrets. Other exceptions apply to information which, if it became known, might have detrimental effects on controlling or regulatory functions of the authorities and to information, the publication of which would cause disproportional harm to involved parties or third parties. Recent case law established that the NMa is subject to the Public Information Act, as the specific provisions of the Dutch Competition Act do not exclude the application of the Act in anti-trust matters. Whilst a large part of the information that the NMa will normally have is likely to be covered by one of the exceptions, the prospects of third parties obtaining such information have nevertheless improved.

Limited waiver

5.137 As indicated above, it is generally possible for third parties with a legitimate interest to gain access to the records of the public prosecutor or a regulator. Access will be granted if there is no compelling need to protect the privacy interests of the affected person. Access will usually be denied if the files contain business secrets of the company concerned. Against this background a company that voluntarily discloses privileged documents to a regulator could mark the documents as 'containing business secrets' and seek to agree with the regulator that these will not be disclosed to any other (private) party. Such an 'agreement' is not, however, binding upon the regulator and a regulator could still decide that the documents can be disclosed to a third party. In practice, a regulator will not elect to disclose documents marked as 'containing business secrets' to a third party before having discussed this issue with the company concerned and will be very careful in making its decision so as to avoid any potential claims for damages.

Privilege pitfalls

5.138 It is important to be sufficiently aware of which documents are privileged, how they are stored and to whom they are given. Even though Dutch law does not require privileged documents to remain with the external legal counsel in order for privilege to apply, best practice would require that such documents would only be given to third parties subject to confidentiality agreements. Furthermore, it is important to be organized in case of on-site inspections or dawn raids by regulators. Though privileged documents may not be seized or reviewed, the question whether or not a certain document is privileged may be subject to debate and regulators may not always be willing to accept on the spot that privilege applies. In such cases, the assistance of an independent third party who can establish the nature of the document may be necessary.

J. Managing Regulators

Dialogue with regulators

Regulated companies often have an informal dialogue with regulators in the **5.139** course of which the regulator may express its view on the interpretation of certain regulatory requirements. Once an investigation has commenced, it is generally advisable that the company under scrutiny communicates to the regulator that it will fully cooperate (as far as feasible), although in principle no company is obliged to do so. Further, the company should set up a clear plan as to who is handling the communication with the regulator.

Engaging proactively with the regulators will normally be beneficial to the com- **5.140** pany. It will reduce the risk of surprises and may help reduce the scope of the potential problem area. Often, the communications with the regulators are managed through external law firms who have a track record of dealing with the regulators.

Use of information by regulators

The exchange of information between regulators, or between regulators and the **5.141** OM, is normally restricted and only allowed if the applicable legislation provides for a specific legal basis or obligation to do so. As a general rule, every person (civil servant or otherwise) who in his involvement with a public task obtains confidential information, is under a legal obligation to keep such information secret.[110] The breach of confidentiality by public servants is a criminal offence.[111] However, specific legislation often contains qualifications and exceptions in respect of confidentiality:

- the Code of Criminal Procedure requires civil servants to report to the OM any criminal offences that they have witnessed and requires civil servants to file formal complaints in case of corruption and bribery;[112]
- under the Public Information Act any third party may request access to information on, essentially, governmental affairs which the public authority who holds this information is obliged to disclose, albeit subject to exceptions aimed at protecting business secrets and other legitimate interests;

---

[110] Section 2:5 General Administrative law act.
[111] Section 272 Dutch Penal Code.
[112] Section 162 Code of Criminal Procedure

- under the relevant tax laws the tax inspector has the right to request and obtain such information as is necessary for the levying of taxes, subject to individual exemptions from the Secretary of Finance;[113]

- the Dutch Competition Act provides that information submitted to the NMa may only be used for the enforcement and execution of the Dutch Competition Act and may only be shared internationally with other competition authorities.[114] In the context of the construction sector investigation, the NMa was confronted with criminal and tax offences (bribery of contracting authorities, falsification of invoices) and took the position that it was obliged to report these matters to the OM. The NMa concluded an agreement on information sharing with the tax authorities, except for information submitted in the context of leniency applications; and

- the confidentiality obligations of the AFM as laid down in the Wft are based on European law and are thus of a higher order than the national tax legislation that imposes an information obligation towards the tax inspector.

Managing multiple regulators

5.142 When under investigation by multiple regulators the company must bear in mind that it may be obliged to share information with other regulators or with the criminal authorities. Therefore, the company must be aware that any information supplied could end up in the hands of other regulators. All the issues of which the company needs to be aware during concurrent investigations, as outlined above, should be considered.

K. Managing Employees During Investigations

Cooperation by the employee

5.143 Dutch labour law does not contain explicit provisions dealing with the rights and obligations of employers and employees in connection with investigations. The general rules of Dutch employment law apply. Under these rules employees and employers are obliged to act as a good employee (*goed werknemer*) and a good employer (*goed werkgever*),[115] respectively. Furthermore, the employer has the right to give individual and collective instructions in respect of the manner in which duties under the employment agreement should be performed and instructions

---

[113] Section 55 General Tax Act (*Algemene wet inzake rijksbelastingen*).
[114] Sections 90 and 91 Dutch Competition Act.
[115] Section 7:611 DCC, *goed werknemerschap en goed werkgeverschap*.

aimed at retaining the proper order within the company[116]. The powers to require employees to cooperate in an investigation and to provide information should generally be based on and are limited by these general principles.

Within larger organizations or organizations that are active in a regulated market, **5.144** often codes of conduct are in place containing rules on the manner in which investigations can be carried out and the level and kind of cooperation that is expected from employees. A code of conduct will generally be considered an internal instruction and, similar to a general instruction, its enforceability is limited by the obligation of the employer to act as a 'good employer'.

The duty to act as a 'good employer' limits the ability of the employer to express **5.145** threats in the context of an investigation. There are no specific statutory rules protecting employees in this respect. A refusal to cooperate in an internal investigation could be a justified ground for dismissal or lead to other liabilities if it is found that the employee did not act as a 'good employee' by failing to cooperate.

In practice, it would be most productive to structure the investigation as a coop- **5.146** erative and mutually beneficial process—to understand the issue at stake in order to be able to address it. If employees are 'forced' to cooperate on the basis of their formal duties as set out in their employment agreement or otherwise, the output of any interviews is unlikely to be very productive. Although the rules of the process could be rather strict, the process itself should be positioned as a collaborative effort.

Representation

There is no specific rule of law requiring that employees should always be repre- **5.147** sented by separate counsel in an investigation. Not advising an employee to retain counsel in a situation where an employee could expose himself to civil or criminal liability by answering questions or by cooperating with an investigation, arguably could constitute a violation of the duty of the employer to conduct himself as a 'good employer'. Counsel to the company does not have a specific duty vis-à-vis employees of the company other than making clear that he or she is acting on behalf of the company.

In practice, companies do recommend that managing directors, and occasionally **5.148** ordinary employees, retain legal counsel. In the Dutch context a managing director will often also have an employment contract with the company on the basis of which he or she is also an employee whose rights and obligations are quite

---

[116] Section 7:660 DCC.

similar to those of ordinary employees. However, a managing director will be subject to a different dismissal and liability regime than ordinary employees.

Assurances as to confidentiality and privilege

5.149 It is essentially up to the company to determine what will happen with the statements of an employee made in the context of an internal investigation. However, the information obtained in the course of an investigation should be treated with due care and only be disclosed in case of a legal necessity, respecting the reasonable interests and privacy of the employee and in line with data protection laws. The employee should be informed that the information may be disclosed pursuant to the company's policy decision or applicable regulations.

Ethical implications for counsel

5.150 Generally there should not be ethical implications for counsel representing a company when dealing with employees during an internal investigation. This could be different if counsel were to act within the company as a person of trust (*vertrouwenspersoon*) or in individual cases if counsel were to have a close personal relationship with an employee under investigation. Depending on how close the relationship between counsel and the relevant employees is, it might be appropriate to have someone else (ie fully independent counsel) represent the company in the investigation.

Investigations and disciplinary process

5.151 Ideally, any (internal) investigation should be completely separate from a disciplinary process. The threat of disciplinary action may make employees reluctant to fully cooperate, to refresh their memories and to think about improved procedures going forward. It is, however, not possible to offer the employees a general 'amnesty' even before the investigation has been commenced. Regulators would generally expect that companies deal adequately with any individuals that were involved in misconduct.

5.152 If the allegations against an employee or director are sufficiently serious or if there is a risk that the company may incur further damages because the employee or director may continue his or her actions, immediate suspension or dismissal may be appropriate.

5.153 Dutch labour law, in principle, requires an employer to act immediately if it becomes clear that there is urgent cause[117] for the dismissal of an employee.

---

[117] *Dringende redenen.*

Notice of summary dismissal has to be given immediately after the discovery of the urgent cause (eg after completion of the investigation). A delay of even a couple of days without justification can make the summary dismissal invalid because such delay could be interpreted as a lack of urgency on the part of the employer to terminate the employment. Dismissal might then still be feasible but interference of the court or the labour office would in that case be required for a valid dismissal.

The employee can be suspended during the investigation if the company has **5.154** severe reasons to do so. The outcome of the investigation needs to be discussed with the relevant employee as soon as possible after it has become known.

A suspension or instant dismissal without sufficient justification can lead to a **5.155** serious increase of the severance payment to be awarded to the employee in dismissal proceedings.

A company can choose not to dismiss an employee with immediate effect, how- **5.156** ever this may not always be to the company's benefit. When high-profile individuals are involved, whose actions may have caused considerable damage to the company, delay of the dismissal may not be advisable or in the interest of the company. In the case of a managing director, the decision not to dismiss or not to pursue claims for damages and to honour any previously agreed severance package, may be subject to scrutiny by the Enterprise Chamber of the Amsterdam Court of Appeals following a petition to commence an inquiry proceeding by shareholders of the company or trade unions.

There is no specific whistle-blower protection law in place in the Netherlands in **5.157** the private sector. Employees are thus faced with a dilemma. On the one hand an employee has the duty of confidentiality vis-à-vis his employer, whereas, on the other hand, there may be a public interest for the employee to speak up about irregularities within the company.[118] In Dutch case law the following factors appear to be relevant when determining whether the employee may seek publicity or withdraw cooperation:

- can the employee assume in good faith that there is indeed an irregularity of which publication is justified in the public interest;
- has the employee followed internal procedures;
- has the employee tried to solve the matter internally;
- how did the company respond; and
- did the employee take precautions to limit damage to the company?

---

[118] Section 7 Dutch Constitution and Art 10 European Convention on Human Rights.

5.158 Depending on the answers to these questions an employee may or may not be granted protection against actions by his or her employer in response to disclosure of irregularities.

Challenges posed by ex-employees

5.159 Dutch law does not provide for any specific tools to force ex-employees to cooperate with an investigation apart from any obligations which may still be in force after the termination of the contract (eg confidentiality as regards any financial or business related data of the company, trade secrets etc). Save in industries that are the frequent subject of investigations, it is not common to impose a duty on employees to cooperate to investigations during the employment or after the termination thereof.

5.160 The basic principles of litigation would apply to the situation where a company would want to force an ex-employee to cooperate with an investigation (eg the employer could, under certain circumstances, force the ex-employee to give a statement in court).[119]

Payment of legal fees/indemnification/fee advances

5.161 The concept of a 'joint defence agreement' is not familiar in the Dutch context. In practice, parties involved in litigation (eg employer and employee(s)) whose interests run parallel often coordinate their defences without making formal arrangements.

5.162 Fee disbursements or fee advance arrangements for the costs of litigation in which (former) managing or supervisory directors are involved as a result of serving on the Management Board or Supervisory Board of the company are fairly common in the Netherlands. Any monies received can be subject to reimbursement obligations depending on what has been agreed between the company/insurer and the recipient. For instance, the arrangement may entail that if it is found that the acts are not covered by the D&O insurance policies, any disbursements received must be returned.

5.163 D&O insurance has become standard practice over the last 15 years. In practical terms, D&O insurance seems to offer relatively strong protection as it would cover a pretty high degree of negligence.

5.164 No special rules apply to the indemnification of employees against costs of defending against regulatory enforcement action or any other litigation costs—including fees of (separate) legal counsel. The company may do so if such is

---

[119] Section 186 Code of Civil Procedure.

deemed to be in the best interest of the company. Reimbursement of costs and expenses may be made conditional on compliance with the pre-agreed litigation strategy. Indemnification and/or reimbursement of costs and expenses would often not—or no longer—be deemed appropriate if there is clear evidence of the relevant employee's personal involvement in misconduct.

Best practices

Companies operating in highly regulated sectors or having a business that is likely **5.165** to be subject to investigations, may have an interest in establishing rules and procedures applicable to such investigations and, possibly, sanctions for failing to cooperate with such investigations. Depending on the contents of such policies the implementation may be subject to prior works council consent.

In an investigation employees should be treated fairly and with due respect and **5.166** care, subject to the employment and data protection laws and applicable corporate policies. This could mean that the employer is responsible for advising the employee to retain separate legal counsel in case the employee could incriminate himself by providing information in the investigation.

Employees should be treated as innocent until proven guilty. In the case of personal **5.167** misconduct of an employee, the employee should be confronted with allegations and be given the opportunity to tell his side of the story and to defend himself. In any event, the employer should carry out a thorough investigation before the employer takes any definitive steps. The employee can be suspended during the investigation, if the employer has severe reasons to do so, either in the interest of the investigation and the related wider corporate interest, or in the event that the preliminary outcome of the investigation would indicate that the relevant employee might be subject to severe sanctions. In the event of a suspension, the outcome of the investigation would need to be discussed with the relevant employee as soon as possible after the outcome is known.

L. Concluding an Investigation

There are various factors that may drive the completion of the internal investiga- **5.168** tion. Often, senior management has set a deadline, taking into account the potential need for (urgent) remedial measures, disclosure obligations, reporting dates or questions from the regulator. In substance, the internal investigation should continue until the company can be confident that 'the bottom of the problem' has been reached, possible management, risk and control failures have been identified and remedial measures can—at least on a preliminary basis—be identified.

5.169 A report setting out the results of the investigation would normally be prepared and submitted to senior management. In the report that summarizes the outcome of the investigation, it may be appropriate to emphasize that the company will fully cooperate with the regulator, has stopped or will stop the misconduct and has a sincere interest in preventing the reoccurrence of the relevant problem. Ideally, a clear proposal must be made for remedial measures and the implementation of new systems or rules to ensure future compliance. If individual persons were engaged in the misconduct, the sanctions taken against them should be highlighted.

5.170 The focus of the report should be on the facts. They should be clearly and comprehensively stated. Contradictions within the report or between various versions, unnecessary comments, legal analysis and self-accusation should be avoided. There may be situations where a proper decision with respect to the scope and format of the report could best be made after a first round of fact-finding.

5.171 In all likelihood the regulator will appreciate the company's efforts in investigating the problem and, thus, facilitating the regulator's job. However, the fact that a voluntary internal investigation was conducted will not necessarily lead to the total absence of a sanction. Nevertheless, a thorough internal investigation is likely to improve the relationship with the regulator and will be to the benefit of the company.

5.172 Whether or not the results of an internal investigation should be communicated to the public at large would depend on the company's overall PR strategy employed in connection with the relevant issue or situation. If the market is aware that an internal investigation has been initiated and if during the course of the investigation the underlying problem has been the subject of news coverage, the company should probably inform the public of the outcome of the investigation. Any public statement should be as general as possible and avoid any details of negative findings. If there were findings indicating a breach of law, the focus should be on the company's commitment to cooperate with the authorities and to remedy any problems from the past and the interim measures taken by management to stop the problem and to prevent similar problems occurring in the future.

5.173 Privilege will be waived if the company voluntarily provides the regulator with the report itself and/or privileged documents as part of a report. Consequently, before submitting the report, the company should consider whether or not to refer to the content of the privileged documents in the report or to even provide the privileged documents to the regulator.

M. Litigation Risks

Risks of criminal litigation commenced by regulators

Under Dutch law, most of the 'serious' corporate violations fall into the category **5.174** of criminal offences. Regulatory authorities in the Netherlands do not have the power to conduct criminal investigations. Instead, whenever a regulatory authority learns of facts which indicate that it is reasonably likely that a criminal offence may have been committed, it is required to hand over the respective information to the OM.

Corporates can be criminally liable under Dutch law according to section 51 of **5.175** the Dutch Penal Code. As corporates perform their actions through individuals, a two-element test was traditionally applied in order to establish whether acts of individuals could be attributed to corporates: (i) could the company control the action; and (ii) did it actively or passively accept such actions or generally tend to accept similar types of action. More recent case law has shifted towards a more general criterion that revolves around the question whether the relevant action can 'reasonably' be attributed to the company.[120] Relevant circumstances to determine whether actions may 'reasonably be attributed' include the nature of the action, whether the action took place in the normal course of business of the company, and whether the company actually benefited from the action.

Both the corporation and the persons that ordered the infringing actions[121] or **5.176** were de facto supervising the execution of such actions[122] may be prosecuted. This includes passive behaviour, in case the person concerned, although authorized and reasonably obliged to do so, failed to take action and consciously accepted the risk that criminal offences would occur.[123] The OM may decide to prosecute only the corporate alone, the persons that ordered or supervised the performance of the illegal actions, or both.

Many criminal offences require intent[124] on the part of the perpetrator, or treat **5.177** intent as an aggravating factor (the element of intent is usually what distinguishes crimes from misdemeanours). The prosecution would thus need to demonstrate intent. If members of the Management Board were involved or failed to take action, evidence of 'intent' can likely be construed. If involvement of members of the Management Board cannot be established, intent may still be determined in

---

[120] Dutch Supreme Court, 13 November 2001, NJ 2002, 219.
[121] *Opdrachtgever.*
[122] *Feitelijk leidinggevende.*
[123] Dutch Supreme Court, 16 December 1986, NJ 1987, 321 and 322.
[124] *Opzet.*

case the intentions of an individual can be attributed to the corporate. Whether such intent can be construed, will often depend on the internal organization of the company and the position of the relevant individual within the organization.

Risks of civil litigation commenced by regulators

5.178 Regulators in the Netherlands do not have civil enforcement powers, such as the powers that are available to certain regulators in the US. In general, the use by regulators of civil litigation to ensure compliance is considered ineffective and inappropriate as this would amount to circumvention of the due process safeguards in relation to their enforcement powers. However, the OM may in certain cases seek the disgorgement of criminal gains on top of any criminal sanctions.[125]

Risks of private civil litigation

5.179 Plaintiffs can bring civil actions based on the published results of regulatory investigations conducted by the AFM, DNB or NMa.

5.180 As outlined above, Dutch administrative law enables interested parties to request regulatory authorities to commence an investigation and impose a fine. There is some uncertainty as to the legal implications of an administrative fine for civil liability. An order or fine imposed by a regulator is not the same as a court order. Any order or fine imposed by a regulator is subject to judicial review. If an administrative order or fine is not appealed, it will become final.[126]

5.181 It seems probable that a decision by an administrative court on the question whether a fine was correctly imposed will be followed by the civil court in which private litigants litigate their claims. This may, however, be different for the order of a regulator by which a fine was imposed and which has only become final as a result of the expiry of the appeal period. By deciding not to appeal an administrative order or fine, the relevant defendant cannot automatically be deemed to have accepted the relevant fact pattern as the basis for civil liability vis-à-vis a third party.

5.182 The legal implications of a criminal conviction for civil litigation are determined by section 161 of the Dutch Code of Civil Procedure. It stipulates that in any subsequent civil litigation the court is bound by the final criminal conviction; save for proof to the contrary the conviction would constitute evidence in the civil case.

---

[125] Section 36a and further of the Dutch Penal Code.
[126] This is called the principle of '*formele rechtskracht*' (formal judicial force).

Claims may be based on tort, as any person who fails to comply with the law may **5.183**
be liable on the basis of tort.[127] Any claim on the basis of tort would presuppose
that the specific action constituting the breach of law has at the same time prejudiced the interests of the relevant plaintiff (the so-called 'relevance requirement'[128]). For instance, if the law or regulation that was breached was not aimed
at protecting the plaintiff, there would be no liability on the basis of tort.

Considering that a large number of the provisions of the Wft are aimed at pro- **5.184**
tecting the interests of investors, the requirement that the relevant law or regulation must protect the interests of the plaintiff will often be met in case of an
infringement of the Wft.

Failure to comply with the law may also affect the validity of legal acts, such as a **5.185**
contract between a financial institution and a client. In the event that a contract
is found to be invalid because the seller of a financial product did not comply with
the requirements of the Wft, a plaintiff may request that all transactions performed under the contract be unwound.

The *ABP/Poot* case[129] severely limits the possibility of derivative law suits in the **5.186**
Netherlands. Essentially, the *ABP/Poot* ruling prevents shareholders from claiming damages on the basis that the value of their shares was depreciated as a result
of mismanagement. The prevailing doctrine in the Netherlands is still that damages suffered by a company as a result of mismanagement should be claimed and
recovered by the company itself (or its bankruptcy trustees). Distribution of any
litigation proceeds should be the result of a corporate decision, not the result of a
decision to litigate taken by individual shareholders.

Shareholders may, however, independently seek to recover damages if a managing **5.187**
director has personally acted wrongfully vis-à-vis shareholders. Any such action
would presuppose that the norm that was breached by the managing director was
aimed at protecting shareholders against depreciation of their shares, for instance
in case a managing director provided false information about the company or
created an incorrect market perception. This was the position that was argued in
the *Royal Philips* case[130] and the *Baan Company* case.

---

127 Under s 6:162 of the Dutch Civil Code (DCC) an act may constitute tort when it is in breach
of a statute. Other actions may also qualify as tort—for instance where an act is committed by disregarding a duty of care (*zorgvuldigheidsnorm*).

128 *Relativiteitsvereiste.*

129 Dutch Supreme Court, 2 December 1994, NJ 1995, 288.

130 VEB/Philips, Dutch Supreme Court, 7 November 1997, JOR 1998/9. The case was eventually settled out of court and the investors received compensation. The rule that can be taken away
from the case is that if investors claim that the information provided was incorrect at the time it was
provided by the company, the company is obliged to provide evidence that proves otherwise. In
addition the case indeed seems to confirm that if incorrect information is provided by management,

5.188 Currently, Dutch law has no legal concept similar to the US class action. In practice it is possible to achieve some similar effects with the help of section 3:305a of the DCC. This allows public interest organizations, including special purpose trusts formed to represent the interests of a particular group of plaintiffs, to file a collective suit. However, in such collective suits no monetary damages can be claimed only so-called 'declarations for justice',[131] for instance a ruling by the court that the company acted wrongfully by making misleading statements to the market. A collective claim for monetary compensation for damages resulting from any such misleading statements could, in principle, not be included in any such section 305a action.[132]

Relevance of investigation report

5.189 A regulatory decision establishing a breach of law may be used in the course of a civil action. If such a decision is not challenged—or, if challenged, confirmed in appeal proceedings—it will become final and binding. In such a case, the regulatory findings will be vested with a presumption of validity that could only be revised under extraordinary circumstances. This does not necessarily imply that a civil court is legally bound to accept the regulatory findings as binding evidence of the facts, though the evidential value of a decision from a specialized regulator based on an extensive investigation will in practice often be significant.

N. Settlement with Regulators

Process

5.190 There is no established practice or process in the Netherlands for entering into settlements with regulators. The leniency programme as run by the NMa provides an example of a policy whereby the regulator agrees not to impose sanctions in return for information. The applicant will have to admit its involvement in the infringement and may not contest the facts. The applicant will also be faced with an infringement decision, and to that extent the term 'settlement' is perhaps less appropriate.

---

this can qualify as a wrongful act of the company itself resulting in liability of the company pursuant to s 6:162 DCC.

131 *Verklaringen voor recht.*

132 In practice various constructions have been used to enable large groups of plaintiffs to claim damages, including the assignment of claims by individual plaintiffs to a foundation that subsequently files suit on their behalf. However, from a technical legal point of view each claim remains a separate claim and action, thus requiring that with respect to each of the claimants the basis of liability of the defendants vis-à-vis the plaintiff is established, as well as the presence of a causal chain between the acts that caused the damages, the damages and the appropriate amount of compensation. In practice, this can be rather complicated.

A new instrument under competition law (both EU and Dutch competition law) is the decision to give binding effect to commitments of companies subject to investigation, where these companies commit to stop infringing behaviour or take other measures, allowing the Commission or the NMa to end the infringement procedure.

The OM has wide discretion in deciding which matters to prosecute and which **5.191** not to. Entering into a settlement falls within this discretionary power. The OM has developed policy guidelines for the settlement of criminal charges. A settlement[133] is only possible for criminal offences that carry a maximum prison sentence of six years or less.

The OM's decision to prosecute a company depends on several factors, including: **5.192**

- the nature of the crime;
- the circumstances under which the crime was committed;
- the consequences of the crime, including its impact on the public at large;
- the personal circumstances of the suspect; and
- the ability of the OM to obtain the required evidence to secure a conviction.

Under the current guidelines, high profile cases that have drawn significant pub- **5.193** lic attention and resulted in broad public indignation are not likely to be settled. This does not mean that high profile cases cannot and in practice are not settled. However, if the OM intended to settle a high profile case it would need to find pretty persuasive arguments to justify its decision. In addition, with respect to these matters there is a formal approval trajectory within the OM, involving approval by the *college van procureurs generaal* (a national steering committee of senior prosecutors) and the Attorney General.[134] A similar approval procedure applies to settlements involving a settlement amount in excess of €50,000.

In practice the OM has been willing to settle various high profile cases, such as **5.194** cases involving price-fixing in the building industry and fraudulent invoicing in large infrastructural projects, stating as reasons for doing so: the complexity of the case and the difficulty of putting together the evidence required for a conviction.

In regulatory matters, there is no court involvement in a settlement. Essentially, **5.195** settlement means that the case is not prosecuted. A settlement involving no admission of guilt seems to give the best possible protection in subsequent civil litigation, as a settlement has no formal status under the Dutch Code of Civil Procedure unlike a criminal conviction.

---

133 *Transactie.*
134 *Minister van Justitie.*

Impact if under investigation by multiple regulators

5.196 A settlement agreement with one regulator does in principle not affect the authority granted to other administrative authorities. However, a settlement with the OM would preclude the possibility to impose administrative fines for the same infringement.

Plea bargaining and amnesty arrangements

5.197 Plea bargaining is not allowed as a matter of strict policy of the OM. The NMa's leniency programme, however, provides a clear example of a regulatory amnesty arrangement.

O. Conclusion

5.198 Regulatory enforcement in the Netherlands has increased dramatically over the past years, as is evidenced by numerous high-profile investigations by the AFM and the NMa and by the increasing number of independent regulatory bodies and agencies. Compliance is likely to remain of key importance for companies operating in the Netherlands, who not only face regulatory and criminal law exposure but also—in particular in the field of competition law—private enforcement via civil damage claims. A proactive response to irregularities and proper structuring of voluntary investigations will therefore be key in protecting the integrity, sustainability and value of corporates and businesses in the Netherlands.

6

INVESTIGATIONS IN GERMANY

A. Introduction[1]

6.01 Recent internal and regulatory investigations into German companies illustrate three main developments.

6.02 First, the establishment of the Federal Financial Supervisory Authority[2] (BaFin) as Germany's integrated financial supervisory authority in May 2002 as well as the most recent legislation in the area of securities law, in particular the Act on the Improvement of Investor Protection,[3] have led to stricter regulation and closer supervision of listed corporations in Germany in the field of securities trading.

6.03 Secondly, an increasing number of German companies have faced corruption allegations following more stringent German and European laws on corporate conduct and anti-bribery laws in the late 1990s.

6.04 Thirdly, the ongoing extension of leniency programmes in the area of competition law has improved the incentives for members of a cartel to disclose their misconduct to the authorities and to fully cooperate with them.

6.05 At the core of the new legislation in the area of securities law was a revision of the Securities Trading Act (WpHG)[4] and its provisions governing insider trading,[5]

---

[1] Contributors: Hanna Blanz, Anke Meier, Julia Strese, Carolin Weide, Martina de Lind van Wijngaarden and Alfried Heidbrink.

[2] *Bundesanstalt für Finanzdienstleistungsaufsicht.*

[3] *Anlegerschutzverbesserungsgesetz.*

[4] *Wertpapierhandelsgesetz.*

[5] WpHG, s 14.

ad hoc disclosure of material facts which may have a substantial impact on stock price,[6] notifying all transactions in securities and derivatives conducted by any member of the executive board or supervisory board (directors' dealings),[7] and market manipulation.[8] While most violations of these provisions qualify as 'administrative offences',[9] some severe violations are classified as criminal acts which are prosecuted by the prosecutor's office.[10]

In 2006,[11] BaFin commenced 51 new investigations into suspected insider trad- **6.06** ing and filed complaints with the prosecutor's office in 24 cases against 106 implicated persons. At the end of 2006, 106 investigations, including investigations that had been commenced in prior years, were pending.[12] BaFin also initiated 30 new cases of suspected violations of the ad hoc disclosure obligation,[13] and commenced 11 new investigations into directors' dealings, while it concluded 79 pending investigations.[14] Further, BaFin launched investigations into 53 suspected cases of possible market manipulation and filed complaints with the prosecutor's office in 15 cases against 38 implicated persons. At the year end, 103 investigations relating to market manipulation were still pending.[15]

In 1999, the Organization for Economic Co-operation and Development Anti- **6.07** Bribery Convention came into effect in Germany. It criminalizes bribery of overseas public officials. Until that point, the German government allowed tax deductions for bribery of officials overseas. In 2002, the prohibition of bribery was extended to include bribes to foreign private companies. Since then, a batch of corruption scandals has created widespread media attention in Germany. The most prominent cases of allegations of bribery involved Siemens, Volkswagen and Daimler Chrysler. In each case, independent internal investigations were undertaken.

Generally, the risk of bribery being discovered has increased since 1999 **6.08** when company auditors were given a statutory obligation to report suspected criminal acts to the public prosecutor. Further, the anti-money laundering departments of banks have to report suspicious transactions. These reports are automatically forwarded to the financial intelligence unit of the local public prosecutor.

---

6 WpHG, s 15.
7 WpHG, s 15a.
8 WpHG, s 20a.
9 *Ordnungswidrigkeiten*, WpHG, s 39.
10 WpHG, s 38.
11 As of April 2008, the most recent Annual Report of *BaFin* available was the 2006 Annual Report <http://www.bafin.de>.
12 Annual Report of BaFin (2006), 163.
13 Annual Report of BaFin (2006), 177.
14 Annual Report of BaFin (2006), 177.
15 Annual Report of BaFin (2006), 170.

The accusations against Siemens, for example, were triggered by the suspicious transaction report of a Swiss bank.

6.09 As a result of the changes in the laws on corporate conduct, an increasing number of German listed corporations have recently established the position of a chief compliance officer (CCO).[16] The CCO is charged with uncovering and preventing weaknesses in the compliance system. The CCO also typically leads internal investigations into suspected cases of regulatory or criminal offences and engages the authorities whenever necessary.

6.10 In the area of competition law, the German Federal Cartel Office (*Bundeskartellamt*) as well as the EC Commission[17] have extended their leniency programmes in recent years. The *Bundeskartellamt* issued a revised leniency programme on the immunity from and reduction of fines in cartel cases[18] on 7 March 2006.[19] Contrary to the prior leniency programme of 2000, it automatically grants complete immunity to the participant in a cartel which is the first to provide the *Bundeskartellamt* with relevant information, provided it cooperates fully and certain other requirements are met. Even once the *Bundeskartellamt* is in a position to obtain a search warrant, complete immunity may still be achieved. The second and third participants in a cartel which fully cooperate may still achieve a reduction of the fine by up to 50 per cent. Finally, a participant in a cartel can now contact the *Bundeskartellamt* and declare its willingness to cooperate to save its place in the queue until it files an application for leniency and submits the relevant information.

6.11 In order to benefit from the leniency programme, the cartel participants have to collect and present the relevant information to the *Bundeskartellamt*. This has considerably increased the practical relevance of internal investigations in this field.

B. Regulators

Key regulators

6.12 In Germany, there is no single regulator with comprehensive authority over listed corporations. Different authorities have jurisdiction for the supervision of the

---

[16] A recent example is Deutsche Bahn which hired the chief state prosecutor of Frankfurt to become the CCO of the company (see 'Bahn holt Korruptionsexperten', *Financial Times Deutschland* (30 May 2007), 1).

[17] European Commission Leniency Programme of 1996 OJ C207, 18 July 1996, 4; European Commission Leniency Programme of 2002 OJ C45, 19 February 2002, 3; European Commission Leniency Programme of 2006 OJ C298, 8 December 2006, 17.

[18] *Bonusregelung.*

[19] Available at <http://www.bundeskartellamt.de/wDeutsch/download/pdf/Merkblaetter/Merkblaetter_deutsch/06_Bonusregelung.pdf>.

various activities of listed corporations and their employees. Administrative agencies supervise the listed corporations' compliance with the applicable regulatory regime and pursue so-called administrative offences.[20] Whereas criminal offences committed by directors, officers, and employees of listed corporations are exclusively prosecuted by the public prosecutor's office.

BaFin

BaFin is the key regulator in the fields of securities trading, banking, and the **6.13** insurance industry. It was established on 1 May 2002 through a merger of the former federal supervisory authorities for securities trading,[21] banking,[22] and the insurance industry.[23] In addition to these three main pillars of supervision, BaFin's organizational structure includes three cross-sectoral departments[24] and an anti-money laundering/anti-terrorism funding group.

BaFin also ensures listed companies' compliance with the rules of the WpHG, **6.14** the Securities Acquisition and Takeover Act (WpÜG),[25] and the Securities Prospectus Act (WpPG).[26]

In addition to handling cases of insider trading, director's dealing, ad hoc publi- **6.15** cations and market manipulation already described above, BaFin's responsibilities under the WpHG include the supervision of listed companies' compliance with their obligations with regard to notifications of changes in respect of shareholding or voting rights,[27] and the rules of conduct and organizational duties of investment services providers.[28]

As mentioned above, violations of the WpHG constitute at the least an adminis- **6.16** trative offence and can be sanctioned with an administrative fine of up to €1m.[29] However, the fines reported in the 2006 annual report of BaFin were considerably lower.[30] Severe cases of insider trading and market manipulation may also constitute criminal offences and are punishable by up to five years of imprisonment.[31]

---

[20] *Ordnungswidrigkeiten.*
[21] *Bundesaufsichtsamt für den Wertpapierhandel.*
[22] *Bundesaufsichtsamt für das Kreditwesen.*
[23] *Bundesaufsichtsamt für das Versicherungswesen.*
[24] Financial Markets and International; Consumer and Investor Protection, Certification of Private Pension Plan Contracts, and Legal Unit; Integrity of the Financial System.
[25] *Wertpapiererwerbs- und Übernahmegesetz.*
[26] *Wertpapierprospektgesetz.*
[27] See WpHG, s 21 sub.
[28] See WpHG, s 31 sub.
[29] WpHG, s 39.
[30] Annual Report of BaFin (2006): €80,000 for failure to report inside information (p 177), €5,000 for director's dealing (p 177); €3,750 for attempted market manipulation (p 171); €20,000 for failure to report change of voting right (p 179).
[31] WpHG, s 38.

BaFin may not prosecute criminal offences itself, but has to hand them over to the state prosecutor's office.

6.17 BaFin is responsible for an enforcement procedure, introduced in July 2005, which subjects the reports of listed companies to an additional external examination. If reporting errors are identified a correction thereof has to be published.[32] This might also trigger an ad hoc disclosure obligation.

6.18 Under the German Banking Act (KWG)[33] BaFin is responsible for monitoring and enforcing solvency requirements; granting and, where applicable, revoking banking licences; examining proposed acquisitions of banks; and ongoing supervision, in particular with respect to risk coverage and liquidity. BaFin's sources of information are special audits, annual audit reports as well as notifications from banking institutions themselves. Its possible reactions range from serious findings and administrative fines to the dismissal of the bank's management. In 2006, 113 special audits resulted in more than 85 serious findings and 17 actions against the management.[34]

6.19 In the insurance sector, BaFin is also responsible for monitoring and enforcing solvency requirements; granting and, where applicable, revoking insurance licences; examining proposed acquisitions of insurance companies, and ongoing supervision. It regularly conducts routine investigations of insurers. Due to Germany's federal system, BaFin shares responsibilities in the area of insurance supervision with the federal states' supervisory authorities.

Bundeskartellamt

6.20 The *Bundeskartellamt* is the most significant subject matter specific regulator that conducts corporate investigations in Germany. Some of the *Bundeskartellamt's* key functions include preventing agreements or concerted conduct by competing enterprises aimed at restraining competition by measures such as non-compete arrangements or price-fixing; preventing abuses of market-dominant positions; monitoring M&A transactions in cases where the offeror and the target have combined worldwide annual sales of €500m or more; and prohibiting such transactions where they are likely to create or strengthen a market-dominant position.

6.21 The *Bundeskartellamt* also applies European competition law in cases where the European Commission, as the competition authority at European level, is not competent under the Merger Control Regulation or, as far as Articles 81 and 82

---

[32] WpHG, s 37q(2).
[33] *Kreditwesengesetz.*
[34] Annual Report of BaFin (2006), 129.

of the EC Treaty are concerned, under Regulation 1/2003 and the case allocation criteria that have been developed.

In 2005 and 2006, the *Bundeskartellamt* conducted ten searches in 79 companies **6.22** and six private premises. It uncovered a number of cartel agreements and conducted several administrative fine proceedings. In 2005, the total amount of fines imposed on the respective companies was approximately €163.9m. In 2006 the *Bundeskartellamt* imposed fines of approximately €4.5m. At the same time, the number of the applications for the leniency programme increased. The *Bundeskartellamt* received a total of 76 applications concerning 19 different proceedings in 2005 and 2006.[35]

Bundesbank

In addition to BaFin, the German Central Bank (*Bundesbank*) is involved in ongo- **6.23** ing banking supervision. BaFin and the *Bundesbank* have set out their roles in day-to-day supervision in a Memorandum of Understanding (the Memorandum)[36]. Under the Memorandum, the *Bundesbank* is assigned most of the operational tasks in banking supervision. In particular, the *Bundesbank*'s responsibilities include the evaluation of documents, reports, annual accounts, and auditors' reports submitted to it by the banks.[37] Moreover, the *Bundesbank* and BaFin may both initiate informal regulatory meetings with banks.[38] In practice, the *Bundesbank* holds these individual meetings after assessing the relevant bank's annual accounts, and it invites BaFin to participate. BaFin, on the other hand, is given control over all sovereign measures, including the conduct of regulatory investigations.[39]

Stock exchange supervision

While listed companies' compliance with securities law is monitored by BaFin, **6.24** compliance with applicable statutory provisions as well as listing rules promulgated by the stock exchanges themselves is supervised by the stock exchanges and the federal states' stock exchange supervisory authorities.

Under the German Stock Exchange Act (BörsG),[40] the stock exchanges are under **6.25** a statutory obligation to establish and maintain a market surveillance department (HStÜ)[41]. The HStÜ's mandate includes the monitoring of exchange

---

[35] 2005 and 2006 activity report of the *Bundeskartellamt* (short version), 43 <http://www.bundeskartellamt.de/wEnglisch/download/pdf/07_Kurz_TB_e.pdf>.
[36] An English language version of the Memorandum is available at <http://www.bafin.de/sonstiges/mou_021031_en.htm>.
[37] See Art 3 of the Memorandum.
[38] See Art 4 of the Memorandum.
[39] See Art 5 sub of the Memorandum.
[40] *Börsengesetz.*
[41] *Handelsüberwachungsstelle.* See BörsG, s 4 (1).

trading and clearing;[42] and in particular, price quotations, conduct of trading, and compliance with the rules and regulations set up by the stock exchange. Decisions on admittance to and exclusion from trading are made by the board of the relevant stock exchange.[43]

6.26 The stock exchanges themselves are supervised by the exchange supervisory authorities of the federal states. Supervision of Germany's most important stock exchange, the Frankfurt Stock Exchange, is carried out by the Ministry for Economic Affairs, Transport and Regional Development of the State of Hesse. The exchange supervisory authorities may give instructions to the market surveillance departments and take over investigations that have been initiated by the latter in relation to compliance with the listing rules.

BAFA

6.27 The Federal Office of Economics and Export Control (BAFA)[44] is the central licensing authority responsible for the administrative implementation of the federal government's export control policy. Together with the monitoring and investigating authorities, especially the different customs offices, it supervises a complex export control system. Another task of BAFA is the administrative implementation of the embargo resolutions adopted by international organizations, such as arms embargos imposed by the United Nations or the European Union (EU).

6.28 Infringements of the export control and embargo provisions constitute criminal offences or in less severe cases administrative offences pursuant to sections 33 and 34 respectively of the Foreign Trade and Payments Act (AWG).[45] Internal investigations have become the response of choice to allegations of misconduct in this area. For example, when the Volcker report alleged in autumn 2005 that 263 German companies allegedly violated the Iraq embargo, the most prominent German company affected immediately launched an internal investigation and submitted its investigation report to the public prosecutor before the prosecutor had even commenced proceedings against the suspected company.[46]

Other federal agencies

6.29 There are numerous other federal regulatory agencies in Germany covering areas such as the development of the German energy, telecommunications and railroad

---

[42] See BörsG, s 4 (1).

[43] *'Zulassungsstelle'*, see BörsG, s 31 (admittance) and BörsG, s 43 (exclusion).

[44] *Bundesamt für Wirtschaft und Ausfuhrkontrolle.*

[45] *Außenwirtschaftsgesetz.*

[46] 'Justiz weitet Irak-Ermittlungen aus' (28 February 2008) <http://www.tagesspiegel.de/wirtschaft/; art271,1945774>.

infrastructure markets, food and drug safety, aviation safety, railroad safety, environmental protection etc. These regulatory agencies are separate authorities each of which is supervised by one of the federal ministries.

Self-regulatory organizations

The independent exchange bodies (HStÜ) set up by the various stock exchanges **6.30** in Germany to supervise the markets are semi-self-regulatory organizations which may conduct investigations. The respective HStÜ monitors exchange trading and exchange settlements and conducts the necessary investigations in the event of an infringement. The HStÜ, however, is not truly self-regulatory, as the exchange supervisory authority (in case of the Frankfurt stock exchange the Ministry of Economic Affairs of Hesse) can give instructions to the HStÜ and take over the investigations.

Another self-regulatory body which might conduct investigations into the finan- **6.31** cial statements of a listed corporation is the Financial Reporting Enforcement Panel (DPR).[47] The DPR is a private association; its members include the Federation of German Industries, various associations of the German banking and insurance industries, the German Confederation of Trade Unions, the association of German certified public accountants, and various associations of private investors.

The DPR was established in 2004 in reaction to various financial reporting scan- **6.32** dals in Germany and abroad. It is authorized to conduct supplementary audits of companies' annual statements if specific facts warrant the conclusion that the statutory provisions on accounting may have been violated[48] or if such supplementary audits are requested by BaFin.[49] The DPR may also conduct random supplementary audits.[50] However, it has no coercive authority over companies, and instead has to rely on their voluntary cooperation. If a company refuses to cooperate with the DPR, the DPR is required to report such refusal to BaFin;[51] the latter may then conduct its own supplementary audit.[52] Likewise, BaFin may conduct its own supplementary audit if it has substantial doubts as to the accuracy of a supplementary audit conducted by the DPR.[53]

---

[47] *Deutsche Prüfstelle für Rechnungslegung.*
[48] See the German Commercial Code (*Handelsgesetzbuch*—HGB), s 342b (2) sentence 3 No 1.
[49] See HGB, s 342b(2) sentence 3 No 2.
[50] See HGB, s 342b(2) sentence 3 No 3.
[51] See HGB, s 342b(6).
[52] See WpHG, s 37o and s 37p.
[53] See WpHG, s 37p(1).

The prosecutor's office

6.33 German regulatory agencies do not have the authority to prosecute criminal offences, they may only impose fines for administrative offences. Instead, exclusive jurisdiction for criminal prosecutions lies with the prosecutor's office. Further, legal entities, such as listed corporations, cannot commit crimes. Only individuals, such as directors, officers, or employees of a listed corporation can be prosecuted for them. However, if a director, officer or any other person responsible for the management of a company has committed a criminal offence by which duties of the company have been violated or the company was enriched or was intended to be enriched, this behaviour is attributable to the company as an administrative offence and the company may be fined.[54] This administrative offence is also prosecuted by the prosecutor's office. In general, the amount of the fine is limited to €1m.[55] However, if the economic benefit of the company exceeds this limit, the fine may be higher.[56] In the administrative offence proceedings relating to the corruption allegations against Siemens, the competent court imposed a fine of €201m on Siemens.[57]

6.34 The prosecutor's offices are authorities of the respective federal states. Regulatory authorities, such as BaFin, are required to inform the relevant prosecutor's office if and when they find that a certain breach of law amounts to a criminal offence.[58] For example, section 38 of WpHG enumerates acts and omissions by directors, officers or employees of a listed company in the context of securities trading which qualify to be criminal offences. The regulatory authorities have to provide their factual findings to the prosecutor's office who is then exclusively in charge of the matter.

6.35 The concept of grand juries does not exist under German law. Instead, whenever the prosecutor's office concludes that there are sufficient grounds to suspect that a person has committed a criminal offence, the prosecutor's office itself will hand down the indictment to the court.

Concurrent investigations

6.36 As regulatory jurisdiction under German law relates to the subject matter at issue, there is virtually no overlap between the jurisdictions of various regulatory bodies.

---

[54] See German Regulatory Offences Act (*Gesetz über Ordnungswidrigkeiten*—OWiG), s 30(1).
[55] See OWiG, s 30(2) No 1.
[56] See OWiG, s 17(4).
[57] Frankfurter Allgemeine Zeitung; (6 October 2007) 18.
[58] See WpHG, s 4(5); OWiG, s 41(1).

Although concurrent investigations by different regulators are not excluded **6.37** under German law, they rarely occur in practice and there seems to be no published case in which different regulators investigated a company in respect of the same subject matter at the same time.

Concurrent investigations by regulatory authorities from various states[59] are **6.38** virtually impossible because state regulators by definition do not have jurisdiction in cases with multi-state implications. Also, concurrent investigations by a federal and a state regulator cannot usually occur because the jurisdiction of the federal versus the state regulator is more or less clearly defined by the applicable statutory law.

It is, however, not unusual that the investigation of a regulatory agency, such as **6.39** BaFin, reveals criminal conduct in which case the agency is required to file a criminal complaint with the state prosecutor which then takes over the investigation. For example, in 2006 BaFin submitted 24 cases of suspected insider trading[60] and 15 cases of suspected market manipulation[61] to the prosecutor's office. One of the few published cases in which BaFin continued to be involved in the investigation after it had filed a criminal complaint with the state prosecutor is the recent case of Air Berlin. In June 2007, BaFin concluded its investigation into suspected insider trading at Air Berlin in the context of its takeover of DBA and handed the case over to the state prosecutor. This led to the search of 10 business premises and private residences by approximately 50 police officers who were accompanied by BaFin officials.[62] While the state prosecutor was exclusively in charge of the suspected insider trading, BaFin continued to investigate whether Air Berlin violated ad hoc disclosure obligations in the same context.[63]

Relationship with overseas regulators

If a regulator such as BaFin decides to investigate breaches of law by a non- **6.40** German party, statutory provisions usually allow the regulator to cooperate with its foreign counterparts. BaFin, for example, may request regulators in another member state of the EU to conduct an investigation or to submit information to BaFin and vice versa.[64] In addition, BaFin has concluded a range of bilateral Memoranda of Understanding with the supervisory authorities of non-EU member states which govern the exchange of information and cross-border

---

[59] *Länder.*
[60] Annual report of BaFin (2006) 163.
[61] Annual report of BaFin (2006) 170.
[62] See <http://www.ftd.de/unternehmen/handel_dienstleister/:Razzia%20Air%20Berlin/2148 90.html> (23 June 2007).
[63] <http://www.airlines.de/airlines/nachrichten/article/seite.php?articleid=12285> (24 June 2007).
[64] See WpHG, s 7(2) through (4) (in the area of securities supervision).

cooperation in suspected cases of insider trading, market manipulation or other violations of national law.[65]

6.41 In the case of criminal investigations, the international cooperation is governed by international treaties.

C. Powers of Regulators

Sources of investigations

6.42 In general, regulatory authorities, such as BaFin, will conduct corporate investigations when, based on facts that have come to their attention, there is reason to suspect that an applicable law has been violated. This may be the case if 'suspicious' facts are reported by a third party such as the media or if a private party files a complaint with the regulator, or if the company itself provides information (including in routine filings) which warrants a further investigation.

6.43 The main sources of information for regulators are the reports and filings submitted by the companies themselves. By way of example, financial services institutions which deal in securities are under a far-reaching statutory obligation to report to BaFin their transactions in securities or derivatives no later than the next working day after conclusion of the transaction.[66] Moreover, they are under a statutory obligation to immediately notify BaFin if they become aware of facts that give rise to the suspicion that the statutory provisions on the prohibition of insider dealing and market manipulation may have been violated.[67]

6.44 At present, except for the field of anti-trust violations, whistle-blowing is not a major source of information for regulators. However, in the wake of the whistle-blowing provisions in the Sarbanes-Oxley Act 2002, the topic has been under discussion within the legal community.[68] As a consequence, there have been various proposals that are aimed at providing a safe and structured environment

---

[65] The respective countries/supervisory authorities are (i) in the area of banking supervision: US (FDIC), Dubai, Brazil, Russia, US (OTS), Australia, Canada, Malta, China, Hong Kong (HKMA), Poland, South Africa, US (Fed Board/OCC), Romania, Czech Republic, Estonia, Slovakia, US (NYSBD), Argentina, Lithuania, Slovenia, South Korea, Jersey, Latvia, Hungary, Hong Kong (SFC), Portugal, Finland, Norway, Austria, Sweden, (ii) in the area of insurance supervision: South Korea, Dubai, Australia, Malta, Canada, Romania, Lithuania, Estonia, Czech Republic, Hungary, China, Latvia and Slovakia; (iii) in the area of securities trading: Dubai, Slovakia, Canada (Quebec), Cyprus, Jersey, Russia, South Africa, Austria, Singapore, Turkey, Brazil, Poland, Argentina, Australia, China, Hong Kong, Portugal, Czech Republic, Hungary, Italy, Spain, Taiwan, US (SEC), US (CFTC) and France (see Annual Report of BaFin (2006) 62).

[66] See WpHG, s 9.

[67] See WpHG, s 10.

[68] See Reiter, in Recht der Internationalen Wirtschaft (RIW) (2005) 168 sub; and Berndt/Hoppler, in Betriebs-Berater (BB) (2005) 2623 sub.

for whistle-blowing as a measure of 'good corporate governance'[69] which, if implemented, may potentially yield a valuable source of information on corporate wrongdoing. Further, in the context of the most recent corruption scandals, the introduction of new leniency provisions into the German Penal Code has been discussed.[70] The German Federal Government introduced a draft bill amending the German Penal Code in August 2007.[71] The draft proposes a mitigation or abrogation of a sentence if the offender considerably contributes to the clarification of facts. The mitigation is restricted to a catalogue of certain offences in the case of which the clarification of facts is typically difficult, especially in the areas of white-collar crimes, terrorism and organized crime. In order to avoid abuse, the proposed leniency rule shall only be applied if the offender announces his cooperation before the beginning of the main stage of the criminal proceedings against him. Whistle-blowing has, however, gained increasing importance with the competition authorities. As outlined above, the *Bundeskartellamt* published its revised leniency programme in 2006 according to which cartel participants can obtain complete immunity under certain circumstances or a reduction of fines if they provide relevant information to and fully cooperate with the *Bundeskartellamt*.

6.45 Civil lawsuits are, as a practical matter, not particularly relevant as a source for investigations by regulatory authorities. This is mainly because there is essentially no discovery in German civil procedure; therefore, civil litigation in Germany will not usually uncover information that is not already in the possession of the competent regulator.

Levels of regulatory scrutiny

6.46 Regulators often have informal contact with regulated companies. In particular, the *Bundesbank* and BaFin frequently hold informal regulatory meetings with banks. Furthermore, BaFin, in its capacity as securities regulator, will usually be prepared to discuss certain regulatory matters on an informal basis with a company or its counsel. This also applies to the *Bundeskartellamt* and other regulators. In the course of such a dialogue, a regulator may express the view that particular conduct may constitute a regulatory violation and may request further information from the company at issue. It is essentially a question of semantics whether or not to label such a process an 'informal investigation'. In German

---

[69] See Berndt/Hoppler, in BB (2005) 2623 at 2627 sub.

[70] 'Bund will Korruption international bekämpfen', <http://www.faz.net/s/Rub594835 B672714A1DB1A121534F010EE1/Doc-EC2AF8752DD57410A8FFE71490CBC25F7-ATpl-Ecommon-Scontent.html> (12 June 2007).

[71] See *Gesetzentwurf der Bundesregierung, Entwurf eines Gesetzes zur Änderung des Strafgesetzbuches-Strafzumessung bei Aufklärung- und Präventionshilfe, Drucksache 16/6268 vom 24.8.2007.*

practice, the term 'investigation' in a regulatory context is more likely to be understood as something 'formal', such as official proceedings (with a file and a docket number) conducted subject to, and in accordance with applicable law.

6.47 Even once a formal investigation has commenced, a uniform level of scrutiny may still not be applied, since regulators have a discretion as to what measures to take in order to establish the relevant facts. For example, rather than immediately demanding that the company produce certain documents, the regulator may start by requesting a more 'casual' meeting with the appropriate individuals.

6.48 Enforcement by regulatory authorities includes two main aspects. First, enforcement may be aimed at ensuring future compliance with the applicable regulatory regime. Secondly, enforcement may be effected by levying sanctions for past wrongdoing. German law places the first aspect genuinely and exclusively within the remit of the regulators themselves. By contrast, responsibility for the second aspect is shared by regulators and general law enforcement authorities insofar as criminal investigations and indictments can only be conducted and handed down by the prosecutor's offices. Any enforcement action is preceded by an investigation, although the investigation may of course be rather short if the facts are patently clear.

Investigation tools

6.49 The mechanisms available to regulators under German law for conducting regulatory investigations vary. Most statutes include a general provision according to which the regulator may take such measures that it deems to be 'suitable and necessary'[72] to prevent or remedy infringements of applicable law.[73] Typically, the relevant statutes also set out specific measures which the regulator may take.[74] By way of example, in the areas of securities and banking supervision, BaFin has extensive powers to demand information and documents from regulated corporations and banks, their management and supervisory boards, employees, subordinate and controlled entities, and stockholders.[75] A person may only refuse to provide such information if he or she would otherwise expose himself or herself or his or her spouse, fiancé/e, or certain close relatives to prosecution for a criminal or

---

[72] '*Geeignet und erforderlich*'.

[73] See, eg, WpHG, s 4(1) (in the area of securities supervision); KWG, s 6(3) (in the area of banking supervision); WpÜG, s 4(1) (in the area of takeover supervision).

[74] See WpHG, s 4(2), (3) and (4) (in the area of securities supervision); KWG, s 44(1) (in the area of banking supervision).

[75] See WpHG, s 4(3) (in the area of securities supervision); KWG s 44 sub (in the area of banking supervision).

administrative offence.[76] Moreover, BaFin has subpoena powers[77] and may enter business premises during and, in certain circumstances, outside normal working hours.[78] Most regulators, including BaFin, can only seize documents with a prior court warrant.[79] This rule can be modified in cases of 'imminent danger'.[80] Such 'imminent danger' may be assumed by the regulator if specific facts warrant the conclusion that obtaining a prior court warrant would jeopardize the seizure, for example because the relevant documents or items might be destroyed or disposed of by the target company's personnel.[81] Some regulators, such as the *Bundeskartellamt*, have the general power to proceed without a prior court warrant.

Extra-territorial jurisdiction

As a general rule, German law does not purport to give German regulatory **6.50** authorities jurisdiction over parties or conduct outside Germany. There are, however, some exceptions to this rule where a regulator's jurisdiction includes certain extra-territorial aspects. For example, in securities trading the provisions of the WpHG governing insider dealing, directors' dealings, ad hoc disclosure etc apply whenever the relevant securities are listed on a German stock exchange,[82] regardless of whether the issue or conduct in question is based or takes place in Germany or abroad. If this conduct takes place in a member state of the EU or a contracting state of the European Economic Area (EEA), BaFin will ask the competent regulatory authority of this state to conduct the investigations and to transmit the information that is suitable and necessary for BaFin to meet its statutory tasks.[83] BaFin may request the foreign regulatory authority to allow civil servants of BaFin to participate in the investigations of the foreign authority.[84] If the foreign regulatory authority does not respond to BaFin's request in due course or dismisses its request without sufficient reasons, BaFin may inform the Committee of European Securities Regulators.[85]

---

[76] See WpHG s 4 (9) (in the area of securities supervision); and KWG, s 44(6) (in the area of banking supervision). It is important to note, however, that the right to refuse to provide information is limited to oral information, whereas there is no such right if a regulatory authority requests documents (see 6.110).

[77] See WpHG, s 4(3); such subpoena powers of BaFin, however, are limited to the area of securities supervision.

[78] See WpHG, s 4(4) (in the area of securities supervision); KWG, s 44(1) and (2) (in the area of banking supervision).

[79] See OWiG, s 46(2) and German Code of Criminal Procedure (*Strafprozessordnung*—StPO), s 98(1).

[80] '*Gefahr im Verzug*'; see OWiG, s 46(2) and StPO, s 98(1).

[81] See E Göhler, *Ordnungswidrigkeitengesetz* (14th edn, 2006) Vor § 59 No 84.

[82] See WpHG, s 1(2).

[83] WpHG, s 7(4)1.

[84] WpHG, s 7(4)2.

[85] WpHG, s 7(4)6.

Protections

6.51 As a general rule, the discretion of regulatory authorities to demand information and documents or take other measures in the course of an investigation is limited by the principle of proportionality, which is rooted in German constitutional law and states that the government is not allowed to use disproportionate means to accomplish a given purpose.

6.52 In addition, the Federal Act on Administrative Proceedings (VwVfG),[86] which is generally applicable to investigations by federal agencies, provides for certain protections regarding the regulators' investigatory powers. While a witness is generally obliged to answer questions, he or she may refuse to testify at all if he or she has a close personal relationship to the person under investigation.[87] Further, the testimony may be refused concerning questions the answering of which (i) would cause the witness or a related person an immediate economic disadvantage, (ii) would disgrace the witness or a related person or would involve the jeopardy of the witness' prosecution for a crime or administrative offence, or (iii) would require the witness could not answer without disclosing an art or trade secret.[88]

Sanctions for failure to cooperate

6.53 German law imposes certain statutory obligations on companies to provide information to regulators. Outside the scope of these obligations, regulators as well as the public typically expect that companies adopt a proactive approach towards an investigation that goes beyond statutory requirements and helps regulators to conduct their investigations effectively and efficiently. Accordingly, companies targeted by a regulatory investigation usually publicly announce that they intend to fully cooperate with the regulator.

6.54 Regulatory authorities, on the other hand, may try to set an 'incentive' for cooperation by threatening to seize large amounts of documents if a company fails to provide the relevant documents voluntarily. In general, if a regulatory authority senses that the company under investigation is procrastinating in cooperating with the investigation, it will usually become even more determined to pursue its goal and will be less willing to conduct the investigation in a manner that minimizes disruptions to the company's operations.

6.55 If a corporation fails to cooperate with the investigation, the regulator, such as BaFin, may be authorized, under statutory law, to force cooperation by imposing

---

[86] *Verwaltungsverfahrensgesetz des Bundes.*
[87] See VwVfG, s 65(2) in conjunction with German Code of Civil Procedure (*Zivilprozessordnung*—ZPO), s 383.
[88] See VwVfG, s 65(2) in conjunction with ZPO, s 384.

a 'coercive payment'[89] of up to €250,000.[90] Moreover, failure to comply with a request by BaFin constitutes an administrative offence.[91] For such administrative offences, the authority may levy an administrative fine of up to €150,000.[92]

The coercive payment and the administrative fine are not mutually exclusive. **6.56** Therefore, BaFin may levy an administrative fine even if, upon imposition of a coercive payment, a company produces the documents requested by BaFin. However, as BaFin has discretion whether or not to levy an administrative fine under the general provisions on administrative offences,[93] it may agree not to levy such a fine if a company, upon imposition of a coercive payment, complies with BaFin's request.

As far as BaFin, in particular, is concerned, companies rarely fail to cooperate **6.57** with regulatory investigations in practice. This is because there is a general perception that a good working relationship with BaFin is of vital importance and that endangering this relationship is not usually a wise strategy.

D. Voluntary Investigations

Benefits and risks of voluntary investigations

Voluntary internal investigations are generally welcomed by regulators because **6.58** they demonstrate good faith on the part of the company and may be a valuable source of information. It is often difficult to draw a clear line between active cooperation in an investigation conducted by the regulator and an internal investigation by the company itself. Hence, regulators will perceive an internal investigation as the most advanced form of cooperation, assuming, that the company will share its findings with the regulator.

Although not specifically required under statutory law, dedicated internal audit **6.59** departments are also common in major German companies outside the banking industry. They usually play an active role in conducting internal investigations of possible regulatory violations.

Regulators will not allow internal investigations completely to replace their own **6.60** investigations. Nevertheless, regulators may use the findings of internal investigations

---

[89] *Zwangsgeld.*

[90] See the Act Establishing the Federal Financial Supervisory Authority (*Gesetz über die Bundesanstalt für Finanzdienstleistungsaufsicht*), s 17.

[91] See WpHG, s 39 (3) No 1 lit (a) (in the area of securities supervision) and KWG, s 56(3) No 9 (in the area of banking supervision).

[92] See WpHG, s 39(4) (in the area of securities supervision) and KWG, s 56(4) (in the area of banking supervision).

[93] See OWiG, s 47(1).

particularly as they are generally considered a valuable source of relevant data. In general, authorities will often admit that their investigative role would be much more difficult if the company did not actively participate in the investigation by compiling documents and putting together those materials that may be relevant to the official investigation. For example, in large, complex cases, the authorities will often lack the manpower and other resources necessary to conduct a thorough and comprehensive yet expeditious fact-finding process without help from the company. An internal investigation is therefore often considered beneficial by both the regulators and the company.

6.61 Moreover, companies sometimes conduct an internal investigation before any regulatory activity has been initiated; particularly in cases of suspected anti-trust violations. The company will then keep the internal report on file so that it can be handed over to the *Bundeskartellamt* if, and as soon as, the latter initiates an investigation. The intended result is that the *Bundeskartellamt* curtails the scope and intensity of its own investigation and lets itself be guided to some extent by the findings of the internal investigation.

Events triggering an internal investigation

6.62 In the banking industry, there are express legal requirements to conduct what might be referred to as ongoing internal investigations. The responsibilities of the internal auditing department include, inter alia:[94] conducting subsequent reviews of business transactions and procedures; reviewing the effectiveness of the bank's risk control systems; and ensuring compliance with relevant law. The internal auditing department must record any deficiencies that come to its attention and ensure that they are remedied; if the deficiencies are not remedied, the appropriate member of the bank's senior management must be informed. If the internal auditing department becomes aware of misconduct on the part of a member of the bank's top management, the entire board of management must be informed in writing. BaFin requires that the internal auditing department be independent from, and not bound by, instructions from the bank's management.

6.63 Outside the banking industry various events might cause corporations to consider conducting internal investigations. For example, German corporations are increasingly performing internal investigations to clarify suspected cases of corruption and bribery. In addition, internal investigations may be triggered by suspected violations of the anti-trust laws. However, the use of independent investigations is not limited to these situations. It might also be advisable in any

---

[94] For a discussion of the functions of, and requirements, with respect to internal auditing departments, see U Braun, in Boos, Fischer and Schulte-Mattler, *Kreditwesengesetz* (2nd edn, 2004) § 25 a Nos 129 sub.

case of suspected violation of the law which might result in a regulatory investigation depending on the potential sanctions and the reputational risks involved.

Structuring an internal investigation

If a company decides to conduct a voluntary investigation it does not have to observe any specific mandatory statutory provisions on internal investigations. However, as a matter of course, the company has to comply with all general provisions relevant for its business, for instance, provisions in the area of labour law governing the rights of its employees. Consequently, no internal investigation justifies a violation of any such provisions. **6.64**

As a general rule it is of utmost importance for each company to investigate the issues at stake as quickly but as comprehensively as possible. Therefore, the company's decision-makers must decide within a short period of time as to whether a voluntary investigation shall be conducted and define its purpose. **6.65**

The success of an internal investigation depends upon the effective structuring and management of the investigation process. First, it is necessary to clearly define the aim and issues of the investigation and determine who from the company's personnel shall become part of the team conducting this investigation. Almost every internal investigation will require the involvement of the legal department, and possibly external legal advisers, since there are inevitably a number of legal questions at stake as explained below. Once the team is established, it is necessary to allocate precise roles and functions within the team and determine a team leader who overviews the entire investigation and assumes overall responsibility for managing the team effectively. **6.66**

It is also critical at the start of an investigation to establish the channels of communication between the investigation team and the management. Depending on the sensitivity of the issues at stake, the company must consider whether or not it is preferable to have written reports which outline the provisional and final results of the investigation. It is important to bear in mind that, as described below, the company's internal documents in most cases will not be privileged even if an in-house counsel is involved in the investigation. **6.67**

Each internal investigation should be tailored according to the means that are available, suitable and effective in order to achieve the defined aim of the investigation. This includes considering factors such as whether it is necessary to review documents or examine other employees. In many cases, a large volume of documents will be relevant and material to the investigation. Consequently, it is necessary to implement a well-functioning document management system from the outset and to designate a team member as responsible for all questions concerning document management including dealing with sensitive or secret documents. **6.68**

This person must be experienced in handling multitude and complex data and documents.

6.69 During the course of the investigation, it is advisable to review regularly whether the aim of the investigation can actually be reached by the means available or if it has become necessary to utilize other means or redefine the aim and issues of the investigation. Regular reviews of the provisional results reduce the risks of being sidetracked or investing too much time on irrelevant points. Ideally, in order to avoid such problems, an investigation, if possible, should be structured in different phases which are executed one after the other. Upon completion of each phase it is possible to assess whether the aim of that particular part of the investigation was reached and draw any conclusions from the results for the next phase.

6.70 Once the investigation has been concluded, a prudent company considers whether its conclusions have implications for the company beyond the particular investigation itself. For instance, the team should ask if there are, in general, certain processes that could be optimized or if there are other tools that can be implemented to avoid misconduct or irregularities at a very early stage. The company should then consider implementing or improving a compliance system which aims to ensure that relevant statutory provisions are observed and misconduct of single individuals is avoided, or, at least, that possible irregularities are discovered at an early stage.

Using external advisers

6.71 In general, the role of outside counsel in internal investigations is not yet as important in Germany as it is in the US. In the past, most of the internal investigations, at least those which are now in the public domain, were carried out by in-house personnel.

6.72 There is, however, a recent trend of relying on outside counsel more heavily for internal investigations. The reason for this change may be found to some extent in a general tendency in German corporate and legal communities to adopt US-style methods and practices.

6.73 Further, German companies which are conducting business abroad and are listed in the US also have to comply with US law. If they are under scrutiny by the German authorities as well as the SEC or the DoJ, independent internal investigations will generally be launched because they are such standard practice in the US. It is much easier for companies to avail themselves of legal privilege if the investigation is done by outside counsel rather than in-house personnel (since some jurisdictions do not recognize the privileged position of internal counsel). A report by external counsel is increasingly seen as more credible by regulators, shareholders and the public. This is particularly the case if the company suspects that there are significant and particular sensitive irregularities, for example if the company's higher management is involved in the matter.

There are further reasons why it may be advantageous to engage the services of an **6.74** external lawyer. External lawyers will usually have a wider experience of conducting independent investigations, handling and reconciling the data and conducting the interviews that are necessary. Overall, in a wide-scale investigation comprehensive legal knowledge and experience in the areas of civil law, labour law and criminal law may be required in addition to the legal provisions governing the particular business sector of the company. During an investigation a person with comprehensive legal knowledge can ensure that such provisions are observed. This might be necessary, for example, to ensure that the rights of employees or other persons are not violated during the course of an internal investigation thus preventing any criminal offences being committed.

External advisers, such as lawyers and auditors, have the added advantage of hav- **6.75** ing confidentiality obligations. In contrast to the personnel of the company's legal department an external lawyer has the right to refuse testimony in court proceedings. Furthermore, external lawyers typically are experienced in determining as to how evidence that was obtained during the investigation can be used in subsequent proceedings before courts or any competent authorities. The involvement of external lawyers may also be helpful in cases which reveal that preliminary measures before the courts become necessary, such as garnishment of assets.

When considering the selection of counsel, it is important to note that in the **6.76** German marketplace, law firms to some extent compete with accounting firms. The likelihood that an accounting firm will be retained to conduct, or assist in, the investigation—or parts thereof—is particularly high if the subject matter of the investigation is very 'technical' (eg if it involves details of payments or accounting decisions such as revenue recognition). Under German law, accountants have broadly the same professional secrecy obligations with respect to client-related information as lawyers.[95] Consequently, the law on privilege, or more precisely confidentiality, is also very similar between the two professions.

There is no 'official' standard of independence for law or accounting firms to sat- **6.77** isfy in order to be retained to conduct an internal investigation. Statutory law does not establish any specific requirements in this respect either. Furthermore, regulators will not usually second guess the choice of counsel by the company. However, it is critical, obviously, that a law or accounting firm is retained which,

---

[95] See Act on Auditors' Professional Obligations (*Wirtschaftsprüferordnung*—WPO), s 43(1).

in the regulator's view, cannot have been involved, in any way, in the subject matter of the investigation. For example, if it turns out that a company's financial statements may have been manipulated, regulators—as well as the media and the general public—would not usually welcome the decision to have an internal investigation conducted by the same accounting firm that has audited the incriminated financial statements.

6.78 Often, a company may find that it is in its best interest if the internal investigation is conducted by a firm which has not previously had much involvement in the company's affairs. The obvious reason is that a firm with longstanding ties to the company's management may be, or at least may appear to be, less inclined to expose potential wrongdoing by top company officials. Given the fact that an internal investigation can be a tool for the company to maintain or re-establish credibility in the eyes of regulators as well as the 'court of public opinion', this consideration is usually not taken lightly.

6.79 Obviously, the general rules of professional conduct and, in particular, the rules on conflicts of interests[96] apply. Therefore, if the subject matter of an internal investigation at Company A is a suspected bribe paid by employees of Company A to employees of Company B, a law firm will obviously not be in a position to conduct the investigation for Company A if the same firm represented Company B in the transaction in which the bribe was allegedly paid. If the law firm has represented, or is representing, Company B in other unrelated matters, this will not preclude the law firm from acting for Company A in the investigation. The reason for this is that under German professional conduct rules the concept of a conflict of interest for law firms is rather narrow, as a conflict will only exist where a firm has represented two or more clients in relation to the same matter. Nevertheless, if only for reasons of appearance and reputation, Company A in the above example would be ill-advised to have the internal investigation conducted by a law firm with close ties to Company B.

6.80 While companies would usually argue that a firm's reputation, rather than its size, is the primary consideration in selection of counsel for an internal investigation, it is fair to say that large firms will have a practical competitive advantage over small firms if the subject matter of the internal investigation is particularly complex or voluminous. Moreover, it should be noted that the German market for internal investigations is still in a rather early state of development, and usually only the larger firms have the expertise and manpower to develop such new areas

---

[96] See Act on Attorneys' Professional Obligations (*Bundesrechtsanwaltsordnung*—BRAO), s 43a(4).

of practice. Finally, such exercises can involve numbers of people at short notice; only larger organizations have the ability to meet this need.

In a German corporation, retaining outside counsel for an internal investigation **6.81** is within the remit of the board of management (*Vorstand*).[97] The board of management will usually have delegated the general authority to retain outside counsel to the company's in-house legal department. In most cases, the legal department's staff, particularly the general counsel, will be entitled to make their own assessment and decide on whether or not to hire outside counsel, and such general delegation of authority would include the power to retain outside counsel for an internal investigation. Nevertheless it seems fairly safe to assume that the legal department would usually seek specific approval by the board of management for retaining outside counsel for an internal investigation.

In specific cases, outside counsel may be retained by the (non-executive) supervi- **6.82** sory board. In particular, the supervisory board may hire counsel in cases where potential wrongdoing by and/or claims against members of the board of management are at issue.[98]

Managing illegal activity during internal investigations

There may be a strong case for allowing potentially illegal conduct to continue, **6.83** pending the investigation if it would otherwise be impossible to collect sufficient evidence to punish the perpetrators. Legally speaking, however, an intention to collect evidence will not be a valid excuse for letting unlawful conduct continue. Therefore, if the conduct in question constitutes a criminal or administrative offence, it will usually not be advisable to allow the potentially illegal conduct to continue during the investigation.

E. Self-reporting Obligations

Duty to self-report

German law does not provide for a statutory duty to self-report either general **6.84** regulatory violations, or specific violations of corporate law, regulations or practices. Certain exceptions apply in the fields of securities trading and banking.

---

[97] See German Securities Act (*Aktiengesetz*—AktG), s 78(1), which sets out the general rule that the board of management (*Vorstand*) acts on behalf of stock corporations.

[98] See AktG, s 112, which stipulates that the supervisory board (*Aufsichtsrat*) acts on behalf of stock corporations vis-à-vis the members of the board of management. In context of claims against (members of) the board of management, it is generally acknowledged that the supervisory board may hire counsel, eg for representation in court, or fact-finding, see, eg, U Hüffer, *Aktiengesetz* (6th edn, 2005), s 112 No 3.

For example, financial services institutions have to report suspected instances of insider trading and market manipulation to BaFin pursuant to section 10 of WpHG. In addition, if a bank's internal audit results in severe findings against managers, the management then immediately has to inform the supervisory authorities.[99] Otherwise, German law imposes statutory duties to self-report (regulatory) violations only in particular areas of law, including various environmental regulations and the statutory provisions on product safety.[100]

Culture of self-reporting

6.85 Outside the scope of statutory disclosure obligations, there is no real culture of self-reporting in Germany in connection with corporate misconduct. The only areas in which self-reporting has gained a considerable practical relevance are anti-trust law and tax law. As set out above, both the European Commission in its capacity as anti-trust enforcement authority and the *Bundeskartellamt* have adopted leniency programmes in recent years which reward a member of an unlawful cartel for reporting the cartel and its members to the authorities. The reward may be a reduction of the fine or even full immunity. In the area of tax law, the tax authorities may refrain from imposing a fine or the public prosecutor can refrain from filing charges in the case of tax evasion if the suspect reports the relevant facts himself.

F. Announcements and Public Relations Strategies

Regulatory investigations

External communications

6.86 Under section 15 of WpHG, an issuer of financial instruments admitted to trading on a German stock exchange must disclose information about circumstances which have not been made public without delay, provided that (i) such circumstances have occurred, or are sufficiently probable to occur in the future; and (ii) are likely to have a significant effect on the exchange or market price of such financial instrument. This obligation is limited to inside information directly concerning the issuer. BaFin has published a set of *Issuer Guidelines* clarifying the provisions of the WpHG, in particular the provisions on inside information and ad hoc disclosure.[101] In accordance with the recommendations by the Committee

---

[99] Section BT 2.3.4(4) of BaFin circular 18/2005 on Minimum Requirements for Risk Management (MaRisk).

[100] See Devices and Safety Act (*Geräte- und Produktsicherheitsgesetz*—GPSG), s 5(2).

[101] BaFin Issuer Guideline dated 15 July 2005, an English translation can be found at <http://www.bafin.de/EN/Home/homepage__node.html?__nnn=true>.

of European Securities Regulators (CESR), the BaFin *Issuer Guidelines* enumerate the inside information that only indirectly concerns the issuer and thus does not trigger a disclosure obligation.[102] However, it also contains a catalogue of inside information invoking a disclosure obligation.[103]

According to the CESR recommendations, significant action taken by public authorities or other public institutions (for instance the information that the competent authority has initiated investigations regarding the issuer's shares, given alleged violations of the WpHG) does not establish an ad hoc disclosure obligation.[104] However, according to the BaFin *Issuer Guidelines*, the ad hoc disclosure provision applies to administrative and court proceedings which involve and directly relate to the issuer. The disclosure obligation is invoked as soon as such proceedings are deemed to have the potential to significantly affect prices. The point in time at which a disclosure obligation materializes is generally the moment from which it is sufficiently probable that such proceedings will have a significant effect on prices. However, the disclosure obligation may also materialize if the issuer takes measures (such as setting aside provisions), which, by their very nature, have a significant effect on prices—regardless of the result of the proceeding.[105]   **6.87**

However, in case of investigations relating to a defect in a product, the company may be under a contractual and statutory obligation to report the potential defect to its customers and alert them of potential risks to prevent damage.   **6.88**

In general, BaFin does not make public announcements when it initiates investigations into companies. However, if journalists call BaFin and ask whether a certain company is under investigation BaFin will answer this request and will also indicate the general subject matter of the investigation.   **6.89**

As the public, shareholders or customers thus might become aware of the investigation anyway, each company should have an emergency plan in place on how to deal with the media and requests for information in such a situation.   **6.90**

Internal communications

Under German law, there is no general duty to inform employees of regulatory or criminal investigations. However, the work council[106] of the company should   **6.91**

---

102 BaFin Issuer Guideline, 41.
103 BaFin Issuer Guideline, 43.
104 BaFin Issuer Guideline, 41.
105 BaFin Issuer Guideline, 50.
106 *Betriebsrat*. Under the applicable statutory provisions, a *Betriebsrat* may be established by the employees in any operation (*Betrieb*) in Germany with at least five employees, even if the company that maintains the relevant operation has its seat outside Germany. However, it is not the company's responsibility to set up a work council or to advise employees on the election procedure.

be informed. The time and scope of such communication should be determined according to the circumstances of each individual case.

6.92 Although there is no general duty to inform employees of regulatory or criminal investigations it might be nevertheless advisable to do so if they will hear of the investigation from other sources of information anyway. By communicating that an investigation is underway and explaining the strategy as to how to deal with the situation, the management can demonstrate leadership and prevent rumours and insecurity among the employees.

Voluntary investigations

External communications

6.93 In the era of modern mass communication it is likely that information communicated to employees (particularly in large organizations) will almost immediately reach the public domain. However, as far as disclosure to the public is concerned, certain companies will also have to bear in mind the applicable legal requirements. Listed companies (as well as companies that have issued other securities such as bonds) are under a statutory obligation to make ad hoc disclosures of material facts that are likely to have a substantial effect on the stock price (or the market price of the other securities).[107] While an internal investigation as such will not usually require ad hoc disclosure, the opposite may be true for the underlying events that have triggered the investigation. Whether this is the case will depend on the individual circumstances. If the company has to disclose these circumstances, it will usually make sense also to disclose the fact that an internal investigation has been launched at the same time.

Internal communications

6.94 German law does not provide rules regarding if and when employees should be notified of a voluntary internal investigation.

6.95 However, the work council (*Betriebsrat*) of the company should be informed of the internal investigation. Time and scope depend on the circumstances of the case. The purpose of the work council's right of being informed is that the work council shall be in a position to determine whether its participation rights

---

The *Betriebsrat*'s rights include 'cooperation rights', including rights to information, hearings/initiatives, consultation and vetoes as well as rights to consent to employers' decisions, and 'co-determination' rights, under which the *Betriebsrat* may participate in the decision-making process within the operation. If a *Betriebsrat* was established in the relevant operation, suspension of certain employees during an internal investigation would be likely to require the *Betriebsrat*'s consent as a consequence of the latter's 'cooperation rights'.

107 See WpHG, s 15.

are concerned.[108] If the investigation involves the review of written or electronic documents the work council has to ensure that the employee protection laws, such as data protection laws and the Telecommunication Act (TKG),[109] are observed. Whether in addition to the work council's right to being informed, the work council also has a right to have a say in specific measures to be taken in the course of the internal investigation depends on the scope of the measure.

If, for example, employees are interviewed using questionnaires, depending on **6.96** the content of questions, such questionnaires might be deemed to be personal questionnaires[110] within the meaning of section 94 of *BetrVG*, the use of which requires the consent of the work council. Further, if the investigation is into either email traffic which is not exclusively limited to business purposes or private documents, the consent of the work council is also required.[111] By contrast, if written documents and/or emails to be scrutinized are purely business related, then the consent of the work council is not required.

Finally, if the internal investigation exclusively relates to the wrongdoing of direc- **6.97** tors[112] and officers the work council's right to being informed is reduced, as the *BetrVG* does not protect such persons.

Otherwise, a company's decision on whether and when to inform its employees **6.98** about an upcoming or ongoing internal investigation will usually be driven by the objectives of the internal investigation.

If the primary objective is to provide information to a regulator or a prosecutor's **6.99** office, it may be wise to conduct the investigation with as much secrecy as possible, at least during the initial stages. If, by contrast, the investigation is predominantly aimed at maintaining or re-establishing the company's reputation as a 'good' corporate citizen, it would seem natural for the company to communicate the fact that the investigation is under way to the employees and to the general public at a much earlier stage. The same consideration applies to the extent that the investigation serves other publicity purposes, such as paving the way for a company's new management to pursue claims against the former management.

Even if the purpose of the internal investigation calls for more, rather than less **6.100** secrecy, the company may determine that it will be impossible to keep the investigation completely confidential. This may prompt the company to disclose the fact that an investigation is to be launched to some or all employees.

---

[108] Work Council Constitution Act (Betriebsverfassungsgesetz—BetrVG), s 80(2).
[109] *Telekommunikationsgesetz.*
[110] *Personalfragebögen.*
[111] BetrVG, s 87(1) No 1.
[112] *Leitende Angestellte.*

6.101 Preventing the creation of false information and rumours can be very challenging, particularly since it has become very easy to spread information by email or similar means. This difficulty may be another reason for a company to take a more proactive approach in informing its employees about the investigation.

G. Key Points for Public Relations Strategies

6.102 The BaFin *Issuer Guidelines* set out the requirements of the form and structure of ad hoc disclosures[113] as well as the forms and structures of preliminary notices which have to be submitted 30 minutes prior to the ad hoc disclosure to BaFin and to the management of the exchanges on which the financial instruments issued by the company are traded.[114] The *Issuer Guidelines* further describe the publication channels and the language requirements and explain under which circumstances an ad hoc publication is considered immediate.[115] In Germany, certain service providers specialize in the technical implementation of ad hoc disclosures, such as Deutsche Gesellschaft für Ad-hoc Publizität, euro adhoc and Hugin IR Services Deutschland GmbH.

6.103 Each company should have a designated emergency team and an emergency plan in place on how to deal with the media and requests for information in case of a crisis and/or investigation. The emergency team should consist of members of the top management of the company, and be available to be summoned on short notice. The email addresses, addresses, and telephone numbers of the team members should be kept up to date at all times (ie at weekends, during vacations, business trips etc). Only the person designated by the emergency team should engage in any internal or external communications. Ideally, this person alone should perform the entire communication to demonstrate that the company is focused and the responsibilities are clear.

6.104 If the company does not have a special PR department, obtaining professional PR support from outside consultants should be considered. Together with the company's counsel they can create a legally correct and media suitable concept of communication which can help to avoid negative publicity to the widest extent possible.

6.105 Further, no statement should be issued prior to a first analysis of the situation. Even if journalists notice the search of the company's premises and suddenly confront the management with questions, the management should not give in to

---

[113] BaFin Issuer Guideline, 56.
[114] BaFin Issuer Guideline, 61.
[115] BaFin Issuer Guideline, 64 sub.

this pressure. Rather, nothing spontaneous should be said and reference should be made to a press conference that is in the process of being set up. In addition, all other employees should be explicitly asked to refrain from public statements. In especially critical situations, having them sign written confidentiality agreements should be considered.

Any statement by the company's spokesperson should be brief and comprehensible and should contain only confirmed facts. The emergency plan should list the most dangerous mistakes of conduct such as (i) complete silence, (ii) giving of no comment answers, (iii) hesitation, (iv) defending oneself, (v) minimizing of the problem. **6.106**

H. Best Practices in Document Gathering and Preservation

Expectations of regulators and courts

Under German law, there is no general obligation for companies or individuals to preserve documents once a regulatory or internal investigation has begun or is likely to begin. There are, however, some provisions that give regulatory authorities the power to specifically demand that certain documents be preserved. For example, in securities supervision, BaFin may demand that a securities trading firm preserve its existing telecommunication records with respect to particular individuals if there is reason to suspect that the individuals have violated the provisions of the WpHG on insider trading or market manipulation.[116] **6.107**

Furthermore, some statutory provisions require companies to preserve certain types of documents for certain periods of time regardless of whether an investigation has commenced, or is likely to do so. For example, securities trading firms must keep records on buyers and sellers of securities and must preserve such records for six years.[117] Likewise, the statutory provisions on the prevention of money laundering require banks and insurers to verify their clients' identity, and to preserve their records of such verification for six years.[118] A failure to comply with these provisions constitutes an administrative offence.[119] **6.108**

Irrespective of any legal obligation under German law, adverse inferences may be drawn by regulators if documents are destroyed or missing. In addition, if parallel **6.109**

---

[116] See WpHG, s 16b.
[117] See WpHG, s 16.
[118] See the German Money Laundering Act (*Geldwäschegesetz*—GwG), s 9.
[119] See WpHG, s 39(2) No 10 (in the area of securities supervision); GwG, s 17(1) Nos 2 and 3 (in the area of money laundering).

investigations of German and foreign regulators are imminent, the best practice for the foreign regulators should be observed.

Rights over documents and confidentiality

6.110 In the areas of securities and banking supervision, BaFin has far-reaching powers to demand documents and emails from both companies and their employees.[120] Employees must comply with such requests even if, by doing so, they may expose themselves to a possible prosecution for a criminal or an administrative offence.[121] Failure to comply with a demand by BaFin constitutes a separate administrative offence.[122]

6.111 In anti-trust law enforcement, the *Bundeskartellamt* has the power to demand documents which may be relevant to its investigations. However, the relevant statute does not specifically authorize the *Bundeskartellamt* to demand such documents from employees, and instead, the *Bundeskartellamt* must make its request to the company (meaning, for practical purposes, its senior management).[123] It is then up to the senior management to obtain such documents from the company's employees.[124] It is unclear as to whether management can refuse to hand over incriminating documents.[125] However, if the *Bundeskartellamt* performs a search on the premises of the company in lieu of, or addition to, submitting a document request list, it may seize any document which might potentially serve as a means of evidence.

6.112 Similar rules apply to BaFin's ability to secure documents in the area of insurance supervision. Under the applicable statutes, the authority must make its demand to the insurance company's board of management which, if necessary, has to obtain the relevant documents from the company's employees.[126] Again, management must honour such a demand even if, by doing so, they expose themselves to a possible prosecution for a criminal or administrative offence.[127] Failure to comply with a demand by BaFin constitutes an administrative offence.[128]

---

[120] See WpHG, s 4(3) (in the area of securities supervision); KWG, s 44(1) (in the area of banking supervision).

[121] See U Braun, in Boos, Fischer and Schulte-Mattler, *Kreditwesengesetz* (2nd edn, 2004) § 44 No 64; S Kümpel and H-D Assmann, in Assmann and Schneider, *Wertpapierhandelsgesetz* (3rd edn, 2003) § 15 No 242.

[122] See WpHG, s 39(4) No 1 lit (a) (in the area of securities supervision); KWG, s 56(3) No 9 (in the area of banking supervision).

[123] See Act against Restraints of Competition (*Gesetz gegen Wettbewerbsbeschränkungen*—GWB), s 59(1).

[124] See GWB, s 59(2).

[125] For an overview of the discussion see S Klaue, in Immenga andMestmäcker, *Gesetz gegen Wettbewerbsbeschränkungen* (3rd edn, 2001) § 59 No 54.

[126] See German Insurance Supervision Act (*Versicherungsaufsichtsgesetz*—VAG), s 83(1) No 1.

[127] H Kollhosser, in Prölss, *Versicherungsaufsichtsgesetz* (12th edn, 2005), § 83 No 28.

[128] See VAG, s 144(1a) No 5.

However, BaFin has no power to seize the requested documents if they are **6.113** not handed over by the company.[129] The *Bundeskartellamt* however, may seize documents even without a warrant. It must obtain a subsequent confirmation from the court if the company or the individual from whom items have been seized objects to the seizure.[130]

If the offices of a company are searched for documents in the course of an investi- **6.114** gation no document should voluntarily be handed over to the authorities without being actually seized. This is because judicial review can only be obtained in the event of a seizure. If documents are voluntarily handed over judicial review is excluded.[131] Further, if documents are about to be seized, it should be ensured that a list of the seized documents is prepared. This list should be as detailed as possible. For example, the list should contain a description of the content of each individual binder.

If possible, photocopies of the seized documents should be made. If the scope of **6.115** the documents so allows, important documents should be photocopied prior to the seizure. If the documents to be seized are so voluminous that they cannot be photocopied easily, the company should offer to preliminarily store them in a separate room and to have it sealed by the authorities. The documents can then subsequently be photocopied under the supervision of the authorities. Especially, if the search cannot be completed within one day, the authorities might be open for such a solution. However, the searched company does not have a right to such a solution.

If the original documents are essential for the operation of the company, a **6.116** reasonable solution should be negotiated with the authorities. This may be necessary if, for example, the authorities threaten to seize a computer hard drive which exclusively contains the data on all suppliers and customers. In this case, at an absolute minimum, an early date for the return of the computer should be negotiated.

Alternatively, and especially if the investigation also focuses on the content of **6.117** emails and other electronic documents, the seizure of computer hard drives and the on-site search of the IT network can sometimes be prevented if the company and/or its counsel offer to do the search for the authorities. In such a case, the company and/or its counsel can ask the authorities to prepare a list of search terms.

---

129 See GWB, s 58(1).

130 See GWB, s 58(2) and (3).

131 If a seizure of documents was performed in a way that violated the principle of proportionality or was otherwise unlawful, the person affected thereby can seek judicial review of the process and might obtain a ruling prohibiting the regulatory authority from making use of the seized documents. If the documents are handed over voluntarily, the regulatory authority may always exploit them.

The company then searches the computer hard drives and servers for documents containing the relevant words and hands over to the authorities CDs and/or printouts of the found documents.

6.118 If the seizure of documents cannot be avoided, the investigators should be asked not to visibly carry boxes of documents outside, but to park their cars in the company's garage and load the cars there in order to avoid any unnecessary publicity. Again, there is no right to such a treatment.

6.119 In an internal investigation, the company has an unlimited right to demand documents and emails from its employees insofar as such documents and emails are work-related (especially if they are the employee's work product).[132]

6.120 In the case of personal documents and emails (particularly in the case of personal emails sent from or received on the employee's company email account), the situation is less clear. In general, the company is required to observe the employee's privacy rights.[133] This puts certain limitations on a company's power to demand personal (electronic) documents or emails from the employee. Despite its increasing practical relevance, there is relatively little case law on this point. With regard to electronic documents and emails, the courts have considered whether the company has permitted the respective employee to use his or her computer for private purposes.[134] In a case in which such private use had been expressly forbidden in the employment contract, a lower labour court held that any data stored on the employee's computer could not be deemed to be part of the employee's private sphere.[135] Consequently, the court assumed that the company could have unlimited access to the employee's computer.

6.121 There appears to be no authority on cases in which private use of computers had been permitted or at least, not expressly forbidden.[136] The prevailing opinion among legal scholars seems to be that access to data stored on the employee's computer is subject to the employee's consent, and that the company's request for such consent is subject to the weighing-of-interests test.

---

[132] See W Blomeyer, in Münchener, *Handbuch des Arbeitsrechts* (2nd edn, 2000) § 53 Nos 47 sub (Protection of the employer's property).

[133] See W Blomeyer, in Münchener, *Handbuch des Arbeitsrechts* (2nd edn, 2000) § 97 No 1 (Basic principles of personal rights).

[134] See R Wank, in Erfurter, *Kommentar zum Arbeitsrecht* (7th edn, 2007) BDSG, § 28 recitals 20 with further references.

[135] See Arbeitsgericht Frankfurt am Main (Local Labor Court), in MMR (2004) 829 at 830; Arbeitsgericht Frankfurt am Main (Local Labor Court), in Neue Zeitschrift für Arbeitsrecht ('NZA') (2002) 1093 at 1095 sub.

[136] See R Wank, in Erfurter, *Kommentar zum Arbeitsrecht* (7th edn, 2007) BDSG, § 28 recitals 20 with further references.

I. Data Protection

Authorities often request information containing data relating to an identified or **6.122** identifiable individual. Such data is protected under the German Data Protection Act (BDSG)[137] if it is either processed or used by means of electronic data processing systems[138] or collected for such purposes (personal data). As a general rule, the company that is the holder of personal data (eg of their employees, customers, business partners[139]) may transfer such data to third parties[140] only subject to the affected person's consent or if the BDSG or any other legal permission allows such transfer.[141] When assessing whether a data transfer requested by an authority is admissible, one must differentiate on the one hand between mandatory requests of an authority and the voluntary cooperation with authorities and on the other hand—within these categories—whether the requesting authority is located in Germany or another EU-member state or outside the EU:

Mandatory official inquiries

In case a German authority requests information containing personal data (infor- **6.123** mation) on the basis of a statutory authorization, the transmission of that information is permissible since it is based on a legal justification. However, the requesting authority has a duty to inform the recipient of the request and of the statutory provision on which it is based.[142] Where the authority fails to comply with such duty, it is advisable to first inquire as to the legal basis for the request. Furthermore, if, in the end, it turns out that there is no legal provision supporting the request, the information cannot be transmitted to the requesting authority.

In case the delivery of information is directly requested by authorities of EU **6.124** member states other than German authorities, the delivery is generally voluntary since non-German authorities of EU member states generally do not have any direct statutory powers in this respect. In such a case, if obtaining the consent of

---

[137] *Bundesdatenschutzgesetz.*

[138] BDSG, s 1(2) No 3. The applicability of the BDSG in the event of non-automated processing or use of data (eg with respect to data stored in paper form) depends on whether the data is processed or used in a 'filing system' or collected for that purpose. This is the case for any non-automated compilation of personal data that is structured uniformly and can be accessed and analysed by certain features. The legal concept of a 'filing system' is, however, not very clear and requires interpretation. Generally, as soon as data can more easily be accessed or analysed as a result of their logical and organizational context, they are included within the scope of protection of the BDSG and therefore fulfil the criteria of a 'filing system' (eg a compilation of questionnaires that have to be completed by employees in the context of an investigation).

[139] The BDSG only protects information relating to natural persons.

[140] 'Third parties' in the meaning of the BDSG are also entities of one group of companies since the BDSG does not know a 'group privilege', BDSG, s 4(4) No 3, s 3(8).

[141] BDSG, s 4(1).

[142] BDSG, s 13(1a).

the person concerned is not practical, as a rule a legal justification for the data transfer can be found only in the BDSG according to which the transfer of the information would, amongst other things, be permissible if such transfer is necessary to protect the rightful interests of the company and if there is no reason to assume that protected interests of the affected person precluding the transfer of its personal data outweigh the interests of the company.[143] Accordingly, the permissibility of the transmission of the information to the requesting authority depends on a balancing of interests. The outcome of that balancing of interests, however, depends on each individual case and its specific circumstances. However, where the authorities of EU member states operate on the basis of administrative assistance and consult the responsible German authorities which then officially submit the request to the respective company by an administrative act,[144] the transmission of the information to the German authority is permissible.

6.125 In cases where a non-EU member state authority requests information directly from the company there is generally no official process for such requests and they will not be considered mandatory under German data protection law. Accordingly compliance is voluntary. Something different would only apply, if the requesting non-EU member state authority were to ask a German authority for help on the basis of international cooperation agreements (eg between tax and customs authorities, or between government services responsible for public safety) and the responsible German authority then officially asks the company for the information by an administrative act. In that case the transmission of the information to the German authority is also permissible.

Voluntary cooperation with authorities in Germany and EU member states

6.126 If companies intend to voluntarily cooperate with authorities in Germany or another EU member state requesting information, the information may, as outlined above, be transferred only with either the concerned person's consent or if the balancing of the company's interest in cooperating and transmitting the information to the requesting authority with the interests of the affected persons comes to the result that the latter do not outweigh the company's legitimate cooperation interests.

---

[143] BDSG, s 28(1) No 2. Another legal justification that comes into consideration in such cases is BDSG, s 28(1) No 1, according to which the transfer of personal data is also permissible if doing so is conducive to achievement of the purpose of an agreement between the responsible party and the affected person (eg the employment contract).

[144] WpHG, s 7.

Such interest meriting protection is the informational right to self-determination[145] **6.127**
of each individual data subject, which has to be balanced against aspects such as
economic or professional disadvantages to be feared by the company as a
consequence of the non-cooperation with the requesting authority or the
company's legitimate interest to prove that the suspicious facts which have led to
the investigation are (partly) not correct. In addition, it must be considered
whether there is an alternative to the transmission of personal data.[146] One
approach, for example, could be to anonymize the personal data or to create
pseudonyms for it. The result of such balancing of interests, which must be carried out by the holder of the personal data (ie the company that is the subject of
the investigation or request), very much depends on the specific circumstances of
each individual case.[147] However, with respect to personal data of employees, it
can, as a general rule, be assumed that protecting employee interests can include
voluntary cooperation with authorities with the objective to dispel accusations
against the company justifying the transfer unless specific circumstances
(eg severe sanctions imposed on employee v marginal interest of company to
cooperate) indicate an overriding interest of the employee not to disclose the
data.

As regards the voluntary transmission of information to authorities for the **6.128**
purpose of supporting investigations that are not directed at the company
itself, but at third parties, the interest of the company to voluntarily cooperate
with the authority is considered not legitimate when balanced with the interests
of the concerned data subjects worthy of being protected. Also balancing
the interests of the authority with the interests of the data subjects according
to the aforementioned criteria[148] will usually not turn out in favour of the
authority and can, therefore, not justify the transmission of personal data to the
authority.

Special requirements in relation to authorities of non-EU member states

If and to the extent the information is requested by authorities of non-EU mem- **6.129**
ber states, the transfer is permitted only under certain conditions which are more
stringent than in the case of a transfer to authorities of EU member states.

---

[145] The informational right to self-determination is the right of each individual derived from the
general right to privacy (German Basic Law (*Grundgesetz*—GG), Art 1, 2) to principally control the
disclosure and use of one's personal data oneself.

[146] P Gola and R Schomerus, *Bundesdatenschutzgesetz* (9th edn, 2007) para 28 n 34.

[147] In cases of doubt it might be recommendable to ask the responsible German data protection
authority (ie the authority of the federal state in which the company is located) for a (preliminary)
evaluation of the specific question on an anonymized basis. In some cases this approach has proven
to be very helpful.

[148] BDSG, s 28 (3) No 1.

Background is that in such countries the data protection level is generally not considered to be adequate in comparison with the data protection standard in the EU. An adequate level of data protection has been determined by the EU Commission[149] only for a small number of non-EU member states.[150] Other than for the 'Safe-Harbor–Program',[151] the US is not among these nations. We are not aware of any US authorities having joined this programme.

6.130 As a general rule, the transfer of personal data to countries without an adequate level of data protection is only permissible if either:

    (i) the affected person has consented to the transfer of its personal data;

    (ii) the transfer is necessary for the performance of an agreement between the affected person and the responsible party; or

    (iii) the transfer is necessary for the protection of an important public interest or to assert, exercise or defend any legal rights or claims in court.[152]

6.131 If it is not feasible to obtain the affected person's consent, in practice, it is in most instances very difficult to affirm that the exemptions as described under (ii) or (iii) are given in case the requesting authority is not a court. The reasons are as follows.

6.132 The contracts with affected employees or customers normally do not fulfil the requirements under (ii). Also, a broad interpretation of the term 'court' as referred to in the second alternative of (iii) that would encompass 'government agencies' is implausible since such interpretation would be inconsistent with the character of the provision as an exception, which generally requires a narrow interpretation. Additionally, as regards the first alternative as described under (iii), the public interest of a non-EU member state, in and of itself, does not qualify as a public interest within this meaning. The relevant public interest is purely national in nature (ie it must be a public interest of the country from which the data is transferred).

---

[149] Pursuant to Art 25(6) of Council Directive (EC) 95/46 on data protection [1995] OJ L281/31, the Commission may bindingly determine within the framework of proceedings regulated according to Art 31(2) of Dir 95/46 that a 'third country' provides for an appropriate level of data protection.

[150] Argentina, Canada, Switzerland, Guernsey and the Isle of Man. Information may be transferred to the authorities of these countries, provided that the other requirements for transfer under the BDSG are satisfied, without any special review of whether the level of data protection is adequate.

[151] 'Safe-Harbor' is a data protection package negotiated by the Commission with the US Ministry of Trade obliging the recipient vis-à-vis the US authority in charge to comply with certain principles of data protection, see P Räther and N Seitz, 'Übermittlung personenbezogener Daten in Drittstaaten - Angemessenheitsklausel, Safe Harbor und die Einwilligung', MMR (2002) 425.

[152] See BDSG, s 4c(1) Nos 1–4 and BDSG, s 4c(1) Nos 5 and 6 for further exemptions.

Recently, the Article 29 Working Party expressly noted that a government agency   **6.133**
located in the EU and responsible for the protection of personal data may not
invoke the laws of foreign jurisdictions when reviewing the permissibility of data
transfers. Only if such foreign laws reflect a public interest that is recognized in
the European country of the party exporting data, may such laws be taken into
consideration for purposes of balancing the interests of the party exporting data
against the privacy rights of the affected person.[153] As an example of a public
interest, the official rationale for the European Data Protection Directive cites
the public interest in international cooperation (eg the fight against money laundering, the supervision of institutional institutions, or international cooperation
between tax and customs authorities, or between government services responsible for public safety).[154]

If one of the above-described requirements is not given, the transfer of the infor-   **6.134**
mation is only permissible if the authorities to which the information is to be
submitted can guarantee an adequate data protection level[155] and if the balancing
of interests of the company and the affected person comes to the result that the
latter does not predominate. Besides joining the 'Safe-Harbor-Program' another
possibility to guarantee an adequate data protection level is, in principle, the
conclusion of the so-called standard contractual clauses adopted by the EU
Commission[156] which provide for various obligations of the party exporting
personal data and the party importing personal data, to guarantee the protection
of personal data.

However, such standard contractual clauses have been developed for transfers   **6.135**
serving private purposes and not public purposes, which would mostly be given
in case of requests of authorities, so that in this case the agreement must be
submitted to the competent German regulatory agency for review and approval.
According to information from several State Data Protection Supervisory
Authorities no such agreement between a foreign government agency and a
private company has ever been reviewed or approved. Part of the reason may be

---

[153] See s 4.6.3.4. WP 128, Opinion 10/2006, on the processing of personal data by the Society
for Worldwide Interbank Financial Telecommunications (SWIFT), adopted on 22 November
2006, 01935/06/EN; see also WP 117, Opinion 1/2006 on the application of EU data protection
rules to internal whistle-blowing schemes in the fields of accounting, internal accounting controls,
auditing matters, fight against bribery, banking and financial crime, adopted on 1 February 2006
00195/06/EN.

[154] Against this background, a public interest would not exist in case the SEC asks a German
company for information in context with an investigation because of the violation of US insider
trading laws with regard to a company that is only listed in the US and not traded on the over-the-
counter market in Germany or another EU member state so that German or European insider trading laws are not concerned.

[155] BDSG, s 4b(2) and (3).

[156] Commission Decision C (2004) 5271 OJ L385/74.

that it is generally not the practice of foreign government agencies to submit to regulation by a regulatory agency of another country.[157]

6.136 In summary, it can be said that—if the exceptions as described above are not given—and the requesting authority cannot guarantee an adequate data protection level, the transmission of the information is in the final analysis not permissible.

Further restrictions arising out of the principle of telecommunication secrecy

6.137 Further restrictions to the investigation and transmission of information regardless of whether they contain personal data within the meaning of the BDSG may arise from the principle of telecommunication secrecy if the requested information (or a part of it) can be obtained by the company only by searching the business email accounts of employees. If the employees are allowed to use the companies telecommunication facilities including the employer's email system for private purposes the prevailing literature considers the employer to be a telecommunication service provider[158] that is obliged to preserve the telecommunication secrecy[159] which is also protected under constitutional law.

6.138 The principle of telecommunication secrecy protects the content of the telecommunication, in particular, whether someone has participated in the communication. In general, providers of telecommunication (ie employers in the above-mentioned case) are not allowed to obtain knowledge about the content of the telecommunication or its closer circumstance beyond what is necessary for the commercial provision of the telecommunication services including the protection of its technical systems. To use such knowledge for other purposes, particularly the disclosure to others is only permissible if the TKG or another legal provision allows such use and explicitly refers to telecommunication processes. Overall, the described problem is very complex and controversially discussed in literature. Case law which deals with this specific question in employment relationships does not exist as yet.

6.139 In summary, it can be said that, according to the current legal situation, from a strict point of view, companies are principally not allowed to search through employees' emails without the consent of the employee and the communication

---

157 International law, too, raises substantial concerns as to whether any German data protection agency would have jurisdiction to approve such a data protection agreement.

158 Telecommunication Act (*Telekommunikationsgesetz*—TKG), s 3 No 6a and 10. S Ernst, 'Der Arbeitgeber, die E-Mail und das Internet', NZA (2002) 585. E Weißnicht, 'Die Nutzung des Internet am Arbeitsplatz', MMR (2003) 448.

159 TKG, s 88(2) sentence 1.

partner concerned (which is normally the case) or the existence of a legal justification which fulfils the above-described requirements.[160] The violation of the telecommunication secrecy can even lead to a criminal offence under German criminal law[161] if the person who carried out the search transfers such email or information contained in it to 'another person'[162] (eg the requesting authority).

If, in contrast, the employees are not allowed to use the telecommunication services **6.140** provided by the company for private purposes, the employer does not qualify as a telecommunications provider. The employer thus may principally assume that access to and transfer of personal data (eg stored on the computer or in an email) is lawful.[163] However, the mere prohibition to allow such devices for private purposes is not sufficient in order not to qualify as a telecommunications provider. The employer must monitor and enforce the compliance with this prohibition; otherwise, the private use is considered to be tolerated and all restrictions as described above apply.

Violations of the provisions of the BDSG can be punished by administrative fines **6.141** of up to €250,000, alternatively imprisonment of up to two years or fines if committed with the intent to make a commercial profit or to infringe on a third person's rights.[164]

The violation of telecommunication secrecy can be punished by imprisonment **6.142** of up to five years or pecuniary penalty.[165]

Practical considerations

When setting up a policy relating to the private use of computers and email by **6.143** employees, each company should consider the effect this might have on the possibilities to search documents and emails in the course of an internal investigation without the employee's consent. If the company does not want to avail itself of this possibility it should consider implementing a policy which explicitly prohibits any private use of business computers and email and monitor the compliance of such prohibition.

---

[160] Such a justification would be, eg, StPO, s 100a according to which providers of telecommunication on basis of a warrant are obliged to enable the responsible judge, the prosecutor and its bodies the monitoring and recording of the telecommunication.

[161] German Criminal Code (*Strafgesetzbuch*—StGB), s 206(1).

[162] The term 'another person' does not necessarily mean a person outside the respective company. A transfer of information from, eg, the IT administrator to another person which is employed in the company will also be considered as a transfer to 'another person' in the meaning of StGB, s 206(1).

[163] Labour Court of Frankfurt/Main (*Arbeitsgericht Frankfurt am Main*), MMR (2004) 829.

[164] BDSG, ss 43, 44.

[165] StGB, s 206(1).

J. Dealing with Privileged Documents

General rules on privilege

6.144 The work product of attorneys, patent attorneys, tax advisers and auditors, as well as their communications with their clients, are protected under German law and cannot be seized according to the relevant provisions of the German Code of Criminal Procedure (StPO).[166] However, these restrictions on seizure only apply if the documents are in the possession of the attorney, tax adviser or auditor. In a criminal investigation, the prosecutors therefore have no authority to request work product and communication from attorneys, tax advisers and auditors. These professionals also cannot be made to testify (in court or outside court) against their clients,[167] except if the client waives the privilege.[168] The same rules apply in the regulatory context, either by virtue of a specific statutory reference to the appropriate procedural rules[169] or as an unwritten but universally observed limitation of the regulator's powers.

6.145 While German law provides broad protection of attorney work product and correspondence in the attorney's possession, such protection does not apply to the work product and correspondence in the client's possession (with the exception of work product of, and correspondence with, criminal defence attorneys in the possession of a suspect in a criminal investigation). This has the effect that attorney work product and communications in the possession of the client are not privileged and can generally be seized by the prosecutor.

6.146 The privilege position regarding attorney work product and communications in the possession of the client can be stronger, however, if the documents are in the sole custody of in-house lawyers. In-house lawyers generally enjoy the same privilege as outside attorneys, if and to the extent they are lawyers admitted to the bar and have performed typical tasks of an attorney in the relevant case.[170] Not every in-house lawyer in Germany is an 'attorney' in this sense. An in-house lawyer can be admitted to the bar only if he or she has some degree of autonomy in the corporate organization. As a result, junior in-house lawyers often do not qualify as 'attorneys', whereas the more senior members of the legal department (and, in particular, the general counsel) usually do. In the individual case, it can be very difficult to decide whether or not an in-house lawyer, who is admitted to the bar, has performed typical tasks of an attorney. Currently there are no clear rules available for this differentiation.[171]

---

[166] *Strafprozessordnung.* See StPO, s 97(1) Nos 1 and 2 and StPO, s 53(1) No 3.
[167] See StPO, s 53(1) No 3.
[168] See StPO, s 53(2).
[169] See WpHG, s 4(3) sentence 3 (in the area of securities supervision).
[170] See LG Berlin, NStZ (2006) 470 with further citations.
[171] See LG Berlin, NStZ (2006) 470 with further citations.

If the aforementioned requirements are fulfilled, in-house attorneys enjoy the **6.147** same privilege as outside attorneys as long as the work product and other documents at issue are within the sole custody of the legal department.[172] This means that documents will not be privileged if management has unhindered physical access to them.[173] By contrast, if the respective documents are kept in a separate file room etc to which only the legal staff has direct access, the custody requirement will be deemed to have been fulfilled, and the documents will be privileged.[174]

There is a widespread perception among companies that in-house privilege does **6.148** not work well in reality as, more often than not, searches and seizures by authorities include documents in the possession of the legal department. In this context, it is feared that once privileged documents are in the regulator's hands, the regulator will be unable to ignore such information, even if it is later established that the documents were privileged and should not have been seized. This is a driving force for the increase in use of outside counsel for internal investigations.

Attorney work product in the possession of a third party, which does not have the **6.149** right to refuse to testify, such as an external expert, will never be privileged under German law and can therefore be seized by the prosecutor.

With regard to privilege rules in Germany, it should be noted for the sake of **6.150** completeness that there is no concept of pre-trial discovery or disclosure under German law. There is no general obligation for a party to civil proceedings to disclose documents. However, a party must prove any fact it asserts and the other side contests. Therefore, the parties will generally produce evidence, including documents on which they rely in support of their case. Only in very exceptional circumstances will the parties have an obligation to produce documents in civil proceedings. Recent reforms to the German Code of Civil Procedure (*Zivilprozessordnung*—ZPO)[175] enable a court to order the parties or a third party to submit documents to which the parties have referred to in the proceedings.

If the court orders a party to the proceedings to produce documents, the party **6.151** can withhold documents the submission of which would violate its constitutional rights (eg diaries under certain circumstances as part of the inviolable private sphere or papers containing business secrets). A third party can withhold documents if it were to be unreasonably burdened by the production thereof or if he or she is entitled to refuse to testify according to sections 383 and 384 of ZPO. Under section 383 of ZPO, inter alia any person who, in the course of his office,

---

[172] See Roxin, in Neue Juristische Wochenschrift (NJW) (1995) 17 at 22.
[173] See Roxin, in NJW (1995) 17 at 22.
[174] See Roxin, in NJW (1995) 17 at 22.
[175] See ZPO, s 142.

profession or trade, receives information that is confidential by law or by its nature may decline to answer questions and produce documents in civil proceedings. People covered by this 'professional privilege' include inter alia board members, lawyers, auditors, doctors, journalists, translators, arbitrators and bankers.

6.152 Attorney-client privilege in Germany requires lawyers to keep confidential all information that has been obtained in the course of professional activities for a specific client, regardless of the nature of the information or the manner in which they obtained it. Lawyers are not even allowed to reveal that they are acting for a specific client. Therefore, all communications between a client and his or her legal representatives are privileged.

6.153 According to section 384 of ZPO, a person is also entitled to refuse to testify if answering the questions were to result in direct financial damage to, or criminal liability on himself or herself or his or her close relatives, or were to require the disclosure of business secrets. This provision should protect the witness or a third party against occupational or commercial damage due to the testimony. The term 'business secrets' is not defined in the various statutes, but has been established by the courts.[176] A 'business secret' is any fact in connection with a business that is not apparent but only known to a limited number of people and that should be kept secret according to the intention of the owner of the business.

Waiving privilege

6.154 Privilege can be waived if the company provides a third party (including a regulator) voluntarily with privileged documents. Privilege can also be explicitly waived if an attorney or any other person covered by 'professional privilege' is formally excused from the obligation of secrecy so that they are free to be a witness in civil proceedings or to provide a third party with documents, which are privileged. Explicitly waiving privilege only poses a limited risk to the company as it can control if and to what extent the privilege is waived.

6.155 Once a private civil litigant has lawfully gained access to privileged information or work product, the private civil litigant is free to use such information or work product in the litigation and is not bound by privilege. Therefore, it must be considered to what extent private civil litigants can obtain access to such information or work product. Obtaining such information directly from the company under investigation is very difficult for private litigants because, as described above, there is no concept of US style discovery in German civil procedure. In fact, the German law of civil procedure expressly disallows 'fishing expeditions'.[177]

---

[176] Eg German Federal Court (BGH), 7 November 2002, GRUR (2003) 356, 358.
[177] Zekoll/Bolt, in NJW (2002) 3129 at 3133.

Private litigants can only request access to documents to which the opponent referred to in the proceedings pursuant to section 142 of ZPO (see para 150 sub above) or to the authorities' (especially the prosecutor's) files (see para 6.158 below).

Under German law, private civil litigants have traditionally had very limited **6.156** access to information disclosed to, or seized by, regulators. However, this changed greatly after 1 January 2006, when Germany's newly adopted Federal Freedom of Information Act (FOIA) entered into force (see para 6.160 below).

Under general administrative law, access to official records must, subject to some **6.157** exceptions, be granted to parties whose legal interests are directly affected by the outcome of the administrative proceedings.[178] In most regulatory contexts, this is hard to demonstrate for third parties. For example, a plaintiff in a securities litigation case based on an incorrect disclosure of material facts will not usually be able to show that his or her legal interests depend on the outcome of BaFin's proceedings and whether BaFin imposes a fine on the issuer of securities.

In criminal cases, however, where the prosecutor's office conducts an investigation, **6.158** potential civil litigants can request access to the files if they pursue a legitimate interest that requires such access. Access will be denied if the interests of the affected person that should be protected outweigh those of the civil litigant, for example if the files contain business secrets. Access is granted at the discretion of the prosecutor's office.[179] Practical experience shows that the prosecutor's office will usually be willing to grant such access if it is sought in order to prepare a private civil action. In practice, however, the prosecutors will put their own interest in dealing with the matter quickly and efficiently and the defendant's interest in being able to mount an effective defence first.[180] They will usually therefore grant private claimants access to the files only when both the prosecutors themselves and the defence counsel have had sufficient time and opportunity to review the files.

Somewhat more 'liberal' rules apply in proceedings of the *Bundeskartellamt*. **6.159** Here, a competitor that has initiated the investigation (eg by tipping off the *Bundeskartellamt* as to potentially unlawful conduct) may be granted access to the files.[181] Business secrets of the company under investigation, however, are excluded from such access rights.[182] Nevertheless, obtaining access to the files of the *Bundeskartellamt* can be a powerful tool for preparing a private civil action

---

[178] See s 29.
[179] See StPO, s 475(1) and Nos 182 sub of the Guidelines on Criminal Proceedings and Administrative Proceedings (*Richtlinien für das Strafverfahren und das Bußgeldverfahren*—RiStBV).
[180] See StPO, s 475(1) and RiStBV No 184, according to which the prosecutor's office's and the regulatory authority's interest in conducting their investigations outweigh applicants' interest in being granted access to the files.
[181] See VwVfG, s 29 and GWB, s 72(3).
[182] See GWB, s 72(2).

for damages. A competitor that has not initiated the investigation does not have these statutory rights.

6.160 The FOIA brought about a considerable expansion of private parties' information rights over and above these rights under general administrative law, taking effect 1 January 2006. This new law grants anyone, whether or not his or her legal rights are directly affected by the outcome of a given administrative proceeding, access to official information in the possession of federal authorities (either by inspecting the files or by obtaining oral information).[183] Some exceptions apply, most notably with respect to information which, if it became known, 'may have detrimental effects on controlling or regulatory functions of the tax, competition and regulatory authorities'[184] and with respect to business secrets.[185] It remains to be seen how this new statute will be implemented in practice. Nevertheless, private parties will, in all likelihood, have greatly increased prospects of gathering relevant information to be used in the pursuit of their civil claims.

6.161 A company disclosing privileged documents to a regulator could mark the documents as 'containing business secrets' and agree with the regulator not to disclose them to any other (private) party. However, such an 'agreement' is not binding upon the regulator and a regulator could still decide that the documents can be disclosed to a third party. In practice, a regulator will not elect to disclose documents marked as 'containing business secrets' to a third party before having discussed this issue with the company concerned and will be very careful in making its decision so as to avoid any potential claims for damages against the regulator by the affected company.

Privilege pitfalls

6.162 The main danger area, in practice, where privilege can be waived accidentally is the circulation of privileged documents within a company. Critical documents should therefore remain in the sole possession of an in-house counsel if at all possible. A further risk area is the disclosure of privileged documents to a third party, such as an external technical expert. As the privilege rules do not apply to documents in the possession of such external experts, the documents can be seized by the public prosecutor. It is therefore crucial to only provide third parties such as external experts with such documents that the company would generally also disclose to the regulator.

---

[183] See FOIA, s 1(1) and (2).
[184] See FOIA, s 3 No 1 lit (d).
[185] See FOIA, s 6.

K. Managing Regulators

Dialogue with regulators

Regulated companies often have an informal dialogue with regulators in the course of which the regulator may express its view on the interpretation of certain regulatory requirements. Once an investigation has commenced, it is generally advisable that the company under scrutiny communicates to the regulator that it will fully cooperate, although, in principle, no company is obliged to do so. The company should be very precise as to who is handling the communication with the regulator, the scope of authority that he has and as to why that person is appropriate. The right relationship with a regulator can be critical. **6.163**

Control of scope of investigation

By communicating to the regulator at an early stage of the investigation that the company will fully cooperate and by offering to perform the (time consuming and labour intensive) investigation itself or through independent counsel, a company under investigation can try to limit the scope of the investigation and keep the regulator focused on the original subject of investigation without expanding the scope of it. If the regulator performs the document search and interviews various persons at the company under scrutiny, it might discover other potential breaches of law unrelated to the original subject matter. **6.164**

Use of information by regulators

The fact that a regulator has obtained certain information from the company as the result of an internal investigation has no official relevance. Regulators have the right to use any information that is lawfully obtained in any way that they see fit. **6.165**

To the extent that informal 'settlement' arrangements are an option, it is possible for the company and the regulator to reach an agreement that certain information provided by the company may be used only for specific purposes. Such agreements, however, are not common as regulators in Germany are generally reluctant to impose such restrictions on themselves and possibly fetter their discretion with regard to future proceedings. **6.166**

L. Managing Employees During Investigations

Powers to compel cooperation

German employment law does not contain specific provisions governing employees' duties and rights in, or companies' powers to induce or compel cooperation **6.167** with, an internal investigation. Instead, the general rules of German employment law apply.

6.168 Under these rules, the company will usually have the right to require from its employees that they cooperate with an internal investigation. While written employment contracts do not usually contain specific provisions addressing this issue, it is fair to say that the employee will be bound by an unwritten ancillary obligation to the company to disclose and make available to it information which relates to the company and its operations and of which the employee has become aware in the course of his or her employment.[186] The company may also resort to general statutory information rights applicable to any service relationship (*Auftrag*) under German law (section 666, 675 of the German Civil Code (*Bürgerliches Gesetzbuch*—BGB)). On these grounds, the company is only entitled to information regarding the employee's individual responsibilities and activities; any request to disclose information beyond this rather narrow scope cannot be based on the relevant statutes. The employee, in turn, is fully obliged to cooperate since these information rights concern the work performance itself owed under the employment contract; it is hardly permissible to dismiss the company's request as unreasonable. In particular, the employee remains bound to provide full information to the company even if he or she would have to accuse oneself of wrongdoings in such statement.

6.169 Employees who have reason to fear that full cooperation will give rise to adverse consequences typically will not openly refuse to cooperate but will instead try to undermine the investigation by withholding key information. It is worth noting, however, that real life experience often shows the opposite. Employees often tend to be rather talkative in an attempt, which may or may not be legitimate in the relevant case, to shift the blame from themselves and claim that any potentially unlawful activity was not their own initiative but was devised and overseen by their superiors.

Control on threats

6.170 If employees refuse to cooperate, even though they are effectively ordered to help with the investigation, the employer may consider legal consequences. Refusing to disclose information to which the employer is entitled is deemed to be a breach of duty under the employment contract and may trigger various sanctions which are subject to the general rules of German employment law.

---

[186] See W Blomeyer, in Münchener, *Handbuch des Arbeitsrechts* (2nd edn, 2000) (Handbook), § 54 Nos 10 sub. and § 54 No 8 for a general discussion of employees' ancillary duty to provide the employer with information relating to the employment.

In most cases the employer is well advised to give the employee a formal warning letter demanding that he or she complies with the duty to provide information and pointing out that the employment might be terminated if the employee persistently refuses to cooperate and to disclose information. **6.171**

Depending on the circumstances of the individual case, the employer might, however, be entitled to dismiss the employee with notice or, more unusually, with immediate effect if the employee continues to refuse to disclose information. In the case of an 'ordinary' termination with notice, it is usually necessary for the company to first issue a formal warning to the employee, demanding that he or she changes his or her conduct. Furthermore, an ordinary termination requires observing the applicable notice period (which may, under statutory law, be up to seven months depending on the employee's tenure with the company, or possibly even longer under the employment contract). **6.172**

Employees enjoy, however, a wide range of protection against dismissals. In case of termination, an employee may file a complaint with the labour court, which may review all grounds upon which the employer based the termination. As a general rule, German labour courts tend to be fairly restrictive in upholding terminations by employers. It is therefore hard to predict whether in a given case an employee's failure to cooperate with an internal investigation would entitle the company to terminate the employment for cause with immediate effect or whether the termination would have to be 'ordinary' and subject to the applicable notice period. Given the restrictive attitude often displayed by German labour courts in connection with terminations, it is not even guaranteed that a termination based on the employee's failure to cooperate with the internal investigation will be upheld at all. **6.173**

Accordingly, employers should not enforce cooperation by illegally threatening an employee. However, it is fair if the employee is made aware of potential and legal consequences (ie a suspension or a dismissal). There is no special protection against dismissals for whistle-blowers. **6.174**

Representation

In an internal investigation in Germany, an employee is only represented by separate counsel if he or she may be liable to the company for breach of duty under his or her employment relationship, or the regulatory or criminal liability of the employee is at issue. In such cases, the company is free to recommend separate counsel for the employee. However, more often than not, this simply involves a general suggestion to the employee to retain his or her own counsel; the company would not typically involve itself in the employee's decision of whether to hire counsel and whom to select. In some investigations, the company yet insisted on proper representation of employees (or even provided for a lawyer); this approach **6.175** is meant in order to render the evidence produced more credible and less vulnerable in a future court proceeding. The company's counsel is under no legal or ethical obligation to encourage separate representation of the employee.

Assurances as to confidentiality and privilege

6.176 Counsel representing a company conducting an investigation will be able to assure employees that the discussions will be kept confidential only if the company and its counsel have agreed that, in order to foster candour and openness on the part of the employees, certain specific information provided by the employees is to be kept confidential. To this end, information would also be kept confidential from the company. If there is no such agreement, the investigating counsel will be obliged to report all relevant information to its client, the company. There is no formal warning required in the process of internal investigations. At times, the company does not even inform employees about the scope of the investigation as such disclosure might reduce willingness to cooperate.

6.177 When the matter is being investigated by a regulator or the prosecutor's office, the decisive factor is whether, and to what extent, the company is under a legal obligation to provide information. If there is such an obligation, the company (as well as the investigating counsel, who in this respect might be deemed to act on the company's behalf vis-à-vis the employees) will not be able to guarantee confidential treatment to the employees.

6.178 An employee may refuse to testify in both civil and criminal proceedings as far as a (true) statement implies the risk that the employee himself or herself or close relatives will be prosecuted for a felony or misdemeanour. However, this privilege against self-incrimination does neither excuse the employee from appearing in court nor from generally making a statement. The employee can only refuse to answer incriminating questions; the court has to check carefully whether a testimony actually poses a risk for the employee himself or herself or may only result in disadvantages for a third party. Furthermore, the privilege does not release the employee from his contractual and/or statutory obligation to disclose information to the employer who, subsequently, may also introduce this material in a court proceeding.

Ethical implications for counsel

6.179 Ethical implications for counsel conducting an internal investigation could arise if counsel exposed himself or herself to a conflict of interest. The investigating counsel is usually retained by the company alone. While the investigation may greatly benefit from a friendly and mutually supportive relationship between the investigating counsel and the employees from whom information is sought, counsel must at all times bear in mind that he or she owes a duty of loyalty to the company alone. Therefore, counsel must be extremely cautious in making statements to employees that might be construed to be legal advice.

Investigation and disciplinary process

The employees' obligation to disclose and make available information to the **6.180** company is part of their duties under the employment contract; thus, employees have to furnish full and correct information. In case of failure to comply with this obligation, the employer may consider taking disciplinary measures (formal warning letter, notice for behavioural reasons). To the extent that non-cooperation with an internal investigation causes a demonstrable loss to the company, the company will be entitled to seek damages from the employee.

Any assurances made by counsel to employees of continued employment are **6.181** deemed to be given with the tacit consent of the company and are considered to be legally binding on the company. Therefore, companies and counsel usually define in advance those assurances which counsel may give during the course of their interviews with the company's employees. In particular, companies often use a strategy of granting their employees a limited immunity by promising them that no adverse employment measures will be taken (especially that no notice of termination will be given) on the basis of facts disclosed by the employee by a certain deadline.

The company may consider suspending the employee during the course of the **6.182** investigation. Obviously, this is a temporary measure which can be feasible if the employee shall be denied access to the company premises or if evidence gathered does not yet suffice to support a termination of employment. Under German employment law, suspension of an employee 'without pay' is permitted only with the employee's, and in certain cases, the work council's, consent.

A suspension 'with pay' will usually, although not always, be possible. German **6.183** employment law has long recognized that, in principle, an employee has a 'right to work' which places limits on the employer's ability to suspend him or her even with continued compensation. The employee's right to work is, however, subject to a balancing test. If the employer has a legitimate interest in suspending the employee, this interest must be weighed against the employee's interest in being able to continue working. In this weighing process, a court would usually take note of the fact that a suspension (even a suspension 'with pay') may have a stigmatizing effect on the employee.

In general, it seems reasonable to assume that in cases where there is an internal **6.184** investigation of a potential wrongdoing in which a given employee appears to be implicated, the company's interest in suspending the employee will usually be deemed to outweigh the employee's interest in being able to continue working. However, if the employee challenges the suspension in court, the burden will be on the employer to show that the suspension was indeed justified by a legitimate interest (eg an interest in preventing the employee from obstructing or otherwise interfering with the investigation).

6.185 Whether a given employee should be suspended is a question to be addressed in light of all circumstances of the case. For example, the company will have to consider whether the employee could potentially interfere with the investigation such as by trying to influence other employees or by obstructing access to important documents. Evidence of suspensions may help underline the company's claim that it is vigorously pursuing the allegations of wrongdoing and help protect its public profile.

Challenges posed by ex-employees[187]

6.186 Former employees have only very limited obligations to their former employer. Without a continuing employment contract, employees will generally have no obligation to provide further information; at times, a termination agreement may stipulate a post-contractual obligation to furnish information. One possible option is to ask employees to cooperate voluntarily with internal investigations. Details of the cooperation such as reimbursement of expenses, expected timing and duration of availability can be governed by a cooperation agreement and increase the chance that the former employee is willing to cooperate.

6.187 Former employees can be named as witnesses in legal proceedings before a German court. Unless there is a case of self-incrimination, former employees are bound to attend court proceedings and to give testimony. Former employees are generally bound to secrecy about their former employment relationship. Specific obligations might be imposed by the employment contract. The former employee is nevertheless obliged to cooperate with a witness summons but may limit any testimony to facts, which do not lead to self-incrimination or which are in breach of his confidentiality duty, at least where business secrets would have to be disclosed.

Payment of legal fees/indemnification/fee advances

6.188 There is nothing in German law that would prevent companies from indemnifying their officers and employees for their legal fees in connection with internal or regulatory investigations.

---

[187] See U Preis, in Erfurter, *Kommentar zum Arbeitsrecht*, BGB, s 611 recitals 916 ff; M Diller, *Der Betrieb* (2004) 318.

Such indemnification is possible either by advancing legal fees to the respective **6.189** officer or employee, or by providing reimbursement. The most common way for companies to provide indemnification is by taking out a specific insurance (usually referred to as 'legal protection insurance') that covers the employee's legal fees and, where applicable, court costs. However, this method of indemnification is a special privilege and not a standard feature of employment contracts.

In the event the employment contract does not include an indemnification **6.190** clause, the company might offer a formal agreement providing for certain benefits. This is a way to encourage cooperation of current employees and the only means to involve former employees. However, any payments beyond a mere reimbursement of costs are viewed critically; such payments may also raise doubts regarding the contents of a statement. An agreement providing for a contractual penalty in case the employee does not make use of his or her privilege against self-incrimination is most likely null and void. It is advisable for the company to think carefully before agreeing to provide such indemnification, as doing so might be considered an unlawful payment at the expense of the company which exposes the directors and officers agreeing to provide such indemnification to a personal liability. In particular, this is the case if the company prematurely waives potential claims for damages against the employee.

Where officers or employees are entitled to an indemnity for their legal fees, **6.191** the employment agreement sometimes states that the right to such indemnification is forfeited if the officer or employee is found to have engaged in improper conduct. Furthermore, in cases where 'legal protection insurance' has been taken out, the insurance policy will usually contain an exclusion for wilful conduct.

At present, it is not common practice in 'corporate Germany' to indemnify **6.192** employees for legal fees incurred.

Joint defence agreements

Joint defence agreements are not widespread practice in Germany. They will, how- **6.193** ever, often be problematic from a legal ethics standpoint, as they may expose counsel to a conflict of interests. Therefore, in such situations, the parties would pursue a joint defence strategy rather than entering into a 'formal' joint defence agreement.

Best practices

Employees should be clearly instructed to cooperate with the investigations. The **6.194** employer should treat the employees fairly and with due respect and care. An employee must be treated as not guilty, subject to the results of the investigations. The measures to be taken by the employer should be adjusted according to the individual circumstances.

6.195 It is vital to find a way of investigating which does not prevent employees from contributing. The employer must comply with the company's policies and rules on data protection, the use of email correspondence and other relevant provisions. Furthermore, employers must follow the respective procedure prescribed by law, by works agreement or other internal rules.

M. Winding up an Internal Investigation

Managing expectations

6.196 When managing the expectations of the regulators at the end of an internal investigation, emphasis should be made of the fact that the company fully cooperated with the regulator, stopped the misconduct and has a sincere interest in preventing the reoccurrence of the problem triggering the internal investigation. Ideally, a clear proposal for internal measures and the implementations thereof to guarantee future compliance with the law should be made. If individual persons were engaged in the wrongdoing the sanctions taken against them should be highlighted.

6.197 In all likelihood, the regulator will appreciate the company's efforts in investigating the problem and, thus, facilitating the regulator's job. However, the fact that a voluntary internal investigation was conducted does not necessarily lead to the absence of a sanction under German law. Nevertheless, a thorough internal investigation will usually improve the relationship with the regulator and will be to the benefit of the company. The quality of the cooperation from the company will be considered when determining the level (and proportionality) of any administrative fine.

6.198 If the internal investigation uncovers criminal conduct and the results thereof are revealed, the prosecutor's office is legally required to file an indictment if, in its assessment, there is a 'sufficient likelihood'[188] that a crime has been committed. However, limited by specific guidelines, the prosecutor's office has the discretion to drop minor charges. Usually this requires court approval and the indicted person has to make a specific payment to the state.[189] In the best case, the internal investigation can cause the prosecutor's office to make use of the aforementioned discretion. However, this should not be taken for granted.

6.199 When a company first approaches a regulator to find out whether it might grant immunity or reduction from fines for regulatory misconduct, it is advisable to limit the initial information provided to the regulator to the basic facts of the issue.

---

[188] *'Hinreichender Tatverdacht'*, see StPO, s 170(1).
[189] See StPO, s 153 and StPO, s 153a.

It can be further advisable to communicate only orally with the regulator at this stage because of the admission/litigation risk. The leniency programme of the *Bundeskartellamt* explicitly allows oral leniency applications. Leniency is generally subject to the condition that the company cooperates fully and on an ongoing basis with the regulator. If the regulator requests the company to provide additional information and/or to conduct further investigations the company should answer these information requests and perform these investigations as thoroughly as possible. If things that were initially unknown come to light in the course thereof they should be presented without undue delay to avoid any disappointments of the regulator, thereby undermining the value of the exercise. Usually, the regulator expects to be provided with a written final report which wraps up all prior submissions. If new material facts come to light after the report was finalized, regulators usually expect to receive an update.

Coordinating with Public Relations strategy

Whether the results of an internal investigation should be communicated to the **6.200** public depends on the company's overall PR strategy taken in connection with the individual problem triggering the internal investigation. If the public is aware that the internal investigation was initiated and if during the course of the investigation the underlying problem was the subject of constant news coverage, the company should consider informing the public of the end of the investigation. It is acceptable in Germany for such a statement to be very general and to avoid the details of negative findings. If there were findings indicating a breach of law, the focus should be on the company's commitment to cooperate with the authorities. Further emphasis should be on the interim measures taken by the management to stop the problem and prevent similar problems in the future. However, clearly, any statement cannot be misleading and it is an exercise in careful judgement to be accurate and meet expectations without unnecessarily damaging the company position both in terms of reputation and legal exposure to third parties, as an admission in such a statement could be pleaded against a company in litigation.

N. Reporting Obligations

Although unusual in Germany, if different authorities are conducting, or may **6.201** conduct, investigations which have certain factual background in common, it is very important that the reports are consistent in approach. Any such report needs to take account of the wider circumstances in which it may be read.

6.202 In Germany, it is usual, when submitting a report that the focus will be on the facts alone. They should be clearly and comprehensively stated. However, it is perfectly acceptable, and indeed, recommended to avoid all unnecessary commentary, drawing of causal connections, making of legal evaluations and admissions of legal responsibility and the like. Any report needs to be very carefully reviewed from this perspective.

6.203 Regulators usually expect a written final report. If prior submissions setting forth answers to specific information requests contained any ambiguities, the final report provides the opportunity to clarify them. To a German board, the results of an internal investigation can be generally presented in an oral report. There is no general statutory requirement that this has to be done in writing.[190] However, the board members should consider to request a written report to exclude their own potential liability arising from the events leading up to the internal investigation. A written report will facilitate to demonstrate that they managed the crisis on the basis of appropriate information and exercised sound business judgment in handling it thereby providing a safe harbour from liability.

O. Litigation Risks

Risks of criminal litigation commenced by regulators

6.204 Under German law, most of the 'serious' corporate violations fall into the category of criminal offences. Regulatory authorities in Germany do not have the power to conduct criminal investigations. Instead, whenever a regulatory authority learns of facts which indicate that it is reasonably likely that a crime may have been committed, it is required to hand over the respective information to the competent prosecutor's office.[191] In turn, the prosecutors' offices are under an obligation to update BaFin on the status of their proceedings.[192] Once the prosecutor's office has initiated a criminal investigation, jurisdiction to prosecute a related administrative offence also passes to the prosecutor's office by operation of law.[193] However, various applicable statutes provide for a mutual exchange of information between the regulators and the prosecutor's office.[194] Moreover, in

---

[190] Exceptions apply, inter alia, in the banking industry (see para. 6.62).

[191] See, eg, WpHG, s 4(5) (in the area of securities supervision); OWiG, s 41(1) (in general).

[192] See WpHG, s 40a (in the area of securities supervision); KWG, s 60a (in the area of banking supervision).

[193] See OWiG, s 40.

[194] See, eg, WpHG, s 40a(1) (in the area of securities supervision); KWG, s 60a (in the area of banking supervision).

the area of securities supervision, the prosecutor's office may consult BaFin in order to benefit from the latter's expertise.[195]

Corporations and other entities cannot be subject to criminal liability under German law. However, the criminal authorities can prosecute a company because of an administrative offence and impose a fine on the company if a director, officer or any other person responsible for the management of the company has committed a criminal offence by which duties of the company have been violated or the company was enriched or was intended to be enriched[196] or if the company is responsible for this behaviour.[197] The criminal proceedings against the individual and the administrative offence proceedings against the company usually run parallel without the criminal offence proceedings taking priority. In the Siemens corruption case, for example, the administrative offence proceedings against the company leading to a €201m fine were concluded while the criminal proceedings against the individual officers were still pending.[198] **6.205**

The most likely corporate offences which could result in criminal litigation or administrative offence proceedings include: **6.206**

- unlawful insider trading[199] (criminal offence, punishable by up to five years' imprisonment or a fine);
- various other insider violations[200] (administrative offence, carrying a fine of up to €200,000);
- misrepresentations by board members in relation to the shareholders' general meeting or auditors or in the company's financial statements[201] (criminal offence, punishable by up to three years' imprisonment or a fine);
- various bankruptcy offences, including bankruptcy fraud, preferential treatment of creditors or debtors, failure to file a petition for the opening of insolvency proceedings after the company has become illiquid or over indebted[202] (criminal offence, punishable by up to five years' imprisonment or a fine);
- intentional market manipulation in relation to securities[203] (criminal offences, punishable by up to five years' imprisonment);

---

195 See WpHG, s 40a(1).
196 See OWiG, s 30(1).
197 See OWiG, s 130.
198 Frankfurter Allgemeine Zeitung, 6 October 2007, 18.
199 See WpHG, s 38(1).
200 See WpHG, s 39(2) No 3 and No 4.
201 See AktG, s 400(1).
202 See AktG, s 401(1).
203 See WpHG, s 38(2).

- failure to make a requisite ad hoc disclosure of material facts[204] (administrative offence, carrying a fine of up to €1m);
- dishonest dealing[205] (criminal offence, punishable by up to five years' imprisonment or a fine);
- corruption[206] (criminal offence in respect of natural persons, punishable by up to three years' imprisonment or a fine; administrative offence in respect of the company if the corruptive behaviour of its employees is attributable to it or if the company is responsible for this behaviour[207]); and
- bid-rigging[208] (criminal offence, punishable by up to five years' imprisonment or a fine).

6.207 It is worth noting that in Germany, as in other jurisdictions, the criminal offence of making misrepresentations to the shareholders' general meeting or in the company's financial statements has been of increasing relevance in the recent past in connection with 'securities scandals' involving overstated revenues and similar issues.

6.208 In order to put the criminal sanctions into context, German courts hardly ever impose maximum criminal sentences. While there are no formal sentencing guidelines, there are certain customary sentencing standards, which may vary from region to region, for the more frequent crimes.

6.209 In the case of white-collar crimes, defendants, who typically are first time offenders, are usually fined or given a suspended jail sentence. Finally, if a criminal defendant is found guilty on various counts, the jail terms for each count are not consecutive; instead, the jail term for the most serious count is increased somewhat to reflect the other counts. Unless a defendant is sentenced to life imprisonment, which is, for all practical purposes, reserved to the crime of first-degree murder, the maximum possible jail sentence is 15 years in general.[209]

6.210 Moreover, the offences listed above are still (or at least not yet) not prosecuted very frequently.

---

[204] See WpHG, s 39(2) No 5 lit (a) and No 6.

[205] See the German Criminal Code (*Strafgesetzbuch*—StGB), s 268. One of the most prominent cases in recent years involving accusations of dishonest dealing was the criminal case against members of the supervisory board of Mannesmann AG because of allegations of dishonest dealings in the context of the takeover by Vodafone. The accusation was that remunerations paid to the management board of Mannesmann AG were allegedly granted in breach of the AktG. At the end, the case was concluded without a sentence being rendered against the payment of a stipulated amount of money.

[206] See StGB, s 299 and 333.

[207] See OWiG, s 30 and 130.

[208] See StGB, s 298.

[209] See StGB, s 38(2).

Risks of civil litigation commenced by regulators

The concept of 'civil' enforcement is unknown in the German regulatory con- **6.211**
text. Instead, an actionable violation of the law that does not constitute a criminal
act is considered an administrative offence, which may trigger a fine to be levied
by the regulatory authority or, if the prosecutor's office has taken over the prosecution, by the court.

Consequently, regulators will consider whether certain misconduct constitutes a **6.212**
criminal offence or merely an administrative offence. In the former case, the
prosecutor's office is legally required to file an indictment if, in its assessment,
there is a 'sufficient likelihood'[210] that a crime has been committed, save that
there is discretion to drop minor charges (which usually requires court approval).[211]
Even in these cases, the discretion is limited by the guidelines defined by the state
ministries of justice (which act as supervising entities for the local prosecutor's
offices).[212]

If only an administrative offence is at issue, the authorities have discretion as to **6.213**
whether or not to pursue the matter.[213] Here again, the discretion is limited by
precedent and guidelines. Generally speaking, a decision not to prosecute an
administrative offence will usually require a finding that the perpetrator acted
with only a slight degree of negligence and/or did not cause substantial harm to
third parties or the general public.[214]

Risks of private civil litigation

Any civil plaintiff will have to prove a private cause of action against the defen- **6.214**
dant. The fact that a regulatory investigation or other action has taken place or
has even yielded a particular result, does not necessarily mean that all elements
of the private cause of action are present. Nevertheless, private plaintiffs may use
information obtained from regulatory actions to bolster their civil cases to the
extent that the plaintiffs can obtain lawful access to such information. Areas such
as securities and anti-trust, regulatory, or criminal investigations often arouse the
interest of private parties and trigger civil actions.

---

210 *'Hinreichender Tatverdacht'*, see StPO, s 170(1).
211 See StPO, s 153 and StPO, s 153a.
212 Guidelines on Criminal Proceedings and Administrative Proceedings (*Richtlinien für das
Strafverfahren und das Bußgeldverfahren*—RiStBV).
213 See OWiG, s 47(1).
214 See L Meyer-Goßner, *Strafprozessordnung* (48th edn, 2005), s 153 No 1 sub and s 153a No 8.

6.215 Under German civil procedure law, civil courts are generally not bound by the findings of regulators or criminal courts.[215] An exception to this rule applies in the field of competition law.[216] Nevertheless, as a practical matter, it is fair to say that a court in a civil case will usually, perhaps even subconsciously, accord substantial or even controlling weight to such regulatory or criminal findings in determining whether there was a breach of law.

6.216 Nonetheless, a civil claimant has to fully substantiate its claim. In order to obtain the required information it will often try to obtain access to files of the regulators or the criminal court. In order to be given access the civil claimant will have to demonstrate a 'justified interest'.[217] Where a cartel participant has filed an application for immunity or reduction of a fine, however, the *Bundeskartellamt* will use its statutory limits of its discretionary powers to refuse such an application by private third parties.[218]

6.217 With the exception of perhaps the files of the *Bundeskartellamt*, civil claimants who assert that they are entitled to damages because of the misconduct that was at the centre of the regulator's or the criminal court's decision and who allege that they will need access to the information in the files to substantiate the basis and the amount of their claim will generally be granted such access. Therefore, a company has to carefully weigh the potential benefits of its full cooperation with the regulator or prosecutor's office to obtain a reduced sanction against the potential risk involved that civil litigants might obtain access to information otherwise unavailable to them to bolster their claims.

P. Settlement with Regulators

Process

6.218 German regulators do not enter into formal settlement agreements with regulated companies, as German law does not provide an official settlement mechanism for regulatory actions. Nevertheless, it is common for companies facing a regulatory investigation to have a dialogue with the regulator with a view

---

[215] See the Introductory Act for the Code of Civil Procedure (*Einführungsgesetz zur Zivilprozessordnung—EGZPO*), s 14(2) No 1.

[216] See GBW, s 33(4) pursuant to which a civil court is bound by the findings of the cartel authority where a private claimant seeks damages from a cartel participant.

[217] See StPO, s 406e relating to access to criminal court files, OWiG, s 46(3) relating to access to the files regarding administrative offences; VwVfG, s 40 relating to access to the files of regulatory authorities.

[218] Section FI of the Notice no 9/2006 of the *Bundeskartellamt* on the immunity from and reduction of fines in cartel cases of 7 March 2006.

to conveying their arguments and to convince the regulator that its initial suspicion may be unfounded as a whole or in part. As a result, informal agreements under which the company accepts a given sanction or agrees to conduct itself in a certain way in exchange for having the regulatory action discontinued are often reached.

However, subject to certain exceptions in the field of competition law, there is no **6.219** general practice according to which a thorough voluntary internal investigation would, of itself, cause the regulator to abstain from any sanction. If a breach of law has been established this will be sanctioned in accordance with the statutory requirements. The fact that the company fully cooperated will generally influence the regulator's discretion when it decides on which sanction to apply. However, the regulator will still impose a proportional sanction once a breach of law is established.

Informal arrangements are more difficult to achieve where a criminal offence is at **6.220** issue. This is because, under German law, criminal prosecutors do not have discretion as to whether or not to prosecute.[219] Instead, whenever a criminal investigation has shown a sufficient likelihood that a crime may have been committed, the prosecutor's office is legally required to file an indictment with the court of competent jurisdiction.[220] Only in narrow circumstances, such as if the criminal offence is of minor seriousness and gravity, does the prosecutor's office have discretion to drop the charge.[221] In most cases, this will require court approval.[222]

Plea bargaining and amnesty arrangements

German criminal procedure law does not expressly permit plea bargains. **6.221** Nevertheless, the issue of plea bargains, often referred to as deals, was widely discussed amongst the judiciary, attorneys and practitioners in Germany in the late 1990s. The situation remained unclear until 1997, when the German Federal Supreme Court[223] held that an 'understanding'[224] in a criminal proceeding between the court, the prosecutor's office and the defendant under which the defendant confesses to the prosecutor's allegations is not prohibited by German law. The prerequisites of such an agreement are as follows:[225]

• The court, the prosecutor and the defendant must enter into the agreement in the courtroom (ie in public). They may, however, discuss the terms of the agreement in advance, in private.

---

[219] See StPO, s 152(2).
[220] See StPO, s 170(1).
[221] See StPO, s 153 sub.
[222] See StPO, s 153a and StPO, s 153b.
[223] *Bundesgerichtshof* (BGH).
[224] '*Verständigung*'.
[225] See BGH, NJW (1998) 86 at 88 sub.

- The court must not commit to a specific sentence in advance. In the event that the defendant confesses, however, the court may commit to a specific upper limit of the sentence which it will not exceed.

- Despite the understanding and despite the defendant's confession, the court must weigh all relevant circumstances and hand down an appropriate sentence on that basis.

- In the agreement, the parties cannot exclude the defendant's right to appeal against the judgment rendered by the court.

6.222 If the prerequisites described above are met, the court is bound by the understanding in general. It may deviate only in exceptional circumstances, for example if, on the basis of the defendant's confession, it finds that the crime committed is more serious than (or even entirely different from) the crime which the defendant was charged by the prosecutor's office.[226] If the court intends to deviate from the understanding, it must inform the defendant of such an intention.[227]

Q. Conclusion

6.223 The number of publicly discussed internal and regulatory investigations into German listed corporations has increased steadily over recent years. While an independent internal investigation does not guarantee that the authorities will refrain from any sanctions for regulatory or criminal misbehaviour, the fact that an internal investigation was undertaken (and as a result irregularities were stopped, the processes within the company were improved and future irregularities were prevented) will generally be favourably taken into consideration when determining the sanction to be imposed on the company. As recent examples demonstrate, independent internal investigations have increasingly become the response of choice for many German corporations when faced with regulatory as well as criminal issues. This trend is likely to continue in the future.

---

[226] See BGH, NJW (1998) 86 at 89.
[227] See BGH, NJW (1998) 86 at 89.

7

INVESTIGATIONS IN FRANCE

A. Introduction[1]

7.01 Over the last few years, France has turned its focus to improving the efficiency of its regulatory system. This has resulted in the reinforcement of pre-existing powers through the creation of new independent bodies empowered with extensive investigation and sanction procedures, which have willingly engaged in an increased number of regulatory investigations.

7.02 The merger of previous independent bodies, under the 2003 Financial Security Act[2] established two new powerful independent authorities: the Financial Market Authority (AMF)[3] and the Insurance Regulatory Authority (ACAM). The AMF is currently the most active regulator in France, supervising approximately 1,000 listed companies and almost as many investment service providers, as well as all financial instruments, which are traded on the Paris Stock Exchange.[4]

7.03 In 2006, 1,500 market incidents were examined by the AMF, resulting in 500 requests for information to financial services providers, and 61 requests to foreign regulators.[5] In 2006, the AMF made 105 on-site investigations of investment service providers, followed by 88 investigations. The enforcement committee completed 30 proceedings, 25 people were punished and 20 legal entities were sanctioned.

---

[1] Contributors: Elie Kleiman, Pascal Lagesse, Jérôme Philippe, Marine Lallemand, Jérémie Fierville, Nicolas Léger.

[2] *Loi de sécurité financière*, 1 August 2003.

[3] *Authorité des Marchés Financiers*.

[4] *2006 Annual report*, Autorité des Marchés Financiers, 210 and 213.

[5] *2006 Annual report*, Autorité des Marchés Financiers, 215.

These punishments have included fines of between €750,000 and €1.5m   **7.04**
against a number of capital management firms and banks for insider trading, a
€500,000 fine against a distribution company and a €1m fine against its former
CEO for disclosure of false information to the market, and several decisions
where fines amounted to €1.5m such as the *Altran* decision in March 2007.[6]
The fines awarded by the AMF amount to €18,018,148 for the year 2006.

The French Competition Council[7] has also demonstrated a greater commitment   **7.05**
to investigating and sanctioning anti-competitive practices in recent years. In
2006, 75 cases were referred to the Council, which rendered 111 decisions and
opinions, including 13 decisions sanctioning cartels and abuses of dominant
position, for a total of fines above €128m.[8]

This trend towards increased investigations with greater fines seems set to increase   **7.06**
in the near future with the AMF placing greater emphasis on the duration of
investigations (due to last up to a maximum of 12 months) and creating a charter
explaining the investigation practices.[9]

B. Regulators

Key regulators

There are three key regulators in France: the AMF, the Competition Council[10]   **7.07**
and the Directorate General for Competition, Consumer Affairs and Fraud
Repression (DGCCRF).[11]

Financial market regulation

Regulation of financial markets in France is largely the responsibility of the   **7.08**
AMF. The AMF[12] is currently the most active regulator in France, empowered by
the Financial Security Act with extensive investigation and sanction powers.
It is a public body mandated with: (i) safeguarding investments in financial
instruments; (ii) maintaining orderly financial markets; and (iii) ensuring that

---

   [6] Altran Technologies was fined €1.5m and each member of the board was fined €1m for the
dissemination of false information and organization of a mechanism in order to falsely inflate the
turnover.
   [7] *Conseil de la concurrence.*
   [8] In 2005, the total of fines was above €754m, in particular because of fines imposed to mobile
operators (combined amount of €534m for three operators).
   [9] *Pour une meilleure régulation*, Autorité des Marchés Financiers, November 2006, 15.
   [10] *Conseil de la concurrence.*
   [11] *Direction Générale de la Concurrence, de la Consommation et de la Répression des Fraudes.*
   [12] For further information, see <http://www.amf-france.org>.

investors receive material and accurate information.[13] The AMF also lends its support to financial market regulation at the European and international level.

7.09 The AMF has four main areas of responsibility through which it oversees corporate finance activity (ie securities trading and compliance of listed companies and financial institutions to financial regulations): (i) regulation; (ii) authorization; (iii) supervision; and (iv) enforcement.

7.10 More specifically, the AMF sets rules for, and monitors, transactions involving the securities of publicly traded companies (initial public offerings, capital increases, mergers etc), and ensures that tender offers are conducted in an orderly fashion. It also monitors companies to ensure that they provide complete and relevant information on a timely basis and in an equitable manner to all market participants (the public investors, analysts, fund managers, the press etc).

7.11 The AMF also authorizes the formation of collective investment schemes (SICAVs and FCPs) as well as ensuring that special characteristics of complex products are adequately explained to potential investors. It also establishes principles of organization and operation for market undertakings (such as Euronext Paris) and settlement systems (eg Euroclear France). It approves the rules of clearing houses (eg Clearnet) and sets conduct-of-business rules for their members. It monitors the markets and the transactions that take place in them.

7.12 The AMF establishes conduct of business rules and professional obligations that must be observed by persons authorized to provide investment services or advise on financial investments (credit institutions authorized to provide investment services, investment firms, investment management companies, financial investment advisers, direct marketers). It registers and approves investment management companies at the incorporation stage, assessing the skills, fitness and propriety of corporate officers as well as the adequacy and suitability of the company's resources. The AMF also establishes conduct-of-business rules for custody and administration of financial instruments.

7.13 The AMF supervises financial investment advisers, a new legal category established by the Financial Security Act. The AMF bears the responsibility of ensuring that financial investment advisers honour their professional obligations. Any breach of the laws, regulations or professional obligations applicable to advisers is subject to sanctions imposed by the AMF.

7.14 The AMF may also conduct inspections and investigations; and, when practices are found to contravene its General Regulation or professional obligations,

---

[13] Art L 621-1 of the French Monetary and Financial Code (*Code Monétaire et Financier*, (CMF)).

its Enforcement Committee[14] may impose sanctions or penalties. When the facts of a case suggest a criminal offence, the AMF Board[15] transmits the report of its inspection or investigation to the public prosecutor.

There are four stages involved in the AMF enforcement process: (i) supervision **7.15** and investigations: initiated and conducted under the direction of the AMF Secretary General;[16] (ii) opening of sanction proceedings: decided by the AMF Board, which serves a statement of complaints[17] and refers the case to the Enforcement Committee after examining the inspection or investigation report; (iii) documentation of the sanction proceedings: conducted by a member of the Enforcement Committee serving as *Rapporteur*; and (iv) imposition of sanctions or penalties: ordered by the Enforcement Committee, after hearings during which the parties are entitled to submit their defence. However, the Enforcement Committee may not hear a case based on facts that occurred more than three years prior to the report being made if no act contributing to the uncovering, declaration or punishment of those facts took place during that period.

The Committee may impose sanctions or penalties on: (i) professional entities under **7.16** the supervision of the AMF, for any breach of professional obligations established by law, regulations or rules of professional conduct approved by the AMF; (ii) individuals under the authority of or acting on behalf of such entities; and (iii) any other person whose practices contravene legislative or regulatory provisions, when such practices infringe upon investors' rights or impair the orderly operation of markets.

Professional entities may be subject to sanctions related to the conduct of their **7.17** business activity (warning, reprimand, temporary or permanent prohibition on providing all or part of the services previously provided) as well as fines up to €1.5m or ten times the unlawful profits earned (€300,000 or five times when the professional in question is an individual, except in cases of market abuse practices as defined in Article L. 621.14 of the CMF). Other persons may be subject to fines not exceeding €1.5m or ten times the amount of profits earned. The amount of the fine is set based on the seriousness of the acts committed and in proportion to the profits made or other advantages gained by virtue of those acts.

Appeals from the AMF's decisions and sanctions are brought before the Paris **7.18** Court of Appeal,[18] except when these decisions and sanctions relate to professionals under the supervision of the AMF, in which case the French Supreme Court for administrative matters, the Council of State,[19] has exclusive jurisdiction.

---

[14] *Commission des sanctions.*
[15] *Collège de l'AMF.*
[16] *Secrétaire Général de l'AMF.*
[17] *Notification des Griefs.*
[18] *Cour d'appel de Paris.*
[19] *Conseil d'Etat.*

7.19   Due to the peculiarities of the French legal system, a single act may face dual punishment, such as criminal sanctions imposed by criminal courts, and disciplinary/administrative sanctions imposed by regulators such as the AMF.

7.20   While the AMF's enforcement role is confined to the imposition of disciplinary/administrative sanctions and/or fines, the Public Prosecutor and third parties may initiate criminal proceedings where corporate and/or white collar crimes are committed. The Public Prosecutor[20] enjoys a discretionary power to decide whether criminal proceedings should be initiated. Third parties who may be victims of the criminal activity may, by filing a complaint with the competent investigating magistrate[21] force the Public Prosecutor to initiate criminal proceedings.[22]

7.21   When the facts of a case suggest that a criminal offence has been committed, the Board of the AMF must hand the matter over to the Public Prosecutor and pass on its inspection or investigation report.[23]

Competition regulation

7.22   The Directorate General for Competition, Consumer Affairs and Fraud Repression (DGCCRF),[24] and the French Competition Council[25] are both responsible for regulating competition issues in France.

7.23   The DGCCRF is a directorate within the French Ministry of the Economy, which has primary responsibility for the enforcement of competition law. It investigates, among other issues, anti-competitive practices, such as cartel agreements and abuses of dominant positions[26] and can advise the Minister of the Economy, Finance and Industry to refer such practices to the Competition Council for decision and potentially, sanctions.

7.24   In addition, the DGCCRF is in charge of detecting competition restrictive practices[27] for which it can bring claims in the French civil or commercial courts.[28] The DGCCRF also ensures that public procurement procedures comply with competition rules. Finally, the DGCCRF is in charge of assessing the

---

[20] *Ministère public.*
[21] *Juge d'instruction.*
[22] Art 1, § 2 of the French Code of Criminal Procedure ('*Code de procédure pénale*').
[23] Art L. 621-20-1 of the CMF.
[24] *Direction Générale de la Concurrence, de la Consommation et de la Répression des Fraudes.* For further information, see <http://www.finances.gouv.fr/DGCCRF>.
[25] *Conseil de la Concurrence.* For further information see <http://www.conseil-concurrence.fr>.
[26] Arts L. 420-1 and L. 420-2 of the French Commercial Code (*Code de commerce*).
[27] Art L. 442-1 et seq of the French Commercial Code.
[28] Restrictive practices include discriminatory practices, certain behavioral abuses, sudden breach of established commercial relationships as well as other practices (see notably Art L. 422-6 of the French Commercial Code).

concentrations (mergers and acquisitions), which trigger the French merger control thresholds.

The Competition Council ('the Council') is an independent administrative body **7.25** created in 1986 that is not under the authority of the government and has the power to impose quite severe penalties. The Council may take action to suppress anti-competitive practices and intervene, either at the request of complainants or at the request of the French Minister of the Economy, whenever competition is likely to be distorted on a market, irrespective of the business concerned or whether the operators involved are public or private entities. In this context, the Council may order emergency interim measures, injunctions and/or fines.[29] The Council, however, does not deal with commercial practices that are deemed to be pernicious or unfair, or with disputes between parties seeking damages as such actions fall within the jurisdiction of the judicial courts. The Council's decisions are subject to scrutiny by the Paris Court of Appeal.[30]

The Council has the power to impose substantial penalties including heavy fines up **7.26** to a maximum of a 10 per cent of a company's worldwide pre-tax turnover (€3m if the offender is not a company).[31] This prevents companies from attempting to reduce the prosecuted legal entity's turnover during proceedings. In addition to fines, the Council may also issue injunctions requiring the parties to alter their behaviour. The details of Council decisions may also be published in the press.[32]

If the Council deems it appropriate, it may choose to refer a matter to the Public **7.27** Prosecutor.[33] This allows for criminal sanctions which may be imposed for an infringement of competition law:

> if any natural person fraudulently takes a personal and decisive part in the conception, organisation or implementation of the practices referred to in Articles L. 420-1 and L. 420-2, this can be punished by a prison sentence of up to four years and a fine of up to 75,000 Euros.

Although this theoretically could lead to a great number of criminal proceedings **7.28** against the most serious anti-competitive behaviour, practice tends to indicate that it is difficult to show the 'personal and decisive part' taken by the concerned person in the conception, organization or implementation of the practices. However, the number of cases passed on to the Public Prosecutor seems to be on the increase.

---

[29] Art L. 464-2 of the French Commercial Code.
[30] Art L. 464-8 al 1 of the French Commercial Code.
[31] Art L. 464-2 I al 4 of the French Commercial Code.
[32] Art L. 464-2 I al 5 of the French Commercial Code.
[33] Art L. 462-6 al 2 of the French Commercial Code.

7.29 It is important to note that, in a recent communication regarding its leniency policy, the Council committed not to transfer to the criminal prosecution cases of individuals employed by or affiliated with a company benefiting from the leniency programme.

Other regulators

7.30 Numerous industry-specific regulatory bodies and authorities may also conduct investigations and impose sanctions.

Insurance market regulation

7.31 The ACAM[34] is a new independent regulatory body with legal personality created by the Financial Security Act 2003, dealing with the regulation of the insurance sector. It has its own budget and sanction proceedings, and is likely to become an increasingly important regulator over the next few years, although in 2006 it pronounced only nine sanction decisions.[35]

7.32 The ACAM's main function is to control the proper application of relevant laws and regulations by insurance companies, mutual insurance companies and specific retirement institutions, and their ability to enforce at all times their contractual obligations towards their policyholders. In order to achieve these goals, the ACAM has been granted with investigation, injunction and safeguard powers. Most of its decisions are not published, especially when dealing with facts regarding individuals, which fall under professional secrecy rules. The ACAM can issue fines up to 3 per cent of the overall pre-VAT turnover of the last fiscal year of the sanctioned company, and/or issue disciplinary sanctions. Moreover, the same facts can lead at the same time to (i) administrative fines given by ACAM and (ii) criminal sanctions awarded by criminal courts.[36]

The Banking Commission

7.33 The French Banking Commission[37] is charged with monitoring credit institutions and investment firms' observance of the laws and regulations applying to them.[38] It also examines the conditions under which these institutions operate and monitors the soundness of their financial position. It ensures that the

---

34 For further information, see <http://www.ccamip.fr>.

35 *2006 Annual Report*, ACAM, 30.

36 *2006 Annual Report*, ACAM, 31.

37 *Commission bancaire*. For further information, see <http://www.banque-france.fr>.

38 Art L. 613-1 et seq of the CMF. Another financial regulator, the CECEI, is responsible for authorizing the activity in France of (i) credit institutions conducting banking operations as their business on a regular basis and offering investment services; and (ii) investment firms, except portfolio management companies which are under the jurisdiction of the AMF.

standards of sound banking practice are observed, without prejudice to the powers of the AMF.

To carry out its tasks, the Banking Commission has extensive administrative **7.34** jurisdiction supplemented by judicial powers. In order to be able to exercise these administrative powers, the Banking Commission can conduct off-site monitoring[39] and on-site inspections[40] in the institutions subject to its control. In addition to routine inspections, the Banking Commission conducts targeted inspections of institutions which may be vulnerable. It also organizes inspections of certain sectors of the banking industry in order to increase its knowledge of a specific sector.

In the framework of its judicial power, the Banking Commission may decide to **7.35** institute disciplinary proceedings under the terms of Article L. 613-21 of the Monetary and Financial Code.[41] If a credit institution or investment firm has contravened a law or regulation relating to its business activity, has failed to respond to a recommendation or comply with an injunction, has not heeded a cautionary notice or even failed to honour the commitments made on the occasion of an application for authorization or a permit or dispensation provided for by the laws and regulations that apply to credit institutions and investment firms, the Banking Commission may, without prejudice to the powers of the AMF, impose various sanctions which may be published at the expense of the firm or institution.

In this respect, the Banking Commission may issue a warning, reprimand, prohi- **7.36** bition on the execution of certain transactions and any other restriction on the conducting of its business, temporary suspension or automatic dismissal of managers and deletion of the credit institution or investment firm from the list of authorized credit institutions or investment firms. Moreover, the Banking Commission may issue, either instead of, or in addition to such sanctions, a financial penalty at least equal to the minimum capital which the legal entity sanctioned is required to maintain. The Banking Commission may also decide, either instead of, or in addition to such sanctions, to prohibit or limit the distribution of a dividend to the shareholders, or a return to the holders of membership shares.

---

[39] Off-site monitoring is based on the General Secretariat's examination of accounting and prudential documents and on regular contacts with the senior managers of the institutions.

[40] Through on-site inspections, the Banking Commission ascertains that the information disclosed by the institutions is an accurate reflection of their situation.

[41] When the Banking Commission makes a ruling under the terms of Art L. 613-21 of the Monetary and Financial Code, it is acting as an administrative court.

7.37   Although the law entrusts great responsibilities to the Banking Commission, its effectiveness is dependent upon working closely and cooperating with the other authorities which have jurisdiction in banking and financial matters.

7.38   When the facts of a case suggest that a criminal offence has been committed, the Banking Commission must hand the matter over to the Public Prosecutor and pass on its inspection or investigation report.[42]

The Electronic Communications and Post Regulation Authority (ARCEP)[43]

7.39   ARCEP regulates competition in the area of telecommunication and postal services.[44] It has investigative powers and can impose a graduated range of sanctions that may be applied to operators which do not respect the operating framework of the postal activities market. It also has the power to rule on disputes between postal and telecommunications operators, and the power to sanction operators that do not fulfil their obligations. It may remove their frequency and numbering resources and, in case of emergency, take interim measures. It can also impose fines on operators that can amount to up to 5 per cent of their yearly turnover.

The Superior Council of Audiovisual (CSA)[45]

7.40   The CSA is the regulator for the audiovisual industries in France, with responsibility for television and radio services. The CSA ensures that broadcasters (i) comply with relevant regulations (ie regarding advertising, support to the French movie industry and child protection) and (ii) do not infringe upon fundamental principles (ie human dignity and public order).

7.41   In order to fully carry out its mission, the CSA has the power to control broadcasters and issue administrative sanctions, including: (i) suspension of the licence (after formal notice); (ii) reduction of the licence term; and (iii) withdrawal of the licence (in the most serious cases). The CSA can also fine broadcasters or request a communiqué to be broadcast on the broadcaster's channel or station. The level of the fines depends on the seriousness of the offence committed and the profit earned as a result of the offence, without exceeding 3 per cent of the tax-free turnover realized during the previous year. However, except in cases where particularly

---

[42] Art 40 of the Code of Criminal Procedure. According to the 2006 Annual Report of the Banking Commission (161), five matters have been handed over to the Public Prosecutor in that year.

[43] *Autorité de Régulation des Communications Électroniques et des Postes*. For further information, see <http://www.arcep.fr>.

[44] The *ARCEP* was set up by the Regulation of Postal Activities Act 2005 ('*Loi relative à la régulation des activités postales*') and replaces the Telecommunications Regulation Authority ('*Autorité de régulation des télécommunications*'). The latter had a narrower ambit as it was only charged with regulating telecommunication services and not postal activities.

[45] *Conseil Supérieur de l'Audiovisuel*. For further information, see <http://www.csa.fr>.

serious or repeated offences have been committed and a sanction is unavoidable, the CSA always prefers dialogue and prevention.

In addition, in cases of criminal offence such as unauthorized radio and television **7.42** broadcasts, or the non-compliance of a radio station with the technical aspects of its licence agreement, the CSA can refer matters to the Public Prosecutor.

The Commission for the Regulation of Energy (CRE)[46]

The CRE is the regulator for gas and electricity industries, mandated to guarantee **7.43** the right of access to public electricity grids and to natural gas facilities and systems; ensure the smooth running and development of the electricity and natural gas facilities and systems; guarantee the independence of system operators; and ensure that the progressive opening of the market functions by uniting the introduction of competition with the fulfilment of public service missions.

The CRE can open investigations, led by competent officials, who can gather **7.44** elements and information through on-site investigations. The CRE can impose two main types of sanctions: (i) prohibition to access to electric and gas networks for up to one year, and/or (ii) financial sanction of up to 3 per cent of the company's turnover.

Concurrent investigations

A company in France could be the subject of several investigations being **7.45** conducted simultaneously on different grounds. For instance, the AMF can investigate a company about insider trading issues, while competition authorities are also investigating the same company for anti-competitive practices.

There are, however, a number of safeguards that protect a company from being **7.46** subject to concurrent investigations by different regulators on the same grounds.

For instance, regulators such as ARCEP, the CRE, the CSA, have the power to **7.47** settle disputes in situations that may sometimes involve competition issues. The risk that the Competition *Council*'s rulings may conflict with those of the industrial regulators is limited by the existence of so-called 'bridges' reciprocal consultation procedures.

In such a case, if for instance the Chairman of ARCEP has to inform the **7.48** Competition Council of any abuses of a dominant position and practices which hamper the free exercise of competition of which it becomes aware in the area of postal activities, it may also call on the Competition Council for an opinion on

---

[46] *Commission de régulation de l'énergie*. For further information, see <http://www.cre.fr>.

any other question under its jurisdiction. Similarly, the Competition Council informs ARCEP of any case within its jurisdiction and requests its opinion on cases in the area of postal activities on which it is asked to rule.[47]

7.49 With regards to financial regulation, the Board of Supervisory Authorities of businesses in the financial sector is composed of the Chairman of the three main regulators of the financial sector (AMF, the Banking Commission and ACAM) and chaired by the Minister of Economy. This board facilitates the exchange of information between the supervisory authorities of financial groups and addresses any questions of common interest relating to the coordination of the supervision of these groups.[48]

7.50 When investigations by regulators reveal that a criminal offence has been committed, the matter shall be referred to the Public Prosecutor. In particular, concurrent investigations can be simultaneously conducted by the AMF and the Public Prosecutor where issues regarding market abuses are under scrutiny. In cases of market abuses, the same facts may indeed lead to two sanctions being awarded by both the AMF and criminal courts on two different grounds (eg (i) breach of financial regulations regarding insider trading and (ii) commission of the offence of insider trading).[49] Therefore, the general principle according to which criminal procedure takes precedence does not apply, and no rule limits or regulates concurrent investigations. In practice, the Public Prosecutor tends to await the results of the inquiry conducted by technically skilled investigators of the AMF before pursuing its own investigation. The Public Prosecutor can also conduct a concurrent investigation or await the end of the enforcement proceedings before the AMF before deciding whether to launch criminal proceedings. In 2006, 23 inquiry reports were handed over by the AMF to the Public Prosecutor.[50]

Relationships with overseas regulators

7.51 The AMF and the Banking Commission may request any document, information or explanation necessary to complete their assignments, whether those documents or information are held by the company under the investigation or its parent companies or subsidiaries, and whether those companies are located in an EU member state or in a country party to the European Economic Area (EEA) Agreement. For instance, the AMF can directly request a financial institution based in London to disclose the name of one of its clients suspected of market manipulation in France.

---

[47] Art L. 5-8 of the Postal and Electronic Communications Code ('*Code des postes et des Communications électroniques*').
[48] Art L. 631-2 of the CMF.
[49] *Manquement d'initié et délit d'initié.*
[50] AMF, 2006 annual report, 223.

Moreover, the AMF and the Banking Commission can enter into cooperation **7.52** and information-sharing agreements with non-EEA countries.[51]

In 2006, the AMF addressed 277 requests for assistance and received 163. **7.53**

An administrative or criminal investigation may also be opened by French **7.54** Regulators or by the Public Prosecutor upon request of a foreign authority with equivalent jurisdiction, based in the EU, in an EEA member state or in any other state when these states are subject to cooperation agreements.

The Competition Council and the DGCCRF both belong to the European **7.55** Competition Network (ECN)[52] and have also been members of the International Competition Network (ICN) since the end of 2001.[53]

The ECN is composed of the European Commission and member states' com- **7.56** petition authorities. They form a network of public authorities, which cooperate closely in order to protect competition. The network is a forum for discussion and cooperation for the application and enforcement of the European competition policy. It provides a framework for the cooperation of European competition authorities, notably in cases where Articles 81 and 82 of the EC Treaty are applied.

In the same way, the Competition Council and the DGCCRF are active mem- **7.57** bers of the ICN[54] that seeks to provide competition authorities with a specialized yet informal venue for maintaining regular contacts and addressing practical competition concerns. It is focused on improving worldwide cooperation and enhancing convergence through dialogue.

C. Powers of Regulators

Sources of investigations

An investigation of a company for financial offences is usually opened (i) as a **7.58** result of observations made in the course of market surveillance or monitoring of

---

[51] For instance, in the US, the AMF negotiated a cooperation agreement with the Securities and Exchange Commission (SEC), and the Banking Commission negotiated cooperation agreements with the FED, the FDIC, the OCC, and the New York State Banking Department.

[52] Created by the Council Regulation No 1/2003 of 16 December 2002. French competition authorities have been involved in the ECN since the Ordinance of 4 November 2004 (Ordinance n° 2004-1173 of 4 November 2004 which was transposed in the Arts L. 450-1 al 3 and L. 462-9 II of the French Commercial Code (for the ECN)).

[53] The ICN is the only international body devoted exclusively to competition law enforcement. Membership is voluntary and open to any national or multinational competition authority entrusted with the enforcement of anti-trust laws.

[54] France was one of the first states which launched the ICN in October 2001.

listed companies, (ii) in response to complaints, or (iii) following a request addressed by the judicial authorities to the regulator. Investigations may also be opened at the request of foreign authorities with equivalent jurisdiction.

7.59 The Competition Council takes action to suppress anti-competitive practices and intervenes, either on its own initiative or, at the request of complainants or at the request of the Minister of the Economy, whenever competition is likely to be distorted on a market, irrespective of the business concerned or whether the operators involved are public or private entities.

7.60 Investigations may also be launched following information provided under the leniency procedure. The leniency procedure encourages companies engaged in anti-competitive agreements to inform the *Competition Council of such agreements* providing evidence, identifying the parties responsible for the agreement. In exchange, the *Competition Council* may exonerate them from all or part of the fines that may be imposed.[55]

Levels of regulatory scrutiny

7.61 As the AMF has a wide area of responsibility covering oversight of the markets and must ensure that listed companies comply with applicable laws, regulations and practices, it exercises three levels of scrutiny in the course of monitoring listed companies and financial institutions: (i) market surveillance (ie systematic and automatic surveillance of ordering of securities); (ii) controls over investment services providers and market infrastructures (ie on-site and off-site controls regarding the compliance of financial institutions with applicable financial regulations); and (iii) investigations over market abuses or over financial information.[56] The General Regulation of the AMF draws a distinction between the 'inspection' of a company (see 7.62 below) and the 'investigation' into the company's practices (see 7.67 et seq below).

7.62 Within the scope of its inspection functions,[57] the General Secretary of the AMF issues an inspection order to the agents who conduct the inspection.[58] The head inspector then notifies the company or person under the AMF's scrutiny of the type of information, documents and evidence that the AMF requires. Inspectors are allowed to hear any person that works under the authority of the suspected person or acting on their behalf who may be in a position to provide information

---

[55] Art L. 464-2 IV of the French Commercial Code.
[56] AMF, 2006 Annual Report, ch 5.
[57] Pursuant to Arts 143-1 et seq of the General Regulation of the AMF.
[58] An order contains the name of the entity or corporate body to be investigated, the identity of the head inspector and the purpose of the inspection.

that is deemed useful to complete their inspection.[59] The inspectors then draft a report, which is communicated to the company.[60]

AMF investigators tend to request or seize a large variety of documents in order **7.63** to establish the facts of a particular case. The company under investigation can, for instance, be requested to respond to an initial questionnaire. The answers given can lead to wider requests and/or searching of premises. A company investigated by the AMF must therefore ensure that the investigators permanently act within the scope of the investigation order issued by the General Secretary of the AMF.

The DGCCRF officials have wide investigation powers which can be used to **7.64** investigate competition law related issues, but also consumer law related topics and more general 'fraud' issues as well as competition related issues. Officials are notably allowed to hear any person, to ask questions and make clarifications, to copy documents etc, depending on the kind of investigation. The DGCCRF officials can act directly on behalf of the Minister for the Economy, as well as pursuant to the request of the Competition Council in the scope of an ongoing investigation.

Investigation tools

The AMF enjoys a wide array of powers and procedural tools in order to conduct **7.65** investigations. The AMF investigators are usually either AMF staff, or members of supervisory authorities other than the AMF such as experts listed in judicial experts lists, statutory auditors or chartered accountants, persons specializing in financial sector studies, market executive bodies or clearing houses.[61] The scope of these investigatory powers depends on the purpose of the inquiry.

In the case of standards investigations, the AMF investigators may ask to be pro- **7.66** vided with any documents or records in any medium and obtain copies of them; summon and hear any persons likely to provide information; and access the work premises.[62] Any person obstructing an investigation or providing inaccurate information to AMF investigators is subject to criminal prosecutions.

---

[59] Pursuant to the last paragraph of Art 143-3 of the General Regulation of the AMF, any such person is bound to defer to any request from the AMF and to cooperate in a diligent and honest manner.

[60] Except where there is evidence of behavior which may give rise to criminal sanctions in which case communicating the report to the company may interfere with judicial proceedings (Art 143-5 of the General Regulation of the AMF).

[61] Art L. 621-9-1 of the CMF.

[62] Art L. 621-10 of the CMF.

7.67 The AMF's powers of investigation are increased where the inquiry is conducted to search for market abuses (insider trading, disclosure of false or deceptive information to the market, or market manipulation).[63]

7.68 In the scope of this procedure, the General Secretary of the AMF may ask the Presiding Judge of the Civil Court[64] in the jurisdiction where the premises are located, further to a substantiated application, to grant authorization to allow coercive measures to obtain the information.[65] This allows investigators to visit all premises between 6.00 am and 9.00 pm and seize documents. A company can appeal the order before the French Supreme Court,[66] however, it cannot suspend the order.

7.69 Such an investigation must be conducted in the presence of the occupier of the premises or its representative, or if they are absent, in the presence of two witnesses.[67] A judicial police officer[68] must also be present during the operation and keeps the Presiding Judge of the Civil Court informed of the investigation. The judicial police officer ensures that professional secrecy and defence rights are observed.[69]

7.70 A list is drawn up of the items seized. If drawing up the list at the company's premises causes problems, the evidence and documents shall be placed under official seals. In the event that official seals are used, all employees, including cleaning staff, have to make sure that the official seals are not damaged.

7.71 Investigators are bound by a specific confidentiality obligation. Any communication or disclosure of a document obtained from a search to a person, who is not authorized by law, by the signatory or the recipient of the document, may be penalized by a maximum fine of €4,500 and two years imprisonment. Evidence and documents that are not useful for demonstrating the truth must be returned to the occupier of the premises.

7.72 Given the AMF's wide-ranging powers and, more generally, the powers of any judicial police investigator in the context of a criminal investigation, any person called upon to take part in an investigation conducted by a regulator should receive appropriate training.

7.73 In particular, all receptionists must be informed of the procedure to follow and must have an up-to-date list of the managers to contact. The investigation order

---

[63] Art L. 621-12 of the CMF.
[64] *Président du Tribunal de Grande Instance.*
[65] Art L. 621-12 of the CMF.
[66] *Cour de cassation.*
[67] Art L. 621-12 of the CMF.
[68] *Officier de police judiciaire.*
[69] Art L. 621-12 of the CMF.

must be delivered to the manager in charge of the investigation. The manager in charge should contact the in-house lawyers, external counsel, executives of the company and the department in charge of corporate communications to the media. The manager in charge must take note of all the investigators' questions to staff members, as well as the answers provided. Following the investigators' visit, the manager in charge must make a statement in the minutes regarding the company and its staff's level of cooperation during the visit and, as the case may be, any disagreements.

Infringements of competition rules are often the result of complicated practices, **7.74** which can only be proven by the use of extensive investigations or even expert resources. Following the examples of procedures employed in the US or by the European Commission, the French legislator has introduced new competition law procedures, in order to facilitate the task of gathering evidence and shorten the time necessary to deal with certain cases (negotiated 'settlement', leniency and commitments).[70]

The Commercial Code gives case handlers of the Competition Council and of **7.75** the DGCCRF power to launch investigations. Two types of investigations can be conducted, either ordinary investigations[71] or in-depth investigations.[72]

When conducting an ordinary investigation, officials are not obliged to present **7.76** any document indicating the subject and scope of the investigation, but they must state them orally at the beginning of the investigation. They do not have to give prior notice before proceeding with an investigation. Officials are allowed access to all professional premises and business documents and may request copies, however they are not entitled to seize original documents.

In-depth investigations may be launched only once the competent judge[73] within **7.77** the relevant local civil court of first instance[74] (has granted a formal authorization (in an *ordonnance*) to proceed with the investigation. This authorization must be notified to the company prior to the effective beginning of the investigation and be annexed to the minutes of the investigation.

One or several members of the police must be present during an in-depth investi- **7.78** gation. Officials are allowed to search and to seal premises, to seize and seal original documents (memoranda, notes, correspondence, minutes, diaries etc) and computers (they usually take copies of relevant electronic files, including emails).

---

[70] Art L. 464-2 III and IV of the French Commercial Code.
[71] *Enquêtes simples.*
[72] *Enquêtes lourdes.*
[73] *Juge des libertés et de la detention.*
[74] *Tribunal de Grande Instance.*

7.79 In such investigations, subject to the approval of the competent judge, officials may also access private homes and documents.

Extra-territorial jurisdiction

7.80 The AMF has jurisdiction over all companies whose securities have been offered to the public, and have been listed and admitted to trading on a French regulated market, regardless of the location of the registered office of the issuer, whether in France, a European member state or in any other country. Therefore, all companies that are listed in France are subject to the AMF's jurisdiction and are bound to comply with applicable laws and regulations.

7.81 The AMF also has jurisdiction over all financial institutions authorized in France or acting in France via the EU freedom to provide services' principle.

7.82 The AMF can also directly request information from investment services providers that are members of a regulated market and are based in any EU member state when, for instance, one of their clients has committed an insider trading breach.[75]

7.83 The AMF can investigate market abuse practices—carried out in France or abroad—concerning securities admitted to trade in a French regulated market. The AMF also has the power to investigate acts carried out in France when they relate to securities admitted to trade on a regulated market of any EU member state, any state member of the EEA Agreement, or any state party to a cooperation agreement with France.

7.84 The AMF may penalize any person, in France or abroad, who has acted in breach of the applicable laws and regulations or professional rules that protect investors against insider trading, market manipulation or the disclosure of false or misleading information to the market, or when that breach may affect the security of investors or the proper functioning of the market.[76]

7.85 French competition rules apply only to practices that have or are likely to have effects in France.[77] However, for the application of Articles 81 and 82 of the EC Treaty, the Competition Council can act upon requests from other national competition authorities of member states or from the European Commission.

7.86 French criminal law is applicable (i) to all offences committed within the territory of the French Republic (ie where one of the elements characterizing the offence

---

[75] Art L. 632-10 of the CMF.
[76] Art L. 621-14 of the CMF.
[77] Paris Court of Appeal, 15 September 1993, *Société Brasseler*; Competition Council decision 89-D-22 of 13 June 1989, *Société Phinelec*.

can be located in France); (ii) to any person who, within the territory of the French Republic, is found guilty of being an accomplice to a criminal offence committed abroad—if this offence is punishable under both French and foreign law, and if it has been established by a final decision of a foreign court; (iii) to any criminal offence committed by a French national outside the territory of the French Republic if the conduct is punishable under the legislation of the country in which it was committed; and (iv) to any criminal offence punishable by imprisonment, committed by a French or foreign national outside the territory of the French Republic and where the victim was a French national at the time of the offence.

For instance, the French Public Prosecutor can initiate criminal proceedings against a foreign company manipulating securities listed on a French regulated market. **7.87**

Protections

While financial regulators and the Public Prosecutor have wide investigative powers, companies and employees enjoy few protections when under investigation. There are no general protections from self-incrimination in France. Moreover, information cannot be withheld from financial and criminal investigators on grounds of professional privilege[78] except representatives of the law,[79] including French lawyers.[80] As a result, French lawyers can invoke the professional secrecy rule to refuse to provide privileged documents. Moreover, under French criminal law, an indicted person[81] or assisted witness[82] can remain silent when appearing before the investigating judge.[83] **7.88**

Similarly, French competition legislation provides few protections for companies under investigation. While under French competition law, there is no provision protecting companies from self-incrimination,[84] limited protection has been acknowledged at the European level.[85] **7.89**

---

[78] With respect to the AMF proceedings, see Art L. 621-9-3 of the CMF, and with respect to Banking commission, *Banque de France* or any judicial authority acting in the context of criminal proceedings, see Art L. 511-33 of the CMF.

[79] *Auxiliaires de justice*

[80] *Avocats.*

[81] *Mis en examen.*

[82] *Témoin assisté.*

[83] Arts 116 and 113-7 of the French Code of Criminal Procedure.

[84] Self-incrimination is the act of accusing oneself of a crime for which a person can then be prosecuted. In competition law, the main problem lies in the application of Art 6(1) of the European Convention of Human Rights.

[85] See Case 374/87 *Orkem SA v Commission*; T-112/98, *Mannesmannröhren-Werke AG v Commission.*

Sanctions for failure to cooperate

7.90 Investigators may for the purposes of their investigation, request the person under investigation to disclose documents, in any form, including data held and processed by telecommunication operators. They may obtain copies of such documents. The AMF can also directly request information from an investment services provider located in an EU member state.

7.91 During the process of collecting evidence, the investigators can directly search the premises without prior contact with the company or request general information on a case by way of questionnaire. In the latter case, answers will lead to further questions until the investigators have a clear understanding of the facts and information from several sources. In this case, the cooperation tends to shift the burden of collecting facts (emails, phone calls etc) to the company.

7.92 When AMF investigators request documents, the person under investigation is under an obligation to disclose such documents, and more generally to cooperate. Hindering an AMF audit or investigation or providing inaccurate information is penalized by two years' imprisonment and a maximum fine of €300,000.[86] AMF investigators may mention in their investigation report any failure to cooperate they have encountered during their investigations. Such failure to cooperate may be considered by the Board of the AMF when deciding whether or not to launch sanction proceedings.

7.93 Under Article L. 450-8 of the French Commercial Code, any action that prevents officials, such as DGCCRF investigators and Competition Council case-handlers, from fulfilling their investigation powers, can be punished by an imprisonment sentence of up to six months and/or a fine of up to €7,500 for natural persons (up to €37,500 for companies).

D. Voluntary Investigations

Benefits and risks of voluntary investigations

7.94 The practice of conducting voluntary internal investigations is still limited in France. The financial regulators and criminal investigators do not generally expect companies to voluntarily communicate the findings of an internal investigation.

7.95 Internal investigations can be initiated at an early stage and before any prosecution or external investigation has been conducted, in cases where facts are discovered

---

[86] Art L. 642-2 of the CMF.

which might result in criminal, civil or regulatory sanctions. The aim is to collect evidence internally in order to obtain a clear picture of the factual situation, assess the consequent legal risks, and take any relevant action (ie taking measures to stop the activity that has produced the risk, identifying and possibly sanctioning the responsible parties, elaborating a strategy of communication, and possibly informing relevant authorities etc).

The main benefit is therefore that of keeping the situation under control by being **7.96** proactive, rather than enduring an external investigation by remaining passive. The main risk for the company is that it might be prosecuted afterwards for not having taken appropriate measures as soon as it had knowledge of the facts. Moreover, the company will have to disclose to the Public Prosecutor any serious crime[87] that has been revealed by a voluntary investigation, if the effects of this serious crime can still be prevented or limited. Failing to do so would be subject to a fine of up to €45,000 and three years of imprisonment.

Finally, as under French law most regulators cannot settle cases, there is a high **7.97** risk that disclosing the results of an internal investigation and evidence of a breach would lead to a regulatory investigation and, as the case may be, to sanctions. Moreover, as a general rule, investigators or prosecutors bear the burden of proving that a breach has been committed. Therefore persons under investigation do not have a general duty to communicate documents or other information to the AMF without prior request. However, companies should be aware that any documents disclosed might provide investigators with sufficient evidence to require the company's further cooperation. Therefore disclosure of any potentially incriminating document or information gathered during an internal audit should be carefully considered, unless it is specifically requested by the investigators.

Ultimately, it will be up to the AMF to decide whether the company's explanations **7.98** are sufficient, or whether it needs to conduct its own investigations and, as the case may be, launch enforcement proceedings. Therefore, conducting an internal investigation may enable the listed company to persuade the AMF, from the first steps of an investigation, that no breach of the relevant rules occurred. If the enforcement committee finally highlights breaches of regulations, an early internal investigation followed by compliance actions prior to an external investigation could lead to lower sanctions.

Events triggering a voluntary investigation

A voluntary investigation will generally result (i) from the internal procedures **7.99** put in place within the company to identify potential wrongdoings ('red flags'),

---

[87] *'Crime'* ie offence punished by at least 10 years' imprisonment.

or (ii) from the fortuitous revelation of facts which could lead to a civil, criminal or regulatory sanction, and therefore need clarification.

7.100 Under French law, the chairman of the board of directors of companies making public offerings shall report to the general meetings internal proceedings put in place by the company. Therefore, such companies will be required to conduct internal investigations. However, companies, even though not making public offerings, tend to voluntarily undertake such investigations in order to improve their internal organization and consequently their performances.

7.101 The costs of internal investigations have to be balanced against the benefits in the light of the concerns as to misbehaviour. Internal investigations are aimed not only at conforming to laws, but also at improving the internal functioning of the company. Non-quoted companies have a greater degree of flexibility in deciding whether to hold a voluntary investigation than French quoted companies which may have little choice in the light of their listing obligations.

7.102 In criminal matters, internal investigations can be conducted in order to assess if a criminal risk exists, that is, whether a criminal offence has been committed, where facts are discovered that might lead to criminal sanctions.

Structuring an internal investigation

7.103 There are no rules in France regulating internal proceedings or investigations. Each internal investigation is therefore structured in order to reach a particular goal. However, several basic principles are most of the time followed when structuring an investigation.

7.104 First, clear direction must be set from the top management: the aims and the means of the investigation must be clear to all participants.

7.105 Secondly, a carefully selected team must be put in place that will be supported by the top management. This core investigation team gathers experts from the company that are independent from the department under investigation, and is led by a manager vested with clear powers to achieve its mission. Most of the time this manager and a senior in-house lawyer will liaise with external counsel during the investigation and will provide them with requested documents.

7.106 Thirdly, a team of dedicated internal experts and external counsel will collect and analyse documents in order to assess the factual situation and will then, on the basis of their findings, conduct any necessary interviews. The choice to have external counsel participate or conduct the interviews will be made on a case-by-case basis. External experts can be appointed at any time to provide further or parallel technical analysis, which can be provided to clients or external investigators at a later stage.

Fourthly, the lawyers will assess the legal risks and provide the top management **7.107** with recommendations as to further steps to be taken.

Apart from internal investigations ordered to cope with a specific crisis, legal pro- **7.108** visions require the structuring of internal controls. Some private organizations, such as the AFEP[88] and the MEDEF,[89] have published documents providing helpful advice such as summarizing in the introduction the various aims of inter- nal proceedings, or a list of subjects that should be mentioned in the report.

In October 2006, the AMF established a working group in order to establish a **7.109** framework of reference for listed companies compelled to set up internal con- trols.[90] The group's guidelines are defined as grounded on general principles aimed at homogenizing practices on an incentive basis but are not binding. For instance, it suggests that the board of the company should be informed of major issues likely to challenge the continuity of operations so that they can check with directors whether the proceedings are reliable.

Using external advisers

In conducting an internal investigation, a company may seek to demonstrate, for **7.110** example, that it takes reasonable care in establishing and maintaining adequate procedures, systems and controls to enable it to comply with its obligations. Furthermore, in the case of crisis, it enables the company to fully assess the seri- ousness of the situation in order to determine what course of action, if any, needs be taken in order to remedy it.

For the purpose of an internal investigation conducted to prevent or manage a **7.111** crisis, a mixed team of experts and external counsel will usually be set up in order to investigate the factual situation, assess the risks, and provide recommendations (see section 'Structuring an internal investigation', 7.103 et seq). Indeed, external advisers often have greater experience than the company itself in conducting investigations as well as the additional resources and manpower necessary to con- duct an investigation efficiently and rapidly. Moreover an external lawyer can offer privileged protection to correspondences exchanged with the company due to its professional secrecy.

In the case where the internal investigation does not aim to address a particular **7.112** crisis, it is often led by members of the committees of a company's Board of Direc- tors. These can include members of any audit, remuneration, or appointment

---

[88] *Association française des entreprises privées.*
[89] *Mouvement des entreprises de France.* AFEP and MEDEF communication, 17 December 2003, available on <http://www.medef.fr/medias/upload/58136_FICHIER.pdf>.
[90] AMF communication dated 31 October 2006. This group issued a report on January 2007 <http://www.amf-france.org/styles/default/documents/general/7602_1.pdf>.

committee. The assistance of external advisers can be requested to establish a general framework laying out how the investigation should be conducted and specifying the applicable legal requirements.

7.113 A market practice has emerged amongst listed companies in France to set up specialized committees to deal with strategic investment, environment and sustainable development issues. Therefore, any of these specialized committees can be mandated to undertake periodic or punctual internal audits to ensure compliance with applicable laws and regulations, and improve the management of the company.

7.114 Even though the practice that has developed is intended to create and maintain a certain percentage of independent directors within these committees, not all potential auditors are or need to be entirely independent of the company.

7.115 A company may also carry out internal investigations by calling upon the company's statutory auditors. In such instances, the auditors' independence from the company is a pre-condition to their carrying out any such investigation.[91] The Financial Security Act has made it clear that statutory auditors must be independent of the company they audit and that they cannot therefore have any interest in the company, its parent company or the companies it controls. In addition, in order to guarantee their independence, individual statutory auditors and members of auditing firms are prohibited from auditing the accounts of listed companies for more than six consecutive financial years.[92] Hence, internal investigations led by statutory auditors are a means of ensuring that such internal audits are carried out as impartially as possible.

7.116 Companies may also launch internal investigations by making use of independent third parties such as lawyers, experts or specialized auditing and advisory firms. In doing so, companies will seek to satisfy themselves as to the competence, efficiency, and independence of the person or company in charge of conducting such investigations. This assures the company that careful scrutiny will be exercised over the matter at hand and that any findings will be reported in a clear and presentable manner. Obviously, outsourcing internal investigations may ensure greater impartiality.

---

[91] Under Art 4 of the Statutory Auditors' Ethical Rules, (*'Code de déontologie'*), independence is a state of mind which is revealed by evidence of integrity, objectivity, competence and the absence of situations that may lead third parties to doubt such independence.
[92] Art L. 822-14 of the French Commercial Code.

Illegal activity during investigations

There is no general rule that prohibits the continuation of potentially illegal con- **7.117**
duct while such conduct or related activity is under investigation. However, naturally once there is concern that illegal conduct has been identified with sufficient
detail, immediate cessation of the relevant activity is the recommended course of
action. To knowingly pursue illegal conduct indeed entails the risk that those
who were aware of the conduct and allowed it to continue become themselves
susceptible of being sanctioned both directly and as accomplices—broadening
the scope of potentially liable parties and increasing the risk of civil liability.

E. Self-reporting

Duty to self-report

While listed companies are under a general obligation to comply with their **7.118**
reporting requirements to the AMF, there is no express obligation to self-report
breaches of corporate laws, regulations or practices under French law.

However, listed companies in France are coming under an increasingly heavy **7.119**
burden to disclose the measures they have implemented to ensure good corporate
governance practices.

The Financial Security Act makes it mandatory for the Board of Directors of a **7.120**
listed company, in addition to its annual general report to the shareholders, to
provide a report to the shareholders meeting on the internal control procedures
put in place by the company[93] and the work accomplished by the Board of
Directors in relation to the internal report.

The specific obligation to report on the preparation and organization of the **7.121**
Board's work is limited to companies making public offerings.[94] The French
Commercial Code[95] provides that, concerning companies making public offerings, the Chairman of the Board of Directors shall describe the preparation and
organization of the Board's work in a report attached to the annual report. This
report shall also include any restrictions made by the Board of Directors to the
Chairman's powers, and the principles and rules issued by the Board of Directors
in order to determine wages and advantages awarded to members of the Board.[96]

---

[93] Arts L. 225-37 and L. 225-68 of the French Commercial Code.
[94] Loi 2005-842, 26 July 2005.
[95] Art L. 225-37 para 6.
[96] Para 7 added pursuant to an act dated 30 December 2006, Art L 225-37 of the Commercial
Code also provides that in listed companies [*sociétés dont les titres sont admis aux négociations sur un
marché réglementé*].

MEDEF and AFEP, and the AMF have also published similar guidance. This reporting obligation is however specific and does not intend to reveal breaches of law or regulation to the shareholders meeting.

Culture of self-reporting

7.122 Despite the absence of a statutory duty to self-report violations of corporate laws, regulations or practices, a culture of self-reporting has nevertheless increasingly developed in France in the area of competition law.

7.123 Competition law has set up a specific leniency procedure which encourages companies engaged in anti-competitive agreements to inform the Competition Council of such agreements, providing evidence and identifying the parties responsible for the agreement. In exchange, the Competition Council may exonerate them from all or part of the fines that may be imposed.

F. Announcements and Public Relations Strategies

Regulatory investigations

External communications

7.124 Unlike in criminal investigations, no provisions define the legal framework governing the status and consequences of the rule of secrecy governing AMF investigations.

7.125 Professional secrecy is imposed, by a specific provision, on the AMF employees, investigators, and experts[97] but not on third parties who would in the course of the AMF's investigation obtain information concerning the investigation. However, an isolated and unpublished decision rendered by the French Supreme Court on 31 May 2005 considered that when a bank, in the course of its professional activities, receives information covered by the professional secrecy binding AMF employees/investigators, this professional secrecy is extended to the bank itself. The Court therefore considered that the bank had rightfully refused to communicate documents concerning the AMF investigation to one of its former employees, who requested them for the purpose of an action against the bank.

7.126 Although this decision is isolated and has not been published by the French Supreme Court, and therefore cannot be considered as stating a clear principle on this issue according to which any communication about an AMF investigation by a company would automatically lead to criminal prosecutions for breach of professional secrecy, it cannot be excluded that all information concerning an AMF investigation could in the future be considered by Courts as being covered by

---

[97] Art L. 621-4 II of the CMF.

professional secrecy and that such secrecy would be imposed on third parties. If this were to be the case, a company would not be entitled to reveal the fact that it is being investigated by the AMF or the details of the investigation, at least on a proactive basis.

However, where the investigation is already known by the public, a few mediatized **7.127** examples demonstrated that, in case of crisis, companies have set up press conferences in order to control the consequences of this revelation. To our knowledge, this external communication did not lead to prosecutions for breach of professional secrecy.

Nevertheless, no general acceptance of external communication regarding AMF **7.128** investigations can be inferred from these exceptional examples. A company which is facing an AMF investigation and wishes to issue external communication on it should deal with this issue very carefully and contact legal counsels prior to any contact with the press, either formal or informal.

Internal communications

When faced with a regulatory investigation the company will need to inform those **7.129** persons who, inside the company, will be required to provide information to the investigators. There is no general obligation to inform all the employees of the existence of an investigation, but it is necessary that those who will be confronted with the investigators be informed as to what precisely is being investigated while avoiding potential accusations of tipping-off or interfering with the investigation. Those employees should also be made aware of their duty to cooperate with the investigators and to not hinder the investigation.

Internal communications must be discreet. No more than a few senior executives **7.130** and in-house lawyers should be in charge of communicating with the employees for the purpose of cooperating with the AMF investigators.

Internal investigations

External communications

A company has no statutory obligations to report or announce an internal investi- **7.131** gation to the market, to its clients or to the public authorities unless a serious crime, which effects could still be prevented or limited has been revealed (see 7.96).[98]

In practice, companies will prefer to keep the internal investigation secret at least **7.132** until the end of the investigation. Depending on the result of the internal investigation, the company will decide whether it might announce it to the market, its clients or the public authorities.

---

[98] Art L. 434-1 of the French Criminal Code.

7.133 From a regulatory perspective, the fact that settlements cannot be reached with the AMF implies that companies are not encouraged to disclose possible breaches to regulations. Indeed, the disclosure of such information could lead the AMF to launch an investigation which could end in a sanction for the company.

7.134 Notwithstanding this, companies may want to inform the AMF, and through their external counsel, that they have reasons to suspect that an illegal practice has been committed and thus inform the AMF that they are beginning an internal investigation. In doing so, the company will be trying to obtain the support of the AMF in order to control the potential consequences of the suspected breach.

7.135 This decision to inform the AMF, which needs to be taken very carefully since it will not be possible to anticipate the reaction of the AMF, will depend in particular on the company's appreciation of whether there is a risk that the suspected illegal practice will be leaked to the market through one source or another (eg by a former employee).

7.136 Finally, the enforcement committee of the AMF might take into account, during the enforcement proceedings on a case-by-case basis, the proactive behaviour of the company which decided to disclose an internal investigation.

Internal communications

7.137 When faced with a regulatory investigation, the company will need to inform those persons who, inside the company, will be required to provide information to the auditors or independent investigators. Those employees who need to be informed, should be informed of their obligations to cooperate and should not be provided with any information or incentives that could hinder the proper conduct of the internal investigation.

Key points for Public Relations strategies

7.138 Because there is no statutory or regulatory obligation to disclose the existence of an internal investigation, the PR strategy will be more a function of the risk, as perceived by the company, that the internal investigation will become public, such as through leaks to the press. When faced with this type of risk, it is generally in the best interest of the company to disclose the existence of the investigation and to assure the market and the public that it is cooperating with the regulatory body or that it has put in place the necessary control procedures that will allow the company to precisely determine the issues at stake and the ways and means of preventing these in the future.

7.139 Public relations should not normally be the determining factor in elaborating the company's strategy regarding the disclosure of voluntary investigations. Those responsible for public relations should defer to senior management and to those in charge of supervising the investigation and ensure that nothing is communicated without the approval of these persons.

A successful public relations campaign ensures that the regulatory body is not **7.140** taken by surprise: when opportune, unofficial contact should be made with the relevant regulator.

G. Best Practices in Document Gathering and Preservation

Expectations of regulators and courts

There is no express general requirement for the company to preserve documents **7.141** even once a regulatory or internal investigation is under way.

However, tampering with evidence, deliberately withholding, falsifying or **7.142** destroying documents that the regulators or other public authorities seek to obtain, will be considered an obstruction of the investigation.

In case of an AMF investigation, any persons involved in, and found guilty of **7.143** such activity including the company itself, may be fined up to €300,000 and/or be sentenced to up to two years' imprisonment.

With regard to criminal investigations, such conduct may be sanctioned by a fine **7.144** of up to €45,000 for an individual and €225,000 for a company, and/or by three years' imprisonment. Thus, prudence is essential, irrespective of any wider concerns associated with evidence destruction.[99]

From a purely commercial perspective the company may find itself in an embarrass- **7.145** ing position if documents are not preserved and the market or judicial authorities may become more suspicious and draw adverse inferences from such conduct. In any event, there is a presumption that companies are aware of their internal affairs.

Rights over documents and confidentiality

Regulators and criminal authorities have different document gathering powers **7.146** from those of an employer. Whereas regulators and public authorities can obtain documents from a company through warrants, and judges can request documents in the course of a hearing, employers do not necessarily have those powers.

While an employee is under a duty to respond to a regulator or to criminal inves- **7.147** tigators, whether or not he responds to his employer depends on his particular duties, as the extent of his cooperation must be commensurate with his position

---

[99] Art L. 434-4 of the French Criminal Code and Art 55 of the French Code of Criminal Procedure.

within the company. For example, cooperation expectations would not be the same for a CFO and a secretary. This idea is based partially on the French principle that the company is presumed to have knowledge of its internal affairs. While there is no case law concerning this point, where an employee's position is such that he would be expected to provide documents, and he refuses to do so, this could result in disciplinary action.

7.148 The key regulators and criminal authorities are provided with extensive investigating powers to carry out their assignments. Therefore, a company can resist an investigator's request when this request is outside the scope of the investigators' assignment order. Hence, when an on-site investigation is conducted, the first reflex is to ask for the investigators' assignment order and to circulate it to senior executives, in-house lawyers and external counsels.

7.149 For the purposes of their investigations, the investigators may require the provision of any records in any medium whatsoever, including data kept and processed by telecommunications operators, and are entitled to obtain copies of such records or data belonging either to the company or to the employees, subject to the reservation that documents concerning employee's privacy are not subject to review.[100]

7.150 A regulator must be duly authorized before it can conduct searches and seizure of documents. Thus, the President of the *Tribunal de grande instance* in whose jurisdiction the relevant premises are located, may, after receiving a reasoned request from the General Secretary of the AMF, authorize such a search.

7.151 In practice, regulatory and criminal investigators may choose either to seize hard disks or to copy them during the investigation, with the assistance of IT experts. However, the company's lawyers will ensure that the investigators comply with privacy rules and erase from the hard disks all personal data concerning the company's employees.

7.152 All materials seized will be protected by the secrecy rules applying to all AMF employees. However, relevant information can be disclosed to foreign regulators in the context of international cooperation.[101]

7.153 Members of the AMF are subject to professional secrecy for all facts, acts or information that they may come across in the course of their activities.[102]

7.154 Similarly, 'members of the AMF shall take steps to ensure that the oral or written information transmitted to them in connection with their functions at the AMF

---

[100] Art L. 621-10 of the CMF.
[101] Art L. 632-16 of the CMF.
[102] Art L. 621-4 II of the CMF and Art 111-9 of the General Regulation of the AMF.

remains strictly confidential'.[103] This duty also applies to the experts appointed in the AMF's Consultative Commissions. Therefore, any discussions with members of the AMF in the course of an investigation must be treated as confidential. Failure by a member of the AMF to respect professional secrecy can give rise to criminal sanctions, namely a fine of up to €15,000 and imprisonment for the term of one year.[104]

Distinction between private and professional information

Hardcopy or electronic files, documents, or emails are deemed to be professional. **7.155** Consequently, the employer may in principle access all employee files, documents and emails except those which the employee has marked as 'private' or 'personal'. Employers cannot, however, access data stored by their employees at home or on a personal PDA.

Employers may only access the employee's hard copy or electronic files or documents **7.156** labelled 'private' or 'personal' in the employee's presence, or after having duly convoked the employee's presence.

Personal or private documents can only be accessed without the employee's permission **7.157** or without duly convening him when a risk or 'particular event' so justifies. The French Supreme Court has not defined such a risk or 'particular event' and it is uncertain whether requests to access personal or private information by public authorities qualify as such.[105]

The situation is different with regard to emails. Emails labelled 'private' or 'personal' **7.158** in the heading, or which are stored in a special folder, cannot be accessed without the employee's express prior consent, as they are covered by the 'secrecy of correspondence' principle. Opening them may constitute a criminal offence. If, in the course of an investigation, an email deemed 'professional' proves in fact to be 'personal' and/or 'private' once the body of the text has been read, the employer is bound to cease reading the email. Accessing information in this manner does not, however, constitute a criminal offence as there is no criminal intent.

Data protection

French law n° 2004-801 of 6 August 2004 has amended French law n° 78-17 **7.159** of 6 January 1978 on Data Processing, Data Files and Individual Liberties

---

[103] Art 111-9 of the General Regulation of the AMF.
[104] Art L. 226-13 of the French Criminal Code.
[105] French Supreme Court, Labor Section, 17 May 2005, n° 1089 FS-PBRI, *Klajer v Sté Cathnet-Science.*

('the French Data Protection Law') in order to implement Directive EC/95/46 on the protection of individuals with regard to the processing of personal data.

7.160   As a result, French Data Protection Law is now in line with the principles set forth in the European Directive. However, two issues, also amended by the law of 6 August 2004, remain specific to France: the strong formalities to be fulfilled prior to implementing a processing of personal data and the wide range of powers granted to the French Data Protection Authority.[106]

Prior formalities

7.161   One of the unique aspects of data protection in France is that the law requires compliance with strong, and sometimes cumbersome, prior formalities obligations.

7.162   According to French Data Protection Law, any automatic processing of personal data must be notified to the CNIL prior to their implementation.[107] No processing of personal data can be performed before such prior notification is filed with the CNIL and the CNIL has issued a formal acknowledgement of receipt.[108] In the context of this notification, the data controller must supply certain details to the CNIL, including the purposes for which the data will be processed and the persons to whom the data might be disclosed.

7.163   However, this prior notification is not required in certain circumstances such as, for example, (i) in case of a CNIL's decision of exemption or (ii) provided certain conditions are met, when a personal data protection officer has been appointed.[109]

7.164   On the contrary, in certain cases, the implementation of personal data processing requires a prior authorization from the CNIL. Such prior authorization is notably required in case of implementation of whistle-blowing systems or biometric data processing.

7.165   Data controllers have to inform and/or to consult works councils in accordance with the provisions of the French Labour Code of any such data processing activity. Pursuant to French Law, the works council must be informed before the implementation of any automatic processing of personal data within the company.

---

106 The *Commission Nationale de l'Informatique et des Libertés*—CNIL.

107 Processing of personal data means any operation or set of operations in relation to such data, and will for instance cover access to employees' communications.

108 *Récépissé de déclaration.*

109 To compensate the absence of notification, data protection officers must hold an updated list of all data processing implemented by their company. They also control compliance of their company with the French Data Protection Law and make an annual report to the CNIL of their activities throughout the year. They cannot be sanctioned by their employer on the grounds of their activities as data protection officers.

This means that the employer is under a duty to inform the works council of the contemplated scheme he or she is about to implement and the purposes thereof. The works council must be informed and consulted before the implementation of any system designed to monitor employees. This means that the employer is under a duty to provide the works council with sufficient information, to enable it to render an opinion on the employer's project.[110] For instance, the implementation of a whistle-blowing system requires the prior consultation of the works council.

CNIL's powers

The wide range of powers granted to the national data protection authority, the **7.166** CNIL, is another peculiarity of the French Data Protection regime.

The CNIL is empowered to supervise compliance with the French Data Protection **7.167** Law. In this respect, to exercise their functions, members of the CNIL are entitled, from 6 am to 9 pm, to access any places, premises, surroundings, equipment or buildings used for the processing of personal data for professional purposes. They equally have the right to request and obtain a copy of all documents necessary for the performance of their mission, regardless of the medium.

The CNIL is also entitled to impose sanctions on any data controller who does not **7.168** comply with French Data Protection Law. The CNIL may therefore issue a formal warning to such data controller and even order a cessation of the breach within a specified time limit. If the data controller does not comply with this order, the CNIL may impose (i) a financial penalty or (ii) an injunction to stop or to interrupt the processing, after fair proceedings. The amount of the financial penalty may be up to €150,000 or, in the event of a repeated breach within five years from the date on which the preceding financial penalty became definitive, up to €300,000.[111]

Moreover, under certain circumstances, non-compliance with the French Data **7.169** Protection Law (such as failure to comply with prior notification/authorization obligations) can amount to a criminal offence, which can trigger sanctions of up to five years' imprisonment and a fine of up to €300,000, for individuals, and €1.5m for legal entities. The CNIL may inform the Public Prosecutor of any offences of which it has knowledge.

---

110 Non-compliance with the obligation to consult with the works council prior to making a decision may be considered obstructing the proper operations of the works council. This is a criminal offence which is punishable by a maximum fine of €3,750 and/or a maximum one year prison term. The works council may also bring a claim against the company in civil court in order to obtain compensation for the violation of its right to be consulted.

111 The CNIL first used this power in a decision of 28 June 2006, the CNIL and imposed upon the French banking group *Crédit Lyonnais* a €45,000 penalty. Several other financial penalties have been issued thereafter (11 financial penalties have been imposed in 2006 for a total amount of €168,300 and 6 between January and June 2007 for a total amount of €120,000).

7.170 As a consequence, the CNIL must be notified of all operation on data (data processing), including transfers of data to regulators or to external advisers. In addition, pursuant to Articles 68 and 69 of the French Data Protection Law, transfers of personal data to countries outside of the EU must be specifically authorized by the CNIL when the recipient countries have not been recognized by the European Commission as providing an adequate level of protection for personal data.

Practical considerations

7.171 When faced with an investigation by a regulator, the company should gather and preserve all potentially relevant documents in an orderly fashion. Before disclosing documents to the regulator, the company must: (i) check that each document relates to the purpose of the inquiry; (ii) make note of all documents requested, presented or checked; (iii) record the source of the document copied by the regulator; (iv) submit voluntarily some professional books or documents which have not been requested by the regulator but that may be favourable to the company's defence (taking legal advice beforehand); and (v) take three copies of each document handed over to the regulator: one copy for the regulator, one for the company and one for the lawyer.

H. Dealing with Privileged Documents

General rules on privilege

7.172 Key regulators and investigators in the context of a criminal investigation enjoy wide investigatory powers that extend to the search of premises and the seizure of documents under certain conditions. Notably, professional secrecy does not protect a company from the financial authorities such as the AMF,[112] the Banking commission or any judicial authority acting in the context of a criminal investigation.[113] AMF's investigators and duly authorized judicial investigators may therefore examine and make copies of the following types of documents: personal calendars, internal reports, diaries (including electronic diaries), external correspondence, company's books, electronic documents, and emails.

7.173 However, all attorney-client correspondence is confidential. Seizure or examination, even brief, of such documents is, in principle, prohibited. When subject to an investigation, the manager in charge of dealing with the investigators will have to pay particular attention to the documents that the investigators want to seize or review. The presence of an external lawyer, when possible, for example when the investigation is conducted by the AMF, should ensure that secrecy is respected.

---

[112] Art L. 621-9-3 of the CMF.
[113] Art L. 511-33 of the CMF.

Legal privilege, as it is known in common law jurisdictions, is a concept foreign to **7.174** French law. This does not mean however that the attorney-client relationship is not protected from intrusions. In fact, French law protects these relationships to a far greater extent than most common law jurisdictions. Attorney-client relationships are in effect covered by professional secrecy rules which extend, inter alia, to any legal advice given by a lawyer to his client, any correspondence between them, as well as any revelations made in the course of their client-attorney relationship. Correspondence between French lawyers is also covered by the professional secrecy rule, unless that correspondence was marked 'non-confidential' or 'official' by its author. But when a lawyer marks correspondence 'non-confidential' or 'official', such correspondence cannot refer to prior correspondence that was not marked 'non-confidential' or 'official'.[114] 'Non–confidential' or 'official' correspondence between French lawyers can be communicated to third parties voluntarily.

The professional secrecy rule is general, unconditional, and unlimited in time. **7.175** Breaching the professional secrecy rule is a criminal offence[115] and any person in possession of such confidential information who discloses such information may be fined up to €15,000 and sentenced to one year's imprisonment.[116]

Specific rules apply to searches of lawyers' offices or homes. These can only be **7.176** carried out where the lawyer's participation in an offence is suspected and if prior judicial authorization is obtained. They must be conducted by an investigating judge (ie in the context of a criminal investigation) in the presence of the *Bâtonnier* (the Chairman of the relevant Bar). Consequently, no search and seizure can be carried out on the premises of a lawyer by the AMF.

It is important to note that written correspondence with in-house counsel is not **7.177** protected by the professional secrecy rule described above. Indeed in-house counsels are not members of the bar. They are therefore not subject to the rules of ethics of the relevant bar. Moreover, as employees of the companies for which they work, they are not independent; they therefore cannot invoke and are not subject to the professional secrecy rule and legal privilege.

Waiving privilege

Whilst a lawyer cannot at any time disclose documents covered by attorney-client **7.178** confidentiality (a client may not even ask his lawyer to disclose on his behalf correspondence covered by the secrecy rule nor can he waive the rule and require that his lawyer, say, testify in an investigation), a client can decide to voluntarily

---

[114] Art 3.2 internal rules of the Paris Bar.
[115] Art 226-13 of the French Criminal Code.
[116] For lawyers, such disclosure will be regarded as both a criminal offence and a disciplinary breach.

disclose correspondence otherwise covered by the secrecy rule to third parties, including a regulator. A client who has decided to voluntarily disclose correspondence otherwise covered by the secrecy rule cannot subsequently invoke this rule in respect of such correspondence. The document that was so disclosed can be used in subsequent proceedings subject to the professional secrecy to which it is bound by the relevant regulator.

Limited waiver

7.179 Although a company may disclose to the AMF documents covered by attorney-client confidentiality, the AMF is bound by professional secrecy and cannot subsequently provide the documents it received from the company to other parties (ie other than the Public Prosecutor or foreign regulators via international cooperation). Therefore, any waiver of privilege to the AMF is in fact a limited waiver.

7.180 A company may also voluntarily disclose documents protected by attorney-client confidentiality to the competition authorities. However, in such a case, it cannot be excluded that the authorities include these documents in their file for use during the investigation. Therefore, they may very well become available to the parties involved in the matter.

Privilege pitfalls

7.181 In order to ensure that all attorney-client correspondence remains confidential and avoid potential pitfalls, it is generally recommended that:

- all privileged documents be clearly marked 'protected by attorney-client confidentiality';
- privileged documents be kept in a secure file marked 'documents protected by attorney-client confidentiality';
- copies of privileged documents not be distributed internally; and
- the company always bears in mind that written correspondence with in-house counsel is not protected by the professional secrecy rule.

I. Managing Regulators

Dialogue with regulators

7.182 It is generally beneficial for companies to maintain open channels of communication with regulators. It could be in the company's interest to take the initiative to inform the AMF of any potential suspicions raised in the course of an internal investigation. By doing so, the company could try to limit the scope of a potential subsequent investigation by the AMF. These types of unofficial discussions should nonetheless be discussed with the company's in-house and external lawyers and their presence at these discussions is often advised. Indeed, since there are no rules concerning dialogue with regulators and it is not possible to settle with the AMF, the risk of the disclosure of information leading to an AMF investigation must be balanced against and the benefit of informing the regulators of a possible situation and thus obtaining their support. An outside counsel's knowledge and expertise of regulator practices could be quite useful in these types of situation.

Control of scope of investigation

The scope of the investigation conducted by the AMF is generally limited to a **7.183** specific stock and time period. Once launched, the scope of the investigation is very hard to control. Moreover, the investigation, whether it is conducted by a regulator or takes place in the context of a criminal investigation, is secret and the company cannot have access to any information relating to the investigation while it is on-going, unless it is considered as an indicted person[117] during a criminal investigation.

Cooperating with the investigators, as described in the previous sections, is prob- **7.184** ably the best way to ensure that regulatory investigations remain focused on the issue in question.

Use of information by regulators

Members of the AMF are subject to professional secrecy for all facts, acts or infor- **7.185** mation that they may come across in the course of their activities.[118]

Similarly, 'members of the AMF shall take steps to ensure that the oral or written **7.186** information transmitted to them in connection with their functions at the AMF remains strictly confidential'.[119] This secrecy is also imposed on the experts appointed in the AMF's Consultative Commissions.[120] Therefore, the AMF cannot disclose, to third parties, any information obtained from outside counsel or the company itself, during the course of an investigation. Failure by a member of the AMF to respect such professional secrecy can give rise to a fine of up to €15,000 and to one year's imprisonment.[121]

---

[117] *Mis en examen.*
[118] Art L. 621-4 II of the CMF and Art 111-9 of the General Regulation of the AMF.
[119] Art 111-9 of the General Regulation of the AMF.
[120] The AMF itself is however not bound by professional secrecy.
[121] Art 226-13 of the French Criminal Code.

Managing multiple regulators

7.187 When a company is the subject of investigations by several national regulators, there are a number of safeguards that protect the company from being subject to concurrent investigations by different regulators on the same matter. For instance, industrial regulators such as the ARCEP, the CRE and the CSA have the power to settle disputes in situations that involve competition issues. The risk of the Competition *Council*'s rulings conflicting with those of the industrial regulators is therefore limited by the existence of so-called 'bridges', reciprocal consultation procedures.[122]

7.188 With regards to French financial regulators (the AMF, the Banking Commission and ACAM), the Supervisory Authorities Board[123] of the financial sector businesses facilitates the exchange of information between the supervisory authorities of financial groups and addresses any questions of common interest relating to the coordination of the control of these groups.[124] However, this exchange of information and coordination does not mean that concurrent investigations cannot be conducted at the same time for different breaches by different regulators.

7.189 When investigations by regulators reveal that a criminal offence has been committed, the matter shall be referred to the Public Prosecutor. Therefore, concurrent investigations can be simultaneously conducted by the AMF, for instance, and the Public Prosecutor where issues regarding market abuses are under scrutiny.

7.190 When a company is the subject of different investigations by regulators from different jurisdictions, concurrent investigations can be conducted at the same time. In this case, foreign regulators tend to directly request information from the company.

7.191 However, under French law, disclosure of financial, economic, commercial or industrial information in view of foreign administrative or judicial proceedings, outside the procedures set forth in international judicial assistance treaties (Law of 26 July 1968) is a criminal offence sanctioned by six months' imprisonment and a fine of up to €18,000. Therefore, a company is under the obligation to refuse any direct communication to foreign regulators, the later being compelled to request information through international cooperation means.

---

[122] See 7.45 on 'Concurrent investigations'.
[123] *Collège des autorités de contrôle des entreprises du secteur financier.*
[124] Art L. 631-2 of the CMF.

J. Managing Employees During Investigations

Powers to compel cooperation

When AMF investigators request documents, the person under investigation is **7.192** under an obligation to disclose such documents, and more generally to cooperate. Hindering an AMF audit or investigation or providing inaccurate information is penalized by two years' imprisonment and a maximum fine of €300,000.[125]

Besides, and as a general rule, evidence must be collected fairly. Thus, evidence **7.193** obtained from employees through threats, during an internal investigation, would be considered as having been obtained illegally and could not be relied upon in the course of disciplinary proceedings.[126]

This principle is less strictly appreciated by criminal courts, as they cannot set **7.194** aside evidence on the sole basis that it has not been collected fairly. Hence, evidence obtained from employees through threats will not necessarily be set aside by criminal courts.[127]

During the course of an investigation, an employer is entitled to ask the employ- **7.195** ees to cooperate within the normal scope of their contractual duties under their employment contracts. The fact that the company is subject to an inquiry does not change the scope of an employee's duties

There is no case law on the specific point of whether employers can require full **7.196** cooperation from an employee during the course of a company investigation. As a general rule, the extent to which an employee must cooperate with his employer will depend on his particular position. Furthermore, French employment law contains a specific principle of loyalty, whereby an employee must perform his contract loyally and in good faith. This loyalty duty could be interpreted as including full cooperation with the AMF, for example.

Often, employees are not directly approached by public authorities with requests **7.197** for evidence. Rather, in the course of an investigation, public authorities may require companies to produce specific documents. Therefore, it would be plausible for employers to serve the role of evidence collectors and request information from their employees to the extent this is commensurate with their duties.

---

[125] Art L. 642-2 of the CMF.

[126] Art 9 of the French Code of Civil Procedure provides that 'it shall be incumbent on each party to prove *in accordance with the law* the constituent facts in view of the success of his claim'.

[127] Art 427 of the French Code of Criminal Procedure provides that 'except where the law otherwise provides, offences may be proved by any means of evidence and the judge decides according to his innermost conviction'.

Again, while there is no case law on this point, where an employee's position is such that he would be expected to provide documents, and he refuses to do so, this could result in disciplinary action being taken by the employer.[128]

Whistle-blowing

7.198 For historical reasons, whistle-blowing is not a culturally accepted practice in France and is generally frowned upon. In addition, France's data collection laws are stricter than EU guidelines on that matter. By way of illustration, since a whistle-blowing procedure involves the collection and processing of employee data, CNIL must be involved whenever a whistle-blowing system is set up in order to ensure data protection and compliance with the French law.

7.199 Pursuant to CNIL guidelines,[129] a whistle-blowing system may only be considered legitimate if it is put in place in order to comply with a legal obligation (statutory or regulatory) or if it is necessary in order to realize a legitimate interest where this legitimate interest is qualified and its realization does not imply any overriding of the interests or fundamental rights and freedoms of the data subjects.[130]

7.200 Under the first consideration, a whistle-blowing system is justified where it is designed to establish internal controls in specific areas. Such an obligation clearly results, for example, from provisions relating to internal controls within credit and investment companies.[131]

7.201 Under the second consideration, French companies listed in the US, or French subsidiaries of US listed companies, which must certify their accounts with the US stock market authorities, clearly have a legitimate interest in setting up whistle-blowing procedures in order to report alleged inappropriate accounting or auditing practices.

7.202 On the other hand, for whistle-blowing systems that are not set up pursuant to statutory or regulatory obligations, which require the establishment of internal controls in financial, accounting, banking and anti-bribery areas, the CNIL will carry out a case-by-case assessment of the legitimacy of the proposed whistle-blowing system. It is difficult, however, to prove that there is a legitimate interest in setting up a whistle-blowing system that falls outside of the above scope.

---

128 Art 427 of the French Code of Criminal Procedure provides that 'except where the law otherwise provides, offences may be proved by any means of evidence and the judge decides according to his innermost conviction'.

129 CNIL's orientation document dated 10 November 2005.

130 French Data Protection Act of 6 January 1978, Art 7(5).

131 Regulation of 31 March 2005 amending Regulation by the Banking and Financial Regulatory Committee, 'Comité de réglementation bancaire et financière', NR 97-02 of 2 February 1997.

Protecting the whistle-blower is a requirement inherent to any whistle-blowing **7.203** system. It is the CNIL's responsibility to ensure that such protection is granted to the whistle-blower under the whistle-blowing system. In particular, pursuant to the Data Protection Act, the whistle-blower's identity must be processed confidentially so that the individual does not suffer any retaliatory action such as termination of employment or a lesser sanction.

Control on threats

According to a recently amended section of the French Labour Code, 'no **7.204** employee may be punished, discharged, or subject to discriminatory measures, directly or indirectly [. . .] for having reported in good faith, to his employer or to a law enforcement or administrative agency acts of corruption that he had knowledge of in the course of his employment'.[132]

As a general principle, employees are protected against disciplinary sanctions fol- **7.205** lowing disclosures to regulators (and more broadly to any public authority) or the employer of acts that might be considered unlawful (such as acts of thefts, corruption, harassment etc), provided that the disclosure was done in good faith.[133] If the disclosure was found to have be done with the sole intent to harm the company or one of its employees, no protection applies.

As a general rule, regulatory authorities conduct their own investigations[134] and **7.206** the employer merely cooperates with the authorities by providing the requested information.[135] For the purposes of the investigation, the regulatory authorities may ask to interview employees of the company, and may also ask that all relevant documentation be made available. Preparing and advising staff prior to or in the course of an investigation conducted by the regulators could be regarded as an obstruction to the investigation. Thus, the need as well as the relevance of preparing the employees should be evaluated carefully on a case-by-case basis.

---

[132] Section L 1161 of the French Labour Code.

[133] French Supreme Court, Labor Section, 14 March 2000, n° 1285 P, *Pitron v Cunéaz* and Section L 1161 of the French Labour Code.

[134] For example, Art 143-1 of the General Regulation of the AMF: 'To ensure the good performance of the market and the conformity of activities of entities or persons mentioned at II of Article L.629-9 of the French Monetary and Financial Code (*"Code monétaire et financier"*) with professional obligations resulting from laws, regulations and professional rules approved by it, the AMF performs controls on documents and at the professional premises of said entities or persons.'

[135] For example, Art 143-3 of the General Regulation of the AMF: 'Persons charged with the mission of control indicate to the entity or the person controlled the nature of the requested information, documents and justifications. They may hear any person acting for or under the authority of the person controlled and likely to furnish information they believe will be useful to their mission. They may verify information transmitted by comparing it with the information obtained from third parties.'

7.207   If an employer conducts an internal investigation at the request of a regulatory authority, whether French or foreign,[136] or on its own volition, it is inconceivable for the employer to take disciplinary action against an employee who disclosed information at his employer's request.[137] As a matter of practice, an employer who wants to conduct an investigation cannot compel the employees to cooperate outside the provisions of their employment contracts.

Representation

7.208   An employee may be assisted during a disciplinary proceeding by an employee of the company (an ordinary employee or a staff representative).

7.209   There is no legal obligation for an employee to appoint his or her own counsel in the case of an investigation conducted by a regulator. Employees are entitled to appoint their own lawyers for assistance and guidance during the procedure, although this is not a common practice since the employees are usually not personally involved. The employee suspected of having committed the wrongdoing that triggered the investigation does, however, have a vested interest in appointing his own lawyer.

7.210   There is no legal provision prohibiting a company from recommending separate counsel for their employees, although this is not common under French law. In any event, the employee's counsel must ensure that he remains independent from his client's employer so as not to breach his professional obligation of maintaining external representation.

Assurances as to confidentiality and privilege

7.211   Information discovered in the course of an investigation can warrant disciplinary action against an employee. In order to ensure full cooperation, individuals participating in the investigation can be reassured that the responses they give will not be used against them in the future, although no formal assurances can be given to the employees that, if the investigation reveals their personal involvement in any wrongdoings, they will not be dismissed. Except if agreed otherwise, there is no special confidentiality guarantee granted to the employees during interviews. As mentioned previously, evidence obtained from employees through threats would be considered as having been obtained illegally and could not be relied upon in the course of disciplinary proceedings.[138] Consequently, the interviews with the employees should be conducted carefully.

---

136 For example, French subsidiaries of US companies that are subject to the reporting and disclosure procedures of the 2002 Sarbanes-Oxley law are likely to conduct internal investigations to determine their conformity with the US legislation.

137 French Supreme Court, Labor Section, 14 March 2000, *Pitron v Cunéaz*.

138 Art 9 of the French Code of Civil Procedure.

However, if the employer asks his corporate counsel to conduct an internal inves- **7.212**
tigation, the lawyer will be subject to its professional ethical rules, in particular to
its professional secrecy rules. As a result, the attorney cannot disclose to a third
party information that he obtained from the company's employees in connection
with advising or defending the company. However, the company's lawyers can
disclose to the company the information he or she obtained from the employee
during the internal investigation.

Ethical implications for counsel

Except where otherwise agreed by the parties, lawyers must not act for several cli- **7.213**
ents where there is a conflict of interest, a risk that professional secrecy will be
breached, or a risk that their independence will be compromised.[139] Thus, where
there is a serious risk of conflict of interest, such as between a company and its
employees, lawyers must obtain the agreement of all the parties involved before
agreeing to assist more than one party.[140]

Conflicts of interest can arise, for example, when the lawyer cannot carry out his **7.214**
work without jeopardizing the interests of one or more of his clients. Accordingly,
when acting for the company's employees, lawyers must ensure that there is no
conflict of interest and no risk of such conflict.

Lawyers are prohibited from taking advantage of the fact that the other party has **7.215**
not appointed and is not assisted by a lawyer. Therefore, the employer's lawyer
must act very cautiously if he or she appears to intervene directly during the investigation. Notably, it is the lawyer's responsibility to ask the unrepresented employee
to appoint his or her own lawyer as soon as he or she feels that the interests of the
employee conflict with those of the company. If the employee chooses not to
appoint his or her own lawyer, he or she must be made aware of the fact that all
information that he or she provides to the company's lawyer will be disclosed to the
company. This might convince the employee to reconsider his or her decision.

Investigations and disciplinary process

The concept of 'gardening leave' does not exist in France. Under French law, an **7.216**
employer can suspend an employee's employment contract in two situations: if the
employee has committed misconduct[141] or pending an investigation into alleged
misconduct.[142] This last type of suspension allows the company to conduct the

---

[139] Art 4.3 of the Internal rules of the Paris Bar Association ('*Règlement intérieur du Barreau de Paris*').

[140] Art 4.4 of the Internal rules of the Paris Bar Association.

[141] *Mise à pied disciplinaire.*

[142] *Mise à pied conservatoire.*

investigation without the possibility of the employee intimidating other employees or destroying evidence. This is generally done in more serious cases, the idea being that it will be possible to conduct the investigation more effectively if the employee is removed from the premises.

7.217   During a suspension, an employee's salary is also suspended. If, following the investigation, the employee is not found to have engaged in misconduct, the employer will be required to compensate the employee for the loss of income during the period of the suspension and will be required to reinstate the employee. However, if the employee is indeed found to have engaged in misconduct, and he is dismissed for gross or wilful misconduct, he will not be paid during the suspension period.

7.218   Employers in France are thus able to retain disciplinary authority over their employees while at the same time complying with an AMF or other investigation. In addition, by suspending an employee, this enables employers to demonstrate to the authorities that they took appropriate action as soon as they became aware of the situation and that they did everything in their power to cooperate with the authorities.

Challenges posed by ex-employees

7.219   In the context of an internal investigation, an employer wishing to obtain information from former employees regarding facts they might have learned during their employment cannot compel cooperation. The former employee, who is no longer in a subordinate relationship with the employer, has no obligation to respond to the employer's demands.

7.220   In the context of a regulatory investigation, regulatory authorities, as a general matter, have broad powers and are authorized to conduct investigations in application of their powers. They may interrogate anyone who is likely to furnish information deemed useful to their investigation, including former employees of the company.

7.221   For example, AMF investigators may verify information it received by comparing it with the information obtained from a third party.[143] In this particular situation, former employees are required to answer the questions of the AMF investigators.[144] Further, the former employee has to be considered free from any contractual obligation of secrecy vis-à-vis the employer and cannot be judicially pursued for the disclosure of confidential information.[145] Any contractual provision to the contrary is without legal effect.

---

[143] Art 143-3 of the General Regulation of the AMF.
[144] Art 143-4 of the General Regulation of the AMF.
[145] Application of the theory of Legitimate Authority (*'Autorité Légitime'*).

Payment of legal fees/indemnification/fee advances

Companies may indemnify employees for the cost of representation by separate **7.222**
legal counsel, as long as this does not infringe on the counsel's independence.
Potential infringements are to be appreciated on a case-by-case basis. In order to
avoid any risk, it is recommended that the company not indemnify the employees for their legal costs before the matter is fully completed. In practice, the
employer usually agrees to bear the financial responsibility for the expenses of the
employees' representatives including the employee's lawyer's fees.

French rules of ethics require lawyers to refuse to allow their fees to be paid by a **7.223**
third party if they know that the third party is not informed of the circumstances
of payment, or if, by making payment, the third party would act in violation of
the law, regulations or its articles of incorporation.[146] Thus, companies will only
be authorized to advance fees for representation by separate legal counsel in connection with internal or regulatory investigations if they are aware of the consequences of such payment, and if by proceeding with such payment, they do not
violate the law, regulations or their articles of incorporation.

If an employee is found guilty of a legal offence that was prejudicial to the **7.224**
employer, the employer cannot be reimbursed by withholding the attorney's fees
from the employee's salary. This would be in violation of the legal prohibition
against pecuniary punishment.[147] However, in the event that the employee has
committed wilful misconduct (*Faute lourde*),[148] the employer may be able to take
legal action against the employee to obtain damages to repair any injury resulting
from the employee's conduct. Damages may include attorney's fees paid by the
company for the defence of the employee. It is important to note that this payment must be ordered by a judge.

Joint defence agreements can be concluded between a company and its **7.225**
employees.

Best practices

In the context of an internal investigation, by or at the initiative of a regulatory **7.226**
authority, several precautions should be taken.

In practice, as the investigation will affect the general functioning of the com- **7.227**
pany,[149] it is necessary to inform the works council of the nature and scope of the

---

[146] Art 11.7 of the Internal Rules of the Paris Bar Association.
[147] Court of Appeals of Dijon, Labour Section, 23 May 1995, *Mourey v SA MFLS Forézienne*.
[148] French Supreme Court, Labor Section, 4 February 1988, *SARL Le Cabinet J & F Athenoux v Boukris*.
[149] Art L. 432-1 Para 1 of the French Labor Code.

investigations to be conducted at the company's premises. It is recommend to strengthen the legal confidentiality obligation of the works council members by entering into specific non-disclosure agreements, even though the enforceability of such documents could be difficult. The works council should also be informed and consulted if the employer intends to install a system (or modify an existing system) to monitor the activities of employees.[150]

7.228 If the investigators access files stored on the company's computers during the investigation, the employer is not exempt from his obligation to respect the individual freedoms and liberties of the employees. The employer may not access files marked 'personal' without the employee being present. However, all other files may be accessed by the employer as they are presumed to be professional.[151]

7.229 If investigators collect personal data regarding the employees, the investigation should be declared to the National Commission of Data Processing and Liberties[152] to guarantee the protection of personal information and obtain the Commission's opinion.[153]

7.230 There is utmost difficulty in properly advising companies which are subject to an investigation. It is essential to stress that each case must be dealt with on a case-by-case basis, bearing in mind that one must not obstruct an investigation by regulating authorities, whose powers are granted by law.

K. Winding up an Investigation

7.231 The company has no general statutory obligations to report or announce an external or voluntary internal investigation to the market. The issue is rather whether the substantive position (rather than the fact of an investigation) could have a material effect on the share price such that exchange requirements mandate a statement to the market.

7.232 The decision to disclose the report or the conclusion, in full or in part, either to the regulator (if purely internal) or to the public is, therefore, a question that needs to be dealt with on a case-by-case basis. It will depend largely on what is discovered, the nature of public interest and any commitments made at the outset. However, as always, a report is a potentially dangerous document: if there is a problem and the report is honest, it will be extremely valuable to any hostile party and it is, therefore, important to take extreme care as to what is prepared and what commitments are made as to what will be produced.

---

150 Art L. 432-2-1 Final Para of the French Labor Code.
151 French Supreme Court, Labor Section, 18 October 2006, *Le Fur v Sté Techni-Soft*.
152 *Commission nationale d'information et des libertés*.
153 Arts 15 et seq of the Decree N° 2005-1309 dated 20 October 2005.

If, at the outset of its voluntary investigation, the company decided to inform the **7.233** AMF of its decision to carry out a voluntary investigation, it will need to inform the AMF of the outcome. Typically, this will have been done if the company believed that there was a risk of uncontrolled disclosure of the investigation to the market. In this situation, the ways and means through which the market will be informed will be determined by agreement with the AMF (eg disclosed in the next AMF filing—a more discreet option—or will be the subject of a specific release).

If the investigation was not disclosed at the outset, the outcome will dictate the **7.234** company's attitude going forward. If the findings are that no wrongdoings have been committed, then no information is required. However, if the results are likely to affect a company's share price, then the company will need to inform the AMF and the market. Practically speaking, the company will usually have identified the probable outcome of the investigation well before a final report is issued. An investigation is usually a rather long process and the company will have been monitoring its progress throughout, such that, when it appears that there were wrongdoings that would impact the share price, the company does not have the luxury of waiting for the final report but may well have to inform the market in advance. Moreover, it may be sensible to keep the AMF informed of the likely outcome so that there are no last minute surprises.

It is usually important to consider internally well in advance whether a formal **7.235** report will be necessary, and if so, in what form this should be done. There may well be differing views within the company, and it is usually prudent to discuss this issue at an early stage—not least because it may inform the level of detail to which work is done in the investigation.

Public expectations and reactions also need to be managed. The PR strategy **7.236** should ensure that capital markets and the press are well prepared for any announcement, again in order to avoid any last-minute surprise. Perhaps even more importantly regulators should not be taken by surprise by any public announcements. When opportune, unofficial contact should be made with the relevant regulator to alert them to potential public developments.

L. Litigation Risks

Risks of criminal litigation commenced by regulators

Although the AMF may conclude in the course of its supervisory and investiga- **7.237** tive work that a criminal offence may have been committed, it does not have the authority to investigate criminal matters.

Consequently, when the facts of a case investigated by the AMF suggest that a **7.238** criminal offence has been committed, the Board of the AMF must disclose its investigation report to the Public Prosecutor. The Public Prosecutor is entitled to obtain all information obtained by the AMF in connection with its investigation, and must examine the AMF's report and decide whether or not to pursue the matter and bring criminal proceedings.

7.239 A person may therefore face both AMF enforcement proceedings and criminal proceedings for the same act.

7.240 For example, the followings facts are subject to two separate sets of rules (criminal and administrative): insider trading,[154] market manipulation,[155] and the dissemination of false or deceptive information.[156] Hence, a person guilty of such practices may be liable to the AMF for sanctions as well as a fine of up to €1.5m or ten times the profit resulting from the prohibited trading and/or two years' imprisonment under criminal law. This combination of sanctions has been criticized for being in conflict with the rule *non bis in idem*, under which a person cannot be sanctioned twice for the same offence.[157]

7.241 However, French criminal courts are not bound by the AMF's interpretation of the facts and may take a different view, even though the AMF's recommendation or decision is likely to be taken into account for the purposes of determining whether a criminal offence has been committed. For example, French criminal courts tend to prosecute individuals rather than legal entities, while the AMF tends to initiate enforcement proceedings against both, when both are involved. Moreover, the Criminal Court may order the deduction of the amount of the fine already imposed by the AMF from the one this Court awards.[158]

7.242 The AMF may also forward its investigation report to other regulatory authorities such as the ACAM or foreign regulators if the case falls within their jurisdiction.

Risks of other proceedings being commenced by regulators

7.243 The AMF has discretion as to whether or not to pursue an enforcement action against a corporation. However, the AMF will be time-barred from bringing any enforcement action if more than three years have elapsed since the alleged breach,

---

[154] Art 622-1 of the General regulation of the AMF and Arts L. 465-1 et seq of the CMF.

[155] Art 631-1 of the General regulation of the AMF and Art L. 465-2 s 1 of the CMF.

[156] Art 632-1 of the General regulation of the AMF and Art L. 465-2 s 2 of the CMF.

[157] However, the EU Directive 2003/6 on market abuses provides that administrative sanctions for market abuses must be implemented without prejudice of the states' rights to impose criminal sanctions. Moreover, France considers that the *non bis in idem* principle only applies where two sanctions are awarded for the same facts by criminal Courts, according to the saving clause (*réserve*) made by the French Republic to the European Convention of Human Rights.

[158] Art L. 621-16 of the CMF.

and no action was taken by the AMF to detect, record or sanction this breach during that period.[159]

The Board of the AMF considers the following factors when deciding whether to **7.244** initiate enforcement proceedings against a company:[160] whether the practices are likely to: jeopardize the rights of investors; disrupt the normal functioning of the market through market manipulation;[161] procure an unfair advantage for the parties having a direct or indirect interest in the company; jeopardize equal disclosure of information to investors, or the treatment of investors or their interests; or enable the issuer or investors to benefit from misconduct on the part of financial intermediaries.

The Board may also bring enforcement proceedings if a professional on the finan- **7.245** cial market breached a disciplinary or professional rule. When pursuing an administrative or a disciplinary action against an individual for corporate misconduct, the AMF will rely on the same criteria used for companies.

Risks of private civil litigation

Since regulatory enquiries and investigations by the AMF are confidential, civil **7.246** plaintiffs will in practice find it difficult to bring an action based on the AMF's investigations alone.

However, the AMF generally publishes its decisions. This makes them available **7.247** to civil plaintiffs who are therefore free to use them as evidence.

For example, if an investigation has determined that the company's accounts do **7.248** not reflect the true financial situation of the company, a third party who, say, underwrote a bond issue based on those accounts could bring an action in tort against the company in order to obtain compensation for the losses sustained as a result of the misleading information contained in its accounts. The same would be true of a bank that lent money on the basis of inaccurate accounts.

Relevance of investigation report

A company does not have, as a matter of principle, a duty to disclose its internal **7.249** investigations' reports to the regulators.[162] However, these reports could be seized during a dawn raid. Moreover, the regulator or the judge may take into account the fact that a company decided to voluntarily disclose such reports. As the best behaviour will depend on the facts of each particular case, companies should

---

[159] Art L. 621-15 of the CMF.
[160] Art L. 621-14 of the CMF.
[161] *Manipulation de cours.*
[162] See section on external communication.

contact their counsel in order to assess the situation and determine whether they should disclose internal investigations' reports to the investigators on a proactive basis.

7.250 In a civil action, the plaintiffs would not have access to the report or, more generally, to the AMF or any other regulator's case file. Moreover, nothing contained therein may be disclosed. The only document in fact available to the plaintiff will be the regulatory decision (which is, with respect to the AMF, generally published) but which, as a matter of law, is not res judicata as concerns the Civil Courts. As a practical matter, its weight should not be neglected. Indeed, regulators are viewed by French courts as specialists in their area and are therefore considered reliable.

7.251 However, in criminal matters, which may include civil claims for compensation brought within criminal matters, the investigation report will be communicated by the regulator to the Public Prosecutor. Where the facts reveal that a criminal offence has been committed, the investigation report would then become part of the criminal file.

M. Settlement with Regulators

Process

7.252 The question as to whether the AMF should be authorized to settle in the framework of disciplinary or administrative proceedings has been debated on a number of occasions in recent years. However, for the time being, the AMF is not authorized to enter into settlements.

7.253 The Public Prosecutor[163] enjoys discretionary power to decide whether criminal proceedings should be initiated, after having analysed the seriousness of the potential offence and the evidence of the facts at his disposal. In France, criminal actions emerging from a regulatory investigation are not likely to be settled: if the regulator considers that an offence has been committed and therefore refers it to the Public Prosecutor, a prosecution is likely to be undertaken.

7.254 In addition to the 'leniency procedure' (see 7.60), there exists, under French competition law, a 'settlement procedure', which allows parties to anti-competitive practices to benefit from reduced fines if they do not object to the allegations made against them and if they undertake to alter their conduct in the future. In such cases, the maximum amount of the penalty incurred is reduced by half.[164]

---

163 *Ministère public.*
164 See Art L. 464-2 III of the French Commercial Code.

Admission is a fundamental part of the leniency procedure. As far as the 'settle- **7.255**
ment procedure' is concerned, the parties must not be opposed to objections by
the competition authority. Finally, formal admission is not as such requested in
the 'commitments' procedure, although it could be argued that agreeing to
undertake certain commitments could lead, to a certain extent, to an admission
of guilt.

Impact if under investigation by multiple regulators

In principle, a formal settlement or informal arrangement with a regulator will **7.256**
have no impact on other regulators which are investigating different breaches
which fall within their jurisdiction. Therefore, reaching an arrangement with one
regulator does not have any impact on the approach taken by another.

As indicated above, on 11 April 2006, regarding its leniency policy, the French **7.257**
Competition Council agreed not to transfer to the criminal prosecution cases of
individuals employed by or affiliated with a company benefiting from the leniency
programme. Thus a competition leniency agreement, albeit short of a formal
'settlement' should prevent criminal proceedings against employees. However, a
criminal prosecution could have been conducted in this case if a complaint had
been filed before an Investigating Judge. If criminal offences had been committed, the leniency proceedings under competition law would not have hindered a
criminal judge to award criminal sanctions.

Plea bargaining and amnesty arrangements

A French version of plea bargaining or *comparution sur reconnaissance préalable de* **7.258**
culpabilité (CRPC) was recently introduced. This procedure is not available to
companies in proceedings before the *Commission des Sanctions* of the AMF—as
set out above, there is no ability of the AMF to settle matters. Rather, it is only
available when criminal proceedings have been initiated. Where an accused party
admits that he or she is guilty of a criminal offence punishable by a fine or a jail
sentence not exceeding five years, the Public Prosecutor[165] may, on his or her own
motion or at the request of the accused party or his or her lawyer, have recourse
to plea bargaining. If the accused party agrees to the sanction proposed by the
Public Prosecutor, he or she must appear before the President of the *Tribunal de
grande instasnce*, who decides whether or not to approve the 'agreement'.[166] The
agreement only concerns the sentence, and the scope of the offence is
non-negotiable.

---

[165] Pursuant to Art L. 621-20-1 of the CMF.
[166] Art 495-7 et seq of the French Code of Criminal Procedure.

7.259 Insider trading,[167] market manipulation,[168] and dissemination of false or deceptive information[169] are subject to fines of up to €1.5m or ten times the profit resulting from the prohibited dealing and/or two years' imprisonment. Therefore, plea bargains would be possible for these offences.

N. Conclusion

7.260 The AMF is a powerful institution. Unlike its counterparts in other countries, the AMF not only investigates and prosecutes but also imposes sanctions which can amount to €1.5m or ten times the profits resulting from the commission of market abuses.

7.261 Sanctions imposed by the AMF do not preclude subsequent criminal proceedings if the facts of the case fall within the scope of a defined criminal offence, although the sanction imposed by the AMF may be discounted from the fine imposed by the criminal courts.

7.262 In recent public declarations, the Chairman of the AMF has stated that the AMF will lobby to have the ceiling on sanctions raised and to be allowed to settle matters.

7.263 A report dated January 2008 requested by the Ministry of Justice on the decriminalization of business law reopened the discussions regarding concurrent proceedings leading to two different sanctions (criminal and administrative) for the same facts. The report proposes (i) to create joint investigation teams composed of AMF investigators and criminal investigators under the authority of the Public Prosecutor and (ii) to vest the Public Prosecutor with the power to direct each case before a criminal court or the AMF (the AMF would have to stay the administrative proceedings during this preliminary stage). As a consequence, the same facts would not lead to two different sanctions. However, the implementation of these proposals remains uncertain.

7.264 Nonetheless, the general trend is that of increasing severity in dealing with market offences, and nothing seems to suggest that this trend will be reversed in the coming years.

7.265 The amount of the fines imposed by the French competition authorities has also increased, and this trend will continue. In addition, the new leniency and settlement procedures encourage companies to better cooperate with the

---

[167] Art 622-1 of the General regulation of the AMF and Arts L. 465-1 et seq of the CMF.
[168] Art 631-1 of the General regulation of the AMF and Art L. 465-2 s 1 of the CMF.
[169] Art 632-1 of the General regulation of the AMF and Art L. 465-2 s 2 of the CMF.

competition authorities. In this respect, the leniency procedure inter alia provides a new option for companies which, following an internal investigation, 'realize' that they have already infringed on or are currently infringing on competition rules.

Given this increased regulatory scrutiny in France together with increasingly **7.266** severe penalties, companies are becoming more aware of the need to institute stringent checks and balances and ensure compliance with all regulatory requirements. Companies are becoming more proactive in investigating their own affairs in order to keep regulators at bay or be treated more leniently. This trend, whilst not as developed as in the US and UK, looks likely to gather momentum over the next few years, and companies will be more inclined to react to any discovery of misconduct and control the investigation process themselves.

8

INVESTIGATIONS IN SPAIN

A. Introduction[1]

8.01 Over the last few years, Spain has seen a marked increase in regulatory investigations. International corporate scandals, such as Enron and Parmalat, have led to a number of legal reforms (including the enactment of soft law on corporate governance), which have resulted in stricter regulation and closer supervision of listed companies and their personnel.

8.02 Law 44/2002, of 22 November 2002, on Reforms in the Financial System, designed to increase the efficiency and competitiveness of the Spanish finance system and to implement the EU Directive on market abuse, has had a significant role in bringing about this increased regulation. Furthermore, Law 26/2003, of 17 July 2003, which modified Law 24/1988, of 28 June 1988, on the Securities Market and the Public Limited Company Law, introduced a number of important measures to help ensure transparency in public corporations, in light of the recommendations of the Winter Report.[2] Finally, Law 6/2007, of 12 April 2007, and Law 47/2007, of 19 December 2007, have also made material amendments to the Securities Market legislation, enhancing the transparency of the markets and the investigating powers of the National Securities Market Commission (CNMV).[3]

---

[1] Contributors: Javier Bau, Fernando Bedoya, Christian Castellá, Raquel Florez, Sergio Miralles, Rafael Murillo.

[2] The Winter Report or Report of the High Level Group of Company Law Experts chaired by Jaap Winter, presented on 4 November 2002, which focused on corporate governance in the EU and the modernization of European company law.

[3] *Comisión Nacional del Mercado de Valores.*

Royal Decree 1333/2005, of 11 November 2005, built upon Law 24/1988 on **8.03** market abuse in the stock market, to complete the implementation in Spanish Legislation of the new EU regulation on market abuse, and was further instrumental in creating this new regulatory regime.

The CNMV, responsible for the supervision, inspection, and discipline of the **8.04** securities market, is the key regulatory authority likely to conduct investigations in Spain.[4]

The introduction in 2005 of new internal regulations has provided the **8.05** CNMV with the power to investigate and pursue infringements on the basis of accusations from members of the public. This initiative allows reports of violations to be treated separately from claims, complaints and other written communications to the CNMV, which are managed by the Investors Assistance Office and generally relate to deficiencies at investment firms, thus enabling it to discharge its role of ensuring market supervision and discipline more effectively.

However, the investigation tools and the material and human resources of the **8.06** CNMV are still insufficient given the number of entities and activities subject to its supervision.[5]

In 2006, the number of investigations leading to penalty procedures dropped for **8.07** the second year in a row. However, as in 2005, the complexity and relevance of the cases were certainly high. Ten penalty procedures[6] commenced in 2006 investigating 13 alleged violations. Moreover, the CNMV concluded 14 investigations of cases related to 22 violations.

Thirty penalties were imposed, comprising 29 economic sanctions (for an aggre- **8.08** gate amount of more than €2.3m) and a suspension in respect of certain investment services. The most relevant were the penalties imposed upon Deutsche Bank AG London for insider trading in the acquisition of shares of Ebro Puleva, SA, which included a fine of €1m and a three-month suspension in respect of certain investment services.

---

4 See the chart summarizing the cases investigated by the CNMV in 2005 and 2006 annexed to this chapter.

5 According to the statements of the president of the CNMV, Mr Julio Segura, in a conference of 18 February 2008.

6 Under Spanish law, an administrative penalty procedure generally commences with a resolution of the instructing body of an administration informing of the facts and the legal merits that may lead to a penalty. The entity the subject of such penalty procedure should then have the opportunity to make relevant representations in its defence. Afterwards, the instructing body may issue a proposal for a sanction, which may be confirmed by the sanctioning body of the relevant administration after reviewing further representations made by the subject of the penalty procedure.

8.09 Investigations conducted by the Bank of Spain (BS) in 2006 led to 17 proceedings being commenced against supervised institutions[7] and individuals and 46 proceedings against the directors or managers of such institutions.

8.10 In July 2007, the new Competition Act[8] was finally approved by the Spanish Parliament, and entered into force on 1 September 2007. The main principle that has inspired the whole reform process is the closer alignment of the Spanish anti-trust regime to European Community rules. One of the most important changes brought about by the new Competition Act is the introduction of a leniency programme similar to the existing leniency system under EU law, which is expected to lead to more investigations by the Spanish competition authorities.

8.11 Finally, the Executive Service for the Prevention of Money Laundering and Monetary Offences (SEPBLAC), carried out 33 inspections while reviewing the procedures and bodies in charge of the internal control systems of obliged entities aimed at the prevention of money laundering. These inspections led to 206 correction measures. The number of inspections in this particular area is still not very high given the number of entities subject to money laundering obligations (8,990 in 2006).

8.12 Despite the increase of legislation in respect of regulated activities, the new regulations do not create any obligations to notify to the authorities possible infringements, or provide for the possibility of avoiding or reducing eventual sanctions by self-reporting the infringements. Moreover, although the general law on administrative bodies[9] provides for the possibility of reaching settlement agreements with public bodies as a way of ending an administrative procedure, this option is not available in the case of regulatory investigations.

8.13 The lack of any mechanism to communicate and negotiate with regulators following a voluntary internal investigation is slowing the trend for companies to conduct voluntary internal investigations in Spain. Although companies may choose to conduct internal investigations if they discover signs of infringements, this practice is still not as widespread as in countries such as the US and UK and its focus is purely internal governance or preparatory work in reaction to, or in anticipation of, proposed regulatory action.

---

[7] These included proceedings against one bank, one branch of an EU credit entity operating in Spain, one credit financing entity (*establecimiento financiero de crédito*) two appraisal companies (*sociedades de tasación*), five currency exchange bureaux, two non-authorized currency exchange bureaux and five proceedings for infringements of the duties regarding minimum reserves ratios.

[8] *Ley 15/2007, de 3 de julio, de Defensa de la Competencia.*

[9] Act 30/1992, of 26 November, on the Legal Regime of the Public Administrations and Common Administrative Procedure.

B. Regulators

Spain has several regulatory bodies empowered to carry out corporate investiga- **8.14**
tions. All of these entities are public bodies with wide-ranging powers to investigate, control and penalize the companies that fall under their jurisdiction.

Key regulators

National Securities Market Commission (CNMV)

The CNMV is the public body responsible for supervising and inspecting the **8.15**
Spanish securities markets and the activities of all the participants (both legal
entities and individuals) in those markets.

The purpose of the CNMV is to ensure the transparency of the Spanish securities **8.16**
markets, the correct formation of prices in it, and to protect investors. The CNMV
promotes the disclosure of any information required to achieve these goals.

The entities that are subject to the supervision of the CNMV are referred to in **8.17**
Article 84 of the Securities Market Act 24/1998, of 28 July 1998 (SMA), and can
be summarized in the following outline.

Table 8.1 Entities supervised by the CNMV

Entities directly regulated by the SMA	Number
Official markets	8
Central counterparties, settlement and clearing systems of markets created according to the provisions of the SMA	5
Spanish and non-communitarian investment services firms operating in Spain	120
Investment funds and their managing companies	6.141
Private equity firms and their managing companies	221
Managing entities of the securitization funds	8
Entities regulated by way of their transactions connected with the securities market	**Number**
Securities issuers	680
Banks and savings banks	204
Investment services firms operating in Spain which are authorized by another EU member state	973
Funds operating in Spain which are authorized by another EU member state	340
Investors, and in general terms, any individual company	N/A

Source: CNMV

8.18   The CNMV exercises power both over the legal entities themselves and directors, executives and people with similar positions within these firms.

8.19   The CNMV has the power to impose sanctions for infringements of the rules over which it presides. The sanctions available to the CNMV in respect of an infringement depend on the nature of the infringement. An infringement may be a 'very serious infringement', a 'serious infringement' or a 'minor infringement'.

8.20   Very serious infringements[10] by persons within the CNMV's jurisdiction include, among others:

- failure to comply with rules governing the markets in which they operate or disregarding instructions given by the CNMV;
- deficiencies in the management or accounting structure or in the internal control procedures within firms subject to prudential supervision by the CNMV, if such deficiencies endanger the solvency or viability of the firm;
- infringements of the prohibition established in paragraph 4 of Article 12 of the Securities Market Act;[11]
- failure to disclose, or incorrect disclosure of, significant holdings;
- market manipulation inducing a significant alteration in the quotation of securities;
- insider dealing;[12] and
- obstruction of inspections.

8.21   Sanctions for very serious infringements include:[13]

- suspension or restriction of the type or volume of securities market transactions or business that the offender may carry out for a period not greater than five years;
- suspension of membership of an official or unofficial secondary market for a period not greater than five years;

---

[10] The SMA, Art 99, sets out the complete list of very serious infringements.

[11] Entities entrusted with keeping book entry records and members of securities markets may not process transfers or pledges nor make the relevant entries until the person making the disposition returns the certificates previously issued to him. The obligation to return the certificate lapses when the certificate has expired.

[12] Insider dealing will be a very serious infringement when the volume of funds, securities or financial instruments used in committing the infringement is significant, or where the offender acquired the information through membership of the issuer's governing, management or controlling bodies or in the course of his or her profession, work or functions, or where the party appears or should have appeared in the registers referred to in the SMA, Arts 83 and 83 *bis*.

[13] The SMA, Art 102, sets out the full list of available sanctions for very serious infringements.

- withdrawal of authorization in the case of investment services firms, public debt market registered dealers and other firms registered with the CNMV;[14]
- public reprimand;
- removal from office and disqualification of the offender from holding directorships or executive posts at the same firm for a period not greater than five years; and
- removal from office and disqualification of the offender from holding directorships or executive posts at any other financial institution of the same kind for a term not greater than ten years.

Serious infringements[15] include: **8.22**

- failure to disclose, deposit or publish a significant fact as required by Article 112.2 of the SMA;[16]
- failure to make required filings with the CNMV in a timely manner;
- failure to draft or publish the annual report on corporate governance referred to in Article 116[17] of the SMA;
- failure by firms[18] to comply with regulations regarding the accounting of transactions, the preparation of accounts and the way in which books and records must be kept, and with the rules on consolidation;
- breach of the rules of conduct;
- market manipulation (where not considered very serious); and
- insider dealing (where not considered very serious).

Sanctions for serious infringements[19] include: **8.23**

- public reprimand;
- suspension or restriction of the type or volume of securities market transactions or business that the offender may undertake for a period not greater than one year;

---

[14] Branches of investment services firms authorized by another EU member state can be prohibited from commencing new operations in Spanish territory in place of withdrawal of CNMV authorization.

[15] The SMA, Art 100.

[16] The SMA, Art 112.2, establishes:

The signing, extension, modification of a shareholder agreement which addresses the exercise of voting rights in Shareholders' Meetings, or which restricts or conditions the free transferability of shares or convertible or exchangeable bonds of listed companies, must be disclosed immediately to the company in question and to the National Securities Market Commission, accompanied by a copy of the clauses of the shareholder agreement itself which affect the voting rights or which restrict or condition the free transferability of the shares or convertible or exchangeable bonds. Once these disclosures have been made, the document containing the shareholder agreement must be recorded in the Mercantile Registry in which the company is registered. The shareholder agreement must be published as a significant disclosure. Until the disclosure, deposit and publication as a significant event occur, the shareholder agreement shall have no effect on the aforementioned matters, without prejudice to the remaining applicable regulations.

[17] The SMA, Art 116, establishes the rules on when and how the annual report on corporate governance should be published.

[18] As envisaged by the SMA, Art 86.

[19] The SMA, Art 103, sets out the full list of available sanctions for serious infringements.

- suspension of membership of an official or unofficial secondary market for a period not greater than one year; and
- disqualification for a period not greater than one year from holding executive office in the firm where the infringement occurred.

8.24 Sanctions imposed for serious infringements are published in the Official State Gazette once they have become final.

8.25 Minor infringements[20] can also result in CNMV sanctions. Breaches of obligations envisaged in the regulations concerning organization and control of the securities market which are not serious or very serious infringements constitute minor infringements. The sanctions for minor infringements can include a private reprimand and fine of up to €30,000.[21]

8.26 It should be noted that when the offending firm is a credit institution, a report from the Bank of Spain is an obligatory prerequisite for imposing sanctions.[22]

Bank of Spain (BS)[23]

8.27 The start of Stage Three of the Economic and Monetary Union (EMU) on 1 January 1999 and the creation of the European System of Central Banks (ESCB) and the European Central Bank (ECB) have meant that several of the functions traditionally performed by the BS have had to be redefined.[24]

8.28 The BS adopts regulations relating to monetary policy, the promotion of stability and proper functioning of the financial system and other regulations for the exercise of the rest of its powers, which provide the framework for the exercise of its functions.

8.29 The BS regulates the elements of the finance industry, seeking to make it more stable. It supervises the solvency and specific regulatory compliance of credit institutions, savings banks, credit cooperative banks, the branches of foreign credit institutions, specialized credit institutions and electronic money issuers.[25] It also supervises mutual guarantee and re-guarantee companies, currency exchange bureaux and appraisal companies. The BS also cooperates with the

---

[20] The SMA, Art 101, sets out the full list of minor infringements.
[21] The SMA, Art 104.
[22] The SMA, Art 97.1.
[23] *Banco de España.*
[24] Act 13/1994 of Autonomy of the Bank of Spain was amended by Act 66/1997, of 30 December, and Act 12/1998, of 28 April, so as to ensure the full integration of the BS into the ESCB. Therefore, in the exercise of the functions arising from its status as an integral part of the ESCB, the BS follows guidelines and instructions from the ECB.
[25] In accordance with Law 13/1994, of 1 June 1994, on the autonomy of the BS and other provisions, Art 7.6.

other national supervisory authorities, such as the CNMV, DGIPF,[26] SEPBLAC,[27] and with the authorities of the autonomous regions of Spain that have powers in financial matters.

It can pursue certain infringements committed by the credit institutions and impose sanctions. The BS, like the CNMV, classifies infringements into very serious, serious and minor infringements. **8.30**

Very serious infringements by credit institutions and other entities subject to the supervision of the BS include, among others: **8.31**

- rejection of or resistance to inspection requested expressly and in writing;
- the pursuit of activities not included within their legally determined and exclusive corporate objectives;
- execution of acts without authorization, where such authorization is required;
- failure to maintain the legally required accounts; and
- breach of the obligation to submit the annual accounts to audit in accordance with the current legislation.[28]

Sanctions for very serious infringements include a fine of up to either 2 per cent of an institution's capital or €300,000, whichever is the greater; revocation of the institution's authorization, and public reprimand.[29] **8.32**

Serious infringements which the BS can pursue include, among others: **8.33**

- failure to submit required filings on time or falsifying filings;
- breaching statutory rules on booking transactions and preparing balance sheets, profit and loss accounts, and financial statements;
- failure to report in general meeting orders of authorizing bodies;
- occasional or sporadic pursuit of activities outside the legally determined and exclusive corporate objectives; and
- breaching rules on risk limits on the volume of certain lending or deposit-taking operations.[30]

Sanctions which can be imposed by the BS for serious infringements include a fine of up to either 0.5 per cent of an institution's capital or €150,000, whichever is the greater, and public reprimand published in the Official State Gazette.[31] **8.34**

---

[26] *Dirección General de Seguros y Fondos de Pensiones* (General Directorate of Insurance and Pension Funds).

[27] *Servicio Especial Para el Blanqueo de Capitales Executive* (Service for the Prevention of Money Laundering and Monetary Offences).

[28] In accordance with Law 26/1988, of 29 July 1988, on discipline and intervention of credit entities, Art 4.

[29] In accordance with Law 26/1988, Art 9.

[30] In accordance with Law 26/1988, Art 5.

[31] In accordance with Law 26/1988, Art 10.

8.35   Minor infringements are violations of compulsory rules for credit institutions contained in regulatory and disciplinary provisions that are not considered serious or very serious. These are penalized by either private reprimand, or a fine of up to €60,000.[32]

Executive Service for the Prevention of Money Laundering and Monetary Offences (SEPBLAC)

8.36   SEPBLAC is an administrative body within the Ministry of Economy and Finance charged with preventing the use of the financial systems for money laundering. It also oversees the prevention of monetary offences of a criminal nature and non-criminal infringements of foreign economic transactions regulations.

8.37   SEPBLAC assists the judicial bodies, the Public Prosecution Department, the police and relevant administrative bodies by providing information on possible criminal offences or administrative infringements. It is the initial contact point for information relating to possible suspicious transactions, and can decide to take further action as it sees fit.

8.38   The entities subject to SEPBLAC's jurisdiction are stated in Article 2.1 of Law 19/1993, of 28 December 1993, on certain measures for the prevention of money laundering (the Anti-Money Laundering Act), which include, among others: financial entities, lawyers, auditors, notaries and casinos. Such entities must report any suspicious transactions that they become aware of to SEPBLAC, which may start to investigate the individuals or entities involved in such suspicious transactions and report to the relevant administrative or judicial bodies.

8.39   SEPBLAC can impose sanctions for very serious infringements such as tipping-off; failure to self-report suspicious activities to SEPBLAC; and failure to cooperate adequately with SEPBLAC.[33] Sanctions include a fine of no less than €90,152

---

[32] In accordance with Law 26/1988, Arts 6 and 11.

[33] The Anti-Money Laundering Act (as developed by Royal Decree 925/1995, of 9 June 1995, on measures for the prevention of money laundering), Art 5, considers the following to be serious infringements:
- breach of the duty of confidentiality;
- breach of the duty to communicate any operation related to money laundering or operations showing lack of correspondence with the nature, activity, volume, or operative records of the clients;
- the unjustified breach of the duty to communicate any operation related to money laundering or operations showing lack of correspondence with the nature, activity, volume, or operative records of the clients, when any employee or director of the obliged entity had declared the existence of evidence or the certainty that an operation was related to money laundering;
- refusal to provide any concrete information requested by SEPBLAC by means of a written demand; and
- infringements classified as serious if in any of the five previous years the offender was convicted by final judgment for crimes under Art 344 *bis*, h or I of the Spanish Criminal Act or crimes of covering up activities.

and no more than the higher of the following amounts: (i) 5 per cent of the entity's capital; (ii) twice the economic value of the operation; or (iii) €1,502,530; public reprimand; and/or revocation of authorization of the institution.[34]

SEPBLAC can also sanction serious infringements[35] with either a public or private reprimand and/or a fine of between €6,010 and the higher of: (i) 1 per cent of the entity's capital; (ii) the amount of the economic value of the operation involved, and an additional 50 per cent; or (iii) €150,253. Generally, entities found committing a serious infringement will be fined.[36]   **8.40**

Other regulators

The Spanish special prosecutor's office for the fight against white-collar crimes related to corruption ('the Special Prosecutor's Office')

The Special Prosecutor's Office is one of the bodies of the Prosecutor's Ministry, and, while not a regulator, has broad investigation powers in relation to financial crimes. It is included in this section since some of the matters it deals with are those that may be investigated by regulators. It has at its disposal a Special Unit of the Police ('Special Unit') and as many experts and professionals as considered necessary to achieve its aims. Therefore, there are also a number of Tax Inspectors and Audit Officials that work for the Special Prosecutor's Office.   **8.41**

The list of economic crimes investigated by the Special Prosecutor's Office is broad enough to allow the Special Unit to inquire into any of the relevant situations that might be related to corruption, and it includes, among others: economic fraud, smuggling, and criminal offences against the public treasury. In addition, the General Prosecutor can authorize the participation of the Special Prosecutor's Office in any other kind of proceedings, even if they relate to other kinds of criminal offences, if it is deemed expedient.   **8.42**

To these ends, the Special Prosecutor's Office has powers to require a person to answer questions, provide information, or produce documents for the purposes of an investigation. In the event that a person refuses to produce documents, the Special Prosecutor's Office may decide whether to propose to the relevant Criminal court the initiation of proceedings against the investigated party.   **8.43**

---

[34] In accordance with the Anti-Money Laundering Act, Art 9.2.

[35] These include failure to follow proper client verification procedures; failure to be alert to potentially suspicious transactions; failure to preserve documents adequately; failure to establish a proper system of internal controls to prevent money laundering; allowing suspicious activity to continue without notifying SEPBLAC; and failure to adopt the corrective measures proposed by SEPBLAC (Anti-Money Laundering Act, Art 5).

[36] In accordance with the Anti-Money Laundering Act, Art 8.

8.44 As mentioned at 8.41, the matters that can be investigated by the Special Prosecutor's Office overlap with those that can be investigated by regulators. Where in the course of an investigation, a regulator obtains evidence relating to one of the crimes contained in the Spanish Criminal Code the regulator must communicate such circumstances to the Public Prosecutor's Office and suspend the administrative proceedings until a judgment is passed by the relevant criminal court.[37]

Spanish tax authorities (STA)[38]

8.45 Although, strictly speaking, the STA are not regulators, they are involved in investigating and confirming that taxpayers comply with their tax obligations. The STA can review and correct tax returns filed by a party. To these ends, the STA's investigations may involve third parties, for example employees, suppliers or clients.

Spanish competition authority (CNC)[39]

8.46 The *Comisión Nacional de Competencia* (CNC) acts as the competition watchdog under the Spanish Competition Act.[40] It has far reaching powers of investigation and is also the decision-making authority for restrictive practices and abuses of dominant positions.

8.47 The CNC is responsible for ensuring that entities comply with the provisions of the Spanish Competition Act. In many cases, the CNC's functions overlap with other industry-specific regulatory bodies, such as the Telecommunications Market Commission[41] and the National Energy Commission.[42] When this happens, the CNC has stated that the industry-specific regulators will ensure that the provisions of their sectors' legislation are complied with, whilst the CNC will ensure compliance with the general competition provisions established in the Competition Act.

Self-regulatory organizations

8.48 In Spain, there are no self-regulatory organizations,[43] as all regulatory bodies are public bodies subject to administrative law—pursuant to Article 2 of Act 30/1992, of 26 November 1992, on the Legal Regime of the Public Administrations and Common Administrative Procedure (Act 30/1992),

---

[37] In accordance with Royal Decree 1398/1993, of 4 August 1993, on Procedures for the Exercise of Sanctioning Powers and similar provisions contained in the special regulation of each regulator.
[38] *Agencia Española de Administración Tributaria (AEAT).*
[39] *Comisión Nacional de Competencia (CNC).*
[40] *Ley de Defensa de la Competencia.*
[41] *Comisión del Mercado de las Telecomunicaciones.*
[42] *Comisión Nacional de la Energía.*
[43] *Régimen Jurídico de las Administraciones Públicas y del Procedimiento Administrativo Común.*

entities subject to public law with legal personality which are ancillary to any public body shall be treated as public bodies. When any such entities use their discretionary authority they are subject to Act 30/1992, at all other times they are subject to the rules set out in their own constitutional documents. Consequently, all entities that exercise public law are subject to administrative law.

Concurrent investigations

Even though each regulatory body has its own functions and carries out its own investigations into discrete aspects of a corporate or its activities, sometimes the powers of one regulator may overlap with those of other regulators. In such instances, Article 4 of Act 30/1992, which sets out the general principle of cooperation between public bodies, requires regulators to cooperate with one another. **8.49**

For example, a listed company may come under the authority and supervision of both the CNMV and the BS. As a general rule, both regulators coordinate their actions on the understanding that the monitoring of the relevant financial institution's solvency rests with the BS, and that the monitoring of its operations in the securities markets rests with the CNMV. In order to coordinate their powers of surveillance and supervision, the CNMV and the BS should coordinate their actions, according to Article 88 of the SMA, on the principle that (i) the final guardianship of the solvency of the financial entity rests with the institution holding the corresponding Register (the BS); and (ii) the good working of the stock markets rests with the CNMV. **8.50**

The CNMV also has an obligation to cooperate with the courts and the Public Prosecutor's Office in order to clarify events relating to the securities markets which may be of a criminal nature. Some recent instances of such cooperation include the *AVA* case and the *Gescartera* case. **8.51**

AVA was a Spanish investment firm which offered its clients a financial product that had a return of 10 per cent per year. It achieved this level of return through investing in futures in emerging economies' markets. However, AVA did not advise its clients of the full risks related to such investments. In February 1998, while AVA was being investigated by the CNMV, it declared its insolvency causing losses of more than €138m to nearly 10,000 investors. The Public Prosecutor continued the investigations and instigated prosecutions: the trial has still to take place. **8.52**

Gescartera was a Spanish investment firm who defrauded its investors by taking their money out of the country where it could not be recovered. This case achieved widespread notoriety as a number of town councils and the Church were linked to the case, and the former president and founder of the company had an information source inside the CNMV. As with the *AVA* case, the investigations were **8.53** initiated by the CNMV (in 2001) and continued by the public prosecutor. Approximately 4,000 investors were defrauded of an aggregate amount in excess of €52m.

8.54 More recently, regulators have been clamping down on various investment schemes which are defrauding investors by exploiting investments in tangible assets, which are not subject to CNMV supervision. Such schemes included the pyramid schemes set up by Afinsa and Forum Filatélico, in which they defrauded investors by purchasing stamps valued at higher than their market price (overvalued by up to 800 per cent), and which were maintained by attracting new clients and the entering into new contracts with them. The authorities have been criticized for the lack of supervision for this type of 'investment firm', which will presumably be resolved in the near future, by, perhaps, the creation of a specific regulator for such investment firms.

Relationships with overseas regulators

8.55 The CNMV is empowered[44] to supervise and carry out inspections of all of the companies that operate in the Spanish securities market, regardless of their nationality. As long as they participate in the Spanish securities markets, the CNMV is entitled to exercise its inspection powers over them.

8.56 In this regard, please note that, according to Article 97.1.a of the SMA, the commencement of proceedings which affect an investment services firm authorized by another EU member state is required to be notified to the relevant overseas supervisory authority so that, without prejudice to the adoption of the appropriate precautionary measures and sanctions in accordance with the SMA, such overseas authority may adopt any measures which it deems appropriate to stop any infringement and prevent its recurrence.

8.57 Cooperation with foreign regulators is governed by the SMA,[45] which as a result of the transposition of Directive 39/2004/EC, on Markets in Financial Instruments, has strengthened the cooperation of the CNMV with the relevant authorities of other EU members states in the following areas: (i) cooperation in investigations; (ii) *in situ* verification or supervision; and (iii) information exchange.

8.58 Furthermore, the CNMV may only refuse to cooperate with other EU member states in these areas when: (i) such cooperation may jeopardize sovereignty, security or public order; (ii) a judicial proceeding has commenced due to the same facts and against the same persons; or (iii) a final and unchallengeable judgment has been passed in respect of the same persons and facts.

---

[44] In accordance with the SMA, Art 84.
[45] The SMA, Arts 91 and 91 *bis*.

As for cooperation with non-EU member states, Article 91, Quarter 1 of the **8.59** SMA provides for the possibility of signing Cooperation Agreements on information exchange with their relevant authorities.

In this regard, since 2003, the CNMV has formed part of the IOSCO Multilateral **8.60** Cooperation and Exchange of Information which, in 2006, included 35 subscribers. In 2006, 39 collaboration requests were sent by the CNMV to foreign regulators, and 46 were sent to the CNMV. Approximately half of the requests for cooperation (both received and sent) related to investigations into market abuse, while the other half related to investigations into activities performed in the securities market without due authorization.

According to Article 91, Quarter 2 of the SMA, the information received (both **8.61** from EU member states and non-EU member states) can only can be disclosed with the express consent of the authority who has provided the information, and only for the purposes stated in the consent.

The BS cooperates closely with foreign supervisory authorities, especially with **8.62** those of the Latin-American countries. To date, the BS has signed Cooperation Agreements with the central banks of Argentina, Brazil, Chile, Colombia, Mexico, Peru, Uruguay, and Venezuela. Under the terms of these agreements, the foreign supervisor is unrestricted and is mandated to provide the BS with all the relevant information about the subsidiaries of Spanish companies that the BS requests.

C. Powers of Regulators

Sources of investigation

The CNMV may commence an investigation if any of the persons or firms that, **8.63** directly or indirectly, perform activities related to the securities market engage in practices aimed at, or with the effect of, significantly influencing the value of securities on the securities market (such as front running or large orders executed in the closing session); or if they behave to the detriment of their client (such as allocating one or more securities to themselves when the clients have requested those securities on the same or better conditions).

The CNMV usually also investigates significant transactions made prior to a **8.64** significant event that affects the value of shares as there is a suspicion that they could be made with inside information.

In 2005, a new internal regulation was introduced which provides for the CNMV **8.65** to pursue possible infringements of regulations reported by members of the public. It is hoped that this will establish a more efficient procedure for investigations commenced by public reporting.

8.66 The CNC may initiate an anti-trust investigation *ex officio* or pursuant to a complaint by a third party. These investigations will be carried out by the Directorate for Investigations within the CNC. Pursuant to the Spanish Competition Act, the CNC may decide to initiate investigation proceedings *ex-officio* when there are sufficient reasons to believe that the Spanish Competition Act has been infringed. However, in practice, most of the investigation proceedings are initiated on the basis of informal complaints by third parties or press speculation evidencing anti-trust infringements.

Levels of regulatory scrutiny

8.67 There are different levels of regulatory scrutiny among investigations conducted by Spanish regulators. CNMV investigations may start in an informal manner such as arising out of the analysis of documents filed with the CNMV by the individuals or companies for other purposes; or from cross-checking documents filed by third companies with the ones filed by the relevant company. The investigation may then continue through personal interviews with directors, managers, or auditors as well as the inspection of the company premises.

8.68 For instance, in 2006, the Market Surveillance Unit (*Unidad de Vigilancia de los Mercados*) (UVM), the body of the CNMV in charge of analysing the existence of market abuse practices, investigated 415 persons.

8.69 Within these investigations, 2,227 actions were taken, of which 2,128 were formal requests for documentation and other types of information, 29 were collaboration requests to foreign organs, 48 were requests for formal statements and 22 were inspections.

8.70 CNC anti-trust investigation proceedings are divided into two phases. The Directorate for Investigation will carry out a preliminary investigation where it will decide to open a formal investigation, if there is sufficient evidence of a potential infringement, or to shelve the proceedings, if there isn't.

8.71 If a formal investigation is opened, the Directorate will refer the file to the main chamber of the CNC, which can carry out further investigation work deemed necessary for the proceedings.

Investigation tools

8.72 The CNMV has wide investigative powers under the SMA[46] such as the capacity to request any kind of information or document or carry out dawn raids in order to seize documentary evidence. In this regard, the amendment to the SMA made

---

[46] The SMA, Art 85.

by the Law 47/2007, of 19 December 2007, has improved the investigation tools of the CNMV, by strengthening mechanisms of cooperation, both national and international, with other supervisors.[47]

The investigation tools can be used directly by the CNMV, in collaboration with **8.73** other authorities (Spanish or foreign), or, for certain measures, following a request to the courts (eg the seizure of assets).

The CNMV is entitled to request as much information as it deems necessary **8.74** from individuals and firms operating in the Spanish market. In order to obtain such information and to verify it, the individuals and firms subject to an investigation are obliged to supply any books, registers, and documents, whatever their format, which the CNMV deems pertinent. Information is generally provided in documents and interviews are less common. However, Article 85.2 of the SMA entitles the CNMV to take statements, and even request records or transcripts of the communications of the investigated entity. Failure to provide the CNMV with the information requested constitutes a very serious infringement.

Investigations may take place in any office, department or, premises of the firm **8.75** being inspected, provided that regular working hours are observed, at any offices of its representative, or at the premises of the CNMV.

The BS is entitled, when carrying out its investigation activities, to obtain from **8.76** the entities subject to its supervision any books, registers, and documents it deems necessary, including software and databases, whatever their format.[48]

Similarly, SEPBLAC is empowered to compel 'obliged entities'[49] to provide **8.77** information requested in the execution of its functions.[50] There are some exceptions to this power in relation to notaries, lawyers, *procurators*, auditors, accountants, and tax advisers when they are representing or defending a client in an administrative or court procedure.

The CNC, through the Directorate for Investigations, also has wide investigatory **8.78** powers which include requiring any representative or employee of the company or group of companies to provide explanations of facts or documents related to the inspection and keeping records of the answers and explanations given; requesting information from any person or entity; hearing those companies which may be affected by the alleged infringement; and carrying out on-the-spot inspections of the alleged infringing company's premises (dawn raids).

---

[47] Considered at 8.57.
[48] Pursuant to Art 43 *bis* 1bis of Law 26/1988.
[49] Obliged entities are discussed at 8.38.
[50] Under Art 3.4.b of the Anti-Money Laundering Act.

8.79   Neither the CNMV, the BS, SEPBLAC, or the CNC have direct powers in criminal matters such as corruption, although SEPBLAC and the CNMV[51] have specific legal obligations to cooperate with the Judiciary and the Public Prosecutor's Office.

Extra-territorial jurisdiction

8.80   The CNMV is empowered to supervise and carry out inspections of all of the companies that operate in the Spanish securities markets, regardless of their nationality.[52] Moreover, pursuant to Article 84 of the SMA, the CNMV has jurisdiction to supervise and sanction Spanish investment firms, including their offices and centres located abroad. However, the CNMV can only operate extra-territorially through the cooperation of the relevant authorities in other countries.

8.81   The CNMV can request EU member states' cooperation to carry out *in situ* verifications or investigations in respect of matters regulated by Directive 2004/39/EC, on Markets in Financial Instruments.[53]

8.82   In respect of any non-EU member states, the inspection powers of the CNMV are governed by any Cooperation Agreement on information exchange signed with the non-EU member state in question.[54]

8.83   The BS is also empowered to inspect the premises of Spanish entities subject to its supervision located in other member states. Furthermore, under Article 43 bis of Law 26/1988[55] the BS has the power to supervise and inspect credit entities, which power covers all branches of credit entities whether located inside or outside of Spain. However, the BS must give the relevant authorities of the foreign territories prior notification of any inspections. Under Article 6.1 of Royal Decree Legislative 1298/1986, of 28 June 1986, Adapting the Spanish Legal System in relation to Credit Entities to the EU Legal System,[56] the BS, in the exercise of its duties of supervision and inspection of credit entities, is required to cooperate with the relevant authorities of the foreign country.

8.84   The CNC has no extra-territorial jurisdiction. However, it could potentially investigate any competition infringement having an effect within the Spanish territory. Generally, the CNC will only investigate companies whose registered office is within the Spanish territory.

---

[51] In the case of the CNMV in order 'to clarify events related to securities markets which may be of a criminal nature' further to Art 88 of the SMA.

[52] Discussed at 8.55.

[53] The SMA, Art 91.4.

[54] Discussed at 8.59.

[55] *Ley de Disciplina e Intervención de las Entidades de Crédito.*

[56] *Sobre Adaptación del Derecho Vigente en Materia de Entidades de Crédito al de las Comunidades Europeas.*

Spain has been a member of the Financial Action Task Force on Money Launder-   **8.85**
ing (FATF) since 1994. The FATF was established by the G-7 Summit held in
Paris in July 1989 to examine measures to combat money laundering. Its purpose
is the development and promotion of measures to combat money laundering and
terrorist financing. Nowadays, the FATF has a membership of 31 countries and
two international organizations.

Protections

Generally, the powers of the Spanish regulators are very far reaching and there are   **8.86**
few protections available. Company employees, however, may invoke the privilege
against self-incrimination when interviewed as part of an investigation. This is
more likely to be permitted in investigations with criminal implications rather
than purely administrative proceedings.

Additionally, lawyers working for a company under investigation are bound by   **8.87**
their obligation to keep confidential all facts and matters that they come to know
through the conduct of their professional obligations. This is reinforced by their
duty not to disclose facts and documents that have come into their possession as
a result of their professional activities.[57] Consequently, lawyers cannot be forced
to share information about the company during the course of an investigation.
Moreover, documents that are protected by attorney-client confidentiality that
are in the client's possession preserve their confidentiality and do not have to be
disclosed to the investigatory bodies.

In this regard, Spanish law does not treat in-house lawyers differently to external   **8.88**
lawyers—in-house lawyers have the same duties of confidentiality, and communications with in-house lawyers are protected by attorney-client confidentiality
in the same way as are communications with external lawyers. However, it is not
clear whether communications with in-house lawyers will continue to be
protected under Spanish law following a decision of the European Court of
Justice (in its judgment in the *Akzo Nobel* case), which decided that they should
not be, albeit in the context of competition investigations.

In addition, Spanish case law in respect of privilege and confidentiality is not   **8.89**
always clear and, therefore, it is important to analyse each situation on a case-by-
case basis, and to consider not only rules on privilege, but also constitutional
rights which may be affected, including the right to an appropriate legal defence,
the right to avoid self-incrimination, rights over private property, and rights to
personal privacy.

---

[57] Spanish Professional Code of Conduct, June 2000 and the General Statute for Spanish lawyers
approved by Royal Decree 658/2001, of 20 June 2001.

Sanctions for failure to cooperate

8.90 All entities have an obligation to cooperate with the regulators in the course of regulatory investigations. A party under investigation must disclose all the documents required by the regulator, including those that might adversely affect its case. If the party chooses not to cooperate with the regulator, it will be penalized.

8.91 Under Article 99(t) of the SMA, the CNMV can impose sanctions for non-cooperation by individuals and legal entities which are legally obliged to submit to inspection by the CNMV, provided that clear written instructions have first been served.

8.92 The failure to cooperate with the CNMV amounts to a very serious infringement which may be penalized under Article 103 of the SMA with a fine of up to €300,000 or 2 per cent of the equity capital, whichever is the greater.

8.93 The sanctions that may be imposed by other regulators for failure to cooperate are as follows:

- *BS*—a failure to comply with the obligation to provide documents and information to the BS may be considered a severe offence. Pursuant to Article 10 of Law 26/1988, if a credit entity commits a severe offence, the BS can impose on it a fine of up to €150,000 or 0.5 per cent of the equity capital, whichever is the greater.

- *SEPBLAC*—in the event that SEPBLAC requests a document from a party and that party refuses to comply with its duty to produce the document, SEPBLAC can impose a fine of between €6,010 and the higher of (i) 1 per cent of the entity's capital, (ii) the amount of the economic value of the operation involved, and an additional 50 per cent or (iii) €150,253.[58]

- *CNC*—under the Spanish Competition Act, failure to comply with the duty to provide information to CNC can be sanctioned with a fine of up to 1 per cent of the total turnover of the company (Articles 62.2(a) and 63.1(c)). In addition, the CNC can impose a fine of up to €12,000 on companies refusing to collaborate with it when legally obliged to do so (Article 67).

D. Voluntary Investigations

Benefits and risks of voluntary investigations

8.94 Although companies in Spain may conduct voluntary internal investigations when they discover indications of possible infringements or misconduct, or even

---

[58] Pursuant to Art 8 of the Anti-Money Laundering Act.

in application of an internal policy, there are still no effective mechanisms to communicate the results of such voluntary investigations to the regulators.

Spanish legislation does not contemplate the possibility of conducting a voluntary investigation as a tool to avoid an investigation by a regulator and/or to obtain a lower sanction. Furthermore, with one exception, there are no rules requiring the discovery of any infringements to be reported. **8.95**

In addition, while the general law on administrative bodies provides for the possibility of concluding an administrative procedure by way of a settlement agreement, this option is not available to companies under investigation. **8.96**

In light of the current legislation and attitudes of the regulators, voluntary investigations do not accord companies any special benefit and therefore have not yet become common practice in Spain. **8.97**

The Anti-Money Laundering Act is the exception to the general rule that Spanish law does not impose on companies a duty to self-report. It establishes the duty to report to the relevant authorities any suspected money laundering activity. In practice, however, companies are more likely to report infringements committed by third parties than those committed by themselves. **8.98**

If a company decides to communicate to a regulator a report generated as a result of an internal investigation, it would be treated as a private document. As a consequence, such report would not have conclusive evidentiary value in front of a court (unless it has been legally acknowledged)[59] but would be taken into account. **8.99**

Although documents produced to regulators may not have conclusive evidential value, they can be an important source of information which they may decide to use at their discretion. Moreover, such documents could contain statements that may be difficult to refute at a later stage. **8.100**

Apart from cases of suspected money laundering, regulators do not expect companies to undertake internal investigations and therefore do not have pre-established criteria in respect of them so a company conducting an internal investigation can take whatever steps it feels are appropriate. **8.101**

---

[59] Pursuant to Art 1225 of the Spanish Civil Code, a 'legally acknowledged' private document shall have the same evidential value as a document produced by a public body. Acknowledgement, in this context, means that none of the parties (the public body and the company submitting the report) challenge its content.

Events triggering considering conducting a voluntary investigation

8.102 Despite the lack of a culture of conducting voluntary investigations and report-ing the results to a regulator, there are certain cases where carrying out an investi-gation would be advisable, even if for internal purposes only. For instance, if senior management discovers a potential infringement of which a regulator is not aware, they should initiate an investigation in order to understand the problem and what internal steps need to be taken. Likewise, if the audit committee of the Board of Directors of a listed company receives a report regarding an irregularity in the company's conduct from a 'whistle-blower', an investigation should be undertaken and the necessary steps, if any, taken.

8.103 Moreover, a company should consider initiating an internal investigation if it believes it is about to become the subject of an imminent investigation by a regu-lator, or if evidence of misconduct is leaked to the press or other opinion formers, in order to prepare to defend itself before the regulator or show the public that appropriate internal action is being taken.

8.104 It is also generally advisable for a company to conduct a voluntary investigation whenever it suspects that a possible fraud has taken place or confidential informa-tion has been leaked.

8.105 When a company becomes aware of suspicious activity, it is important that it understands fully what has occurred. Conducting an internal investigation is an effective mechanism to determine if an infringement has taken place and any relevant measures required in order to minimize its impact, as well as to identify those responsible for the infringement.

8.106 Internal investigations are often carried out after a merger or an acquisition, as a protective measure against any infringement committed by the previous owners of the company; or after a change of directors, especially if the previous manage-ment are suspected of any improper conduct.

8.107 Finally, the Unified Good Governance Code (the Conthe Report)[60] includes a recommendation that listed companies establish a 'whistle-blowing' procedure under the supervision of the audit committee of the Board of Directors. Through these procedures, employees can confidentially or, where appropriate, even anon-ymously report any irregularities they observe in the company's conduct.[61] It is

---

[60] Passed by a resolution of the Council of the CNMV approving the single text of corporate governance recommendations of 22 May 2006.

[61] The working group which drafted this code understands that the cases dealt with will mainly refer to financial or accounting matters, and that companies establishing such mechanisms will do so in strict adherence with the terms of data protection legislation.

foreseeable that these whistle-blowing procedures will lead to investigations into listed companies.

Structuring an internal investigation

As there is no widespread practice of conducting internal investigations in Spain, **8.108** there are no consolidated principles as to how to structure an internal investigation. However, there are a number of general principles that should be considered when conducting any type of investigation.

In order for a company to investigate thoroughly any suspicious activity and deter- **8.109** mine the exact details of what may have transpired, it is usually effective to assemble a small investigation team with appropriately balanced skills and authority. This team should draw on personnel from all areas of the company's business and avoid includ- ing, or reporting to, any persons potentially involved in the alleged misconduct.

The investigation team should ensure that the investigation is sufficiently thor- **8.110** ough to gain a complete picture of any suspicious activity and misconduct. The internal investigation should be at least as comprehensive as an investigation conducted by a regulator.

Using external advisers

In most significant cases, it is advisable to engage the services of external advisers **8.111** to support the internal investigation team. The type of external adviser best suited to this task varies according to the circumstances prompting the investigation but may include forensic accountants, computer forensic specialists, and external lawyers with experience of investigations.

External advisers often provide an objective and experienced perspective, assist- **8.112** ing in the rapid identification of any infringements committed and in determin- ing the action required to rectify the situation.

Managing illegal activity during investigations

If potentially illegal conduct is discovered during the course of an investigation, **8.113** the most common action would be to suspend such conduct as soon as possible whilst analysing it and determining whether it is legally permitted. If the analysis reveals that the conduct can be modified so that it complies with all Spanish leg- islation, then the company will normally modify the conduct to make it legal irrespective of the implied concern that it might previously have been illegal.

Failure to suspend or modify potentially illegal conduct once it has been deter- **8.114** mined to be illegal could have severe consequences for a company including increased sanctions.

E. Self-reporting

Duty to self-report

8.115 Under Spanish law there is no general legal duty to self-report violations of corporate law, regulations or practices, except for the breach of certain environmental obligations[62] and money laundering legislation.

8.116 As discussed above,[63] the Anti-Money Laundering Act is the exception to the general rule that Spanish law does not impose on companies a duty to self-report. It establishes the duty (on 'obliged subjects'[64] only) to report to the relevant authorities any suspected money laundering activity. In practice, however, companies are more likely to report infringements committed by third parties than those committed by themselves.

8.117 A company so obliged may not execute any transaction suspected of being related to money laundering activities without first communicating it to SEPBLAC.

8.118 If it is impossible to refrain from executing such a transaction prior to contacting SEPBLAC, or if such restraint is likely to frustrate efforts to pursue the beneficiaries of a suspected money laundering operation, the communication to SEPBLAC may be made immediately after the execution of the transaction (but must be made then, if not earlier).

8.119 Although there is no formal obligation to self-report competition related infringements, the leniency programmes established by the new Competition Act provides incentives for companies that may be members of a cartel to self-report any abuses or misconduct. These can include partial or even total immunity from penalties for such transgression.

Culture of self-reporting

8.120 Although there is no general legal duty to self-report violations of corporate law, regulations or practices, the Olivencia,[65] the Aldama,[66] and the Conthe[67] Reports (which have led to the Unified Good Governance Code) dealing with corporate

---

[62] It is a general principle of the Spanish environmental legislation that corporations that violate the provisions of such legislation are obliged to self-report such violations to the relevant environmental authorities.

[63] At 8.98.

[64] As defined in the Anti-Money Laundering Act.

[65] *El Gobierno de las Sociedades Cotizadas of 26 February de 1998.*

[66] *Informe de la Comisión Especial para el fomento de la transparencia y seguridad en los mercados y en las sociedades cotizadas of 8 January 2003.*

[67] *Código Unificado de Buen Gobierno, aprobado por el Consejo de la CNMV el 22 de mayo de 2006.* The Conthe Report is a harmonization and an update of the Olivencia and Aldama Report with

governance encourage transparency by companies.[68] Although this code is non-binding, failure to implement the recommendations could have negative ramifications for companies, including sanctions (for omissions, mistakes or misleading data contained in their Corporate Governance Reports), further monitoring, and public statements by the CNMV regarding compliance with the corporate governance rules. In addition, it could have a negative impact on the market value and image of the company, as the Corporate Governance Reports are publicly disclosed.

Article 116 of the SMA sets out the 'comply or explain' principle that requires **8.121** listed Spanish firms to specify their 'degree of compliance with corporate governance recommendations, justifying any failure to comply' in their Annual Corporate Governance Reports. The Unified Good Governance Code sets out the recommendations to be considered by listed companies when fulfilling their disclosure requirements under the SMA.

These disclosure requirements mainly refer to the Corporate Governance Report, **8.122** which should contain the following:[69]

(a) the company's ownership structure;
(b) the company's administrative structure, with information relating to the composition and the organization and functioning rules of the Board of Directors and its committees;
(c) related-party transactions between company and its shareholders and directors and executives and intra-group transactions;
(d) risk control system;s
(e) functioning of the Shareholders' Meeting; and
(f) the extent to which corporate governance recommendations are followed and, where appropriate, an explanation of why they have not been followed.

Spanish legislation, therefore, leaves it to companies to decide whether or not to **8.123** follow corporate governance recommendations, but requires them to give a reasoned explanation for any deviation, so that shareholders, investors, and the markets in general can arrive at an informed judgment.

It will be left to shareholders, investors and the markets in general to evaluate the **8.124** explanations companies give of their degree of compliance with Unified Good

---

supplementary recommendations that it considered to be warranted and has led to the Unified Good Governance Code.

[68] These reports were commissioned to analyse the criteria and guidelines that should apply to companies which issue securities and instruments admitted to listing on organized markets in their relations with consultants, financial analysts, and other companies, persons, or entities which assist them or provide professional services to them, and those which should apply among the latter, in order to increase the transparency and security of the financial markets.

[69] Referred to in the SMA, Art 116.

Governance Code recommendations. The extent of compliance or the quality of explanations will not give rise to any actions by the CNMV, as this would directly invalidate the voluntary nature of the Unified Good Governance Code.[70] However, regulators generally regard the failure to self-report unfavourably as it does not allow the markets to assess the degree of fulfilment of the corporate governance recommendations.

F. Announcements and Public Relations Strategies

Regulatory investigations

External communications

8.125 There is no obligation under Spanish Law compelling a company to externally communicate that a regulatory investigation is underway. Nevertheless, listed companies have an obligation to disclose information about activities related to, or having an influence on, the equities market (price-sensitive information).[71] Issuers of securities are obliged to disclose all price-sensitive information to the market immediately, by means of a communication to the CNMV.

8.126 Such communication must take place before the information is disclosed by any other means and as soon as it becomes known. The contents of the communication must be honest, clear, complete, and, when the nature of the information so demands, quantified, in such a way that does not lead to misunderstanding or deception. The issuers of securities shall also disseminate the same information on their websites. If the companies do not make such information public, the CNMV may do so itself.[72]

8.127 If the issuer considers that the information should not be made public because publicity could affect the issuer's legitimate interests, it must immediately inform the CNMV of this. The CNMV may release the issuer from its disclosure obligation, if it deems that disclosure of such information would be contrary to the public interest or would be seriously detrimental to the party making the disclosure, provided that, in the latter case, such an omission would be unlikely to mislead

---

[70] This would not, of course, prevent the CNMV from pursuing a company for any breaches of the non-voluntary rules arising out of the same facts which amounted to non-compliance with the United Good Governance Code.

[71] Price-sensitive information is defined as all information whose knowledge may reasonably encourage an investor to acquire or transfer securities and, therefore, which may have a significant influence on the security's price on a secondary market. Where price-sensitive information is known to the corporation but has not yet been disclosed to the CNMV (eg because it is in the process of being disclosed, it is a future operation etc), generally, persons with knowledge of it cannot use it in the market.

[72] The SMA, Art 89.

the public with respect to events and circumstances the knowledge of which is essential for assessing the securities in question.

Although it would be reasonable to assume that the fact that a company is under **8.128** investigation falls within the definition of price-sensitive information (as it constitutes a significant fact), whether it does depends on the potential significance of the matter being investigated. If it is sufficiently significant, it is, however, likely that the CNMV would deem that the disclosure of such information would be contrary to the public interest or would be seriously detrimental to the party making the disclosure, and therefore would dispense with the obligation to disclose, under Article 82 of the SMA, until the investigation has been completed.

Generally, no official public communications are made by the CNMV or by the **8.129** company during investigations. Unless a company finds itself in a position that it is required to make a public announcement, it is generally advisable that it should not publicly disclose that it is facing or conducting an investigation. However, the company must be prepared for possible leaks to the press, which can often be inaccurate.

It is always advisable to try to keep open channels of communication with the **8.130** regulator in question and request its views prior to making any communication that could possibly affect the price of the company's securities. If the press has revealed any relevant information regarding the investigation, the company, together with the regulator, should consider the appropriateness of making an official communication to clarify the situation.

Internal communications

Currently, there is no legislation or market practice in relation to whether, when, **8.131** and how a listed corporation or any other 'regulated' entity should make its own personnel aware of an internal or external investigation.

As mentioned above,[73] as an investigation could be considered to be price-sensi- **8.132** tive information, a company that decides not to disclose that an investigation is underway should remind the employees with knowledge of the investigation of the rules on inside information set out in Article 81 of the SMA and its subsequent regulations.

If necessary, the company will have to consider whether it is more beneficial to **8.133** make a general disclosure to employees and the general public that an investigation is underway in order to limit the impact of uncontrolled rumours on the share price and to dispel possible allegations of abuse in relation to trading activities.

---

[73] At 8.128.

8.134 In any event, it may be necessary to disclose the fact that an investigation is underway to a sufficient number of employees to ensure preservation of all relevant documents and/or suspension of routine destruction of documents, and, consequently, a wider announcement may become inevitable.

8.135 The Employment Act[74] sets out a list of cases in which a company's employees' committee should be made aware of certain information regarding the company, its sector and any information concerning employment matters.[75] However, these do not include regulatory or internal investigations or corrupt practices.

Internal investigations

8.136 Communicating the commencement of an internal investigation either internally or externally is not common practice in Spain. However, in some cases of extreme gravity involving listed companies, it could be considered price-sensitive information subject to the obligation of disclosure to the CNMV.[76] When deciding whether to inform its employees of an internal investigation a company should weigh up the same considerations as when facing a regulatory investigation.

8.137 Evidence suggests that listed corporations have often taken the approach that an internal investigation is more effective if kept confidential as much as possible and employees are informed on a 'need to know' basis only.

Key points for Public Relations strategies

8.138 Where in respect of a listed company an investigation constitutes price-sensitive information, or where it is otherwise appropriate for a company to make an external disclosure of facts relating to an investigation, it is generally advisable to make the necessary disclosures in tandem with a wider PR strategy to avoid potentially negative PR. The content of a PR strategy depends on the specific circumstances of the case, however, as a general rule, the following key points should be taken into account:

Before an investigation:

- Put in place an emergency crisis management plan just in case the investigation become public with negative ramifications for the company.
- Keep a good, open relationship with the media.

---

[74] Royal Decree 1/1995, of 24 March 1995 (*Real Decreto Legislativo 1/1995, de 24 de marzo, por el que se aprueba el texto refundido de la Ley del Estatuto de los Trabajadores*).

[75] Such information includes three monthly general updates on the company's industry sector, the company's production programme, changes to the company's employment policies and strategies, and the company's forecasts regarding the hiring of new employees. The company's employees' committee also has the right to receive a copy of the annual financial statements and, in the case of limited liability companies, it can also access all the documents provided to the shareholders.

[76] Considered at 8.128.

- Consider the investigation specific PR issues carefully in the context of the overall PR positioning of the company and by reference to the experiences of other companies that have been in similar positions. Many press reactions include references to comparators.

During an investigation:

- Appoint a single spokesperson.
- Identify the issues that cannot be given to the media, with explanations as to why such information is not available and the measures underway in order to show that the situation is under control.
- Ensure that everyone else in the company knows that they are not authorized to make statements regarding the investigation or its results.
- Cooperate and cultivate good relations with the media—use all the possible media available to communicate to the public.
- Focus on a few key messages and consistently communicate them, in plain language without the use of jargon.
- Everything disclosed must be true and accurate; contradictions must be avoided.
- Show that the company wants always to solve potential irregularities.
- Take the initiative: it is better to create an image than modify an existing one.
- Rehearse public statements and comply with media requirements.
- Make arrangements to monitor media activity and rapidly correct any inaccuracies that are published.

Things to avoid:

- Avoid incriminating statements and admissions of liability that could be used against the company in any further litigation.
- Avoid speculations as to what has happened.
- Avoid 'no comment' statements.
- Avoid any 'off the record' conversations. Requests to the media to not disclose parts of the statements made can be prejudicial in the medium/long term.

G. Best Practices in Document Gathering and Preservation

Expectations of regulators and courts

While there is no specific duty in Spanish law to preserve documents once a regu- **8.139**
latory or internal investigation is underway, Spanish legislation contains multiple
provisions imposing a duty to cooperate with regulators by providing them with
all the information that they may request during a regulatory investigation.[77]

---

[77] This is considered further from 8.72.

8.140 Therefore, if the company under investigation fails to provide regulators with the information requested, whether because the documents have not been duly preserved or otherwise, the regulators may impose administrative sanctions for failure to comply with the legislation. Moreover, in most cases companies have an interest in preserving documents, since these may serve as evidence to prove that they have acted properly and within the law.

8.141 In addition, there are legal obligations requiring certain categories of documents to be retained including:

- documents relating to tax obligations, which must be retained for four years;
- companies' accounting books, correspondence, documentation, and receipts for their business, must be retained, duly arranged, for six years;[78] and
- where an entity is subject to the requirements of the Anti-Money Laundering Act,[79] documents relating to certain transactions must be retained for a minimum of six years.[80] In addition, in certain circumstances, such entities must retain details of those persons that have participated in the transactions. Failure to comply with this duty may give rise to sanctions.

8.142 Furthermore, in Spain, destruction of evidence of a crime by a third party, in order to avoid the discovery of the crime, will constitute a criminal offence punishable with imprisonment of between six months and three years.[81] The commission of this crime requires knowledge of the commission of the crime being concealed and cannot be committed by mere negligence. There must be the intent to cover up a crime.

8.143 A failure to preserve documents or the destruction of any documents when proceedings or investigations are underway or imminent could be considered by the regulator to be a breach of the duty to cooperate.

8.144 Therefore, it is advisable to adopt and adhere to a formal document management policy to ensure compliance with all statutory obligations and any ad hoc regulatory requests.

---

[78] In accordance with the Commercial Code, Art 30.

[79] Such entities are detailed in Art 2 of the Anti-Money Laundering Act, and include financial entities and other bodies acting in the financial markets, as well as other professionals such as notaries, lawyers, and auditors.

[80] The Anti-Money Laundering Act, Art 3.3. Originally, the obligation was for five years but was increased to six years by Royal Decree 925/1995, of 9 June 1995, on measures for the prevention of money laundering.

[81] The Criminal Code, Art 451.

Rights of documents and confidentiality

Regulators have far reaching powers to request documents and information dur- **8.145** ing investigations. Regulators in Spain are generally empowered to request any document in any medium related to the scope of their jurisdiction.

For example, the CNMV can request any information it considers to fall within the **8.146** scope of the SMA. Therefore the entity under investigation (or its administrators, managers, and other similar persons) can be compelled to deliver the books, records, and documents, in any medium, that the CNMV deems necessary, including computer programs and hard drives, CDs/DVDs, or any other types of archives.

Exceptionally, when conducting an investigation, the regulator or the employer **8.147** is not permitted to access materials that are considered to be the employee's private property as this would infringe the employee's right to privacy.[82]

Under the Employment Act, the employer has a legal right to monitor its employ- **8.148** ees 'in order to verify that the employee complies with his/her employment duties' provided that it respects the employee's human dignity.

Monitoring activity is limited by fundamental rights set out by the Spanish **8.149** Constitution, such as the right to privacy, right to honour, right to confidentiality of communications, and the freedom of speech of employees, all of which must be respected by the employer.

Since there is no specific legislation on the fundamental rights of employees, **8.150** employment courts have stated that the company's right to monitor and disclose a specific employee's electronic communications should be assessed on a case-by-case basis. In general terms, employment tribunals have deemed valid the monitoring of email and voice mail communications, Internet access, and other stored information under the following circumstances:

- the employee is aware of the possibility of monitoring and the employer's policy is clear in this regard;[83]
- the existence of a clear, express, and lawful reason for the monitoring;
- the degree of monitoring is proportionate to the eventual risk;
- the measures are necessary in order to illicit the required information; and
- there is minimum impact on the employee's privacy rights.

---

[82] The right to privacy is a constitutional right established by Art 18.1 of the Spanish Constitution, which relates to and derives from Art 10.1 of the Spanish Constitution (human dignity). These rights have been analysed and determined by the Courts in the following cases: SSTC 209/1988, of 10 November 1988; 197/1991, of 17 October 1991; 143/1994, of 9 May 1994; and 156/2001, of 2 July 2001, among others.

[83] There is an obligation to inform the employee of the possibility of the monitoring activity.

8.151 Therefore, since a company may well want to access employees' email and voice mail communications (etc), particularly during an investigation, it is advisable for companies, together with the employees' representatives or directly with the employees, to set out an express policy regarding employees' use of email and Internet, making express reference to the possibility of the employer accessing the employees' emails, or even monitoring the employees' use of the Internet or telephone, under specific circumstances.

8.152 In those cases where the information is protected by the employee's right to privacy the regulator would not be able to gain access to the information without a court order.

8.153 As outlined below,[84] Article 37 of Act 30/1992 provides private individuals and corporations with the right to access registers and documentation resulting from an administrative investigation once it is finished. However, Article 37(5) provides an exception by which documents protected by trade or industrial secrecy or privilege cannot be disclosed. Moreover, the special rules governing investigations by the CNMV, SEPBLAC, the Competition Authorities, and other regulators have specific provisions regarding the confidentiality of the information obtained in the execution of their activities.

Data protection

8.154 When gathering documents containing personal information for the purpose of an investigation (either internal or external), a company must bear in mind any restrictions applicable under the Spanish data protection regulations (mainly, Basic Act 15/1999 on Personal Data Protection ('the Data Protection Act')).

8.155 The Spanish Constitutional Court ruled in a landmark decision of 2000[85] that the right of privacy should be differentiated from the law of personal data protection, with the latter laying down the broader right of the individual to control the processing of his or her personal data by third parties (whether this personal data pertains to the private sphere of the individual or not). Hence the Data Protection Act should be taken into account in addition to privacy law considerations (see 8.147 above).

8.156 In general terms, the collection and processing of personal data by the company must be for specified, explicit, and legitimate purposes and such data must not be further processed in any way that is incompatible with those purposes. Generally, the processing by an employer of personal data of employees for the purpose of conducting an (internal or external) investigation should be considered lawful

---

[84] At 8.172.
[85] STC 292/2000, of 30 November 2000.

processing of data based on the right of the employer to monitor its employees (see 8.148). In order to avoid any possible infringement of the Data Protection Act, some companies include data protection wording in employment agreements whereby the employees consent to the processing of their data for investigation and monitoring purposes.

When a regulator requests information that incorporates personal data of employees, **8.157** clients, suppliers etc of the company in the context of an investigation, the company may find itself obliged to communicate personal data to a 'third party'. Under Spanish law, personal data may be communicated to third parties only for purposes directly related to the legitimate functions of the transferor and transferee with the prior consent of the data subject (the employee, the client the supplier etc). Such prior consent will not be required if the communication is destined for the Ombudsman, the Public Prosecution, judges, courts, or the Court of Auditors in the exercise of their functions.

Where the regulator in question does not belong to any of the aforementioned **8.158** entities, the communication of personal data to that regulator must always be preceded by the consent of the data subject. If consent is not obtained, and the regulator insists on gathering the documentation, the company should oppose this and, if necessary, make the information anonymous. If the regulator continues to insist on obtaining the documentation containing personal data, it is advisable for the company to set down in the inspection record its express opposition to the disclosure of personal data. This could avoid the potential liability of the company for breaches of the Data Protection Act.

Any intra-group communication of personal data by a company will be consid- **8.159** ered a communication of such data to a third party. The consent of the data subject to such communication, however, will not be required if the third party is a 'data processor' in relation to the company making the communication (ie the recipient of the data will process it on behalf of the transferor), provided that, inter alia, the communication of personal data is necessary for the provision of a service to the company by the data processor.

Processing by third party data processors must be regulated in a written contract **8.160** between the data processor and the company, or a contract in any other form that allows its performance and content to be assessed, which expressly states that the processor shall process the data only in accordance with the instructions of the company, shall not apply or use the data for a purpose other than that set out in the said contract, and shall not communicate the data to other persons even for their preservation. Once the contractual service has been provided, the personal data must be destroyed or returned to the controller, together with any media or documents which contain processed personal data.

8.161 A company subject to an investigation may need to transfer personal data out of Spain (eg in the case of an investigation conducted overseas). Although generally such international transfer will be exempted from authorization by the Spanish data protection authorities, it is advisable to discuss the specific circumstances of the transfer with a data protection specialist before conducting it.

8.162 Other issues related to personal data that may be worth considering in the context of an investigation are as follows:

- The scope of the Data Protection Act covers the processing of personal data of individuals, whether the processing is done in an automated form or not. Consequently, paper-based filing systems containing personal data fall under the scope of the regulations.

- A company targeted by an investigation should be careful about the transfer of personal data which it is processing on behalf of third parties (eg a data processing centre being requested to disclose information from one of its clients which is under investigation). In these circumstances, it is important that the controller of the data be informed of the investigation by the data processor and of the request to transfer the personal data.

- Breach of the data protection regulations may lead to economic fines. Proceedings for sanctions may be brought by a data subject filing a claim, or by the Spanish Data Protection Agency (SDPA) on its own initiative. The level of fines which can be imposed for breach of the regulations varies according to the gravity of the breach and the damage caused. Note that the level of fines set out in the Data Protection Act is amongst the highest in Europe.[86]

- The SDPA has conducted a number of inspections on its own initiative (*ex officio*) in various sectors (hotels, schools, telecommunications etc). Upon completion of the exercise, the SDPA issues summary documents setting out guidelines for better compliance of the different sectors.

Practical considerations

8.163 A company facing an investigation or initiating a voluntary internal investigation in Spain should take the following action:

- Give clear instructions to employees to ensure that no documents are destroyed that might be relevant to the investigation. Steps should also be taken to make sure that these instructions are followed. Failure to preserve relevant documents could amount to a criminal offence.

---

[86] For example, transferring personal data without consent of the data subject, when required, is a very serious breach resulting in a fine of between €300,506 and €601,012.

- Inform employees that care needs to be taken when creating documents, to avoid speculation, exaggeration, and to limit the scope for misinterpretation. It should be made clear that this caution extends to internal emails and notes, not just formal memos and letters.

- Record key decisions taken by the company in investigating the problem and formulating its response.

Document management is especially important during a voluntary investiga- **8.164**
tion, as civil liability claims and criminal and regulatory actions will be difficult to defend if the company cannot produce good records to show that it acted responsibly in trying to investigate any possible infringements and amend the eventual damages caused. It is crucial to have records showing who did what, when, and how and why they did it.

H. Dealing with Privileged Documents

General rules on privilege

Legal privilege, in particular the duty of confidentiality that lawyers and court **8.165**
representatives[87] owe in respect of any information received from their clients while acting in their professional activities, is expressly regulated under Spanish law.[88] In Spain, only lawyers with a law degree and registered as active[89] members of the relevant Bar Association are bound by a duty of confidentiality. In addition, Spanish law prohibits lawyers and court representatives from making depositions about information obtained in the course of their professional activity. The breach of such obligations can result in administrative and, if applicable, criminal liability.

The Spanish Supreme Court has rendered a number of judgments[90] stating that **8.166**
attorney-client communications are privileged, as their confidentiality is essential for protecting the rights of defence of the client set forth in Article 24 of the Spanish Constitution. Although these judgments were handed down in criminal cases, where the protection of the right of defence is more critical than in the rest of the legal system, the same principles are applicable to civil and administrative cases.

---

[87] Court representatives are the representatives of the parties to a claim in their relations with the Courts. Their intervention, in ordinary proceedings and some verbal proceedings is compulsory.

[88] The general rules on privileged information and lawyers are set out in Art 542 of Organic Act 6/1985, of 1 July 1985, on the Judiciary Power, and in the Deontological Code that develops the General Statute of the Legal Practice.

[89] *Ejerciente*.

[90] Judgments of the Spanish Supreme Court of 17 February 1998 (RJ 1998, 1633) and 13 May 1999, amongst others.

8.167 There is no clear position in Spain as to whether communications between a company and in-house counsel are privileged under Spanish law. All lawyers have to be members of a Bar in order legally to act as lawyers in Spain. The implication is that all lawyers (including in-house lawyers) are subject to, and hence benefit from, the same rules of professional conduct. In addition, under Spanish law, the purpose of legal privilege is to protect the client's right of defence. It is therefore arguable that legal privilege should apply to documents from and communications with in-house counsel when such in-house counsel is clearly acting for the defence of the company in legal proceedings, in order to ensure the right of defence of the company.

8.168 In relation to competition investigations, the Spanish Competition authorities have followed the resolutions of the European Court of Justice (ECJ) and the Court of First Instance, which determine that the principle of confidentiality of written communications between lawyer and client has to be respected when requesting a party to produce documents in the context of an administrative or judicial proceeding. This protection is extended to earlier written communications relating to the subject matter of such proceedings. This protection is not lost when the legal advice is reported in internal documents, including internal notes, when these internal documents are confined to reporting the text or the content of those communications.

8.169 In the context of competition investigations, to benefit from the duty of confidentiality, the Courts require that (i) communications between lawyer and client are made for the purposes and in the interests of the client's right of defence and (ii) they emanate from independent lawyers, that is to say, lawyers who are not bound to the client by a relationship of employment.

8.170 There may be instances where a company may deem it necessary to disclose attorney-client communications as part of a defence strategy. However, the conditions under which a client can refuse to produce documents as a result of them being privileged are not expressly regulated and the case law is not too wide.

Waiving privilege

8.171 The legal privilege protecting information obtained by lawyers in the execution of their activities is both a professional right and an obligation. Lawyers cannot lawfully disclose any of the information received from, or communications between them and, their clients except in certain extraordinary cases.[91] The consent of the

---

[91] Art 5.8 of the Deontological Code that applies the General Statute of the Legal Practice sets out that in exceptional cases of great gravity, in which the observance of the obligation to keep the professional secret could cause irreparable damages or flagrant injustices, the Dean of the relevant Bar Association can advise the lawyer in order to guide him or her, and if possible, determine alternative means and procedures taking into account the legal rights in conflict.

client does not release the lawyer from his duty of professional confidentiality. Therefore, privilege cannot generally be lawfully waived under Spanish law by a lawyer, even with client consent.

However, the client, who is not subject to the duty of professional confidentiality, **8.172** can disclose the information produced by the lawyer if the client deems it necessary for its right of defence. Thus, material that is only in the possession of an external lawyer (or, possibly, an internal lawyer) cannot be disclosed directly by the lawyer, without breaching his or her bar obligations.

Limited waiver

Generally, providing privileged information to a regulator will not result in a **8.173** waiver of privilege over that information in relation to private civil litigants. Under Article 37 of Act 30/1992, private individuals and corporations have the right to access registers and documentation resulting from an administrative investigation, once such procedure is concluded. However, Article 37, at paragraph 5, provides an exception by which documents protected by trade or industrial secrecy[92] or privilege cannot be disclosed.

This protection cannot prevent documents from being disclosed to courts or **8.174** administrative authorities, but prevents commercially sensitive documents being disclosed to the public and, in particular, to competitors.

Moreover, Spanish regulators usually have specific duties of confidentiality set out **8.175** in legislation that prevents them from disclosing any confidential information that comes into their possession during an investigation. Whilst there are a number of exceptions to these duties,[93] disclosing confidential or privileged information to regulators does not necessarily constitute a complete waiver of a company's rights in this respect.

---

[92] There is no single piece of Spanish legislation that clearly defines what should be deemed to be a trade secret. However, there are a number of legal provisions which recognize the existence of trade secrets and grant them some protection. In addition, a number of pieces of legislation acknowledge the right of a company to protect its trade secrets except in the case of compulsory disclosure to an administrative authority. For example:
- Law 3/1991, of 10 January 1991, on Unfair Competition provides that it is uncompetitive behaviour to disclose or exploit, without appropriate authorization, industrial secrets or any kind of business secrets which have been accessed legitimately, but subject to a duty of secrecy, or illegitimately, as a consequence of espionage or a similar process or by inducing employees, suppliers, clients, or other obliged subjects to break their basic contractual obligations.
- The Spanish Criminal Code considers that the 'spreading, disclosure, or transfer of a business secret by the subject who was legally or contractually obliged to keep this secret' is a criminal offence—should this offence be committed, the subject shall be liable to imprisonment for between two and four years and a fine.

[93] The SMA, Art 90.4.

8.176 The SMA contains specific provisions regarding the confidentiality of the information received by the CNMV (or other competent authorities) when exercising its supervision and investigation powers. Under Article 90.2 of the SMA, any information gathered is protected by professional secrecy and, subject to certain exceptions,[94] may not be disclosed to any person or authority. This duty of secrecy ceases once the related information is voluntarily disclosed by the company under investigation.

8.177 The CNMV's obligations of confidentiality extend to all current or former employees of the CNMV and those who have had knowledge of inside information. Such persons may not give evidence or testify and may not publish, disclose, or display inside information or documents, even after they have left office, without the express consent of the CNMV. If consent is not given, the person concerned shall maintain secrecy and shall be exempt from any responsibility arising from it.[95] Failure to comply with this duty of confidentiality can result in criminal and other sanctions.

8.178 Article 90 of the SMA also sets out a number of situations in which the CNMV's duty of confidentiality is considered to be waived. These include[96] when the interested party expressly consents to the dissemination, publication, or disclosure of the data, where it is demanded by competent judicial authorities in criminal proceedings or in a civil suit, and where the CNMV is required to produce the information to fulfil obligations to foreign authorities or bodies responsible for the surveillance of financial institutions and investor protection.[97]

8.179 However, under Article 90.5, courts which receive confidential information in respect of a company from the CNMV (eg as a consequence of the obligation to collaborate with the Courts and the public prosecutors set out in Article 88 of the SMA) are obliged to adopt adequate measures to ensure that the information remains confidential for the duration of the relevant proceedings. Other authorities, persons or, firms which receive such information are also subject to professional secrecy and cannot use the information except to fulfil their legally established functions.

8.180 Similarly, Law 13/1994, of 1 June 1994, of the Autonomy of the Bank of Spain, imposes an obligation on members of the BS to treat confidential information[98]

---

[94] Considered at 8.177.

[95] The SMA, Art 90.3.

[96] Art 90.4 of the SMA provides for other situations in which the CNMV can waive its duty of confidentiality.

[97] The CNMV will only disclose the information to such authorities if a reciprocal arrangement is in place and those authorities and bodies are bound by a duty of confidentiality that is at least equivalent to that established under Spanish law.

[98] According to Art 6 of the Royal Legislative Decree 1298/1986, of 28 June 1986, on the adaptation of the law in force regarding credit entities, to the law of the European Communities, data, documents and information, which are in possession of the BS, are considered confidential.

as professional secrets, even after they have left the BS. Breach of this obligation will be sanctioned.[99]

SEPBLAC's duty of confidentiality is set out in Article 26 of the Royal Decree **8.181** 925/1995, which enacts Spain's anti-money laundering legislation. According to this Article, anyone who carries out or has carried out an activity for the Commission for the Prevention of Money Laundering and Monetary Offences and has had access to confidential information is compelled to keep such information secret, and may only disclose it with the express permission of such Commission. As with the CNMV, SEPBLAC can be compelled to disclose such confidential information in certain circumstances.

Public authorities or entities receiving confidential information from the **8.182** Commission for the Prevention of Money Laundering and Monetary Offences are also bound by duties of confidentiality and cannot use such information other than in accordance with their functions established by law.

Finally, Law 15/2007, of 3 July 2007, on Defence of Competition, allows Spanish **8.183** Competition Authorities to declare, *ex officio* or following the request of a party, certain information to be confidential and non-disclosable to other parties in the proceedings.

In practice, these confidentiality obligations are duly observed by the regulators. **8.184** However, in the past there have been cases of leakage of confidential information by the CNMV.

Privilege pitfalls

The risks associated with privilege are relatively predictable in Spain. Whilst it is **8.185** unclear whether communications with in-house lawyers will continue to enjoy legal privilege to the same extent as communications with external lawyers have done (aside from in EU Competition proceedings, where they do not), the privilege of external lawyers is as robust as ever. Moreover, the release of otherwise privileged documents to a regulator does not generally make them vulnerable to inspection by third parties or potential litigants. Spain does not have a general disclosure or discovery procedure and hence the issue of whether a document that would otherwise have been privileged loses its protection because it has been disclosed to a regulator is not relevant in practice.

---

99 However, this obligation does not apply if the Spanish Parliament requests access to the information covered by the duty of confidentiality. Any requests for such information must be made to the Governor of the Bank of Spain, who can require detailed explanation of the reasons for the request, which can be considered at either a specially convened confidential meeting or through the normal proceedings for dealing with access to classified matters.

I. Managing Regulators

Dialogue with regulators

8.186 Spanish corporations have no legal obligation to maintain an open dialogue with regulators. However, in practice they will comply with all requests for information from a regulator. Consequently, some large corporations have designated employees generally responsible for relationships with regulators or departments in charge of communications with them.[100]

8.187 If a corporation anticipates an investigation, it should communicate to regulators in advance any details of the activity subject to investigation, particularly in the case of activities associated with eligible assets, regulatory capital, or late transactions, which frequently attract regulatory attention. It is generally better in Spain to take the initiative and to have a proactive relationship with a regulator, particularly when some form of relationship is inevitable.

8.188 It should be noted that some institutions are obliged to have a dedicated internal representative for money laundering matters.[101] This representative manages all requests and requirements from, and communications to, SEPBLAC.

8.189 It is generally recommended to maintain open and fluent channels of communication with the regulators, if possible by assigning experts who deal with and manage the relationship with them. This can decrease the likelihood or severity of investigations, as the company will have a better opportunity to explain the actions taken and the rationale behind them with more detail than would otherwise be the case.

Control of scope of investigation

8.190 Each of the Spanish regulators has a defined mandate and will limit its investigation to the scope of its jurisdiction. However, the powers of the regulators are so wide that, in practice, once a regulator has determined that it has jurisdiction to investigate a matter, it is very difficult to limit the scope of its investigation.

8.191 Regulators have the discretion to determine the information they need for their investigations, and are entitled to request whatever information they deem pertinent

---

[100] These are usually known as the Institutional Relationships Department (*Departamento de Relaciones Institucionales*) in the banking area or the Investors Relationship Department (*Departamento de Relaciones con los Inversores*) in the securities and markets area, but it can even be run by the Financial Department (*Dirección Financiera*).

[101] Royal Decree 925/1995, of 9 June 1995, developing Law 19/1993, of 28 December 1993, of certain measures for the prevention of money laundering (the Money Laundering Act), (the Money Laundering Regulation), Art 12.2.

for their purposes (which are usually defined in very broad terms). Regulators are not limited to investigating a specific allegation at hand, they can investigate whatever action falls within their mandates.

Moreover, failure to provide the relevant regulator with the information it requests, **8.192** in most cases, constitutes a very serious infringement leading to considerable sanctions. Therefore, although in theory a company could refuse to produce a specific document alleging that it is not pertinent to matters within the scope of the requesting regulator's mandate, this would only be advisable in very exceptional cases as it could lead to very serious sanctions and, moreover, the company would have the difficult task of having to prove that the regulator is exceeding its mandate.

Use of information by regulators

During an investigation, regulators can demand as much information as they **8.193** deem necessary. Corporations are obliged to cooperate and share with the regulators all the information that they require, except for that information which is legally privileged.

Although regulators are not generally entitled to disclose to third parties the infor- **8.194** mation that they have been given[102] (and can only make use of such for the purposes of the investigation) information can, in certain circumstances, be shared between regulators. As detailed above,[103] all the information disclosed to regulators must be treated as confidential, except when wider dissemination is the purpose of the disclosure (eg disclosure of price-sensitive information) or the information disclosed is not privileged or confidential (eg corporate governance reports).

Managing multiple regulators

Although Articles 87[104] and 88[105] of the SMA impose obligations on the CNMV **8.195** to coordinate with other regulatory bodies in the investigation of an entity, in

---

[102] Act 30/1992, Art 37.5; Royal Decree 1298/1986, of 28 June 1986, Art 6; the SMA, Art 89; and the Resolution of the Bank of Spain's Government, dated 28 March 2000, approving the internal regulation of the Bank of Spain, Art 17.

[103] Discussed at 8.172.

[104] The SMA, Art 87.5: 'Whenever firms which are individually supervised by a body other than the National Securities Market Commission form part of a consolidated group of investment services firms, the National Securities Market Commission, in exercising the powers attributed to it by this Law regarding such firms, must coordinate its actions with the respective supervisory body in each case.'

[105] The SMA, Art 88:

In all cases where the powers of surveillance and supervision of the National Securities Market Commission and the Bank of Spain overlap, both institutions shall coordinate their actions on the understanding that oversight of the relevant financial institutions' solvency rests with the institution keeping the respective register and that oversight of the operation of the securities markets rests with the National Securities Market Commission. In order to coordinate their respective powers of surveillance and supervision, the National Securities Market Commission and the Bank of Spain shall sign agreements specifying their respective responsibilities.

practice this process has been found to be deficient. It is, therefore, generally recommended that corporations communicate with each regulator separately.

8.196 It will usually (and particularly when dealing with especially technical matters) be advisable to tailor a specific report for each regulator instead of submitting the same report to all regulators. This does involve an element of duplication but leads to a more precise product focused on the legal concerns of each regulator.[106] It is, clearly, critical that such reports are consistent and are structured as part of a suite of reports, working together to deal with issues comprehensively, since they may well be exchanged between regulators.

J. Managing Employees During Investigations

Powers to compel cooperation

8.197 Spanish employment legislation is very protective towards employees, especially when it comes to constitutional rights such as the right to privacy, the right to honour, and the right to dignity.

8.198 The Employment Act establishes the general basic legal framework for employment matters. However, it should be noted that almost every industry has its own collective bargaining agreement in place between employers and employees, which may establish rules that differ from the general legislation. Therefore, the Employment Act should not be treated as containing the entire universe of legal rights and obligations governing the employer/employee relationship.

8.199 In general terms, a company's employees have the legal obligation to follow the employer's instructions (or those of the person designated by the employer) when carrying out the job for which they have been hired.[107] The employee has a duty of diligence and cooperation towards the employer as set out in the law, collective bargaining agreements, and the orders and instructions adopted by the employer in the regular exercise of his or her management faculties.

8.200 The employer may adopt the most appropriate monitoring and control measures in order to verify that the employee is complying with his or her job's obligations and duties,[108] particularly against the backdrop of an investigation. If an employee does not comply with his or her legal obligation to cooperate with the employer, then the employee may be penalized according to the law and/or the collective bargaining agreement that governs the relevant industry.

---

[106] Guidelines relating to the tailoring of the report are set out further at 8.236.
[107] The Employment Act, Arts 20.1 and 20.2.
[108] The Employment Act, Art 20.3.

A company should not threaten its employees. Moreover, whilst a company can, **8.201** in principle, compel its employees to cooperate with an ongoing investigation on the grounds of the employees' obligation to follow the employer's instructions, a company's ability to monitor and compel cooperation from its employees is limited by the fundamental rights set out by the Spanish Constitution. These include the right to privacy, right to honour, right to confidentiality of communications, and freedom of speech of employees, which must be respected by the employer.

Although there is no specific legislation regarding powers of employers during **8.202** investigations, it is likely that the case law on the powers of companies to monitor employees (ie monitoring the use of email and voice mail communications, Internet access and other stored information) will be applicable. The case law indicates that control or monitoring measures taken by an employer may be lawful in some circumstances, if certain requirements are met.[109]

Therefore, if the employer requests the employee's cooperation in the course of **8.203** an internal investigation that is related to the job for which the employee has been hired, then the employee should cooperate. In the case where an employee refuses to participate, and such participation is considered within his employment duties, the company could penalize the employee with disciplinary measures including, where appropriate, dismissal alleging misconduct and disobedience of the employer's management powers.[110]

Employees are entitled to refuse to respond to those questions which are not related **8.204** with their employment, such as personal, family related, or other questions, unless the company demonstrates that such queries are clearly related with the investigation. The company shall consider in any case that employees' fundamental rights to privacy must be respected.

Control on threats

Under the Spanish Employment Act, employees are required to comply with the **8.205** instructions given by their employer within the regular exercise of its managing powers. However, the employer is obliged to respect the employee's dignity and fundamental rights.

In light of the above, any requests for cooperation made by an employer to an **8.206** employee should be made in a way that does not amount to threatening the employee, respects the employee's dignity, and is non-discriminatory and justified.

---

109 This is considered further at 8.150.
110 The Employment Act, Art 54.2(b).

8.207 An employer's actions which breach an employee's rights of dignity and privacy may be considered by a social court as very serious infringements and may be sanctioned with a fine of up to €187,515 and, as the case may be, considered null and void.

8.208 In addition, there is a possibility that an employee may file a claim either asking for termination of his or her employment relationship or claiming damages on the basis that the employer has breached his or her fundamental right to privacy. In the event that the court upholds the employee's claim:

- to terminate the employment agreement, the relevant employee will be entitled to compensation equal to 45 days of salary per year of service up to 42 months' salary (pursuant to current employment case law no additional compensations should be granted); or

- for damages (for breach of fundamental rights), the relevant court will assess their amount on a case-by-case basis (there are no clear criteria for the determination of the relevant compensation).

Representation

8.209 There are no specific provisions prohibiting corporations from recommending separate counsel for their employees during an investigation. In cases where an employee may be liable separately from its corporate employer, it might be advisable from a practical point of view to recommend separate counsel. In order to avoid infringing the defence rights of the employee or the company, as the case may be, such recommendation should be made prior to commencing the investigation.

8.210 In any event, advising both the employee and the company may have some ethical implications for counsel. This is the case when, during an investigation, it becomes apparent that the interests of the employee are not in line with those of the company and, consequently, there is a conflict of interest. In such circumstances, counsel should cease acting for (at least) one of the parties. This notwithstanding, if counsel has confidential information relating to both parties, it would be necessary for counsel to stop rendering services to both of them.

8.211 Employees do not have an express right to be assisted by a lawyer when they attend any investigation related meetings. However, a refusal to allow an employee to appear assisted by a lawyer may be seen as bad faith on the part of the company and, accordingly, may be counter-productive.

The conduct of the interview

8.212 During the course of an investigation, there may be situations where counsel is required to interview employees. Handling such interviews adequately may be critical in obtaining a useful outcome in relation to the investigation. Accordingly, the interview should be prepared carefully and sufficiently in advance and the interviewer should be provided with any available information material to the investigation.

At the beginning of the interview it may be advisable for counsel to introduce **8.213** himself or herself as counsel for the company. Additionally, any rules applicable to the meeting (eg confidentiality) must be made clear at this stage of the conversation. Particularly, if records or notes of the interview are being taken, it is necessary to disclose such fact to the employee, and explain who will have access to them.

Counsel should explain to the employee that he or she is advising the company **8.214** and that he or she is under no obligation to maintain professional secrecy over the contents of the interview. This notwithstanding, it may be useful to give an assurance that information disclosed by the employee will be treated as confidential and not be made public or disclosed without the consent of the employee. However, it is advisable to expressly allow for the possibility of using the information obtained in an interview in a disciplinary procedure against the relevant employee or disclosing it to any regulator or judicial authority if so requested.

Spanish legal deontology codes do not provide for specific rules regarding the **8.215** relationship between counsel and the company's employees. However, there is a general obligation on Spanish lawyers to act at any time with due respect to 'honesty, integrity, probity'.[111] Accordingly, any relations between counsel and the employees of a company must be based on truth, mutual respect, and politeness. Besides ethical considerations, keeping a cordial and professional approach will increase the responsiveness and cooperativeness of the employee. It is essential to avoid using lies or creating confusion to obtain information. This may generate distrust between the employee and counsel and would clearly make future communications between them more difficult.

Investigations and disciplinary process

The execution of an investigation may unveil new facts, previously unknown to **8.216** the company, which may give rise to disciplinary action. Accordingly, the company should avoid giving assurances to the employees involved in an investigation process that they will not be subject to disciplinary procedures.

Whilst it is uncommon to do so in Spain, the company may decide to grant an **8.217** amnesty to an employee in exchange for full collaboration with the investigation process. However, the company cannot offer protection against administrative sanctions imposed by regulators or any personal civil or criminal liability deriving

---

[111] Spanish Code of Deontology for the Legal Profession.

from third party claims. Additionally, it should be noted that, under certain circumstances, the company might be obliged to take action against an employee. This is particularly the case in the following cases:

- in certain regulated industries (eg financial entities or insurance companies), where employees in key positions are required to meet certain standards of 'honour'. If the acts committed by an employee in such a position give rise to regulatory or criminal liability, the employee may no longer be suitable for that post; and

- where a criminal sanction against an employee automatically disqualifies the employee from its post without the need for employer intervention (ie in regulated industries where the body overseeing the industry requires certain standards to be maintained by persons filling particular posts within supervised firms).

8.218 If an employee has been, or if there is a reasonable suspicion that he or she may have been, involved in conduct which is the subject of the investigation, the employee may, as a precautionary measure, be suspended with or without pay. Such a measure would be exceptional, and subject to reasonable limits, in particular on the time and scope of the suspension. In practice, it might be easier to justify a precautionary suspension if the relevant employee continues to receive full pay and benefits, whilst the company is carrying out the investigation.

8.219 In this regard, and in particular when considering the term of the suspension, it should be noted that under Spanish law employees have a right to effective occupation, which they may try to enforce if they feel the suspension is breaching it. Unjustified breach of this right may entitle the employee to terminate the employment agreement with a right to compensation equivalent to 45 days of salary per year of service, up to 42 months. Accordingly, any suspension should be no longer than the period of time that is actually necessary to carry out the investigation.

8.220 It is important to be aware that any applicable collective bargaining agreement may include specific procedures that must be followed when a company intends to take precautionary or disciplinary measures. The application of a collective bargaining agreement is mandatory and not the choice of a company subject to it.

8.221 Under Spanish law, employee related disciplinary measures are subject to particularly tight limitation periods.[112] Accordingly, it is very important to take appropriate steps to ensure that any investigation is carried out sufficiently fast and undue delays are avoided.

---

[112] Employment disciplinary measures for infringements are time-barred after ten days (for minor infringements), 20 days (for serious infringements), or 60 days (for very serious infringements), from the date on which the company first knew of the existence of the breach. Additionally, no employment disciplinary measures can be adopted against an employee in respect of an infringement after six months from the date on which it took place.

Challenges posed by ex-employees

Generally, aside from any obligations which may remain in force after the termi- **8.222**
nation of a contract of employment (eg confidentiality clauses, trade secrets etc),
a company will have no tools or legally enforceable rights at its disposal to induce
former employees to cooperate with an investigation. Consequently, it is very
difficult in practice to obtain evidence from former employees.

It is therefore advisable to, where the termination of an employee's employment **8.223**
involves a degree of negotiation, include a cooperation covenant in the termination agreement (especially where the employee occupies a sensitive post). Pursuant to such covenant, a former employee would be bound to participate in an
investigation process. However, it is necessary to bear in mind that such covenant
has limited effect—it cannot be used to compel a former employee to cooperate
against his or her will.

Payment of legal fees/indemnification/fee advances

There are no specific provisions governing whether corporations can indemnify **8.224**
or advance fees to employees for separate legal representation in internal and/or
regulatory investigations. Although not prohibited by the employment regulations, the practical consequences of such a course of action should be reviewed on
a case-by-case basis.

Joint defence agreements between and among a corporation and its employees **8.225**
are permitted under Spanish employment legislation. However, once again, the
risks attaching to their use should be reviewed on a case-by-case basis, since in
some cases they may give rise to conflicts (eg if sanctions may be imposed on both
the company and the employee separately). In such cases, it is not advisable for
the parties to agree on a joint defence (particularly if only one of the parties is to
lead the conduct of the defence).

On the other hand, joint defence agreements may be useful in certain circum- **8.226**
stances to ensure the full cooperation of employees, access to all available information, and the coordination of defence strategies. Additionally, joint defence
agreements between the company and its employees may be perceived by staff as
evidence of the company's commitment to its employees and, consequently,
facilitate the company's own defence.

There are alternative coordinated defence mechanisms available to companies **8.227**
and employees. Where joint defence agreements are not possible due to conflicts
of interest, it may be possible to establish collaboration or coordination undertakings between the company and its employees (eg covering information
exchange, or coordinating strategies). However, this is normally carried out on an
informal basis and coordinated by legal counsel.

8.228 It should also be noted that, pursuant to the codes of conduct[113] of most of the Spanish bar associations,[114] lawyers are under an obligation to give up a case as soon as they identify a conflict of interest. This must be done in such a way as to minimize the negative effects on the right to defence of the parties involved. Although not specifically regulated, counsel could simply give up one of the parties unless he or she has obtained relevant information from such party, which could be used against it, therefore infringing its right to defence.[115] In order to avoid the likelihood of this occurring, counsel should, when dealing with employees, clearly indicate from the outset that he or she is acting for the company.[116]

Best practices

8.229 In order to facilitate the cooperation of employees and to minimize the risk of any eventual breach of employment legislation, an 'information letter' should be addressed to employees involved in an investigation, requesting their cooperation, explaining the reasons for the investigation, and limiting any requests to those which are of a professional nature and relate to the subject matter of the investigation.

Where an investigation involves a high number of employees, the Works Council (or the relevant employees' representatives) should be informed about the investigation, before any actions are taken or interviews performed, even though this may slow down the investigation process.

Generally, meetings and interviews may not be recorded and/or transcribed unless the employee gives his or her express, voluntary, and unequivocal consent.

This notwithstanding, it is necessary to point out that internal investigation procedures in Spain are uncommon and are generally carried out in an informal manner. Accordingly, it is not possible to identify any accepted or common practices in this regard.

K. Winding up an Investigation

Managing expectations

8.230 As internal investigations are not yet a widespread practice in Spain, there are no consolidated principles regarding the winding up of an investigation.

---

113 *Códigos deontológicos.*
114 *Colegios de abogados.*
115 In which case, counsel should give up the case.
116 Considered further at 8.212.

The investigation team should ensure that the investigation has been sufficient to **8.231** have obtained full details of the actions taken and the eventual infringements committed (if any). An internal investigation should be at least as comprehensive as an investigation taken by a regulator.

Once the investigation team has concluded an investigation, it should consider **8.232** whether it is appropriate or useful to draft a written report. The corporate management, assessing the circumstances of the case, should decide if a PR strategy is needed, the type of PR strategy that should be adopted, and whether the regulator should be made aware of the results of the investigation.

When assessing the appropriate type of action to take on conclusion of an inves- **8.233** tigation it is always advisable to seek the advice of a PR agency with crisis management expertise, as well as that of independent legal experts to assess the gravity of the results of the investigation, in order to coordinate a PR Strategy.

Coordinating a Public Relations strategy

If it is decided that it is beneficial to disclose the results of an investigation, the **8.234** statements made by the company should be clear, true, mindful of the shareholders' interests, and avoid any incrimination. The company will usually demonstrate its concern regarding the situation and its intention to compensate any damage caused and avoid future infringement, and communicate the measures taken to rectify any issues.

It is essential that the company does not contradict itself—everything said has to **8.235** be consistent with any final report that could be made publicly available, and should be true and accurate.

To this end, whilst it is important to maintain good relations with the media, it is **8.236** also important not to disclose any final conclusions until the report on the investigation is finished and the company has decided the position it will take towards the general public.

L. Reporting Obligations

Tailoring the report

There are no specific requirements under Spanish law regarding the content of **8.237** any report to the regulators. If the company decides to submit a report of an internal investigation to regulators, it is free to decide whether to submit a full report or to tailor the report to the interests of each individual regulator.

There are both advantages and risks to tailoring reports, which should be weighed **8.238** carefully before deciding on an ultimate course of action.

8.239 Tailoring an internal report allows the report to be modified to use more appropriate language and be more descriptive: an internal report is an internal document aimed at people with good knowledge of the company; it will not always give clear explanations; it may use company jargon; and it may be less accurate in describing the facts and circumstances of the case—this could leave the report open to misinterpretation if it is submitted in an unedited form.

8.240 However, tailoring a report runs the risk of creating contradictions with the internal report, which could at a later date create problems for the company if it was perceived that the company had not been entirely transparent. In order to avoid this situation, the drafters of a tailored report for a regulator should tailor the report knowing that the regulator could likely gain access to the original internal document if it so wished. Therefore, if any change is introduced in the tailored report, the company should take care to ensure that such changes, when compared with the original report, do not produce mismatches of information or misunderstandings, or indicate an intention to hide facts or circumstances.

Coordinating with Public Relations strategy

8.241 As internal investigations and the subsequent submissions of reports are not common practice in Spain, there are no particular principles to be observed when coordinating the submission of an investigation report with any PR strategy. Spanish law does not hinder the disclosure of an investigation report. Nevertheless, it is not normal practice to make a wider disclosure of a report submitted to a regulator, and a company would not usually even publicize that an internal investigation had taken place or that a report had been submitted to the relevant regulator.

8.242 However, a company should consider the expediency of submitting a report of an internal investigation if it fits in with the company's general PR strategy, as it may serve as evidence of the company's corporate responsibility, its intention to follow good practices, and of its general approach of rectifying issues swiftly and effectively. In practice, the disclosure of a report or of the fact that a report has been submitted to a regulator, as a general rule, is only advisable if it aims to correct any inaccuracy already published or prevents the spread of rumours or any speculation prejudicial to the company which does not correspond to the reality of the facts.

8.243 Main index listed Corporations (known in Spain as Ibex 35), use slogans referring to corporate governance compliance to attract possible investors. The market appears to regard highly transparency and compliance with the corporate governance code. Therefore, disclosing investigation reports could be highly beneficial to such companies.

M. Litigation Risks

Risks of criminal litigation commenced by regulators

Regulators have a wide range of powers and can begin and conduct administrative **8.244** procedures and investigations, as well as impose administrative sanctions for administrative infringements. However, in the Spanish legal framework, regulators cannot pursue a corporation for criminal liability. As soon as a regulator, in the course of an investigation, obtains evidence that may be related to one of the crimes contained in the Spanish Criminal Code, it should suspend its investigation and inform the judicial authorities in charge of investigating and adjudicating the suspected crime.[117]

In practice, it is common for the Special Prosecutor's Office,[118] one of the bodies **8.245** of the Prosecutor's Ministry, to initiate a criminal investigation based on an initial regulatory investigation carried out by the CNMV. In this regard, pursuant to Article 88 of the SMA, the CNMV 'shall provide such cooperation as may be requested by the Judiciary or the Public Prosecutor's office in order to clarify events relating to the securities markets which may be of a criminal nature'.

This has occurred in a number of cases, including the *Xfera* case, in which a **8.246** number of the directors of Abengoa were prosecuted by the Special Prosecutor's Office following a CNMV investigation.[119]

Risks of civil litigation commenced by regulators

Under the Spanish legal framework, regulators are not empowered to pursue cor- **8.247** porations under civil jurisdiction. Pursuant to the provisions of Act 30/1992, regulators are only entitled to pursue those actions or omissions that may be considered to be infringements of the administrative legislation in order to impose administrative sanctions.[120] However, the sanctions imposed by a regulator can be challenged before the contentious administrative courts.

---

[117] Pursuant to the SMA, Art 96, the 'exercise of the authority to penalise referred to in this Law shall be independent of any possible concurrent liability for criminal offences or misdemeanours. However, when criminal proceedings are underway for the same events or for other events that cannot rationally be separated from the events punishable under this Law, the proceedings relating to such events shall be suspended pending the court's final decision. On resumption of the proceedings, if applicable, any resolution made must respect the court's findings of fact.'

[118] Considered at 8.41.

[119] The investigation was a result of the transfer (in December 2002) of the interests in Xfera held by a company owned by the majority shareholders of Abengoa to an affiliate of Abengoa for a price far over its market price. The National Audience finally dismissed the case in March 2007.

[120] Act 30/1992, Art 4; and Royal Decree 1398/1993, Art 1.

8.248 It should be noted that individuals and entities subject to the provisions of the SMA, and the persons managing them, could be sanctioned by the CNMV for infringements of the rules governing the securities market.[121]

Risks of private civil litigation

8.249 There is no prohibition in Spanish law preventing civil plaintiffs from bringing actions based upon regulatory investigations and actions.

8.250 Third parties (eg investors) who have suffered damage due to a regulatory breach discovered by way of an investigation may seek compensation through civil proceedings. The relevant facts discovered during the investigation can be used as evidence of the misconduct in question. However, the regular standards of proof would continue to apply, such as those regarding misconduct, damages, and the causal relationship.

Relevance of investigation report

8.251 Pursuant to Spanish legislation,[122] administrative acts of public bodies are vested with a presumption of validity. Therefore, a regulatory finding or pronouncement will be considered valid, and could be used in the course of a civil procedure by the civil litigant.[123] However, a regulatory act or finding following an investigation is an administrative act that can be challenged by the company if it considers that it is unlawful.

8.252 Administrative acts can be challenged in some cases directly before the contentious administrative courts, while in other cases they have to be first challenged before the public body itself (eg resolutions of the BS issued further to its investigation activities have to be challenged before the Ministry of Economy)[124] and, following the conclusion of the administrative procedure, then before the courts.

8.253 If the resolutions of the regulator are not challenged within the statutory time limits, they will become final and unchallengeable. In these circumstances, the administrative acts will be vested with a presumption of validity that could only be revised under extraordinary circumstances such as where: factual mistakes

---

[121] The SMA, Art 95.

[122] Act 30/1992, Art 57.1, establishes that 'all acts of the administrative authorities will be valid and display their effects from the day they are enacted'; and RD 1398/1993, Art 17.5, states that 'the facts that have been confirmed by authorised public employees and that have been formalised in a public document complying with all the legal requirements, will be considered as a valid piece of evidence, without prejudice to those pieces of evidence that the concerned parties may propose'.

[123] The Civil Procedure Act, Art 319.1 (*Ley 1/2000, de 7 Enero, de Enjuiciamiento Civil*).

[124] Law 26/1988, Art 43 *bis* 7.

are apparent in the file documents; essential documents are discovered that demonstrate a mistake; there is an unchangeable and final judgement declaring documents or statements on which the resolution is based to be false; or there is an unchangeable and final judgement stating that the resolution was passed as a consequence of violence, bribery, or other punishable behaviour.

N. Settlement with Regulators

Process

Pursuant to Article 88 of Act 30/1992, one of the ways for a company to terminate an administrative procedure carried out by regulators is to reach a settlement agreement with them. **8.254**

This option is, however, only available when the requirements stated in that Article are met, that is to say that the settlement agreement (i) cannot be unlawful; (ii) cannot be related to a subject on which legislation prohibits settlement agreements; and (iii) must contain certain minimum information regarding the parties concerned, the personal, functional, and territorial scope, and term of validity of the agreement. **8.255**

In connection with the second requirement, Spanish case law[125] has specified that those administrative powers whose exercise is rigorously regulated, such as sanctioning powers, fall outside the scope of legal transaction, and thus cannot be the object of a settlement agreement, except when otherwise provided by special law. Where so provided, a regulator should take into account the general interest and the specific circumstances of the case before reaching a settlement agreement. In this regard, it is worth noting that settlement agreements are provided for in the anti-trust regulations, but there are no similar provisions in the specific regulations applicable to the sanctioning procedures followed by the CNMV and BS. **8.256**

However, the payment of economic sanctions imposed by the CNMV may be partially or fully dismissed, or deferred, by the Minister for the Economy and the Treasury, on the basis of a report compiled by the CNMV, provided that the enforcement of the penalty in its original terms would be unfair or contrary to the general interest due to: (i) a change of control following the commission of the infringement; (ii) an insolvency proceeding; or (iii) other exceptional circumstances. **8.257**

These measures, governed by Law 37/1998, of 16 November 1998, which modified Directive 93/22, of 10 May 1993, were introduced to counteract the problem **8.258**

---

[125] Judgment of the Supreme Court of Canary Islands, N° 853/1998 of 7 September (RJCA 1998\3083) and Judgment of the Spanish Supreme Court of 30 April 1979 (RJ 1979\1592).

of high economic fines being imposed on companies that had, since the infringement in question, been absorbed by other corporate groups, which usually resulted in the change of the entire governing body of the corporate in question. In these circumstances, the new management team would be unrelated to the former one, which was after all responsible for the infringements that gave rise to the economic fines. In such cases, it did not seem fair to impose the burden of a huge economic sanction, since it would have had a very negative impact on the new management team and new shareholders.

8.259 For these reasons, Spanish legislation decided to provide the Minister for the Economy and the Treasury with the necessary powers to analyse on a case-by-case basis the potential impact of any economic sanctions imposed and to tailor the measures to each situation in order to reach a fair result.

8.260 These exceptional measures will not be extended under any circumstances to the former directors or members of the former management team that were responsible for carrying out the infringing actions that gave rise to the administrative sanctions.

8.261 Moreover, neither the dismissal nor deferral of a penalty is possible, under any circumstances, where, on the sale of a company, any penalty, incurred or prospective, arising as a result of a prior infringement by the company, is effectively discounted from the consideration due to the vendor or where the vendor offers an indemnity to the purchaser in respect of such penalty.

Is admission necessary?

8.262 Admission is not a requisite element of the settlement processes regulated by Article 88 of Act 30/1992. Neither is it required in settlement procedures with the Competition regulators. In fact, this is one of its key advantages as the allegedly infracting company undertakes to change its conduct without admitting a prior infringement.

8.263 As there are no settlement processes available in respect of the other regulators such as the CNMV, BS and SEPBLAC, the question of the admission of a previous wrongdoing is not applicable. However, it should be noted that Article 8 of the Royal Decree 1398/1993, of 4 August 1993 (RD 1398/1993), approving the Ruling on the procedure of the sanctioning procedures, envisages that sanction proceedings are resolved, if the infringing party admits its responsibility with the imposition of the sanction.

8.264 Where a sanction is monetary, admission can lead to a reduction in the final amount, provided that this is specified in any applicable regulations. However, no such regulations apply to sanctions of the CNMV, BS or SEPBLAC.

Impact if under investigation by multiple regulators

Pursuant to Article 88.4 of Act 30/1992, a settlement agreement reached with **8.265** one regulator would not alter the competences granted to other administrative authorities. Therefore, a settlement agreement reached with one of the regulators investigating the company should not affect the ability of other regulators to investigate and, where applicable, sanction such company.

Plea bargaining and amnesty arrangements

Plea bargaining under Spanish law is considerably different to that regulated in **8.266** other legal systems (such as the UK and US, for example).

In criminal procedures, the public prosecutor (and, where applicable, the **8.267** private prosecutor, or both) is responsible for pursuing a criminal action against offenders. At the beginning of a trial, the prosecutor will file a writ of criminal charges establishing the specific penalty that should be imposed on the offenders.

Pursuant to the Spanish Criminal Procedural Act 1882,[126] if the offender **8.268** agrees with the highest penalty as stated in the writ of criminal charges and admits his guilt, a judgment would be passed 'in conformity', therefore avoiding the trial.

In practice, this implies that prosecutors may negotiate the final sanction to be **8.269** imposed with the offender.

There are three requirements that a court would have to verify before passing **8.270** a 'conformity judgment': (i) that the agreed penalty is appropriate according to the criminal offence charged, that is, the penalty is within the limits set out in the Spanish Criminal Code for the offence being prosecuted; (ii) that the penalty is less than six years' imprisonment; and (iii) that the defendant has acted voluntarily, that is, knowing the consequences deriving from his conformity.

If such requirements are met, then the judge must pass judgment 'in conformity' **8.271** establishing the agreed penalty and is not able to impose a higher one.

Therefore, under Spanish law, strictly speaking there is no 'plea bargaining', but **8.272** the defendant can negotiate and accept the penalty requested in the writ of criminal charges in certain cases.

---

[126] Art 655 for ordinary proceedings and 784.3 and 787 for abbreviated proceedings.

O. Conclusion

8.273 The Spanish investigations regime is almost exclusively based on regulatory investigations. Voluntary internal investigations remain a developing practice.

8.274 Despite the recent legal reforms towards stricter regulation and closer supervision of companies (especially listed companies), the new rules do not contemplate the obligation to communicate infringements to the regulators, or the possibility of avoiding or reducing sanctions by self-reporting them.

8.275 Moreover, although the general law on administrative bodies contemplates the possibility of reaching settlement agreements as a way of ending of an administrative procedure, the specific regulations governing most of the individual regulators do not provide for this option.

8.276 Therefore, although companies conduct their own investigations when there are signs of possible infringements; the fact is that there are still no mechanisms enhancing the communication of the results of such to the regulators.

8.277 The only exceptions to this would be the Anti-Money Laundering Act, which establishes the duty on 'obliged subjects' to self-report to the relevant authorities any suspected money laundering activity, and the obligation for listed companies to disclose information about activities related with, or having an influence on, the equities market (price-sensitive information).

8.278 On the other hand, as we have seen, regulatory investigations have become more common in recent years due to the recent legal reforms which set out further obligations on companies.

8.279 Regulators have far reaching powers to investigate and the different specific investigation procedures contemplate severe sanctions for those companies that do not cooperate with regulators during investigations.

8.280 It is likely that following the recent Afinsa and Forum Filatélico scandals stricter measures will be adopted in the future in order to avoid frauds related to tangible assets. To this end, the Ministry of Health and Consumer Protection has already prepared a bill of law on tangible assets companies, which increases the transparency obligations of such companies.

8.281 There is currently no legislation being prepared regarding a substantial amendment of the current regime on investigations, therefore it is expected that in the short to medium term the investigations will continue to be commenced by the regulators and there will remain less of an impetus for companies to initiate their own internal investigations.

Annex 8.1

Penalty procedures taken by the CNMV

	Cases opened		Cases closed	
	2005	2006	2005	2006
Very serious infringements	15	9	25	11
Failure to disclose/incorrect disclosure of significant holdings	—	3	13	1
Engaging in prohibited activities	3	2	3	1
Market manipulation	1	—	—	1
Breach of coefficients	—	—	—	—
Failure to disclose significant events/provision of misleading, incorrect or materially incomplete information	—	—	—	—
Violation of general securities market regulations	3	—	5	3
Violation of general IIC regulations	—	—	—	—
Accounting irregularities	2	1	—	—
Unregistered issues	—	—	—	—
Insider dealing	6	3	2	5
Obstruction of inspections	—	—	2	—
Serious infringements	9	4	11	11
Accounting irregularities	—	—	3	—
Engaging in prohibited activities	—	—	1	1
Breach of coefficients	—	—	1	—
Violation of general securities market regulations	4	—	—	—
Violation of general IIC regulations	1	—	1	—
Breach of rules of conduct	3	—	5	3
Market manipulation	1	—	—	1
Insider trading	—	1	—	—
Lack of compliance in filing publications of the relevant reports	—	3	—	6

Source: CNMV

9

INVESTIGATIONS IN ITALY

A. Introduction[1]

9.01 The Italian regulatory climate and the approach to corporate investigations have been in a state of flux in recent years, largely due to a series of financial scandals and corporate collapses in 2002–2005 involving companies such as Cirio, Parmalat, Giacomelli, Banca Popolare di Lodi and Unipol as well as other Italian corporates and financial institutions. A host of legal reforms were enacted between 1998 and 2007, starting with the Financial Services Consolidating Act (FLCA)[2] and its implementing regulations, followed by Legislative Decree no 231 of July 2001 ('Decree 231') on the 'quasi-criminal' liability of corporations and by a comprehensive reform of Italian corporate law that entered into force on 1 January 2004. The new regulatory regime was also bolstered by the market abuse provisions enacted on 18 April 2005, the Law on Public Savings of 28 December 2005, later coordinated with the FLCA and the Italian Banking Act by Legislative Decree no 303 of 29 December 2006. This new legislation has been supplemented by the new Self-Regulatory Code on Corporate Governance for listed companies, adopted in March 2006.

9.02 The last few months have seen a wave of activism, by large (and mostly foreign) institutional investors, on corporate governance issues. The tangible increase in

---

[1] Contributors: Fabrizio Arossa, Grazia Bonante, Giovanni Barone, Andrea Marega, Maria Tecla Rodi and Elena Pagnoni.

[2] Legislative Decree no 58 of 24 February 1998, as amended.

shareholder and consumer activism will be further facilitated by the recent intro-duction into Italian law of collective actions for damages effective from 29 June 2008. Furthermore, Italian prosecutors have stepped up their fight against white collar financial crime associated with cases of insolvency, fraud, market abuse, investor harm and obstruction of regulators. These are all contributing to the dramatic change to the Italian legal and regulatory landscape, which until now was something of a paradox: the (possibly unrivalled) panoply of statutory and regulatory checks and balances did not translate into a systematic enforcement of investigative powers by the various 'controlling bodies'.

An ever-increasing focus on pre-emptive controls over corporate activities, in **9.03** order to allow for better monitoring and avoidance of irregularities, has in fact resulted in a number of changes in the areas of corporate governance, financial reports, internal auditing,[3] minority shareholders and conflicts of interest in Italian listed companies. The combination of pre-existing and new statutory and regulatory provisions has led to a proliferation of internal and external corporate 'controls'—the efficiency and effectiveness of which, however, remain to be evaluated.

Historically, both independent directors and those individuals exercising various **9.04** internal control functions, including statutory auditors, were effectively appointed by the top management, often also the dominant shareholders.[4] Frequently these independent individuals did not carry out their functions proac-tively and incisively. The Commissione Nazionale per la Società e la Borsa (Consob),[5] at that time lacking the currently available investigative and enforce-ment powers, could not investigate frauds or irregularities before they became public knowledge, usually as a result of criminal prosecutions following whistle-blowing, the emergence of fraud, or corporate collapse.

Traditionally, the extent and frequency of investigations and the overall climate **9.05** depended, to a large extent, on the type of supervisory scrutiny to which the rele-vant corporations were subject. This was in turn greatly influenced by the resources available to the relevant supervisory authority or regulator. The Bank of Italy devoted a large part of its resources to conducting regular inspections of banks and intermediaries (although not always with consistent effectiveness). By contrast, Consob and the Istituto per la vigilanza sulle assicurazioni private

---

[3] In Italy corporate bodies have an internal 'watchdog' known as *collegio sindacale*, or board of statutory auditors, which does not have an equivalent in other jurisdictions.

[4] The Law on Public Savings of 28 December 2005, as amended on 29 December 2006, has required listed companies to effectively enable the appointment of minority and independent directors.

[5] The Financial Services, Capital Markets and Stock Exchange Regulator.

e di interesse collectivo (ISVAP),[6] with fewer personnel, carried out inspections less frequently. The Bank of Italy also made wide use of its so-called 'moral influence' and preliminary powers as an *ex ante* measure of prevention, whilst Consob used such powers less frequently.

9.06 Change is gaining momentum in light of Consob's new investigative powers and its recent tendency to flex its muscles. Indeed, following the implementation of the Market Abuse Directive, Consob has been more proactive than in the past in commencing investigations for market abuse cases.[7] It more frequently approaches corporations and financial intermediaries to obtain clarifications over transactions and has shown a tendency to encourage cooperation in terms of reporting possible breaches and volunteering information. Ultimately, this change is likely to enhance the reputations and be economically beneficial to corporations whose shares are traded in Italy as it eliminates a certain element of unreliability.

9.07 It is now expected that the combination of new statutory and regulatory provisions, increased powers and independence attributed to various controlling bodies and regulators, as well as a heightened awareness following the string of financial scandals, will all contribute to make the overall process of corporate control more effective and to step up the intensity and frequency of investigations.[8] This is

---

[6] The Insurance Sector Regulator.

[7] This change of attitude was highlighted, for instance, in the 2006 Consob investigation of the 'Fiat-Ifil-Exor' case. The investigation proceedings, initiated in September 2005, concerned an undisclosed equity swap contract executed between Exor SA and Merrill Lynch following which Exor (and its parent Ifil) managed to keep effective control over Fiat through a certain percentage ownership of the share capital in spite of an ostensible dilution arising out of the conversion into equity of certain bank debentures. The inquiries began after Fiat and Ifil denied that Ifil would regain such percentage ownership and Consob also examined a query regarding the applicability of the rules on mandatory tender offers to the restructuring of the shareholdings of the Ifil-Fiat group.

At the end of the investigation proceedings, Consob forwarded to the judicial authorities reports on various aspects of the case (including possible market abuses and obstruction to the supervision of regulators), together with documentation gathered during the inquiries, partly in response to requests received from the criminal prosecutors. Consob also issued hefty fines on the entities and individuals involved.

More recently (eg in connection with the *Banca Popolare di Lodi-Antonveneta* case), there have also been 'whistle-blowers' and third party allegations in civil lawsuits and criminal proceedings which effectively contributed to the launch or increased scrutiny of regulatory investigations.

[8] Direct investigative and sanctioning powers over supervised companies enabled Consob on February 2007 to fine Ifil, the holding company of the Fiat group, and three of its directors, who were also temporary suspended from their appointments, for market manipulation, in the total amount of €16m in connection with the misleading communications released in August 2005. In March 2007, Consob used, for the first time, its 'new' power to freeze assets of a listed company illicitly purchased, sanctioning Mr Lonati for insider trading in addition to a fine of €1.5m.

Furthermore, in the last years there has been a significant consolidation in the Italian banking industry. Such consolidation has often resulted in a change in the corporate governance system of the relevant banks. They have often adopted a two-tier 'dual' system of governance that is designed to ensure a clear division of responsibility between the management board and the supervisory board.

already reflected in the way banks and corporates have started to conduct systematic internal investigations to an unprecedented degree (and indeed, some of the banks and companies involved in recent scandals have conducted their own internal investigations on past irregularities, often as a basis for subsequent damage claims against former directors and auditors). Ultimately, a radical shift may grow out of the marked increased trend of criminal courts and prosecutors to utilize Decree 231, on the 'quasi-criminal' liability of corporations, to sanction the inertia of Italian and foreign businesses in monitoring their internal affairs in Italy, with harsh penalties including suspension of trade.[9]

B. Regulators

Key regulators

In Italy, there is no single regulator or authority with comprehensive jurisdiction over the behaviour of corporations. The Italian regulatory system is based on the combined supervision of a number of independent authorities and governmental entities acting as regulators, notably in relation to specific industries (financial services being the most tightly regulated) or based on the 'supervision by objectives' model (whereby regulated entities may be subject to the control of more than one authority, each authority being responsible for one objective of regulation regardless of the legal form and the activities of the regulated entity). Italy's system is generally described as a mixed model of supervision, especially of financial market activities, as opposed to the centralized model adopted by other legal systems.[10]

9.08

The Bank of Italy's Governor has emphasized the need to pay particular attention to internal controls and improvement of risk management systems at the group level. New supervision rules will be issued in order to make similar controls over financial intermediaries and banks, avoiding inspections in favour of more frequent requests of information: Bank of Italy, Annual Report for 2006, dated 31 May 2007.

[9] In a number of cases foreign companies (such as Siemens in the public procurement cases) and banks (such as UBS and Deutsche Bank by a Milan Court decision of 13 June 2007 in the Parmalat judicial proceedings) have been held liable under Decree 231. A significant body of case law now shows that a foreign company/bank does not need to have branch offices or any permanent establishment in Italy for Decree 231 to apply. As long as the entity engages in business in Italy, the decree will apply. In June 2007, a criminal judge in Naples froze €175m worth of assets of Impregilo (a company listed in Milan) and suspended it from any waste management activity for one year.

[10] Bibliographical references on Italian regulators and respective procedural features include:

N Longobardi, 'Autorità amministrative indipendenti e diritti: la tutela dei cittadini e delle imprese', *Il Foro amministrativo TAR* (2007); A Rinaldi Alma, 'Coordinamento fra autorità dei mercati finanziati nell'evoluzione della normativa italiana e internazionale', *Le Società: rivista di diritto e pratica commerciale, societaria e fiscale* (2007); L Cuocolo and G Lembeck, 'Le autorità di regolazione e controllo dei servizi di interesse generale in Europa: una prospettiva comparata', *Diritto pubblico comparato ed europeo* (2007); M Poto, 'Autorità amministrative indipendenti e garanzie partecipative', *Responsabilità civile e previdenza* (2007); A Colombo, 'Giurisdizione, autorità di vigilanza e

9.09   Consob, the Bank of Italy and the Italian Antitrust Authority (IAA) are considered to be the key regulators within this system. A crucial role in the Italian regulatory landscape, however, continues to be played by the activism of public prosecutors.

Consob

9.10   Consob, established in 1974, is the principal regulator of listed corporations, capital markets and the finance industry in Italy. It supervises financial intermediaries, listed issuers and regulated markets and has broad supervisory and investigative powers over these entities' compliance with applicable laws and regulations as well as enforcement and regulatory powers.

9.11   Financial intermediaries falling under Consob's supervision include securities broker/dealers and investment firms (SIM),[11] asset management companies (SGRs),[12] investment funds and SICAVs,[13] banks, financial intermediaries with limited banking licences[14] providing investment services ('107 Intermediaries') and central depositaries. Consob aims to ensure disclosure, transparency, behavioural fairness and compliance by financial intermediaries with applicable laws and regulations.[15]

9.12   Consob supervises listed issuers to ensure that investors are protected and to maintain the efficiency and transparency of markets. This includes regulating and supervising the offering of securities, public takeover bids, disclosure of

---

responsabilità amministrativa ex delicto degli intermediari finanziari', *Banca impresa società* (2007); S Screpanti, 'La partecipazione ai procedimenti regolatori delle autorità indipendenti', *Giornale di diritto amministrativo* (2007); E Freni, 'I nuovi poteri dell'autorità garante delle concorrenza e del mercato', *Obbligazioni e contratti* (2007); A Pera, 'Appunti sulla riforma delle Autorità: regolazione e concorrenza', *Mercato, concorrenza, regole* (2002); L Radicati di Brozolo, 'Il nuovo quadro delle comunicazioni elettroniche', *Mercato, concorrenza, regole* (2002); G Scarselli, 'Brevi note sui procedimenti amministrativi che si svolgono dinanzi alle autorità garanti e sui loro controlli giurisdizionali', *Foro Italiano*, (2002); G Amato, 'Autorità semi-indipendenti e autorità di garanzia', *Rivista trimestrale di diritto pubblico* (1997); F Merusi, 'Autorità indipendenti', *Enciclopedia del diritto* (6th Update, 2002); F A Grassini (ed.), *L'indipendenza delle autorità* (2001); F Caringella and R Garofoli (eds), *Le Autorità indipendenti* (2000); G Scarselli, *La tutela dei diritti dinanzi alle Autorità garanti* (2000); Various authors, *Il procedimento davanti alle Autorità indipendenti*, Quaderni del Consiglio di Stato (1999); A Predieri (ed.), *Le autorità indipendenti nei sistemi istituzionali ed economici* (1997); S Cassese and C Franchini (eds), *I garanti delle regole* (1996); OECD, *Distributed Public governance. Agencies, Authorities and other Government Bodies* (2002); OECD, *Flagship Report on Regulatory Quality* (2001); OECD, *Review of Regulatory Reform in Italy* (2001).

   [11] *'Società di Investimento Mobiliare'.*
   [12] *'Società di Gestione del Risparmio'.*
   [13] SICAV is the acronym for *Società di Investimento a Capitale Variabile ie*, an investment company that is an investment vehicle set up in corporate form with variable capital.
   [14] Intermediaries enrolled in a special register which is maintained pursuant to Art 107 of the Consolidated Banking Law of 1993.
   [15] See Arts 5 and 6 of the FLCA.

shareholdings, disclosure of other information, corporate organization and governance of the issuers and market abuse. Consob's jurisdiction for all matters, other
than aspects of the issuer's corporate organization and governance, extends to both
Italian and foreign issuers of financial instruments listed on any Italian regulated
market.[16] Furthermore, Consob authorizes the setting up of such markets and
supervises market management companies.[17]

Consob's investigative powers are aimed at detecting both criminal and adminis-   **9.13**
trative infringements with the peculiarity that it has direct sanctioning powers in
case of administrative offences (notably, those connected with market abuse).[18]
Infringements may be committed by intermediaries, listed companies or auditing
firms and can include, inter alia, malpractice or irregularities in the performance
of investment services, obstruction of Consob's supervisory functions, false statements in prospectuses and in auditing firms' reports, failure to disclose relevant
shareholdings, miscommunication regarding price-sensitive information or code
of conducts compliance, breach of rules on takeover or exchange offers, insider
dealing and market manipulation.

Sanctions have been greatly increased by the Law on Public Savings, which quin-   **9.14**
tupled all the administrative fines provided for by the FLCA.[19]

The Bank of Italy

The Bank of Italy supervises the Italian banking system in accordance with the   **9.15**
Banking Consolidated Act (BCA).[20] It is responsible for all aspects of banking
conduct, including granting or revoking banking licences, solvency requirements, regulatory capital monitoring and bank liquidation proceedings.

The Bank of Italy also exercises supervisory powers in relation to the financial   **9.16**
stability and limitation of risks of securities broker/dealers and investment firms,

---

[16] With reference to inside information duties, any foreign persons issuing financial instruments,
for which an application has been made for admission to trading on Italian regulated markets, are
also included.

[17] In particular, Consob may require market management companies to communicate data
and information and to transmit documents and records. It may also (i) carry out inspections
of such companies; (ii) require the exhibition of documents and the adoption of any
measures deemed necessary. In case of urgency, Consob itself may adopt any measures deemed
necessary.

[18] In the Italian legal system the two existing forms of market abuse (insider trading and market
manipulation) are subject to a dual track regime which gives rise to both criminal and administrative
liability.

[19] The Law on Public Savings also doubled criminal sanctions. The administrative sanctions can
range from €200/300 to €300,000/500,000 and in some cases can reach some millions of euros. In
market abuse cases sanctions can go up to €25m and up to 12 year's of imprisonment.

[20] Legislative Decree no 385 of 1 September 1993, as amended (*Testo Unico delle leggi in materia
Bancaria e Creditizia*).

investment funds and SICAVs and 107 Intermediaries. These powers are exercised jointly with Consob, each one dealing with its specific area of responsibility. The Bank of Italy's other responsibilities include regulating solvency and financial requirements, risk management, accounting, control and organizational structure of the financial intermediaries, as well as obligations related to the custody of financial instruments and monies.[21] In addition, the Bank of Italy supervises banking groups on a consolidated basis.[22]

9.17   The Bank of Italy can pursue infringements including unauthorized fund-raising, banking activity, issue of electronic money, and financial activity. Whenever there is a grounded suspicion that a company engages in such activities without being authorized, the Bank of Italy may file a report with the public prosecutor or may petition the court to adopt the relevant measures. Additionally, administrative infringements pursued by the Bank of Italy can vary from unauthorized banking or financial activity, unauthorized acquisition of shareholdings, to the breach of the rule of corporate representatives, and omission of communication for relevant holdings.

Italian Antitrust Authority (IAA)

9.18   The IAA was instituted in 1990 by Law no 287 of 1990. The IAA shares its duties with the European Commission in relation to anti-trust issues impacting the EU and has a primary responsibility for the Italian market. The IAA's main responsibilities in relation to competition law include:

  i.   enforcing Italian competition law (Law no 287of 1990);
  ii. enforcing EU competition law, and namely Article 81 and Article 82 of the EC Treaty;
  iii. assisting the European Commission or other national competition authorities of EU member states in the enforcement of EU competition law; and
  iv. overseeing the Italian pre-merger notification system for mergers and acquisitions that do not have a Community dimension.

9.19   Following the entry into force of the Law on Public Savings, as amended, at the end of 2006, the anti-trust enforcement powers in the banking sector, formerly granted to the Bank of Italy, have now been effectively transferred to the IAA. As a result, anti-competitive agreements and/or concerted practices as well as abuses

---

[21]   The Bank of Italy is also responsible for issuing asset management licences to SGRs.

[22]   The system provided for by Italian law sets out that the parent company represents the point of reference for the Bank of Italy in relation to consolidated supervision issues and it must ensure that the bylaws of any of its subsidiaries include a specific provision that acknowledges the role of the parent company in relation to the consolidated supervision of the group and contains an undertaking to provide any form of cooperation, which is not therefore limited to the provision of information.

of dominant positions in the banking and finance sector, currently fall within the exclusive jurisdiction of the IAA.[23]

Other regulators

The national government also plays a limited regulatory role in the Italian system. For example the Treasury establishes certain requirements (such as regarding the 'honour' and 'professionalism') for qualified shareholders, directors, auditors and managers of financial intermediaries, banks and market management companies. The Treasury also authorizes and regulates the bulk market for Treasury bonds. Similarly, the Ministry of Justice draws the 'black list' of countries that do not have sufficient corporate transparency. **9.20**

Italy also has a number of industry specific regulators including the following authorities: **9.21**

ISVAP

ISVAP is responsible for the supervision of national and foreign insurance companies carrying out insurance activities in Italy, which includes the authorization and revocation of relevant authorizations and the monitoring and inspections of such companies. ISVAP regulates the insurance market with an aim of ensuring **9.22**

---

[23] In the most serious and urgent cases, where the IAA, after a preliminary assessment, considers that the likelihood of an infringement of competition law is high (so-called *'fumus boni iuris'*) and that there is the urgency to halt an irreparable damage to competition (so called *'periculum in mora'*), it may adopt, even *ex officio*, interim measures aiming at preventing further prejudice to the competition. If at the end of the investigation the IAA ascertains a breach of competition rules, the IAA can order the undertakings concerned to refrain from the infringing activity as well as impose a monetary fine. The fines can amount to up to 10 per cent of the worldwide turnover of the undertakings involved. The IAA may also pursue failure to provide notifications of mergers, with a maximum potential liability of up to 1 per cent of the turnover of the undertaking(s) acquiring control, although as a matter of practice the fines for such violations have been generally modest, ranging from €5,000 to €50,000.

In cases where the IAA is investigating an alleged abuse of dominance or a restrictive agreement/concerted practice (ie practices in violation of Arts 2 or 3 of Italian competition law no 287 of 90 or Arts 81 or 82 of the EC Treaty), the undertakings under investigation may avoid the adoption of a decision finding a breach of the said Italian or EC anti-trust rules by offering, within three months from the notification of the launch of the investigation by the IAA, structural and/or behavioural commitments that are capable of resolving the anti-competitive conduct at issue alleged by the IAA. If the proposed commitments, after having been formally market-tested, are satisfactory to the IAA, the latter may make them binding upon the investigated undertakings and close the proceedings without ascertaining whether there has been any infringement. Furthermore, since February 2007 undertakings participating in horizontal cartels may apply for immunity or reduction of fines by submitting to the IAA substantial evidence and information on the cartel at issue, in a way similar to what is foreseen by the EU Leniency Programme. Immunity may be available only to the first 'whistle-blower', whilst reductions of fines may be granted to more than one undertaking provided that they submit to the IAA evidence and information which significantly strengthen the evidence already in the possession of the IAA. Immunity/leniency applicants will also have to continuously and closely cooperate with the IAA until the end of the investigation.

the efficiency, stability and financial soundness of the companies and of protecting policyholders.

9.23 When exercising its general power to request information from the supervised entities, ISVAP is under a duty to keep Consob informed of any requests regarding listed companies and may ask Consob for assistance when carrying out investigations.[24]

9.24 ISVAP also provides advice to the IAA on anti-trust issues relating to the insurance sector.

Autorità per l'energia elettrica ed il gas (AEEG)

9.25 The AEEG is the gas and electricity industry regulator. The AEEG's responsibilities includes setting tariffs, defining service quality standards, and overseeing the technical and economic conditions governing access and interconnections to the networks for those services. It prevents technical, legal or other constraints interfering with normal competitive market conditions and the ability of the market to protect the interests of users and consumers. The AEEG liaises with the IAA to protect areas of common interest.

Autorità per la vigilanza sui contratti pubblici di lavori, servizi e forniture

9.26 The *Autorità per la Vigilanza sui Contratti Pubblici di Lavori, Servizi e Forniture* supervises public works and ensures compliance with the tender procedures for the award of public works' contracts and the consistency of the execution of such contracts with the goal of containment of public expenditure.

COVIP

9.27 COVIP regulates Italian pension funds by ensuring the transparency and proper functioning of the funds in order to protect social security savings. COVIP authorizes the setting up of pension funds and approves their constitutional documents and internal regulations. It also approves the agreements for the management of the pension funds' assets and supervises compliance with transparency requirements in dealings with participants, as well as the technical, financial and accounting management of pension funds. COVIP exchanges information with the Bank of Italy, Consob and ISVAP.

Autorità per le garanzie nelle comunicazioni (AGCOM)

9.28 AGCOM works with the IAA to ensure level playing field conditions for fair market competition and for the protection of consumers in the telecom and media sector.

---

[24] See Art 71 of Legislative Decree no 209 of 2005 ('the Insurance Code').

Self-regulatory initiatives

Borsa Italiana SpA is the market management company responsible for the **9.29** organization and management of the Italian stock exchange. Its functions include:

i. defining and organizing the functioning of the market;
ii. defining the rules and procedures for admission and listing on the market for issuing companies and dealers;
iii. managing and overseeing the market; and
iv. supervising disclosure by listed companies.

Borsa Italiana carries out tasks relating to the examination of listing prospectuses **9.30** or applications for listing on its regulated markets.[25] Borsa Italiana and Consob coordinate closely when dealing with listing procedures allowing for a wide oversight of listed companies.

Borsa Italiana oversees the reporting and disclosure to the market of inside infor- **9.31** mation.[26] It is also empowered to request and obtain from listed issuers any information that it deems useful, whether occasionally or regularly, to allow the correct functioning of the market.[27]

Borsa Italiana adopted a 'Self-Regulatory Code for Listed Companies'. This **9.32** Code, drafted by an ad hoc Corporate Governance Committee, sets out recommendations introducing a best practice model for the organization, governance, control and functioning of Italian listed companies, based on a 'comply or explain' model.[28]

Pursuant to Article 124-*bis* of the FLCA,[29] listed companies must annually com- **9.33** municate information outlining their adoption of, and compliance with, the Self-Regulatory Code for Listed Companies or any other codes of conduct promoted by market operators and/or trade associations and related recommendations, explaining the reasons for any failure to comply therewith ('comply or explain').

---

[25] Arts 62, 64 and 94-*bis* of the FLCA.

[26] In accordance with Art 181 of the FLCA, 'price-sensitive' information shall mean any 'information which, if made public, would be likely to have a significant effect on the prices of financial instruments ... [ie] information a reasonable investor would be likely to use as part of the basis of his investment decisions'.

[27] Paras 2.6.1, 2.6.2, 2.6.3 and 2.6.4 of the Regulations of Markets Regulated and Managed by Borsa Italiana.

[28] To this end, listed companies must issue a report on their compliance with the Self-Regulatory Code when they release their financial statements. This report shall be at the shareholders' disposal and shall be transmitted to Borsa Italiana, for its dissemination to the public.

[29] Introduced by the Law on Public Savings.

9.34 Consob sets out how to communicate compliance with any such Self-Regulatory Code and monitors the accuracy of the information concerning the compliance. Consob imposes sanctions in the event of finding inaccuracies or breaches of these requirements.[30]

9.35 Borsa Italiana's authority over listed companies, shared with Consob, consists of admission to trading of financial instruments and suspension or exclusion of financial instruments from trading. It is also responsible for admitting, suspending and excluding dealers from trading.

Concurrent investigations

9.36 Regulators, whether independent bodies or governmental institutions, may ask the public prosecutors to commence a criminal investigation but otherwise they have no jurisdiction over such prosecutions. Therefore, there is always a possibility of an overlap or coexistence of regulatory and criminal investigations. Some breaches of the law may only have regulatory consequences, including administrative fines or penalties, while others may also constitute a criminal offence. The public prosecutor is exclusively responsible for the prosecution of regulatory breaches that also constitute criminal offences in Italy.

9.37 In the past, Italian prosecutors, who are, effectively, independent of the government, have often been more proactive than regulators in enforcing the law, including in connection with market abuse cases. Following the implementation of the Market Abuse Directive, Consob has made wide use of its regulatory powers and is now more proactive in commencing investigations for market abuse cases. One feature of such new powers that deserves attention is the fact that Consob, when summoning an individual for an interview, is not required to disclose whether he or she is being interviewed as witness or a suspect. This has major practical implications. Furthermore, owing to the fact that Consob has a duty to cooperate with the public prosecutor, there is a risk that documents or information given to Consob will be passed to the public prosecutor and acquire relevance in the context of criminal proceedings (including in respect of a company) which might be triggered by the regulatory investigations. Therefore, it is of paramount importance for anyone receiving requests for information by Consob to devise from the outset a proper defensive strategy and to conduct an internal investigation on the facts.

9.38 There is also the possibility of overlapping regulatory investigations. In Italy there are a number of regulators that each have different supervisory responsibilities, one legal entity may be subject to the regulatory and supervisory powers of a

---

[30] Art 124-*ter* of the FLCA.

number of authorities. This can result in a number of practical issues. As a matter of practice, regulators tend to avoid conducting concurrent investigations in an attempt to minimize the impairment of the company's day-to-day operations.

The FLCA, the BCA and the Insurance Code require close collaboration among **9.39** the regulators responsible for the supervision of banks, investment firms and insurance undertakings. They are obliged to reciprocate and exchange information without raising any objections as to professional secrecy.[31]

As the Bank of Italy and Consob jointly supervise financial services, each regulated **9.40** entity in these industries is simultaneously subject to both the Bank of Italy's and Consob's supervisory powers, which are carried out independently. Consob focuses on investor protection and fair conduct rules, while the Bank of Italy concentrates on economic stability issues. The cooperation obligation between the Bank of Italy and Consob is expressly set out in Article 5 of the FLCA, which provides that the Bank of Italy and Consob have to operate in a coordinated manner, in order to minimize the costs incurred by authorized intermediaries. To this end, on 31 October 2007, the Bank of Italy and Consob executed a Memorandum of Understanding setting out their respective roles and responsibilities.

Overlaps may also arise in the procedure for the clearance of the acquisition of **9.41** qualified holdings in banks, financial intermediaries and insurance companies.

Article 10, paragraph 2 of the FLCA also requires Consob and the Bank of Italy to **9.42** notify each other of the inspections that they carry out. This allows for requests to be made to the body carrying out the inspection to carry out on-the-spot verifications of matters falling within the authority of the other body. In practice, each regulator informs the others *before* undertaking inspections, thereby enabling the others to adopt any relevant measure falling within their scope of authority.

Relationship with overseas regulators

The Bank of Italy, Consob and ISVAP may also carry out on-the-spot verifications **9.43** on EU financial intermediaries' Italian branches where the competent authorities of other EU countries so request, or agree upon other methods of inspection. Analogous procedures may be agreed upon with non-EU regulators.

The Bank of Italy, Consob and ISVAP have a general duty of cooperation with **9.44** EU regulators. In particular, the Bank of Italy may conclude agreements sharing responsibilities for consolidated supervision over multinational banking groups.

---

[31] Otherwise, Consob and its officials, consultants and experts are bound by professional secrecy even vis-à-vis any public authority with the exception of the Ministry of Economy and Finance. In the event of criminally relevant breaches, they refer to the five-member governing bodies and the Chairman would then inform the prosecutor's office.

9.45 Conversely, the Bank of Italy, Consob and ISVAP may, but do not have a positive duty to, cooperate with non-EU regulators, provided that such non-EU regulators are subject to requirements of professional secrecy.

9.46 Cooperation procedures among regulatory authorities play a pivotal role in the investigations for regulatory breaches by foreign entities.[32]

9.47 To this end Consob has recently entered into a number of Memoranda of Understanding (MoU) on the Exchange of Information and Surveillance of Securities Activities with foreign regulators of the US, Argentina, Hungary, Albany, Romania, Turkey, Taiwan and South Africa in order to ensure an effective cooperation for multi-jurisdictional supervision. In addition, Italy adheres to the policies of the CESR (the Committee of European Securities Regulators), the CEBS (the Committee of European Banking Supervisors) and of the CEIOPS (the Committee of European Insurance and Occupational Pensions Supervisors).

9.48 Cooperation with foreign regulators is essential in the context of supervision of multinational groups. Directive 2002/87/EC which provides a regulatory framework for conglomerates with multinational dimensions was implemented in Italy by Legislative Decree no 142 of 2005. This allows for a further and additional form of supervision, mainly characterized by 'prudential' controls and encompasses groups with international presence. It also sets out cooperation arrangements among regulators of the countries involved. By providing a notion of financial conglomerates, and by identifying the competent authorities for their supervision, this legislation fills the existing gaps in the context of supervision over international groups.

C. Powers of Regulators

Sources of information

9.49 Historically, the main sources of regulatory investigations into corporations have been market information (including media and analysts' reports and share price movements), 'prosecution' initiatives[33] (at times, following some whistle-blowing

---

[32] As outlined above, Community legislation provides for positive duties of cooperation among EU regulators in the form of exchange of information and assistance in the carrying out of regulatory inspections. However, any form of cooperation with non-EU regulators requires the execution of specific agreements. This type of cooperation has proved particularly useful in connection with the blocking of Internet sites used for investment solicitations in contravention of the relevant securities laws and with market abuse cases.

[33] Ie information received by Consob from public prosecutors carrying out criminal investigations concerning listed corporations. For example, in 1993 Consob's comprehensive investigation over listed corporate group Montedison-Ferruzzi Finanziaria and its then auditors PriceWaterhouse effectively started only after material misrepresentations in the financial statements began to surface following, in particular, the action of Milan prosecutors who arrested and/or interrogated several

like in the 2005 investigation concerning Banca Popolare di Lodi) and, to a lesser extent, information obtained through routine filings, regulatory reporting, public companies' auditors and qualified investors with substantiated complaints (whereas allegations by other third parties have played a minor role). This is in spite of the fact that the Italian legal framework was, even prior to the new legislation, designed to create a regular flow of information, and to maintain a complex system of 'internal controls' and of 'gatekeepers' (including statutory auditors, accounting firms, the independent directors, the internal auditors, the supervisory body set forth by Decree 231, and others) mandated to monitor and enquire and, in some instances, to report to the regulator (Consob) and the judiciary. In fact, Italy's recent economic history has shown, as in other countries, some gatekeeper failures and regulatory investigations have often been initiated after the facts have come to light. Some of the most notorious examples are the Ferruzzi-Montedison case (1993), the Cirio and Parmalat collapses (2003) and the Italease bank crisis (2007), where major frauds were first discovered and investigated by the public prosecutors and only thereafter by the regulator.

It is expected that the sources of regulatory investigations in Italy will increase in **9.50** the future and encompass information and reports arising out of a more stringent and effective exercise of the internal audit functions and reporting requirements, increased shareholder and investor activism with associated allegations, a more rigorous and quasi-investigative approach adopted by Italian specialized media and market analysts, and Consob's more proactive stance and effective use of its increased powers.

Levels of regulatory scrutiny

There may be different levels of regulatory scrutiny within investigations con- **9.51** ducted by Italian regulators. Investigations may start somewhat informally, by scrutinizing any of the information delivered as a result of mandatory reporting requirements, or received from other sources as described above, and may continue, or escalate, through personal interviews and/or inspections of corporate premises.

---

corporate officers and directors of the group. Equally, financial statements of listed corporate group Cirio Del Monte, previously approved and not challenged by Consob, started to be significantly questioned and then judicially challenged at the beginning of 2003 after the group admitted its insolvency and various prosecutors initiated actions against its directors, officers and bankers. Similarly, in other recent cases (Banca Popolare di Lodi, Unipol) Consob has somehow 'followed' the initiatives of investigative magistrates (albeit showing a higher degree of proactivism) in connection with allegations of fraud and market manipulation.

Often, Consob is also requested by public prosecutors to advise on technical issues arising in the context of the criminal investigations.

9.52 The IAA tends to skip any initial informal stage in competition enquiries, other than internally within the IAA itself (although, once the investigation has started, there is a degree of informality in subsequent stages). Conversely, the first stage of an investigation by other regulators may involve a degree of informal scrutiny. This can include meetings with directors, senior managers and auditors. In reality, there is a fine line between the informal and formal stages.

Investigation tools

Requesting information

9.53 In addition to continuing statutory reporting requirements, the Bank of Italy, the IAA and Consob may request data, information, documents and records from entities subject to their supervision. They may also issue ad hoc administrative measures.

9.54 They can demand information such as accounting or statistical data, or specific information pertaining to any event or circumstance considered to be relevant, and/or pertaining to specific requirements from any authority relating to the need to assess whether the data and information reported are complete and correct.

Inspections and other tools

9.55 The Bank of Italy and Consob can send officers to any legal entity's premises in order to verify whether that entity complied with the relevant legal and regulatory provisions falling within the scope of their respective jurisdiction and to assess whether business activities are carried out in compliance with applicable rules.

9.56 The Bank of Italy and Consob may require the adoption of measures, including any relevant corporate resolutions, deemed to be necessary to facilitate the regulator in carrying out the inspections.

9.57 Consob has specific mechanisms for it to investigate, notably in order to verify the accuracy of the corporate information distributed to the public or in order to ascertain any market abuse. Under Articles 115 and 187-*octies* of the FLCA, Consob may require further information and documents from any foreign or Italian corporation whose securities are listed in Italy and from any of their controlling parent entities or persons, interview any of their directors, auditors, officers, managers, carry out inspections at any of such entities' or persons' premises and take copies of documents. It can also demand production of existing telephone and banking records, personal data, and may have access to databases, such as those of the tax administration and the Bank of Italy's central 'credit risk' database. Furthermore, Consob may also, with prior authorization of the prosecutor, seize assets, forcibly search persons or premises and obtain any other telecommunication records and data and, in case of market abuse, order to stop any conduct.

The IAA may initiate investigations, either *ex officio* or prompted by a third **9.58** party's complaint, against a party suspected of violating competition law. In the context of such proceedings, the IAA has significant investigative powers, including powers to conduct raids[34] with the assistance of the Finance Police.[35]

Also Consob and Bank of Italy (as well as COVIP, ISVAP and IAA) may avail **9.59** themselves of the cooperation of the Finance Police in carrying out any regulatory investigations. Data and information obtained by the Finance Police is protected by secrecy and can only be communicated to the relevant regulatory authority.

If the regulatory investigation is being conducted simultaneously or in tandem **9.60** with a criminal investigation, the criminal prosecutor may enable the regulator to piggyback on all mechanisms available to prosecutors. This includes the prosecuting authority's power to summon any individual for the purposes of supplying information or responding to queries. To this end, regulatory authorities often apply for, and obtain, the recognition of being a 'victim of the crime', enabling them to access the criminal file and the option to become a civil party in the criminal proceedings.

Extra-territorial jurisdiction

Italian regulators generally have jurisdiction over Italian corporations and foreign **9.61** issuers of securities traded in any Italian regulated market. However, there is statutory authority to provide the regulators with some form of extra-territorial reach.

---

[34] The IAA can issue written requests for documents and impose penalties for non-compliance. Oral requests for documents may be made during raids or at hearings before the IAA.

During inspections and raids, IAA officials may examine, take and obtain copies of documents and conduct electronic searches of files, subject to relevance and usefulness. Usefulness is defined broadly, with reference to the scope and purpose of the investigation.

[35] The Finance Police has a merely supporting role. All documents copied during the raid remain exclusively with the IAA and can be used as evidence exclusively in relation to anti-trust proceedings (ie not for tax purposes). Clearly, if during a search it emerges that a criminal offence may have been committed, the Finance Police must take action and transmit the relevant evidence to the public prosecutors. More generally, it should be noted that, as the IAA's case team members are public officials, they are also under the obligation to report to the public prosecutors any evidence they have come across involving criminal liability (ie in case of bid-rigging).

9.62 Extra-territoriality issues particularly come into play in connection with the powers of the Bank of Italy, Consob and ISVAP over financial, banking and insurance entities operating internationally.

9.63 The Bank of Italy, Consob and ISVAP have supervisory powers over foreign branches of Italian banks and investment firms and may request regulators in other EU countries to carry out inspections or agree on other verification methods[36] over such branches. Analogous procedures may be agreed upon with non-EU regulators.

9.64 Under Article 114 of the FLCA, any Italian and foreign entities having applied for admission of securities to trading in Italy, as well as any issuers of securities listed in Italy and their 'parents', that is, controlling entities or persons, wherever they are located, have an obligation to disclose to the public and Consob any price-sensitive information.[37] Article 115 empowers Consob to carry out inspections and remove copies of documents from the offices of any such persons and entities (including abroad) and to search, seize, access telephone and banking records and issue interim measures. Consob would require assistance from local authorities and rely on international treaties to enforce the disclosure or other requirements.

9.65 Any crime and/or offence arising from market abuse is punishable in Italy, even if committed abroad, in instances where the relevant behaviour concerns securities admitted to trading, or for which an application has been made to be admitted for trading, on an Italian regulated market. In addition, the criminal sanctions for market abuse committed in Italy apply to behaviours relating to securities admitted to trading, or for which an application has been made to be admitted to trading, on an Italian regulated market as well as on a regulated market in other EU countries.[38]

9.66 In its turn, the IAA has jurisdiction over any infringement of Italian and EC competition law that may have an effect on the Italian territory.

9.67 Finally, criminal courts have established the 'quasi criminal' liability of foreign corporations and banks, based on Decree 231, even where they do not have branch or other offices in Italy, as long as some business is transacted in Italy.

---

[36] See Art 10 of the FLCA, paras 3, 4 and 5.

[37] Consob may require the disclosure of any relevant document and data to any of such persons or entities as well as any of their directors, auditors, senior executives (*dirigenti*) and qualified shareholders (holding more than 2 per cent of voting rights), or parties to shareholder agreements concerning such listed securities, in all such cases irrespective of the nationality of the person or entity involved.

[38] Art 182 of the FLCA.

Protections

Based on the constitutional principles of the right of defence and fair trial, Italian **9.68**
law recognizes the right against self-incrimination. However, this principle does
not entail that companies under investigation have an absolute right to elude
such investigations on the ground that they may result in regulatory or criminal
actions being taken against them. In contrast they have a positive duty to cooperate with the regulator and, as noted, Italian regulators have the power to compel
individuals to be interviewed and companies to provide documents and information that are deemed to be useful for the carrying out of investigations. Their
refusal to cooperate may amount to both a criminal and administrative offence
(as better detailed below). Therefore, while as a general rule individuals may not
be compelled to answer leading or self-incriminatory questions which may trigger criminal charges, in the context of regulatory investigations there is a requirement to disclose all documents requested, regardless of whether or not they may
adversely affect the case of the persons under investigation.

Sanctions for failure to cooperate

Article 2638 of the Italian Civil Code (ICC) punishes, by imprisonment for a **9.69**
term of one to four years,[39] any directors, including the managing director/CEO,
auditors, general managers, COOs, or managers in charge of preparing draft
accounts/financial statements, who intentionally or consciously obstruct the regulators' exercise of their functions. Action that constitutes obstruction includes
the intentional failure to make required disclosures or purportedly misrepresent-
ing or concealing any facts that should have been reported.[40] The Italian Civil
Supreme Court[41] stated in 2005 that in principle such provision applies to all
public supervision authorities and/or regulators. On such basis, it would seem
that such provision could also apply in relation to the IAA.

Furthermore, anyone factually obstructing Consob's supervisory functions can **9.70**
be punished by imprisonment for up to two years and a fine up to €200,000.[42]
The mere failure or delay to respond to Consob's requests for information can
result in a fine of between €50,000 and €1m.[43]

---

[39] Or two to eight years, in case of corporations with shares 'widespread among the public' or
listed on a regulated stock exchange.
[40] These sanctions are in addition to those provided for in relation to misrepresentations in
financial statements.
[41] Judgment by the Italian Supreme Court Corte di Cassazione of 24 October 2005, no 44234.
[42] Art 170-*bis* of the FLCA.
[43] Art 187-*quinquiesdecies* of the FLCA.

9.71 Corporations and other entities suspected of anti-trust infringements have an additional specific duty to cooperate with the IAA.[44]

9.72 Failure by companies to cooperate with regulatory inquiries may amount to an obstruction of the exercise of the regulators' functions, which represents a crime under the above mentioned Article 2638 of the ICC and other laws including the FLCA and the Insurance Code. Regulators can also impose administrative sanctions for failure to comply with a regulatory investigation.

9.73 Obstruction of the exercise of Bank of Italy's functions can also amount to a crime and incur penalties pursuant to Article 2638 of the ICC and/or an administrative breach pursuant to Article 144 of the BCA.[45]

9.74 Obstruction of the exercise of ISVAP's functions may amount to a crime pursuant to Article 2638 of the ICC; a crime pursuant to Article 306, paragraph 1, of the Insurance Code;[46] and/or an administrative breach pursuant to Article 306, paragraph 2, of the Insurance Code.[47] This can result in either imprisonment and a fine of between €10,000 and €100,000, or an administrative sanction of €10,000 to €100,000.

---

[44] See Art 10 of the IAA Regulation no 217 of 1998. This is subject to the conditions that the documents requested by the IAA be deemed 'useful' to the investigation and concern (i) the proceedings (the element of objective relevance) and (ii) an undertaking involved in the proceedings (the element of subjective relevance). When these conditions are met, the relevant entities must disclose all documents requested where they are subject to an IAA investigation, including those documents that adversely affect their case. They may also hand over any documents on which they rely, as long as they are relevant (objectively and subjectively) to the case. It is to be noted that, in practice, the ability to raise professional secrecy or privilege of certain documentation has been undermined by the IAA.

[45] Pursuant to Art 144 of the BCA, persons performing administrative or managerial functions in a company, as well as its employees, that obstruct the carrying out by the Bank of Italy of certain supervisory powers, may be liable to an administrative fine of up to €250,000. Alternatively, the Bank of Italy may increase any fine it imposes on the matter under investigation, or impose *interim* measures, including suspension of operating licences or temporary closure of premises.

[46] Pursuant to Art 306, para 1, of the Insurance Code, which is applicable under circumstances that do not trigger the application of Art 2638 of the ICC—any person who hinders the exercise of ISVAP supervisory functions by (i) refusing the access by ISVAP functionaries to the company's premises or (ii) refusing to exhibit any documentation concerning the insurance activity upon request of the ISVAP functionaries in charge of assessing any breach of Art 305 of the Insurance Code (which prevents any possible provision of insurance activities without the prescribed authorizations) is punished by imprisonment up to two years and by a pecuniary administrative sanction of between €10,000 and €100,000.

[47] Pursuant to Art 306, para 2, of the Insurance Code, which is applicable under circumstances that do not trigger the application neither of Art 2638 of the ICC nor of Art 306, para 1, of the Insurance Code, whoever does not comply with ISVAP requests or delays the exercise of ISVAP functions shall be punished by a pecuniary administrative sanction of between €10,000 and €100,000.

Companies are subject to the same penalties when consciously hindering Consob's **9.75** supervisory functions in any manner, including omitting to make any required communications and disclosures.[48]

With regard to Italian competition law, Article 14 of Law no 287 of 1990 pro- **9.76** vides that the IAA, where its order to exhibit documents or information is not complied with, may, by means of a decision, impose an administrative fine of up to €25,821 in case of refusals to provide the documents without a legitimate reason, or a fine up to €51,643 when false information or documents are submitted. On the other hand, failure to cooperate with the IAA in the course of a dawn raid may also result in an aggravating circumstance capable of increasing any fine that could be imposed for the matter under investigation. Where such obstructive conduct is adopted by an entity that has applied for immunity and/or fine reduction, it may cause the loss of the applicant's right to benefit from the immunity or the fine reduction. The obstruction of the exercise of the IAA's investigative activity may amount to a crime pursuant to Article 2638 of the ICC.

D. Voluntary Investigations

Benefits and risks of voluntary investigations

Despite the statutory proliferation of stringent internal control systems, serious **9.77** and independent internal investigations are a relatively recent phenomenon in Italy and have not been widely adopted. They have been rare outside the Italian subsidiaries of large multinational groups and have only had a lukewarm reception from regulators.[49] In other words, until fairly recently the Italian corporate environment was not particularly inclined to foster a culture of voluntary investigations by giving real teeth to its internal watchdogs, the benefit of which was largely unnoticed. Accordingly, but further diminishing the perceived benefits, Italian regulators did not historically attach great importance to unsolicited internal investigations, even if delegated to outside counsel, but tended to initiate and carry out their own inspections to which, possibly, the internal, parallel investigation would contribute useful elements, as a form of active cooperation. This is also driven by the fact that regulators can be subject to sanctions if they refrain from performing their duties, which include investigating regulatory breaches.

---

[48] The sanctions are doubled, where the supervised entity issues securities listed on any Italian or EU regulated markets or widely distributed among the public.
[49] Other than, to a degree, the IAA's attitude toward anti-trust/competition compliance programmes.

9.78 Recently, however, Italian regulators (notably Consob) have shown a change of attitude toward voluntary internal investigations. Moreover, Italian corporates increasingly recognize the 'hard' and 'soft' benefits of pervasive internal investigations. The most important 'hard' benefit can be the avoidance of quasi-criminal liability of companies under Decree 231 (which may entail suspension from business) if (but only if) the criminal judge finds that the Supervisory Body entrusted with the task of monitoring and preventing the commission of certain crimes was effectively delegated pervasive powers to investigate the affairs of the company (with associated resources and even to interfere with senior management) and has actually made use of such powers (including by carrying out internal dawn raids and other inspections).

9.79 The 'soft' benefits include a reputational enhancement which is increasingly perceived by the Italian business community as a competitive advantage over other corporates, thus potentially triggering (in a globalized economy) an investors' 'flight to quality' as well as a magnet for talent (recruitment and retention); hence, an increased focus on corporate governance reports and awards. Furthermore, the raising of behavioural standards and their effective enforcement would have a positive impact on the internal culture, thus further reducing the risk of wrongdoings and further increasing the credibility with regulators of the corporate governance inclusive of systematic internal investigations.

9.80 Indeed, regulators in the past have also relied on and valued the information provided, and/or the enquiries (if any) conducted, by statutory auditors (*collegio sindacale*) who have been historically assigned by the Italian statutory framework an ongoing role as watchdog.[50] The Bank of Italy and Consob, in particular, rely on information provided by statutory and external auditors for the purposes of the companies' reporting requirements. As noted, auditors of a listed corporation are under a duty to inform Consob, without delay, of all the facts or matters found in the performance of their duties which may amount to management irregularities or violations of laws and regulations.[51] Similar provisions apply to the Bank of Italy.[52] It is generally agreed that the auditors can informally liaise with the Bank

---

[50] The majority of statutory auditors may be de facto chosen and appointed by controlling shareholders and management of the corporation they should audit, and in any event regulators would still carry on their own investigation, but the extent of the statutory auditors' duties and their personal features (ie their being outside professionals) normally yields a (not negligible) weight to their findings and reports. Furthermore, the Law on Public Savings now requires the Chairman of the statutory auditors to be appointed by minority shareholders in listed companies and requires all statutory auditors to comply with stringent independence requirements.

[51] See Art 149, para 3 of the FLCA. In case of serious irregularities, statutory auditors and Consob may inform judicial authorities under Art 152 of the FLCA.

[52] See Art 52 of the BCA.

of Italy and/or Consob regarding relevant facts and matters, especially where the information to be communicated is urgent.[53]

Due to its functions and responsibilities, the board of auditors should be constantly in contact with the managers of the relevant company. The control of the board of auditors is expected to be proactive and aimed at assessing any irregularity which has occurred and/or is likely to occur.[54] The Supervisory Body contemplated by Decree 231 is also expected to be similarly proactive within its remit (which is to monitor and prevent the commission of certain crimes such as, for instance, corruption, money laundering or market abuse). **9.81**

Therefore, it is reasonable to assume that, whenever outside counsels are requested to carry out ad hoc investigations and their activities are performed under the control of the auditors and/or supervisory bodies (which is also a possibility contemplated by the Self Regulatory Code of Corporate Governance of Listed Companies), Italian regulators would give weight to their findings, and at the very least value the cooperation. **9.82**

Regulators would expect such investigations to provide at least a preliminary or partial analysis of the facts in order to assess whether to proceed with further actions or not. As noted above, the Bank of Italy and Consob would normally start their own further investigations before the end of the internal investigation, and always do so in the most serious cases, in order to verify the reliability of the information provided. Nevertheless, the regulators would look at the outcome of such internal investigations, where conducted by, or under the supervision also of, statutory auditors or other persons or entities presenting and commanding a high degree of independence as a valuable source of relevant information. The fact that an internal investigation has been conducted may impact upon the size of the fine or other sanctions. **9.83**

Events triggering considering conducting an internal investigation

A fairly wide range of events would likely trigger a company in Italy to initiate an internal investigation. Often internal investigations can be triggered by press rumours, interest or specific requests for information by the regulators. A number of internal investigations in Italy have been triggered in such circumstances. **9.84**

---

[53] See Bank of Italy Supervisory Instructions, Chapter XXXIX.
[54] Furthermore, firms that audit the accounts of Italian investment firms and management companies and SICAVs shall notify the Bank of Italy and Consob without delay of the facts or matters found in the audit that may constitute a serious violation of the laws governing the activity of the audited companies, jeopardize the continued existence of the undertaking or result in a negative or qualified opinion on the annual accounts or interim financial statements or in a disclaimer.

9.85 In high-profile cases such as Unipol, Banca Popolare di Lodi and Italease, internal investigations followed the enquiries by prosecutors and regulators (which were in turn, at least in one case, prompted or accelerated by whistle-blowing). Often, once public prosecutors have begun to investigate allegations of corruption, the companies involved have engaged promptly thereafter in large scale internal investigations (with a view to containing damage, establishing facts and punishing responsible individuals): this, however, would not exclude quasi-criminal liability of the company. In other cases, voluntary investigations have somewhat preceded the start of an official probe by outside forces. In both scenarios, there has been an overlapping and parallel conduct of the internal and external investigations. As noted, where for example individuals are summoned by Consob in connection with possible market abuse cases of sizeable magnitude, it is advisable to commence a fully fledged internal investigation with a view to establishing the facts as soon as possible and devising a proper and effective defensive strategy, hopefully before the commencement of criminal proceedings.

9.86 Where the underlying facts are not publicized, investigations have been triggered at times by events at competitors or other businesses: for example, sometimes the discovery within a supplier of goods or services of undisclosed, illicit payments to the buyer or procurement officer (or other members of the senior management) of a customer aimed at 'facilitating' the award of contracts has given rise to an investigation and dismissals of executives both at the level of the suppliers and thereafter, following an exchange of calls between the respective CEOs, at the level of the customer.

9.87 Normally, however, an ad hoc investigation should be triggered by the results of regular checks or internal audits and other institutional oversight activities (notably where significant unusual patters are detected) and/or be a natural part, or corollary, of such regular audits, especially in industries where corruption, fraud, financial irregularities have traditionally constituted a risk (eg construction, defence and other public contractors, banking). In other words, the primary trigger of dedicated internal investigations should be the proper functioning of the gatekeepers' mechanisms and flow of information among gatekeepers/internal control bodies contemplated by Italian law. For instance in the field of financial intermediaries, internal control functions pursue any irregularity in relation to compliance with 'prudential' rules, internal organization provisions and conduct of business rules.

Structuring an internal investigation

9.88 The recent laws and regulations[55] introduced or reinforced so many 'internal controls' mechanisms that many of them overlap, and companies are still getting

---

[55] Decree 231, Bank of Italy and Consob regulations, Corporate Law Reform, Law on Public Savings, Self Regulatory Code on Corporate Governance for listed companies.

to grips with how to enforce them correctly. As internal investigations have not yet become commonplace in Italy it is difficult to identify a full set of Italy-specific rules or precedents or guidance tips as to how investigations should be structured (other than by following best practice developed in other jurisdictions and by taking into consideration the factors illustrated in the chapter, for example, concerning the UK). However, any investigation should be conducted in accordance with any Italian legal and regulatory requirements (notably on privacy and employment law), as better described below, and by taking into account Italian peculiarities.

For example, given the proliferation of internal audit and watchdog functions, **9.89** responsibility for a voluntary investigation should lie with one of the corporate bodies contemplated by Italian law, rather than creating a new, ad hoc, committee: for example, either the board of statutory auditors or the Supervisory Body under Decree 231. This may depend on the nature of the irregularities potentially involved: if they represent one or more of the crimes that might trigger the quasi-criminal liability of the legal entity, the latter would be the appropriate body responsible for the investigation process.

Furthermore, proper attention should be paid to the need to avoid duplication of **9.90** work and appropriate coordination among these bodies and functions. In fact, efficiency would be maximized and overlapping or loophole risks would be minimized by reorganizing the entire corporate governance along lines that are allowed for by Italian laws and regulations. For example, the company could adopt a governance and control system (so-called *monistico*) whereby both the functions of the board of statutory auditors (which would disappear) and those of the Supervisory Body under Decree 231 would be attributed to an audit committee constituted within the board of directors and entirely consisting of independent directors meeting the relevant requirements. The audit committee could also oversee the internal audit organization and could outsource specific investigations to outside firms, or combination of firms (eg forensic accountants, lawyers, investigators). This structure would appear to be the most efficient being the one envisaged by experienced commentators and the Self Regulatory Code of Corporate Governance for Listed Companies.

In order for this governance to be functional and meet the goals required (also **9.91** under Decree 231), the audit committee should be delegated wide-ranging authority and powers, including appropriate resources to carry out its functions.

Criminal case law has confirmed that quasi-criminal liability of the corporation **9.92** cannot be avoided unless the Supervisory Body (or audit committee) has all necessary resources and means to inspect, verify and possibly stop at any time any corporate action (including by senior management) and does so independently and through urgent mechanisms.

Using external advisers

9.93 Hiring outside counsel to conduct internal investigations is not very common in Italy and there are no generally applicable rules as to when they might be engaged.[56] The practice of involving outside advisers in the context of internal investigations has up to now revolved around internal audits carried out by large independent auditors, often, the big accounting firms or affiliated entities, who are instructed by the company. Albeit there are just a few public examples of internal investigations to date, an increased tendency to use external counsel in future investigations is to be expected along with an increase in internal investigations.

9.94 Independent advisers including external counsel are often used in order to design and implement organizational structures for the purposes of Decree 231.

9.95 Decree 231 gives the company a chance to be exempted from quasi-criminal administrative liability if it gives evidence, inter alia: (i) that the company has adopted and effectively implemented 'Organizational Models'[57] (or compliance programmes) capable of preventing the commission of unlawful acts; and (ii) that the Supervisory Body has been granted with independent powers of initiative and controls. Therefore, companies frequently hire outside advisers as individual members of the Supervisory Body to shore its expertise and independence. Such external members are often lawyers, accountants and academics.

Managing illegal activity during investigations

9.96 Under Italian law corporate bodies are under a statutory obligation to take immediate action to stop any illegal activity as soon as it is discovered and to minimize its adverse consequences.[58]

9.97 From a practical point of view, it is extremely unlikely that an entity under investigation will continue to carry out any conduct or related activity if this is regarded

---

[56] The Self Regulatory Code of Corporate Governance of Listed Companies envisages the possibility to wholly or partially 'outsource' certain audit/control functions to external advisers.

[57] The effectiveness of an organizational model is proved when it:
- identifies the activities in the context of which offences may be committed;
- provides protocols for the programming of the formation and implementation of decisions of the company relating to the prevention of crimes;
- identifies activities relating to the management of financial resources which are capable of preventing crimes being committed;
- provides information as to persons supervising the operation of and the compliance with the model; and
- introduces disciplinary measures in case of failure to comply with provisions of the model.

[58] The corporation itself may be even criminally liable if, for example, the Organizational Model described has not functioned in a manner as to halt certain illegal activities of which it has become aware or should have been aware.

by the regulator as illegal. In theory, it may be possible for a company under investigation to continue to undertake potentially illegal conduct if the company believes that such conduct or related activity does not infringe any laws. In such cases, however, the regulator may issue a restraint order prohibiting the continuation of the illegal conduct.

No illegal conduct will be allowed to continue, with or without permission of the **9.98** regulator, as a means to discover the perpetrator of the illegal activity.

E. Self-reporting

Duty to self-report

There is no general, open-ended and express obligation under Italian law for **9.99** listed companies, banks or other regulated entities or persons to 'self-report' any violations of laws and regulations. However, corporations, banks, and other entities have a system of internal controls designed to prevent and discover corporate irregularities, or violations of laws and/or regulations, and to report on these as necessary. Certain reporting obligations insist upon the internal control bodies.

The main corporate bodies involved in the internal controls system of any joint **9.100** stock corporation, including unlisted corporations, are:

i. the board of statutory auditors (or equivalent corporate body, such as the audit committee within the board of directors or the *consiglio di sorveglianza* in the two-tier governance system);
ii. the board of directors, as much as it supervises the activities carried out by any executive director/persons; and
iii. the Supervisory Body contemplated by Decree 231.

The board of statutory auditors, composed of independent individuals selected from **9.101** certain professional categories, supervises the proper management of the company and its compliance with any applicable laws and the bylaws.[59] In particular, they monitor the effectiveness of the administrative and accounting organization

---

[59] Art 2403 of the ICC. Unlisted corporations can also entrust statutory auditors, under Art 2409-*bis*, with the functions of accounting control, otherwise assigned to an outside auditing firm. Under Art 2397 of the ICC, the board of statutory auditors can have three or five effective members (and two alternate members), of which one effective and one alternate must be chosen among individuals registered in a special list of 'auditors' maintained at the Ministry of Justice while the others must be chosen among certain professional categories or university professors. Each statutory auditor is subject to stringent impendence requirements under Art 2399 of the ICC (eg they may not be related to any directors nor perform consultancy or other such continuing services or be linked by such other relationship, as to compromise their independence).

of the company and whether it is adequate to ensure full compliance with the laws.

9.102 To this end, they are entitled to demand any relevant information from directors and subsidiaries' auditors and each auditor within the board is individually empowered to carry out internal inspections and controls. The auditors may enlist the help of third parties, however these can be refused access to information constituting trade secrets.[60] Furthermore, the board of statutory auditors has a duty to investigate, notably, any matters or suspected irregularities which are brought to its attention by minority shareholders representing at least 5 per cent of the share capital (2 per cent in listed corporations). This could lead it to report the matters to the Court or the prosecutor.

9.103 Under Article 2408 of the ICC each individual shareholder is entitled to report any suspected irregularities to the board of statutory auditors. The board of statutory auditors shall record the shareholder's complaint in the report that it must submit to the shareholders on the occasion of the meeting convened to approve the company's accounts.[61]

9.104 Under the FLCA, the board of statutory auditors of a listed company monitors:

  i. the compliance with any laws and the bylaws and with the principles of correct management; and
  ii. the adequacy of:
    • the organizational structure;
    • the internal control function; and
    • the corporate administrative and accounting system.

9.105 The board of statutory auditors has wide-ranging powers to obtain information from directors and persons performing any internal control functions. It may at any time carry out internal inspections, availing itself of the company's employees if necessary.[62]

9.106 The board of statutory auditors is under an obligation to notify Consob of any irregularities found in the context of its supervisory activity.[63]

---

[60] Art 2403-*bis* of the ICC.

[61] The board of auditors is bound to investigate any suspected irregularities brought to its attention by minority shareholders.

[62] The board of statutory auditors may also obtain by the external auditors data and information necessary for the carrying out of its duties. It shall report on the supervisory activity performed and on any censurable irregularities found to the shareholders' meeting called to approve the annual accounts.

[63] See Art 149 of the FLCA. Where it has a well-founded suspicion that the directors, in breach of their duties, have incurred serious irregularities, that may cause injury to the company or one or more of its subsidiaries, the board of statutory auditors *may* also report the facts to the Court.

Furthermore, the law expressly provides for listed companies to operate an internal audit system similar to the internal audit systems provided for banks and financial intermediaries and, in addition, the establishment of an ad hoc internal audit structure is strongly recommended by the Self-Regulatory Code for Listed Companies, where it is defined as 'the set of procedures to monitor the efficiency of the company's operations, the reliability of financial information, compliance with laws and regulations and the preservation of the company's assets'.[64] **9.107**

It is also important to note that the external auditors themselves are under an obligation to inform the board of statutory auditors and Consob of any misconduct that should be censured. **9.108**

Culture of self-reporting

There is not as yet a widespread culture of self-reporting in Italy other than those duties assigned to auditors. However, a combination of long-standing remedies and recent developments, such as leniency regimes in anti-trust and other areas, including de facto leniency in cases of cooperation with investigating magistrates/prosecutors, coupled with the implementation of certain statutory reforms such as Decree 231 which fosters a degree of cooperation or self-reporting, should reverse this trend and introduce a higher degree of self-reporting. **9.109**

F. Announcements and Public Relations

Obligations when facing a regulatory investigation

A company does not have any specific obligations to make announcements to the market or the stock exchange when facing a regulatory investigation. However, whenever any of the facts under the investigation or the investigation itself are of a price-sensitive nature they may have to be disclosed under general rules, notably Articles 114 and 181 of FLCA, and its implementing regulations.[65] A disclosure will need to be made 'promptly' as soon as there is a sufficient degree of certainty about the issues discovered. Consob's Regulations no 11971 of 14 May 1999, as amended, ('the Issuers Regulation') and its Notice on market disclosures of 28 March 2006 do not specifically address internal or regulatory investigations as **9.110**

---

[64] According to the provisions of the Self-Regulatory Code for Listed Companies, responsibility for the internal audit system lies with the board of directors. To properly discharge its duties, the board of directors may appoint an 'Internal Audit Committee'. The appointment of such Committee is recommended by the Code.

[65] These define (by setting out broad parameters) where a specific fact should be disclosed as price-sensitive.

facts requiring disclosure. It is, therefore, crucial to assess the possible impact on the share price of public knowledge of the investigation.

9.111 This can be done with Consob's consent if an early or premature disclosure of the fact that a price sensitive investigation is underway might prejudice the listed corporation's legitimate interests. This might be permitted in the event that the outcome of the investigation is still unclear and, while the corporation is ascertaining the extent of the problem, the disclosure would not enable the public at large to fully evaluate the facts.[66] Consob has permitted delays in the disclosure of information in several cases when it was deemed that the information could materially change and could therefore be misleading.

9.112 In the event of deferred disclosure, strict confidentiality must be then ensured, by adopting effective measures which would restrict access to any information concerning the investigations only to those persons who 'need to know' in connection with the performance of their functions and who would have formally to acknowledge all the relevant confidentiality duties and the sanctions for breach of these duties.

9.113 As soon as confidentiality may no longer be maintained, a full public disclosure must be made:[67] Consob may make the disclosure on its own initiative, at the expense of the issuer (or its parent, as the case may be).

9.114 Therefore, it is generally advisable to consult with Consob, whenever there is doubt, to determine whether and when to publicly disclose the fact of an investigation.[68] In practice, however, there is a certain cultural 'resistance' among a number of Italian companies to involve Consob, and engage in a dialogue, to make that determination.

Internal communications

9.115 There are no statutory or regulatory provisions nor market practice which has emerged in relation to whether, when and how a listed corporation or any other 'regulated' entity should make its personnel aware of a specific (voluntary or regulatory) investigation.

9.116 Obviously, the obligation of listed issuers and its parents to communicate any price-sensitive information to the market under Article 114 of the FLCA may

---

[66] Art 66-*bis*, first and second para of the Issuers Regulation.

[67] Art 66-*bis*, third para, (c) and fifth para, of the Issuers Regulation.

[68] On their side, the Bank of Italy or Consob are not required, under Italian law, to inform the public of investigations they are carrying out while the investigations are under way, unless a fine is eventually imposed. Only a limited number of decisions adopted by Consob are subject to publication on the Consob Bullettin, while the determination on which decisions may be considered remarkable for publication purposes is entirely within the discretion of Consob.

lead to a general disclosure to the employees and the public of the existence of an investigation, in order to avoid the undue impact of uncontrolled rumours on the share price and possible allegations of abuse or, conversely, to the maximum confidentiality under Article 66-*bis* of Consob's Issuers Regulation.

It may also be necessary to disclose the fact that an investigation is underway to all or some of the employees in certain circumstances, such as where it is advisable to ensure preservation of all relevant documents and/or suspension of routine destruction of documents. **9.117**

Voluntary investigations

External communications

As voluntary investigations are still a growing field in Italy there are few precedents of communication to the public, stock exchange or customers that would be appropriate in the event of an internal investigation. Disclosure would only become necessary where the information of the incoming investigation is of a price-sensitive nature. However, external communication of a voluntary internal investigation can be utilized as a marketing tool or a way to reassure various stakeholders that the company or bank is taking the matter seriously by assuming a proactive stance. **9.118**

Internal communications

Similarly, there are no duties of internal communications when dealing with a voluntary investigation. Evidence suggests that, in a number of cases, Italian listed corporations have taken the approach that an internal investigation would be more effective if kept confidential to the extent possible and employees are informed on a 'need to know' basis only. However, it may be advisable to inform employees of an investigation in order to implement document preservation policies or to prevent unfounded rumours from reaching the marketplace. Furthermore, privacy and criminal law considerations, as illustrated below, may dictate a degree of communication with respect to certain access to employee computers and correspondence. **9.119**

Key points for Public Relations strategies

A PR/communication strategy should also be factored into the overall process of reacting to a regulatory investigation or announcing an internal investigation. The reputation of the corporate and some of its key players, as well as the loyalty of some key customers, may be at stake. Increasingly companies are engaging investor relation (IR) functions or PR/communication firms to work with lawyers and other advisers, with a view to coordinating and managing PR campaigns and overall PR strategy with the applicable laws and regulations. The IR **9.120** function, in particular, ensures the correct communication to the market of the relevant events and the fair representation of the situation. The need for ensuring that all communication is tied to an effective PR strategy is even more acute in Italy due to the open channel of communication between the press and prosecutors and the frequency of leaks to the press from regulatory and criminal investigations, making the need for mitigating the PR damage all the more pressing.

9.121 It is key to coordinate any PR-driven communication with the legal constraints, notably those arising out of disclosure requirements and statutory provisions on the fairness and accuracy of corporate statements. In light of some tendency of the IR/PR people to prioritize the preservation of crucial relationships with stakeholders and the corporate image, which sometimes leads to somewhat inaccurate statements, it is essential to validate any such statements with legal counsel prior to their release to the market.

G. Best Practices in Document Gathering and Preservation

Expectations of regulators and courts

9.122 There is no specific statutory or regulatory positive requirement generally to preserve documents once a regulatory investigation is underway.[69] However, the destruction of documents could constitute a criminal offence under a number of broad statutory provisions[70] as it may be seen as obstruction of justice or of the regulator's investigation or as conduct instrumental to a crime.

9.123 Further, while there is no standing duty to preserve all documents at all times, companies have general obligations to keep accounting records, invoices and correspondence for a ten-year period under Article 2220 of the ICC or until the limitation period for tax claims expires,[71] and special obligations to keep records on securities trades and other transactions. Failure to preserve other documents and/ or the deliberate destruction of any documents when proceedings or investigations

---

[69] It is worth noting that pre-trial discovery or broad disclosure duties do not exist in Italy.

[70] See, eg, as repeatedly noted, Art 2638 of the ICC (which provides that it is a criminal offence to 'fraudulently hide, in whole or in part, facts concerning the company's economic, financial or net worth situation which were to be disclosed' to the regulators), Art 170-*bis* of the FLCA (on the obstruction of the regulator's investigation) and Art 10 of Legislative Decree no 74 of 2000 (providing for the crime of destruction of accounting documents for the purposes of evading taxation).

[71] This general term could be extended if the Financial Administration in a proceeding makes a petition for accounting records disclosure (see, eg, Italian Supreme Court (Corte di Cassazione) no 9797 of 19 November 1994). In specific cases the duty to preserve accounting records is statutorily extended, over the time provided for by Art 2220 of the ICC, until the assessment proceeding is not concluded (see Art 22 of the Presidential Decree no 600 of 29 September 1973).

are underway or imminent may nonetheless be considered by the regulator as evidence against the company in connection with establishing a breach and the duty to cooperate and may therefore prove detrimental to the company.

It is therefore advisable to adopt and adhere to a formal document management **9.124** policy in addition to the statutory obligation pertaining to accounting and other records to be kept. It is believed that ground preservation systems put in place by the company will help manage the relationship with the regulators.

Rights over documents and confidentiality

As illustrated above, the regulator has far-reaching powers to require any employee, **9.125** and any other person potentially informed about the facts under regulatory investigation, to provide relevant information, data and documents both in paper and electronic format. Employees have a duty to the company to cooperate with any regulatory investigation, and with any internal investigation aimed at establishing whether the corporation is in breach or compliance with applicable laws and regulations.[72]

Certain limitations apply to the regulators' powers of investigation with respect **9.126** to employees' personal items or their ability to collect documents in the custody of employees without their cooperation. Further, the duty of cooperation does not oblige the investigated company's employees to provide answers that would lead to self-incrimination.[73] Under Article 220 of the implementing provisions of the Code of Criminal Procedure, whenever in the course of a regulatory investigation facts emerge which might form the basis of criminal allegations, there must be compliance with the due process safeguards provided for by the Code of Criminal Procedure.

Also during inspections by the IAA, officials have the right to access any premises **9.127** of the company under investigation, for one or more days. In particular, they can access any area of the premises (including remote electronic servers and other IT equipment) as well as vehicles and other means of transportation, with the exclusion of places of residence or domicile (including private cars) that are not related

---

[72] In addition, the regulator may request the public administration to reveal personal data and information (by derogation to the legal provisions on data protection and privacy), have access to tax records, telecommunication data, bank or postal accounts and the Bank of Italy's centralized automated credit risk database. The exercise of some investigation powers by the regulator, as explained above, is subject to prior authorization of by the public prosecutor.

[73] See the decisions of the Administrative Regional Court (TAR) of Lazio, no 6139 of 5 July 2001 and of the Supreme Administrative Court (Consiglio di Stato), Sec VI, no 2199 of 23 April 2002.

to the business of the concerned undertaking.[74] The right of access to records also applies to third parties that are in possession of the undertaking's business documents and files (eg book-keeping that has been outsourced to a third party), provided that those documents and files are located outside of private homes. Unlike the European Commission, the IAA is not entitled to enter private homes or other places that are not connected with the activity of the undertaking.[75] Disclosure of documents may also be orally requested in the course of the dawn raids or during hearings before the IAA, provided that such request is recorded in the minutes of the inspection/hearing. During the dawn raids, the IAA officials may also ask for verbal clarifications with regard to the seized documents; both the questions posed by the IAA officials and the related answers by the representatives of the undertaking under inspection must be recorded in the minutes of the inspection.

9.128 Regulators are bound by professional secrecy, and cannot disclose the documentation obtained to third parties, other than the public prosecutor (whenever any facts emerged in the context of the investigation may lead to the commencement of criminal proceedings) and other regulatory authorities.

Data protection, employment and criminal law

9.129 Article 1 of the Legislative Decree no 196 of 30 June 2003, ('the Data Protection Code' or 'the Privacy Law') sets out the general principle that 'everyone has the right to protection of the personal data concerning him or her'.

9.130 Article 4, paragraph 1(b), of the Data Protection Code defines 'personal data' as 'any information relating to natural or legal persons, bodies or associations that are or can be identified, even indirectly, by reference to any other information including a personal identification number'. Paragraph 1(d) of the same article defines 'sensitive data' as 'personal data allowing the disclosure of racial or ethnic origin, religious, philosophical or other beliefs, political opinions, membership of parties, trade unions, associations or organizations of a religious, philosophical, political or trade-unionist character, as well as personal data disclosing health and sex life'.

---

[74] IAA officials can only request access to records which are currently located at business premises in Italy or which are available to an undertaking that is domiciled in Italy.

[75] The IAA, assisted by the Fiscal Police (*Guardia di Finanza*), may also seal premises during an inspection. This may mean that computers or entire rooms may be inaccessible until the investigation is over.

The IAA officials may examine documents belonging to, or concerning, the undertaking under investigation and take copies of the same, provided that such documents are 'useful' to the investigation (such 'usefulness' is generally construed extensively, in relation to the object and the scope of the investigation).

The Data Protection Code specifically contemplates the means by which the per- **9.131**
sonal data concerning a specific individual may be used or 'processed' (meaning
the 'collection, recording, organization, keeping . . . elaboration, modification,
selection, retrieval, comparison, utilization, interconnection, blocking, communication, dissemination, erasure and destruction of data')[76] and does so by setting
forth certain notice and consent requirements.

The Data Protection Code does not expressly contemplate the issue of internal **9.132**
investigations; therefore, the privacy law implications of processing 'personal
data' during the investigation is normally assessed against the specific provision
that the individual's consent shall not be required if the processing of the data is
necessary in connection with certain defensive investigations or 'to establish or
defend a legal claim, provided that the data are processed exclusively for said purposes and for no longer than is necessary thereof [and] by complying with the
legislation in force concerning business and industrial secrecy, dissemination of
the data being ruled out'.[77] In other words, processing (including disclosure to
regulators and courts) of employee personal emails, data and documents is lawful
where proportionate and necessary for purposes of investigating, or establishing,
or defending against, legal claims and is limited to the timeframe required for
such purposes.

The above principles have also been clarified by the Italian Data Protection **9.133**
Authority. On one occasion, the Data Protection Authority held that computer
searches made by the employer on the employee's computer must be relevant to
the investigation at stake and should not exceed its intended purpose. In that
case, the employee was alleged to access the Internet during office hours for personal purposes. The Data Protection Authority observed that it would have been
sufficient for the employer to provide evidence of web access and its duration,
without investigating the specific nature and contents of the websites visited by

---

[76] See Art 4(1)(a) of the Data Protection Code.
[77] Art 24, para 1(f) of Data Protection Code. See also Tribunal of Milan, 20 March 2006, which
after having recalled the provisions of Art 24, para 1(f), of the Data Protection Code, held that the
Italian legislator 'has clearly recognised as a general rule that the right to an effective defence provided for by Art 24, para 2, of the Italian Constitution shall prevail on the privacy rights of any individual related to the processing of personal data and of certain sensitive data'.

However, a ruling of the Privacy Authority (dated 2 February 2006 and published on 14 February
2006) held that computer searches made by the employer on the employee's computer must be relevant to the investigation at hand and should not exceed their intended purpose. In that specific case,
the breach attributed to the employee was the access to Internet during office hours, to which access
he was not entitled. The Authority observed that it would have been sufficient for the employer to
provide evidence of the web access and their duration, without investigating the specific nature and
contents of the websites visited by the employee, entailing the processing of sensitive data such as
religious beliefs, trade union affiliations and 'sexual tastes'. Such sensitive data could be processed
without the employee's consent only if they were 'essential' to establish the employer's claim, which
was not the case.

the employee, entailing the processing of sensitive data (such as religious beliefs, trade union affiliations and 'sexual tastes'). Such sensitive data could have been processed without the employee's consent only if they were 'essential' to establish the employer's claim, which was not the case.[78]

9.134 The above provisions are substantially replicated at Article 26, paragraph 4, of the Data Protection Code, in relation to 'sensitive data'[79] and at Article 13, paragraph 5(b), in relation to personal data not collected from the data subject.

9.135 Nevertheless, in order to avoid a misuse of investigation powers and an unlawful infringement of the employee privacy in personal and professional relationships, the Privacy Authority provided, as described below, some guidelines so that processing of data by electronic network could be brought into line with respect for fundamental rights and freedoms and data subjects' dignity.

9.136 Furthermore, in the course of investigations which are considered to be necessary to establish or defend a legal claim, employers should bear in mind that, as a general principle, any personal correspondence, whether by post or email, as well as phone conversations, sent or received by the employee, are in principle not accessible under constitutional,[80] labour[81] and criminal law.[82]

---

[78] Data Protection Authority, decision of 2 February 2006.

[79] Sensitive data 'may also be processed without consent, subject to the Grantee's authorisation [...] if the processing is necessary to establish or defend a legal claim, provided that the data are processed exclusively for said purposes and for no longer that is necessary thereof. Said claim must not be overridden by the data subject's claim, or else must consist in a personal right or another fundamental, inviolable right or freedom, if the data can disclose health or sex life'. The same exception applies in relation to certain defensive investigations and the compliance with legal or regulatory obligations. Therefore, the judge in charge of the case, should balance, in case of a conflict, one party's defence rights with the other party's privacy rights whenever data concerning health or sexual life are involved (see Tribunale Bari, decree 12 July 2000, in *Foro it*, 2000, I, 2989. See also A Palmieri, *Il contemperamento tra 'privacy' e diritto di difesa: pluralità di criteri in relazione alla natura dei dati*, comment to the decision of Tribunal of Bari).

[80] Art 15 of the Italian Constitution.

[81] Italian scholars have clarified that the application of Art 4 of Law no 300 of 20 May 1970, the main regulation regarding the Italian Labour matter ('the Workers Statute') presupposes that the employer sets up and uses a device with the exclusive purpose of controlling the employee's activity (see G Cian and A Trabucchi, *Commentario breve alle leggi sul lavoro* (Padova, 2001), 664). For example, Italian case law held that the controls forbidden by Art 4 of the Workers Statute must concern the working activity of the employee whereas the so-called defensive controls aimed at ascertaining unlawful conducts of the employees (as unjustified phone calls) are out of the scope of the provision (Tribunal of Turin, 9 January 2004, in *'Giurisprudenza piemontese'*, 2004, 131; in the same sense see Italian Supreme Court (Corte di Cassazione), Labour Division, 3 April 2002, no 4746, in *'Giust civ Mass'*, 2002, 576; Tribunal of Teramo, 12 May 2006, in *'Notiziario Giurisprudenza lav'*, 2006, 345). For more details, see 'Managing Employees During Investigations' and 'Control on Threats'.

[82] Arts 616 et seq of Italian Criminal Code, dealing with 'access' to 'correspondence' (including emails), provide that:

Anyone who takes knowledge of the content of any closed correspondence which is not addressed to him, or hides or embezzles, in order to take or let others take such knowledge,

Since, until recently, it was not clear to what extent this principle applied to email **9.137**

any closed or open correspondence not addressed to him or destroys or shreds it, in whole or in part, is punished, unless the fact is contemplated as a crime by another statutory provision, by imprisonment up to one year or by a fine from €30 to €516.

In this connection a very recent judgment of the Supreme Court (Decision of 19 December 2007, no 47096, of the Italian Supreme Court (Corte di Cassazione) has held that any electronic correspondence (ie emails) can be considered 'closed' only for people who do not have free and lawful access to the IT system for sending or receiving emails. In that case, access was deemed to be lawful as the employer had received the specific password from the employee, who knew that it could be used in her absence and/or for disciplinary reasons.

Therefore, the criminal liability of those individuals who had 'access' to the emails (or other correspondence) sitting on, or accessible through, the employer computer systems, can be excluded if such correspondence was 'open' prior to the access by any unauthorized non-addressee and this could be finally verified by checking what were the employment arrangement (or policies) regarding access or if there are individual passwords.

The second paragraph of Art 616 of the Criminal Code, dealing with 'disclosure' provides that:

If the guilty party discloses, without cause, in whole or in part, the contents of the correspondence is punished, if such disclosure is prejudicial and unless it constitutes a more serious crime, by imprisonment up to three years.

Therefore, a requirement for making any unauthorized disclosure of private correspondence illegal under Art 616 is the absence of 'cause'. Furthermore, disclosure must be done 'by the guilty party' (ie the individual having unlawfully accessed the private correspondence) and be prejudicial to the interest of the addressee (or, as noted the sender).

Art 618 of the Criminal Code provides that:

Anyone having, outside the cases provided for by Art 616, unlawfully [literally: 'abusively'] known the content of correspondence not addressed to him which was intended to remain secret, discloses it partially or entirely without justifying reasons, shall be punished if harm is caused, by imprisonment until 6 months or by a fine of between €1,003 and €516.

This provision offers some protection whenever it is not possible to apply Art 616 of the Criminal Code, including where the correspondence is not closed (eg where the correspondence was already read or opened by the addressee) or where disclosure is made by individuals not guilty of having made the original 'access' to the correspondence. The cumulative elements that must be taken into consideration for valuating if a disclosure of correspondence can be considered a crime under Art 618 are:

(i) the secret nature of the content of the correspondence;
(ii) the unlawful (or 'abusive') knowledge of the correspondence;
(iii) the absence of a justified reason for the disclosure.

As far as point (i) is concerned, the analysis regarding the nature (secret or not secret) of the correspondence has to be carried out taking into consideration its content and the intention of the sender or of the addressee. In this connection, legal scholars maintained that the secrecy of the correspondence can be excluded in presence of any explicit or implicit declarations or behaviours. For instance, the secrecy could be excluded if the addressee left the correspondence unattended (V Manzini, *Trattato di diritto penale italiano*, vol. VIII (Torino, 1986) 977; R Garofoli, *Manuale di diritto penale, Parte Speciale II* (Milano, 2006) 287).

As for point (ii), this test should be broadly the same as the defined in the above mentioned decision of the Supreme Court: the knowledge of emails' content would be lawfully (and not abusively) acquired by the relevant company if it had the right to read these emails by accessing the system where they were filed under the employment arrangement (or policies) regarding access at the time. The Supreme Court, in fact, held that people having the right to access their computer systems are entitled to know about the information included.

As far as point (iii) is concerned, the concept of 'justified reason' is quite wide. Legal commentators hold that the judge can maintain the existence of a justified reason considering the opposite interests: on one hand, the interest of a party in not disclosing the correspondence and, on the other hand, the interest of a party in disclosing it in order to obtain a result that it is impossible to get in accounts (and computer systems) provided by the employer,[83] in March 2007 the Privacy Authority issued its guidelines on Internet and email communications which helped to clarify the issue ('the Guidelines').[84]

9.138 Essentially, the employer must now establish and clarify whether the company's email account can be used by the employees only for business reasons or both for private and business reasons. If the corporate email account can be used for both private and business reasons, the Guidelines suggest that the electronic correspondence would be deemed comparable to personal correspondence because the personal data may concern, in addition to work-related information, the private life and/or personal sphere of both employees and third parties and thus would be considered inviolable.[85]

---

any different way (R Garofoli, *Manuale di diritto penale, Parte Speciale, II* (Milano, 2006) 274). There is some case law considering as a justified reason for the disclosure of correspondence the production thereof in a proceeding in order to establish one's claims or defences.

[83] By Law no 547 of 23 December 1993 the definition of correspondence has been also extended to any 'correspondence electronic or carried out through any other type of communication at a distance'.

[84] See Guidelines of 1 March 2007. The Privacy Authority recognized that 'the contents of email messages as well as the external communication data and attachments are a type of correspondence that is subject to confidentiality safeguards and also to Constitutional principles. The rationale of such safeguards consists of protecting the essential core of human dignity and fostering the full development of one's personality in the social context. Additional safeguards are afforded by the criminal provisions protecting inviolability of secrets (Arts 2 and 15 of the Constitution; Judgment no 281 of the Constitutional Court dated 17 July 1998, and no 81 of 11 March 1993; s 616(4) of the Criminal Code; s 49 of the Digital Administration Code)'.

[85] Under such Guidelines, the employer:
has to adopt and publicize internal policies, illustrating to all employees, inter alia, (i) the types of conduct which are not permitted, (ii) to what extent it is allowed to use email and network services also for personal purposes, (iii) what information is recorded on a temporary basis and who is lawfully entitled to access such information, (iv) whether and if so, what information is kept for longer in a centralized manner also for backup copies, technical management of the network and/or log files, (v) whether and to what extent the employer reserves the right to carry out controls in pursuance of the laws, on an occasional and/or non-regular basis, whereby the legitimate grounds on which such controls would be carried out will have to be specified in detail and (vi) which consequences, also of a disciplinary nature, may be drawn by the employer where the latter establishes that email and Internet services are misused; has to adopt organizational and technological measures to prevent the risk of misuse and minimize the use of employee related data, for instance, by making available an ad hoc account to be used by an employee for private purposes, providing for a layered approach to control and allowing, where it is necessary to assess the contents of email messages on account of pressing requirements related to work, and the relevant employee is absent from work unexpectedly and/or for prolonged period, the data subject to entrust another employee with checking the content of his or her email messages.

Once these conditions are met, the employer may lawfully process personal, *non-sensitive* data if the data subject has given him or her free consent thereto in a valid manner, or without the data subject's consent, in pursuance of the agreements with trade union representatives; failing the latter agreement, the authorization by a peripheral branch of the labour management agency will be necessary. *Sensitive data* may be processed with the data subjects' consent.

In particular, several mandatory and optional measures were indicated in the **9.139** Guidelines above: among them, the adoption by employers of an internal policy (which shall be adequately publicized and regularly updated) illustrating and clarifying, with detailed information:

(i) the appropriate usage applied to the equipment; and
(ii) whether and how controls are carried out.

Therefore, personal data processing carried out by employers in the context of **9.140** internal investigations must be compliant with data protection safeguards and rules, notably: the *principles of necessity* (ie information systems and software must be configured by minimizing use of personal and/or identification data in view of the purpose to be achieved); *fairness* (ie the fundamental features of the processing must be disclosed to employee in the context of the employment arrangement); and proportionality, *relevance and non-excessiveness* (ie the processing must be carried out for specific, explicit and legitimate purposes) and must be compliant with the Guidelines, in order to be entirely lawful as to the access to employee emails and documents in the search for wrongdoings, whether or not following up initial evidence.

If the employer does not comply with these requirements and/or recommenda- **9.141** tions set out in these Guidelines and most notably does not specify to its employees the terms of use of the companies' computer systems, it would be possible that the control of electronic correspondence by the employer be deemed protected by the constitutional right of secrecy, violation of which may trigger labour and criminal liability challenges.

An important issue is represented by the transfer of worker's data to third coun- **9.142** tries. Pursuant to Opinion no 8 of 2001 on the processing of personal data in the employment context adopted by the Privacy Authority on 13 September 2001 and in compliance with Article 25 of the Directive 95/46/EC, the transfers of personal data to a third country outside the EU can only take place where the third country ensures an adequate level of protection for the data and if the data processing and the data transfer satisfy all the other provisions of the above Directive.[86]

---

[86] Moreover, as it was pointed out by the Privacy Authority in the aforementioned Opinion, in light of Art 26 of Directive 95/46/EC, it is possible to derogate from the said general rule in the following cases and, in particular, when: (i) the data subject has given his or her consent unambiguously to the proposed transfer (the same considerations of chapter 10 of the Opinion no 8 of 2001 remain applicable here), or (ii) the transfer is necessary for the performance of a contract between the data subject and the controller, or (iii) the transfer is necessary or legally required on important public interest grounds, or (iv) for the establishment, exercise or defence of legal claims, or (v) the transfer is on the basis of contractual solutions as authorized by a member state as providing adequate safeguards, or (vi) the transfer is on the basis of standard contractual clauses approved by the Commission as providing adequate safeguards.

9.143 On the contrary, the processing of third parties data without satisfying the requirements described above, shall be considered unlawful. As a consequence, the collected data cannot be used during the investigation; moreover, the Data Protection Code provides for monetary sanctions up to €54,000 if the relevant employees are not properly informed about the data processing in the context of the investigation and criminal liability (with imprisonment of up to three years) and if the employer processes the employees' personal data outside the limits set forth above without obtaining an express consent from the relevant employee.

Practical considerations

9.144 From a data protection perspective, when conducting an investigation it is recommended to inform the data subjects (including employees) on a aggregate basis that an investigation is being carried out as a consequence of an alleged misconduct and that certain personal data may be collected and processed in the context of such investigation (by way of example, email communications sent by the employees).

9.145 Moreover, when conducting an investigation it is often recommended to pass copies of sensitive documents to an independent lawyer to be stored, since they would be able to refuse their disclosure on the basis of professional secrecy (*segreto professionale*), should they prove that they received the documents for reasons related to their profession and not purely for 'storage'.

H. Dealing with Privileged Documents

General rules on privilege

9.146 Under Italian law, members of certain professions, including lawyers, notaries, consultants and accountants, must keep confidential all documents and information sent to them in the context of their professional activities.[87] In particular, documents handled by or to a lawyer in the context of their professional activities are protected by professional secrecy (*segreto professionale*).

9.147 During investigations carried out by judicial or regulatory authorities on the premises of a lawyer, a lawyer can refuse to hand over documents or any other object provided by the client by claiming professional secrecy. In such cases, a judge has the authority to verify whether there are any grounds to oppose the professional secrecy.

---

[87] Arts 200 et seq and 256 of Italian Code of Criminal Procedure.

A judge should thoroughly investigate the matter prior to authorizing the seizure **9.148** of the allegedly 'privileged'/confidential documents. Such investigation should be aimed also at assessing whether the requirements of *segreto professionale* exist, that is if the lawyers involved have obtained or drafted a certain document in relation to their jobs or for unrelated reasons. There would be no privilege if the documents were obtained or drafted for unrelated reasons. In practice, some judges tend to be less rigorous than they should be and often grant the prosecutors' request to forcibly seize certain documents (eg contracts) in the lawyers' hands where they appear to be crucial to the criminal investigation.

If professional secrecy is not invoked, lawyers have to hand over any document **9.149** received by or drafted for their client in the original, if so required.

Producing documents covered by *segreto professionale* constitutes a criminal **9.150** offence and damages can be sought, unless there is *cause*.[88] In addition, it should be noted that the *Codice Deontologico del Consiglio Nazionale Forense* (Professional Code of Conduct) reaffirms the rule of professional secrecy and requires a lawyer to maintain absolute secrecy regarding his services and information provided by the client or which has become known to him or her in the course of the legal assistance. This duty extends to former clients and to persons who have consulted the lawyer without formally retaining him or her.

Segreto professionale applies only to lawyers who are members of the Italian bar, **9.151** most of whom are self-employed. In-house lawyers who are employed by a company or a bank and who cannot therefore be members of the bar are not subject to, and not protected by, *segreto professionale*.

In principle, therefore, this attorney-client confidentiality applies to any profes- **9.152** sional communication between the corporate client and its outside counsel, as well as to any document produced by the outside lawyer in connection with the assistance provided to the client, and, as a result, attorney work product should be protected in the context of an investigation, including market abuse investigations.[89] In practice, certain regulatory authorities, such as the IAA, and some prosecutors have shown a penchant for disregarding the privilege which should be attached to the attorney work product in the hands of the corporate client during dawn raids. In some instances the IAA has simply seized the privileged document irrespective of its nature, whilst in some other cases the IAA and the EU Commission have not materially seized the document but nonetheless read its content during the inspection in order to get a picture of the object of the legal

---

[88] Cause normally exists in extreme cases such as the actual danger of physical harm to a third party.
[89] In market abuse investigations the relevant directive specifically defers to the national professional secrecy provisions.

opinion and possibly clarify some relevant issues/facts. In order to avoid such situations, it is common practice amongst anti-trust practitioners to have attorneys closely shadowing the inspectors (from the IAA, the European Commission and/or the local police) during all phases of the investigation so as to be able to immediately oppose the seizure (and even their analysis if the intervention is prompt) of privileged documents.

9.153 Furthermore, as noted, there is no legal privilege over internal communications with the in-house legal or compliance department regardless of the qualifications of the staff. Any documents held by in-house lawyers, other than those communications from outside counsel, may have to be handed over to the regulator.[90] In Italy, unlike some other EU Countries, in-house counsels' professional activity is not recognized nor regulated by any legal norm or statute. As of today, Italian law considers legal counsels working inside a company as direct employees of the same. It results that, even if possessing all requirements to be registered with the Bar, an in-house legal counsel cannot be admitted to it (with some limited exceptions) and is thus deprived of all rights and privileges attached to independent lawyers registered therewith.

9.154 Furthermore, as noted, there is no legal privilege over internal communications with the in-house legal or compliance department regardless of the qualifications of the staff. Any documents held by in-house lawyers may have to be handed over to the regulator.

Waiving privilege

9.155 In practice, withholding allegedly privileged documents from regulators inspecting the premises, as noted above, can be somewhat difficult. In the light of the Italian regulators' far-reaching powers to require any document in the course of a regulatory investigation and the related duty to disclose all documents requested, including those that may adversely affect the case of the entity under investigation, and given the regulators' own duty of maintaining secrecy, they have often adopted the approach, particularly during raids or inspections at the corporate premises, to take any document, including those that are covered by privilege with the promise to somehow exclude them later from the file. For instance, in one case the IAA openly admitted that among the evidence gathered during its investigation there was a legal opinion drafted by one of the parties' counsel.[91]

---

[90] Judgment of the Court of First Instance of 17 September 2007, joined cases T-125/03 and T-253/03 *Akzo Nobel Chemicals Ltd and Akcros Chemicals Ltd v Commission of the European Communities.*

[91] Resolution no 6662 of IAA relating to the proceedings involving two Italian broadcasting companies.

Consob has, in the past, obtained and made some use in the course of investigations of memoranda and notes drafted by legal counsel, despite attorney-client privilege.

The legitimacy of this practice can be disputed: however, it is important to take **9.156** it into account and store, to the extent possible, any legally privileged documents in separate archives preferably at outside counsel's premises and, in any event, to call outside counsel to oversee any raid or inspection by regulators.

As a result, legal privilege does not enjoy, as a matter of practice, the same effective **9.157** protection as afforded by other jurisdictions. It is hoped that, in the future, Italian regulators will comply at least with the principles set out in EU case law by which the principle of lawyer-client confidentiality strictly covers correspondence between a client and an independent lawyer established within the EU.[92] This only applies to correspondence exchanged (i) after the initiation of proceedings by the European Commission and related to the defence of the client and/or (ii) prior to the initiation of proceedings, but in this case only if it is closely linked to the proceedings.[93]

According to some legal scholars, in Italy the correspondence exchanged with the **9.158** lawyers should not be seized during raids in the light of the broad constitutional right of legal defence established in Article 24 of the Constitution. However, this theory (albeit legally persuasive) has not yet been supported by case law and appears to be, as noted, somewhat neglected by regulators.

If a privileged/confidential document is shared with a third party, the privilege **9.159** for that document may be lost. Courts and regulators may ask the third party to produce the document(s) and the third party will generally have less interest in protecting the document from disclosure by objecting to the request. Furthermore, a corporate client can authorize its lawyer to disclose one or more documents which would otherwise be protected from disclosure.

Limited waiver

As a general rule, the disclosure of any privileged documents or confidential **9.160** information to a regulator does not constitute a waiver of privilege or any confidentiality right vis-à-vis any third party. The information provided should remain

---

[92] European Court of Justice, judgment of 18 May 1982, case no 155/79, *AM & S Europe Limited v Commission of the European Communities*; see also judgments by the Court of First Instance of the European Communities of 30 October 2002, case nos 125/03 R and 253/03 R; judgment of 17 September 2007, joined cases T-125/03 and T-253/03 *Akzo Nobel Chemicals Ltd and Akcros Chemicals Ltd v Commission of the European Communities*.

[93] Correspondence between a client and an independent lawyer established in a non-member state and correspondence with an in-house lawyer are excluded.

confidential and not accessible from private civil litigants, even if the regulator discloses the information to other regulators and/or to the prosecutors in the context of criminal proceedings. Regulators are under an obligation to keep information gained in the course of an investigation confidential and to refrain from disclosing or giving access to it.

9.161 However, in practice, once a document has been obtained by a regulator, there is a degree of risk that it could become available to a third party such as a civil litigant, particularly if a civil litigant manages to gain access to the file: this would be the case, for example, where documents are acquired by a prosecutor's file and the third party becomes a civil party within criminal proceedings. There have been instances of documents prepared by outside counsel, normally excluding legal advice, that have found their way into the files of aggrieved parties in criminal proceedings. Once a private litigant has so gained access to 'privileged' documents, such party is not bound by privilege and would normally use the document in litigation.

Privilege pitfalls

9.162 Companies facing regulatory investigation must always be aware that there is a danger that any documents drafted by lawyers are kept on the premises of the company, including hardware, and could be seized by a regulator in the context of administrative proceedings, and the company cannot claim the attorney-client confidentiality which can be invoked only by lawyers.

9.163 Moreover, even though, as a general rule, private citizens have no access to documents and information obtained by the regulator in the course of an investigation, litigants (or, to a degree, those who show they have an interest) may be granted access to the administrative file and/or (if they are recognized as 'victims' of the crime) to the criminal file, which may provide access to some or all of these documents.

I. Managing Regulators

Dialogue with regulators

9.164 Requests for information by regulators should be promptly satisfied, particularly in light of the sanctions for non-compliance. Historically, the attitude toward regulators was less cooperative in Italy than in other jurisdictions, such as the UK. However, this is changing, primarily due to the developments in the regulatory framework, and related criminal enforcement, whereby conduct may be considered obstructive to the regulators.

9.165 It is generally preferable to be assisted by expert external lawyers when dealing with the competent authorities concerned. However, in some instances, the authorities' prefer to deal directly with the company; in such cases the role of the external counsel should be to work behind the scenes, advising the clients and guiding them through the dialogue.

The approach in replying should always be respectful and formal. It is crucial to **9.166** maintain a favourable environment for the company when there is an ongoing investigation.

Controlling the scope of the investigation

Generally all answers to enquiries by the regulators should be clear and focused **9.167** so to avoid further inquiries likely to enlarge the scope of investigations.

In Italy, the inspection procedures applicable to listed companies, banks and **9.168** other intermediaries are specified in the laws and regulations and do not provide the regulators with much leeway to expand the scope of their investigation beyond the matter at hand. However, the regulators wide inspection powers provide them with the authority to conduct general inspections, the scope of which are very difficult to limit or control.

Use of information by regulators

Under Italian law, regulators are generally bound by a professional secrecy/confi- **9.169** dentiality duty which prevents them, in principle, from disclosing any information concerning and/or obtained in connection with their investigations. Pursuant to Article 4, paragraph 10, of the FLCA, information obtained by Consob in connection with the exercise of its supervisory powers is covered by secrecy vis-à-vis any public authority, with the exception of the Ministry of Economy and the other regulators among which a duty of cooperation applies.

Therefore, information obtained in the context of an investigation cannot, in **9.170** principle, be disclosed to private parties nor used by them subsequently. However, there is an exception to this rule in the context of the process for the adoption of administrative sanctions commenced against the private parties themselves. Irrespective of the wording of the relevant provisions, the persons against whom a sanctions process is commenced shall have access to certain documents collected by Consob in order to exercise their right of defence. However, Consob has determined a list of documents which are considered to be highly confidential and to which access should nevertheless be denied in all cases.[94] These documents include legal memoranda of external counsel requested by Consob with respect to specific investigations unless they have formed the basis of Consob's

---

[94] See Consob resolution no 9641 dated 13 December 1995.

final decision or were referred to in the decision underlying the imposition of administrative measures or provisions, and Consob's resolutions concerning documents to which access is denied.

9.171   According to Article 12, Regulation no 217 of 1998, save in case of criminal offences, the information collected by the IAA in the course of an investigation must be kept confidential and cannot be transmitted to any third party, including other public authorities. Whilst the parties being investigated as well as qualified third parties may have the right to access the case file, this is assessed by the IAA on a case-by-case basis, balancing out the right of defence of such undertakings (or possible third party claims) with the need to maintain confidential business and commercial secrets. Clearly, most of the information gathered during the investigation, which represents the factual basis for the IAA's final decision (after a statement of objections), will find its way into this IAA document. Further, legal memoranda through which the investigated parties have exercised their right of defence may also be illustrated in the final decision, although the IAA may agree to publish only a redacted version of the decision in case of business/commercial secrets.

9.172   In any other case, access by third parties to documents gathered during an investigation should be denied by way of specific decision of the courts.[95]

Managing multiple regulators

9.173   Although there is a risk that a company in Italy could be exposed to a number of different regulators with overlapping jurisdiction, it is fairly uncommon that more than one regulator actively investigates the same company at the same time.

---

[95] This principle has been reaffirmed by a major precedent where the investigated party, an auditing firm, suspected of having breached certain provisions of law in carrying out its auditing activities over a listed company, requested access to the documentation collected by Consob in the course of a proceeding which had not resulted in the adoption of a sanction in order to make use of it in the context of civil proceedings that the audited listed company had commenced against the auditing firm. Consob refused any access to the documentation, on the grounds of secrecy.

The Supreme Administrative Court (Consiglio di Stato) (the competent jurisdictional authority) asked the Constitutional Court (Corte Costituzionale) to determine whether the relevant provisions of the FLCA preventing any form of disclosure by Consob of the information obtained in the exercise of its supervisory powers were to be considered consistent with certain principles of the Italian Constitutional Chart, when they result in the impossibility for a party subject to investigation to have access to the documents collected by the regulator, other than in the context of proceedings commenced against it by the regulator (see Order, Administrative Supreme Court (Consiglio di Stato), 5 July 2002 on the action no 680 of 2002 brought by Arthur Andersen SpA against Consob).

The Constitutional Court deemed that the constitutional claim had no grounds (Constitutional Court no 32 of 2005), and thereby indirectly confirmed the legitimacy of Consob's refusal to give access to documentation obtained in the course of investigations other than to recognize the investigated party's right of defense vis-à-vis Consob itself.

It is much more frequent, on the other hand to have parallel investigations conducted simultaneously by one regulator and one or more criminal prosecutors. In any event considering that all regulators are under a duty to collaborate and exchange information, it is important to be even handed and not to withhold documents or information from one authority while providing it to another unless there is a compelling reason for doing so.

The 'real-life' risk of facing both criminal prosecution (at the company level under **9.174** Decree 231 as well as at the individual or executive level) and regulatory investigation(s) triggers a practical problem of coordinating the various defences. This is made somewhat easier by the fact that the criminal defence counsel appointed by the company executives is paid for by the company, until individual guilt is finally established. However, it is obvious that the respective interests may not necessarily be aligned and that the criminal counsel's professional duties are owed to his client. Tensions may particularly explode where individual executives are suspended or dismissed but also where they choose plea-bargaining or other available 'fast' routes under Italian criminal procedure. Furthermore, defence against a regulatory investigation can be more difficult if the company does not know all the information available to the prosecutor. One recommendable avenue, also in fraud/corruption cases, could be to explore whether the company (under different management, possibly) can be a recognized 'victim of the crime' in criminal proceedings, thus having access to the prosecutor's file and establishing cooperation.

J. Managing Employees During Investigations

Powers to compel cooperation

Articles 2094, 2104, 2105 and 2106 of the ICC provide that employees are sub- **9.175** ject to the employer's control and direction. Moreover, employees are bound by a general duty of loyalty to the employer and to carry out their work with due diligence. These obligations require employees to cooperate in a loyal and fair manner with both internal and regulatory investigations, although internal investigation may be subject to a 'reasonableness' test.

The employer, in order to induce or compel cooperation from its employee, can **9.176** remind the employee that he or she can be sanctioned or ultimately dismissed if he or she substantially fails to cooperate in a loyal and fair manner in any reasonable internal and/or regulatory investigations.

Control on threats

As stated above, it is established by Italian law that employees will cooperate with **9.177** reasonable orders from their employers and this extends to requests to cooperate with internal investigations unless these are only directed at undermining, persecuting or targeting the employee. This does not apply to regulatory investigations, as there are specific provisions and sanctions effectively imposing a duty to cooperate upon entities and individuals with regulators.

9.178 Other than the abovementioned general rules referring to the duty of loyalty and obedience laid down by Articles 2104 and 2105 of the ICC, there is no specific law which enables the employer to exert pressure upon an employee in order to gain his cooperation in the context of internal investigations.

9.179 An employee only has a duty to comply with orders or requests which are legitimate, therefore it is crucial that during an internal investigation cooperation is properly requested. In this respect, employers in Italy must abide by some limits established by the law (in addition to data protection legislation) when either collecting information about any employees or investigating any employees' activity in and/or out of the workplace. The employer is restricted in the subject matter of the investigation and the way in which it can conduct the investigation.

9.180 Article 8 of Law no 300 of 20 May 1970 ('the Workers' Statute') prohibits employers from investigating the political, religious or trade union opinions of their workers, and in general any matter which is irrelevant for the purposes of assessing their professional skills and aptitudes. Article 8 is split into two parts. The first part is a clear prohibition against investigating particular aspects of the employee's private life.[96] The second part is a general clause that basically allows the employer to investigate any other aspects, provided that they are relevant in order to evaluate the employee's professional abilities.[97]

9.181 In addition to the data protection issues outlined above, a company conducting an internal investigation must ensure that it complies with Articles 4 and 7 of the Workers' Statute. Article 4 prohibits the use of cameras and similar audiovisual media to control work activity at a distance, any such surveillance activity can be punished as a criminal violation.[98] Originally, this rule was introduced in order to prevent employers from controlling work activity with the indiscriminate use of the video cameras situated in the workplace. Italian case law has expanded the

---

[96] Data that cannot be collected include information that refers to the religious, political beliefs or other elements considered irrelevant for the purposes of evaluating the employees' skills.

[97] For instance, Italian Courts held lawful, in light of Art 8 of the Workers' Statute, investigations conducted with reference to employee's previous convictions, provided that there is a connection with the tasks entrusted (Italian Supreme Court (Corte di Cassazione) no 2225, 2 March 1988; Tribunal of Palermo, 18 November 1983; Tribunal of Naples (*Pretura*) 24 July 1977).

[98] Workers' Statute, Art 4, para 1.

interpretation of this provision[99] to include the use of telephone devices, which can record the telephone number and the length of the employees' calls. As noted, this prohibition now extends to any system through which the employer can control work activity and therefore also the firm's electronic information system.[100]

In essence, employers are allowed to carry out general and/or preventive controls **9.182** over employees as long as they comply with the specific restrictions set out by the Worker's Statute and, as noted above, the Data Protection Authority's guidelines and to the extent agreed upon with the work councils, as the case may be. Moreover, before adopting any disciplinary measures, employers must follow the procedure provided for by law to that effect.

However, employers are allowed to carry out 'defensive' controls to verify (*ex post*) **9.183** if the employees carried out unlawful conduct, regardless of the strict restrictions provided by the Worker's Statute and the Data Protection Code, as far as they have to establish or defend a legal claim.

Representation

There is a fine line between investigating a matter and starting disciplinary pro- **9.184** ceedings against an employee involved with the facts, in which case, the positions of the corporation and the employee might be in conflict. Whether or not employees should be independently represented at an interview or otherwise in an investigation, ultimately, depends upon the circumstances. For example, whether there is any suggestion that the breach may have resulted from deliberate action by an employee, whether there is a risk of the employee facing a criminal prosecution or whether there is a risk that the interests of the employee and the interests of the company may conflict.[101]

---

99 Tribunal of Milan, 2 March 2004; Tribunal of Milan, 2 May 2002; Tribunal of Milan, 15 January 2001, no 2330; Tribunal of Turin, 9 January 2004, in '*Giur Piemontese*' (2004) 131; Italian Supreme Court (Corte di Cassazione), sez lav, 3 April 2002, no 4746, in '*Giust civ Mass*' (2002) 576; Tribunal of Teramo, 12 May 2006, in '*Notiziario Giurisprudenza lav*' (2006) 345.

100 It is important to highlight that Art 4, para 2, of the Workers' Statute provides that whether the fixtures and fittings, through which it is possible to remotely control work activities, are needed for organizational and productive requirements or for security at work, the employer's power to control is not negated, but only limited by a specific and compulsory procedure described under para 2 of Art 4. According to this procedure, the installation of these instruments must be necessarily agreed with the work councils. In the absence of agreement with the work councils, the employer files a request with the local Work Inspectorate, which directs, if it is needed, the way to use these instruments. Therefore, if the employer wants to inspect the employees' use of the Internet or the activity of any particular employees through computers or phones, the adoption of internal policies is not enough. It is necessary to execute the procedure mentioned above.

101 If there is no conflict, or no significant risk of conflict, one counsel may act for both a listed corporate and its employees.

9.185 In these circumstances, it may be appropriate for the employer to take immediate action to suspend the employee or remove him or her from sensitive positions. Not only is this a matter of common sense, but it may also be viewed by the investigating regulatory authority as a positive step taken by the company in response to the breach, to ensure that the breach is not repeated in the short term and to protect the evidence. In doing so, the company should ensure that it complies with compulsory disciplinary procedures under Italian law, in order to reduce the risk of an employee successfully challenging the removal. In certain cases, the employee may accept to be moved to other, non-line functions (eg this is common where environmental violations may affect the individual position of the plant manager).

9.186 In any event, if the individual asks to bring a lawyer to an interview, it is usually imprudent as well as counter-productive to refuse, especially if the employer is already represented by counsel.

Assurances as to confidentiality and privilege

9.187 Counsel should not give employees any absolute assurances about the confidentiality of their discussions with investigating counsel. The discussions could reveal matters that may result in disciplinary proceedings being instigated against the interviewee or another person. Secondly, the company's counsel is not bound to professional secrecy vis-à-vis employees as such and therefore the information disclosed to counsel, if not conflicting with the professional secrecy owed to the company, may be revealed to the regulatory authority or to a public prosecutor. Counsel may, at best, assure the employee that there will be efforts, within the law, to minimize adverse consequences and unnecessary publicity.

Ethical implications for counsel

9.188 As in other jurisdictions, counsel should always treat employees with respect, introduce him or herself, indicate that he or she is acting on behalf of the employer whilst maintaining privilege and confidentiality, and explain the purpose of what is happening in a polite fashion. It will rarely be productive to conduct an interview in a heated manner. Usually, given the need for objectivity, it will normally be sensible for the interviewer not to have been involved in the events in issue. No matter how polite or experienced the counsel is, chances are that some of the Italian employees will become somewhat defensive, or aggressive, during the interview. The most senior executives would normally resent being questioned by a lawyer, as opposed to their ultimate boss. The latter's presence would be advisable in those cases. It is essential that interviewers are properly trained.

It should be noted that, as soon as the facts unveiled give rise to an employee **9.189** being subject to disciplinary sanctions, the employer must notify the employee in writing that disciplinary proceedings have been commenced. Therefore, an ethical issue may arise for the counsel if he or she does not promptly advise the employer, at the end or during the interview, that the employee is likely to face disciplinary proceedings.

Investigation and disciplinary process

Counsel should not give an employee assurances about his continued employ- **9.190** ment given that, until the interview has taken place and its outcome fully evaluated, the employer will not know the extent of the employee's participation in the suspected conduct. Moreover, depending on the factual circumstances, for example in the case of an employee's regulatory or criminal liability, the employer may find itself in a position of having to dismiss the employee, whether or not under regulators' pressure, perhaps in order to avoid being viewed as aiding and abetting the regulatory or criminal breach made by the employee. Finally, it is possible in the financial services industry that the employee's conduct would result in losing the necessary licence to continue his or her job. Notwithstanding the above, the employer may remind the employee that he or she can be sanctioned or dismissed in relation to the circumstances arising during the investigation only to the extent that such circumstances qualify as misconduct by the employee.

The procedure for suspension from work and the applicable limits are regulated **9.191** by Article 7 of the Workers' Statute and usually also by the applicable national collective bargaining agreement. An employee can be suspended pending the outcome of the investigation, provided that the violations for which the employee is charged are formally notified to the employee in compliance with the law and reasonably appear to be serious enough to potentially justify a dismissal for just cause. The employee can only be suspended for the limited period of time strictly required to complete the disciplinary process regulated by the law.

The procedure for imposing disciplinary sanctions and, in the most serious cases, **9.192** dismissal, must comply with certain mandatory rules and requirements imposed by Italian labour law and national collective bargaining agreements. These set out that the employer is obliged to inform the employee in a timely manner and in writing of the breach, and that the employee has the right to explain his actions within five days from receipt of the written notice. Some national collective bargaining agreements require that any disciplinary sanction must be imposed by and not later than ten days from receipt of the employee's explanations.

9.193 Failure by the company to comply with these rules may entitle the employee to challenge any disciplinary sanction taken and have it nullified.[102]

9.194 Dismissal of employees is governed in Italy by Law no 604 of 1966 and the Workers' Statute, as amended. Moreover, the applicable national collective bargaining agreements usually set out additional rules, with which the employer needs to comply.

9.195 As stated above, failure by an employee to comply with the obligations to cooperate in a loyal and fair manner in both internal and regulatory investigations may enable the employer to lawfully impose disciplinary sanctions and possibly terminate the employment relationship. However, an employee may seek to make a claim against the company for wrongful and/or unfair application of disciplinary sanctions or dismissal if the company were to impose sanctions on, or dismiss, him, for failing to cooperate with an internal investigation, or were to take action that ultimately caused the employee to resign. The success of such a claim will depend upon whether or not the employee's failure to cooperate with the investigation could be deemed to be misconduct.

Challenges posed by former employees

9.196 Once the employment contract has terminated, as a matter of fact it is extremely difficult for an employer to gain information or documents from former employees. After the termination of the employment the employees are no longer bound to any loyalty duty and they cannot be forced to cooperate with the former employer with reference to a potential investigation.

9.197 The employer might only keep reviewing the documents (digital and hard copies) stored by the former employee, which have to be considered the employer's

---

[102] If the employee commits an infringement, employers must follow the procedure outlined in Art 7 of the Workers' Statute prior to taking disciplinary action.

Art 7 provides that, in order to proceed with any kind of disciplinary action, including dismissal, the following procedure must be met: the employer has to adopt a Code of Conduct on the use of Internet and email; the employer has to adequately publicize the disciplinary rules (ie violations, relevant sanctions and disciplinary procedures) by affixing them in a place which is accessible to all employees. No other way of communication is allowed, including a personal delivery of the text to the employee. Besides, the employer cannot take any sanctions without first communicating and specifically indicating the grounds for them to the employee concerned and hearing his defence.

Sanctions which are more serious than a verbal reprimand cannot be taken until five days have elapsed since the employee was provided with written grounds.

Reprimands (written and verbal), fines and suspension are the usual sanctions and, in any case, Art 7 prohibits taking sanctions which cause definitive modifications of the employment relationship (ie transfers or change of job content). Finally, the employer must inform the employee of the sanctions.

The same procedure must be followed also when the employer inflicts the most severe sanction of dismissal.

property, subject to the restrictions set out by Privacy Law (for instance it would be possible to check the emails stored in the employer's server, to the extent that the proportionality and necessity tests are met and that an appropriate policy on emails monitoring has been put in place, but the investigation should not address emails of a purely private nature which are not relevant to the investigation).

Payment of legal fees/indemnification/fee advances

Only in the case of criminal investigations or proceedings brought against an **9.198** employee in connection with the duties he or she carries out for the employer, under some collective bargaining agreements, are certain employees, usually, executives (*dirigenti*), middle-managers (*quadri*) and sometimes also employees with lower profiles (*operai* and *impiegati*) entitled to be indemnified by the employer for any expenses incurred (including attorneys' fees), until and unless individual guilt is finally established. Additional entitlements to reimbursement are sometimes established by internal company policy and individual employment agreements. *Dirigenti* are usually covered by insurance policies paid for by the employer for any risks and disbursements, including compensation for damages, related to the performance of their working duties. Such reimbursement provisions also apply when the company itself is subject to a regulatory investigation.

Employees may also be advanced fees for representation by separate legal counsel. **9.199** However, some collective bargaining agreements set out the employer's right to recover expenses incurred in favour of the employee in the case that he or she is definitively found guilty for gross misconduct or fraud. Moreover, company regulations and/or individual agreements can set out the employer's right to recover expenses incurred in favour of the employee under certain circumstances, such as if the employee is ultimately found to have engaged in improper conduct also pursuant to internal or regulatory investigations.

Joint defence agreements

Joint defence agreements are not common in Italy. However, sometimes, when **9.200** the employer's and employee's interests do not conflict, they may and do appoint the same attorney and follow the same defence strategy. It is to be noted, though, that, under Italian law and Bar regulations, the attorney is always bound to act in the best interests of each client and therefore, if there is an actual or potential conflict of interests between the company and the employee, the attorney has an obligation to choose for which of the two clients he or she will continue to act. Moreover, in the case of a joint defence agreement, both parties, at all times, reserve the right to choose a different attorney and follow an independent defence strategy. If the employer or the employee decides to terminate the joint defence agreement and to be assisted by a different attorney, attorney-client privilege shall not be affected and the previous attorney will not be able to use or disclose any privileged document or information with which he or she has become acquainted of by virtue of his or her being the attorney of the employee or the employer.

K. Winding up an Internal Investigation

Managing expectations

9.201 Internal investigations in Italy are conducted essentially by a company's relevant corporate bodies in compliance with applicable rules and are generally not addressed to the regulators. Therefore, reports are filed and kept internally to demonstrate that all 'internal controls' have been duly complied with and are kept available for any judicial authority or regulatory formal investigation. This is particularly relevant as a tool to avoid quasi-criminal liability of the corporation under Decree 231.

9.202 Culturally, there is still a high degree of resistance to disclose to the public the results of an internal, voluntary investigation. Aside from the mandatory, above mentioned, reporting requirements (as to price-sensitive facts) under securities law (FLCA) and implementing regulations, Italian companies prefer to 'put their house in order' rather than to report. A limited exception may be represented by the 'corporate governance' report which listed companies should disclose annually: this may be a forum where to disclose the frequency, and possibly results, of internal investigations: where results have unveiled crimes, care should be taken to address any possible aspects of aiding and abetting, removing the consequences and addressing the coordination with any criminal proceedings.

L. Reporting Obligations

Tailoring the report

9.203 In Italy, generally speaking there are no obligations to submit reports of internal investigations to the regulators. However, there are legal and regulatory provisions governing the required content in any mandatory reports to be submitted to regulators.

Coordinating with Public Relations strategy

9.204 As there are no obligations to report to the authorities, it is unlikely that any reports would be released that would require and accompany PR effort. In other words, the PR strategy in relation to voluntary investigations can be determined freely.

Beware of waiving privilege

As anticipated, legal privilege may in principle be invoked in connection with **9.205**
any document produced by counsels in providing their assistance to corporate
clients, including any assistance in connection with an internal investigation.
Since it is unusual that a company would share the results of an internal investigation with regulators, it is unlikely that there is a risk of privilege being waived in
this manner.

It is understood that should the corporate investigation be carried out only with **9.206**
the assistance of in-house counsels (and its resulting reports) it will not be covered
by legal privilege. Furthermore, even if drafted by external counsel, should the
report of the investigation be attached to the minutes of the meeting of any
corporate body of the company, the privilege would be waived.

M. Litigation Risks

Risks of criminal litigation commenced by regulators

Regulators may not pursue crimes but instead must report the case to the Public **9.207**
Prosecutor and prompt a criminal investigation conducted by the Prosecutor.
However, they can pursue and sanction administrative offences.

Consob is entitled to pursue corporate violations that amount to regulatory **9.208**
breaches, including breaches of disclosure requirements,[103] breaches of takeover
(tender offers) rules, false communications on adoption or compliance with
codes of conduct for listed issuers, and can impose administrative fines. Consob
also pursues corporate violations, such as market abuses or misrepresentations in
financial statements, which may constitute both regulatory and criminal breaches,
in relation to the regulatory sanctions.

Likewise, both the Bank of Italy and ISVAP are entitled to pursue corporate **9.209**
violations that amount to regulatory breaches with administrative fines only.[104]

Reciprocally, pursuant to Article 187-*decies* of the FLCA, once it receives infor- **9.210**
mation indicating that a criminal offence has been committed in connection
with market abuse such as insider trading or market manipulation, the public
prosecutor has to immediately inform the Chairman of Consob. Consob and the

---

[103] In connection with, eg, holdings in listed companies and with shareholders agreements.

[104] Major corporate violations that amount to criminal breaches, and therefore cannot be pursued by the regulators, include the following: dissemination by the company of false corporate
information and false financial statements; publication of a prospectus containing false information;
undue return of contributions to the capital of the company; illegal allocation of profits and reserves;
illegal transactions in shares of the company or the holding company; illegal transactions to the detriment of creditors; exercise of illegal influence on shareholders' meetings.

judicial authorities cooperate with each other through the exchange of information in order to facilitate the investigation. This also applies in relation to administrative sanctions.

Risks of civil litigation commenced by regulators

9.211 The US concept of civil enforcement, as such, is alien to the Italian legal system. Any violation or breach of applicable laws or regulations falling within the remit of a regulator would trigger administrative enforcement, and the imposition of fines, by the regulator. Fines and the regulator's decisions may be challenged before the Administrative Court. However, Consob and other regulators may ask to be recognized as 'victims of the crime' and bring civil claims for damages in criminal proceedings. This has been done recently in some high profile cases. Notably, a statutory provision[105] allows Consob to join in criminal proceedings relating to market abuse and insider trading and to seek monetary damages relating to any 'violation of integrity of the market'.

Risks of private civil litigation

9.212 Third parties, such as investors, who have suffered damages may seek compensation through a civil action, whether (most commonly) in tort or in contract. In the course of such action, they may make reference to the results of regulatory investigations and/or any order given by the regulator as evidence of the misconduct. However, claimants will have to give evidence that the damages suffered by them arose as a direct consequence of the regulatory breaches.

9.213 In the *Parmalat* and *Cirio* cases, a large number of investors (over 30,000 in the *Parmalat* case) have joined in the criminal proceedings and claimed monetary damages (each, by way of an individual claim brought through common representation by a handful of lawyers). In other cases, such as the *Banca Popolare di Lodi*, the regulatory and criminal investigations have been followed by the bank/corporate lawsuit for damages against former directors.

9.214 With Law no 244 of 21 December 2007, the Italian Parliament approved the introduction of collective actions for damages in the Italian judicial system,[106]

---

[105] Art 187-*undecies* of the FLCA.

[106] At the end of December 2007 the Italian Parliament passed the Budget Law and Financial Act 2008 and so finally introduced a specific statutory provision (Art 140-*bis*) into the Consumer Code that contemplates an opt-in collective action for damages arising out of: liability in connection with mass contracts; torts; unlawful commercial practices; or anti-competitive behaviour. The new law became effective on 29 June 2008.

Under the new collective action (which is somewhat limited in scope), bodies acting on behalf of consumers or investors (previously entitled to seek injunctive relief) will be able to obtain a declaratory judgment of the right to obtain compensation and the refund of sums due (although the collective action will not necessarily lead to a direct order to pay this money).

which should make it somewhat easier for aggrieved investors or consumers to ask for damages on a 'group' basis consisting in collective claims for the restoration of damages suffered by consumers from an unlawful conduct put forward by a company. As indicated, the new law will enter into force on 30 June 2008.

Relevance of investigation reports

As a matter of practice, Italian case law tends to attribute strong evidentiary **9.215** value in civil proceedings to the results of inspections carried out by the Bank of Italy and Consob. Accordingly, any findings by regulators may be deemed to constitute evidence, or initial evidence and/or basis for presumptions, of misconduct and therefore form the basis for any application for damages. The evidentiary weight of the regulatory findings and pronouncements is further increased where such findings have withstood any challenge in Court such as whenever the regulated entity has appealed against the relevant findings before the competent Administrative Court and the latter has rejected the appeal and has thus upheld the regulatory judgment. Nonetheless, all the other requisite elements of a private civil action, particularly causation and damages, must be established.

N. Settlement with Regulators

Process

Theoretically, no regulator has any discretion as to whether or not to pursue **9.216** enforcement actions, since the regulator should in principle pursue any alleged

---

Standing to bring such a claim to protect consumers' interests has been granted to a few entities, namely:
- consumer associations with nationwide presence, and
- any other consumer group, investor group or association sufficiently representative of collective interests (as assessed by the judge).

First, a court will filter the claim to assess admissibility; the second phase will consist of a fully-fledged trial to obtain the substantive declaration, and the criteria for calculating loss; then there will be further, separate individual procedures to determine damages for each claimant.

If the action is declared admissible, the plaintiff must proceed with suitable advertising to inform all of the class members of the collective action, enabling them to opt in to the action and take part in the proceedings. Consumers may opt in to the collective action by a simple written notice (without any particular formality) to the group plaintiff which must be sent by (and no later than) the penultimate hearing (ie the post-trial hearing at which the relief sought is finally set out). They will then be bound by the result.

Individual consumers that do not opt-in to the collective action still have the alternative option to bring individual claims against the defendant either by joining proceedings in the traditional way or by separate proceedings.

There are two special procedures to assist with the binding determination of individual damages which can either be out of court; or, in whole or in part, before a judicial 'chamber of conciliation'.

breach of laws and/or regulations falling within their jurisdiction. However, in practice, given the regulators' heavy workload and backlog of work they may and do prioritize certain actions and efforts over others on the basis of the importance, size and media coverage.

9.217 There are no formal guidelines as to when a regulator would consider active enforcement but they would take into account elements such as the seriousness of the potential offence, its size, public importance, and media coverage.

9.218 Regulatory actions cannot be formally settled. Rather an understanding is reached, which may not be documented, that no further action will be taken. Civil litigation arising from regulatory actions can in theory be settled, to the extent that damages or other rights or interest may be waived, or disposed of, by private parties.

Is admission necessary?

9.219 An admission would be viewed by the regulator as cooperative behaviour possibly resulting in a decrease of the amount of the sanction. However, as there are no prescribed rules on settlement with regulators, an admission could not be considered a necessary prerequisite for a settlement.

Impact if under investigation by multiple authorities

9.220 As settlement agreements are not commonplace and there are no rules governing the circumstances under which they occur, there is little evidence as to the extent that a settlement agreement with one regulator would impact upon investigations being conducted by other authorities or regulators.

Plea bargaining and amnesty arrangements

9.221 Criminal actions can be settled through plea bargaining, which under Italian law does not necessarily imply any recognition/admission of liability (although the issue is debated) but merely an agreement on the applicable criminal sanction, particularly for the purposes of compensating third parties for damages arising from the conduct.

9.222 Plea bargains are permitted only where the punishment actually applicable to the crime being considered does not exceed five years of imprisonment. Moreover, plea bargains exclude the application of additional penalties, the payment of additional charges as well as mention in the criminal records. One of the key elements considered is the partial or total indemnification of the damages caused.

O. Conclusion

A history of financial scandals, defrauding investors and corporate crashes has pro- **9.223**
duced a legal framework that places a heavy emphasis on regulatory and internal
controls over corporations and financial institutions. It is expected that, at both
levels, control will be more effective than in the past and will boost the frequency
and intensity of investigations. Italian regulators have been given new and pervasive
powers[107] and, just like prosecutors, have recently been flexing their muscles.[108]

A definitive turning point is evident from the increased tendency of prosecutors **9.224**
and criminal judges to make enormous use of the Decree 231 on quasi-criminal
liability of legal entities and to apply its sanctions, ranging from hefty fines to
freezing orders and suspension of trade, or ban on any transaction with governmental entities, against foreign and domestic corporations and banks.[109] Since
the only way to avoid the sanctions is to show that an effective 'organizational
model', including a compliance programme, has been put in place and monitored by an internal supervisory body empowered with adequate resources and
investigative tools, it is a fair assumption that this should trigger a higher number
of more effective internal investigations than in the past.

The new legislation on collective actions for damages effective from 29 June **9.225**
2008 provides a further platform for an increase of corporate awareness of the
need for investigating internally any fact that might give rise to corporate exposure to third party claims.

In this respect, it is important to bear in mind that, for internal investigations to run **9.226**
smoothly, certain practices must be adopted, which include, at least as a precautionary
move against possible employee complaints, appropriate disclosure of policies such
as on access to emails and seeking union consent. Conversely, it is important to appreciate that, with respect to regulatory investigations, certain barriers to regulators such
as legal privilege may not function as effectively in Italy as in other jurisdictions.

---

[107] These powers, all point to a strengthening of their investigative activities, which the regulators
are in fact beefing up. Consob, for example, has set up a dedicated investigative department (*Divisione
Ispettorato*), operative as from April 2007.

[108] Traditionally, regulatory investigations primarily affected regulated entities, mostly in the
financial services industry and in connection with their compliance with industry-specific rules, eg on
ratios, conduct of business and internal organization. The current trend is to increase investigations
into any listed corporation as well as any other person or entity possibly under regulatory control.

[109] In early July 2007, a criminal judge in Pescara has frozen assets and pursued an investigation
under Decree 231 against foreign banks including Citigroup, Goldman Sachs, JP Morgan and
Lehman Brothers in relation to a tax-avoidance scheme known as dividend washing. The banks are
said to be cooperating with the judicial authorities, as they otherwise risk being banned from advising or assisting the Italian national and local government in the lucrative areas of bond placement,
privatizations and corporate finance.

10

INVESTIGATIONS IN HONG KONG

A. Introduction[1]

10.01 Securities regulation and market infrastructure in Hong Kong has been overhauled in recent years, first in 2000 with the listing of Hong Kong's stock exchange company, and then in 2003 with the most significant regulatory development in 20 years, the implementation of the Securities and Futures Ordinance (Cap 571) (SFO).

10.02 It is widely agreed in the regulatory community that the enactment of the SFO has brought securities laws in Hong Kong in line with those of the other main financial centres of the world.[2] As a result of this, Hong Kong has been in an optimal position to take advantage of the enormous opportunities that have arisen since the recovery of global equities markets in 2003, and has been able successfully to serve as a platform bridging the international marketplace and the fast-growing Chinese economy.

10.03 The SFO regime is underpinned by the main regulator of financial services in Hong Kong, the Securities and Futures Commission (SFC). The role of the SFC is to ensure that the provisions of the SFO are followed by all market participants,

---

[1] Contributors: Patrick Swain and Peter Yuen.

[2] 'An Overview of the Major Events and Regulation of the Securities and Futures Markets between 1997 and 2007', found at <http://www.sfc.hk/sfcPressRelease/EN/sfcOpenDocServlet?docno=07PR108>.

and it has been granted a wide range of investigatory and enforcement powers in order to ensure that this happens.

As a result of these reforms, issuers, intermediaries and investors have shown their **10.04** confidence in Hong Kong's regulatory regime by making Hong Kong the third international financial centre in the world in 2007.[3]

B. Regulators

Key regulators

Hong Kong's listed corporations are predominantly regulated under a 'three- **10.05** tiered regulatory structure'.[4] The government stands at the apex of the regulatory structure and, by Article 109 of the Hong Kong Basic Law, has responsibility for the overall development of Hong Kong's financial markets and for the setting of broad economic policies that affect the economy at large. In the run-up to the transfer of sovereignty over Hong Kong from the UK to the People's Republic of China, there was some concern expressed that there would be greater interven-tion by the government in the corporate sector and that as a result Hong Kong's competitive advantage would be eroded. This concern has, to date, proved to be misplaced.

At the next two tiers of the regulatory structure are the SFC and the Hong Kong **10.06** Exchanges and Clearing Limited (HKEx).[5] These are the principal regulators of Hong Kong listed corporations.

Aside from the SFC and HKEx, there are a number of industry-specific regula- **10.07** tors in the banking, insurance and telecommunications sectors, whilst investiga-tions into serious fraud/white collar crime and corruption are handled by the Commercial Crimes Bureau of the Police force (CCB), and the Independent Commission Against Corruption (ICAC).

The SFC

The SFC is an independent statutory body with overall responsibility for the reg- **10.08** ulation and development of Hong Kong listed securities and futures markets. The SFC aims to balance effective implementation of its regulatory objectives

---

[3] Global Financial Centre Index, see <http://www.zyen.com>.
[4] See generally, the following for further discussion of the 'three-tiered regulatory structure': R Kotewall and G Kwong, 'Report of the Panel of Inquiry on the Penny Stocks Incident' (September 2002) 13–23. The exceptions to this are corporations in the banking and insurance sector which are predominantly regulated by the Hong Kong Monetary Authority and the Insurance Authority.
[5] The HKEx is the parent company of the Hong Kong Stock Exchange.

with the maintenance of the international nature of Hong Kong's securities and futures industry and the competitiveness of Hong Kong as a financial centre.

10.09 The SFC derives its regulatory powers from the SFO, the main piece of legislation in Hong Kong dealing with the regulation of the securities and futures market, and its mandate is to provide a regulatory framework establishing a transparent, fair and efficient market.

10.10 The SFC is divided into four operational divisions:

i. the **Corporate Finance Division** reviews listing documents under the 'dual filing' system (with the Stock Exchange) in relation to listing matters, administers the *Takeovers and Mergers Code and Share Repurchases Code*, oversees the Stock Exchange's listing-related functions and responsibilities, and administers securities and company legislation, including the *Companies Ordinance* (Cap. 32), which provides for registration, regulation and administration of listed and unlisted companies. Under the 'dual filing' system, which has been in place since 1 April 2003, listed applicants and listed companies are required to file their disclosure and listing application materials with both the SFC and the Stock Exchange;

ii. the **Intermediaries and Investment Products Division** devises and administers licensing requirements for intermediaries (regulated entities include corporations licensed under the SFO) to carry out 'regulated activities', and financial institutions authorized by the Hong Kong Monetary Authority (HKMA) who are registered with the SFC to carry out 'regulated activities', supervises and monitors intermediaries' conduct and financial resources, and regulates the public marketing of investment products;

iii. the **Enforcement Division** conducts market surveillance to identify market misconduct for further investigation, enquires into alleged breaches of relevant ordinances and codes, including insider dealing and market manipulation, and institutes disciplinary procedures for misconduct by licensed intermediaries; and

iv. the **Supervision of Markets Division** supervises and monitors the activities of exchanges and clearing houses, encourages development of the securities and futures markets and promotes and develops self-regulation by market bodies.

10.11 The SFC's enforcement-related aims are to protect investors and to maintain market integrity and confidence.[6] Where market participants fail to comply with the relevant laws and regulations, the SFC seeks to take appropriate steps through

---

[6] Derived from the Objectives and Principles of Securities Regulation of the International Organization of Securities Commissions.

surveillance and enforcement. Further, the SFC attempts to ensure that the persons responsible for wrongdoing are held accountable.

These aims are, however, also balanced against making efficient use of SFC's **10.12** resources.[7] As it is a public body, the SFC is accountable for the use of its financial resources. It has therefore established detailed financial and budgetary control measures by using a risk-based approach to prioritize the allocation of its resources. For example, in respect of the supervision of intermediaries, the SFC focuses its resources on resolving issues which have substantial market impact and which may have a flow-on effect or result in significant investor losses.

If the SFC suspects that there has been a breach of relevant laws or standards it **10.13** will investigate what has happened and will consider whether there is any evidence of wrongdoing.

As can be seen from the table below, the investigatory and enforcement activities **10.14** of the SFC have increased significantly over the last five years.[8]

	2001-02	2002-03	2003-04	2004-05	2005-06	2006-07
Investigation cases opened	311	391	1223	501	524	620
Total investigations handled	492	657	1536	1047	1018	1068
Investigations concluded	226	344	990	553	570	N/A
Investigations completed within 12 months	148	276	910	394	427	N/A
Disciplinary inquiries conducted	143	163	167	209	206	211
Disciplinary inquiries concluded	92	90	69	99	84	N/A
Entities and individuals disciplined	105	86	78	88	98	80
Cases of fraud and corruption referred to Police (CCB) and ICAC	N/A	15	32	31	27	16

Source: SFC Annual Reports

The levels of penalties that the SFC is entitled to impose on market participants **10.15** for violations of the SFO have, however, remained the same since the SFO was implemented in 2003. Even then it was commented by some observers that the penalties were not high enough to deter market participants from breaching the SFO.

---

[7] SFO, s 6(2).
[8] Information derived from SFC Annual Reports 2001 to 2006.

Certainly the penalty levels are not linked to (and notably bear little resemblance to) the level of profit derived from the relevant breach. As such, the SFC is now considering a review of the current penalty levels against comparable foreign markets to assess whether they should be increased.

10.16   The SFC pursues a range of corporate violations of the SFO. Some of the categories of violations pursued by the SFC in 2005–06 were in connection with disclosure of interests, cold calling and unlicensed activities. The SFC is equally committed to preventing market misconduct. Penalties for market misconduct offences under the SFO[9] including insider dealing; false trading; price-rigging; disclosure of false or misleading information inducing transactions; disclosure of information about prohibited transactions; and market manipulation can be given by either the courts or the Market Misconduct Tribunal (MMT). Orders which can be imposed by the courts include a fine of HK$10m and imprisonment for ten years on conviction or indictment; or a fine of HK$1m and imprisonment for three years on summary conviction.[10] Under the terms of the SFO, the MMT[11] can impose a range of orders such as:

   i.   an order against being a director, liquidator or receiver of the property or business of a corporation for up to five years;
   ii. an order against dealing with securities for up to five years;
   iii. an order against engaging in market misconduct again;
   iv. an order to pay a fine;
   v.   an order to pay costs to the government and/or MMT; and
   vi. an order for another body to take disciplinary action.

10.17   In the period between April 2005 and March 2006, the SFC successfully prosecuted eight persons in the courts in respect of market manipulation.[12] The more severe of the penalties in respect of these convictions included a seven-month prison sentence and payment for the costs of the investigation in the amount of approximately HK$10,000 and a six-month prison sentence (suspended for two years) with a fine of HK$20,000 as well as payment for the costs of the investigation in the amount of HK$25,000. These levels of fine (if not the custodial sentence) reflect the perceived weaknesses in the SFO's penalty regime. Similar penalties have continued to date.

10.18   According to the SFC's Annual Report of 2005–06, disciplinary action against sponsors, investment advisers, fund managers and in respect of serious conflicts

---

9   SFO, ss 291, 295–99.
10 SFO, s 303.
11 SFO, s 257.
12 SFC Annual Report 2005–06.

of interest was also a priority. The relevant enforcement actions resulted in several suspensions and settlements.

The Hong Kong stock exchange ('the stock exchange')

The Stock Exchange conducts enquiries and investigations into potential breaches **10.19** of *The Rules Governing the Listing of Securities on the Stock Exchange* ('the Listing Rules'),[13] and is empowered to take disciplinary action in respect of any breach. As the frontline regulator of listed companies regarding trading matters, the main aim of the Stock Exchange's enforcement strategy is to influence the future behaviour of companies and individuals by conveying the message to companies and individuals that breaches of the Listing Rules will be identified and that the sanction imposed will have a cost or other adverse impact.

As with the SFC, the Stock Exchange attempts to ensure the efficient use of **10.20** resources. The Stock Exchange therefore generally focuses its resources on the most serious breaches of the Listing Rules, being those for which public sanctions would usually be imposed on errant companies and/or their directors.

The Listing Committee of the Stock Exchange generally deals with disciplinary **10.21** matters such as failures to publish annual and interim accounts, failures to obtain shareholder approval for connected or other transactions, and failures to disclose price-sensitive information, at specially convened meetings. For example, 19 disciplinary meetings were held between May 2005 and May 2006. The disciplinary process is based on written representations and usually involves two rounds of written submissions from the Listing Division and those against whom the action is being brought. Oral representations are then allowed at the hearing.

In the recent *New World Development* case,[14] the Court of Final Appeal[15] held that **10.22** the Listing Committee's Disciplinary Committee is not a 'court' within the meaning of Article 35 of the Hong Kong Basic Law. Parties to proceedings therefore have no automatic right for their legal advisers to address the Listing Committee and permission for such representation has seldom been given in practice.

In its 2006 Annual Report, the Listing Committee has indicated that the impli- **10.23** cations of the *New World* decision are still being assessed. It has, however, acknowledged that it is bound to observe the common law principles of fairness when

---

[13] See the Listing Committee Annual Report 2006 and the HKSE's Strategy for Enforcing the Listing Rules.
[14] *The Stock Exchange of Hong Kong Ltd v New World Development Co Ltd and Others* [2006] 2 HKLRD 518.
[15] Hong Kong's highest appellate Court.

discharging its disciplinary role, and that it will continue to adopt appropriate procedures to ensure the fair disposal of matters for all parties.[16]

10.24 The Stock Exchange and the SFC may also take joint action against wrongdoers. For example, in 2006 the SFC and the Stock Exchange took joint disciplinary action against Deloitte & Touche Corporate Finance Limited ('Deloitte') and its responsible officer over sponsor failures in connection with the listing of the shares of Codebank Limited on the Growth Enterprise Market (GEM). This resulted in a settlement between Deloitte, the SFC and the Stock Exchange where Deloitte, without admitting liability, agreed voluntarily to refrain from acting as sponsor for GEM and Main Board Listings for a period of nine months and the responsible officer, again without admitting liability, agreed not to act as supervisor to any sponsorship mandate for a period of six months.[17]

Other regulators

10.25 The Hong Kong Monetary Authority (HKMA) maintains monetary and banking stability by authorizing institutions that carry on banking business and the business of taking deposits, and by supervising these authorized institutions (banks, restricted licence banks and deposit-taking companies). It is also responsible for the day-to-day supervision of regulated activities by such institutions.[18] Its main responsibilities are governed by the *Exchange Fund Ordinance* (Cap 66) and the *Banking Ordinance* (Cap 155).

10.26 The ICAC is a statutory body established under the *Independent Commission Against Corruption Ordinance* (Cap 204) (ICACO). The ICAC is empowered to investigate allegations, and suspicions, of offences and conspiracies to commit offences. The ICAC's remit also includes the power to investigate offences under the *Prevention of Bribery Ordinance* (Cap 201) (POBO) and the ICACO.

10.27 Where it appears to the Commissioner of the ICAC that a person has committed an offence under the POBO, the Commissioner has the power to authorize an officer ('an Authorized Officer') to require production by that person of, inter alia, accounts, books, other documents and articles belonging or relating to

---

[16] The Listing Committee commented that the established and overriding principle in respect of disciplinary proceedings coming before it is that the proceedings are intended to be informal. As such, although the Listing Committee will continue to consider any procedural points that are legitimately raised, it considers that these types of applications are likely to delay and increase the costs of the matter. It 'take[s] a dim view of those applications which appear to have no other purpose than to delay the process and take appropriate action where it appears that the application is being made simply for tactical reasons.' (Listing Committee Annual Report 2006, 21).

[17] SFC's Enforcement News of 27 June 2006.

[18] Memorandum of Understanding between the Securities and Futures Commission and the Hong Kong Monetary Authority, 12 December 2002, 7.2.

that person.[19] Authorized Officers also have power to seize and hold anything which may be evidence of offences that they reasonably suspect have been committed under the POBO and the ICACO.

A person may also be subject to an investigation by the Commercial Crimes **10.28** Bureau of the Hong Kong Police Force (CCB). The CCB handles cases relating to serious commercial fraud (usually over HK$5m), computer crime, and counterfeiting of currency, monetary instruments, identity documents and credit cards.

The Hong Kong Inland Revenue Department has powers under the Inland **10.29** Revenue Ordinance to investigate tax evasion. These powers include the ability to require listed companies to produce documents and to compel company officers to attend at interview. In practice these powers have seldom been used in the context of limited companies—reflecting Hong Kong's simple, low-tax environment for business.

Hong Kong has a number of other industry-specific regulators including: **10.30**

i. the Office of the Commissioner of Insurance ('the Insurance Authority')[20] is the insurance industry regulator. Its role is to promote the general stability of the insurance industry and to protect existing and potential policyholders. The Insurance Authority is empowered to investigate and to take appropriate actions against an insurer (or insurance intermediary) where there are causes for concern over that insurer. These actions include restrictions on investments, custody of assets by an approved trustee, and the ability to assume control over insurers;

ii. the Office of the Telecommunications Authority (OFTA) is the executive arm of the Telecommunications Authority,[21] the statutory body responsible for regulating the telecommunications industry in Hong Kong. OFTA's main duties are to regulate public telecommunications services, enforce fair competition in the telecommunications sector, and to enforce the Unsolicited Electronic Messages Ordinance. OFTA is empowered to issue directions to holders of telecommunications licences, impose financial penalties if directions are not complied with, and obtain information from any person whom the OFTA is satisfied is in possession of information relevant to any of its investigations; and

iii. the Broadcasting Authority (BA)[22] is the broadcasting industry regulator in Hong Kong. The BA is supported by the Television and Entertainment

---

[19] POBO, s 13(1).
[20] Insurance Authority's powers emanate from the Insurance Companies Ordinance (Cap 41).
[21] Appointed under the Telecommunications Ordinance (Cap 106).
[22] Established under the Broadcasting Authority Ordinance (Cap 391).

Authority (TELA). The BA grants licences to broadcasters in Hong Kong, formulates broadcasting codes of practice, conducts inquiries, and reports its conclusions to the Chief Executive in Council. To enforce the underlying legislation, the BA is empowered to sanction licensees for breaches. Licensees are always given the opportunity to submit representations before the BA makes a decision on the sanction. Licensees can appear to the Chief Executive in Council if they are aggrieved by a decision of the BA.

No general regulation of anti-trust issues

10.31 Both OFTA and the BA is empowered to enforce fair competition in their relevant business sectors in Hong Kong. At present, however, no other competition related legislation is in force in Hong Kong and as a consequence there are no investigative powers applicable to competition issues. There are however, proposals to introduce a market-wide competition law in Hong Kong.[23]

Self-regulatory organizations

10.32 The HKEx owns and operates the Stock Exchange, the Hong Kong Futures Exchange ('the Futures Exchange') and their related clearing houses. The Stock Exchange maintains the stock market in Hong Kong and is the primary regulator of stock exchange participants and persons who trade on or through the Exchange in relation to the trading matters and companies listed on its Main Board and the Growth Enterprise Market.

10.33 As a self-regulatory body, the Stock Exchange does not have any statutory regulatory powers and instead relies on the contractual agreements between itself and the corporations listed on it to regulate those same corporations. The Listing Rules are the main set of rules regulating listed corporations and are binding on all corporations listed on the Hong Kong stock market, regardless of where they are domiciled or incorporated.

10.34 The Listing Rules stipulate the minimum standards of behaviour with which listed corporations are expected to comply. They also include direction as to the corporate governance practices that corporations should adopt, the public disclosures that should be made by listed companies, and the rights of shareholders and investors in listed corporations. The Listing Rules can only be enforced by the Stock Exchange and not by other regulatory bodies, shareholders or investors.

---

[23] For further information see <http://www.cedb.gov.hk/citb/ehtml/Consultation_Paper_Eng.pdf>.

Breaches of the Listing Rules can attract consequences ranging from reprimands[24] to the suspension or withdrawal of a corporation's listing.[25]

The Code on Corporate Governance Practices also contains recommendations **10.35** for listed corporations. Although compliance with this code is not mandatory, the Stock Exchange does require listed corporations to disclose in their annual reports whether or not they have complied with its provisions.[26]

Concurrent investigations

As a private regulator, the Stock Exchange is independent of the jurisdiction of **10.36** other regulators. Equally, in most circumstances it can investigate matters concurrently with other regulators. The Stock Exchange has frontline responsibility for regulating companies seeking admission to the Hong Kong markets and for the supervision of companies listed on the Hong Kong markets. It has sole responsibility for investigating suspected cases of non-compliance with the Listing Rules and, where relevant, initiating disciplinary action.

However, the SFC also has some power to regulate the disclosures made by listed **10.37** corporations under the 'dual-filing' system,[27] and is able to take enforcement action if it finds that the disclosures made are false or misleading.[28] This gives rise to an overlap in jurisdiction with the Stock Exchange.

In light of this overlap in jurisdiction, the SFC and the Stock Exchange have clari- **10.38** fied that they will use their best endeavours to inform each other of any complaint they receive or of any alleged or suspected misconduct that may relate to the other entity's regulatory functions,[29] and liaise in relation to this. For example, where the SFC begins an investigation in relation to the disclosure of documents filed containing false or misleading information, the SFC will inform the Stock Exchange.[30] Insofar as this matter involves the Listing Rules, the Stock Exchange

---

[24] Rule 2A.09 of the Listing Rules.
[25] Rule 2A.08 of the Listing Rules.
[26] Ibid, Appendix 23, 2.
[27] This system was initiated under the Securities and Futures (Stock Market Listing) Rules (Cap 571V) (SFR). Section 5 of the SFR states that applications for the listing of any securities issued or to be issued shall be filed with the SFC within one business day after the day on which the application is submitted to the HKEx. Furthermore, under s 7 of the SFR, a copy of all ongoing disclosure materials issued by a listed company under the Listing Rules must also be filed with the SFC within one business day after the day on which the disclosure is made and issued.
[28] SFO, s 384O.
[29] Securities and Futures Commission and the Stock Exchange of Hong Kong Limited, Memorandum of Understanding Governing Listing Matters, 28 January 2003, at 9.2(e).
[30] Securities and Futures Commission and the Stock Exchange of Hong Kong Limited, Memorandum of Understanding Governing Listing Matters, 28 January 2003, at 9.2(c).

may then deal with the matter or suspend its work, wholly or partly, pending the outcome of the SFC investigation.[31]

10.39 There is also a certain level of overlap between the regulatory responsibilities of the SFC and the HKMA. The SFC is entrusted with the job of regulating institutions that carry on regulated activities (including banks), whilst the HKMA is responsible for regulating banking business, which necessarily includes regulating the behaviour of authorized institutions such as banks.

10.40 In order to clarify the regulatory roles of the HKMA and the SFC, the two regulators entered into a Memorandum of Understanding on 12 December 2002 setting out their regulatory and supervisory roles and responsibilities.[32] Clarifications include that:

  i. the HKMA will keep the SFC informed of any investigations that it conducts into the regulated activities of registered institutions. The SFC will also consult with the HKMA before it commences any investigation into the affairs of an authorized institution pursuant to section 182(1)(e) of the SFO and will keep the HKMA informed of findings of its investigations;[33] and
  ii. the SFC and the HKMA will consult with each other before taking any disciplinary action.[34]

10.41 The SFC is also required to consult the HKMA in respect of the SFC's exercise of certain powers under the SFO.[35]

10.42 The SFO imposes a dual civil and criminal regime for market misconduct. There are six categories of market misconduct under the SFO namely: (i) false trading; (ii) price-rigging; (iii) stock market manipulation; (iv) disclosure of information about prohibited transactions; (v) disclosure of false or misleading information inducing transactions; and (vi) insider dealing.

10.43 Where it appears to the Financial Secretary that market misconduct has or may have taken place, he may institute proceedings before the MMT. The MMT was established under the SFO[36] and is a civil tribunal with the jurisdiction to hear

---

[31] Securities and Futures Commission and the Stock Exchange of Hong Kong Limited, Memorandum of Understanding Governing Listing Matters, 28 January 2003, 9.2(d).

[32] See <http://www.info.gov.hk/hkma> for copy of the Memorandum of Understanding between the Securities and Futures Commission and the Hong Kong Monetary Authority, 12 December 2002.

[33] Memorandum of Understanding between the Securities and Futures Commission and the Hong Kong Monetary Authority, 12 December 2002, 9.

[34] Memorandum of Understanding between the Securities and Futures Commission and the Hong Kong Monetary Authority, 12 December 2002, 10.

[35] See, eg, SFO, ss 119, 134, 135, 159, 180 and 182.

[36] SFO, s 251.

and determine cases falling within the ambit of any of the six categories of market misconduct listed above.

Aside from pursuing civil proceedings before the MMT, the SFC can also pursue **10.44** criminal sanctions against the wrongdoer. However, the same market misconduct activity cannot be subject to both a civil action in the MMT and a criminal action in the courts.[37]

If it wishes to take criminal action, the SFC can prosecute offences under **10.45** the provisions of the SFO in a Magistrates' Court summarily[38] following the Department of Justice's Prosecution Policy.[39] Cases may also be referred to the Department of Justice, which has broad powers to prosecute any criminal offence.

Furthermore, the Listing Committee may conduct a disciplinary hearing in rela- **10.46** tion to any matter relating to or arising out of the Listing Rules.

Given the regulatory overlaps that exist in Hong Kong, circumstances may often **10.47** arise where more than one regulatory authority has powers and/or interests in investigating a matter involving suspected or alleged misconduct. In many cases, the SFC will refer investigations to other regulatory authorities where it believes that such other authorities, such as the CCB or ICAC, are more suited to continuing the investigations. In cases involving registered financial institutions, the SFC and HKMA will also cooperate with each other in conducting investigations.[40]

For example, in July 2006 the SFC commenced an inquiry into the affairs of **10.48** Ocean Grand Holdings Ltd and Ocean Grand Chemical Holdings Ltd to establish whether the business of these collapsed companies had been conducted for any fraudulent or unlawful purpose. In its 2007 annual report, the SFC states that it is presently liaising closely with the CCB in its investigations into these companies, and that it is also liaising closely in this case with the SFC's mainland China counterpart.

---

[37] SFO, ss 283 and 307. See also Consultation Document on the Securities and Futures Bill, The Government of the Hong Kong Administrative Region, April 2000, at 11.21.

[38] SFO, s 388.

[39] Before an offender is convicted, the Judge must be sure that the available evidence is sufficient to prosecute, and also that it is in the public interest to prosecute. One of the factors to be taken into account when considering whether it is in the public interest to prosecute is whether there is a civil remedy available, and if so, whether adopting this would be a more appropriate way of settling the issues in the case than pursuing the criminal prosecution. For the full text of the Department of Justice's Prosecution Policy see <http://www.doj.gov.hk/eng/public/pub20021031toc.htm>.

[40] Memorandum of Understanding between the Securities and Futures Commission and the Hong Kong Monetary Authority, 12 December 2002.

Relationships with overseas regulators

10.49 The SFC has power under section 186 of the SFO, in prescribed circumstances, to provide assistance to overseas authorities, regulators, or company inspectors outside Hong Kong. The SFC can provide such assistance where it is of the opinion that it is desirable or expedient to do so and that it is in the interest of the investing public or in the public interest generally. Alternatively, the SFC may also provide this assistance if it considers that the assistance will enable the recipient to perform its functions, and that the type of assistance provided is not contrary to the interests of the investing public, or the public interest in general.

10.50 The SFC has concluded a number of formal cooperative arrangements with overseas regulators for the purposes of exchange of information and/or investigatory assistance.[41] In particular, in light of the recent amendments to PRC securities laws enabling the China Securities Regulatory Commission (CSRC) to provide assistance to non-mainland regulators, the SFC has been focused on improving cooperation with this body. For example, during 2005–06, the SFC worked with the CSRC on nine occasions (both providing and receiving assistance). The SFC has commented, however, that often the CSRC has not been able to provide sufficient investigatory assistance to the SFC in order to enable the SFC to bring enforcement proceedings. The SFC hopes that closer cooperation between the CSRC and the SFC will be possible in the future.

10.51 The SFC is also a signatory to the International Organization of Securities Commissions Multilateral Memorandum of Understanding Concerning Consultation and Cooperation and the Exchange of Information (IOSCO MOU). In light of the increasing international activity in the securities and derivatives markets, the purpose of the IOSCO MOU is to set up an information sharing arrangement to provide mutual assistance to ensure compliance with, and enforcement of, the securities and derivatives laws and regulations of the respective signatories.

C. Powers of Regulators

Sources of investigation

10.52 Many of the cases that the SFC investigates arise from referrals by external sources including the public, foreign regulators, local regulators, law enforcement agencies, and the Stock Exchange.[42] The SFC maintains close relations with these parties in order to combat international financial crime and misconduct.

---

[41] These overseas regulators include for example, the Financial Services Authority, Australian Securities and Investments Commission; Monetary Authority of Singapore; Securities and Exchange Commission; and the China Securities Regulatory Commission.

[42] SFC Annual report 2004–05, 48.

The SFC also investigates cases arising from its own surveillance activities. Since **10.53** the introduction of the 'dual filing' system, for example, the SFC has commenced cases based on its own scrutiny of listed corporations' disclosure documents.[43] The SFC's Enforcement Division has a surveillance team to monitor companies' websites for the purpose of identifying abnormal behaviour and monitoring the media for reports of improper activities.[44]

Although the level of shareholder activism is generally low in Hong Kong, insti- **10.54** tutional shareholders are increasingly becoming more active. Furthermore, prominent shareholder activists visibly promote corporate governance in Hong Kong and, on occasions, alert the public to issues that lead to investigation.

Similarly, there are also a variety of ways by which potential breaches of the Listing **10.55** Rules may come to the attention of the Stock Exchange. Investigations may be triggered as a result of the Listing Division's surveillance activities, research and data analysis, as well as through external sources such as tip-offs and complaints from the public and media.

Levels of regulatory scrutiny

The SFC will generally make preliminary inquiries before deciding whether its **10.56** Investigation Department should launch a full investigation. For example, in respect of suspected cases of market manipulation, insider dealing, dissemination of false or misleading information, or other trading malpractice, the SFC obtains trading details from brokers in order to conduct a preliminary assessment before referring cases to the Investigation Department. The SFC considers that, on many occasions, such preliminary inquiries have prevented potentially improper trading activities.[45]

Investigation tools

The SFC has broad powers of investigation under section 182 of the SFO particu- **10.57** larly where it has reasonable cause to believe an offence may have been committed under the SFO or the Companies Ordinance. The SFC can, in relation to an investigation, require any person whom it believes has in its possession any document containing information relevant to the investigation to:

i. produce the relevant record or document;
ii. explain the relevant record or document;
iii. attend before the investigator and answer any questions relating to the matters under investigation; and

---

[43] SFC Annual Report 2004–05, 49.
[44] SFC Annual Report 2003–04, 49.
[45] SFC Annual Report 2005–06.

iv. give the investigator all assistance in connection with the investigation which he or she is reasonably able to give, including responding to any written questions raised by the investigator.[46]

10.58 The Stock Exchange may also order an investigation or conduct disciplinary hearings into the affairs of any exchange participant, their authorized clerks, registered users or responsible officers who are suspected of violating relevant rules and legislation. The Stock Exchange can demand production and inspection of books, accounts, records and any other documents it deems necessary.

10.59 It may also expel exchange participants, suspend exchange participants, impose fines on exchange participants, or suspend or revoke registrations. The Stock Exchange can also publish details of the expulsions and suspensions in any way it thinks fit.[47] The Stock Exchange does not have the power to bring prosecutions or commence civil litigation in relation to any breach of the Listing Rules. Where a case involves suspected breaches of civil or criminal laws, the Stock Exchange will refer the matters to an appropriate statutory agency and will provide cooperation as requested.

10.60 The ICAC is given specific legal powers to investigate corruption and to facilitate the prosecution of corrupt persons under three separate ordinances: the ICACO, the POBO, and the Elections (Corrupt and Illegal Conduct) Ordinance (ECICO).[48] The ICACO gives the ICAC powers of arrest, detention, bail, and search and seizure. The POBO gives the ICAC powers of investigation to unravel and identify the transactions and assets concealed in different guises by the corrupt party, confers on the ICAC the power to detain travel documents, restrain disposal of property, and the power to protect the confidentiality of an investigation. Finally, the ECICO gives the ICAC the power to prevent corrupt and illegal conduct at elections.

Extra-territorial jurisdiction

10.61 In line with international practice, the SFO has an extra-territorial element in respect of its provisions on certain market misconduct offences, including the offences of false trading, price-rigging, disclosure of false or misleading information inducing transactions, and market manipulation.[49] As such, these provisions will cover activities outside of Hong Kong associated with Hong Kong traded securities and futures. Market misconduct within Hong Kong but affecting securities

---

[46] SFO, s 183.

[47] Chapter 7 of the Rules of the Exchange can be found at <http://www.hkex.com.hk/rule/exrule/exrule.htm>.

[48] Cap 554.

[49] SFO, ss 295, 296, 298, 299.

that are not traded in Hong Kong will, however, only be considered an offence if it is an offence in the foreign jurisdiction in which the affected securities are traded.[50]

Under Hong Kong law, the SFC can therefore conduct investigations relating to **10.62** activities outside Hong Kong. In order to implement this aspect of its jurisdiction, the SFC has entered into a number of cooperative arrangements with both mainland China and overseas regulators for the purpose of investigatory assistance. These agreements are mainly in the form of Memoranda of Understanding (MOUs), which set out the procedures that need to be followed if one authority ('the Requesting Authority') wishes to request the assistance of the other authority to obtain information in relation to an investigation the Requesting Authority is carrying out.[51] There are usually confidentiality provisions in the MOUs which seek to ensure that the information obtained pursuant to the procedures set out in these documents will be used solely for taking action in relation to the breach of law specified in the request.

As mentioned above, the SFC is also a signatory to the IOSCO MOU. This **10.63** provides for information sharing among securities regulators globally and sets out the procedures that each signatory must follow when requesting information or investigative assistance from other signatories.[52]

Protections

There are relatively few protections available from SFC investigations. There is **10.64** no general right to refuse to answer questions asked by the SFC in the course of its investigations on the ground of any privilege against self-incrimination. However, information obtained from the investigations is generally not admissible as evidence in most criminal proceedings.[53] No privilege against self-incrimination is applicable to the production of documents required under the SFO.

However, an authorized financial institution is not required to disclose any infor- **10.65** mation or produce any record or document relating to the affairs of one of its customers unless the investigator has reasonable cause to believe that the customer has information relevant to the investigation and the SFC certifies that discovery is necessary for the purposes of the investigation.[54]

---

[50] SFO, s 306(3).
[51] For a list of these Memorandums of Understanding together with the full text of each document see <http://www.sfc.hk/sfc/html/EN/aboutsfc/cooperation/cooperation.html>.
[52] Please see <http://www.sfc.hk/sfc/html/EN/aboutsfc/cooperation/cooperation.html> for a list of signatories.
[53] SFO, s 187. Perjury is one of the exceptions.
[54] SFO, s 179(6).

Sanctions for failure to cooperate

10.66 Failure to comply with the SFC's requests without reasonable excuse constitutes a criminal offence[55] and the SFC will not hesitate to prosecute those who fail to cooperate. In 2004, two people were convicted of failing to cooperate with SFC investigations and were fined HK$30,000 and HK$40,000 each, plus the costs of the investigation.[56] However, as mentioned above, the fact that the penalties that the SFC is able to impose on offenders are relatively low may mean that the penalty level in itself does not act as an effective deterrent for potential offenders.

10.67 The MMT enjoys similar powers to compel cooperation under the SFO.[57] A person who fails to comply with the direction of the MMT may be subject to a fine of HK$1m and imprisonment of two years.[58] During 2005–06, the SFC referred one case to the Financial Secretary to consider instituting proceedings before the MMT regarding dissemination of false or misleading information.[59]

D. Voluntary Investigations

Benefits and risks of voluntary investigations

10.68 There is no requirement under the SFO for a listed corporation to conduct an investigation when it identifies that there might be a rule breach or other problem. The SFC's Code of Conduct does, however, provide that licensed or registered persons should ensure that steps are taken to investigate complaints made by clients.[60] Investigations of such complaints can be a source for identifying any potential breach of laws or regulations.

10.69 To encourage auditors to act as whistle-blowers, the SFO provides auditors with statutory immunity against any civil claim that may arise under common law in connection with reports of suspected fraud and other misconduct that they make to the SFC.[61]

10.70 The maintenance of good internal control procedures by listed corporations is likely to assist in identifying potential problems such as suspected breaches of

---

[55] SFO, s 184.
[56] SFC Annual Report 2004–05.
[57] SFO, s 254.
[58] SFO, s 254.
[59] According to the SFC Annual Report 2005–06, this matter was under review by the Department of Justice.
[60] The SFC's Code of Conduct (the Code of Conduct) for Persons Licensed by or Registered with the Securities and Futures Commission, May 2006, 12.3, 21.
[61] SFO, s 381.

laws and rules and regulations. Listed corporations are required to maintain good internal control procedures. For example, under the SFC's Code of Conduct: the Stock Exchange's Code on Corporate Governance Practices:[62]

i. licensed or registered persons are expected to install and maintain internal control procedures which can be reasonably expected to protect its operations, clients, and other licensed or registered persons from financial loss arising from theft, fraud, other dishonest acts, professional misconduct or omissions;[63] and

ii. listed corporations are expected to maintain sound and effective internal controls to safeguard shareholders' investments and the corporation's assets.[64]

Where there has been a suspected breach of laws, rules or regulations, one way of demonstrating good internal control procedures is to commence an internal investigation. This will allow listed corporations to review their internal control systems, identify any weaknesses, rectify existing problems and prevent future problems from occurring. Where an internal investigation is properly conducted, this may assist in demonstrating to the SFC and Stock Exchange that the listed corporation has put adequate internal control procedures in place. Nonetheless, the question of whether a listed corporation decides to launch an internal investigation will depend on the circumstances of each particular case. **10.71**

Where a listed corporation does decide to proceed with an internal investigation, it is important for it to be aware that any documents produced during the course of the investigation, including any notes (typed or handwritten) of discussions with the staff involved, may be at risk of being disclosed to third parties if legal proceedings arise from the matter. As such, where an investigation is conducted internally, the listed corporation should carefully consider whether the creation of any particular document is necessary. Given the risk of disclosure, it may be prudent for a listed corporation to employ internal or external legal counsel at an early stage to handle any internal investigation, and in order to maximize the chances of successfully claiming legal privilege. **10.72**

Where a listed corporation has already conducted an internal investigation into a suspected breach, there is no general rule about the extent to which the SFC and the Stock Exchange will rely on this to determine the extent of their own investigations. In some circumstances, a corporation may (on the basis of an objective, well run internal investigation and follow-up activities) be able to convince the **10.73**

---

[62] The Code on Corporate Governance Practices sets out the principles of good corporate governance.
[63] Code of Conduct, 4.3, 8.
[64] Code of Corporate Governance Practices, C.2.

regulators that no breach of the relevant rules has occurred, or that enforcement action is not necessary. In other circumstances, the regulators may take the view that their own independent investigation is required. It is ultimately for the SFC or the Stock Exchange to decide whether or not, and to what extent, they can rely on a corporation's own internal investigations. One of the factors that may affect this is the identity and standing of the person/firm carrying out the internal investigation.

Events triggering a possible voluntary investigation

10.74 Investigations should be carried out where suspected internal irregularities arise from routine compliance checks or audits. Any external complaints received by the company should also be investigated, if only to determine that the complaint bears no merit.

10.75 Where any incident concerning the company, such as a recent commercial transaction, has attracted a considerable amount of negative public interest, or if the company is the subject of specific adverse press comment, an investigation should generally be initiated.

Structuring an internal investigation

10.76 The first issue to consider in conducting an internal investigation is the choice of investigator. A good investigator is trained and preferably experienced in conducting interviews. Most importantly, the investigator must have a high level of personal integrity and be neutral and objective. For this reason, it may be time and cost efficient to employ an external person or firm to conduct the investigation. Using an external investigator will also allay any concerns of bias and will bring a fresh perspective to bear on an issue.

10.77 An inappropriate investigator may delay the investigation process or produce inaccurate and incomplete information on which decisions, including disciplinary or reporting decisions, will be made by management.

10.78 A decision-maker should also be assigned to the investigation to consider the materials gathered by the investigator, and to draw conclusions. Again, the decision-maker should be independent in order to avoid any allegations of bias.

10.79 When structuring an internal investigation, a listed corporate may also wish to consider:

i. what, if any, action it should take in respect of any employees who were involved;
ii. whether it should report the matter to its insurers;
iii. whether it should voluntarily compensate those who have suffered loss arising from its actions;

iv. whether the matter potentially gives rise to any criminal proceedings;

v. whether the matter potentially gives rise to any civil claims;

vi. what steps it should take to safeguard documents. Any document destruction policies should be reviewed as soon as possible after the decision to launch an investigation has been made in order to consider whether these will impact on the preservation of materials relevant to the investigation. If in doubt, these policies should be temporarily suspended;

vii. what steps it should take to ensure that further documents are not created; and

viii. whether the investigation needs to be announced.

Using external advisers

In the absence of regulatory rules governing the conduct of internal investiga- **10.80**
tions, listed corporations are free to appoint internal or external counsel to conduct internal investigations. Where external counsel is to be appointed, except insofar as stipulated under internal policies, there is no particular requirement as to who should be responsible for carrying out this appointment. It is, however, in the corporation's best interests, especially if it is attempting to use the results of its investigation to persuade the regulators that no breach of rules has occurred or that no enforcement action needs to be taken, to appoint a body which is objectively removed from the matter being investigated to assume the responsibility of hiring external counsel. This would most likely be the listed company's audit committee (assuming it is not audit issues that are under investigation), or a committee led by a senior non-executive director of the listed corporate. This will have the effect of lending greater credibility to the investigation.

There are no set criteria provided by the SFC or the Stock Exchange in relation **10.81**
to choosing external counsel. The body responsible for selecting external counsel should first and foremost ensure that it takes into account whether the firm is able to assess and conduct the investigation expertly and objectively, and thereby produce a robust and reliable report. If there has been no breach of a rule or requirement, a reliable report can be useful to show the SFC or the HKSE that the listed corporation maintains adequate internal controls and ultimately may persuade them that no separate investigation of the matter is necessary.

Other matters to take into consideration in respect of the choice of external coun- **10.82**
sel include:

i. whether the external counsel has sufficient resources (locally or otherwise) to properly manage the relevant scope of the internal investigation (eg to handle any document management exercise or conduct staff interviews);

    ii. whether the external counsel has relevant experience, and therefore the result-
       ing strong reputation, in relation to SFC and HKSE related matters; and

    iii. if the matter involves cross-border extra-territorial elements, whether the
       external counsel has real, integrated multi-jurisdictional capability.

10.83 In some circumstances, a listed corporation may prefer to employ one of its usual external counsel to conduct an internal investigation as they will have good knowledge of the internal operations of the listed corporation. However, external counsel with such a good institutional knowledge of the listed corporation's internal operations may, in some circumstances, be seen as lacking in independence, and in cases such as these, the firm's ability to carry out an objective investigation may be questioned.

10.84 Consideration should also be given as to whether external counsel should be assisted in the investigation by other external professionals, such as forensic accountants.

Managing illegal activity during investigations

10.85 A listed corporation should take immediate steps to cease any suspicious activity which may constitute criminal activity or a regulatory breach. Such steps might include suspending suspect employee(s), or setting up control measures to prevent employees under suspicion from continuing to carry on the alleged misconduct. Failure to take appropriate steps may lead to adverse implications, such as extended liability for the listed company or, in the regulatory context, the conclusion that the company's internal control measures are either absent or compromised. These in turn can cause serious reputational repercussions.

10.86 Directors and responsible officers are required to take all reasonable measures to ensure that proper safeguards exist to prevent the corporation from acting in a way which constitutes market misconduct. Where no steps are taken to prevent an employee from continuing to engage in suspicious activity, directors and responsible officers may be personally liable. This may also impact on their suitability to hold office or their continued employment.

E. Self-reporting

Duty to self-report

10.87 In Hong Kong, there is no general statutory obligation for listed corporations to 'self-report' violations of corporate laws, regulations or practices. However, under the *Code of Conduct for Persons Licensed by or Registered with the Securities and*

Futures Commission ('the Code of Conduct'),[65] registered or licensed persons are required immediately to report to the SFC when:

> ... any material breach, infringement of or non-compliance with any law, rules, regulations and codes administered or issued by the SFC, the rules of any exchange of which it is a member or participant, and the requirements of any regulatory authority which apply to the registered or licensed person, or where it suspects any such breach, infringement or non-compliance whether by:
> (i) itself; or
> (ii) persons it employs or appoints to conduct business with clients or other licensed or registered persons,
> (iii) giving particulars of the breach, infringement or non-compliance, or suspected breach, infringement or non-compliance, and relevant information and documents.[66]

Culture of self-reporting

Traditionally, there has been no strong culture of self-reporting in Hong Kong. **10.88** This reflected the predominance of family-controlled listed companies in the market. However, there has been a push in recent years to encourage 'management responsibility' to enhance investor protection. Under the SFO,[67] every officer of a corporation is required to take all reasonable measures to ensure that proper safeguards exist to prevent the corporation from acting in a manner that would result in market misconduct. Although the complexity of this test makes it difficult to enforce, the spectre of civil and criminal liability for directors and officers acts as motivation to improve internal procedures so as to prevent market misconduct.

Auditors are also now being encouraged to take a more proactive stance in report- **10.89** ing any suspected fraudulent activities to regulatory authorities. By virtue of their work and the access they have to confidential information, auditors are in a strong position to identify possible misconduct, and they therefore can assist the regulatory authorities in their efforts. Many auditors may, however, be unwilling to report suspected fraudulent activities to authorities for fear of exposing themselves to civil claims by their clients.[68] To alleviate such concerns, and to encourage auditors to 'blow the whistle', the SFO provides auditors with statutory immunity

---

[65] The Code of Conduct does not have the force of law but the Commission is guided by it in considering whether a licensed or registered person satisfies the requirement that it is fit and proper to remain licensed or registered.

[66] Code of Conduct, 12.5.

[67] SFO, s 279.

[68] S H Goo and A Carver, *Corporate Governance: The Hong Kong Debate* (Hong Kong: Sweet & Maxwell, 2003), 146.

against any civil claim that may arise in connection with reports of suspected fraud and other misconduct that they may make to the SFC.[69]

F. Announcements and Stock Exchange Obligations

Obligations when facing a regulatory investigation

10.90   There is no specific requirement under the SFO or the Listing Rules for a listed corporation to disclose the fact that it is under regulatory investigation. However, the corporation may be obliged to disclose this information under the general disclosure obligation in the Listing Rules that requires a listed corporation to keep its members, the Stock Exchange, and any other holders of its listed securities informed as soon as reasonably practicable of any information relating to the group (including information on any new developments in the group's sphere of activity which is not public knowledge) and which:

i.   is necessary to enable the holders of its securities and the public to appraise the position of the group; or

ii.   is necessary to avoid the establishment of a false market in its securities; or

iii.   might be reasonably expected materially to affect market activity and the price of its securities.

10.91   Where the subject matter or existence of a regulatory investigation falls into any of these categories, a listed corporation will be under an obligation to disclose the regulatory investigation.

10.92   It is critical, however, that the content of any such disclosure must be considered in the light of the secrecy obligations under the SFO.[70] The SFO imposes obligations on those assisting in investigations under the SFO to aid and preserve secrecy in relation to any matter that is learned of during the investigation. This includes an obligation not to communicate any such matter to any other person or to disclose any documents they have access to by virtue of the investigation unless the SFC gives permission.[71] Breach of the secrecy obligations is a criminal offence. The scope of the provision is broad enough to cover the fact of the investigation itself or the fact that the SFC has a regulatory issue in a particular topic.

10.93   This potentially leads to a 'catch-22' situation for the listed company. By law it is prevented from making a disclosure; under the Listing Rules it is obliged to make a disclosure. In such situations, a prompt dialogue with the regulator (having first

---

[69] SFO, s 381.
[70] SFO, s 378.
[71] Further discussed below at 'Waiving Privilege'.

taken detailed legal advice[72]) is generally the prudent approach, particularly where the company is as a result able to obtain the consent of the SFC to making the disclosure (such a disclosure being protected by a 'safe harbour' in the legislation).

Obligations when conducting an internal investigation

When a listed corporate is carrying out a voluntary internal investigation, the **10.94** main regulatory concern will be to ensure that it complies with its disclosure obligations under the Listing Rules (as described above). One issue that arises in this context is whether the listed corporate needs to put in place a process through which it is informed by its investigating team of any material findings that come to their knowledge. Such a process potentially avoids a situation developing where a listed corporate is criticized for failure to disclose such information to the market.[73] This is a further factor that weighs in favour of the company retaining experienced investigation counsel who will be able to exercise sound judgment over whether and how to raise such issues with the company (while preserving the integrity of the investigation process).

Incorporating obligations into a general Public Relations strategy

If, having considered the circumstances of the investigation, the company **10.95** is of the view that disclosure of the fact of the investigation by way of market announcement should be made, the company should in the first instance discuss with the Stock Exchange and the SFC its intentions, and seek any necessary approvals. Where relevant, the obligations of secrecy under the SFO must be considered.

If a Stock Exchange announcement is to be made, the company should consider **10.96** issuing a press release at the same time in order to avoid any potentially negative reporting on the issue. If the matter is sufficiently serious and has attracted or is anticipated to attract, much public interest, the company should also consider whether it is useful to hold a press conference.

The content of information disclosed to the Stock Exchange and the press must **10.97** be consistent, and the content of the information disclosed should be discussed with the Stock Exchange or the SFC and the legal advisers prior to publication. In particular, it is important that the press is given only such material information as has been disclosed by way of an announcement.

---

[72] Communications for the purpose of seeking professional legal advice in relation to any matter arising under the SFO are exempt from the secrecy obligation.

[73] Or, possibly, becomes liable as a result of a false market in its securities having arisen.

G. Public Relations Considerations and Strategies

Regulatory investigations

External communications

10.98 As mentioned above, when considering how best to approach its PR strategy in relation to a regulatory investigation, a company will be constrained by the secrecy obligations in the SFO, and also by the need to ensure that no more information than has already been disclosed by way of public announcement is given to the press. Indeed, the fact that the outcome of any regulatory investigation into a company's affairs will be unknown and uncertain at the time that the investigation is commenced means that it is preferable for a company to be cautious in making any comment to the press in this context and at this stage. In practice, where any comment is made it will usually be restricted to confirming, where appropriate, that an investigation is in process and that the company is providing appropriate cooperation with the regulator. It is prudent to clear in advance (if possible) with the regulator any comment that it is intended to make.

10.99 At the concluding stage of an investigation, the external PR strategy typically is driven by the outcome of the investigation and (if relevant) by previous communications. If the investigation has concluded without any adverse consequences for the company or any of its stakeholders and without public attention then invariably it is preferable to maintain silence about the investigation. If however the investigation is public knowledge and/or it will lead to such consequences, some communication is likely to be necessary. Judgment of what should be said and how it will in large part be dictated by the prevailing circumstances but must also take into account disclosure obligations, the secrecy obligation and any commitments made to regulators during the course of the investigation.

Internal communications

10.100 Any internal disclosure of the fact of a regulatory investigation should be considered in light of the secrecy provisions under the SFO referred to above, and the privilege issues discussed below.[74] There are no legal rules or regulations that govern the question of whether a listed corporation should inform its

---

[74] See 'Privilege pitfalls' at 10.146.

employees of the fact of a regulatory investigation. Ultimately this is a decision for the listed corporation to make having considered various factors, including:

i. the risk of obstruction to an investigation that may arise from informing the corporation's employees, especially if those employees are subject to the investigation;

ii. the opportunity for a more efficient and thorough investigation that may result from informing employees of the fact of the investigation, and enlisting their assistance should they have relevant information;

iii. the risk of rumours developing and false information being circulated, and the effect on the investigation (including leaks leading to the risk of bad publicity or further regulatory attention); and

iv. the effect on the perceived quality and reliability of the investigation.

Furthermore, any dissemination of information relating to regulatory investigations to a company's employees should be carefully considered, as there is a risk that the employees may misuse the information or may disclose this outside the company. **10.101**

Voluntary investigations

External communications

As discussed above, there is no positive obligation for a company to make a public announcement of the fact of an internal investigation. However, any information that is released should be consistent and the contents of this should be approved by the company and its in-house or external counsel. **10.102**

The key factor that will dictate to a large extent the strategy for external communications in the context of a voluntary investigation is the factual background and thus the purpose of the investigation. **10.103**

If the investigation is reactive to outside criticism or has been convened in response to a specific incident, it will typically be necessary to have a proactive communications strategy. In taking such an approach however, it is wise to be cautious and to avoid making hasty comments/announcements that may sit badly once all facts are known. By contrast where an investigation is purely internal in its focus on an issue that is not the subject of external scrutiny, it will normally be preferable to eliminate external communication unless or until a disclosure is required for legal/regulatory reasons. **10.104**

If the matter is to be communicated outside the company, it is also best practice to nominate one person or, where available, a corporate communications team to handle any follow-up enquiries. These enquiries and the company's responses to **10.105** them should be documented to ensure that the company is clear as to what information is in the public domain in relation to the internal investigation. It is also advisable to adhere to a set of standard responses, any deviation from which should be checked with in-house or external counsel prior to release.

Internal communications

10.106 Similar issues arise in relation to internal communications on a voluntary investigation as described above for regulatory investigation (save that the SFO secrecy requirement is not applicable). Typically the presence of an investigation team within a company's office will create a fertile ground for rumour and speculation unless some explanation is provided to staff. In some circumstances the company will find it necessary to communicate with its staff in order to avoid potential damage to its business as a result of fear or demotivation. This becomes critical in circumstances where the investigation is reactive to external criticism or another visible problem.

Key points for Public Relations strategies

Dealing with the press

10.107 In some circumstances, as described above, the company needs to consider being proactive and to seek to manage the press rather than allowing the press to discover or investigate particular incidents and report on them. Positive action may create a favourable impression in the media that the company is being frank and open about an issue.

10.108 It is also important to take care when such information is disclosed to the press. The company must take care when making any statements to ensure that they are consistent with what the company reports to the regulators. Relevant information that has not been disclosed to the regulators and, where appropriate, to the market, should not first be disclosed to the press. The company should always consult their legal advisers in tandem with their PR team.

10.109 Generally, where a problem arises which affects customers, the company must take, and must be seen to be taking, steps to look after the interests of those customers. This is particularly the case where the company deals directly with consumers. The exact steps to be taken will depend on the circumstances but generally the company should:

   i. keep its customers informed;

  ii. safeguard its customers' interests. For example, by taking steps to secure assets, to remedy the problem or to ensure that no further losses are suffered; and

iii. identify, or take steps to identify what losses have been suffered. The company should also at the earliest opportunity make clear its intended approach with regard to paying compensation.

H. Best Practices in Document Gathering and Preservation

Expectations of regulators and courts

Documents, including emails, must be preserved as soon as an entity or individual becomes, or is likely to become, subject to a regulatory or criminal investigation. It is an offence to destroy, falsify, conceal or dispose of any document with intent to conceal facts relevant to an SFC investigation.[75] If in doubt, legal advice should be sought immediately.   **10.110**

As a matter of caution, any routine destruction of potentially relevant documents should be immediately suspended and measures to ensure that documents are not inadvertently destroyed should be put in place. It is also advisable not to rearrange original documents or files so as not to risk any allegation of tampering with relevant documents.   **10.111**

In the absence of any regulatory investigation, relevant legislative provisions and regulatory guidelines in respect of the preservation of documents must be observed. For example, for entities regulated by the SFC, all records of transactions (which must be sufficient to permit reconstruction of individual transactions) both domestic and international, should be maintained for at least seven years. Records on customer identification, account files and business correspondence should be kept for at least five years after the account is closed.   **10.112**

Where no time limit for retention of certain documents is stipulated in legislation, regulations or other guidelines, it is prudent to retain documents for a reasonable period (ideally not less than seven years). Records relevant to investigations and transactions which have been the subject of regulatory inquiry or investigation should be retained until it is confirmed that the relevant case has been closed.   **10.113**

It is advisable for a listed corporation to have a reasonable document retention policy which is set out clearly in writing and made known to all employees. This policy should be reviewed regularly and adjusted where necessary. A good document retention policy will be consistent and will not have different retention periods or destruction criteria for similar or comparable classes of documents unless they can be objectively justified. If possible, privileged and non-privileged   **10.114**

---

[75] SFO, s 192.

documents should be stored separately. Documents should never be destroyed other than in accordance with the document retention policy.

Rights to documents and confidentiality

10.115 The SFC can require any party under investigation or any person who the SFC has reasonable cause to believe has in his possession *any* record or document[76] which contains, or is likely to contain, information relevant to an investigation,[77] to produce such document or record.[78] In respect of a corporation which is or was listed, the SFC may also require it to produce any document or record where it has reasonable cause to believe that the record or document relates to the affairs of the corporation.[79]

10.116 In respect of Stock Exchange investigations or disciplinary hearings, the Stock Exchange can require a listed corporation to produce any document (including electronic documents) which it deems relevant and appropriate.[80]

10.117 Documents located at the company's office will either belong to the company or to employees. In the former case, no issue arises over the listed company's obligation (or its ability to comply). In the latter case, a corporation may be able to secure such documents from its employees under the implied and express terms of their employment contracts. First, there may be an obligation for employees to produce certain documents under an employee's implied duty of good faith, which may extend to employees assisting their employers with investigations. Secondly, there may be an express term in an employment contract to the effect that an employee must assist the employer with investigations by, among other things, producing relevant documents where appropriate. An employment contract can also stipulate that all documents (including electronic documents and email) created in the course of employment and relating to the employment belong to the corporation, such that employees who are in possession of such documents are required to produce them when so requested.

Data protection

10.118 Issues relating to personal data arise in a number of ways in the investigation context. Hong Kong introduced legislation in 1995 (the Personal Data (Privacy)

---

[76] Pursuant to SFO, s 102, 'document' includes that produced mechanically, electronically, magnetically, optically, manually, or by other means.
[77] Investigations under SFO, s 182.
[78] SFO, s 183(1)(a).
[79] SFO, s 179.
[80] Rule 2B.02 of the Listing Rules.

Ordinance (Cap. 486) (PD(P)O)[81] that was designed to provide a comprehensive code for dealing with data protection issues.

In the context of a regulatory investigation, the legislation permits Hong Kong **10.119** based regulators[82] to collect and process personal data for the purpose of their investigation and provides authority for listed corporates to release such information (although necessary procedural steps must still be followed).

The extent to which corporations can compel the production of personal docu- **10.120** ments in the context of a voluntary investigation is more complex. The answer will depend on the terms of relevant employment contracts, company policies, the nature of the documents and the impact of the PD(P)O. To illustrate this issue, a useful example is the review of emails sent and received by employees. Under the PD(P)O, monitoring employee activity at work in this way may amount to the collection of personal data,[83] and the legislation requires that such data must be collected in a way that is lawful and fair in the circumstances.[84] Guidelines on how to achieve this are contained in the Hong Kong Office of the Privacy Commissioner for Personal Data's 'Privacy Guidelines: Monitoring and Personal Privacy at Work'[85] ('the Privacy Guidelines').

According to the Privacy Guidelines, employers should implement a written **10.121** privacy policy that governs personal data management practices relating to employee monitoring.[86] In relation to the monitoring of email communications, employers should also include a clear statement regarding the conditions of use of email.[87] By implementing a clear privacy policy which employees clearly understand and to which they have access, it is less likely that employees can raise objections to monitoring activities such as email communications, in the context of an investigation. In the absence of such a policy it would be necessary to obtain the consent of the employee prior to reviewing the relevant communication.

---

[81] See also Art 14 of the Hong Kong Bill of Rights.

[82] Regulators include the SFC, HKSE and the HKMA; PS(P)O, s 58.

[83] See PD(P)O, s 2; *Employment Law Asia*, Vol 1 (Netherlands: Kluwer Law International, 1st edn, 2005), at 50–681.

[84] PD(P)O, ss 4 and 2 and Sch 1 ; see also *Employment Law Asia*, Vol 1 (Netherlands: Kluwer Law International, 1st edn, 2005), at 50–681.

[85] Published in December 2004; a copy of these guidelines can be found at: <http://www.pco. org.hk/english/ordinance/files/monguide_e.pdf>; According to these guidelines, employers should implement a written privacy policy that governs personal data management practices relating to employee monitoring. In relation to the monitoring of email communications, employers should also include a clear statement regarding the conditions of use of email. By implementing a clear privacy policy which employees clearly understand and have agreed to it, it is less likely that employees can raise objections to monitoring activities such as email communications.

[86] Privacy Guidelines at 3.2.1.

[87] Privacy Guidelines at 3.2.4.

10.122 It is therefore good practice to obtain and record the employee's consent to carry out necessary investigatory work that involves the collection of personal data. This ideally is obtained in advance by way of an express provision in employment contracts to permit access to an employee's documents without prior notification. Such a provision in an employment contract is legally enforceable in Hong Kong.

10.123 A further issue arises where it is necessary to send or review any personal data outside Hong Kong. Section 33 of the PD(P)O prohibits the transfer of personal data outside Hong Kong, subject to applicable exemptions. One practical solution to this issue may be to transfer any such data in a redacted or anonymized form such that it does not permit the identity of the employee to be ascertained.

Practical considerations

10.124 When gathering and disclosing documents a key issue that may arise is dealing with privileged documents. Care must be taken to ensure that all such documents are identified as privileged and to either avoid disclosing such documents, or to ensure that the regulator is aware of the privileged nature of the documents and keeps them confidential (and to make it clear on disclosure that no general or wider waiver of privilege is intended).[88]

I. Dealing with Privileged Documents

General rules on privilege

10.125 The existence of privileged documents must be disclosed if they are relevant to investigations; however, these documents may be protected from production unless the privilege in them is waived. There are two limbs of legal professional privilege in Hong Kong:

i. Legal advice privilege relates to confidential communications between a legal adviser and his or her client and other documents created by the client for the dominant purpose of giving or receiving legal advice. Such communications are not confined to telling the client the law, but include advice as to what should prudently and sensibly be done in the relevant legal context.

ii. Litigation privilege relates to confidential communications between a legal adviser and his or her client, as well as communications between a legal adviser or client and third parties in contemplation of, and for the dominant purpose of, litigation.[89]

---

[88] *B and RMV v Auckland District Law Society* [2003] 2 AC 736.
[89] In determining the dominant purpose, the intention of the person creating the document, as well as that of the intended recipient, is considered.

Without prejudice communications may also be privileged. These communica- **10.126**
tions, which evidence settlement negotiations, are not discloseable, regardless of
whether they are actually marked 'Without Prejudice'. Although the existence of
without prejudice communications should be disclosed, production of these
documents may be withheld on the grounds of privilege.

When conducting an internal investigation or faced with a regulatory investiga- **10.127**
tion companies should be aware[90] of a number of key issues. First, litigation
privilege does not necessarily embrace material produced for the purpose of a
regulatory investigation. The relevant test is whether adversarial proceedings are
in existence or are anticipated. At the stage of commencement of an investigation
by a regulator, it will typically be difficult to argue that proceedings are anticipated. Such a conclusion is typically formed subsequent to the investigation
when a regulator has written to the company notifying its intention to take
proceedings or where it otherwise makes clear such intention. Listed corporations
should therefore be alert to the fact that the only possible protection available for
documents produced in the context of regulatory proceedings is legal advice
privilege.

For the purposes of legal advice privilege, the 'client' means only those individuals **10.128**
within the client's organization who are specifically responsible for instructing
the relevant legal advisers and obtaining their advice on the issues.[91] There is
therefore some uncertainty as to who the client is for the purposes of legal advice
privilege, and it cannot be assumed that all communications between legal advisers and all employees of a company will be protected by the privilege. This is
another important limitation in practice and is likely to mean, for example, that
notes of interviews with witnesses conducted for the purposes of an internal
investigation may not be privileged, even if those notes are prepared by lawyers.

The purpose for which the document was produced is also critical. Material pro- **10.129**
duced internally to enable the company to take legal advice[92] may well be privileged. However, companies should be wary of creating purely internal documents
analysing what went wrong since these are unlikely to be privileged unless they
are prepared by lawyers or they are prepared directly in order to enable the company to take legal advice. Therefore companies need to be very careful about who

---

[90] See also the UK chapter, Chapter 4. Hong Kong law as it applies to legal professional privilege
mirrors English law.

[91] *Three Rivers District Council and others v Governor and Company of the Bank of England (No 5)*
[2003] 3 WLR 667, Court of Appeal.

[92] Legal advice is interpreted fairly widely, to include all communication within the continuum
aimed at keeping legal adviser and client informed, but it may not include the legal adviser's advice
on purely commercial or business matters: *Three Rivers District Council and others v Governor and
Company of the Bank of England)* [2004] UKHL 48, House of Lords.

creates documents and the purpose for which documents are created. For example, where a document recording legal advice is created by non-legal employees for the board of directors, the document will not attract legal advice privilege.

10.130 As a general rule, privileged documents should always be clearly marked and extreme care should be taken when sharing documents with other parties. This is because third parties have less interest in protecting privilege than the listed company and may volunteer documents to the SFC or Stock Exchange.

Waiving privilege

10.131 Once privilege is lost, it cannot be regained. Privilege may be lost in the following circumstances:

i. where the conditions necessary for a claim to privilege no longer apply, for example, if confidentiality in the document is lost;
ii. where the privilege is waived, either by the listed corporation itself or its counsel, either intentionally or inadvertently. A waiver of privilege in relation to a single document may result in privilege being waived over other documents in the same category/class; and
iii. where a third party is able to adduce secondary (non-privileged) evidence of the contents of a privileged communication.

10.132 The exception might be where privileged material is produced by one party to another within a confidential relationship. In those circumstances, provided there is no intention to waive privilege, the privilege can, potentially, still be maintained against other third parties.

10.133 This may assist in circumstances where corporations disclose certain privileged materials to the SFC because the SFC has demanded production of the material, or because a corporation considers it to be in its best interests to disclose it to the SFC.

10.134 As the SFC is generally required to maintain the confidentiality of disclosures made to it,[93] it is arguable that where a corporation produces privileged material to the SFC it does so within a confidential relationship which is necessary for maintaining the privileged nature of the material.

10.135 Where a listed corporation decides to produce privileged documents to the SFC, it should clearly demonstrate its intention to maintain the privilege over the material provided. The listed corporation should make it clear that the material is and remains confidential and privileged, that it only intends such materials to be used for the purposes of the SFC's regulatory functions, and that it is not waiving the legal professional privilege attaching to the material.

---

[93] SFO, s 378.

The provisions of the SFO generally require the SFC and persons appointed to **10.136** assist it to preserve confidentiality. In particular, the SFC should:

i. preserve and aid in preserving secrecy with regard to any matter coming to its knowledge in the course of performing its regulatory work and functions;
ii. refrain from communicating any such matter to any other person; and
iii. not permit any other person to have access to any record or document which is in its possession by virtue of itsregulatory work and functions.[94]

There are a number of carve-outs to the requirement for the SFC to maintain **10.137** secrecy over the matters it is investigating.[95] If one of these applies, then neither the privilege nor the confidentiality in the relevant documents will be preserved. These include:

i. the disclosure of information which has already been made available to the public;
ii. the disclosure of information for the purposes of any criminal proceedings, or any investigation carried out under Hong Kong's laws in Hong Kong;
iii. the disclosure of information for the purpose of seeking or receiving advice from counsel or a solicitor or other professional adviser acting or proposing to act in a professional capacity in connection with any matters arising under relevant provisions of the SFO;
iv. the disclosure of information by a person in connection with any judicial or other proceedings to which that person is a party; and
v. the disclosure of information in accordance with a court order or in accordance with law.[96]

In the above circumstances, the SFC is not under a duty to maintain the confi- **10.138** dentiality of information given to it in connection with an investigation.

Pursuant to section 378(3) of the SFO, the SFC is also permitted to disclose **10.139** information to, inter alia, the following persons:

i. a liquidator appointed under the Companies Ordinance;
ii. the MMT;
iii. the Securities and Futures Appeals Tribunal; and
iv. other regulatory bodies, such as the HKMA and Insurance Authority.[97]

Notably, private civil litigants are not included in this list. The SFC might not **10.140** therefore be able to disclose information to them under this subsection unless

---

[94] SFO, s 378(1).
[95] SFO, s 378(2).
[96] SFO, s 378(2).
[97] SFO, s 378(3).

consent is obtained. Under section 378(3)(k) of the SFO, the SFC is permitted to disclose information to third parties if it obtains the consent of the person from whom the information was obtained or received and, if applicable, the consent of any other person, to whom the information relates.[98] Where such consent is obtained, the SFC might be able to disclose information to a private civil litigant.

10.141 Finally, it should be noted that it is an offence for a person to disclose information in breach of the restrictions laid down in the SFO.[99]

Limited waiver

10.142 As highlighted above the SFC is generally required to maintain the confidentiality of disclosures made to it. Privileged material is therefore provided to it within the context of a confidential relationship. However, as also noted above, there are circumstances under which the SFC may break this duty of confidentiality.

10.143 The SFC has issued a Guidance Note on Cooperation with the SFC[100] ('the Guidance Note on Cooperation'). This clarifies the practice of giving credit to regulated persons for their cooperation with the SFC, and demonstrates that the SFC may impose lighter disciplinary actions on people who cooperate with it than it would otherwise impose in the absence of cooperation.

10.144 One of the forms of cooperation listed by the SFC includes the waiver of the legal professional privilege attaching to any document provided to the SFC. In return, depending on a number of factors such as the usefulness of the document to the investigation, the SFC will give an appropriate discount in penalty to the alleged wrongdoer.

10.145 Any waiver of legal professional privilege is voluntary. In contrast to the position in some other jurisdictions, the SFC has clarified that refusal to do so will not be considered as an aggravating factor in assessing the appropriate disciplinary penalty.[101]

Privilege pitfalls

10.146 Once an investigation has started it is important that care is taken when creating new documents. As discussed above, a firm's right to refuse the production of documents which are protected by legal professional privilege is preserved. Ideally, new documents should not be created unless they are protected by legal professional privilege.

---

[98] SFO, s 378(3)(k).
[99] SFO, s 378(10).
[100] March 2006.
[101] Guidance Note on Cooperation, 15–16.

Companies may undermine their position if they create documents after an **10.147** investigation has commenced which are not privileged. Ideally, any documents that are produced should be prepared by the company's internal or external lawyers. If that is not practicable, at the very least they should be clearly prepared for the purpose of seeking advice from the company's internal or external lawyers or at the request of such lawyers.

The documents should be marked 'Privileged and Confidential' whenever appro- **10.148** priate. If litigation is contemplated, the document should clearly be marked to show that the document is prepared for this purpose.

If there is to be an internal investigation it is advisable to make sure that recollec- **10.149** tions from relevant employees are given, in the first instance, orally to in-house or external counsel, who will then record such recollections in writing as appropriate. This is because:

  i. notes created by the company's officers or staff (excluding legal) are generally not privileged;
  ii. investigation reports produced by the company's officers, staff or other advisers (eg accountants or investment banks) without the involvement of the company's lawyers are not privileged; and
  iii. lawyers' interviews with witnesses and notes of the meeting may be privileged.

Similar care also needs to be taken when obtaining copies of documents from third **10.150** parties. If the company does not have possession of such documents, or the legal right to obtain such documents, it cannot be compelled to disclose them. It may make such documents vulnerable by bringing them into its possession or control.

With regard to circulating documents, a 'need to know' approach should ideally be **10.151** adopted. The wider the group of recipients, the more likely it is that any privileged status which that document enjoys will be waived. It is therefore important that the company sets out in writing and informs external counsel as soon as possible in the investigation process which individuals in the firm are to be considered as the points of communication for the purpose of dealing with the investigation (this may include the CEO, in-house counsel, members of the compliance team in charge of the investigation, and other selected employees). Members of the team should be constantly informed as to any updates. Furthermore, any legal advice should only be circulated on the request of and for the benefit of these individuals.

Finally, those employees providing assistance to the SFC in an investigation or **10.152** inquiry should be reminded that under their secrecy obligations pursuant to the SFO, they cannot disclose to any other person any information regarding the matters under inquiry, including information disclosed during an interview with the SFC.

J. Managing Regulators

Dialogue with regulators

10.153 When an investigation is being conducted by the SFC, Stock Exchange or other regulator, it is important for the listed corporation to establish lines of communication with those conducting it. It would be prudent to centralize communications with the regulator through one person or a small team (such as, where applicable, an investigations team set up within the Legal and Compliance Department) to liaise with the regulators and ensure that enquiries are handled in a timely manner and that responses are consistent. In any event, this will assist the listed corporation to understand what the regulator requires and enable better management of the process.

10.154 Pursuant to the Guidance Note on Cooperation, one of the factors to which the SFC will have regard when considering the level of sanctions to impose on a listed company is the extent to which the senior management of the company has been involved in liaising with the SFC including the extent to which they have instructed staff to cooperate fully with the SFC.

10.155 It is generally good practice to keep the regulators informed of how the responses are being handled. For example, under the Guidance Note on Cooperation, some forms of cooperation include:

i. taking all practical steps to contain and rectify the matter within the constraints the company faces in terms of resources and time;
ii. taking the initiative to undertake a credible review to identify, for example, the source of the matter, the means by which it was perpetrated, how it escaped discovery and any appropriate remedial actions that should be taken to prevent its recurrence; and
iii. devoting manpower and resources to assist the SFC in its evaluation or investigation of the matter.

10.156 Sufficient time should also be allowed for the internal review of the materials to be handed over to the regulator in order to ensure that privileged and irrelevant documents are removed. A more proactive approach to an issue in which the regulator has indicated its intention to investigate is for the corporate to undertake to investigate the matter in full, proactively itself and to provide a report to the regulator. This may have the advantage of controlling the negative impact on the company's business during the investigation phase and obtaining leniency from the regulator. It is critical that any such investigation is carried out responsibly and robustly in order to avoid the regulator subsequently discovering an issue has not been properly looked into and consequently hardening its position. If such an approach is to work (and it is not an approach that is typically used in the Hong Kong market) it is essential to retain experienced investigation counsel and to ensure that a dialogue is maintained with the regulator at an appropriate level. The scope of the investigation should be identified at the outset of such an investigation. This will depend on the nature and seriousness of the matter to be investigated, but should also be a matter to which consideration is given in discussions with the regulator.

Control of scope of investigation

In order for a company to ensure that regulators do not, impermissibly, extend the scope of investigation, it is important, first and foremost, to be familiar with the precise scope of the particular regulatory and investigatory powers. In practice this will require advice from experienced counsel. If a company believes the regulator is exceeding its powers then this concern is usually outlined in correspondence with the regulator by seeking explanation as to the regulator's reasons for asking for the relevant evidence. In some circumstances, an informal discussion with the regulator will be a useful preliminary start. **10.157**

If it is still believed that the regulator's requests are outside its remit a company can either decline to give the evidence that the regulator has requested (thus forcing the regulator to make an application to the court) or may be able to proactively apply itself to court, for example seeking a clarification order. **10.158**

Use of information by regulators

As outlined above,[102] the SFC is generally required to maintain the confidentiality of disclosures made to it.[103] **10.159**

The SFC and its employees have a general obligation to keep confidential all matters associated with its regulatory work and functions, and not to communicate any such information to others, or to provide others with access to documents gained as a result of their employment. **10.160**

These confidentiality obligations do not apply in certain circumstances, such as in relation to criminal proceedings or other investigations under Hong Kong's laws. The SFC's confidentiality obligations also fall away if it is compelled to produce the information by order of the court.[104] **10.161**

---

[102] See 10.131, on 'Waiving Privilege'.
[103] SFO, s 378.
[104] See section on 'Waiving Privilege' for the complete list of circumstances under which the SFO can waive its confidentiality obligations.

10.162 The SFC can also disclose information to a number of regulatory bodies including the MMT, the HKMA and the Securities and Futures Appeals Tribunal. However, it may not disclose information to private civil litigants without the consent of the person to whom the information relates.

10.163 The SFC is also empowered to conduct investigations where requested to do so by equivalent international regulators and is permitted to pass such information as it obtains to such regulatory authorities.

Managing multiple regulators

10.164 As discussed in the Concurrent Investigations section above, the SFC has entered into arrangements with the HKMA and the Stock Exchange respectively to minimize duplication of work.

10.165 However, where concurrent investigations are being conducted, it is important from the outset to organize the manner in which communications between the various regulators should be conducted. Other useful steps include:

 i. coordinating internally the various requests from different regulators in order to minimize unnecessary duplication of work in response to similar requests;

 ii. ensuring that each team member handling the investigations keeps abreast of all developments in the investigation from each regulator in order to maximize the opportunity to obtain leverage from work already performed in response to requests from other regulators;

 iii. working from a single theme or theory of case to ensure consistency amongst the responses to different regulators;

 iv. continually assessing whether the responses are accurate and sufficient and provided in a timely fashion; and

 v. negotiating with the regulators as to which investigating body will have priority in the investigation. This is an area that requires experience and tact in negotiating. It may also be necessary to update regulators on material provided to others.

K. Managing Employees During Investigations

Powers to compel cooperation

10.166 An employee may be compelled to cooperate with an internal investigation by virtue of the implied or express terms of his or her employment contract. A breach of an implied or express term of the employment contract may result in an employer taking disciplinary action against the employee, and in some cases in the dismissal of the employee.

In Hong Kong, an employee has an implied contractual obligation to carry out **10.167** lawful orders given by employers which are within the scope of the employment contract. An employee is also under an implied duty of good faith during the duration of his or her employment contract. This duty of good faith requires an employee to act in the best interests of the employer and an employee may therefore be under a duty to disclose certain matters including an employee's own misconduct (where it has been fraudulently concealed), and in some circumstances, the misconduct of other employees.[105] Depending on the circumstances, therefore, it may be reasonable to compel an employee to assist in an internal investigation.

Listed companies in some cases will also impose express terms in employment **10.168** contracts requiring employees to cooperate with investigations carried out by regulators/their employers. An employee may be more cooperative with a listed corporation's internal investigation where this obligation is expressly stated in his or her employment contract.

Where an employee is dismissed (or is forced to resign) for failure to cooperate **10.169** with an internal investigation, an employee may seek to claim damages against the corporation for wrongful termination of employment. Whether or not such a claim will be successful will depend upon the terms of the relevant employee's employment contract, and whether or not the employee's failure to cooperate with the investigation could be deemed to be misconduct. There is currently no legal structure supporting amnesty arrangements for employees in Hong Kong. Whistle-blowing employees have no specific status in Hong Kong employment law. Such arrangements are therefore left to negotiation between the employee and company.

Suspension

A further option for listed corporates to consider is to suspend an employee dur- **10.170** ing the investigation process (either with or without pay). This may be of assistance if the corporate does not want the employee to be in a position to hinder the investigation or to cover tracks. Whether this option can be used will depend upon the relevant terms of employment and the company's disciplinary policy. A statutory right to suspend employees exists but it contains restrictions of scope and duration such that in practice it is of limited use in the context of major investigations.

---

[105] *Employment Law Asia*, Vol 1(Netherlands: Kluwer Law International, 1st edn, 2005), 40–231; for example, where a fellow employee has been giving orders amounting to fraud or dishonesty or has advised their position for personal gain.

Representation

10.171 Whether separate counsel for employees and the company should be retained depends on the particular circumstances of the situation. Where a clear conflict of interests between the employee and the company is envisaged, and in circumstances where the employee faces personal liability/reputation damage, it is likely to be appropriate for the employee to engage separate counsel at the outset. It is important that investigating counsel is aware of this issue and it is appropriate to inform an employee of his right to separate counsel in this situation.

10.172 Other than in the context of a conflict of interests, it is not common market practice to engage separate counsel in cases of internal investigations. However, if the employee asks to bring a lawyer to an interview, it is usually imprudent as well as counter-productive to refuse. The company may wish to seek to reserve the right to approve, or veto the choice of external counsel.

10.173 Whether or not employees should be independently represented at an interview or otherwise in an investigation ultimately depends upon the circumstances, for example whether there is any suggestion that the breach may have resulted from deliberate action by an employee, whether there is a risk of the employee facing a criminal prosecution[106] or whether there is a risk that the interests of the employee and the interests of the company may conflict.[107]

Assurances as to confidentiality and privilege

10.174 In conducting interviews with employees, the interviewing counsel should explain the purpose of the interview including that it is not a disciplinary hearing. Guidance should also be given to the employee as to whether the meeting is confidential or (more frequently) not. Where the employer may wish to take disciplinary or other action against the employee, certainly no assurances should be given to the employee about the confidentiality of their discussions or about the employee's continued employment. It may be appropriate also to explain to the employee that the discussion is covered by privilege. This needs to be judged carefully. As discussed above, the interview discussions may not be privileged and may reveal evidence of misconduct of the employee. In such cases, the interviewing

---

[106] In these circumstances, it may be appropriate for the company to take immediate action to suspend the employee or remove him or her from sensitive positions. Not only is this a matter of common sense, but it may also be viewed by the SFC and HKSE as a positive step taken by the company in response to the breach, to ensure that the breach is not repeated in the short term and to protect the evidence. In doing so, the company should ensure that it complies with its disciplinary procedures, in order to reduce the risk of an employee successfully claiming that he or she has been treated unfairly.

[107] If there is no conflict, or no significant risk of conflict, one counsel may theoretically act for both a listed corporate and its employees but see Ethical Implications for Counsel below.

counsel should also explain that, where relevant, any information obtained may be used for the purposes of disciplinary hearings.

The interviewing counsel should also stipulate to the employee that he or she **10.175** cannot talk about what was discussed during the interview with others[108] and that this in itself may be a disciplinary issue.

Ethical implications for counsel

Where external counsel has been engaged by the company to interview employees **10.176** for the purposes of an internal investigation and the employee is not separately represented, if he or she envisages a conflict of interest between the company and the employee, he or she should make it clear that the employee should take his or her own independent legal advice. In practice this may involve employees requesting the company to indemnify them for legal costs. This issue is better addressed at the outset of the investigation as it can impact on the timeliness and effectiveness of an investigation.

It will be rare in the context of an internal investigation that counsel should agree **10.177** to represent both the company or one of its governance entities and the employee(s). Such a duality of roles would be likely to compromise the independence of the investigations.

Where external counsel is considering acting for both the company and an **10.178** employee in an external investigation, they should also ensure that they do not place themselves in a position where their duty under the SFO not to disclose information[109] conflicts with the duty to disclose and use for the benefit of one client information derived from acting for the other client.[110] This will typically involve investigating counsel obtaining written consent from both clients waiving obligations to pass on information received from other clients.

Investigations and disciplinary process

Any disciplinary measures taken by a company against an employee should be **10.179** consistent with the company's internal disciplinary policy and/or the terms of the employment agreement. Possible measures may typically include suspension from work during the period of the investigation, for example, if the employee may be conflicted from continuing work during this period. Where it has been

---

[108] Although it is not standard practice to request confidentiality assurances, it often occurs in practice. This is especially relevant where fellow employees are also being interviewed.

[109] SFO, s 378.

[110] Solicitors Code of Conduct Principle 9.2 commentary 8. See also commentary 7 to principle 8.03.

found that the employee has committed a criminal offence such as fraud, termination of his or her employment may result.

Challenges posed by ex-employees

10.180 Ideally, all information and documents required from an employee should be obtained prior to the employee's departure from the company, as it is often very difficult to obtain an employee's cooperation after his or her employment has ended, whatever cooperation obligations have been negotiated. Nonetheless, the human resources department should obtain the employee's most up-to-date contact details prior to their departure from the company.

10.181 A further complication exists where an ex-employee has commenced new employment, particularly where this is for a competitor to the listed company. It will be necessary for the listed company to balance the need to maintain confidentiality in relation to the investigation against the risk that the investigation may be 'hamstrung' if the relevant ex-employee is not interviewed.

Payment of legal fees/indemnification/fee advances

10.182 Companies are generally permitted under Hong Kong law to indemnify employees for the costs that employees have incurred in connection with internal and/or regulatory investigations and against any liability incurred by them in defending any civil or criminal proceedings in which judgment is given in their favour or in which they are acquitted.[111]

10.183 It is also possible for companies to purchase insurance for its officers or auditors against any liability to the company in respect of any negligence, default, breach of duty or breach of trust, and against liability incurred by the company in respect of defending any such proceedings.[112]

10.184 Companies are generally able to lend funds to employees to pay for representation by separate legal counsel in connection with investigations. However, if a court decision is ultimately not made in favour of an officer of a company, that company would not be able to indemnify the officer and any funds advanced should be repaid.

10.185 Joint defence agreements[113] between companies and their employees are permitted, but not common, in Hong Kong. However, a formal joint defence agreement

---

111 Companies Ordinance, s 165(2)(a).

112 Companies Ordinance, s 165(3).

113 Parties with a common interest in a particular matter agree that they may exchange confidential and privileged information for their mutual benefit, without waiving either the confidentiality or the privilege.

which identifies the common interest of the parties and expressly provides that the documents are being shared between the parties under the protection of common interest privilege, may assist in evidencing the common interest and therefore limiting the risk that privilege is considered to have been waived by the exchange of documents or information between the company and its employee.

It is important to note that, given that common interest privilege is held jointly, **10.186** it must be waived jointly and not by one party alone.[114] This may cause a problem if one party and not the other wishes to waive the privilege in a document protected by common interest privilege.

It is best practice for the fee arrangement to be recorded in a letter or other written **10.187** document.

Best practices

Where an employee has been served with a notice to attend an interview with a reg- **10.188** ulator, it is compulsory that he or she attends. Company policy should be that any person asked to attend an interview with the SFC consults with the Legal or Compliance Department or equivalent before the interview. The employee should also inform his or her line manager that he or she has been requested to attend an interview, but should not reveal the subject matter of the interview to his or her line manager. If he or she encounters persistent requests for information from the line manager, he or she should raise the matter with the company's internal counsel.

The employee should typically prepare before the interview to become familiar **10.189** with any relevant documents which he or she has seen, but in order to ensure the accuracy and integrity of any answers, he or she should generally avoid reviewing documents which were not seen at the time of the events to be discussed. There are no ethical rules that prevent an employee from being advised by counsel during the preparatory phase. Coaching of answers is, however, ethically dubious, is not market practice and is likely to be counter-productive if detected by the regulator.

If there are no real issues in relation to the individual's conduct, it is not essential **10.190** for the individual to be accompanied to the interview. To do so may be interpreted by the regulators as being over-defensive as it is not typically business culture in Hong Kong for employees to be legally represented. This is, however, an area of flux and, particularly in the case of employees of multinational corporates, such representation is becoming more commonplace. Clearly if there is reason to suspect that some misconduct has occurred, the employee should be accompanied by external counsel.

---

114 *The Sagheera* [1997] 1 Lloyd's Rep 160.

10.191 In any situation, if the employee feels uncomfortable in attending on his or her own and requests accompanying counsel, this should be considered. However, where the interests of the firm and the individual attending the interview may conflict (eg if there is a possibility that the individual is guilty of misconduct), then the firm will need to consider recommending that the individual take separate legal advice.

10.192 In respect of internal investigations, good practice when dealing with employees during the investigation is to:

  i. ensure the employee is treated with courtesy and dignity;
 ii. tell the employee in advance why he or she is being interviewed and what the issues are so that he or she has a chance to prepare;
iii. explain that any information obtained may be used for the purpose of disciplinary proceedings if they should result; and
 iv. explain that the employee has no right to control the use of the information disclosed, and that this is a matter purely for the company.

L. Winding up an Investigation

Managing expectations

10.193 Ideally, an investigation should only be concluded after ensuring that the information obtained during its course is sufficient to address the concerns of the regulator or shareholders.

10.194 According to the Guidance Note on Cooperation, swift and appropriate remedial and preventative action taken by the company is also a form of cooperation which the SFC will consider in reducing any disciplinary sanction against the company.

Coordinating a Public Relations strategy

10.195 Where the results of the investigation reveal that there has been no wrongdoing on the part of the company or its employees, and where the fact of the investigation is not in the public domain, there is little benefit in disclosing the matter to the public. However, it may be advisable to inform those in the company (such as employees) who assisted in the investigation of the result of the process or at least that the process has concluded.

10.196 Where the results of the investigation identify wrongdoing on the part of the company or its employees, the relevant regulators should be informed and, where appropriate, remedies should be put in place to rectify the issue. In such circumstances or where the matter is already public, it will be necessary to make an appropriate public announcement. The issues to be taken into account when considering whether it is appropriate to make any public announcement are similar to the issues identified above.[115]

M. Reporting Obligations

Tailoring the report

Any report submitted to the regulators should be checked to ensure no documents covered by legal professional privilege are inadvertently disclosed. Generally the issue of waiver of privilege needs to be considered (and discussed with the company) and if appropriate protective wording will need to be included in the report and if possible undertakings obtained from the regulator not to disclose the report. The report should also accurately state the factual outcome of the investigation.[116]   **10.197**

According to the Guidance Note on Cooperation, one of the factors to which the SFC will have regard when considering sanctions is the results of any independent or internal review, and not only information requested or required, but also other relevant information which the SFC might not otherwise have known about are supplied to it. Therefore, in some cases, it may be beneficial for the listed company to provide additional information to the SFC.   **10.198**

Coordinating with Public Relations strategy

When reporting to the regulator, companies should consider carefully whether to disclose the existence and content of any report to the press. If the existence of the regulatory investigation is already in the public domain, then a company may wish to convey to the general public the fact that it is cooperating with the regulator in this manner. On the other hand, companies may also be worried that there is a risk that the regulator might impose sanctions on the company as a result of the information reported by the company.   **10.199**

It is very important to bear in mind that the outcome of the investigation will still be uncertain at this stage. Companies should therefore remain cautious about what they choose to disclose to the press about their cooperation with the regulators, and how they present these disclosures. As mentioned above, in practice any comment made will usually be restricted to confirming, where appropriate, that an investigation is taking place and that the company is cooperating with the regulator.   **10.200**

---

115 See 'Obligations When Facing a Regulatory Investigation and Obligations When Conducting and Internal Investigation'. As discussed, any press release and HKSE announcement must be coordinated in terms of timing and content.
116 Please refer to 10.146 'Privilege pitfalls' above.

10.201 Even if the existence and outcome of a regulatory investigation is not in the public domain, there is still a possibility that the regulator could decide that it is in the public interest to disclose facts resulting from the investigation.[117] Accordingly, companies subject to regulatory investigations should ensure that they build good working relationships with the relevant regulator, and that they monitor the press carefully on a daily basis so that they are alerted to any press reports of the investigation, and can initiate an appropriate PR strategy in response as soon as possible. It is, however, very unusual for the SFC or other regulators to pursue an active media strategy at this stage of an investigation as opposed to when they take action or obtain a sanction. It is more likely that if the regulator considers that matters should be disclosed about 'issues' affecting listed companies during an investigation, then the regulator will require the company to issue an announcement through the Stock Exchange.

Beware of waiving privilege

10.202 As outlined earlier in this chapter,[118] many regulators do not have a duty of confidentiality, and the SFC's duty of confidentiality can be waived in a number of circumstances. Care must therefore be taken before including confidential or privileged documents and information in the investigation report.

N. Litigation Risks

Risks of criminal litigation commenced by regulators

10.203 Market misconduct offences under the SFO can attract both civil and criminal liability. However, the same market misconduct cannot be subject to both a civil action in the MMT and a criminal action in the courts.[119] The SFC must therefore decide whether to pursue a matter by way of civil or criminal action.

10.204 In making this decision, the SFC will have regard to the guidelines in the 'Department of Justice Prosecution Policy: Guidance for Government Counsel', which requires two basic factors to be considered:

i. the strength of the SFC's case. The burden of proof is greater in criminal proceedings and the SFC will generally only recommend criminal proceedings where there is admissible, substantial and reliable evidence that an offence has

---

[117] For example, see SFO, s 5(g) which gives the SFC the power, in the interests of maintaining and promoting public confidence in the securities and futures industry to exercise its discretion to 'disclose to the public any matter relating or incidental to the performance of any of its functions.'

[118] Please refer to section 10.131, 'Waiving privilege', and 10.146, 'Privilege pitfalls'.

[119] SFO, ss 283 and 307; see also the Government of the Hong Kong Administrative Region Consultation Document on the Securities and Futures Bill, April 2000, 11.21.

been committed and there is a reasonable prospect of a conviction.[120] Where there is a lack of sufficient evidence to meet the criminal burden of proof, the SFC would generally prefer civil proceedings; and

ii. whether, taking into account the circumstances of a particular case, it is in the public interest to bring prosecution before the courts.[121]

Where the SFC believes that a serious criminal offence may have been commit- **10.205**
ted, it will refer the matter t o the Secretary for Justice for criminal prosecution on indictment and/or refer the matter to the Hong Kong Police or the ICAC for further investigation.[122] For breaches of a less serious nature, it can, and does, prosecute the matter itself summarily in the Magistrates' Court.[123]

Risks of civil litigation commenced by regulators

Where the SFC decides that civil proceedings are appropriate, it can make an ini- **10.206**
tial decision to refer the matter to the Finance Secretary for referral to the courts or the MMT.[124] The SFC can also take other action such as applying for an injunction to stop the wrongdoing,[125] disciplining licensed intermediaries,[126] and restricting the business of licensed intermediaries.[127]

It is important to note that where the SFC refers matters to the Finance Secretary **10.207**
to recommend the commencement of civil proceedings, or to the Secretary for Justice for the commencement of criminal proceedings, either the Finance Secretary and the Secretary for Justice can redirect the matter if they disagree with the SFC's referral.[128] In making their decision, the two ministers are likely to consider whether there is sufficient evidence to prove the case, and whether it is in the public interest for criminal action to be taken.[129]

Although the SFC is not required under the SFO to report any matter to either **10.208**
of these ministers, pursuant to its 'Regulatory Philosophy',[130] and in the spirit of its primary role to enforce the laws governing the securities and futures markets, the SFC will always consider whether it should take this action.

---

[120] The Government of the Hong Kong Administrative Region, Consultation Document on the Securities and Futures Bill, April 2000, 23 and 11.18–11.19.
[121] Ibid 11.18–11.19.
[122] Ibid.
[123] SFO, s 388.
[124] Consultation Document on the Securities and Futures Bill, The Government of the Hong Kong Administrative Region, April 2000, 11.17; SFO, s 252.
[125] SFO, s 213.
[126] SFO, Part IX.
[127] SFO, ss 204–09.
[128] SFO, s 252(9) and (10); Consultation Document on the Securities and Futures Bill, The Government of the Hong Kong Administrative Region, April 2000, 11.17.
[129] The Government of the Hong Kong Administrative Region, Consultation Document on the Securities and Futures Bill, April 2000, 11.18.
[130] SFC Regulatory Handbook, Vol 1, Chapter 4.

10.209 In deciding whether or not to take enforcement action, the SFC will consider the following factors:

> i. its principles of regulation. When making decisions or taking action, the SFC is guided by its principles of regulation, namely: firmness; fairness; consistency; proportionality; and a 'negotiate not dictate' policy which encourages open dialogue and negotiation wherever possible;[131]
>
> ii. the need to punish wrongdoers and to deter others. Punishment may deter wrongdoers from further wrongdoing as well as serve as a deterrent to others. The SFC generally publicizes its enforcement sanctions wherever appropriate; and
>
> iii. the costs and benefits of any action that it proposes to take. As the SFC acknowledges, limited resources mean that it must set priorities and may not take enforcement action for all breaches.[132] In practice, this means that the SFC may concentrate on taking action in relation to more serious matters. The SFC has indicated, for example, that it is generally unlikely to take enforcement action on a case concerning a minor technical breach that is unlikely to be repeated and that has resulted in very little or no loss to investors.[133]

Risks of private civil litigation

10.210 Civil plaintiffs are able to bring actions based upon regulatory investigations and actions. However, given the SFC's general confidentiality obligations, civil plaintiffs may encounter some difficulties in obtaining the information that they need to frame their cases from the SFC. Civil litigants may be able to obtain information under section 378(3)(k) of the SFO, whereby the SFC is permitted to disclose information to third parties if it obtains the consent of the person from whom the information was obtained or received and, if applicable, the consent of any other person, to whom the information relates.[134] In practice it may be unrealistic to expect such consent to be given by a prospective defendant.

10.211 However, under the provisions of the SFO, a finding by the MMT that a person is guilty of market misconduct *can* be admitted into evidence in a private civil action.[135] Any judicial finding of criminal market misconduct can similarly be adduced as evidence in a private civil action.[136]

---

131 SFC Regulatory Handbook, Vol 1, Chapter 2.
132 SFC Regulatory Handbook, Vol 1, Chapter 4.
133 Ibid.
134 SFO, s 378(3)(k).
135 SFO, ss 281(7) and 305(6); see also s 401.
136 Evidence Ordinance (Cap. 8), s 62.

Relevance of investigation report

An SFC investigator is under an obligation to make a final report on the results **10.212** of his or her investigations,[137] and the SFC may, with the permission of the Secretary for Justice, cause these reports to be published,[138] although this is typically not the case. There is no guidance in the legislation in relation to the admissibility of such reports in court or in relation to the weight that a court will place on these reports. If the report is relevant to any of the matters in issue between the parties to a court action it is likely to be admitted as hearsay evidence of these issues in the usual way.

In addition, if the SFC decides not to publish the investigator's report, it is possi- **10.213** ble for a party to the investigation to request the SFC to disclose the report to them (using the section 378 procedure referred to above). This provision may, however, be of limited use in the context of adversarial court proceedings, as the person whose consent to disclosure is required under section 378 may well be one of the parties to the court action themselves. In such circumstances, it may be possible for a litigant to obtain the report by way of a subpoena. In either of these cases, if the SFC considers that disclosure of the report in the civil litigation is contrary to the public interest then it can claim public interest immunity over the report, and prevent its disclosure.

The MMT is also under an obligation pursuant to the SFO to prepare a written **10.214** report of its proceedings,[139] and unless the tribunal sat in private for the whole or part of its proceedings, the MMT is required to publish this report.[140] The contents of the MMT's reports are admissible in court as evidence of the tribunal's determination or for the purpose of identifying the facts on which the tribunal's determination was based.[141] As with the investigator's reports to the SFC, there is no guidance in the legislation in relation to the weight that a court will place on these reports.

O. Settlement with Regulators

Process

Regulatory actions by the SFC can be, and are commonly, settled. Between **10.215** 2005–06, the SFC entered into settlements with 67 entities.

---

[137] SFO, s 183(5).
[138] SFO, s 183(6).
[139] SFO, s 262(1).
[140] SFO, s 262(2).
[141] SFO, s 281(8)(b).

10.216 In determining whether or not to settle an action, the SFC will consider factors such as:

i. whether settlement would be in the public interest or the interest of the investing public;

ii. whether the breach or misconduct was inadvertent or deliberate;

iii. the impact of the breach or misconduct on investors;

iv. whether the party involved in the breach or misconduct had cooperated with the SFC and had shown remorse;[142]

v. whether steps had been taken to rectify the breach or misconduct and prevent it from re-occurring;[143] and

vi. whether there has already been a criminal conviction for the same conduct.[144]

10.217 Having regard to all of the circumstances of the case, the SFC may also allow settlement to take the form of voluntary payments without admission of liability,[145] or without the imposition of formal sanctions.[146]

10.218 Examples of cases that have been settled by the SFC include improper accounts handling;[147] breaches of the SFC's Code of Conduct;[148] unlicensed dealing and aiding and abetting unlicensed dealing;[149] and providing misleading information to the SFC.[150]

10.219 The SFC operates a limited leniency regime. According to the Guidance Note on Cooperation, the maximum reduction of disciplinary sanctions that will be considered by the SFC is either one-third of any applicable fine or a reduction in the seriousness of any other sanction by one order of magnitude.

Is admission necessary?

10.220 Admission of wrongdoing is not a requisite element for any settlement with the SFC or the Stock Exchange. However, the SFC has indicated that as a result of general public concern in the past, it is now more cautious of settling cases on a non-admission basis than previously, and it will only do so in appropriate circumstances.

---

[142] See, eg, the SFC Enforcement Reporter (August 2005) 2–3.
[143] See, eg, the SFC Enforcement Reporter (May 2005), 2.
[144] See, eg, the SFC Enforcement Reporter (November 2005), 4.
[145] See, eg, the SFC Enforcement Reporter (August 2005), 2–3.
[146] See, eg, the SFC Enforcement Reporter (November 2005), 4–5.
[147] See, eg, the SFC Enforcement Reporter (September 2005), 3.
[148] See, eg, the SFC Enforcement Reporter (October 2005), 4.
[149] See, eg, the SFC Enforcement Reporter (November 2005), 4.
[150] See, eg, the SFC Enforcement Reporter (July 2005), 2.

As a recent example of circumstances in which a settlement was obtained without admission of liability the disciplinary action taken by the SFC against Towry Law (Asia) Hong Kong[151] in connection with allegations of mis-selling of hedge fund products to clients was settled without any admission of liability. The settlement amount of HK$400m was the largest to date under the SFO. **10.221**

Impact if under investigation by multiple regulators

As discussed in the Concurrent Investigations and Managing Multiple Regulations sections above, the SFC has entered into arrangements with the HKMA and Stock Exchange respectively to minimize duplication of work. However, if other regulators pursue their own investigations, settlement with the SFC does not prevent other entities who may have an interest in the 'settled' matter from pursuing their own claims. In order to prevent a situation where more than one set of sanctions is imposed on a company under investigation by more than one regulator, the company should consider entering into one global settlement assuming each is willing to enter into discussions. An example of this was the settlement by Deloitte of a joint action brought by the SFC and HKEx in relation to Deloitte acting as a sponsor of a listed company. This coordination is typically easier where the regulators are taking joint action rather than by way of separate cases. It must be borne in mind, however, that any settlement that is reached with the regulators will not prevent criminal charges being brought against the company if these are deemed appropriate.[152] **10.222**

Plea bargaining and amnesty arrangements

Plea bargaining, in the sense that an indication is given by a trial judge that if the defendant pleads guilty he will get one sentence and if he does not and is convicted after trial he will get another more severe sentence, is not a part of Hong Kong jurisprudence.[153] **10.223**

Plea bargaining with the prosecution alone is not considered to be true 'plea bargaining', as there is no certainty that a court will accept the plea offered.[154] Such negotiation does however occur. There are two relevant types of negotiations: evidence bargaining where a defendant may agree to give evidence in return for **10.224**

---

151 Now renamed UKFP (Asia) HK.

152 It should be noted, however, that the same market misconduct activity cannot be subject both to a civil action before the MMT and a criminal action in the courts (Consultation Document on the Securities and Futures Bill, The Government of the Hong Kong Special Administrative Region, April 2000, 11.21).

153 *The Queen v Peter Oswald Scales* [1987] HKLR 583, 587–588; see also Archbold Hong Kong 2007, 4–38.

154 G Heilbronn, *Criminal Procedure in Hong Kong* (Hong Kong: Longman, 3rd edn, 1998), 237.

leniency allowed by the prosecution (including immunity from prosecution); and charge bargaining whereby the type and number of charges are negotiated.

10.225   As discussed above, the SFC can prosecute offences under the provisions of the SFO in a Magistrates' Court summarily,[155] and will follow the Department of Justice's Prosecution Policy in doing so. A case may also be referred to the Department of Justice, which has broad powers to prosecute criminal offences. As such, the above principles should also apply to criminal prosecutions arising from a breach of the SFO.

P. Conclusion

10.226   Hong Kong enjoys the benefit of a relatively open and predictable legal regime that underpins the rules and processes applicable to investigation of listed companies. Many of the 'ground rules' for dealing with investigations have evolved from, or otherwise reflect, practices in other developed economies. The growth in regulatory powers over the past decade since the transfer of sovereignty to the People's Republic of China has not altered substantially the attitude of the authorities who continue to adopt a risk-weighted approach to investigation. Corporate culture in Hong Kong has evolved during this period such that voluntary investigations are becoming more widespread. The presence of leading international professional services firms with substantial longevity in the local marketplace ensures that companies are able to tap in to best-of-class advice in responding to investigations. This remains a competitive advantage for Hong Kong over the fast-emerging mainland Chinese centres (principally Shanghai), where both the applicable rules and the approach of the authorities are less predictable or familiar.

---

[155] SFO, s 388.

11

INVESTIGATIONS IN JAPAN

A. Introduction[1]

11.01   Over the last 10 years, the focus of regulatory policies in Japan has undergone a dynamic transformation. More weight has been imposed increasingly on regulatory controls that are devoted to promoting and maintaining fair market competition, whereas the presence of conventional regulatory straitjackets, which were once praised for playing a role in fostering domestic industries, is decreasing, if not disappearing completely.

11.02   The Japanese Fair Trade Commission (JFTC)[2] is among those regulatory authorities with an increasing presence in this regulatory climate. In the 2006 financial year (between 1 July 2006 and 30 June 2007) (FY 2006), in 13 cases, the JFTC issued cease and desist orders whereby the addressees were required to take certain measures (mostly elimination of illegal conduct) rather than to pay fines, including six orders on bid-rigging, three orders on price cartels, and four orders on unfair trade practices.[3] In the same year, the JFTC issued surcharge orders against 158 entities amounting to approximately JPY9bn; it also filed two criminal complaints based on breaches of the anti-trust regulations.

---

[1] Contributors: Masashi Adachi, Mieko Hosaka, Masahide Fukuda, Kazuki Okada, Jennifer L Raisor, Ryo Suzuki, Kaori Yamada, Akiko Yamakawa, Lisa Yano.

[2] *Kosei torihiki iinkai.*

[3] There was no case of private monopolization.

The Securities and Exchange Surveillance Commission (SESC)[4] is another **11.03** regulatory authority that has recently been taking a more prominent role. In FY 2006, the SESC filed a total of 13 complaints with public prosecutors, making it the highest number of complaints filed by the SESC within one year. These included nine complaints for insider trading; three complaints for manipulating prices; and one complaint for false securities reports. The SESC also filed 14 recommendations for surcharges with the Financial Services Agency ('the FS Agency')[5] in FY 2006. The key, most recent, example of regulatory power exercised by the SESC was the December 2006 case regarding the Nikko Cordial Group, where the SESC conducted an investigation into the company, which was alleged to have made false statements in the supplemental filing to its shelf registration. The SESC recommended a surcharge order of a record high JPY500m be imposed, which the FS Agency issued accordingly.

Other regulatory authorities have also been exercising their regulatory power **11.04** more actively. In FY 2005, the National Tax Agency (NTA)[6] conducted 143,000 examinations related to corporate tax evasions and discovered a total of JPY1,665,400m of unreported income (the total back taxes amounted to JPY395,300m for the year). The revenue officials are also empowered to investigate tax crimes. The NTA commenced 231 and completed 221 criminal investigations, followed by 166 formal criminal complaints with public prosecutors in FY 2006.

In FY 2005, the Labour Standards Bureau (LSB)[7] conducted 122,734 inspections **11.05** into approximately 120,000 business entities. The LSB issued recommendations for remedies in 81,395 cases and reported 1,290 cases to public prosecutors in the same year.

B. Regulators

Key regulators

Entities established or operating in Japan are subject to supervision by a number **11.06** of different Japanese regulators. In exercising their supervisory power, these regulators are entitled to conduct inspections or investigations with a view to ensuring that the target entity complies with applicable laws and regulations and, if appropriate, to request or seize information for this purpose.

---

[4] *Shoken torihiki to kanshi iinkai.*
[5] *Kinyu cho.*
[6] *Kokuzei cho.*
[7] *Rodo kijun kyoku.*

11.07   The following are the major regulatory agencies in Japan.

The JFTC

11.08   The JFTC is an administrative agency, whose major role is to implement the Japanese Anti-Monopoly Act.[8] It is an extra-ministerial body of the Cabinet Office, and an Independent Administrative Commission[9] whose autonomy is highly respected.

11.09   The JFTC implements the Anti-Monopoly Act by: (i) setting guidelines to clarify the definitions of unfair trade practices that are prohibited under the Anti-Monopoly Act; (ii) receiving filings from or conducting prior consultations with companies concerning provisions of the Anti-Monopoly Act, especially merger and acquisition provisions; and (iii) conducting administrative or criminal investigations into violations of the Anti-Monopoly Act.

The FS agency and the SESC

11.10   The FS Agency is primarily responsible for stabilizing the financial market and protecting investors through inspecting and supervising financial institutions such as banks, securities companies and insurance companies. The FS Agency is empowered to take any necessary administrative measures including issuing business improvement or suspension orders in respect of any breaches of laws and regulations which the FS Agency has discovered through such inspections or supervision.

11.11   The SESC, like the FS Agency, is designed to protect investors and maintain the integrity of the Japanese securities market, but it is more focused on individual implementation than the FS Agency. The SESC is empowered to:

- carry out daily surveillance of securities markets;
- conduct inspections of securities companies and other financial institutions;[10]
- examine disclosure documents such as annual securities reports; and
- investigate administrative or criminal offences in relation to securities trading[11] such as insider trading, market manipulation and making false statements in disclosure documents, which are prohibited by the Securities and Exchange Law.[12]

---

   [8] The Act Concerning Prohibition of Private Monopolisation and Maintenance of Fair Trade—
Shiteki dokusen no kinshi oyobi kosei torihiki no kakuho ni kansuru horitsu.

   [9] *Dokuritsu gyosei iinkai.*

   [10] Although this is one of the most important roles of the SESC, this chapter is primarily focused on investigations into listed companies in general and does not address this function in detail.

   [11] The criminal offences which the SESC has the power to investigate are provided for in the Financial Instruments and Exchange Law, the Law Concerning Foreign Securities Firms (*gaikoku shoken gyosha ni kansuru horitsu*), the Financial Futures Trading Law (*kin-yu sakimono torihiki ho*) and the Customer Identification Law (*kin-yu kikan to ni yoru kokyaku to no hon-nin kakunin to oyobi yokin koza to no fusei na riyo no boshi ni kansuru horitsu*).

   [12] *Shoken torihiki ho.* The Securities and Exchange Law was amended and renamed as the Financial Instruments and Exchange Law (*Kinyu shouhin torihiki ho*) as of 30 September 2007.

The SESC is supervised by the FS Agency, but its autonomy is highly respected. **11.12**

The government has been considering strengthening the capacity and functions of **11.13**
the SESC especially since the 'Livedoor scandal', in which executives of an IT
company were alleged to have made false statements in order to inflate the share price
of a group company and thereby violated the Securities and Exchange Law. This case
was handled primarily by the Special Investigation Departments of the District
Public Prosecutor's Offices (SIDs)[13] in Tokyo without significant involvement of the
SESC, which is supposed to be the primary watchdog and regulatory authority
regarding the securities market at least in the initial stages. The lack of the SESC's
involvement in dealing with this scandal triggered moves to improve the regulatory
framework, however no new changes have, as yet, been introduced.

The NTA

The NTA is responsible for the nationwide administration of taxation issues. **11.14**
This includes planning taxation policy; maintaining consistent interpretation of
tax related legislation; and supervising 12 Regional Taxation Bureaus (RTBs)[14] as
well as the 524 Tax Offices.[15] The NTA receives and screens tax returns submitted
by taxpayers via each local tax office.

The LSB

The LSB is part of the Ministry of Health, Labour and Welfare (MHLW)[16] and **11.15**
is responsible for ensuring: the compatibility of working conditions with the
requirements under the Labour Standards Law (LSL)[17] and the related regulations;
the improvement of working conditions; and workers' health and safety and
security. The LSB oversees 343 Labour Standards Inspection Offices (LSIOs)[18]
located throughout Japan.

The Police[19] and SIDs

The Police are primarily responsible for criminal investigations. Almost 99 per **11.16**
cent of criminal investigations are commenced and initiated by the Police,
however the public prosecutors are also empowered to initiate and complete

---

Given that this chapter includes a number of mentions of this law in connection with historical
events before the amendment in which context the old name is more relevant, the old name (the
Securities and Exchange Law) is used consistently throughout the main text to avoid any confusion.
However, where substance of this law is discussed, article numbers and contents are all based on the
new law (the Financial Instruments and Exchange Law).

13 *Chiho kensatsu-cho tokubetsu sosa-bu.*
14 *Kokuzei kyoku and Okinawa kokuzei jimusho.*
15 *Zeimu sho.*
16 *Kosei rodo sho.*
17 *Rodo kijun ho.*
18 *Rodo kijun kantokusho.*
19 *Keisatsu.*

investigations independently of the Police. Public prosecutors often utilize this investigatory authority in complicated economic cases such as bribery or large-scale financial crimes involving politicians, government officials, or executives of large corporate entities. The SIDs, which are departments within the District Public Prosecutor's Offices in Tokyo, Osaka, and Nagoya, are usually the primary sections which conduct investigations into such high profile economic cases. In particular, the SID in Tokyo has historically dealt with a number of investigations into headline news cases, such as the Lockheed Scandal in 1976.[20]

Other regulators

Ministry of Economy, Trade and Industry (METI)

11.17 The METI used to supervise formally and informally the broad range of business activities of the manufacturing and energy industries, but after a series of deregulation measures in these industries, its main focus has shifted to the synchronization of various social infrastructures. However, it continues to be the primary regulator for companies engaged in the energy related sectors such as electricity and gas as well as those engaged in cross-border trading. The METI has the power to inspect the relevant premises and issue business improvement orders and business suspension orders. If the undertakings do not duly observe such orders, the authority may ultimately cancel the relevant business licences.

Ministry of Internal Affairs and Communications (MIAC)

11.18 The MIAC was established in 2001 and succeeded the former Ministry of Home Affairs, the Ministry of Posts and Telecommunications and other related agencies. At present, it is in charge of general issues across administrative agencies, municipal governments, disaster prevention, telecommunication, and postal affairs. As a regulatory authority, the MIAC supervises, among other industries, the information and telecommunication industry, including broadcasting companies, telephone/telegraph companies, Internet providers etc. The MIAC has the power to inspect the relevant premises or issue business improvement orders and business suspension orders. If the undertakings do not duly observe such orders, the authority may ultimately cancel the relevant business licences.

Ministry of the Environment (MOE)

11.19 The MOE is in charge of various environmental issues including waste disposal, environmental pollution, conservation of the natural environment, and protection of wild animals. As a regulatory authority, it supervises the implementation of

---

[20] This was a bribery case involving a number of high-level government officials and politicians including the incumbent prime minister, who took bribes in return for facilitating the sales activities of a major US airplane manufacturer to Japanese airliners.

various cross-industry regulations such as regulations on waste disposal, noise/exhaust control, sewage, control of toxic chemicals etc. The MOE has the power to inspect the relevant premises or issue business improvement orders and business suspension orders. If the undertakings do not duly observe such orders, the authority may ultimately cancel the relevant business licences.

Self-regulatory organizations

The Tokyo Stock Exchange (TSE)[21] is one of the most important self-regulatory organizations for listed companies in Japan. The TSE requires all companies listed on the Exchange to comply with its rules concerning profitability, corporate governance, and disclosure of corporate information, and is empowered to expel any company that fails to do so. **11.20**

In order to ensure fair trading in the Exchange, the TSE investigates instances of unfair or illegal trading such as insider trading or market manipulation. If the TSE finds a violation of laws or regulations, it takes appropriate action to rectify such violations including reporting the company to the SESC or issuing cautions. However, the TSE is not empowered to inspect a listed company's premises or to seize documents. The TSE is supervised by the FS Agency. **11.21**

Concurrent investigations

Some of the regulators are empowered to conduct criminal investigations into violations of matters within their jurisdictions. However, only the SIDs are entitled to conduct a criminal prosecution, which is exclusively the right of the public prosecutors.[22] When an issue-specific regulator concludes, based on its investigations, that an entity has violated the laws and regulations of that regulator's jurisdiction, the regulator may call for a prosecution by filing a formal complaint with the public prosecutor's office. Upon filing such a complaint, all the evidence seized by the relevant regulator in the course of its criminal investigation[23] is handed over to the prosecutors.[24] **11.22**

Due to the unique structure of the Japanese government, which is vertically segmented based on different industries rather than types of issues, respective **11.23**

---

[21] *Tokyo Shoken torihiki sho.*

[22] The Criminal Procedures Law, Art 247.

[23] Evidence collected by the regulatory authority in the course of non-criminal procedures is not allowed to be transferred to the Police or public prosecutors in order to support a criminal prosecution regarding the same case. See, eg, Art 47, para 4 of the Anti-Monopoly Act. The prohibition of transfer of evidence from non-criminal procedures to criminal procedures is ultimately based on the requirement of due process under the Constitution.

[24] The Securities and Exchange Law, Art 226, para 1; the National Tax Violation Control Law, Art 18; the Anti-Monopoly Act, Arts 115 and 116; the LSL, Art 102; and the Criminal Procedures Law, Arts 190 and 246.

agencies are not quite coordinated with each other and as a result it is common for more than one government agency to investigate the same case simultaneously. When multiple agencies are involved in investigating the same matter concurrently, each agency investigates a different aspect of the case from the point of view of its own mandate. In the case of the derailment and crash of a commuter train in Hyogo Prefecture in April 2005, where over 100 people were killed, the MLIT[25] and the MHLW investigated the case independently of the Police. The MLIT inspected the train operator and instructed it to secure the safety of its train services to prevent a recurrence of similar fatal accidents. The MHLW also inspected the operator and other nationwide train operators and required them to take appropriate measures to prevent both physical and mental health problems in employees, which may have caused the Hyogo accident.

Relationships with overseas regulators

11.24 The JFTC is an active member of discussion meetings or workshops in the International Competition Network (ICN), which was established in October 2001 and is aimed at the international harmonization in the implementation of anti-trust legislation of each nation (both as regards procedure and substance).[26] It also has a number of bilateral agreements on anti-trust cooperation with the US, EU, and Canada, and enjoys close relationships with the competition authorities in these countries. This includes mutual reporting systems in respect of the implementation of the Agreements.

11.25 Under these bilateral agreements, the JFTC may request the permission of a counterpart nation to commence a regulatory investigation or other exercise of regulatory power in that nation's territory when anti-competitive activities inside the counterpart nation could have a significantly negative impact on the Japanese market; Japan would reciprocate accordingly.

11.26 The SESC maintains close ties with the securities surveillance authorities of other nations—opinions regarding surveillance of securities markets, implementation of related legislation, and inspections are frequently exchanged. The SESC has been active in cross-governmental interactions, based on various bilateral frameworks, with the US Securities and Exchange Commission (SEC), the US Commodity Futures Trading Commission (CFTC), the UK Financial Services Authority (FSA), the Monetary Authority of Singapore (MAS), and the Hong Kong Securities and Futures Commission (SFC), exchanging views and information on cases alleged to involve unfair trading or on the status of compliance of

---

25 *Kokudo kotsu sho.*
26 Competition authorities from 98 countries are registered as members of the ICN as of August 2006.

internationally active securities companies with relevant regulations. The SESC is also a vocal member of the International Organization of Securities Commissions (IOSCO)[27] (especially in the organization's attempt to set up international rules regarding securities surveillance).

Pursuant to these bilateral frameworks, the SESC may request the authority of **11.27** the counterparty nation to commence a regulatory investigation when unfair trading inside the counterparty nation could have a significantly negative impact on the Japanese market, and vice versa.

Both the Police and the Public Prosecutor's Office maintain close relationships **11.28** with counterpart authorities of other nations through participating in various international forums as well as cooperating in cross-border investigations. The bilateral treaties regarding international cooperation in criminal investigations provide a steady ground for international collaboration in criminal investigations including the sharing of critical evidence. Even without such treaties, the Police and the Public Prosecutor's Office proactively assist counterpart authorities of other nations, if requested, based on the conditions and procedures stipulated in the Act on International Cooperation in Criminal Investigations (Act No 69, 1980). The Act on International Cooperation in Criminal Investigations provides separate procedures for investigations initiated by other nations and those initiated by the International Criminal Police Organization (ICPO), but generally speaking the fundamental procedures are the same as domestic criminal procedures.

C. Powers of Regulators

Sources of investigations

The JFTC initiates investigations when it receives preliminary evidence of conduct **11.29** which is alleged to violate the Anti-Monopoly Act by way of either public reports,[28] its own detection activities,[29] or applications to the leniency programme. There is no public record of the JFTC's own detection methods. The number of investigations initiated by public reports has risen over the last several years (5,250 cases in FY 2006). Although the leniency programme is relatively new, introduced in January 2006, in the first year of its existence, 79 cases were filed.

---

[27] IOSCO is an international forum to promote cross-border harmonization in the regulation of securities and cooperation between regulatory authorities of different nations. As of July 2007, 189 government entities are registered as members of IOSCO.
[28] The Anti-Monopoly Act, Art 45, para 1.
[29] The Anti-Monopoly Act, Art 45, para 4.

11.30 It should be noted that regulators occasionally focus on specific industries or types of activity, as was seen recently in the series of investigations by the JFTC on bid-rigging.

11.31 The SESC conducts day-to-day monitoring of share price transition. When the price of a specific stock surges or plunges, the SESC conducts an investigation (through requesting detailed reports from securities companies) in order to identify the cause and clarify whether or not it was the result of misconduct. The SESC also obtains information from the public. According to the SESC, it received in total 7,526 reports from the public in FY 2005.[30]

11.32 The NTA examines tax returns submitted by individuals and corporate entities, in light of other information that it gathers independently. This includes information exchanged with foreign tax authorities, which is particularly useful in the context of cross-border transactions.[31] According to the NTA, the number of cases, annually, where the authority turned to such outside sources amounts to 158 million on average. Recently, the NTA has focused its investigatory efforts on electronic business transactions and the authority has placed expert investigation teams throughout the country.[32]

11.33 The LSB regularly targets specific industries and/or activities on which the authority should conduct focused investigations and for this purpose investigation plans are drawn up. Apart from inspections conducted based on such plans ('regular inspections'), the LSB conducts ad hoc inspections upon the receipt of information provided by the employees of an entity that is alleged to be involved in illegal activities.[33] In FY 2005, the LSB supervised approximately 41,000 entities following such notices from internal whistle-blowers, and the number of cases revealed by reports from insiders is increasing.

11.34 The TSE conducts market monitoring on a daily basis to detect abnormal or unusual trading, which might constitute insider trading or other violations, using advanced technology such as GENESIS (General Network for Securities Information System) and the Market Analysis & Scan System. It also gathers information via international networks[34] or notices from the public. Once the TSE identifies abnormal or unusual trading patterns, it interviews the trading participant for further information or requests the participant to submit reports.

---

[30] Source <http://www.fsa.go.jp/sesc/english/reports/re2005.pdf>.

[31] National Tax Agency Report 2005 <http://www.nta.go.jp/foreign_language/2005e.pdf>.

[32] *Nikkei*, 3 February 2006.

[33] The LSL, Art 104.

[34] The TSE has concluded a 'Market Surveillance Information Exchange Agreement' with several exchanges, including the New York Stock Exchange, the London International Financial Futures and Options Exchange, and the Hong Kong Exchange, and joined the Intermarket Surveillance Group.

Sometimes, if necessary, the TSE also contacts the issuer of the stocks involved in the alleged transaction. Due to its unique nature as a self-regulatory body, the TSE has no power to conduct a full inspection or investigation.

Levels of regulatory scrutiny

When the JFTC concludes, following an investigation, that a certain activity violates **11.35** the Anti-Monopoly Act, it issues an administrative order including an elimination order and/or a surcharge payment order. In addition, it may call for a prosecution by filing a formal complaint with a public prosecutor. Regarding certain types of violations of the Anti-Monopoly Act[35] ('hard-core violations'),[36] the JFTC has exclusive jurisdiction over the filing of criminal complaints to public prosecutors.

The SESC is empowered to investigate criminal offences relating to securities **11.36** trading. When the SESC concludes that a criminal violation of the Securities and Exchange Law or other regulations may have occurred, it will call for a criminal prosecution by filing a formal complaint with the public prosecutor.

Furthermore, since the beginning of 2005, the SESC has been entrusted with the **11.37** administrative power to investigate violations of the Securities and Exchange Law,[37] which includes the powers to issue administrative penalties and commence investigations against the alleged violator. The activities subject to administrative fines include:

- submission of false statements regarding disclosure documents including securities registration statements and annual securities reports;[38]
- spreading rumours etc with an intention to influence the market price of securities;[39]
- market manipulation;[40] and
- insider trading.[41]

Based on this capacity, the SESC conducts investigations regarding the companies in question and, where appropriate, makes recommendations to the FS Agency to impose a surcharge fine, in response to which the FS Agency decides whether a surcharge order should be issued.

---

[35] Violations of Arts 89 (prohibition of private monopolization and unfair trade restrictions), 90 (prohibition of international agreement including unfair trade restrictions etc), and 91 (prohibition of shareholding etc which restricts competition) of the Anti-Monopoly Act.
[36] The Anti-Monopoly Act, Art 96.
[37] The Financial Instruments and Exchange Law, Arts 177 and 194–6, para 2(7).
[38] The Financial Instruments and Exchange Law, Arts 172 and172-2.
[39] The Financial Instruments and Exchange Law, Arts 158 and 173.
[40] The Financial Instruments and Exchange Law, Arts 159 and 174.
[41] The Financial Instruments and Exchange Law, Arts 166, 167 and 175.

Investigation tools

11.38 The JFTC has the administrative power to request information and require related employees or officers of the alleged entity to be present for questioning, if necessary.[42] It is also empowered to scrutinize the activities of companies under suspicion by collecting and reviewing accounting books and related documents and by interrogating related employees or officers. If the JFTC confirms an allegation, the target companies are subject to administrative sanctions including elimination orders and surcharge payment orders.[43]

11.39 In addition, the JFTC was recently granted additional powers to take coercive measures when necessary to investigate criminal cases of hard-core violations.[44] The JFTC can undertake an investigation by appointing investigators to search the premises of companies under investigation (including conducting so-called 'dawn raids') and seize documents pursuant to a court-issued warrant. The JFTC may request reports, information, or data, inspect materials, and order individuals to appear for questioning.[45]

11.40 When the SESC suspects a criminal offence, it may question the party under investigation and/or related parties, inspect materials held by the party under investigation, and request the party or a third party to submit materials on a voluntary basis.[46] When necessary, the SESC may conduct investigations, pursuant to court-issued warrants, including searching the premises of corporations under suspicion and seizing relevant documents etc.[47]

11.41 In April 2005, the SESC was granted the administrative capacity to investigate offences under the Securities and Exchange Law, including false statements in securities reports, insider trading, and price manipulation. In order to investigate a case of false statements, the SESC can require a company to submit its account statements and any other documents that the SESC considers relevant.[48] These investigation powers extend to documents held by third parties. To investigate other violations, the SESC can search the premises of companies, inspect books and other materials, interrogate individuals having relevant knowledge,

---

[42] The Anti-Monopoly Act, Art 40.

[43] The Anti-Monopoly Act, Art 47.

[44] By way of amendments, in 2005, to the Anti-Monopoly Act, which are to be effective as of 4 January 2006.

[45] The Anti-Monopoly Act, Arts 101–03.

[46] The Financial Instruments and Exchange Law, Art 210, para 1.

[47] The Financial Instruments and Exchange Law, Art 211, para 1.

[48] The Financial Instruments and Exchange Law, Arts 26 and 194–6, para 3. The SESC can also request companies who have launched a tender offer or submitted a significant shareholder's report to submit its account statements and any other documents which the SESC regards appropriate in order to ensure the accuracy of such filing documents (the Financial Instruments and Exchange Law, Arts 27-22, 27–30, and 194–6, para 3).

and request such individuals to submit reports.[49] Based on the results of an administrative investigation, the SESC may, if necessary, send a recommendation to the FS Agency for administrative sanctions to be taken against the companies concerned.

The officials of the NTA, RTBs, and Tax Offices are empowered[50] to visit and conduct voluntary investigations in the offices of taxpayers[51] where they may check the taxpayer's books and other relevant documents and, where appropriate, conduct interviews. RTB officials are usually in charge of important investigations, eg large-scale cases, inter-prefectural, and/or difficult cases, whereas officials of the Tax Offices are in charge of other, relatively minor, cases. **11.42**

When conducting a voluntary tax examination, tax officials should notify the taxpayer in advance of the date of the examination to confirm the taxpayer's availability.[52] For the purpose of the examination, tax officials are empowered to question employees and inspect books and other materials.[53] If the officials find unreported income or inaccurate information in the company's tax return, they recommend that the company should amend accordingly and re-file the tax return. In this case, a tax for delinquency, additional tax for deficit, additional tax for no return, or heavy additional tax may be imposed. **11.43**

Aside from these administrative procedures, revenue officials are empowered to investigate tax crimes, by way of both voluntary investigations[54] and compulsory investigations carried out pursuant to judicial warrants from the court.[55] As a result of such investigations, the NTA may request public prosecutors to prosecute the individual or company for tax evasion. **11.44**

Generally speaking, no procedural requirements are imposed on administrative investigations except for the obligation for individual inspectors to present their identification.[56] Investigations of criminal offences, including searches on premises and seizure of evidence, require a judicial warrant, which must be presented before the search commences. Inspectors must ensure that the relevant employees of the company under investigation are present when executing such warrants.[57] **11.45**

---

[49] The Financial Instruments and Exchange Law, Arts 177 and 194–6, para 2(7).

[50] The Corporate Tax Law, Art 153.

[51] *Zeimu chousa*.

[52] Advance notice is given in approximately 90 per cent of corporation tax examinations. However, no advance notice is given when officials conduct examinations in order to confirm the actual state of the business itself.

[53] The Corporate Tax Law, Art 153.

[54] The National Tax Violation Control Law, Art 1.

[55] The National Tax Violation Control Law, Art 2.

[56] The Anti-Monopoly Act, Art 47, etc.

[57] The Anti-Monopoly Act, Arts 105, 106 and 109; the Financial Instruments and Exchange Law, Arts 213, 214 and 217; and the National Tax Violation Control Law, Arts 4 and 6.

11.46 Some regulators, including the JFTC and the SESC, have civil enforcement powers as well as the power to investigate criminal offences. However, it is strictly prohibited and contrary to due process of law for a regulator to investigate a criminal offence utilizing its administrative power or vice versa. For instance, the JFTC must not file a criminal complaint with the public prosecutor based on evidence collected in the course of an administrative investigation. To facilitate compliance with this requirement, regulators establish Chinese walls[58] between their criminal investigation and civil enforcement departments. These departments have different personnel and the direct exchange of investigation information is strictly prohibited. However, criminal investigation departments can transfer the results of their investigations (eg deposition and material evidence etc) to the public prosecutor when they file a complaint and the prosecutor is allowed to use such information, while the transfer of the results of an administrative investigation to prosecutors is strictly prohibited.

Extra-territorial jurisdiction

11.47 In general, the Japanese regulatory authorities do not have the jurisdiction to assert their authority, or to demand compliance with their investigations, overseas.

11.48 The Anti-Monopoly Act does not specify the extent of the JFTC's administrative investigation capacity regarding overseas entities. The JFTC has thus far kept a self-restrictive view in terms of direct search into overseas business offices and no detailed criteria has yet been defined in this respect, except that each case should be evaluated individually on the merits of its specific circumstances. However, the JFTC's official position is that the authority can conduct investigations in certain exceptional cases, including where the relevant information is collected via Japanese entities, or where the JFTC exchanges the necessary information with counterpart authorities of other nations.

11.49 In contrast, the SESC's position is that it does not have any authority to request or compel cooperation with its investigations extra-territorially, and that the only method of collecting relevant overseas information is by requesting it from the appropriate authorities of the country where such information is available. For example, in December 2006, the SESC passed the investigation of a violation to the Hong Kong Securities and Futures Commission, and the Hong Kong authority took final administrative measures against the offending entity, following collaborative investigations by both authorities.

---

[58] Barriers between different sections within the same organization to stop any information flow between two such sections.

Protections

Under the Criminal Procedures Law, anyone suspected of a criminal offence is **11.50** allowed to remain silent during questioning by the authority,[59] and when an attorney is commissioned to store, for safekeeping, certain evidence, the attorney is entitled to refuse to provide the evidence to the authority except with the consent of the suspect.[60] There are no provisions that specifically address a criminal investigation conducted by the JFTC or the SESC, but it is generally interpreted that these same rights are accorded to the parties involved.

These special rights of defence, including the right to remain silent during **11.51** questions or investigations, which are primarily designed for criminal procedures, are not available during administrative procedures taken by the regulatory authorities. When facing administrative investigations, the right to remain silent does not apply and refusal to answer the questions put by the authority may result in the imposition of sanctions.

It should be noted that the law grants no special protection to any locations **11.52** against investigations or searches by the authorities.

Sanctions for failure to cooperate

Companies are required to cooperate proactively with regulatory investigations. **11.53** A company that refuses to cooperate or interferes with a regulatory inquiry may be liable to criminal sanctions.

In general, cooperation by a party subject to an inquiry is not necessarily rewarded **11.54** with particularly favourable treatment by regulators, except when pursuant to the leniency programme introduced into the Anti-Monopoly Act in 2006.[61] On the contrary, where the law explicitly empowers regulators to conduct administrative investigations to detect administrative offences committed by companies, failure to comply with the requirements of the inspection will constitute a criminal offence.

For example, any person who deliberately fails to appear for questioning when **11.55** summoned by the JFTC or makes a false statement during questioning will be

---

[59] The Constitution, Art 38, para 1.
[60] The Criminal Procedures Law, Art 105.
[61] Under the leniency programme, the first company to report itself as being involved in certain activities, including cartels or bid-rigging, in violation of the Anti-Monopoly Act will receive full immunity from any administrative fines, and will also be saved from criminal sanctions, according to a public statement the JFTC. The second and third companies to admit to the same offence will receive, respectively, a 50 per cent and 30 per cent immunity from the applicable administrative fines; and in respect of these latter companies, the JFTC retains the discretion to file a criminal complaint, which it exercises on a case-by-case basis.

subject to imprisonment for up to one year or a fine of up to JPY3m.[62] Any person who contravenes an order by the SESC to submit a report or makes a false report will be subject to imprisonment for up to six months and/or a fine of up to JPY500,000.[63]

11.56 Sometimes, however, regulators conduct surveillances that are not related to suspected violations or crimes. In such cases there are no obligations on companies to cooperate. It should be noted, however, that an uncooperative attitude might create a negative impression with the regulator involved, suggesting that the company is trying to hide a wrongdoing, which could result in unfavourable treatment by the regulator.

D. Voluntary Investigations

Risks and benefits of voluntary investigations

11.57 In the past, Japan's regulatory and criminal investigation authorities rarely either expected or appreciated formal internal investigations. In regulated industries, it was customary for regulators to request that companies experiencing problems look into the causes of the problems and submit reports to help the regulators determine how to proceed, but this procedure fell short of a fully-fledged internal investigation in the sense in which it is now understood. In recent years, however, following a series of scandals involving financial institutions,[64] financial regulators have begun to insist more firmly that institutions come forward with problems when they discover them, and companies making such reports to the regulators tend naturally to follow up with internal investigations.

11.58 In addition to increased demands from regulators, companies are beginning to come under increased social pressure to conduct internal investigations and publicly report the results. These trends, however, are not yet reflected in Japanese law. The general rule remains that while regulators may request the cooperation of the companies they are investigating, they will conduct the investigations themselves. Criminal investigation authorities, moreover, generally do not permit companies any access to seized evidence once they begin an investigation, often making it impossible, as a practical matter, for the company to carry out an effective internal investigation.

---

[62] The Anti-Monopoly Act, Art 94, item 1.

[63] The Financial Instruments and Exchange Law, Art 205, item 5.

[64] In 1997, Yamaichi Securities announced the closure of its business after a series of *Sokaiya* scandals and accounting frauds. The company completed a detailed internal investigation report, thereafter. In 2007, Nikko Cordial disclosed various accounting problems and an independent internal investigation team completed a report.

In general, Japanese regulators do not expect internal investigations to serve as a **11.59** source of information for the regulators. As discussed above, internal investigations are not generally required or standardized by law in Japan, and regulators ordinarily conduct their own independent investigations, including criminal investigations. In regulated industries, however, when regulators direct companies to conduct investigations and submit reports, regulators may use the results as a source of information. The Basic Financial Inspection Guidelines of the FS Agency, for example, provide that FS Agency officers conducting an inspection should as a general rule use data furnished by financial institutions.[65] When there are risks that, for example, the institution has attempted to delay inspections or committed violations of law, however, this general rule does not apply.

It is, however, common for a company facing a regulatory investigation, or com-   **11.60** ing across a problem, to conduct its own investigation for the purpose of looking into the facts and explaining them to its shareholders and the public, strategizing its defence, or implementing improvement measures.

Events triggering considering conducting a voluntary investigation

New developments in various areas of Japanese law have created situations that   **11.61** provide companies with an incentive to conduct internal investigations to iden-tify possible violations of law. The Anti-Monopoly Act leniency programme, for example, may have the effect of increasing the number of internal investigations conducted, even though the purpose of the programme is to encourage reporting rather than internal investigations. In 2006, the JFTC had received more than 30 self-initiated reports admitting violations and seeking leniency.

Another new piece of legislation that can be expected to promote internal inves-   **11.62** tigations is the Whistleblower Protection Law, which was enacted in 2004 and became effective on 1 April 2006. Under the new law and its guidelines, a com-pany that receives a report of an alleged impropriety from a whistle-blower is expected to investigate the matters described in the report and promptly report to the whistle-blower with respect to the results of the investigation and the neces-sity for corrective measures.[66] Since this legislation was introduced, companies are becoming more adept at handling reports of alleged impropriety.

The Deposit Insurance Law requires the management of a bank to conduct   **11.63** investigations into the suitability of instituting civil proceedings or bringing criminal charges against present or former directors and auditors in situations

---

[65] Basic Financial Inspection Guidelines, II 3-1(3) and II 3-2(4).
[66] Whistleblower Protection Act, Art 9.

where 'violations of their professional obligations'[67] have been discovered. Consequently, some financial institutions have established internal investigation committees that report to the directors and corporate auditors.

11.64 Recently, a trend has emerged that when a scandal has come to light at one company, other companies within the same industry have been requested to conduct voluntary internal inspections, in some cases, by supervisory authorities.

11.65 Media reports also serve as another trigger to conducting internal investigations. When irregularities are reported in the media, the company should quickly respond to the allegations.

11.66 Many Japanese companies undertake regular auditing or inspecting procedures. The Corporate Code requires a company's management to establish an effective internal control system, which should include internal investigation procedures.

11.67 Developments such as these, which encourage companies to conduct internal investigations in order to comply with specific laws or regulations, have increased in recent years in Japan, and it is likely that this tendency will continue to grow in the future.

Structuring an internal investigation

Using external advisers

11.68 Japanese law does not establish any rules as to who in a company has the authority to hire outside counsel to conduct an internal investigation. In the past, it was usual for internal investigations to be carried out by an internal investigation team composed of the company's officers and employees joined, in some cases, by the company's regular outside counsel.[68] Recently, however, in the wake of incidents involving large sums of money and having significant social impact, companies are increasingly inviting independent outside experts, including lawyers and accountants, to participate in their internal investigation teams in order to present the appearance of impartiality to the public.[69] Companies are also in some cases hiring teams of outside experts to conduct independent investigations. In circumstances where there is a concern that violations of law may have occurred, these outside experts are often lawyers. Companies seeking help with an investigation often hire lawyers with whom they have had a long association, but, recently, there have been cases in which companies have hired lawyers with whom they have had no prior connection.

---

[67] Deposit Insurance Law, Art 116.

[68] Due to the relative scarcity of lawyers in Japan and cost considerations, Japanese companies rarely employ lawyers in-house, preferring instead to keep outside counsel on retainer.

[69] SMBC retained outside counsel to conduct an internal investigation upon the JFTC's accusation of SMBC's violation of the Anti-Monopoly Act; and Nikko Cordial retained a former head of the FS Agency to conduct an internal investigation for recent account fraud case.

The company's legal department and internal auditors, as well as the company's regular outside counsel, may be involved in the selection of outside counsel.

There are no clear criteria for hiring outside counsel. Few Japanese companies **11.69** have established board committees; it is most often the board of directors or top-level management who make the decision whether to hire outside counsel. The seriousness and social significance of the matter to be investigated will affect the decision, but the determination will ultimately depend on the judgment of the company's top-level management.

There are no clear criteria for independence and, as noted above, it is only in **11.70** recent years that companies have begun to seek independent counsel. Where a company makes the decision to engage independent outside counsel, the company will wish to present an appearance of impartiality to the general public, and will also take the seriousness and social impact of the matter under investigation into account in making a decision. A firm may be selected because its lawyers have performed well in the past on similar investigations or simply because it is large enough to manage the investigation. In serious matters, legal luminaries such as retired Supreme Court justices and prosecutors, as well as socially prominent figures such as well-known economists, are often selected to chair investigation committees. Companies may also seek recommendations from the Japan Federation of Bar Associations or the Japanese Institute of Certified Public Accountants when selecting independent legal and accounting experts.

Managing illegal activity during investigations

There are no specific rules relating to whether potentially illegal conduct should **11.71** be allowed to continue pending the results of an internal investigation. However, if a violation of law has occurred, the company bears the risk associated with the ongoing conduct, and conduct that continues after an investigation is launched may be more easily characterized as wilful.

E. Self-reporting

Duty to self-report

There is no general law in Japan obliging companies to self-report regulatory vio- **11.72** lations. However, individual laws, such as the Securities and Exchange Law, contain specific requirements to report certain violations.[70]

---

[70] The Financial Instruments and Exchange Law, Art 50, para 1(8); Cabinet Ordinance regarding the Financial Instruments and Trade Business etc, Art 200 para 1(6), requires a securities company to report to the FS Agency when it becomes aware that its employees or officers have breached laws or regulations.

Culture of self-reporting

11.73 There is a culture of self-reporting in Japan if a violation of the law or an accident is likely to have a serious impact on people's lives or interests. For example, quite a few companies, such as NTT Data, Yahoo BB, and Sakura Bank, have disclosed that confidential information has been leaked before they have confirmed whether the leak constituted a violation of law.[71]

F. Announcements and Public Relations Strategies

Regulatory investigations

External communications

11.74 There is no statutory obligation for a company to publicly disclose relevant facts when a regulatory authority investigates. However, it is common practice for a company to make a voluntary public announcement disclosing the results of an investigation, if the investigating authority discovers a breach and imposes certain punitive measures against the company. Listed companies are also subject to the TSE's rules on timely disclosure and must officially announce an investigation or its results within a 'timely' period if it falls into the category of certain important matters that have a significant influence on investors.[72] It is also recommended that a company prepares an overview of any investigation and related facts in case questions are made in this regard by shareholders in a shareholders' meeting following the close of the investigation.

Internal communications

11.75 When a regulatory authority investigates a company, the relevant employees should be properly informed and be requested to cooperate with the regulators. Appropriate measures should be taken to prevent employees from destroying relevant information or hiding it from the regulators. Document destruction may amount to a breach of document retention rules or an offence of obstructing regulatory investigations.

---

[71] A company that uses a personal information database for business is required to adopt measures necessary and appropriate for preventing the unauthorized disclosure, loss, or destruction of personal data (the Personal Data Protection Law (*kojin joho no hogo ni kansuru horitsu*) Art 20). If a company is determined to have failed to do so, a competent minister may recommend that the company take appropriate steps to correct the breach (Art 34).

[72] Rules on the Timely Disclosure of Corporate Information by an Issuer of Listed Securities and the like, Art 2.

Internal investigations

External communications

It is common that a premature report by the media regarding a corporate **11.76** scandal triggers a voluntary internal investigation by the company. For instance, in January 2007, the media disclosed the scandal of a major confectionary manufacturer who had been using expired ingredients, and, subsequently, the manufacturer itself conducted an internal investigation in addition to the investigation performed by the regulatory authority (the MAFF). There are no statutory obligations for a company who has conducted internal investigations to disclose the result of such investigations, but as a normal practice the company concerned would hold a press conference to disclose the related facts, considering the negative reputation and the level of concern that would likely have developed in the course of aggressive media reports.

Listed companies are also subject to the TSE's rules on timely disclosure and must **11.77** officially announce an investigation or its results within a 'timely' period if it falls into the category of certain important matters that have a significant influence on investors. If an announcement is to be made, the timing of the announcement must be considered. The disclosure of important matters during trading hours may lead to a suspension of trading; if possible, therefore, announcements should be made outside trading hours. The announcement must be made through the TSE system. Since most Japanese reporters belong to a press club for each industry, it is common for a company to announce any press release through the relevant press club. Companies should manage the situation by arranging timely press conferences at press clubs and the like.

Internal communications

Employees should be made aware of an internal investigation, at the latest when **11.78** the company announces publicly either the discovery of a problem or the commencement of an internal investigation. Appropriate disclosure of the same information to employees through a communication channel such as a company newsletter may help to quell internal unrest and prevent the spread of rumours and false information.

Prior to any general announcement, any employee involved in the investigation **11.79** should be bound to confidentiality and only a limited number of people should be involved on the investigation team. Even if these steps are taken, however, a significant risk of rumours and information leakage remains, creating a potentially unstable situation. In Japan, board meetings are not always an opportunity for managers to engage in meaningful discussions but often serve only as a gathering of high-ranking employees, including the president and CEO. Although Japanese boards have been shrinking in recent years, it is still not uncommon for there to be as many as 30 to 40 directors on the board of a Japanese company. In such cases, directors may pose the same level of risk as ordinary employees in terms of information leakage. Companies must balance the need to limit the dissemination of sensitive information with the need to maintain compliance with the principles embodied in the Corporate Law involving the duties of the board of directors.[73]

Key points for Public Relations strategies

11.80 When there has been a scandal, the basic PR strategy is not to hide anything or lie but rather to emphasize the sincerity with which the matter is being handled in order to recover public confidence. If a company is being investigated by regulatory authorities, information that might interfere with the investigation should not be disclosed to the public. Regulatory authorities will also disapprove of publicity when a confidential investigation is being carried out.

11.81 When an investigation must be disclosed, the announcement should be limited to the fact that the company is cooperating fully with the authorities. The details of the investigation should be kept confidential, while the authorities are still carrying out their duties. If the matter at issue does become public knowledge, it then becomes necessary to periodically disclose that investigations are being conducted; interim reports, however, should be avoided as they are likely to include inaccuracies.

11.82 The PR strategy should focus on recovering public confidence in the company by making it clear that the company is cooperating fully with the investigation and that it is also conducting a fair, objective, and thorough internal investigation to determine the cause of the incident and prevent reoccurrences. As part of its PR strategy, the company must distinguish the initial problem and how the company handled the problem after it was discovered. Through the conduct of its internal investigation, the company should seek to identify those who should be held responsible.

11.83 The media tends to ask persistently about the progress of internal investigations and when they will be completed. Management should refuse to make half-hearted announcements and instead wait to disclose matters fully when the investigation is complete. Only executive officers should deal with the media. It is important for a company to have its top executive well prepared. Recently, some companies have had their executive take media training.

---

[73] The Corporate Law, Arts 362(2), 362(4) and 363(2).

Japanese companies usually have PR departments that deal with advertising, but **11.84** often do not have departments capable of constructing PR strategies in response to crises. Outside specialists, therefore, should be retained at an early stage to help formulate a media strategy. However, there are only a few specialists and lawyers who have actually managed strategic media relations. It is often difficult to find good specialists and lawyers who can take control of the situation.

G. Dealing with Privileged Documents

General rules on privilege

The Criminal Procedures Law contains the following provision: **11.85**

> A doctor, dentist, midwife, nurse, lawyer (including a registered foreign lawyer), patent agent, notary public, religious functionary, or any person who is or was in these positions may refuse to give testimony of such facts as have come into his knowledge in the course of his business because of the relationship of trust and as have related to the secrets of another person; provided, that this shall not apply if the individual has consented to the disclosure, if the refusal to testify is deemed to constitute the abuse of a right intended only for the accused (excluding cases where the accused is the individual who disclosed the information), or if there exist such causes as specified by the rules of the courts.[74]

In addition, the Civil Procedures Law contains provisions permitting a witness, **11.86** who is or was a doctor, dentist, pharmacist, mid-wife, lawyer (including a registered foreign lawyer), patent agent, advocate, notary, or an occupant of a post connected with religion, prayer, or worship, to refuse to testify in cases where they are questioned as to the knowledge of facts which they have obtained in the exercise of their professional duties and which should remain secret. These provisions do not apply to cases where the witness has been released from the duty of secrecy.[75]

In Japanese civil procedure, there is no general requirement concerning the pro- **11.87** duction of documents. However, there are certain limited and specific circumstances in which a party to a civil procedure or a third party may be required to submit specific documents that are deemed related to the case. In such circumstances, the court or the requesting party must specify and give a general description of the required documents, identify who has the documents, and demonstrate that production is necessary for the purpose of obtaining evidence. If the documents are attorney-client communications, the party seeking production will generally find it difficult to specify the content. Even if he or she is able to do so,

---

[74] The Criminal Procedures Law, Art 149.
[75] The Civil Procedures Law, Art 197.

the recipient of the request may refuse to submit internal documents or documents created solely for personal use. The question as to whether internal investigation reports are internal documents or documents created solely for personal use remains unsettled.

11.88 The Practicing Attorney Law permits attorneys to ask their bar association to request evidence from public offices or public or private organizations for the purpose of document production.[76] This procedure is often used to acquire evidence from third parties independently of the court, but the third parties may refuse production without penalty for reasons of privacy or privilege.

11.89 Under the Criminal Procedures Law, lawyers have rights in addition to the right to refuse to testify. Under Article 105:

> A doctor, dentist, midwife, nurse, lawyer (including a registered foreign lawyer), patent agent/attorney, notary public, religious functionary, or any person who was in these positions may refuse the impoundage of such articles as are kept or held by entrustment made in the course of his business and as related to the secrets of another person.[77]

11.90 In addition, criminal investigation authorities are unlikely to conduct a compulsory criminal investigation of a lawyer's office to gather evidence as long as the lawyer is not directly involved in the alleged illegal conduct.

11.91 However, a company's records of communications with its lawyers, legal memoranda, and internal investigation reports created by or with the participation of lawyers are not within the scope of protection. In criminal proceedings, the public prosecutor generally first requests that the defendant produce documents voluntarily. If the documents are not submitted voluntarily, they will be seized pursuant to a search warrant. Therefore, a company must carefully control records of communications with its lawyers. An argument can be made that companies have the right under Article 38 of the Constitution to refuse to submit evidence of their own guilt, but, in practice, refusal is all but impossible.

11.92 Furthermore, under the Criminal Procedures Law, if the court finds it necessary, it can order defendants and third parties to produce documents.[78] Before making such an order, the court will consider the severity of the offence, the value of the evidence, the interests of justice, and other factors it considers relevant. If the order is not complied with, the court has the authority to directly search for and seize the documents, but this is extremely rare in reality.

---

[76] Practicing Attorney Law, Art 23, para 2.
[77] The Criminal Procedures Law, Art 105.
[78] The Criminal Procedures Law, Art 99.

Under the Civil Procedures Law, one category of documents that the holder may **11.93** refuse to produce is that of documents containing official secrets and held by public officials that, if produced, are likely to harm the public interest or significantly hinder the performance of public duties.[79] To determine whether a document falls within this category, the court must ask for the opinion of the relevant governing authority. If the authority presents an opinion that production of the document is likely to impair national safety, the prevention or prosecution of crime, or the maintenance of public safety, the court may not order the holder to produce the document unless the court finds the opinion insufficient.[80] Another category of documents that the holder may refuse to produce in litigation is that of documents related to or seized for a criminal case.

As can be seen from the above, Japanese law does not provide substantive client- **11.94** attorney privilege as available in other jurisdictions. Information held by lawyers is, however, protected in recognition of the confidentiality obligations imposed upon lawyers. Consequently, information kept by lawyers is generally protected against regulatory and administrative investigations. However, it is important to remember that legal advice held by clients is generally not protected.

Waiving privilege

The Civil Procedures Law provides that when a party to litigation is in possession **11.95** of a document referred to by that party in the course of the litigation, the party may not refuse to produce it.[81] Consequently, if a company brings a suit for damages against a third party based on an internal investigation report, the company cannot refuse to produce that document. However, if the company has not disclosed the existence of such internal investigation report, the opposing party may not specify the documents.[82]

In civil litigation, discovery procedures are extremely limited and the party **11.96** requesting discovery must specify the desired items of evidence in as much detail as possible.[83] Accordingly, to the extent that documents and information disclosed to regulatory authorities cannot be specified, they naturally do not become evidence in a civil suit. In addition, government authorities in some cases refuse to disclose the information they have received relying on public officials' duty of confidentiality. However, in some recent court cases, government authorities have been forced to disclose information which was obtained in the course of a regulatory investigation.

---

[79] The Civil Procedures Law, Art 220, item 4(Ro).
[80] The Civil Procedures Law, Art 223, para 4.
[81] The Civil Procedure Law, Art 220, para 1.
[82] See 11.87, above.
[83] The Civil Procedures Law, Arts 219, 221(1) and 232.

Limited waiver

11.97   As there is no system of discovery in Japan, an order to provide evidence cannot be issued unless the desired evidence can be specified. Furthermore, authorities may refuse to disclose documents to outside parties on grounds of confidentiality. However, following the recent introduction of the system for requesting disclosure of information, there have been cases in which courts have ordered authorities to disclose documents they had in their possession following the authorities' refusal to make disclosure on request. Third parties may thus have a reasonable chance of obtaining documents submitted to authorities and it is therefore becoming more difficult to disclose information to authorities without also risking having to disclose it to third parties. There have also been cases in which, following partial disclosure of a document, the courts have required the remainder to be disclosed. In addition, if a document has been partially disclosed, the requesting party is able to specify the document and ask the court to issue an order to submit the remainder as evidence.

Privilege pitfalls

11.98   In Japan, privilege exists not to protect communications between lawyers and clients but to protect lawyers' duties of confidentiality. Consequently, communications with lawyers employed by a client are not always protected and issues regarding the handling of such client documents may arise. Communications between lawyers and clients may also be the target of a document request if they are in clients' hands. Furthermore, information contained in documents obtained by Japanese investigative or administrative authorities may be exchanged in accordance with agreements with foreign governments. As a result, the protection of communications subject to attorney-client privilege under foreign laws may be undermined, because Japanese authorities may exchange such communications, obtained from the client, pursuant to such agreements.

H. Managing Regulators

Dialogue with regulators

11.99   When, in the process of investigating a company, a regulatory authority's officials enter the company's property for the purpose of conducting a search, an important measure that the company should take is to ask the officials to prove their status and qualification and to confirm the type of procedures that will be followed (eg criminal or administrative). The company is also recommended to take legal advice immediately and to record the officials' questions and any responses given. When the officials request the company to submit documents, only copies of the documents should be handed to the officials—the originals must be kept by the company, unless the requests are based on a court-issued warrant for seizure.

The SESC's 'Basic Guidelines for Securities Inspection', which apply to its **11.100** securities inspections (not investigations into criminal or administrative offences), provide that, when conducting an investigation over an infringement of securities regulations, there should be sufficient discussions between inspectors and the party under investigation as to the factual findings of any inspections. Following the inspections and said discussions, the inspectors will hold a review session to orally communicate to the investigated party the key information developed as a result of the investigation, including factual findings and the clarification of any disagreements between the inspectors and the investigated party as to these, as well as the legal evaluation of the case. In response to this review session, the investigated party may submit an opinion in respect of the investigation to the SESC.

Throughout the securities inspection process, it is important to keep an amicable **11.101** relationship with the SESC, but, at the same time, it is critical to input into the investigation by submitting opinions. One aspect of the investigation the investigated party is likely to find difficult is that the review session takes place orally. A multinational company that requires multilingual translation of the content of the review session often has to produce a transcript and translate it within a very limited space of time, which is clearly not easy.

Control of scope of investigation

In respect of criminal procedures or regulatory investigations leading to criminal **11.102** penalties, it is recommended that the company under investigation confirms that the relevant officials are in possession of the appropriate warrants and reviews and examines the contents of such warrants. In particular, a company should make sure that nothing outside the scope of the search, as stated in the warrant, is searched or seized. That said, the scope of search warrants tends to be broadly defined and identifying such deviation is not always easy.

In the case of administrative investigations, the company under investigation **11.103** should confirm that the scope of any proposed search is confined to what is necessary and is proportionate, and, if necessary, it should enter into negotiations with the relevant authority to so limit the search.

Use of information by regulators

Provided that the regulator in question is appropriately empowered to conduct **11.104** either administrative or criminal investigations and information is collected by due process of law, there are no limitations on how such information may be used, except that there is a strict restriction regarding the exchange of evidence or information obtained by way of a criminal investigation with the civil enforcement authorities.

11.105 However, regulators are only allowed to obtain and use personal information in the course of investigations to the extent necessary for the purpose of pursuing the civil or criminal investigation.[84]

Managing multiple regulators

11.106 In Japan, the different regulatory agencies do not necessarily cooperate with each other when exercising their respective regulatory authority. Each regulation has different legislative purposes, and measures taken by the authorities based on regulatory rules can vary in purpose and coverage, depending on which regulatory law and regulations are the basis for such measures. As a result, when certain activities by a company breach more than one regulatory restriction, each authority with responsibility for one or more of the breached regulations conducts a separate investigation with its own outcomes.

11.107 However, when the SESC, JFTC, or NTA conducts a criminal investigation, the investigation is usually a prelude to a call for a prosecution by a public prosecutor. Therefore, in order to proceed more smoothly, where they are conducting overlapping investigations in respect of the same matter, those regulatory authorities sometimes collaborate or act together with the Public Prosecutor's Office from an early stage in the investigations.

I. Best Practices in Document Gathering and Preservation

Expectations of regulators and courts

11.108 Irrespective of whether any regulatory, criminal, or internal investigation is underway, certain types of documents must by law be preserved for a specified period. For example, the Corporate Law requires companies to preserve commercial books and important materials relating to their business for ten years;[85] income tax regulations and the Company Tax Law Enforcement Regulations require companies to preserve records for seven years;[86] and the LSL requires companies to preserve documents related to human resources for three years.[87]

---

[84] The Law Concerning Protection of Personal Information Held by Governmental Agencies (*gyosei kikan no hoyu suru kojin joho no hogo ni kansuru horitsu*), Arts 3 and 8.

[85] Corporate Law, Art 432, para 2.

[86] Income Tax Law Enforcement Regulation, Art 102(4); and Company Tax Law Enforcement Regulation, Art 67(2).

[87] LSL, Art 109.

Many companies have established rules for preserving documents according to type to meet these legal requirements. In accordance with these rules, companies usually store the relevant documents in off-site warehouses and in many cases they are kept for far longer than the specified period. Destroying documents within the specified retention period may be held unlawful and punished by the applicable law.

There are, however, no legal requirements requiring companies to suspend the **11.109** day-to-day disposal of documents in particular circumstances. In practice, it is recommended that, if a problem is suspected, the company immediately suspends the disposal of documents and email messages that may relate to the problem and preserves the current status of documents. If a criminal investigation later ensues, disposal of documents at a time when the company was aware of the problem may expose the company to criminal charges relating to the destruction of evidence. A company that disposes of documents may be charged with evading inspection, if a regulatory investigation or inspection follows. Recently, a Japanese financial institution that was found to have destroyed internal documents just before an FS Agency inspection became the subject of a regulatory action for evading inspection.[88]

Rights of documents and confidentiality

The extent of regulators' or the company's ability to secure paper and electronic **11.110** documents from employees differs according to whether the investigation is regulatory or criminal.

Essentially, a regulatory investigation[89] consists of a regulator collecting informa- **11.111** tion required to achieve a regulatory objective. Regulatory investigations are divided into two types—pure voluntary investigations and voluntary investigations with sanctions—according to the degree to which regulators can compel document disclosure and utilize specific investigation methods under individual laws. Both types of regulatory investigation rely upon the voluntary cooperation of the subject. Voluntary investigations with sanctions, however, may result in criminal consequences if the subject refuses to cooperate, although regulators cannot conduct the investigation by force if the subject continues

---

[88] On 7 October 2004, the FS Agency ordered UFJ Bank to suspend part of its business operations and filed a criminal complaint on charges of evading inspection. Details of the regulatory action taken against UFJ Bank are available on the FS Agency's website at <http://www.fsa.go.jp/news/newse/e20041007-1.html> and were published in the newspaper, *Nihon Keizai Shimbun*, on 8 October 2004.

[89] *Gyosei chosa.*

to refuse.[90] Pure voluntary investigations, on the other hand, are based on the genuinely voluntary cooperation of the subject, who may freely refuse to cooperate without thereby becoming liable to a prescribed sanction.

11.112 During a regulatory investigation, regulators may request a report on specified matters and impose penalties for failing to respond to the request or submitting false reports.[91] Regulators may, after entry upon land, examine documents, the company's books, and other items and inspect facilities and the condition of property.[92] Regulators only have the authority to inspect; they are not permitted to confiscate items or take copies based on this authority. In some cases, regulators may take samples of certain things for the purpose of inspections.[93] Sampling is limited to the extent necessary to conduct the inspection. The company is typically not compensated for any samples taken, and sampled items are usually not returned. In regulated industries, the company may not resist such requests although this is not a compulsory process.

11.113 Criminal investigations[94] are governed by separate, specific legislation. The JFTC, NTA, and SESC (amongst others) are permitted to conduct criminal investigations.[95] Criminal investigations always carry the threat of possible criminal indictment. Actions such as on-the-spot inspections, search, and, seizure may be carried out with the leave of the court. For example, a criminal investigation pursuant to the National Tax Violations Control Law or the Immigration Control and Refugee Recognition Act may involve on-the-spot inspection, search, and seizure. The FS Agency has entrusted the Chair of the Ministry of Finance Kanto Local Finance Bureau with the administrative authority to order the submission of reports or materials from companies that issue securities and to conduct on-site inspections. The SESC also has authority to conduct criminal investigations of legal offences.[96]

11.114 The April 2005 amendments to the Anti-Monopoly Act authorize the JFTC to conduct compulsory criminal investigations. This amendment was enacted in response to criticism that, with authority to conduct only regulatory investigations, the JFTC could not adequately respond to violations, even in recommendation decisions, and could not obtain evidence without filing a criminal claim

---

[90] Among others, the Income Tax Law, Art 242, para 8; and the Water Pollution Control Law, Art 33, para 4.

[91] Medical Service Law, Art 69; and the Religious Company Law, Art 78-2.

[92] Electricity Utility Law, Art 107; and Fire Service Law, Art 4.

[93] Food Sanitation Law, Art 17, para 1; and Waste Disposal and Public Cleansing Law, Art 19, para 2.

[94] *Hansoku chosa.*

[95] The Anti-Monopoly Act, Arts 101–10; the Financial Instruments and Exchange Law, Arts 210 and 211; and the National Tax Violation Control Law, Arts 1 and 2.

[96] Financial Instruments and Exchange Law, Arts 26, 27-22, 27-30, 210, and 211.

with the Public Prosecutor's Office. Following the 2005 amendments, the JFTC now has the authority to conduct both regulatory and criminal investigations.[97]

In the past, regulators were generally not cooperative when it came to disclosing information. However, following the recent law on information disclosure, courts have ordered disclosure of documents even when the authorities involved had refused. The company may seek court protection of trade secrets. **11.115**

A company's ability to obtain paper and electronic documents from employees will depend upon the rules that most companies have in place covering the preservation of documents. Documents and emails relating to the business of the company are the property of the company and are deemed to be under its control. Office regulations and internal rules relating to email use often limit private email and private storage in desks, drawers, and lockers. Accordingly, companies may demand that employees turn over documents and emails upon the instruction of a supervisor. If the employee refuses, companies sometimes obtain documents and emails without the employee's consent. In some cases, companies explicitly permit, by internal rules and guidelines, supervisors to examine emails written on company computers. Even if there are no such internal guidelines, the company generally has master keys to the office equipment, and in many cases will conduct investigations without the employee's consent. **11.116**

Data protection

Office rules often prohibit employees from taking home materials relating to work and may permit the company to order employees to turn over any such materials. In particular, the recent amendment to the Anti-Monopoly Act[98] prohibits employees and former employees from taking trade secrets outside the company. **11.117**

Any items located inside the workplace, including personal belongings kept inside an employee's desk drawers, would be subject to inspection by the company. In such cases, the company will first ask for the consent of the individual, but even if the employee declines, the company may generally conduct an inspection at its discretion. However, when materials are located outside the workplace, the company has no authority to compel the employee to produce them. It can only use the office rules and a threat of disciplinary action against them as leverage to persuade the employee to submit the materials voluntarily. **11.118**

There are no clear criteria governing the review of private materials located in company housing or company dormitories, which are common in Japan. **11.119**

---

[97] The Anti-Monopoly Act, Art 46, and 101–03.
[98] Art 21(1)–(4).

Companies may have rules relating to the management and maintenance of company housing or company dormitories, but even where such rules permit the company to enter a residence in the resident's absence, the company is expected to do so in the presence of the building manager. Even in such circumstances, however, the company's inspection of desks, drawers, and the like in company housing would raise concerns from the standpoint of protecting privacy and would require the consent of the resident. Materials left in plain view, on the other hand, may be taken by the company if they are corporate documents covered by the prohibition on removing materials from the office.

11.120   The Law Concerning Protection of Personal Information prohibits companies from disclosing an individual's personal information to third parties without obtaining the individual's consent.

Practical considerations

11.121   Although many Japanese companies have official document retention policies, in reality, few companies systematically dispose of documents. Within many companies employee job descriptions are not defined clearly and decision making functions on a collective basis, therefore information may be dispersed widely and documents may be disorganized or over-broad in scope. Nevertheless, documents that may become relevant to an internal investigation should be secured immediately and transferred promptly to the internal investigation team.

11.122   Related departments within the company must cooperate in order to complete the necessary tasks, and outside counsel should be retained in order to ensure objectivity. The company should review its document retention policies and organize documents in its custody. It is also important for the company to require its employees to dispose of documents in accordance with company policy.

J. Managing Employees During Investigations

Powers to compel cooperation

11.123   Most Japanese companies have detailed corporate work rules, typically incorporating a code of conduct stipulating that employees must follow the instructions of their supervisors. In addition, the company itself and supervisors have the general authority to instruct, supervise, and direct employees within the scope of their employment.

11.124   When a company conducts an internal investigation, employees are expected to cooperate with the investigation as part of their day-to-day responsibilities. In the event of an investigation, employees should be instructed in writing or orally by their supervisors to cooperate fully with the investigation team. If employees fail to cooperate, they may be subject to disciplinary action. Employees may initially resist cooperating for fear of subjecting themselves to criminal liability, but the possibility of disciplinary measures, which may entail economic sanctions including the elimination or reduction of retirement and pension benefits, may have the practical effect of compelling cooperation. If a supervisor directs his or her staff not to cooperate, contrary to the company's decision to carry out an investigation, the company may replace or discharge the supervisor.

If an employee facing disciplinary action for failure to cooperate with an investigation believes that the company's action is unreasonable, they can present their case before thei labour union or labour relations committee. If the company fails to take appropriate measures to deal with uncooperative employees, regulatory authorities or the public may claim that the company is not serious in conducting the internal investigation. **11.125**

Control on threats

The company may request its employees to cooperate with internal investigations. If such investigation is closely related to the scope of employment, the employees would be obliged to comply with the company's request for cooperation as a result of the de facto threatening power of disciplinary rules inside the company. There is no particular provision that prevents the company from threatening its employees into cooperating with an investigation. **11.126**

Representation

Although it is not standard practice in Japan for companies to recommend separate counsel for employees who become involved in an internal investigation, companies can do this and they sometimes do so in order to make it clear whether legal counsel is representing the company or the employee and to define the scope of the representation. For example, a company may recommend separate counsel when there is a potential conflict of interest between the company and the employee or when the employee is suspected of a breach of trust. A company may also suggest separate counsel when there is a possibility that criminal or civil liability may attach separately to the company and the employee, as the culpability of the company and that of the individual are not always the same. **11.127**

Separate counsel is likely to be appropriate if the directors and officers of a company are the subjects of an investigation being conducted in anticipation of a future shareholder derivative suit. In particular, if there is a high likelihood of future lawsuits or if there is a possibility that employee statements may be used as influential evidence, employees should be encouraged to have their own counsel. **11.128**

11.129 When taking statements from employees in the course of an investigation, the company should advise employees in advance that the results may be used as evidence against them in a lawsuit, and the company should follow procedures similar to those used when taking a deposition, such as recording the content of statements in detail and requesting the confirmation of attendees.

Assurances as to confidentiality and privilege

11.130 Counsel has no authority to provide any assurances as to confidentiality or privilege to the company's employees unless the company, as counsel's client, so authorizes. Counsel may not be required to disclose to regulators or governmental authorities information or evidence obtained from employees to the extent that such information or evidence is in counsel's custody. There is no established rule on the extent of the company's support to its employees. A Company may give amnesties to an employee who has violated internal rules or reserve the right to report the employee to governmental authorities, depending on matters such as the seriousness of the wrongdoing, the extent of the employee's involvement in it, and the extent of the employee's cooperation with the investigation. The company may pay for the employee's lawyer if it is justified under the relevant circumstances.

Ethical implications for counsel

11.131 Counsel conducts investigations at the company's request and interviews are not conducted for the purpose of protecting the rights of the officers or employees who are interviewed. Depending on the circumstances, officers or employees could be prosecuted. Interviews are conducted on a voluntary basis, but officers and employees who refuse to respond may be reprimanded. There is no legal requirement to make these points clear, but ethics may require that they be explained.

11.132 It is generally advisable that counsel explains to officers and employees that he or she is retained by the company, the interviews are voluntary, and the company may use the results of the interview against employees.[99] If the interests of the employee and the company clearly conflict, it may be advisable to suggest to the employee that he or she has personal and separate representation.

Investigations and disciplinary process

11.133 The Whistleblower Protection Act is intended to protect those employees who bring allegations of wrongdoing to the attention of the company or regulatory authorities, provided that the employee's objective is not an illegal one, such as

---

[99] The draft revision of the law relating to the prevention of money laundering does not impose upon lawyers a duty to report irregularities.

fraudulent gain or harm to others.[100] The protection afforded by the Act is narrow: only workers, retirees, and temporary staff may qualify as whistle-blowers;[101] and the subject matter of a whistle-blower's report, as defined in the Act, is limited to violations of certain enumerated laws including the Penal Code, the Food Sanitation Law, the Securities and Exchange Law, and the Air Pollution Control Law.[102] The Act prohibits companies from reacting to such reports in a manner that disadvantages the whistle-blower, through disciplinary discharge, demotion, or reduction in pay.[103]

Most Japanese companies may have rules concerning disciplinary measures by which a disciplinary committee or board may determine disciplinary actions. Before imposing disciplinary actions on employees who are suspected or found to be involved in the alleged wrongdoing, the company must balance the necessity of disciplinary action against the necessity of gathering information. **11.134**

The investigation process is not necessarily linked with the disciplinary process. Findings from the investigation may be used as a basis for disciplinary action but, depending on the case, disciplinary action may take place before the investigation is completed. It is not uncommon for companies to suspend employees during an investigation if they are suspected of wrongdoing. **11.135**

Challenges posed by ex-employees

Former employees may be considered material witnesses to internal investigations. They may be asked to cooperate voluntarily with investigations, but the company will be unable to rely upon a reprimand or the company's supervisory authority to persuade them. The most effective method of obtaining the cooperation of former employees is to ask for it using the typical Japanese style of interpersonal communication. If that is unsuccessful, it may be necessary to suggest the possibility of a criminal prosecution. The company may seek to impose disciplinary action retroactively and ask the employee to return severance pay etc, but this approach may not be effective. Unless special arrangements are made, it is not common to include cooperation covenants in severance packages since, in practice, it would be difficult to enforce such covenants. **11.136**

---

100 Whistleblower Protection Act, Art 2(1).
101 Whistleblower Protection Act, Art 2(1).
102 Whistleblower Protection Act, Art 2(3).
103 Whistleblower Protection Act, Art 1.

Payment of legal fees/indemnification/fee advances

11.137 Companies can and sometimes do indemnify employees for the cost of representation by separate legal counsel in connection with internal and/or regulatory investigations, particularly if the matter is deemed integral to the business of the company. Indemnification is problematic, however, in circumstances where the employee has actually violated the law. Companies are usually not permitted to indemnify employees who have breached company rules a nd been subjected to discipline. In addition, a company's ability to indemnify an employee for legal fees incurred in connection with a shareholder derivative suit where the defendants are company directors or legal auditors is limited by law.

11.138 Companies can and sometimes do advance fees for representation by separate legal counsel in connection with internal, regulatory, and/or criminal investigations so long as the employee has committed no breach of trust, violation of law, or breach of important company rules and the matter concerns the business of the company. If it is later found that the employee has committed breach of trust or an illegal act, however, the company may bring a claim against the employee for reimbursement of expenses paid on the employee's behalf, including legal fees, as part of a damages claim.

Best practices

11.139 Generally it is good practice to instruct employees that they should cooperate fully with the investigation and put them on notice that if they fail to cooperate, they could be reprimanded. However, it may be difficult to obtain the full cooperation of directors and employees during interviews, as they may attempt to protect themselves or others, and there are limits to internal investigations that are not mandatory.

11.140 There are also psychological factors to consider when employees conduct interviews of other employees. Therefore, it is vitally important to employ outside counsel with expertise in interviewing techniques. On the other hand, interviews by employees may contribute to creating a more friendly atmosphere and extracting more information. How best to combine and coordinate the roles of outside counsel and employees is the key to conducting interviews and internal investigations effectively.

11.141 It is also important to analyse any relevant materials before conducting interviews and then confirm and clarify the facts during the interview.

11.142 It is also important for counsel to explain to the interviewee that the result of the interview may be used against him or her.

K. Winding up an Investigation

Managing expectations

Supervisory authorities expect that an investigation report will be submitted at **11.143**
the conclusion of an internal investigation. They may request that the report follows rules set forth in specific laws. In the past, the opinions of the supervisory authorities were often solicited while the report was in a draft stage and then incorporated into the final report. Recently, however, more companies are preparing reports by themselves. There is a current trend for the authorities to request that those found responsible for the action that is the subject of the investigation be named in the investigation report.

It is important to note that the report requested by the supervisory authorities **11.144**
and the report expected by stakeholders, including investors, may not necessarily focus on the same issues. For example, in a case involving the forgery of data concerning the construction of a dam by an electric power company, the supervisory authorities requested the submission of an investigation report focusing on safety. This report was insufficient for investors, however, as the process through which the data was forged and the governance issues involved were equally important to them.

The media, as well as investors, customers and interested parties, also expect an **11.145**
investigation report. They also want to know who was responsible for the incident.

L. Reporting Obligations

Tailoring the report

Supervisory authorities may request reports to be submitted in accordance with **11.146**
certain legal rules. In other cases, there is no legal obligation to prepare a report simply because an internal investigation was carried out. Supervisory authorities, however, usually request a status report and companies may be requested to report in writing. Furthermore, listed companies may be requested to announce the results of their investigation in accordance with the TSE rules on timely disclosure.

One issue the company may encounter when preparing the investigation report **11.147**
is how much detail should be incorporated with respect to the question of accountability. In the past, it was considered difficult to refer to accountability issues in an investigation report, but recently supervisory authorities have been

requesting companies to include a discussion of accountability. Even in case where the report is not legally required, the public may force the company to submit a written report. The company should carefully examine the pros and cons of disclosing an internal investigation report.

Coordinating with Public Relations strategy

11.148 The public announcement of the results of an investigation is important because it is an opportunity to emphasize the company's sincerity in dealing with a problem. The main purpose of conducting an internal investigation is to discover the cause of the problem, to prevent the problem from recurring, and to recover public confidence. It is important to make it clear that no further problems will arise and that appropriate measures have been taken to prevent the problem from recurring.

11.149 Practical preventative measures must be implemented at the latest by the time an investigation is completed. Furthermore, sufficient evidence should be presented to convince the public that no further problems will arise. If there are issues concerning accountability, an announcement to that effect should be made upon completion of the investigation after reprimanding those responsible. When an investigation is completed, the public may require to see the report and ask who would take responsibility. It is important that the company clearly conveys the message that the investigation was thoroughly and independently conducted and proper measures to prevent similar problems have been undertaken.

11.150 In the case of Japanese companies, the members of management who are dealing with the problem may try to protect their predecessors (who may have appointed them) and may not be adequately able to investigate the cause or pursue the question of who is responsible. In addition, the board of directors may not have sufficient supervisory authority.

11.151 However, when there is a management crisis, management should make the investigation results public unless there is a special reason not to, and it is important for management to fulfil its duty to recover the public's confidence by providing a full explanation to shareholders and other stakeholders. Therefore, the investigation report should be announced at the same time it is submitted to the supervisory authorities and it is vital that management respond to questions at press conferences.

11.152 It is generally recommended for a company to release all the information on the investigation at once. The results of the investigation, responsibilities, and preventative measures should be simultaneously announced. Such announcements are sometimes planned over weekends when business is slow.

Beware of waiving privilege

Companies should be aware that there is a significant risk that an investigation report submitted to the regulatory authorities may be disclosed pursuant to the information disclosure rules of the relevant public office. If the public office refuses to disclose the report, a court can order its disclosure. Furthermore, in civil proceedings, if a party can specify the document, it may request the court to order a submission of such document as evidence. If an investigation report is compiled in a written form, a party can easily specify the document. **11.153**

M. Litigation Risks

Risks of criminal litigation commenced by regulators

In Japan, public prosecutors have the exclusive authority to file criminal cases.[104] Other regulators may only file a complaint with a public prosecutor if they conclude that a company has committed a criminal offence as a result of their investigations. As mentioned above, public prosecutors can use all the evidence seized by the regulators as far as the evidence is collected in the course of criminal investigations conducted by the regulators. It should be noted that with regard to Serious Violations of the Anti-Monopoly Act the JFTC has the exclusive authority to file a criminal complaint and no one may file a criminal case without a complaint by the JFTC. **11.154**

Risks of civil litigation commenced by regulators

Regulators have full discretion in deciding whether or not to pursue administrative procedures against a company in order to enforce a certain regulatory straitjacket. There are no clear guidelines or criteria as to the procedures leading to such decisions, but for the purpose of clarity, regulatory authorities publish annual reports containing summaries of their major cases for the year. These annual reports can help companies, to some extent, develop an insight into the trends of the regulatory authorities. **11.155**

One exception to this absolute discretion of regulatory authorities is the delisting procedures of the TSE. The TSE publishes criteria for a listed company to be delisted, including the making of false statements in annual or interim securities reports and statements of 'an unfair representation' by a certified public accountant.[105] According to the TSE's criteria, a company may also be delisted 'in a case where the TSE considers delisting the shares is appropriate in light of the **11.156**

---

104 The Criminal Procedures Law, Art 247.
105 See 'Criteria for Delisting of Stock' of the TSE, Art 2, para 11.

need for shareholder protection or public interests'.[106] When the TSE considers the possibility of delisting, the shares of the company under consideration are transferred to the 'supervision post'. Subsequently, if the TSE concludes that the delisting criteria have been met, the shares are transferred to the 'liquidation post', which, after one month, is followed by actual delisting. In 2006, the TSE expelled 45 companies from the exchange under the criteria for delisting, some of these cases involved the making of false statements in securities reports and others involved late submission of reports.

Prosecution or civil enforcement action against corporate officers and directors

11.157 Under Japanese law, companies are responsible for their own compliance with regulatory obligations, and therefore they are expected to take self-disciplinary measures on their own in the first place. However, where a corporate executive or an employee in a certain position engages in insider trading or issues false reports for his or her own benefit, such self-control mechanism ceases to function, and the SESC may also take actions against such executive or employee.[107]

11.158 Every corporate criminal offence is inevitably based on the actions of individuals working on behalf of the corporation (eg directors and employees), and with this in mind, the Japanese law regards such individuals as the primary parties responsible for such criminal offences, although the company is also punished along with the responsible individuals provided that the violation was committed with regard to the business or property of the company. Crimes that are subject to such 'double punishment' provisions include cartels,[108] market manipulation[109] and tax evasion.[110]

11.159 Regulators have their own policies and criteria to determine how to classify individual offences into either criminal investigations or administrative investigations. For example, the JFTC will seek criminal penalties when the case is vicious and serious enough to influence significantly the lives of the general public, or when the company or the individual involved in the violations is a persistent offender and a mere administrative measure would not achieve the purpose of the Anti-Monopoly Act.

---

[106] See 'Criteria for Delisting of Stock' of the TSE, Art 2, para 19.
[107] The Financial Instruments and Exchange Law, Arts 172, paras 2 and 5, 166, para 1(1), and 167, para 1(1).
[108] The Anti-Monopoly Act, Arts 89, para 1(1), and 95, para 1(1).
[109] The Financial Instruments and Exchange Law, Arts 159, 197, para 1(5) and 207.
[110] The Corporate Tax Law, Arts 159, para 1, and 164, para 1.

Risks of private civil litigation

Under Japanese law, civil litigants have very limited access to information **11.160** collected by regulators in their inspection procedures.

In the case of a violation of the Anti-Monopoly Act, the parties concerned can ask **11.161** the JFTC to disclose the transcript of the hearing proceedings.[111] In criminal cases, any person can in principle inspect trial records after the trial concludes.[112] Further, after the first trial date in a criminal case, victims of the criminal offence can ask for a copy of trial records and use them for a related damages suit.[113]

Relevance of investigation report

In Japan, the independence of the judiciary is fully secured. Accordingly, in **11.162** principle and in theory, no finding by regulators or other courts' decisions can affect the court involved in civil matters. One exception is that, if an administrative order of the JFTC against a private monopoly, an unfair restraint of trade, or an unfair trade practice has been finalized, the offender will be found liable also in a damages suit whether or not the offender has been negligent.[114]

In practice, it is true that findings by regulators often have a strong influence on **11.163** the courts' decisions regarding facts because the findings are the results of the examination of evidence. However, this practice has no statutory basis and a defendant can challenge a regulator's finding by producing new evidence in court.

N. Settlement with Regulators

Process

Japan has no system for a settlement between companies and regulators regarding **11.164** civil or criminal regulatory actions.

Plea bargaining and amnesty arrangements

Japan has no system allowing plea bargains in criminal actions. Under the leniency **11.165** programme introduced into the Anti-Monopoly Act in 2006, however, a company which first admits to committing unfair restraints of trade such as

---

[111] The Anti-Monopoly Act, Art 70-15.
[112] The Criminal Procedures Law, Art 53
[113] The Law Concerning Measures Associated to Criminal Procedures in Order to Protect Victims etc. of Crimes (*hanzai higaisha to no hogo wo hakaru tameno keiji tetsuzuki ni fuzui suru sochi ni kansuru horitsu*), Art 3.
[114] The Anti-Monopoly Act, Arts 25 and 26.

participation in a cartel or bid-rigging may receive full immunity from any applicable administrative fines as well as from criminal charges.

O. Conclusion

11.166 With sophisticated IT, companies today are always exposed to the critical and watchful eyes of the media and the public. Once a company is involved in a corporate scandal related to regulatory violations, the cost the company must bear both in the short and long run is not limited to the investigation and sanctions imposed by the regulatory authority. The company will also have to face harsh social criticism, which sometimes could result in an immense damage to business operations. Even more grave consequences await the violating company if the company mismanages the scandal by, for example, delaying the disclosure of related information or announcements, or intentionally concealing relevant documents. Along with the recent trend of high expectations for morally and ethically correct corporate activities, the importance of regulatory compliance is more relevant now than ever before for each participant in the market economy.

11.167 The series of recent amendments to regulatory legislation in Japan directly reflects this latest trend, and all these newly introduced rules are designed to enhance the power of regulators to conduct investigations, such as the SESC now being empowered to impose administrative surcharges, which enables the SESC to conduct surveillance for not only serious criminal breaches but also for minor infringements. The JFTC is reinforcing its regulatory competency armed with the new leniency programme and surcharges of greater magnitude. Against this backdrop of regulatory development, companies are strongly recommended to keep pace with the recent and future evolution of regulatory rules and the growing authoritative powers of regulators. To avoid panicking in the face of regulatory officials knocking on the door, it is essential to set up and regularly review internal compliance schemes to update all employees with the latest regulatory requirements.

INTRODUCTION TO ANNEXES

In the Annexes that follow, we have set out checklists of matters that should be considered in an internal investigation. Inevitably, these are very general lists since the details will depend on the specific circumstances and such factors as the governing jurisdiction, whether any regulators are involved—and if so—what their powers and likely next steps will be and the size of the issue giving rise to the investigation. These checklists need, therefore, to be used in connection with the detailed commentaries in the individual chapters.

However, we hope that the checklists, which reflect experience, will be a useful support when reacting to the kinds of incidents that give rise to an investigation and will provide a cross reference to make sure that nothing is missed.

The areas covered are as follows:

1. Crisis Management
2. Disclosures
3. Document Management and Privilege
4. Employee issues
5. Public Relations Issues

ANNEX 1

Crisis Management

Initiating an investigation

The circumstances in which an internal investigation is necessary are, almost by definition, unwelcome. They may be either a 'cold shock' in the sense of dawn raid or a whistle-blower with 'smoking gun' type evidence or a slowly growing concern that something is amiss. In either event, there is an absence of hard information and some form of scramble to understand the issues and to establish hard facts. It is usually a time of confusion.

Which of these steps listed below is required will, naturally, depend on the gravity of the problem. In less serious matters, many of these steps can be swiftly rejected as unnecessary.

First steps
- Identify who in the company will be responsible for the executive management of the matter.
- Identify and free up the necessary internal resources (legal, accounting, PR etc).
- Identify whether external resources are required and who, and what, they should be, taking account of any need to ensure that external advisers are sufficiently independent in the light of the anticipated concerns of the courts, regulators, or capital markets likely to be concerned and any previous involvement they may have had in any related issues.
- Establish an interim management structure with regular reporting arrangements and appropriate timescales for action.
- Identify the repository of all information so that there is one person, or group, who is informed of all matters and can monitor factual developments and report to the wider group.
- Consider whether a disclosure needs to be made to the capital markets (see Annex 2).
- Deal with document preservation and control (see Annex 3).

- Identify whether there is any conduct that needs to be terminated or conducted by a 'clean team'.
- Draft an immediate holding press statement to be used defensively if needed.
- Identify a spokesperson, to be available if needed, and ensure that person is properly briefed and has considered Q&As.
- Identify if any assets or data need to be protected or seized.

In the event of a dawn raid

- Trigger immediately the company's dawn raid procedures.
- Call for specialist advice immediately.
- Identify immediately the identity, authority, powers, scope of investigation or alleged infringement and immediate plans of the regulator concerned.
- Gather as many people with the right skills, including IT staff, as are likely to be needed, with a good safety margin. Experience suggests that there are never enough people responding on the company side to a well planned and unforeseen dawn raid.
- Free up and provide the necessary internal facilities (working space, 'incident rooms', copying, refreshments, secretarial support etc). It will usually assist the relationships with the regulators to be hospitable and these resources will also be needed for the company.
- Plan ahead in terms of document and interview requests. Without, in anyway, doing anything which could constitute interference with a regulator's program or be frustrating action, consider whether relevant staff need to be seen immediately, in advance of regulatory access, to alert them to the process underway and to prepare them (appropriately) for likely urgent interviews.
- Do as much as possible to identify the factual position, in rough outline.
- Consider immediately (ideally with specialist advice) whether it is appropriate to make any application for leniency or offer of full cooperation. This can be a critical strategic issue.
- Consider whether it is appropriate (if given a choice) to allow staff to be interviewed.
- Track as closely as possible the activities of the regulator both as to witness interviews and as to document retrieval. Make sure that the company knows exactly what has happened and what has been said.
- To the extent possible, keep copies of all material seized and notes of all conversations.
- Take great care when making any admissions.

Urgent next steps

- Identify the nature and extent of any self-reporting obligations or tactical opportunities (usually with expert advice), and take the critical strategic decisions that result from this analysis.

- Consider whether it is appropriate to suspend any staff, without any finding of guilt, simply because it is the right step to take as a matter of governance (see Annex 4).

- Ensure that any whistle-blower is treated appropriately.

- Determine, on an initial appraisal of the seriousness of the matter, where the strategic responsibility for the matter should rest (ie the Audit Committee, a particular director, the General Counsel).

- Review insurance policies and consider whether any insurance notifications need to be made. Also ensure that individuals negotiating any policy renewal are aware of the issues under investigations for disclosure purposes.

- Consider if disclosures should be made to third parties.

- Consider any internal communications (see Annex 5).

- Undertake a legal and reputation risk analysis. This would include assessing which regulators or criminal authorities might pursue the matter and which is likely to lead. It would also be critical to assess civil litigation risk and how it can be managed.

- Consider whether a remediation package should be considered and if so when should that decision be taken (when will there be a sufficient understanding of the facts for it to be possible to appraise that issue)? Should any offer be proactive or reactive?

- Consider wider ramifications: could similar issues have arisen elsewhere or on other occasions?

- Establish a formal internal investigation if needed.

Establishing the investigation

- Determine whether it should be external, and if so whom the external adviser should be. This may or may not be the same organization that has given initial advice on the matter. The external recourse is likely to involve at least some of: legal, accounting (systems and controls), forensic accounting and IT, specialist technical (say environmental) or (possibly) private investigators.

- Determine the scope of the investigation, if necessary with written terms of reference and procedures for change control.

- Vest the investigation with sufficient authority and senior management support.

- Form a clear idea on how data is to be managed, where (or if) it is to be data-based and who will have access to what data. This may involve two databases—a wide 'dump' of all potentially relevant material, and a working database, capturing meta-data, constituting more relevant material which has been extracted from the initial database.

- Identify potential Data Protection Act restrictions. Assess the size of any potential risk and the impact on the investigation of any limitations that there may be.

- Define the reporting lines and indicative timeframe for the investigation.

- Establish a joint plan of action for identifying factual issues, legal issues and the likely sources of the factual and evidential material for addressing them. It is usually appropriate to consider carefully whether the investigation process should be document or witness-led, which may alter between different phases. It is important to consider the best order in which to approach witnesses, particularly where the witness work leads the document work and the information is less complete when witness interviews start.

- Adopt a clear policy position as to the expectations of witness cooperation. To ensure that the process is fully supported, address any internal management issues and obtain the necessary HR support.

- Ensure that the investigation (if external) has enough resource from within the company for it to operate effectively. In terms of management recourse, distinguish between executives who are part of the investigation team, those who have executive responsibility for the investigation and those that have strategic oversight for governance reasons.

- Ensure that those executives assisting the investigation or supervising it are, themselves, likely to be free from censure by the investigation so that its output will remain untainted.

- Where there are different advisers involved in the investigation ensure that their respective roles and responsibilities are clearly defined and accepted.

- Ensure confidentiality.

ANNEX 2

Disclosures

A critical issue is that of disclosure to capital markets. Irrespective of the seriousness of the underlying issue, it is critical that there is no secondary liability created by a breach of any market disclosure obligation. Not only can that lead to the imposition of further penalties, but its impact on the company's reputation for good governance, and on the credibility of the board, can be enormous.

The necessary steps for considering such issues are likely already to be built into the processes that govern a company's market relationships, investor relations, governance and disclosure policies generally. Those usual processes should be followed as much as possible. However, some particular issues arise in relation to investigations because the factual position is often uncertain at the critical time.

The following points usually fall for consideration in any case that clearly does not give rise to disclosure obligations.

- Raise the issue at the appropriate level within the company immediately and ensure that it is kept under constant review.

- Take expert advice as necessary. This will usually involve the company's leading corporate or securities lawyers and its corporate broker or lead investment bank. It is usually extremely dangerous not to follow the advice of appropriate external advisers since market authorities will usually take an adverse view of such behaviour.

- Identify the necessary test for public disclosure in each market, including any listed debt securities or ADR type instruments. Some of the issues raised below may be relevant to the application of those tests.

- Form a clear view of the likely securities price impact of the information concerned and, therefore, whether it is price-sensitive. Be alert to whether the mere risk that a particular problem might eventuate is, itself, price-sensitive. In addition, evaluate the more obvious potential financial impact of the matter (including civil litigation, remediation, impact on the business model etc).

- Be alert to the prospect that allegations of criminal activity or unethical or dishonest behaviour, particularly directed at senior staff, may have a more significant impact on share price than the financial impact alone would suggest.

- Consider whether any of the issues being investigated could raise questions as to management integrity, or as to the strength or reliability of systems and controls, such as to have an impact on share price.

- Consider whether there is a wider context, including previous history, which would require a matter to be disclosed on this occasion even if it might not need to be disclosed generally.

- If it is deemed that an announcement is not necessary, keep that decision under review on an ongoing basis.

- Where the facts are uncertain, consider whether it is possible to put out a 'holding' announcement to gain time, or take advantage of a time period to investigate, or obtain some comfort from the market authorities to delay an announcement (although there are few jurisdictions where this is possible or where there is any material latitude).

- If it is thought that a disclosure is required, the drafting clearly needs to consider the views of all those that have responsibility for the matter.

- The actual establishing of an investigation may well be the central part of an announcement, with the company disclosing the broad nature of the issue, explaining that it is being investigated and committing to report in due course.

- Consider carefully whether it is necessary to disclose the terms of reference of the investigation; the risk being that, if they are then changed (as they very possibly will be), there may need to be a further announcement which could be unnecessarily damaging to shareholder value.

- If a decision has been taken to cooperate fully with the authorities, it will usually be considered appropriate to make this plain in any public statement.

- Consider carefully whether it is appropriate to make any commitments either to the facts or as to the future. Almost by definition, an announcement is being made when the facts are uncertain and there is a considerable range of potential outcomes for the investigation. If possible, any statement should not be sufficiently detailed so as to require updates as the company's assessment of the position changes or develops. It is usually in no one's interests for an investigation to be conducted against the background of an ongoing level of transparency as to its progress.

- Moreover, when the facts are uncertain, it is critical to avoid saying anything, in all good faith, which, it subsequently transpires, was inaccurate.

- If it was appropriate to announce the launch of an investigation, it will usually be necessary to make some disclosure to the markets as to the termination of any investigation, together with its conclusions and any steps that the company is then taking. This is, naturally, a matter of sensitive drafting.

- Even if an initial disclosure has been made, it is necessary to keep under review whether an interim disclosure is required because information comes to light which is sufficiently material to pass the relevant price sensitivity test, even against the background of the related information that is already disclosed and 'in the market'.

- In addition, the disclosure policy needs to be considered within the framework of the company's normal auditing and reporting schedule, which includes periodical filings with the market authorities.

- In a similar vein, it is important to consider what is said:
  — at shareholders' meetings;
  — in briefings to analysts;
  — in response to inquiries from shareholders to the investor relations department or to senior executives; and
  — to the press.

- All of these issues are likely to fall within the scope of the normal legal requirements in such circumstances but require sensitive handling in relation to an investigation into the company's behaviour.

ANNEX 3

Document Management and Privilege

This Annex provides a checklist for two related and important topics: how to ensure prudent management of existing documents; and how to optimize privilege protection. Privilege (and its waiver) is a highly sophisticated, and jurisdiction-specific, topic and reference should first be made to the relevant chapter and then, as necessary, to specialist work on the subject. The comments made below are for general guidance only.

Document management

- The specific destruction of relevant documentary evidence, even if not actually an offence or giving rise to regulatory penalties, is invariably prejudicial to the company's position in civil, regulatory or criminal proceedings. The following steps would usually be regarded as standard. Indeed, some regulators, particularly in the US, regard it as problematic if the company has not taken sufficient proactive steps of the nature described below, irrespective of whether there is any positive evidence of document destruction.

- As soon as possible, circulate a Document Preservation Memorandum. (This may also be a vehicle for wider communications about the situation and the process that will be adopted.)

- The Document Preservation Memorandum should be sent to all parties with potentially relevant evidence, and to all related administrative support and IT staff.

- The Document Preservation Memorandum should include a definition of subject matter scope, and an explanation of the material to be preserved. It must also involve a clear definition of what is meant by 'documents', which will include all evidence of all kinds, physical and electronic, drafts, multiple copies, personal notes, diaries, expenses receipts, voice mail files etc.

- It may be appropriate to explain the risks of the company's position being prejudiced, and either disciplinary or external sanctions being imposed on the individual, as a result of any destruction.

- It may be appropriate to obtain sign-off by staff that there has been no destruction.

624

- The Document Preservation Memorandum often addresses document creation going forward, to ensure that new documents do not pose problems (eg by making admissions, commenting inappropriately, or misstating the facts). To that end, consider a complete ban on the creation of any such documents unless they will be privileged.

- There is usually a difficult definitional issue in relation to document creation in that one does not want to inhibit the operations of the business. It is therefore necessary to establish rules on document creation that prevent the creation of problematic documents, yet do not inhibit the efficient day-to-day business. In practice, this can usually be achieved, but it requires careful thought.

- The Document Preservation Memorandum may also make recommendations that staff should not discuss substantive issues between themselves (to avoid the 'reconstruction of memory' and the creation of urban myths). It can also deal with what can and (more often) cannot be said by employees to counterparties or externally.

- It is critical to involve IT staff in this process. It may be appropriate for them to speak to external forensic IT advisers to ensure that the preservation process is comprehensive. It will be necessary to take all steps that the IT system permits to protect data on servers or on individual computers, including from remote access; to preserve back-up tapes and long-term storage media and to image or copy data that could be critical. It is not unknown to remove the access rights of staff who are under particular suspicion.

- It will usually be appropriate to take such preservation steps immediately without considering data protection issues. It is rare that mere preservation without further processing could be a breach of any data protection rights.

- As a general rule, keep written communication, even to top management or the board, to the minimum necessary. This can often be achieved by using presentations based on a mixture of non-privileged existing evidential material and oral explanation.

Privilege

Privilege needs to be considered from the outset, even though it may be deemed necessary to waive it at a later stage, in whole or in part. This involves consideration of the following issues.

- Are in-house lawyers given the benefit of privilege in the relevant jurisdictions and by the relevant regulators?

- Is the level of protection of documents enhanced by using a law firm as an external adviser (and the leader of the investigation) rather than some other adviser (as will almost always be the case)?

- If a law firm is leading the investigation, will its, or the company's, communications with other advisers be protected?

- What privilege assistance can be obtained from proper drafting of the Terms of Reference for the investigation? Are they in a form to assist in ensuring that there is a clearly evidenced obligation to advise on legal issues and not just to consider facts?

- Is litigation sufficiently in prospect to make privilege available? If so, how can the purpose of investigative activities be sufficiently clearly recorded to ensure that the available protection is obtained?

- Who is the client? Is there a risk that communications, even by external lawyers, with some parts of the company, including witnesses, are not protected?

- Is it appropriate for witnesses to receive any written communications in connection with the investigation? Should all written records be retained only in the lawyers' possession? This issue is likely to be resolved by reference to the jurisdiction involved. Some jurisdictions better protect both lawyers' own work product and papers in their possession (particularly some civil law jurisdictions).

- Examine whether communications with others with a common interest (such as insurers) are, or can be, protected by privilege.

- Prior to initiation of any communications with people in a position analogous to 'co-defendants' examine whether this communication would be protected and whether privilege would be waived by communicating privileged documents to them.

- Moreover, ensure—to the degree possible—that comments to 'co-defendants' will not be disclosed to regulators, particularly if those other parties are seeking leniency or similar protection.

- Have sufficiently strong instructions, and procedures, in place, to avoid any unintended waiver of privilege. Particular attention should be given to cases involving multi-jurisdictional investigation as, in these cases, privilege may be waived by disclosure to a regulator by someone handling one part of a multi-jurisdictional issue who may not be sensitive to privilege issues in other jurisdictions.

ANNEX 4

Employee Issues

In any investigation, employee issues will be sensitive and require close management attention. It is critical that collateral damage to employee relationships is avoided, and, equally, that opportunities are taken to reinforce cultural expectations, for example on ethical issues. An investigation is also an opportunity for positive change.

As the country chapters have demonstrated, the rights accorded to employees during an investigation, and the associated culture, vary dramatically across jurisdictions. Moreover, multinational companies (particularly those that have grown by acquisition) often have differing contractual arrangements with staff quite apart from the divergent legal regimes. This makes for additional complexity in international cases.

In this environment, the following issues usually fall for consideration:

- Involve the HR department, at the right level, in the investigation process and ensure that employee issues are considered at an early stage. (Note that it may well be necessary to review an employee's personnel files.)

- Consider retaining specialist employment counsel, particularly in difficult jurisdictions, if the necessary expertise is not available in-house.

- Distinguish the investigation process from any subsequent disciplinary process. For that reason, it is generally not advisable to have a member of the HR department present at any interviews, as the employee could then more easily confuse the meeting with a disciplinary hearing.

- Take advice to ensure that the conduct of the investigation will not unnecessarily prejudice any subsequent disciplinary process (the investigation will usually take priority in the case of any direct conflict).

- Review local whistle-blower protections and ensure that they are observed.

- Check employment contracts and local law to establish duties of cooperation, confidentiality, loyalty etc.

- Take great care with the messaging to, and behaviour towards, employees. This is particularly the case where an employee is in the position of being asked to give evidence against a colleague or friend or superior (including personal assistants or secretaries being asked to give information about the person for whom they work). People have genuine fears about retaliation and they need to be considered seriously and realistically.

- Consider whether any amnesty or assurances can or should be given. This will involve not only a policy decision by the company, but a consideration of local law, staff cultural expectations and regulator reactions.

- Short of amnesty, it will usually be appropriate to emphasize the need to cooperate and, possibly, that failure to cooperate, or actively misleading the investigation can be a disciplinary matter, again within the necessary legal constraints.

- Ensure that there is a clear understanding among the investigation interviewers as to the tone that will be adopted with employees.

- As part of that process, it is prudent to review carefully the nature of warning that will be given to employees as to privilege and confidentiality at the start of each interview. It is clearly critical that employees are not misled as to the use to which any information will be put. It will usually be the case that, whenever a company interviews an employee during an investigation, it makes a clear statement at the beginning of the interview outlining the status of the interview, whether the interview will be privileged and whether the notes of the interview will be provided to the employee after the interview.

- Consider in advance what the policy will be in relation to permitting separate representation, or for paying for it, within the applicable legal constraints. Should it be positively offered and, if so, when?

- Pay close attention to the termination arrangements of any employee who is leaving, both as to cooperation obligations and severance packages. Consider whether the latter will seem appropriate at a later stage, in light of the possible conclusions of the investigation.

- Consider the powers to impose suspension or 'gardening leave' and whether it is appropriate for people who might be the subject of serious allegations. As a general rule, it is better not to break the employment relationship before it is really necessary to do so because of the fiduciary duties owed by staff while they remain employees. However, these are very much matters of judgement to be exercised in the relevant legal, regulatory and cultural context.

- If suspension is used, it is important to clarify both what the relevant employee's role is while on suspension, what contact he or she is allowed with other staff, and what access that person has to the firm's IT systems while he or she is suspended. It is also important to consider how the suspension will be portrayed to regulators, other staff and that employee's counterparties outside the business. It will usually be the case that a suspended employee will be seeking independent advice and that relationships with him or her may become (and possibly should become) more formal and legalistic.

- It may be necessary to notify regulators of the suspension.

- A suspension will usually require careful documentation, the involvement of HR, if not external counsel, and, in some jurisdictions, labour representative bodies.

- It is sensible to give close consideration to data protection issues and how they will affect employees in each jurisdiction.

- Specifically, although a tricky area, it is important to consider, in some jurisdictions, if employee consent is required for data protection law purposes before data processing takes place. Clearly such a requirement (and it is a complex issue as to whether there actually is such a requirement) can impede an investigation dramatically. However, seeking such consent may, itself, be an interesting exercise in the context of the investigation. It may be helpful for senior management to take the lead by agreeing to permit the investigation to review their own data. A solution that some may find reassuring is that the review of data released is conducted by an outside law firm who is under instructions only to bring into the scope of the investigation (and thereby potentially disclose to the company) documents that are actually relevant to the investigation. This can give some comfort that irrelevant personal material will not be deployed by the company inappropriately.

- In some countries, it is necessary to consider whether works councils need to be consulted in connection with any data protection issues.

- The compliance, legal, senior management and HR teams should decide who should be responsible for disciplinary decisions during an investigation and ensure that they are conducted in accordance with the appropriate procedure. There is a risk of an overlap with whistle-blower protection in that an employee can easily claim, without any justification, that the reason for his or her dismissal process is not so much what he or she has done but what he or she has said about others in the investigation process. This risk needs to be carefully managed.

ANNEX 5

Public Relations Issues

Adroit management of the PR issues associated with any crisis giving rise to an investigation is essential. It can save the reputation of senior management, limit damage to the brand and protect shareholder value.

It requires a high priority and skilled resources. Any major company will already have a PR function which understands the company's PR positioning and brand, is sensitive to the wider PR issues that the company faces (outside whatever issue has arisen connected with the investigation) and has its own relationships with the journalists and others who cover that company's affairs. Hopefully, that team also has experience dealing with high profile 'incidents'.

This Annex does not seek to summarize the issues that skilled PR professionals understand better than the authors. However, there are some experiences that are more specific to investigations that it may be useful to summarize.

- One of the key values of an investigation is that it can (and usually will) be announced as part of a response to media inquiries about a particular incident. Whilst it is dangerous to hide behind an investigation, it is such a common approach to initiate an investigation into a problem, that journalists will usually accept that a company is limited in what it can say pending the results of that investigation. However, the concomitants are, inevitably, a focus on the results of the investigation, pressure for the investigation to proceed urgently, and a request for updates on how the investigation is progressing and what, progressively, is being revealed.

- It is not appropriate to use a national investigation as a delaying tactic to keep journalists at arm's length. It has to be a genuine process.

- Similarly, a statement that a company is complying fully with the authorities and their inquiries is often included in a wider statement as to the company's position and may well be appropriate.

- In a major crisis, the PR activity can be intense. Particularly given the increasing part played by online media, stories (accurate or inaccurate) spread and mutate extremely quickly. Care needs to be taken that the attention of the top management team does not become overly focused on the PR side; but the news story does need to be managed on a 24-hour basis.

- The PR function needs to be closely integrated with the top management team dealing with the issue.
- It is also critical that the PR function is working closely with the investor relations team to ensure that messaging is entirely consistent.
- There has to be a very clearly articulated 'message' throughout.
- There should be tight control of the communications with only one person, or a very small group, being allowed to speak to the media and all inquiries referred to that person or team.
- In particular, great care needs to be taken regarding the very senior executives in the company who will usually have direct media contacts and relationships. It is a matter for their judgement as to whether they should speak to the media on the issue of concern. It is usually prudent that they do not, particularly in the early stages when the facts are not clear, say very much that is concrete in nature. Senior executives are usually exposed to questioning on hypothetical issues and requested to speculate. This can be very unattractive, particularly on broadcast media, where they are particularly exposed. However, many executives are highly experienced and skilled at managing the media and there may be circumstances where a firm and clear statement from a senior executive is of great assistance in calming the issue and projecting an atmosphere that matters are under control. This is a decision that is highly dependent on the facts and the personalities involved. Experience suggests that it is frequently better for statements to come 'from the company' and that reserving the deployment of senior executives for very specific matters, when they are on very safe ground, rarely damages a company's position. Clearly if a senior executive is exposed to the media, appropriate preparation and definition of the message, including how to respond to questions on delicate areas, is required.
- In a significant problem, particularly one involving allegations of misbehaviour at a senior level, the demands of the media may overwhelm the company's internal function even if they have the necessary materials and contacts. It is worth considering retaining a PR or media consultancy firm, on a short-term basis, to deal with crisis management. In addition to providing extra resources at a time when the demand may be very heavy, leading firms have a wide experience of other, often similar, crises which can be of great use in preparing a strategy. Further, there is often a 'research' function involved in understanding and analysing the wider media position, in particular that of other commentators or the government. This can be very valuable in the development of a media strategy.
- Moreover, it is possible that the media coverage may treat a story as 'news' and it will be covered by different journalists from those with whom the company usually has contact. Internal communications within a news organization may

not be good and stories may be written by people with no knowledge of the company or the industrial sector, and who may not consult with those who have. It may be difficult for the company to get its message across to news journalists working on a particular line on a story with whom the company has no prior relationship. An agency will often have better contacts with the wider news organizations and be able to assist in managing this process.

- It is critical that the company does not say things, innocently or inadvertently, which are incorrect. This has a very damaging effect on the relationships with the journalists and on the company's reputation. That would be standard practice, of course, for any PR team. But in the context of an investigation, where there is a rapid and detailed uncovering of facts, and where a journalist's inquiries, perhaps based on factual (and possibly accurate) tip-offs from elsewhere, it is particularly important. Very close fact-checking, with those in the investigation team who are best placed to verify matters, is therefore critical. A short delay to allow such checking to occur is often better than a prompt, but wrong, answer.

- A particular difficulty in this respect, and one that can bedevil PR management in an investigation situation, is where the journalist knows more about the issue than the company. This is surprisingly common. There may have been an undercover investigative journalism exercise placing people within the company or a detailed and protracted investigation into a problem. The company may only know part of the story, and the news may be broken progressively over a period of time, building the story. There may be more actors involved than the company and the journalists may have better access to those other parties than the company has. This is particularly so if it is an agency or regulator, perhaps with its own angle, that is feeding information to a journalist. This situation is extremely difficult to manage since the company is 'behind the game'. The only response can be to accelerate the investigation. The company will usually have much of the information, either in documentary form, or in the memories of its staff, to enable it to have a deeper understanding, at least of its own position, than the journalist—but it needs to be extracted, and quickly.

- This situation impacts on the investigation at a factual level. Journalists will have access to different, wider sources of information (an investigation is essentially, at least initially, limited to using internal information). It is important to play back to the investigation team the issues that are being raised by journalists, since they will often raise valuable lines of enquiry, or change the priorities with which issues are addressed.

- It is important to pay close attention to the PR position of other parties.

- Regulators may well put out press releases. Along with the legal advisers, it is important to establish at the outset whether this is likely, and what can and should be done to coordinate in this respect. Quite possibly, there will be a congruence of interest with a regulator on PR issues leading to some loose joint understanding on how they should be handled. However, if that is not possible, care must still be taken not to prejudice a company's position with a regulator by inappropriate comment on the position or on the regulator's actions. There is considerable scope for damaging the regulatory relationship in such circumstances.

- In certain cases, trade bodies can play a useful role, particularly if the issue concerned is industry-wide rather than company-specific. Even the market leader can deploy the trade association as the spokesperson, referring questions to it and deflecting interest from the company.

- In a high profile case, the company's relationships with government may be important and thought needs to be given to the wider political agenda.

- A very important part of PR is internal rather than external. It is clearly valuable in terms of staff morale and the culture of an organization. Despite instructions on confidentiality and not speaking to external parties, there will be a risk of leaks. However, a clear simple line communicated internally, which is consistent with the external message can be valuable. Moreover, since staff are interacting daily with counterparties, it is important that they are projecting the right message, even if they know little of the detail.

- The PR on the conclusion of an investigation is fundamentally important. If there is going to be 'closure' on an issue which has already been the public domain, there will usually be an advantage in some form of public conclusion. This may be difficult to manage in that regulatory processes may not have concluded and hence there is no 'true' finality. However, it may be unattractive to wait to the end of such a process and it prevents the company from taking credit for what it has done itself to resolve the issue. This problem may be managed, to a degree, by an appropriate announcement which enables the public to foresee later regulatory action but which makes it plain that the company has dealt internally with the issue. This can explain that the business should not be troubled by the same concerns in the future, and that what remains is the working through of a regulatory process that will address historical infringements but which should not raise further issues as to the company's ongoing performance.

INDEX

Introductory note: Because the entire volume is about 'investigations', this term has not been used as an entry point. Information will be found under the corresponding detailed topics.